ST. JOHN
OF THE CROSS

BY

Fr. BRUNO, O.D.C.

EDITED BY

Fr. BENEDICT ZIMMERMAN, O.D.C.

WITH AN INTRODUCTION BY

JACQUES MARITAIN

NEW YORK
SHEED & WARD
MCMXXXVI

NIHIL OBSTAT : INNOCENTIUS APAP, S.TH.M., O.P.
CENSOR DEPUTATUS
IMPRIMATUR : ✠ JOSEPH BUTT
VIC. GEN.
WESTMONASTERII, DIE VIIA APRILIS MCMXXXII
PRINTED IN GREAT BRITAIN

CONTENTS

v

LIST OF ILLUSTRATIONS

INTRODUCTION

It has long been a matter of pressing and urgent necessity that someone with the double qualification of membership of the Carmelite Order and sound historical scholarship should produce a life of St. John of the Cross—as a corrective to the strange ideas concerning him that are commonly to be found in the minds of those interested in the mystical life. That necessity is here most adequately met by my old friend Father Bruno of Jesus and Mary.

He recently reminded me—when he honoured me with a request for this preface—that, after a University discussion in which philosophy paid but scant respect to divine wisdom, I wrote to him : "Yet it is not for us laymen to defend your saints." And now, though we still await a definitive, critical edition of the Works of St. John of the Cross,[1] here is the first full-length biography, based on methods of right historical criticism.

It was fitting that it should be produced by one of his sons : spiritual relationship, familiarity with the customs, mode of life, and the means of dying to self laid down by St. John of the Cross, give to a man, who has left all things to endeavour in his footsteps to follow Christ, not only a knowledge of the atmosphere, but a sort of distinctive discernment and spontaneous accuracy of appreciation, which no reconstruction made by an outsider could ever attain—no matter what his learning, lyric sense and philosophical intuition. This does not mean that Father Bruno has yielded to any of the prejudices which are the peril of even the most legitimate family feeling. His study is a model of impartiality, and shows the author's filial piety combined, in the easiest and most natural fashion, with a perfect scientific serenity. Moreover, he has seen too clearly to what distortions a desire—even though unconscious—to defend a thesis may lead, not to have taken as his rule, pure historic exactitude. Our thanks are due to the Carmelite Order for having generously thrown open its archives and shown its desire that everything concerning the Saint's life should be elucidated in detail and with nothing slurred over.

The author of the present work, relying on a new documentation of the first importance (the Carmelite archives have been carefully consulted, the process of beatification examined and photographed), has thus been able to throw light on some disputed points hitherto badly presented through want of sufficient study ; the manner in which the complicated skein of the relations and disputes between the Calced and Discalced Fathers has been unravelled is particularly admirable. Whilst the figure of Rubeo has been preserved in all its greatness and nobility, we are shown in detail the terrible opposition which John of the Cross encountered in the bosom of his own Order, and which, in its essential features, is one more example of the common lot of the contemplative—to be little liked by his brethren. *Ecce somniator venit :* one set of brethren throw Joseph down a well : another throw John of the Cross into prison and shorten his days by their ill-treatment. " The poor Fathers," said St. Teresa of Germain and John, " I would prefer to see them in the hands of the Moors, for they would assuredly find more mercy there." It was in his prison at Toledo that John found a sovereign, interior, liberty ; it was there, it would seem, that he passed through the supreme " horrors " of the night of the spirit that he might be raised to the state of transforming union. It was in this prison that, under divine inspiration [2] (which, as poets will be pleased to note, employs, as *instrument* of expression, the scholarly method of versification learned in the school of Boscan and Garcilaso de la Vega), he composed the *Spiritual Canticle*, and also, no doubt, the stanzas of the *Dark Night*. And it was from this prison that the Blessed Virgin helped him to escape.

Father Bruno has shown, with equal clearness, the essential *rôle* of St. John of the Cross in the reform of Carmel. As we read him we see that historians have often paid too much attention to Father Gracian, and thus falsified their perspective. There can be no doubt that it was John of the Cross who best understood and realised St. Teresa's idea, or, let us rather say, the will of the Holy Spirit working through Teresa. He alone succeeded in carrying it out consistently to the end. It should also be remembered that he destroyed the letters the saint wrote to him : hence, it would be incorrect to imagine, because we possess a large part of the correspondence addressed to Gracian, that she had a greater affection for the latter. Father Bruno is rightly somewhat severe on poor Gracian, rash, charming, too gifted by nature—he paid dearly for it,—and the very delicate and subtly drawn manner in which his book reveals Gracian's part, and responsibilities, in the progress of the reform, will be of special interest to historians. He is also persuaded by a close examination that Teresa esteemed John of the Cross above all others, even Gracian. Gracian was in truth more to the front in the Order : he was more *visible*. John of the Cross was too translucent to the Spirit, too concentrated on his own littleness, too absorbed by love to be visible. He was not a born ruler, even though he showed himself an admirable (and miraculous) prior of the convent of the Martyrs. The one office he was fully qualified to fill (in how masterly a fashion !) was that of forming souls to perfection. It is *normal* that men in whom living, immense, spiritual riches are stored, should be hidden, even in the bowels of the earth, which affords them a protection. When they emerge into the light it is to suffer treatment such as their Master suffered. An example of this truth is the passion of John of the Cross in his prison— " motionless as a stone," he was, no doubt, suffering for those who were to live by his doctrine.

Such men are too wise to have any desire to attract attention. When we reflect on them, we understand that, if silence is the father of preachers, it is also something greater than preaching, and that the function of those who speak in public, those who can be seen, is always, to a certain extent, something smaller, to which greater things must needs be sacrificed. The apostles fulfilled the office of preaching only in union with the Sacrifice of the Cross, and martyrdom awaited them at the end. Their contemplation was even loftier than their words. Christ alone, being the Word and the Splendour, could without any diminution, speak and manifest Himself. It is very probable that we should not have had any of the writings of John of the Cross without the prison and tortures of Toledo (and without his charity for certain holy souls). In any case, he never thought of teaching publicly. St. Teresa, speaking of his imprisonment, and the inexplicable powerlessness of his friends to assist him, made use of a striking phrase when she expressed her astonishment that she never met anyone who seemed to remember him.

Souls whose whole glory is from within—it is so with John of the Cross, as with Teresa of the Child Jesus—are rather discouraging " subjects " for the historian. He is wise, therefore, if he contents himself with elucidating, in as complete a manner as possible, the external circumstances of their lives, collecting with pious care all that can give us an idea of their spiritual likeness ; their inmost life, their thought, their spirit, will be found principally in their writings, and nothing can replace direct contact with the works and the doctrine of John of the Cross. It is one of Father Bruno's merits as an historian that he has, with as much humility as learning, thus regarded his task, and that, as he had to recount most complex events of the widest general bearing, he should untiringly recall our attention to the central figure of the saint. He has succeeded in placing the life of his subject in its exact framework, in reconstituting all the surroundings and circumstances that went to make up its human setting. In order the better to bring it before our eyes he went, never growing weary of the task of verification, to see all the places where the saint lived, and describes them for us ; towns and countrysides pass before our eyes, and, that the picture might be complete, he has attempted, where certain data are lacking, to reconstruct the details of place or circumstance—frankly telling us so, of course—in accordance with the probabilities of the case. May I add that, on this matter of external background, he and I are not in agreement ? I, for my part, have no wish for a colourless and conventional hagiography, but I should like one without the ornament of the picturesque. Yet I realise that many think differently, and that Father Bruno, in any case, always interests and certainly instructs— whether he takes us for a stroll through Salamanca, Avila, Toledo, Granada, Cordova, Seville, Segovia ; depicts the landscapes of Andalusia and Castile ; or faithfully notes every interesting fact, be it the age of a nun or the physical features of a monk, leaving no definite detail in the shade. We should recognise that the basis of this meticulous anxiety to note and tell us everything is a great love of truth, and we are bound to be grateful to the author, who has spent so much time and taken so much trouble to place us in a position to form our own judgments, and communicate to us the rich harvest of facts he has amassed.

One of the advantages of such a method is that, without the slightest preconceived idea on the point, from the mere setting out of facts, we come to see clearly the eminent superiority of John of the Cross when compared with other good and worthy Fathers of the Reform, who, though men of merit and virtue, were smaller men, of no far-reaching significance. (Leave out Nicholas Doria, whose virtues are too human, or, if you prefer, too inhuman !) These other men " suffered for the same cause, but in a different manner, just as they led different lives," as Father Bruno, when speaking of Gracian, very justly remarks.

We are especially grateful to our historian for enabling us to perceive, by brief glimpses through the leafy trellis of events, the real countenance of John in his holy humanity. It is quite enough that he should pass thus before us from time to time, for by the merest glimpse of that face of measureless purity one's soul is illumined and made strong. How wretched does Huysmans' exaggerated and repellent portrait look when confronted with the real man ! Moses, says the Scripture, was the meekest of men. The Doctor of the *Dark Night* was a lamb of meekness and compassion. Inflexible in all that concerned God's interests in souls, but singularly unrigid in method, free as the Spirit of God is free ; moderate, prudent, well aware of the conditions

of human nature, using means, like all great artists, as mere
means, never resting in them as ends—he led souls to the
great holocaust of divine union not by striking them down
like animals for slaughter, but by awakening light and love
within them : detaching them and bringing them to peace,
as we may see, in one instance among many, by the admirable
letter to Juana de Pedraza quoted by Father Bruno. When
he said to Ana de Peñalosa : " Nothing, nothing, nothing ;
even to strip oneself of one's very skin and all else for Christ,"
we should be deaf indeed, if we did not hear in that cry the
voice of Charity itself. It was out of his love and mercy for
souls that he grew indignant with ignorant and presump-
tuous spiritual instructors who " hammer like blacksmiths."

We are so gross-minded that we nearly always interpret
the doctrine of the saints, which is of its very essence spirit,
in an utterly material fashion. The life of St. John of the
Cross will be a great help to the understanding of his
doctrine, for the one is the perfect likeness of the other,
vividly fresh and sensitive—and dripping blood.

Speaking of the sadness John felt on one occasion at being
in Andalusia, and of his lament—" he has filled up the
measure of suffering," as St. Teresa remarked at that time—
Father Bruno refers, with accurate appreciation, to " what
we, in our insensitive language, would call the *weaknesses of
the saints*." " They cry aloud for mercy, and the *fiat* is
already manifested by the greater tenderness of their
heart." Such cries of desolation, echoes of the agony of
Gethsemane, far from revealing an imperfection, such as
may be met with even amongst saints, reveal, on the contrary, a simplicity and a candour in acknowledging what
one is, which are surely pleasing to God, and go to make
up an integral part of sanctity, even when the collapse of
the creature seems to be reaching the verge of despair.
" And my soul is removed far off from peace, I have forgotten good things. And I said, my end and my hope is
perished from the Lord " said Jeremias[3] ; and immediately
added, " The Lord is my portion, therefore I will wait for
Him." [4] Paul gloried in his weakness,[5] and with him all
the saints. In truth, if it be a sign of weakness to know one's

own infirmities fully, to have nothing whatever of one's own, to be vanquished by love, there are none more weak than those heroes of the will. They have dropped all bravado and boasting, they have relinquished all the strength of pride, for pure perfection is not the perfection of human power and striving, of a stoic impassivity, but the perfection of poverty and deprivation : all in order that, within this weakness and negation, there the strength of Him in whom we can do all things should abide in its plenitude, and produce, uphold, call into action a liberty, a resolve for self-mastery, and virtues surpassing all human standards, for they have no other rule and measure than the Spirit of God. That is a mystery which man is called on to live, and on which the saints throw light. And hence it is good for us to know that *Elias was a man like unto us.* But we also need to know, that, in another sense, the saints are not like us, base cowards as we are. Their weakness is not like ours. To be weak as they, to be strong as they, we must, as they did, lose ourselves and become a something that belongs to God, a nothing that is borne away by omnipotent love. " Whither the impulse of the Spirit was to go, thither they went ; and they turned not when they went ! " [6]

Let them be shown to us, then, as human, without diminishing their stature, and with that filial care for exactitude which gives so much worth to Father Bruno's book ; but, out of pity for our souls, do not humanise them as a whole literary school of the present day would have us do. We are dying of complacency and insipidity, of vulgarised and minimised truths, of a religion reduced to our own standards. " Death and destruction rather than sin," John of the Cross cries out to us. What we crave from him is his doctrine in all its severity, the example of his complete self-renouncement, his courage, his awe-inspiring patience, his tranquil tenacity in suffering, his entrance within a super-human world absolutely out of proportion with our standards : for just as the disintegrated atom, disintegrating, releases enormous physical forces, so in that world the soul, pierced through by love, and radiating at the highest pitch of spiritual concentration, releases pure divine energies. That life in spirit and in truth Father Bruno helps us to touch, almost with our hands, when he recounts the saint's last years—"Jesus ! This is what Thou hast done," as John said when he saw the bones and nerves of his leg exposed to the light of day.

As David danced before the Ark, so did John, at Christmas, with a statue of the Child Jesus in his arms ; he beat his fists against the walls that he might not be constantly rapt away in the Spirit ; when he spoke of God to St. Teresa, both of them, with their chairs, were raised aloft to the ceiling ; when a little sister sang, in his presence, of that sorrow which " is the vesture of those who love " he was again raised above the ground. " When he came to himself, he said they should not be surprised : that in his prison he had received so much light on the value of suffering, and had suffered so little for love." He prepared food for the sick with his own hands ; washed their utensils ; scourged himself till the blood came, lay at night on the steps of the altar, and prayed without ceasing : the mere sight of him, the touch of his cloak appeased temptations ; his experimental knowledge of the three Divine Persons caused his heart to faint away ; he knelt in the midst of flames, and commanded them. When Jesus asked him what he desired, he replied, " sufferings to be borne for Thy sake, and that I may be despised and counted as nothing." He asked three favours for his death : " Not to die a prelate ; to die in a place where he was not even known ; and to die after having suffered much " ; and he obtained them : " I shall be thrown into a corner like a rag or a dish-cloth," he said to Mary of the Incarnation. And Nicholas Doria did, in fact, send him to Peñuela in disgrace ; they were even thinking of stripping him of his habit, and expelling him from the Order. It was not from the Observants he had now to suffer, but from the friars of the Reform. An enlightened Job transfigured by the perfect peace and wisdom of Jesus : when we read the precious and terrible pages in which the historian describes his death, amidst tortures of suffering and abandonment, amidst joy and

heavenly illuminations, we see something of the secret of
his strength, and that the Lord shares His power with those
whom He unites to Himself in His own last agony.

    .   .   .   .   .   .

I should be loath, in a preface such as this, to refer to
doctrinal controversies with which I intend to deal elsewhere.
But the easy complaisance shown of late years in certain
learned reviews towards fundamentally erroneous inter-
pretations of the doctrine of St. John of the Cross compels
me briefly to define certain points.

St. John of the Cross, faithful to the apostolic tradition,
sees the whole of our human life here below directed to one
last end—the perfection of charity and transformation in
God by love ; contemplation is not, for him, an end in
itself ; it does not stop at knowledge, it is for the sake of love,
and of a loving union with God, and everything else is
ordained to the actual experience of this union. " There is
no better and no more necessary work than love." [7] " We
have been created only for this Love." [8] " God makes use
of nothing else but love." [9] " As love is the union of the
Father and the Son, so is it the union of the soul and God." [10]
Hence it is love itself that gives rise to contemplation, by the
supernatural love of charity, which brings us into intimate
relations with the Divine persons, and which, under a still
higher movement of the Holy Ghost, renders faith sweet and
penetrating, thereby setting it free from the modality of
human reasoning. And since this love is derived from faith,
which alone, in its superhuman obscurity, unites our
intellect with the abyss of the Deity, with the supernatural
subsistent, we are bound to affirm that a living faith, that
is to say, a faith " informed " by charity and enlightened by
the gifts of the Holy Spirit, is the very principle of mystical
experience, and the sole " proximate and proportionate
means " of divine union. [11] St. John of the Cross is never
wearied of repeating this truth.

His whole teaching is thus bound up with the essentially
supernatural order of faith and the theological virtues ; it
enables us to see that it is pure folly to seek, as so many poor

souls now do, for mystical experience apart from faith, or to imagine a mystical experience independent of theological faith.[12]   And all this doctrine is placed beneath the sign of that πολλὴ ἀγάπη of which St. Paul speaks, that "excess of love" which brought about the Incarnation and the Sacrifice of the Cross.   There is no more violent distortion, no more insupportable paradox, than that which would make St. John of the Cross an intellectualist in search of a highly rarefied and refined form of knowledge, a sort of supermetaphysic necessary to complete him.   What he himself desired for completion was suffering and contempt, for the sake of Him whom he loved.   He is a man transported out of himself by love of the true God, Who abides, by grace, in the soul ; and the wisdom that intoxicated him was derived from a loving union with the Blessed Trinity.[13] For the authentic meaning of his doctrine, ask Brother Albert of the Virgin, the porter of his convent, rather than the doctors of our Sorbonne : " Brother Albert of the Virgin, porter of the Convent of the Martyrs, was on the point of death.   His countenance was aflame, and shone with a celestial light which rendered it so marvellously beautiful that all were enraptured, and silently shed tears of joy. . . . Suddenly Brother Albert cried out in a loud voice : ' Ah ! I have seen it, Ah ! I have seen it, Ah ! I have seen it,' and immediately lowering his arms, crossed them on his breast.   As he was about to close his eyes, our Venerable Father John of the Cross hastened to ask him this question : ' Brother Albert, what have you just seen ? ' and he answered ' Love, love,' and remained in an ecstasy." [14]

   The nothingness, emptiness, night, renouncement of all that can be known and comprehended, of which he unceasingly teaches the necessity, has nothing whatever to do with a dialectical purification in the Neo-Platonist fashion ; it is a matter of becoming *love*.   " The perfect [soul] is wholly and entirely love." [15]   The spiritual doctrine of St. John of the Cross is not metaphysical, but evangelical ; it is the pure corollary and unfolding of the good tidings of our redemption ; the stripping which he preaches, and the emptying of the mind are just fundamental applications—

even in the very heaven of the interior life—of the law of the Cross, and of conformity with Christ, according to the law of the Beatitudes. To abide in utter spiritual poverty " is the soul's absolute duty, according to the counsel of the Son of God : he who does not renounce all that he possesses cannot be My disciple." [16] " Oh ! you souls, who dream of walking tranquilly, and with consolations, in the ways of the Spirit, if you but knew how it behoves you to be tried, and, by suffering, to reach security and consolation. If you only knew how impossible it is to attain without the trial of suffering the end to which your soul aspires, and how much ground the soul loses without this trial, you would never seek consolations, either from God or from creatures. You would prefer to bear the Cross, and, whilst attaching your-selves to it, would only ask vinegar and gall to drink." [17] In this fashion then, to transformation in God, which is the end, there corresponds the necessary means, which is the death and burial of the grain within the ground : *nisi granum frumenti*. . . . The whole supernatural order of the Incarnation and Redemption is bound up with it.

.   .   .   .   .   .

The saints have to do not only with philosophers, but also with—let us not say historians, who are a patient, modest, truthful, kindly and estimable race—but, let us say rather with " historiasters," a brood of parasites who batten on the material elements of texts to empty them of their vital content, and construct, from what remains, their own comfortable and erudite nest of pointless difficulties. Some of these, observing an analogy, and a very remote one at that, between the symbols of lamps and caverns—employed by John of the Cross to illustrate the divine attributes and the relation to them of the faculties of the soul—and the metaphor of light and the niche in the wall, to be found in the Koran (why not Aladdin's lamp also, and the caverns in the *Arabian Nights?*) have discovered Islamic influence in the mysticism of John of the Cross—without remembering, as Father Bruno points out (his acute remarks on Gazzali should likewise be noted), that lamps and caverns occur in

The Canticle of Canticles! And even if the saint did borrow from the Arabs as much of their imagery as you like (I have no desire to deny the value of such researches—in their proper place) the absurdity would still remain of seeing, in such borrowings, the faintest trace of *doctrinal influence*, properly so called. Others, perceiving the numerous differences between St. Thomas Aquinas's method of expression and that of St. John of the Cross, exercise their ingenuity in inventing conflicts of thought between those two doctors. All such attempts are mere word-spinning.

St. John of the Cross is, in reality, both far more independent of St. Thomas, and far more in harmony with him, than they imagine. On the one hand, his intellectual formation, the philosophical and theological structure of his thought, owe so much to the scholastic tradition—and especially to the purely Thomist tradition in Theology—that, to obtain a real understanding of the element of speculative knowledge in his writings, one should relate their essential principles to the teaching of St. Thomas Aquinas, as to their natural system of reference. And this is all the more significant inasmuch as, when St. John of the Cross does have recourse to the explanation of scholastic Theology, it is in a free and easy manner, without technical precision [18]; and, far from excluding the fathers and doctors who follow in the wake of the Angel of the Schools, he certainly and very rightly draws liberally on the common treasury, especially on St. Gregory and St. Bonaventure, whose writings, chiefly because of the devotion that animates them, seemed to him most suitable for the spiritual formation of his novices. It may be added that, if one is seeking for the fundamental roots of his teachings, they will be found in the theses developed (at a later date, and without the least allusion to John of the Cross) by John of St. Thomas—on God's indwelling in the soul of the just, and the gifts of the Holy Ghost, even before those theses are to be met with in the works of Carmelite theologians.[19] On the other hand, his own work and doctrine proceed, above all, from a direct experience of things divine, and are so free from the faintest concern as to their exact place in the comprehensive conspectus of any theological system, that, to judge merely from the surface (especially if the keys of Scholasticism are taken for locks) one might get an impression that he did not know how to adapt himself to the precise bounds of the *Summa Theologica*, and that, he is, at any moment, about to " go out through the roof," as they say ; as if the *Summa* had any other roof than the heavens.

The truth of the matter is this : the point of view of St. John of the Cross and the point of view of St. Thomas are quite different, though they deal with the same divine realities, the same mysteries of grace, the same truths. He was quite well aware of this himself (and, by that very fact, showed he was a good Thomist) when he wrote to Anne of Jesus, in the Prologue to *The Spiritual Canticle* : . . . " I only set about this work in order to be useful to Your Reverence, since you expressed a wish for it, and I know Our Lord has given you the grace to rise above first principles, so that He may introduce you further into the bosom of His love. This permits me to hope that, if I should chance to refer to some points of scholastic Theology concerning the interior relations of the soul with its God, I shall not have laboured in vain, in thus addressing myself to the pure intellect. It is true that Your Reverence is not accustomed to assimilate divine truths according to the method of scholastic Theology, but you are familiar with mystical Theology, which is acquired by love, in which one not only knows, but savours at the same time." [20] Not only, as Father Garrigou-Lagrange has so well shown,[21] is the language of mysticism necessarily different from that of philosophy ; but also the teachings of Thomas Aquinas and John of the Cross are to be referred to two manifestly different types of *science ; practical* science for St. John of the Cross, *speculative* science for St. Thomas.[22] The use of concepts, the mode of dealing with the real,[23] the ends pursued, are very different.

St. John of the Cross pursues an essentially practical end, he teaches " the straight road that leads to union," *el puro y cierto camino de la union*.[24] He speaks only " to say something profitable to the soul." [25] I have not space here to show in detail all the consequences of this difference of view-point. But it must be noted that the differences in the mode of expression between the two doctors can easily be seen in their true sense, and thus seen are instantly resolved into an essential harmony. I have pointed this out elsewhere,[26] when dealing with the character of *non agir* attributed by St. John, and the character of *supreme activity* attributed by St. Thomas, to infused contemplation. To take another example, referred to by Father Bruno in the present work (and the list might easily be prolonged), when John of the Cross in his *Spiritual Warnings* addressed to the Carmelite nuns of Beas, tells them to tear out by the roots all attachment to their families, does anybody imagine that he is here contradicting the common teaching of the Church, and, in particular, that of St. Thomas, on the love we owe our parents? On the contrary, he pre-supposes that teaching; I mean that he is quite well aware that the persons whom he is addressing are in no more danger of falling into hardness of heart than the contemplatives, to whom he teaches the way of nothingness, are in danger of falling into Quietism. He is *sure* of the souls whom he is addressing; they are above, not below, nature; fully prepared for the demands of the spiritual life, they can bear the whole weight of the Gospel, interpreted in all its practical rigour and in accordance with the most divine and secret of those meanings that lie hid beneath the letter. " If any man come to Me and hate not his father and mother . . . he cannot be My disciple." [27] John of the Cross says: " the first precaution is to maintain an equal love, and an equal forgetfulness, of all persons, whether or not they be related to us. . . . Look upon all your relations as strangers. . . . Do not think of them at all, neither well nor ill, avoid them, as far as you reasonably can." These prescriptions should be taken in all their force, without the least watering-down. But they must be rightly understood. They do not demand a mere external detachment, but a radical, internal one, a complete death; a radical renunciation of *proprietorship* in, and of the *purely natural exercise* of, our feelings, a renunciation that will make them live by means of a higher love, and not a radical destruction of the *ontological reality*, if one may so express it, of those feelings. There is all the difference between the superhuman and the inhuman, in those two deaths : for growth in the life of the spirit it is just as disastrous to yield to the second—that is to become hard and cold of heart ("The hearts of the saints," said the Curé of Ars, "were *liquid*")—as not to yield to the first, which would be a refusal of the perfection of love, and the price that must be paid for it.

John of the Cross addressed his *Cautelas* to souls determined to leave all for love, and already entered on the way of the spirit ; his own particular mission, his flaming secret, is to lead such souls straight to the end, and that without the loss of a moment. He knows that, for them, even the most legitimate natural affections, and especially attachments to their own families, are, if not radically renounced, one of the greatest obstacles (St. Philip Neri thought likewise, for he ordered his disciples to separate themselves entirely from their own relations) ; [28] how many religious remain mediocre, more or less deaf to the Spirit of God, and, sometimes, even to the voice of the Church, because they remain, in the cloister, too closely *attached* to family affections and prejudices ! His austere counsels are only the application to a particular case, and in an utterly spiritual sense, of St. Thomas's comment on St. Luke : "Our relations must be hated for God's sake, that is, if they should turn us away from God." [29] As the soul cannot attain the highest degree of charity—in which it loves itself in, and for, God—unless it hates itself,[30] that is to say, strips off its own natural love for personal welfare, in order fully to subordinate such love to supernatural charity,[31] so too, it is bound, not to destroy most assuredly its legitimate love for relations, but to subordinate it completely to charity, and, as far as may be necessary, tear out its own sense of proprietorship. Only then will it arrive at a perfect love of its own, in and for God, loving them indeed as its own, but according to God in a supernatural and incomparably deeper way. "*Detach* your heart from the former, as well as from the latter," St. John of the Cross writes in the same place. "You must, in a way, even detach yourself more from your relations, *fearing lest flesh and blood may come to life again, through the natural love which always exists between members of the same family*, and which must ever be *mortified in order to arrive at spiritual perfection.*" These lines, so definite and delicately shaded, supply, as has been rightly remarked, the true meaning of this first warning.[32] If St. John of the Cross had had to draw up the general laws of Ethics and the hierarchy of duties, he would assuredly not have spoken otherwise than St. Thomas has spoken in the Seventh and Eighth articles of *Quaestio* XXVI of the *Secunda Secundae*. If Thomas Aquinas had had to guide such souls to sanctity, can anyone doubt that he would have given (in another tone, perhaps, and in another style) the same advice as that given by John of the Cross to his spiritual daughters at Beas ?

Accidental and reconcilable differences between witnesses confirm the veracity of their evidence, by showing that their agreement was not premeditated. Both saints were skilled in both sorts of wisdom, the acquired and the infused (for the author of the *Spiritual Canticle* had received from his masters at Salamanca, and acquired for himself a solid knowledge of theology, and the author of the *Summa Theologica* had lived in the light of mystical contemplation), but each had a distinct office : and St. John of the Cross, from the point of view of mystical experience, and St. Thomas, from that of theological science, are witnesses to the same living Truth. Now, John of the Cross did not set himself to do the work of a scholastic theologian, but only to sing of what he knew divinely, and then to set forth in his commentaries the practical science of the way leading to such knowledge (though not without a reference to scholastic theology, as was inevitable) ; the movement of his thought, which is lyrical, concrete, and practical, abounding in psychological intuitions, is the very opposite to that of scholastic exposition ; in matters where a difference between points of view entails apparent contradictions,[33] he does not even dream of explaining these, nor of establishing a correspondence, to him self-evident, between his own language and the language of speculation. For all these reasons his fundamental agreement with St. Thomas is all the more significant. A disciple of the finest scholastic traditions in theology, but a disciple of the Holy Spirit in contemplation, writing only " of an experimental science he had lived," his special work was not to continue that of St. Thomas as a commentator, but rather to confirm it as a witness.

Whether it is a question of the relation between the senses and reason ; the distinction between the presence of immensity, whereby God is present in all things, and the presence of grace, whereby He inhabits the souls of the just ; [34] the efficacy of grace, and the liberty of creative and sanctifying love ; the nature of the end and the perfection of human life ; the nature of theological faith ; the relations of charity with the gifts and virtues ; the nature of mystical contemplation itself, and the primordial *rôle* played therein by love and the gifts of the Holy Spirit conjoined with faith ; [35] whether it be a question of that purity, whereby John of the Cross maintains more vigorously than any other mystic, the transcendence of the " secret " and " sacred wisdom " of infused contemplation in relation to metaphysical or theological speculation—in all that is most essential and fundamental, we have a revelation of the perfect unity existing between the doctrine of St. John of the Cross and the teaching of St. Thomas Aquinas. [36]

.   .   .   .   .   .

Happy they who choose for their masters, after Christ Himself, St. Thomas Aquinas, that they may thus obtain supreme communicable knowledge, and St. John of the Cross, that they may be guided towards supreme, incommunicable knowledge ! The doctrine of St. John of the Cross is the pure Catholic doctrine of the mystical life. We may well believe that, if he has been proclaimed in our own days a Doctor of the Church, it is because, like Thomas Aquinas, he meets a special need of the age. At the present day, Naturalism has so ruined and subverted Nature that there is no possible healing for Nature itself, no possible return to the stable order of reason, save by a full and complete recognition of the rights of the supernatural, the absolute, the demands of the Gospel and of a living faith.

Souls a-hunger for joy no longer hope for it. Dying of a desire to be loved, they sink, in crowds, into a mysticism of the creature, and a homesickness of the damned. What they ask for, without knowing it, is that the true countenance of love may be revealed to them.

In the general break-up of the framework of human society, each of us is called on to add to his own weakness a burden of heroism. We need the sternest secrets of wisdom and strength. The Cross lies heavy, with all the weight of love misunderstood, on an ungrateful world, groaning in vain, and loathing it ; nothing remains but to love the Cross dearly ; it will bear us onwards, as, with swift prow, it cleaves the waters of eternal life. What better pilot than the Doctor of the Dark Night ?

The doctrine—held to-day by the best theologians—that all souls, from the mere fact that they are called to the happiness of Heaven, are also called by a general and common call, to enjoy even whilst on earth, by means of infused contemplation, the first fruits of this beatitude, is in full conformity with the teachings of St. John of the Cross. He does not address himself especially to those who are aided by extraordinary graces to advance more swiftly (but not without danger) in the way of the spirit ; the only *means* demanded by him are first a living faith and that organism of supernatural gifts wherewith every soul in the state of grace is endowed, and then the whole ascetical practice of the virtues (as described in *The Ascent of Mount Carmel*), in terms of the special characteristics it assumes in relation to the contemplative life—a practice which lasts for the whole period of spiritual progress. From this point of view it may be said that he addresses all those who are on the way to Christian perfection, whatever may be their particular path : " To one and all, provided they have made up their mind to pass through nakedness of spirit." [37] But it is only when they have reached a certain stage of their journey, when they have attained a certain degree of perfection that he thus speaks. Bearing this in mind, and he underlines the point on several occasions, we are bound to say that he is speaking only to those souls upon whom the divine life has already been at work, and who—having already practised meditation (which they will one day leave aside) and asceticism (which they never will leave aside)— hear themselves summoned by name, and directly, to contemplation. It has been very properly remarked that " it would be an extremely dangerous error to apply indiscriminately the rules laid down by the Mystical Doctor to every soul, from the very first steps in the spiritual life." [38] To counsel heroic passivity, which is the soul's supreme renouncement, to a person who must act for himself, and who has not been deprived, *by God,* of the " human mode " of acting, would be to ruin his whole spiritual life. It is the mark of the Quietist to place himself, by thus usurping divine action, in such a state of passivity. St. John of the Cross, like Ruysbroeck, as Father Bruno justly remarks, was a pitiless enemy of Quietism, and it was to guard against it (and especially against the Quietism of the *Alumbrados*) that he insists so strongly on the authentic signs indicating the dawn of the mystical life.

But, if there are Christians over whom their God has not sufficiently triumphed, who cannot understand St. John of the Cross, who are frightened at his doctrine, as if it prescribed mutilation or suicide, or who grow deluded by not reading him aright, and manufacture a counterfeit mysticism for themselves, there are other souls, separated from God, and tortured by those evil powers that are overwhelming modern life, who find in him the instrument of their salvation. No doubt, they cannot fully understand his doctrine. But he reveals to them, depicted with strokes of flame, the real way to tear off and cast aside the whole lying pretence of our wretched masquerade, telling them in one word for what they have been created. And that may suffice to save them. I knew a youth of twenty, haunted by the desire of deliverance, knowing not how to attain it, who, urged on by a poetry that was false and of the devil, had gone far in spiritual experiences wherein the soul, emptied and overwhelmed, but not by God, enjoyed a deceptive taste of infinite liberty and domination, an ecstasy of nothingness. A certain person, foreseeing that, as the youth had reached the dark night of the depths, he could only be healed by a vision of the veritable, superhuman night, gave him an abstract of the doctrine of St. John of the Cross, consisting of the most significant and startling passages of the saint's works.[39] A fortnight later the boy was suddenly struck down with illness ; called to his bedside, I saw him, once again, disfigured and dying ; in a few hours his death agony was to begin. He had sent that morning for a priest, and questioned him about religion, for he was anxious to obtain further dogmatic teaching ; he had then made his confession, and received Holy Communion. " What joy ! " he said to me, " I now know what joy means. And it has all come about through St. John of the Cross." Henceforward, for me, the thought of the saint and his doctrine will be inseparable from the image of that predestined soul.

JACQUES MARITAIN.

AUTHOR'S PREFACE

IT may be well, at the beginning of this work, to let the reader know the sources on which I have mainly drawn. M. Jean Baruzi, in an appendix to his scholarly, but exceedingly subjective, book, *St. Jean de la Croix et le problème de l'expérience mystique* (Paris, Alcan, 1924) goes so far as to say that " the primary sources " of a biography of St. John of the Cross are certain manuscripts in the *Biblioteca nacional* at Madrid—especially No. 12738—" which seem to have been composed in the main from evidence collected [1] for the Process of Canonisation " (p. 723, etc.). Whilst recognising the importance of the documents collected by biographers from 1597 onwards, I still think I am right in saying that those preserved at Madrid can in no way be regarded as the " primary source." Rev. Father Florencio del Niño Jesús, who is well acquainted with the Madrid Archives, quite rightly pointed out that the *fuente fundamental* of a " complete and authentic " biography is not to be found in Madrid, but in Rome.[2] I have drawn largely upon these Roman documents.[3] The Archives of the Sacred Congregation of Rites contain both the preliminary process of Inquiry (1614–1618) and the Apostolic Process (1627–1628) for the Beatification of Father John of the Cross. It also contains all the depositions taken, in conformity with the Canonical Laws, before the tribunals set up for that purpose. That fact alone is enough to show their value.

Rev. Father Louis de la Trinité made a full examination of this double process—it had never been done before—and had photographic copies taken of the chief documents in Rome, whilst I was working in Spain. The reader may be referred to his careful study : *Le Procès de Béatification de St. Jean de la Croix et le Cantique spirituel,*[4] in which will be found a short inventory and abstract of the documents as well as a valuable contribution to the critical edition of the Saint's works, now in course of preparation. It is to be hoped that our confrère may, after the appearance of this volume, collaborate effectively by publishing a purely theological study of the doctrine of St. John of the Cross.

The present work is mainly a study of the life and person of the Doctor of the Universal Church. And to see him as he lived helps towards a better grasp of the meaning of his teaching.

Thanks to Father Benedict Mary of the Holy Cross (Zimmerman), to whose indefatigable research so many precious data are owing, it is possible to reconstitute the Carmelite life of John of Yepes before he joined the Reform undertaken by St. Teresa. Amongst the valuable documents, in the absence of which this attempt could never have been made, may be mentioned the *Constitutions of the Reform of R. Nicholas Audet*, prior-general from 1524 to 1562, and those of M. John Baptist Rubeo of Ravenna, who governed the Order from 1562 to 1578. These last are very rare ; there is one copy in the Barberini Library in the Vatican, and another in the Bodleian at Oxford. Finally must be named Rubeo's *Regestum*, containing the official acts of his government of the Order. I must thank R. F. Beltrán de Heredia, professor of the history of theology in the old Dominican Convent of San Esteban at Salamanca, for having kindly given me his advice in regard to the important chapter on Salamancan studies. Thanks to the able directions of Don. Miguel Asín Palacios, professor of the University of Madrid, and M. Louis Massignon, professor of the Collège de France, it has been possible to sketch the world of Granada at the end of the sixteenth century, when John of the Cross was writing his great treatises at the Convent of *Los Martires*.

Thanks are also due to Sr. Gallego Burín, now professor in the University of Salamanca, and to Sr. Torres Balbás, architect-curator of the Alhambra.

Others at home and abroad to whom much gratitude is due are : Father Eliseus of the Nativity—for valuable help given throughout, especially in my study of the process—and my Spanish brothers and sisters in religion for their warm welcome when I was travelling in Castile and Andalusia accompanied by Rev. Father Dominic, especially Father Silverio de Santa Teresa and Father Evaristo de la Virgen del Carmen ; the sisters, too, of the Royal Carmelite Convent in Brussels, the guardians of the body and of the precious memories of the Venerable Anne of Jesus.

Unworthy though I be to trace the portrait of our great father, I have always borne in mind Pope Leo's words : " The first law of History is not to dare to tell a lie ; and the second, not to fear to tell the truth." [5]

FATHER BRUNO OF JESUS-MARY, O.D.C.

PARIS, *February 2nd,* 1929.

EDITOR'S NOTE

It will be noticed that the names of some of the people mentioned in this book are in Spanish, others in English : in this we have in general followed the usage of the original work.

At the moment of the publication of this English translation of the Life of St. John of the Cross a new French edition of the original work is in the Press, of which unfortunately we were unable to obtain an advance copy. We understand that in view of a revised edition of the work of M. Baruzi, the author has altered his remarks concerning the latter's opinions, and also that in consequence of the important essay by Sr. Asín Palacios, *Un précurseur hispano-musulman de saint Jean de la Croix*, which appeared in the *Etudes carmélitaines mystiques et missionnaires* (April, 1932), Fr. Bruno has been able, in the XVIIth chapter of this work, to discriminate with greater precision between true and false mysticism in the centre of Islam.

B. Z.

Kensington, April 26th, 1932.

LIST OF ABBREVIATIONS

I. O.	. .	Preliminary process of Inquiry. (1614–1618).
P.A.	. .	Apostolic process. (1627–1628).
B.N.M.	. .	National Library of Madrid.
Alonso	. .	*Vida virtudes y milagros del Sancto Padre Fray Juan de la Cruz.* Tomo Quinto, por el Padre Fray Alonso de la Madre de Dios Asturicense. B.N.M. MS. 13460. (This MS. *Life*—composed by the Procurator for the Inquiries held in Segovia, Avila, Jaén, Ubeda, Alcaudete, from 1616 to 1618—leaves intact, notwithstanding its importance, the value of the *Life* written by José de Jesús-María, who often quotes from Alonso. MS. 13460 has no pagination. There are 220 leaves, but only 381 pages are written.)
Andrés	. .	*Memorias Ystoriales en Orden a laes Obras de Sta Theresa de Jesus, y San Juan de la Cruz, sacadas de monumentos de nro Archivo gen¹* por Fray Andrés de la Encarnación. B.N.M., MS. 13482 (cuaderno 1⁰), from A to J inclusive, is chiefly concerned with St. John of the Cross.
Vel.	. .	*Vida . . . del Venerable Varon Francisco de Yepes . . .* 1615, by F. José de Velasco. B.N.M. U/9935, libros raros.
Acta Cap. Gen.	.	*Acta Capitulorum Generalium Ordinis Fratrum B.V. Mariae de Monte Carmelo.* Vol. I ab anno 1318 usque ad annum 1593 cum notis praecipue a R.P. Benedicto Zimmerman O.D.C. mutuatis . . . edidit Fr. Gabriel Wessels. (Rome, 1912.)
Quir.	. .	*Historia de la Vida y Virtudes del V.P.F. Juan de la Cruz . . .* by Father Joseph of Jesus Mary (Quiroga) Brussels, 1628.
Cyp.	. .	A translation of the foregoing by Eliseus of St. Bernard and Cyprian of the Nativity. (Paris, 1642.)

Jer. . . .	*Historia del V.P.F. Juan de la Cruz.* . . by F. Jeronimo de S. Josef . . . Madrid, 1641.
Ref. . . .	*Reforma de los Descalzos de Nuestra Señora del Carmen* . . . 7 vols. by different authors. (Madrid, 1655–1739.)
Bibl. Carm. .	*Bibl. Carmelitana*, notis criticis et dissertationibus illustrata, by Father Cosmas de Villiers. (Orleans, 1752.)
Arch. C. R. Bruss.	Archives of the Royal Carmelite Convent of Brussels. (Founded by V. Mother Anne of Jesus.)
Ger. . . .	*Obras del místico Doctor San Juan de la Cruz.* . . Edited by Father Gerardo de San Juan de la Cruz. 3 vols. (Toledo, 1912–1914.)
Subida . .	*The Ascent of Carmel.*
Noche . .	*The Dark Night.*
Cantico . .	*The Spiritual Canticle.*
Llama . .	*The Living Flame of Love.*
Cautelas . .	*Spiritual precautions.*
Avisos . .	*Four Counsels to a Religious.*
Silv. . .	*Obras de Santa Teresa de Jesús.* Edited by Father Silverio de Santa Teresa, 9 vols. (Burgos, 1915–1924.)
C.P. . . .	*Œuvres complètes de Sainte Térèse de Jésus* (a French translation by the Carmelites of the first Monastery of Paris, with the help of Mgr. Polit . . . 6 vols. have appeared. (Paris, 1907–1910.)
Vida . .	*Life* (of St. Teresa), written by herself.
Relaciones .	*Spiritual Relations.*
Camino . .	*The Way of Perfection.*
Moradas . .	*The Interior Castle.*
Fund . .	*The Book of Foundations.*
Greg. . .	*Lettres de St. Thérèse de Jésus* (a translation into French by Father Gregory of St. Joseph, 3 vols.), 2nd ed. (Rome, Pustet, 1905.)
Bar. . .	*St. Jean de la Croix et le problème de l'expérience mystique*, by Jean Baruzi. (Paris, Alcan, 1924.)

ST. JOHN OF THE CROSS

CHAPTER I

FONTIVEROS

THE traveller who goes up from Salamanca to the holy city of Avila crosses the plateau of Old Castile, rich with fields of yellow corn ripening in the June sunshine. Not far from the station of Crespos a village with a population of some 1,600 stands out clear and delicate against the dark-blue twilight sky. A walk of dark poplars, *chopos*, leads up to it and, here and there, a lagoon makes a patch of brightness along the roadside. This is Fontiveros, where St. John of the Cross was born in 1542.[1]

It was amidst the sound of chiming bells that the third son of Gonzalo de Yepes and Catalina Alvarez was carried to the parish church of St. Cyprian.

Nothing really ever changes in this land of traditions. The grey clay street, as hollow as the bed of a river, is the same as ever. It is quite in keeping with all the rest, and goats may skip about in it at their ease. A charming convent for Discalced Carmelites was built in 1723, on the site of St. John's birthplace. But, if we wish to summon up the past, we still have the white line of one-storied little houses, with roofs that are almost completely flat. The window, with its mysterious grille, is deeply embedded in the thick wall. The panelled, pine-wood door still has its worm-eaten wooden lock and the upper and lower leaves that were thrown wide open to receive the child on his return from the baptismal font. The procession passed along the public square, by the palace of the bishop of Jaen, Don Alonso Suarez, which was occupied by the Carmelites de la Madre de Dios from 1603. The little twelve-year-old fellow in front was Francisco, John's elder brother, whom he later loved more than anyone in the world.[2]

Gonzalo had been living in the town for at least thirteen years since his marriage to Catalina, who was, like himself, from Toledo, but not of noble birth. Catalina had been living with a widow, who had taken a fancy to her and brought her to Fontiveros, where she employed her at her own silk looms. Gonzalo knew this lady, and used to stay with her when taking the silks in which his uncle traded to the *ferias* at Medina del Campo.

Thus Gonzalo met Catalina Alvarez. The young girl had no wealth save her beauty and her virtue, but these were out of the common,[3] and it was for them alone that Gonzalo loved her. He was of " rich and noble parentage," [4] but what did that matter? The grandson of the Hidalgo Francisco Garcia de Yepes, man-at-arms to John II, did not think of his *limpia sangre*, his pure blood, of which all Castilians were so proud : he took no pleasure in being reminded that he had one uncle, the *bachiler* de Yepes, an Inquisitor at Toledo, and four more, three of them Canons and the last principal chaplain of the mozarabic chapel, all severe and very strong-minded personages.[5] His hostess knew them well, and the fine plans they had made for their nephew. Gonzalo married the beautiful Catalina and paid dearly for marrying beneath him—his family " abhorred her." [6]

The young couple, who were without means, set up house at Fontiveros and from Catalina Gonzalo bravely took lessons in weaving wool and silk. Henceforward he nobly wore the livery of the poor. Catalina, like a true Toledan, kept her home scrupulously clean. Her clothes were poor, but she took such care of them, and wore them with so much grace that long after she had left the district three old ladies still spoke of her as a " person of quality." [7] The young couple had a hard time of it, for they could rely only on the work of their own hands. The Creator blessed this home so like the home at Nazareth. Francisco and Luis were already growing up when John was born.

Shortly before his birth Gonzalo fell sick ; he may, perhaps, have had a previous illness. Velasco tells us that he suffered patiently for two years. He rests to-day, with Luis, beneath a flagstone in the centre of the Church of St. Cyprian.

After Gonzalo's death Catalina was forced to give black bread to her children, so she made up her mind to try to get help from her husband's people at Toledo. She set out with her three children for Avila, crossed the Sierra de Gredos, and went down to Torrijos. After an unsuccessful attempt with the uncle who was an Archdeacon,[8] she walked on to Galvez, five leagues from Toledo. There was a doctor living there, an uncle of her children, and he at once welcomed Francisco as his son, and promised to help Catalina. Francisco remained only a year with his uncle, and his biographer tells us that " it was a noviciate of work and suffering " for the twelve-year-old child.[9]

On returning to Fontiveros, Catalina at once set to work as weaver in order to earn a living. She sent the three children to school, but as Francisco was not very far advanced for his age, she taught him her own trade. To-day there are no longer any weavers at Fontiveros ; the population is wholly agricultural. And yet it is easy to imagine Catalina Alvarez's humble home. She worked close to the window, in the front room, with its whitewashed walls and ceiling crossed with dark brown beams. In one corner a pitcher of water, and in the other a chest. In the middle, a square table covered with a gaudy cloth, and, underneath it, a copper *brasero* with its protecting network, which shed a penetrating warmth throughout the room during the cold winter months.

Facing the door was a little altar, on which was deposited a statue of Our Blessed Lady, as it went in procession from house to house. Little lamps burned before *Maria Purisima*. It was on his mother's knees, close to this little altar, that the Doctor of the Dark Night, like all little Castilians, learned to love Mary, the Morning Star.[10] " The angels are mine and the Mother of God." * John, as a little boy, behaved, we are told, like an angel.[11]

* " Los angeles son mios y la Madre de Dios." *Aphorisms of St. John of the Cross*, (Andujar text, fo. 5), Baruzi edition. (Paris, Féret, 1924). *Avis et maximes de St. Jean de la Croix.* P. Grégoire de St. Joseph. Rennes, 1919.

In all probability the first event to sadden John de Yepes was the death of Luis.

Shortly after the fire which nearly destroyed the great and noble Church of St. Cyprian, John, who was then four or five years old, set off with his little companions to the outskirts of the village, beyond the *huertas* with their green trees surmounted by grey walls. They began to play not very far from the venerable Carmelite Convent de la Madre de Dios, which the Most Reverend Father Rubeo, general of the order, was to visit on April 10th, 1567, before setting out to see Teresa of Jesus at Avila.[12] There were ponds in the neighbourhood, and the child began to throw sticks into the water, amusing himself by seizing them as they came to the surface. All of a sudden he fell in, and the water reached up to his neck. He was nearly drowned, when a most beautiful lady appeared above him. John knew it was the Queen of the Angels, and Mary lovingly said to him : " Give me your hand, child, and I will take you out."

Forty years after, at Baeza and Granada, Luis de San Angelo often heard the Saint repeat with pleasure, laughing, and making fun of himself, that, seeing such a beautiful, resplendent lady with such lovely shapely hands, he made up his mind not to give her his own grubby little fists, but tucked them under his arms. A workman was passing, goad in hand, and John's little comrades ran up crying : " Pull out the little boy who is drowning in the mud." The man ran up and held out his goad, shouting, " Catch hold of it, child." John did not hesitate, he seized the goad and struggled out. But the lady with the lovely shapely hands had disappeared.[13]

This marvellous event took place when famine and drought were desolating Fontiveros. No doubt people went to pray to Christ Crucified in the parish church. It is likely enough that Catalina took John to these public prayers. The child's dark eyes rested on the face of the Crucified racked with pain, the mouth wide open, and locks of real hair hanging down the cheeks as far as the tortured shoulders. Catalina wept, not so much for the misery that famine brought on herself, as for her children's hunger. The Castilian woman is heroic. She is of the race of Jimena Blasquez and Maria de Padilla, one of whom defended the walls of Avila against the Moors, and the other the walls of Toledo against Charles the Fifth. But she had a tender heart and was passionately fond of her children, like the women of Galicia and the Asturias whose Celtic blood also ran in her veins. Catalina, without work or resources, made up her mind to leave Fontiveros, to which her heart and soul were bound by so many precious memories.

And so little John left his native village. There is no manuscript evidence that he ever returned, but we may safely say that there is no place in Spain that preserves such a tender, living memory of him. The peasants have taken him as the patron saint of their confraternity. Two novenas are held in his honour, one ending on May 1st, and the other, which is more solemn, on his feast day. St. John of the Cross too, sends showers of roses. Late one evening I heard an account of a recent miracle from the Jimenes family. The fine old men who were standing round in a circle recalled the fact that all the lads from Fontiveros, who had gone to the wars in Cuba and Africa, returned safe and sound : their heavenly fellow-citizen had protected them.

But there are other, and still more precious favours. . . . In the peaceful little Carmelite Church, so white and clean, I said Mass on the very spot where John was born. To the clear tones of the convent bell, rung by Bonifacio, men carried in benches, and women and children flocked in. In a few moments not a sound could be heard, not the least murmur ; nothing but a great spiritual silence, that wrapped all things in peace. The flame of a candle planted in the ground lit up those brown, attentive, impassive faces. The priest began : "*Nos autem gloriari oportet in Cruce Domini Nostri Jesu Christi . . .*" [14]

CHAPTER II

THE SERVANT OF THE POOR

It was not till some years after her husband's death that Catalina went to seek employment with a weaver of Arevalo, six leagues from Fontiveros. This piece of information, which Velasco [1] no doubt obtained from Francisco de Yepes himself, is in conformity with local tradition, and seems to be most probable. One cannot imagine Catalina leaving Fontiveros, where the people thought all the more highly of her in proportion to her misfortunes, just as she had made up her mind to persevere in a trade which had hitherto secured a livelihood for her little family. It needed " famine and poverty " [2] to force her to abandon the cottage in which her children had been born, and the spot where Gonzalo and Luis slept in peace.

John found himself in contact with the Castille of soldiers and saints in this medieval city of Arevalo, built on a rock bathed by the Adaja. The five massive towers of the old feudal fortress, the *casas solariegas* of the knights of long ago, spoke sternly to his young soul, whilst his mother and brother bent over the looms of a master who was no longer the gentle Gonzalo, struggling for existence, earning their daily bread.

It was probably during this stay at Arevalo that the child began to learn various trades. He was old enough to be apprenticed and Catalina was too prudent to leave his little hands idle. He was placed in turn with a carpenter, a tailor, a wood carver, and a painter. Although John was brave, and well aware of the dire necessity, he had no great liking for these employments. [3] His mind went out towards spiritual realities, for he was a born contemplative. Divine wisdom alone appealed to him, and it was this " folly of the Cross "—if we are to believe Alonso—that urged the nine-year-old child to sleep at night on vine branches as a penance. [4]

There were several convents and seven parochial churches at Arevalo, and the Yepes frequented them. Two sacristans, who cannot have been up to much, compelled Francisco to steal some bitter almonds. This peccadillo was followed by bitter repentance, and Francisco promised to change his life. At Arevalo he married a respectable girl from Muriel, who was as poor as himself, and whose name was Aña Isquierda. They had eight children, seven of whom died young. One daughter became a Bernardine nun in the Convent of the Holy Ghost at Olmedo. And later on, in the vision at Segovia, a niece of John's will be found sharing in the glory of Catalina Alvarez. Francisco was twenty-one years of age when he went to Medina del Campo, with his mother, wife and brother, in order to set up in business. John,[5] then, must have been twelve years of age—if Velasco's chronology be adopted.

Once more the reason for this new exodus is, perhaps, poverty, for we know from another source that it was a year of *mucha carestia*. John was sent to the College of the Children of Doctrine at Medina del Campo, to be fed not only in mind but in body.[6]

He was very " sweet-tempered and wise " : *muy bonito y muy agudo*," [7] and he learned to read and write—for there was nothing else taught in that primary school—in a very short time. The nuns were amazed at him, and grew very fond of him. John helped by begging alms for the school children, and here too he showed himself " clever and able." [8] This is a valuable piece of information, worth bearing in mind. We are not dealing with a little dreamer, for whom the external world does not exist, for his dark eyes had already penetrated its bitter reality. Nothing matures a child more quickly than the feeling that his own are in need. He reacts instinctively to it, and would like to be grown up in order to face poverty and want. Juan de Yepes stretched out his hand, and it is hard to do that, even when one does it from fraternal charity. But his family circle soaked him in true Christianity. Catalina was " most charitable." One day she picked up a poor child at a church door and kept it as her own until it died.[9]

Francisco brought up foundlings,[10] for this elder brother loved poverty and begged it from God as a favour.[11] Even his home, where everything spoke of poverty, was to make John tender towards those little poor men, his brethren.

Medina was, at this time, one of the most important commercial centres in Spain,[12] and men from Italy to the Low Countries flocked there for the *ferias*. During the ninety days of the great fair there was nothing but an intense, feverish activity, from the heights of the impregnable Castillo de la Mota, through the *Rua* and its surroundings, down to the red and green pillared galleries of the Plaza Mayor. French and Dutch cloth, Flemish tapestries, books printed in Italy, Cordoban leather, silks from Valencia and Granada were unpacked, set out for sale, and purchased all the day long. So great was the business transacted there that a merchant, from profits made during one *feria*, built the Great Hospital. Others, it is true, went bankrupt. There were places reserved in the market-place for English, Dutch and German money-changers and a stone line still marks the site of their booths.

John gazed upon all this prodigious display of the great world's productivity, and his artistic temperament was aroused. His own brother wove linen and silk too, silk especially.[13] It was all beautiful and good, the work of the children of the Creator. But his soul was not attached to it for long. There he stood with outstretched hand, whilst the crowd was preparing to hear Mass, which was celebrated on the balcony of San Antolin. He ceased collecting when the bronze men and woman, a munificent gift from Isabella the Catholic, struck the hour for retiring from the ridge of the Collegiate Church.

Whilst John was at the primary school he used to go to the monastery of Magdalens, not only to serve Mass—which he also did in other churches—but to act as sacristan.[14] The monastery is in the *Calle Santiago* opposite the proudly blazoned *palacio* of its founder, Roderico de Duenas. It is said that Charles the Fifth spent a night there, in 1556, on his way to the Hieronymites at Yuste ; and this is probably true, as Roderico was a member of the Financial Council,

and had often been at court. The Emperor probably heard Mass in the Church, so that John would have seen him at close quarters.

This magnificent palace is now occupied by the poorer classes, and animals—not merely birds—make themselves at home in the *patio* and on the carved staircases of the interior. It is a great pity, but as it still wears its ancient air of grandeur we may be grateful that, at any rate, it has not been destroyed.

The Calle Santiago is a real, authentic, sixteenth-century street: what the Spaniards rightly call "Teresian," a "*sanjuanista*," street. There is a convent founded by St. Teresa close by, but, at this time, she had no thought of making foundations. The young sacristan was only fourteen years of age, and we can walk along this side street with him, between the high, flat, red-brick walls—the Castillo and Collegiate Church are built of the same material—and from them acquire an impression of warmth and force.

Francisco tells us that his brother was at length selected for the service of the poor by a *caballero*, who had left the world and retired to a hospital.[15] Was Alonso Alvarez de Toledo first approached by Catalina, or did he take the preliminary steps himself, and offer John employment in the hospital, of which he was the warden? Had he remarked his skill in begging for the poor? Was it self-interest, personal inclination or just pure charity that led him to Catalina's son?

Juan de Yepes was of low stature. When full grown he was only about five feet two, if we are to judge from the tibia venerated at Ubeda, which is only thirteen and a half inches in length. But this smallness was no great hardship for, it would seem, he was strongly made.

His air of reflection drew men; and still more his face, which was a rather full oval in shape, his complexion a warm brown, lighted up by dark eyes. He had a broad, high forehead, well-marked eyebrows, and an almost aquiline nose. It conveyed an impression of nobility and peace like some of Zurbaran's pictures of Carthusian monks.[16] Juan de Yepes looked his breeding. It is quite possible that Alonso Alvarez de Toledo took a fancy for the youth, both for his spiritual qualities and personal charm.   But, at any rate, Catalina's son worked willingly under his orders[17], either at the hospital of the Conception or at that of San Antonio, until his twenty-first year.   We know from Francisco that John was employed in collecting alms for the poor, and in the small-pox hospital [18] ;   and this sheds a double beam of light, not only on his youth but on his whole life.

From the very springtime of his life, John's heart was wide open to the sufferings of others :   and later, describing the torments of the soul—when, having crucified its appetites, it is passing through the Dark Night, he never lay prostrate within his own interior abyss, insensible to our sufferings. We shall never see him " at the end of the journey, dry-eyed, terrible, bleeding," as Huysmans imagined him.[19]   No : St. John's symbol is not that " ardent and sombre lily of torture," but the burning pomegranate of love.

Even if there were no documents to rely on we might feel certain that his presence in the hospital during the best years of his youth was his own personal wish.   He had " the wisdom of an old man," says Fernandez de Bustillo, who knew him as a child.[20]   Apart from the services John could have rendered in any of the sixteen parishes then in Medina, he might easily have become a monk, from his fifteenth year onward.   Pious and intelligent as he was, he would have been received into any novitiate.   Even in the eighteenth century the city still contained eighteen monasteries.[21] Yet Juan de Yepes did not take the habit until he was twenty-one.   Just now, with the young life bubbling in his veins, he was content to stretch out his hands on behalf of the poor and fever-stricken.

At that time there was a remarkable physician in the hospitals of Medina, Gomez Pereira.   A recent historian of St. John of the Cross [22] has spoken of him at length, though he admits that we have no proof that John had anything to do with him.   This Pereira tells us that the years 1556 and 1557, when John most probably began to work in the hospital, were remarkable for their epidemics of fever, and this fact reveals the generosity of the youth's decision to follow Don Alonso de Toledo.

According to Velasco, Francisco de Yepes placed his young brother in the hospital to further his desire for learning.[23] Did his benefactor make him an actual promise on the matter? In any case, John's services were so highly appreciated that he was " given permission to attend the grammar lessons in the College of the Society of Jesus," [24] established at Medina, in the summer of 1551, at the request of Rodrigo de Dueñas. The college had then been in existence only a few years. Father Maximiliano Capella had begun a course on philosophy, and invited young men to attend without payment. The sons of St. Ignatius, as is their wont, spent themselves generously at Medina. Whilst Capella taught Aristotle, Bautista Sanchez preached fervently in the churches and public squares, taught catechism and visited the prisons and hospitals. Such conduct is not always understood. On November 22nd, 1552, the Abbot of Medina, Diego Ruiz de la Camera, the city's ecclesiastical superior, sent a notary to tell the Jesuits that he forbade them to preach and hear confessions until he had had them examined. Padre Sevillano, the rector, who was not yet a priest, accompanied by Diego Castillo, at once went to the abbot, who, in a rage, and before they opened their lips, called them robbers, brigands and impostors, and ordered his alguazils to take the rector off to the *cepo* for punishment. When this became known, a number of people hastened to the abbot, who little by little let himself be appeased. Indeed, at the beginning of August, 1553, St. Francis Borgia was allowed to lay the first stone of a Church, now the *iglesia Santiago*. Fathers and brothers worked at the building with their own hands, and this so moved the passers-by that knights might have been seen laying aside their golden capes and swords and, clad in their silken doublets, carrying bricks and sand. Peace was fully established in 1555, and the Jesuits began to teach Latin, which was an inestimable boon, seeing the crass ignorance of Medina, both rich and poor.[25]

We know, from Francisco, that John's tutor was Father Bonifacio:[26] this young father, who was still a novice, began teaching the third class in grammar in November or

December, 1557. In 1561, he taught the fourth and fifth classes.[27] It would seem as if these were the years John spent at college. At the earliest, it was 1556 when Don Alvarez de Toledo first noticed the youthful sacristan.

Any attempt to show that Catalina's son had a complete secondary education would be an exaggeration that would not bear the test of fact. Francisco testifies that John attended the lessons in grammar.[28] Another and remoter source amplifies this statement : " *en este Hospital estudio gramatica, Retorica, y curso de Artes.*" [29]

The process of canonisation says " grammar and philosophy." [30] It is possible that John had the benefit of Jesuit teaching till he left the hospital for the Carmelite novitiate in 1563. There is no indication that the permission given him by Alvarez was withdrawn after he had finished his studies in grammar. But against these probabilities is one certain fact. Francisco, who was in John's company during this whole period, tells us that he was allowed " only a few moments " for study " in the morning and evening." [31] He needed only a minute or two, indeed, to reach the end of the Calle Santiago, where the college was situated, especially if the hospital is placed where local tradition asserts there was a well, into which John fell one day, to be rescued by the Blessed Virgin, as he had been at Fontiveros.[32] But, however willing a pupil he may have been, he could not have attended all the classes from the beginning to the end. The classes in grammar, in the Society's colleges, usually lasted for two hours and a quarter, one class in the morning and another in the afternoon. The classes followed by the *artistas* usually lasted for two hours and three quarters in the morning, and the same period in the afternoon. Hence Juan de Yepes did not have a complete secondary education, such as those could who were free to dispose of their time. But his intelligence and memory were so good, if we may judge from his power of memorising Scripture texts, that, as Francisco declares, he learned much in a short time.[33] Hence he left the Jesuit college after a few years, a good Latin scholar.[34] His work in the hospital left him little leisure, and he was not master even of his nights.

Catalina says that when people came looking for him in the middle of the night, they found him studying amidst the faggots.[35]

John, who was fifteen, saw a good deal of Bonifacio, who was nineteen. The young Jesuit must surely have remarked a pupil who was so quick in oral discussion. The Jesuit classes were very lively. The students declaimed, composed, disputed, especially in public, every week and, more formally, every month. These literary tournaments were held in Medina on the first Saturday of the month, and the pupils, who were, in fact, very well coached, spared no trouble. They even acted a piece in verse : *David and Absalom*, at the end of the scholastic year of 1562. It was composed by themselves, partly, no doubt, in Latin and partly in Castilian.[36] It would be in no way surprising if John had a share in writing, and even acting a part in the play. He had literary gifts and might well have danced before the Ark for, later on, at Baeza, he acted religious pieces in the cloisters and danced with the Child Jesus in his arms. In short, *David and Absalom* was a great success ; so great, indeed, that neither Rodrigo de Dueñas, the Abbot of San Antolin, nor the wealthy merchants, nor even the monks and friars who had been invited, could believe that such a masterpiece had been · composed by young amateurs, as Bonifacio says in a letter dated August 31st. The lively interest excited by such teaching will be even better realised when the reader is informed that there were also very attractive prizes, such as a hat, or twelve pairs of gloves, as at Seville in 1562.

Juan Bonifacio was a distinguished humanist, and also an apostle. When St. Francis Borgia, in 1567, asked him if he would not like to give up teaching to study theology, Bonifacio replied that, if he did not choose what he believed to be " most fruitful for his own soul and for the good of others," he would feel he had done wrong.[37] He was not yet a priest, but he considered that the task of teaching, with which he was entrusted, was true apostolate. To what extent, and how, was Juan de Yepes influenced by such a man ? It has been asked if, even at this early period, there was not a conflict between the Ignatian " composition of place " and the method devoid of all imagery, which John of the Cross was, one day, to teach.[38]   Such a question cannot be settled here.   What we do know is that John received his literary formation from eminent Jesuits, and that he did not enter their novitiate.

CHAPTER III

THE BROTHER OF OUR LADY [1]

In 1563 [2], perhaps on the morning of February 24th, the Carmelite Fathers met in the Chapter House of their Monastery of St. Anne in Medina del Campo. Juan de Yepes, accompanied by a brother, advanced towards the altar, clad in a secular cloak worn over a white serge habit [3], with black laced shoes and having his head shaven in the form of a crown. Father Alonso Ruiz, the prior, wearing a stole, asked from the altar steps : " What dost thou desire ? " He answered : " The mercy of God, the poverty of the Order and the Society of the Brethren." The prior then explained the works of the Order, its difficulties and austerities. He repeated officially the twelve questions which had been already put in order to remove all obstacles to his reception. John, still on his knees, answered all the questions. The prior warned him that he should observe poverty, chastity and religious obedience, with devotion and for the love of God, and John joyfully accepted the sacrifice.

The secular dress was at once removed, and the young man, who was now twenty-one years of age, was clad only in his white tunic. The prior—reciting the symbolic prayers, which were responded to by the choir—clothed John in the black cloth habit reaching to the heels, girded him with a broad black leathern cincture, and dressed him in the black scapular and detachable hood of the novice. [4]

Thus in a moment he, who had formerly not dared to touch the beautiful shapely hands of the Virgin with his own little grimy fists, now stood in the full white mantle of the Brothers of Our Lady, just like the kneeling Carmelite painted by Filippino Lippi in the Brancacci chapel of the convent in Florence. The prior intoned the *Veni Creator*, and, at the end of the first verse, the friars went in procession to the church, where Juan de Yepes, now Brother John of St. Mathias, prostrated himself before the altar.

Sit laus Patri cum Filio
Sancto simul Paraclito
Nobisque mittat Filius
Charisma Sancti Spiritus.

The white-robed forms bent down in the stalls ; Brother John rose with joined hands, ascended the steps, kissed the altar, the prior's hand and cheek, and then the brethren in turn. He took up his position in the last stall, nearest the altar, and the morning Mass began. It was the feast of the apostle St. Mathias, whose name John had taken. This was not unusual amongst the Carmelites of that era ; the majority still retained their former names, but we know of the existence of an Andrew of the Cross (1548) and even three Johns of the Cross (1442, 1516, 1559), the last of whom was professed in the Monastery at Avila.

The novice went to Holy Communion during Mass, in accordance with the rule of Blessed John Soreth.

Catalina did not regret having given her son to God. Don Alvarez de Toledo's attractive proposals to John were still-born ; and yet her son's priesthood, after a brief interval, and a chaplaincy in the hospital, would have been very pleasant for Catalina, now in her fiftieth year,[5] for a benefice meant an assured future both for John and herself. But the Yepes family did not bargain with Holy Poverty, and John was dreaming of something quite different—the absolute gift of himself. He desired to get away from the world and concentrate on God.[6] When he prayed, even as a small child, his face was radiant with love ; he had learned since then that the more intimate the union the more absolute the oblation ; hence, when a choice had to be made, he did not choose the lesser thing. " Jesus, what dost Thou wish me to do ? " And Jesus replied : " Thou shalt serve Me in an Order that thou shalt raise to a new perfection." [7] " His ardent love for the Immaculate Virgin Mary, Mother of God, increased daily. So he left the hospital," [8] " very secretly, and asked for the habit of the Order " [9] " which had been established for the honour and service of

Our Lady." [10]   He was so happy and in such great haste to receive the habit that he hurried off that very morning in secular dress to the barber's in order to have his head tonsured.[11] Not indeed that he left his humble home for ever, for he sometimes went there, hooded, and clad in a long, white mantle, just like the other brethren who went around begging alms for the Order. He did not leave Medina—at any rate not permanently—for at that epoch the religious remained attached till death to their particular monastery.

The bell summoned the friars to None and the conventual Mass. In 1563 the feast of St. Mathias was also Ash Wednesday. There was no liturgical difficulty for the feasts of the apostles were then holidays of obligation. Thus the Doctor of *Todo y Nada*, at the dawn of his religious life, heard himself reminded of the nothingness of the creature : *Memento homo quia cinis es et in cinerem reverteris.*

It is somewhat difficult to form a clear picture of the monastery of St. Anne three years after its foundation by Father Diego Rengifo. There is no account either at Rome, Madrid, or even in the local archives of the coming of the Carmelites to Medina del Campo. The restorer of the chapel where the saint probably celebrated his first Mass, is of opinion that this chapel, which is at right angles to the ruin of the church, was used as a conventual church when John of St. Mathias made his novitiate. If this be correct, then Rengifo of Avila had not done things on a very big scale, and Velasco exaggerated when he wrote that " in 1560 the church of the glorious St. Anne was founded in the city— a city of thirty thousand inhabitants." [12] It is true that Master Jean de Salazar, professor at Salamanca, and founder of the Madrid convent, splendidly rebuilt the monastery, certainly before 1597,[13] and this would seem to imply that the monastery was at first a simple enough building.

The painstaking Hye Hoys, in his *Teresian Spain*, has given a sketch of St. Anne's,[14] in which we can see, side by side, the chapel restored by Father Michael in 1909, and the church, so magnificently rebuilt by John de Salazar, of which the Corinthian style and three naves are the pride of the historians of Medina. At the present day this church has fallen into decay ; it was obviously very large, and its ruins, of the same red brick as the Castello and San Antolin, even now have an air of majesty. They consist of the last arch of the central nave in front of the presbyterium, the back wall, the side walls of the high altar, and portion of the side walls of the transept. This fine building forms a right angle with the restored chapel. Both open out on a *patio*, which is now covered in and used as a sawmill. The dimensions of the cloister, and all that now remains of the curved portions of the arches, would seem to suggest a modest, and even primitive building. John had to pass from the strictly enclosed novitiate through this cloister to take part in the community exercises.

    .   .   .   .   .   .

John of St. Mathias, in his solitary cell, opened the little octavo book of the Constitutions of 1462, which are called after Blessed Soreth. The master of novices had just given it to him and, under the heading of *Rubrica prima*, the first page begins :

" What is the answer to be given to those who ask when and how our Order arose ? And why are we called Brothers of the Blessed Virgin Mary of Mount Carmel ? " He read : " We reply, giving testimony to the truth, that, from the time of Elias and his disciple Eliseus, who piously lived on Mount Carmel, not far distant from Achon, many holy Fathers, both of the Old and the New Testament, loved to live in the solitude of that same mountain, and there contemplate heavenly things. There, close to the fountain of Elias, they gloriously and religiously persevered in a life of perpetual penance, as the Sixth Chapter of the Book of Kings bears witness . . ."

" They built an oratory to the Mother of the Saviour, and, for this reason, took the name of Brethren of the Blessed Virgin Mary of Mount Carmel, and have since been called so by Apostolic privilege . . ."

" Albert, patriarch of Jerusalem, legate of the Holy See, gathered them together under a common rule, which he gave them, before the Lateran Council, and this rule was approved of by Honorius III, Gregory IX, and Innocent IV . . ." *Rubrica Secunda* : " The Order is made up of twenty-two provinces : the Holy Land, Sicily, England . . . the provinces of Narbonne, Rome and France. The tenth is the province of Spain," that is to say, Castille, the foundation of which was decided on at the Chapter held in London in 1254.[15]

John paused : his heart was deeply moved. Mount Carmel, bathed by the sea under an Eastern sky ! The hermit of the " Sacrifice " * had gazed from its topmost peak upon the spreading sunny plain of Esdraelon, and the mysterious, shady valleys that concealed the grottoes of his spiritual forebears.

Thabor glowed in the morning sunshine, and he could pick out the hills of lower Galilee that concealed Nazareth, the city of flowers. And when evening came, and the radiant, fiery surface of the sea shaded off into clear shadows, the mountains of Lebanon stood out softly in the twilight before his wondering eyes.

One day, more than three hundred years ago, the hermits, harassed by Saracen invasions, had descended the slope of that mountain from which the Prophet had seen the cloud, and, casting a lingering glance on the beauty of Carmel, had sailed away to distant lands. The first migrations took place in 1238 to the Aygalades of Provence, to Sicily, to Cyprus,[16] the home of the Most Reverend Nicholas Audet.†

In Europe, under the energetic generalship of Simon Stock—through force of circumstances which now seem to us to have been inevitable—Carmel, hitherto eremitical, in 1247 adopted the apostolic life.[17] This was a transformation of which Brother John was probably ignorant, at least in its details. What he heard in the novitiate of St. Anne of the great English Carmelite, was his filial devotion to the Blessed Virgin, and the gift of the Holy Scapular which he

* The spot where Elias had offered sacrifice (1 Kings xviii).
† He died on December 6th, 1562, having ruled the Order for thirty-eight years.

received from her as a reward. Hence John would be instructed never to take off the little habit of the Virgin, not even at night, for death may surprise us, and those who pass away clad in the scapular will not go to hell. Fifty years after the apparition St. Peter Thomas, one of the great glories of his Order, observes the same rule.[18]

Life in a novitiate does not allow for much leisure in one's cell. It is enough to glance through the Acts of Nicholas Audet's Reform, and consult the Ordinal, to see that this life of a Carmelite, and especially of a novice, was weighed down by a multiplicity of liturgical and claustral observances.

In 1562 the daily life of a religious was still, thank God, framed within the austere and sober liturgy of the Holy Sepulchre, sprung from the Gallo-Roman rite, which is of great antiquity, and closely resembles the Carthusian liturgy. St. John of the Cross lived according to its prescriptions up to the decree of August 13th, 1586, in which, as we shall see, he had no share. The *Opus Dei* was chanted, day and night, in every monastery containing six of the brethren. From the fifteenth century onwards the number of saints' offices had been greatly increased at the expense of the ferial office for the day, to such an extent that Audet was forced to issue an order that at least twice a month the ferial office should be recited. But, if the professed religious were dispensed, by the introduction into the calendar of so many saints and offices, from reciting the Office of the Blessed Virgin, the Office of the Dead, the Gradual and Penitential Psalms and the Litany of the Saints, the novices were bound to recite, in the chapter-room, the office *De Beata*, with a commemoration of St. Albert of Sicily, and the Office of the Dead, when these latter were not recited in choir. A plain chant conventual Mass was sung every day, and a second Mass celebrated after Prime. On Sundays this Mass was always that of Easter Sunday, and was chanted. This is the characteristic trait, which differentiates the rite of the Holy Sepulchre from the Gallo-Roman rite, introduced into the Holy Land at the time of the Crusades. In addition requiem Masses were frequently chanted after Sext and None. The dead were not forgotten, and, in conformity with a decree of the Chapter of Treves, held in 1362, every Monday morning a funeral procession, with its four absolutions, took place round the cloisters and cemetery. Nor was this all. If there were more than four novices they were bound to sing, before Prime, a Mass of the Blessed Virgin, together with a short hymn of praise, in the presence of the novice master. And as they had to assemble again in the evening, after the *Salve Regina* which follows Compline, to sing another hymn, we may see how the whole day was set in songs of praise to Mary.

It was a joy and consolation for John of St. Mathias to serve Mass, even though he should spend his whole morning in so doing. Fernandez de Bustillo, who still used to meet John after he had become a Carmelite, admired his humility and the manner in which he carried out very tiring duties.[19]

As the foundation was quite recent it is likely that there were few novices, and consequently not many to help with the work. John was the sixth to make his profession. Apart from this piece of information given by Alonso, we know that of eight pupils of the Jesuits who became religious in 1563, three were Carmelites.[20] We may very well suppose that John's fellow students at Salamanca, Rodrigo Nieto and Pedro de Orozco, made their novitiate with him in 1563, at St. Anne's, since they were both natives of Medina del Campo.

.   .   .   .   .   .

Every day during this year of probation long hours were spent in the choir stalls or facing the lectern, gravely singing or chanting in a subdued voice, marking the pause in the verse, according to rule. At a signal given by Fr. Alonso Ruiz, the novices, followed by the fathers, left the choir after making a profound bow to the tabernacle. They then went to the chapter room where, after they had said the prayer *Praetende*, various claustral rules demanded observance.

Great or small, these took up all the spare time. Each religious was bound to read every day a chapter of the Ordinary, and this was followed by a lecture on the Holy Scriptures, in every monastery where there were at least eight

priests. We may conjecture that John assisted at all these
duties. He may have been dispensed from the grammar
lesson unless, indeed, he gave it himself to those who were
illiterate. Lastly, there was practice in plain chant, to
which Audet attached great importance.

Brother Ass, even if he be a Castilian, needs some repose.
There were but few walks during the winter, but, on fine
days the novice master led his lambs, clothed in white
mantles " that the candour and purity of Our Lady might
appear in them," [21] along the slopes of the Castillo de la
Mota. From the keep one may see the whole plain lying
below, the green meadows intersected by the Zapardiel,
whose waters, as it was said, are only drinkable from Fontiveros to Medina. One may rest there and let one's gaze
wander over the roads alive with traffic, which lead to
Segovia and Avila.

Other physical exercises might be carried on without
leaving the convent. The Father Sacristan, an important
person in those days, for he was appointed by the provincial
Chapter, required the novices twice a week to sweep the
church. But this work had its compensations, even for poor
human nature, for if Catalina Alvarez happened to be
praying in St. Anne's, then her beloved John might speak to
her without committing a fault. Nicholas Audet had foreseen the need for such a permission, and in the presence of
a mother the reformer graciously laid aside—for the moment
—the iron glove.

The novice master at Medina, whose name we shall
probably never know, gathered his disciples together to
explain the ceremonies and initiate them in the customs of the
Order. He spoke of monastic regularity, warned them
against habits engendered by routine, and spoke of very
simple matters in stately fashion. " At the first sound of the
bell . . . " words such as these took on a solemn air as they
fell from his lips. He was, indeed, quite right thus to insist,
for all were bound, under pain of punishment at chapter,
to be in their places in choir before the bell ceased ringing.
At this period the friars went to choir in single file, and the
novice master reminded the feather-headed that, if one made

a mistake during the recitation of the office, then one was bound to admit one's fault by touching the ground with a finger. He constantly recommended perfect silence. Care must be taken not to make a noise by lowering the seat in one's stall and, with all the carefulness of a master of ceremonies—he may perhaps have been one—he told the acolytes again at what precise moment the candles were to be lit and extinguished, and when a light was to be brought to the *absconsoria* for those who needed it. In small convents, such as St. Anne's, the first acolyte was entrusted with this duty for the first three days of the week and the second acolyte from Thursday onwards, having also charge of the thurible. And both of them, after their duties at the altar, were to serve the religious at table.

A Carmelite refectory was no more attractive then than it is now. Every day, before the *prandium* and the *cena,* or collation, the prior asks if any fault has been committed, and it is only after a brief exhortation that he gives the signal to the reader to begin reading the Bible. On Friday, the day fixed for confession, it is *de rigueur* for all to accuse themselves, even more strictly than usual, with downcast eyes and hands folded beneath the scapular, of any faults committed against the Rule.

This Rule is called the rule of Eugenius IV, and was read publicly every Friday during dinner, and, according to Audet's regulation, the reading was followed by a commentary in the Castilian language. We do not know if the novices were asked to preach. John of St. Mathias soon learned that the rule which he followed was the result of a mitigation, obtained by the General, John Faci, in 1432, after the terrible " Black Death," and the universal disorders occasioned by the Great Schism. Thanks to an apostolic privilege meat was allowed three times a week, or even four, if the prior so wished, save in the seasons of Advent, Lent and a certain number of vigils. A still graver point, the principle of retreat, which had been so strongly laid down in the primitive Rule, had been relaxed, but this, thank God, had not lasted very long. John Soreth (1405–1471) after taking his degrees and teaching theology in the University of Paris, had been elected General. In 1462, at a chapter held in Brussels, he had his constitutions approved, and this marked the beginning of a real reform. Audet, *magister in sacra Pagina,* accentuated the return to strict observance. His decrees, which were approved in 1524 by the members of the chapter of Venice, are terribly rigorous. He commanded all provincials and priors to observe them, and see that they were observed, under pain of rebellion, suspension from office, and incapacity for holding any office, rank or dignity. For two or three years, or even longer, successive portions of these decrees were read daily in the refectory. In 1531 Luis Perez de Castro, a Castilian Carmelite, admits, in his *Status Ordinis,* that the greater number of the brethren of his province had left on account of the new reforms *propter reformationem,*[22] and this fact perturbed the Chapter held at Padua in 1532, when it was charitably decreed that, in consequence of this exodus of Spanish Carmelites the provinces of Castile, Aragon and Andalusia should in future only send three, instead of nine, representatives to the General Chapters.[23]

In 1567 St. Teresa was to see the Carmelites of Castile " reduced to such an extent that they are on the point of extinction." [24] What does this imply ? Luis de St. Angelo heard an old Trinitarian monk say that, at this time, the Carmelite provinces of Castile, Andalusia and others were about to perish, and that such was the relaxation that no one in this order troubled to study ; they were satisfied with merely being ordained.[25] This statement calls, however, for qualification. It will be seen from what follows that the *studium generale* at Salamanca was very much alive, and that when Audet's successor, John Baptist Rubeo of Ravenna visited Spain in 1567 he had no difficulties with the Castilians. He imposed, however, as many reforms as could be demanded of religious. There is no document that throws direct light on the community of Medina, but an account of two canonical visitations, held in 1567 and 1568 by the Vicar-General of León, of a recently founded monastery in the province of Castile, Valderas, is extremely illuminating. This unpublished document was discovered in the Simancas archives. Religious observance was austere at Valderas. There was no failing in regard to poverty, and the monks did not leave their convents without good reason, though regret is expressed that the young monks were charged with the duty of begging, as the older ones did not do so. The prior, Alonso Fernandez, although *pater honoris* (this was a new title which, since Audet's time replaced " the jubilee by anticipation ") lived the same life as the others. The Father Preacher, Balthazar Nieto, whom we shall meet later on, only finds fault with the prior for not having reading, during the whole of the meal, on feast days ; so that it would seem as if Audet himself might sleep peacefully in his tomb at San Martino dei Monte.

John the novice seemed to be an angel, say the manu-scripts [26] ; we may well believe it, and the conclusion follows that, like an angel, he had need to live by the spirit. Like a true Castilian he respected the letter of the rule and observed it punctiliously, as taught him by his novice master. It had a value of its own, yet it did not enlarge and expand the soul save under the impulse of the spirit. Where was the spirit of Carmel to be found ?

From 1507, when it was printed in the *Speculum Ordinis*, a work attributed to John XLIV, bishop of Jerusalem, and entitled *A Book of the Institution of the first monks*, spread through all the Spanish convents, became the chief spiritual book of the Order, and was even looked on as the ancient rule of Carmel. Previously, in 1370, a provincial of Catalonia, Philip Riboti, *magister in sacra Pagina*, had had the honour of publishing it in a collection of Carmelite documents.[27] It may be taken as certain that John became acquainted with this work during his novitiate, and hence the whole teaching of the *Ascent of Mount Carmel* and the *Dark Night* were impregnated with the spirituality of the *Institution*, in which he read :

" The Carmelite life has a twofold end. We attain the

first by our own toil and virtuous efforts, aided by divine grace. It consists in offering to God a holy heart, free from all actual stain of sin. . . . The other is communicated to us by a free gift of God, *ex mero Dei dono*, and consists in tasting, in some way, in the heart, and experiencing in the spirit, the strength of the Divine Presence, and the sweetness of the glory from on high. It is with this twofold end in view that the monk should lead an eremitical life, according to the Words of the Prophet : ' In a desert land, and where there is no way, and no water : so in the sanctuary have I come before thee, to see thy power and thy glory.' " [28] (Psalm lxii).

John trembled with joy as he read these lines, which truly convey the mystical traditions of his Order. It was a pure breath from the summit of Mount Carmel coming to refresh his soul. In that age-old ideal he recognised his own, and his heart beat faster as he came upon it. The grandson of the Hidalgo, Garcia de Yepes, was ardent and trained to sacrifice ; he was to become a hero, and never would he allow his life to be lower than his ideal. He would lead a life of austerity and recollection, in accordance with the Primitive Rule, of whose existence he now became aware. Did he inform his novice master of his plan, or did he keep his own secret ? A witness, Father Alonso de Vilalba, who was an *artista* at Salamanca in 1567–1568, tells us that John, after his profession, obtained permission from his superiors to lead a life according to the rule of St. Albert, and hence could abstain from meat from the feast of the Holy Cross in September until Easter. [29]

According to Audet's constitutions every novice was at liberty to pronounce his vows without waiting for the end of his year of probation. It is not known if John availed himself of this privilege, as the book of professions, which was carefully preserved for many years at St. Anne's, has disappeared.

Antonio de Sagrameña declares, in the process of beatification, that one day he took the book containing the profession of St. John of the Cross, and, without the knowledge of anybody, had it elegantly bound in black leather picked out with gold.   He had the arms of the Order engraved on both covers, and a portrait of the saint as a frontispiece, with the following inscription : *Primo incola Carmeli, deinde restitutae observantiae parens ac propagator.   Obiit anno* 1591.   The prior of St. Anne's manifested in this way his own veneration, but may we not say that the whole ancient order of Carmel was with him ? [30]

One day the Father Provincial arrived at Medina del Campo to preside over the ceremony of John's profession. Angel de Salazar [31] is certainly one of the most attractive figures of the Castilian Carmelites of that era.   Professed at Seville, we find him, without any explanation, prior of Toledo in 1555.   In all probability he became provincial in 1561, and became a great help to the reform of St. Teresa. On August 22nd, 1563, de Salazar authorised Doña Teresa de Ahumada to live, with four nuns of the convent of the Incarnation, in the little convent of St. Joseph, which had been founded the year before.   This foundation had caused a great commotion throughout Avila, from the canons to the magistrates of the city ; for to establish a new monastery without any revenues is well known to be foolish !

So, on this morning, the community met in the chapter room before the conventual Mass.   In the presence of Father Alonso Ruiz and the *caballero*, Don Alvarez de Toledo, his benefactor, John promised obedience, poverty and chastity to God, to the Blessed Virgin Mary of Mount Carmel and to the Most Reverend Father, Brother John Baptist Rubeo of Ravenna, Vicar-General of the Order, according to the rule of the Order, until the day of his death.[32]   Father Angel de Salazar, having received the memorandum of profession, clothed him with the scapular, now sewn on to the hood, and the *Te Deum* was chanted.

CHAPTER IV

MENTION is first made of the *studium* of the Carmelites at Salamanca in the acts of the general chapter held at Avignon in 1482. But we know that they arrived in Salamanca about 1306, and established themselves in the south of the city, *extra muros*, near the Puerta San Pablo. They were never to leave this site, which looks down on the fresh blue waters of the River Tormes. When a road was opened up towards the river in 1479 the bishop, Don Gonzalo de Vivero, and the municipal council handed over the parish church of St. Andrew, which was opposite their old residence, to the fathers.

Of that vast Carmelite monastery there remain to-day, within a tannery built against the city walls, some vestiges of a Roman cloister and, at a lower level than the high road, where the church formerly stood, an old wall partly constructed of the pink stone which makes old Salamanca look like a piece of terra-cotta work baked in the sun. The old wall is pierced by a few square windows, framed in blocks of stone. A battered statue of Our Lady of Mount Carmel still stands in one window and is all that now remains of the monastery of el Señor Sant' Andres.

When John of St. Mathias arrived in 1564 the Carmelite College had, for sixteen years, been affiliated to the University as a *studium generale*. The Masters of the Order gave regular courses of instruction to their younger brethren, at which seculars and members of other Orders might assist, with a view to presenting themselves later on before the examining board of the University. The professors themselves were at liberty to stand for professorial chairs, but it does not seem as if the Carmelites occupied any important posts, at any rate at this date.

The intellectual status of the Order had declined (as had that of the other mendicant orders), and this was due not so much to the defection of the large number of religious who had been antagonised by the introduction of the reforms as to the multiplication of universities and the want of money. But we kept intact the treasure of great poverty.[1]

A mastership in theology, when not conferred by papal privilege, required at least ten years' study. At an epoch when masters were few in number they had a right to assist at provincial and even general chapters. When the Chapter of 1503 could say : " To-day there are almost as many graduates as brothers without degrees," [2] their prerogatives were retrenched, merely leaving them precedence in choir and refectory. Why go to so much trouble unless you were out for a professorship ?

There were few Carmelites in Spain, and still fewer who attended the University courses. In fact, during the four years 1564–1568, when John was attending lectures in the University of Salamanca, the College of St. Andrew sent only sixteen students all told, as we see from the matriculation registers, and several of these were not Castilians, but came from Saragossa, Seville and Lisbon. The Chapter held at Venice in 1548 ordered the prior of Salamanca to admit all the students of the other Spanish provinces for a pension of ten crowns a year, and the monastery of St. Andrew thus became the intellectual centre of the Carmelites in the Peninsula. The Father Prior, Ferdinand de Molina, was bound in honour, as well as by rule, to treat his students well : *honeste et copiose*, said the Chapter of 1548 ; and the Chapter held at Rome, in this very year 1564, improved on it by saying : *honeste alantur studentes, nutriantur et conserventur*. So the board and lodging at Carmel was better than that of most university students.

How many hungry *sopistas* had not the brother-porter of Sant' Andres to keep in order with his big ladle as, every morning at the monastery gate, he distributed his thick soup made of fishes' heads. Poor scholars—who did not arrive at Salamanca, like young Don Gaspar de Gusman, with a train of eight pages, ten valets and a head cook—if unable to live in furnished lodgings as free *camaristas*, were forced to seek shelter with " a bachelor of pupils " who fed, lodged and looked after them for a few coins. Don Pablo de Segovia, Quevedo's hero, describing his first meal, paints vividly the extreme poverty of these *picaros*, penniless wooers of the Empress of Intellect, Salamanca with her rose-red walls and her crown of turrets and steeples.

But the time has not yet come for us to mingle in the life of the University. We must linger for a moment within the high walls of the Carmelite College. The statutes, which were enacted by the Vicars-General of the Order, for the College of St. Andrew, and which the Chapter of Venice had also commanded to be faithfully observed, are no longer in existence. Hence no details can be given of the intellectual life led by John of St. Mathias during the four years he spent in his monastery. Nevertheless, we have certain data to go upon.

The Chapter of Venice, in 1548, ordered that, as far as theology was concerned, Michael of Bologna and the other authors of the Order were to be followed (though this did not apply to the provinces of Italy, where Baconthorp was still the authority). The Chapter of Naples, in 1510, had already caused the commentaries of the sentences by those two masters to be distributed throughout the Order and, in 1524, the Capitularies of Venice called for a new edition of their works. In 1540 the Carmelite congregation of Mantua, having first stated that the Summa of St. Thomas, especially the *prima pars*, will be read, goes on to recommend, by special enactments, the works of Michael of Bologna, Baconthorp, and—even more strongly—Thomas Walden. Hence we have a constant century-old tradition. But were the prescriptions of the Chapter of 1548 carried out, even in St. Andrew's ?

We can, of course, compare the teachings of St. Thomas with those of Michael of Bologna and Baconthorp. We can see to what degree they depart from traditional Thomism, and to what degree also John of the Cross has retained some of their formulas on certain points in philosophy.[3] On March 15th, 1581, he was present, as third definitor, at the

Chapter of Alcalá, when the province of Discalced Carmelites was established, and signed the constitutions wherein it was enacted that "the doctrine of the authors of our Order is to be taught and upheld." [4]

But we should not forget that the students, besides the lectures given in their own colleges, followed those of the University, and even those of other colleges, so that it was impossible for them to adhere to one fixed author. Furthermore, the lectors taught, not only for the students of the Order, but for all who wished to hear them ; hence they could scarcely have confined themselves to the teachings of the old Carmelite authors, who were indeed rather eclectic. As the general current, amongst the Salamancan professors, ran direct to Thomism—in the sense in which the word was understood before the advent of Molinism—if the professors at St. Andrew's had taught some special theses of their own we should certainly have echoes of them. They would have been attacked, either at the University or by their neighbours the Dominicans, or even the Augustinians. And, perhaps, we might now know of it from objections included in the *Salmanticenses* when they came to be published. Until we have evidence to the contrary it is wise to believe that John's Carmelite masters accepted—with a certain amount of independence—the teaching of St. Thomas Aquinas.

In Rubeo's constitutions of 1568, drawn up during his canonical visitations of Spain and Italy, there is one whole chapter—an important chapter—dealing with studies, students and universities, but there is no allusion to the authors to be followed. How is this silence to be interpreted ? Were the prescriptions of 1548 so faithfully carried out that the Master-General had no observation to make, no advice to give ? That is not likely. Rubeo, a former professor of the University of Padua and of the Roman "Sapienza," had himself commented on passages from Michael of Bologna.[5] The time had now come for him to insist, following the decisions of the general chapters, on fidelity to the authors of the Order. He did not do so, probably because he knew by experience that it was not practical in face of the prevailing Thomist current. Before leaving Spain, on September 5th, 1567, Rubeo authorised Master Rodrigo, of the province of Portugal, to go on a pilgrimage to Compostella, and to procure the *Summa* of St. Thomas for his own private library.[6]

We have no *official* document to tell us who were the professors at the college of St. Andrew when John was admitted. Possibly Alonso de Villalobos. It is probable that the future provincial, Alonso Gonzales, taught theology : Rubeo granted him the mastership, *honoris causa*, after the Chapter of Avila in 1567.

If Gonzales, that " most estimable and guileless old man," [7] observed the general constitutions of Nicholas Audet, he must have read a commentary on the Sentences of Peter Lombard every day, and presided over the theological disputations. The course for a *Master of Arts*, if we suppose there was one, would have been divided up into three years, as was done in the convent in Paris : one year for logic, one for physics (natural philosophy), and one for ethics. He also was bound to teach every day. Add to this a daily lesson on Sacred Scripture by the Regent, or his delegate, for all the religious, and another daily lesson on moral theology, prescribed by the Chapter of 1564,[8] and we may be sure that " ignorance, the mother of all errors, was," as Audet had hoped, " sternly banished from the cloister." Were the students who followed the University lectures strictly bound to attend these three or four classes at St. Andrew's ? In the absence of a list of the special rules of our *studium* at Salamanca it is impossible to determine with certainty. The point will be further discussed in connection with the extent of the studies of John of St. Mathias.

.   .   .   .   .   .

Every morning, after Prime and, perhaps, after morning Mass,[9] the young Carmelite theologians, two by two, in their long white mantles and with hoods pulled over their heads,[10] set off for the University, to attend the important lecture called " Prime." These students were Fray Juan de Heredia, Fray Antonio de la Luz, Fray Juan de Cepeda,

Fray Bartolomé Sanchez, Fray Hernando de Medina and Fray Hieronimo Brito. They were closely followed by the " artistas " : Fray Sebastian de Oliva, Fray Rodrigo Nieto, Fray Juan de Santo Matia and Fray Pedro de Orozco. They went some little way down the Puerta San Pablo. After a glance to the right, at the magnificent convent of St. Stephen, whither, every year since 1481, the University, by special privilege, adjourned on March 7th to celebrate the feast of St. Thomas Aquinas,[11] the young Carmelites turned to the left into the Calle del Tostado, and came out on the vast square in front of the new Cathedral, behind which stood one of the gates of the greater schools.

According to the first *Libro de Matriculas* that has been preserved, the number of students, from all parts of Spain and abroad, in *Roma la Chica*, or little Rome, as Salamanca was called, reached 5,150 in 1546 ; in 1584 it mounted to 6,778, the highest point attained. Hence motley-coloured, noisy groups flocked together from all directions.

The collegians, more elegant than the poor *camaristas* and *pupileros*, not only wore the square cap, but over their brown mantle they wore the *beca*, three ells of cloth covering both shoulders and falling to the heels. Each of the four great colleges had its own colour, brown for San Bartolomé, blue for Oviedo, scarlet for the Archbishop's, and violet for Cuenca. The students of the military orders of Calatrava and Alcántara wore the red cross of St. James on their breasts. Towards nine o'clock all this lively, many-coloured crowd filled the University cloister, with its ceiling panelled in red, green and yellow. The swallows, sparrows, storks and thrushes, as the Dominicans, Franciscans, Mercedarians and Hieronymites were irreverently nicknamed, crowded around the great double door on which may still be deciphered, in Hebrew and Latin, the Benefits of Sacred Theology.[12] At one side, in the magnificent chapel of the University Council, the chaplains were beginning to celebrate the eight masses said daily " for the conservation and growth of the University, its professors and students." [13] In spite of the beadle's vigilance, cheery and shabby-looking *picaros*, such as were to terrify St. Teresa's companion on All Saints' Night in 1570, were making noisy demonstrations, for they were not held in check by anything like the iron rule of the ten young Carmelites, who were threatened with eight days' imprisonment, the discipline and dry bread, or even a premature return to their home convent, for any failure of discretion whilst attending the University.[14]

The negro on the huge clock struck nine blows with his hammer on the bell ; the two rams rose and fell ; the angels and the three wise kings prostrated themselves at the Virgin's feet [15] : Master Mancio of Corpus Christi entered the theology lecture room, which was 15 yards long and 15 broad. He walked towards his Gothic pulpit at the foot of which sat the *actuante*.*

The scholars took their places on the rough benches, and the less studious began to carve the clumsy wooden desks with their *navajas*. So little light filtered in through the high windows that it was a temptation not to take notes, and, moreover, the professors read rapidly. Still, Mancio took some pains to enable them to follow him.[16] As for Juan de Guevara, too much stress has been laid on the solitary statement of December 15th, 1565, suggesting that it was impossible for John of St. Mathias to take notes of the lectures.[17] Indeed, in May, 1568, while he was still following the course, the licentiate, Zurbano de Vitoria, testifies that Guevara read in such a way that one could write down what he said ; and during the next scholastic year there are two other witnesses to the same effect.[18]

John of St. Mathias is down on the registers as an *artista* for the three scholastic years of 1564–1565, 1565–1566, 1566–1567, and is inscribed as a priest and theologian in 1567–1568.[19]

In spite of the authenticity of this valuable documentary evidence it behoves us to establish, in another fashion, the fact that John actually attended the University lectures during those four years. This may seem strange, but specialists on Salamanca are well aware of the fact that a number of students matriculated in all parts of the Peninsula

* A student who reads out the texts.

and only went to the University to take part in the election of the masters. This is clear from what happened during the vigorous fight between Bañes and Guevara for the Chair of Durandus.[20] It is certain that the young Carmelites took part in these elections and voted for the professors of their choice. (The Constitutions of Alcalá, for the reform, in 1581—constitutions approved of by Father John of the Cross and Father Antonio de Heredia—include a strict prohibition, under pain of excommunication—*latae sententiae ipso facto incurrenda*—not only against canvassing for a chair in any faculty whatsoever, but even against voting for any candidate for a chair.)[21] Hence, when Quiroga tells us that, after his interview with St. Teresa, in September, 1567, John of St. Mathias, on her advice, remained at Medina in order to prepare for an eremitical life,[22] though he misinterprets the Mother's idea—for she was always in favour of studies—yet his statement does not, in itself, contradict the archives of Salamanca. Brother John, already a matriculated student of the University, might have gone there only to take part in the voting of January 12th and 27th, 1568.[23]

But we have seen that the Chapters-General of the Order provided for and desired, the despatch of intelligent young religious to the University. Moreover, two further facts support the view that registered students did actually attend lectures. An examination of the registers shows that the name of John of St. Mathias is not down for the year 1568–1569, although it would have been quite easy to inscribe it with that of his fellow-students for a second year's theology. Another indirect indication comes from the case of Brother Bartholomew Sanchez of Toledo. He suspended his studies in theology during the year 1567–1568, as we know, from a decree of Rubeo, dated May 9th, 1569, authorising him to resume his course, and appointing him Master of Students. Now, he is not registered for the year 1567–1568, but for the three previous years and for 1569–1570. When Carmelite students were registered then, it meant that they were following the lectures. So there can be no doubt that St. John of the Cross, Doctor of the Church, was nourished, not

only *de jure* but *de facto*, on the sound teachings of the professors of the University. Who were these professors ?

It is practically impossible to determine what courses
John followed during the three years he was an *artista*.
Although every student had a month in which to decide
which professor's lectures he proposed to attend,[24] the members of religious orders were probably bound to go to those
selected by their superiors. Moreover, there were a great
number of chairs, five or six series of professors, and thou-
sands of students in arts. We cannot establish any certain
data, and are bound to rely on Dominic de Soto's commentaries for the years 1564 to 1567. To mention only the
principal chairs, the professor of elementary logic, or
Sumulas, was Martin de Peralta, and of major logic, was that
Gaspar de Torres, who, to frighten his pupils one afternoon,
threw an enormous bronze compass, weighing three or four
pounds at least, at an unruly joker ; the scapegrace luckily
dodged it. Enrique Hernandez, whose name is given for
the chair of Aristotelian physics from 1535, must have had
a substitute, of whose name we are ignorant, for the nine
years before the time we are considering. The third year
was devoted to Aristotle's ethics and politics, and the
professor was a canon of Salamanca, Francisco Sanchez, a
commissary of the Inquisitor, who played a prominent part in
the trial of Archbishop Carranza. In 1566 Master Sanchez,
Master Rodriguez and the famous Dominicans, Mancio of
Corpus Christi and Bartholomé de Medina, approved, in
the name of the University, the privileges of the Sabbatine
Bull, which had been contested.[25]

The name of Mancio of Corpus Christi leads us to the
portals of Sacred Theology. The faculty was world-
renowned, but was not so important as that of Law, which
led, as it does to-day, to positions of trust and honour. The
chairs of Theology were not so well endowed.[26] They were
of two kinds : permanent foundations, *cathedras de propriedad*,
and *cathedras menores*. The former consisted of the chairs of
Sacred Scripture and the chairs of Prime and Vespers,
called after the hours when the lectures were delivered.
These two chairs, as well as the *Biblia*, were held for life,

but after twenty years' teaching the holder became a *jubileus*, and could, on payment, select a substitute and hold the chair until he died.

Although we have no definite information as to what lectures John followed during his year at the University as a *teólogo*, we are on safer ground than when dealing with the *Artes*. It seems certain that the young Carmelites attended the morning lecture given by Mancio, and the evening lectures given by the Augustinian, Juan de Guevara, on account of the importance of those two professors, for everyone at Salamanca talked of Mancio, and Guevara's lectures were regarded as absolute miracles.

This first chair of Theology, though open to competition, was held by Dominicans for more than two centuries almost without a break. The fame of this chair dated from Francis de Vitoria. "We know," writes Dominic Bañes, St. Teresa's faithful friend, "we know, from what all our masters have told us, that, sixty years ago, in this University of Salamanca, or, rather in the whole of Spain, the professors of scholastic theology were of no great worth ; and thus it was, until an illustrious man, an eminent Master of the Order, Francis de Vitoria, by the sole influence of his lectures, restored, like another Socrates, all their former splendour to the doctrines of the ancient school." [27]

Vitoria had led back the divine sciences from the hopeless speculations of a decadent scholasticism to their primary sources, the Sacred Scriptures, the definitions of popes and councils, the fathers, and St. Thomas Aquinas. From that day forward the University of Paris, which had been the theological centre since the thirteenth century, yielded pride of place to Salamanca. Thanks to intelligent efforts, especially at Valladolid, where the mode of life was organised with a view to the intellectual development of the most promising students, the Order of St. Dominic provided a succession of real masters. Melchior Cano (1546–1552) succeeded Vitoria ; then came Dominic de Soto (1552–1560), Peter de Sotomayor (1560–1564) and, lastly, Juan Mancio of Corpus Christi (1564–1576). Mancio arrived from Alcalá, where he had occupied Cano's chair from 1550, that is to say, for fourteen years.

Mancio was faithful to the spirit of his Order, as expressed in a General Chapter held at Salamanca in 1551, and a decree issued in 1561, which substituted, for University lectures, the *Summa Theologica* in place of Peter Lombard's *Sentences*. The *Summa*, as we know, was accorded honours similar to those given to the Bible by the Fathers of the Council of Trent. Mancio expounded this code of Thomism, article by article, in accordance with Cajetan's commentaries.[28]

During the scholastic year 1567–1568, whilst John was a *teólogo*, Master Mancio explained the third part of the *Summa*,[29] so that the saint heard the professor setting forth all that the holy doctors of the Church had been able to discover regarding the wonderful mysteries of the Incarnation and Redemption. And yet, despite the theological searchings into those caverns of the rocks, despite all the understanding that holy souls have attained here below, Father John was one day to write, " the greatest part remains unsaid, unknown ; so must we still dig deep in Christ." [30]

The Master of the Vesper Chair, Juan de Guevara, of the Order of St. Augustine, taught, during the year 1567–1568, the beginning of the *Prima Secundae*.[31] From St. Luke's day to December 16th he had only got as far as the fourth article of the third question, and in the following May had only reached the fourth article of the ninth question. Did he ever go any faster ? All that we can say is that, on St. Luke's Day, 1568, he resumed his course with the twentieth question.

It is of interest to note how the author of the *Living Flame of Love* at the end of his commentary on the third stanza, insists on the Thomist doctrine of Beatitude.[32] We know definitely that Juan de Guevara followed the Angelic Doctor's teaching faithfully. His biographer, Gregorio de Santiago Vela, of the Order of St. Augustine, speaks of his " inveterate hostility towards ecclesiastical novelties," and says that he " gave obvious proof of it in the discussions provoked by Molina's *Concordia*." . . . " It cannot be questioned," he adds, '' that he was a disciple of the ancient school of St. Thomas, and completely at one with the Dominican Fathers as to the *Concordia*.'' [33]

When their lectures were over the Salamancan professors were bound *asistir al poste*, that is to say, to go and stand by one of the columns in the cloister in order to give their students an opportunity of putting questions. The young '' Master of the Students '' of St. Andrew's * had full liberty then to question Mancio and Guevara. Mancio was a modest, peaceful man, a lover of Our Lady and of the poor, and a truly spiritual man. Whilst John was attending his lectures Father Ibañes had already laid before him a communication from Doña Teresa de Ahumada.[34] As for Guevara, we know that, later on, he was to observe some striking events in connection with a relic of St. John of the Cross preserved at Medina del Campo.[35]

The Augustinian, Juan de Guevara, was born in 1504, in the neighbourhood of Toledo, and taught in the University of Salamanca from 1556. At first he was *catedrático de Santo Tomás*, and, in 1565, competed successfully for the Vesper Chair in theology against the Dominican, Juan Gallo, who had been a theologian at the Council of Trent and professor of the University at Coimbra. In spite of the lively opposition of the Augustinian professors, a new chair was created in order to retain Gallo at the University. The matter was referred to Madrid, and the king ultimately approved of a salary of two hundred ducats for Juan Gallo, on condition that he delivered a theological lecture every morning, from ten to eleven in winter and nine to ten in summer. In 1567–1568, Gallo had to lecture on three most interesting topics : on the Soul, on Simony, and on States.[36] All these questions were likely to interest the man who, in a few months, was to embrace a poor, humble, solitary and contemplative life at Duruelo. Everyone interested in St. Teresa will remember her intervention when Juan Gallo was dying in 1573.[37]

In 1567–1568, Gaspar Grajal—disciple of Luis de Leon, and, like him, to be imprisoned one fine day by the Inquisi-

---

* We shall see, in Chapter V, the meaning of this title, and when John received it.

tion—taught Scripture, acting as substitute for Gregorio Gallo. Grajal interpreted the Psalms, beginning with the fiftieth.[38]

The courses given by Mancio, Guevara and Gallo were the most important and the best attended, and, as we have already said, they dealt with the *Summa* of St. Thomas. The secondary chairs were those of St. Thomas, Scotus, and a chair of Nominalist Theology. All these chairs were held for only four years.

The chair of St. Thomas was allotted to the Dominican convent, and held by Rodriguez Lencina. As his lectures were given in the morning it was not possible for the young Carmelites to attend them, for they coincided either with the *Prime* or with Gallo's lectures, and, as they had to make a choice, it is more probable that they went to the Greater Schools. It was the duty of Master Rodriguez Lencina to supply, as in Paris, a systematic objective presentation of St. Thomas's teaching. The Scotus chair, in the Franciscan convent, had no students, and there was always talk of suppressing it, but the future Archbishop of Burgos, Cristobal de Vela, saved it. The chair of Gregorio de Arimino y Durando, devoted to the exposition of Nominalism, was held from 1565 to 1573 by Master Luis de Leon, and if St. John of the Cross had any intercourse with the celebrated Augustinian it is not likely to have been as one of his students.

.   .   .   .   .   .

John of St. Mathias was a mystic, not an idealist orientated towards philosophical speculation. He accepted the discipline of the school and had no desire to escape from it. It was useful to him, and he appreciated its solid and harmonious synthesis, its fixed terminology ; and hence, in the prologue to the *Cantico*, he told Mother Anne of Jesus that he was about to employ the scholastic method.[39] His Arts course had been very complete, hence his skill in discussion, where his natural gifts as a psychologist had an opportunity of displaying themselves. His moral theology was acquired from Aristotle's *Ethics*, the daily lesson ordered by the Chapter in 1564, and the *Summa* as taught by Guevara and

Juan Gallo. It is said that he read dogmatic theology for only one year at the University. At first one cannot see why, as he was an *artista* like Rodrigo Nieto and Pedro de Orozco, he should have taken his theological lectures before their time. According to the decrees of 1548, which deal with the Paris *studium generale*, a philosopher did not proceed to theology until he had finished his three years in *Artes*, and then only at the intervention of the Master of Students.[40] And yet, as will be seen in the next chapter, whilst John was still an *artista* at the University, he was also a *teólogo pasante*— repetitor in theology—at St. Andrew's. It was, doubtless, with a view to ordination that he proceeded so rapidly, and led simultaneously the life of a philosopher and the life of a theologian. While living in the University centres of Alcalá and Baeza and during the five years at the Monastery of the Incarnation at Avila he was able to complete his curtailed studies. He never became a Master of theology, no doubt because the University regulations would not allow of his doing so, but also because, in the humility of his heart, he did not trouble to obtain degrees which would add nothing to '' what he not only knew, but likewise savoured.'' [41]

In the light of all this, a reply may now be attempted to a question put by some modern writers. Was the Scholastic-Thomist influence on the intellectual formation of St. John of the Cross freely accepted by him, or merely endured ? Can we not, in fact, '' conceive another John of the Cross, incomparably greater than the one we know, and yet virtually contained in the man who actually existed ? One who would have applied to a philosophy constructed by himself, and not received from without, that organising logic which seems one of the most indisputable gifts of John of the Cross.'' *

The answer surely lies in this, that whereas contact with the University at Salamanca, represented by such masters as Mancio, Guevara and Juan Gallo, did undoubtedly exercise a deep—and happy—influence on St. John of the Cross, yet there is no evidence to show that he had any wish to avoid it. To think of '' another John of the Cross, incomparably

* Baruzi, 129.

greater," is an insult to the John of history, and the holy doctor would have shuddered had he been able to foresee this entirely wanton effort of the imagination.

" A man," we are told, " is only completely great in so far as he escapes the influences inseparable from his intellectual and moral surroundings." *

But does not a genius who dominates such influences most truly escape them ? St. John of the Cross held fast to the scholastic tradition, and was not crushed by it. He employed it not merely as a sure and certain technique, but because it enshrines Christian truth and because mysticism is, above all else, a faith that is lived and not personal metaphysic, as some would seem inclined to believe. One must be wanting in a humble, healthy love of dogma, and have reached a position in which the attitude of the believer is regarded as " the grossest submission to external authority," † to despise Scholasticism—a philosophy that fits revealed truth in its every part. The spirit of revolt does not fit with Scholasticism because it rejects revealed truth ; it stands for the rights of the thinker and the artist to independence. It is afraid lest the crystallisation of a method should freeze the creative impulse ; and in order to bend truth to its own fashion it dismisses a good old servant, Scholasticism, which has served truth for seven or eight centuries, and knows far, far more about it than all our creative impulses.

St. John of the Cross, without minimising the daring features of his art, or blunting the fine point of his lofty mysticism, fitted himself to the Thomist tradition. It has been admitted that " he learned at Salamanca a clear-cut language that afterwards saved him from the flabbiness of so many mystical effusions." ‡ Be it added that there he also learned to find a home for his spirit within the fixed confines of Catholic truth, and thus saved himself from both Illuminism and Quietism. It is sheer fancy " to feel in him a sort of deficiency which impoverished his thought." §

Hence the futility of the search for the so-called liberating

* *Id.*, 456.   † *Id.*, 129.   ‡ Bar., 128.
§ *Ibid.*, 128.

influences which might have been brought to play upon John of St. Mathias, shut up in his Carmelite-Dominican surroundings. There is no historical foundation for an imaginary " drama of Salamanca," a drama played within the restless spirit of the young student of twenty-five, in contact with the innovations to be found at the University, especially the famous Luis de Leon, who was imprisoned for five years by the Inquisition for having translated the Canticle of Canticles into the vulgar tongue. The greater number of Salamancan professors had their own difficulties with the Inquisition, even Mancio, who, though a consultor of the Holy Office, was cautioned twice. That John of the Cross, from his time at Salamanca onwards, appreciated a poet, musician, exegete, and astronomer like Luis de Leon, seems more than probable—but that is all that can be said.*

The dramatic spiritual struggle that went on in John's soul was of quite another nature ; he was not tormented by a desire for intellectual emancipation, but only by a violent longing for the solitary and contemplative life.

* We are happy to see that the Augustinian Fathers agree with us. Speaking of the division that existed between Scholastics and Scripturalists when John was studying at Salamanca, Father Conrado Rodríguez, O.S.A., asks, " what side did John of the Cross take ? Did he fight for Luis de Leon or against him ? *Nada sabemos.* We do not know. There are few blanks in the history of great men so regrettable as those we may observe in documents of the period concerning these decisive moments in the lives of Fray Luis de León and St. John of the Cross. If the young Carmelite allowed himself to be influenced by the tendencies prevailing in his own convent he would have sided with the Scholastics. The energy and holy independence he afterwards displayed during the Reform show that he was not a man who would allow himself to be overpowered by the opinions current among his brethren. Moreover, the reasons militating in favour of a lively sympathy between the Carmelite theologian and the Augustinian poet cannot easily be set aside. Both had a predilection for the vulgar tongue, which they employed in the publication of their mystical and scriptural treatises, a practice which the Scholastics, with Melchior Cano at their head, regarded with very great suspicion. " Homenaje a Fray Luis de Leon en el cuarto centenario de su nacimiento." *Religión y cultura*, June-July, 1928, p. 550.

CHAPTER V

On January 7th, 1566, St. Pius V was elected Pope, and Philip II at once urged him to apply the decrees of the Council of Trent to Spain. On the February 24th following, the Pope deputed, by brief, the Most Reverend Father John Baptist Rubeo of Ravenna to reform his Order. Philip welcomed the Master-General with all the customary honours accorded to Spanish grandees, but, on Rubeo's return from the Chapter of Seville the suspicious monarch, who had been prejudiced by the Carmelites of Andalusia, would not even receive him. Before this indignity befell him the Master-General made a visitation of the convent at Salamanca.[1]

On Tuesday, February 4th, riding on a mule, he crossed the Roman bridge spanning the Tormes (where Teresa of Jesus was one day to spend fourteen *reales* for two pictures of Christ painted in distemper)—and rode up to St. Andrew's, accompanied by Master Bartholomew Ragusius, Master Ambrosio de Castro and, very probably, the Father Provincial, Angel de Salazar, a favourite of the General's.

Whilst the bells were pealing out, the Father Prior, Ferdinand de Molina, introduced John Baptist Rubeo of Ravenna within the walls of the venerable *studium generale* of Salamanca. All the religious were assembled in choir, and after the Father-General had given each of his sons the kiss of peace, all moved off to the cemetery. Rubeo then visited the sick in the infirmary, and only then did he retire to his own apartments.[2]

After resting a little from the fatigue of his journey the illustrious visitor had the community assembled in chapter. We know in a general way from his Constitutions that he was especially severe in all matters concerning religious

44

poverty. " This does not belong to me, but is for my use. A religious discovered possessing property of his own on the day of his death shall be deprived of ecclesiastical burial." Rubeo spoke and acted severely. And then, after his long discourse, in the presence of a notary, one or other of the older fathers had to renounce some comfortable ecclesiastical benefice. Master Bartholomew Ragusius went through all the cells, armed with a pair of scissors, to cut off from the shirts the large metal buttons, and carrying a basket to contain ruffles and collars, then fashionable, because any friar who wore them was ineligible for office. Caps edged with green or saffron-yellow silk, with coloured cords hanging from them, also disappeared into the basket, for the wearing of them was contrary to the spirit of the Chapter of Padua, which forbade even theologians to wear the insignia of their office. Nor were flasks of rose-water tolerated, or secular musical instruments, such as the lyre, the lute or guitar. Not, indeed, that the Master-General disliked music, for on April 24th he gave a warm welcome at Avila to the Portuguese sub-deacon, Gaspar d'Evora, who, *cupiditate musicae*, had twice fled from his own province.*

This sketch, like any other summary, may seem an exaggeration, for the *Actes* of Rubeo's Spanish visitations are lost, and it is based only on the general reforming constitutions of the period. In Rubeo's reliable *Regestum* there is only one decree in connection with the convent of Salamanca ; on February 9th, 1567, he grants Francisco del Ezima, not the possession, but the administration of twenty-five or thirty ducats, that had been given him as an alms for his old age, and also definitely authorises him to go for a walk with a companion chosen by himself, after informing the Prior of St. Andrew's.

But there were saints in the convent of Salamanca, and John of St. Mathias was not the only one living for God alone. During his first two years there, John had been edified by the society of a theologian, a newly-ordained priest, Hieronimo

---

* *Reg. Rubei*, f. 83. It is interesting to note this flight in connection with the appointment of Francisco Salinas, the famous blind musician, to the University of Salamanca in 1567.

Brito, from the convent of Lisbon. This Carmelite's praises of the Blessed Virgin were so tender that after his death, on January 1st, 1583, his tongue remained incorrupt and was preserved in a reliquary.[3]

At the end of the first session the Master-General had sheets of paper distributed containing the questions on which he proposed to examine each of the religious in turn, and he imposed a solemn precept on all to reveal the true state of the monastery.

When John of St. Mathias went back to his cell that evening he approached the little window that opened out on the altar, where the Blessed Sacrament was reserved, and began to pray. The light of Wisdom rose up from the Sacred Host ; it was a light of love ; and John then went from Love to the Cross. He stripped, and inflicted on his young, emaciated frame a scourging far more severe than that given by the *hebdomadarius* three times a week, according to the rule, a violent scourging such as was administered by the most zealous members of the *Cofradía de estudiantes disciplinantes*, who went in procession from St. Stephen's.[4] The blood flowed down on his shirt and drawers, woven of rough grass, which he wore as a penance. He stretched himself out on a sort of chest, his head upon the wood, and dreamed.[5] Through an opening in the roof the moon cast a silver circle of light on the little table where mystical and theological works lay side by side. He dreamed of his student's life, that held no place for recollection, and scarcely any for prayer, except the night hours. Even on Thursdays when, since the Chapter of 1564, the office of the *Corpus* was recited, time was given to study. Was he to lead such a life as this during his four years of theology, and, should his superiors wish, definitely look forward to an academic career, or the work of preaching, like Juan de Heredia and the others? Was this the future he had foreseen at Medina del Campo, when he fled from a chaplaincy at the hospital, in order to lead a life of recollection? And John of St. Mathias, the young Carmelite, twenty-six years of age, turned his mind's eye to the harsh mountain ranges of Castile, far away near Segovia.

In his *De Redditibus Ecclesiasticis,* Doctor Navarro Martin Azpilcueta had written in the preceding year—on July 8th, 1566—from that same Charterhouse of El Paular, on the joy of living in calm and peaceful solitude, the very image of Heaven. *O Bonitas !* was the cry of that son of St. Bruno, a man " like Elias and John the Baptist." [6] How happy a life of solitude and divine contemplation within the massive walls of the Charterhouse at El Paular !

And yet, on that very day, the Master-General of his Order had pointed out with force and conviction the true ideal of Carmel.

" The primitive and principal ideal of the inhabitants of Mount Carmel—which all Carmelites should imitate and pursue—is to devote themselves, day and night, with all their strength, to uniting their souls and spirits with God the Father, by means of prayer, contemplation and uninterrupted love, and that not merely in an habitual, but even actual manner." [7]

Such indeed was the prescription of the Primitive Rule and *The Institution of the first friars.* John of St. Mathias recalled to mind Rubeo's stirring language, for it had captured the heart that beat beneath that rough shirt and woollen scapular. In a short time the bell rang for Matins.

Next day, or the day after, he was called before the Master-General. Rubeo was now sixty years of age ; he had a commanding air, a splendid forehead, and his noble countenance was framed by a slight beard. He was well aware that Brother John´ was in his twenty-fifth year, that he lovingly carried out the Primitive Rule, and that he was a brilliant *artista.* History gives us no details of the interview, which certainly took place between these two illustrious Carmelites of the sixteenth century—a father and son who seem to us to have been so well made to understand each other.*

Did John of St. Mathias speak out ? Did he let the

---

* " Po generalisso . . . conocia al Sto pe frai Joan, aquien avia visto, icomunicado en suconvto de Salamanca, y por el nombre de su santitad, conservaba memoria del." Alonso, Bk. I, c. 7.

Spiritual Father of his Order, this man " so highly favoured by God," [8] hear of his desire for a more perfect, solitary, primitive life ? And if he did, why did the Master-General not allow him, as he had already, on April 3rd, 1563, allowed John de Piedad of Portugal, and as, on July 7th, 1568, he was to allow Albert of St. Augustine of Aragon, to build a hermitage and live there according to the full rigour of the reform ? On November 15th, 1565, in the most affectionate terms he granted Father James Montañés, of the same province of Aragon, permission to build a monastery according to the Primitive Rule at Our Lady of Hope, close to Onda and at no great distance from Valencia. Why did John not go and join his brethren at Onda ? It may be that John de Piedad had established, as he was free to do, his hermitage in Castile, which would be nearer, and in the same province. Who knows whether the Master-General, wishing to retain such a valuable subject for the reformation of the province of Castile, did not bring pressure to bear on the humble religious ? The prudent Rubeo, as we shall see, intended to reform the entire body of the Order, and separate attempts only too often resulted in separating themselves from the parent stock, after rapid growth. In any case, John may, perhaps, have kept his secret, that it might be better realised when God's hour should come.

One fact is certain : John of St. Mathias was appointed Master of Students at St. Andrew's. The constitutions passed at the Chapter of Avila (1567), now lost, lay down, according to Alonso,[9] that, for this office the student best fitted should be elected, that he should teach and direct the scholastic disputations. All this is in complete accord with the decision of the General Chapter of 1548, as also with the future constitutions of Alcalá, of which Father John of the Cross was to approve.[10] The subjects of John's lectures were decided by the Regent. Since Velasco testifies that when John came to Medina —which he did a few months later—he was a *teólogo pasante*,[11] it is clear he was entrusted with the duty of giving private lessons in dogmatic or moral theology after his appointment, which was in all probability made by Rubeo himself.*

But it is on mystical theology that we should love to hear of him speaking to his brethren.   And indeed, he may have done so, for the constitutions of the Blessed Soreth enact that the Master of Students (at that epoch a young bachelor of theology who was lecturing on the *Sentences*) should not only lecture on natural and moral philosophy and take part in scholastic disputations inside and outside the monastery, but also, once a week, thrash out some special problem.[12] Now Quiroga tells us that, when John of St. Mathias was at Salamanca " he read those authors who treat of the perfect life of our ancient solitaries, whose ordinary exercise was divine contemplation " ; and also that he read St. Denis and St. Gregory ; but he found their doctrine, and that of other saints whom the Church regards as luminaries on these matters, " so contrary to the new opinions," that is, to certain methods of prayer " invented and introduced by various spiritual masters, and founded on artifice and human industry rather than on what we receive from the divine operation," that he treated this delicate problem " in an excellent discourse." [13]   This is a valuable piece of information, but it was probably later, especially during the five years spent at the Incarnation in Avila, that John really got into touch with the past and elaborated his mystical synthesis.   It would be of interest to know who were the spiritual masters in Salamanca during this period. We know, at any rate, that, in 1564–1565, Alfonso Rodriguez, the future author of the *Practice of Christian Perfection* (he was then twenty-seven years of age), was master of the young scholastics of the Society of Jesus, and that Francisco Suarez was beginning his course as an *artista*.[14] Did Brother John of St. Mathias come into contact with them ? We do not know, but the mere possibility is thrilling enough.

·   ·   ·   ·   ·   ·

* There is no absolute certainty on this point ; but we know that, on March 9th, 1569, from Santa Maria in Trastevere (Rome) the General appointed Bartholomew Sanchez as Master of Students at St. Andrew's. *Regestum Rubei* 358, f. 195.

" *Studentes sunt viscera Ordinis nostri,*" students are the very
heart of our Order,[15] was undoubtedly the last piece of
advice given by the Master-General before he left Salamanca.
Brother John of St. Mathias took good care not to forget it.
He was not the Father Master of Students, for this office was
held by Martin de Santillana, who was also appointed
sub-prior after the Chapter held at Avila on April 12th.
But John could not dissociate his intellect from his heart,
and if he exercised influence over others, in virtue of his
position, it was through his soul, utterly athirst for divine
union. The saints do not offer part, but make a full and
complete gift of themselves to God. By his assiduity in
prayer, his constant recollection, John showed those around
him that it was not enough to follow out Rubeo's constitutions to the letter ; as, for instance, by attending Compline
and the solemn *Salve* only on Saturdays. The Master-
General's express wish, indeed, was rather to diminish than
increase dispensations. Some found the young Master of
Students' teaching too severe, and a few malcontents went
even so far as to whisper at his approach : " Let us get away
from here before the devil comes." [16] Alonso de Vilalba
mentions this incident, which must have taken place whilst
John was Master of Students, because Alonso did not begin
his course in Arts at Salamanca until the scholastic year of
1567–1568. We should not forget that John was only
twenty-five, and was not yet registered as a *teólogo* in the
University ; he may have been only a deacon, and there
he was, charged with presiding over theses, perhaps even
lecturing to priests and theologians older than himself—to
Sebastian de Oliva, for instance, who became prior of
Toledo in 1579, and confessor to Cardinal Quiroga ; or to
the bachelor, John of Heredia, who was one day to be a
doctor of theology, professor of the sacred sciences, a most
famous preacher all over Spain, twice prior of Valencia,
twice provincial of Aragon and rector of Saragossa for ten
years. This Heredia was a man so brilliant in intellect that
he publicly defended a thesis at the Chapter of Avila, and,
as the *Acts* tell us, in such fashion that those who objected
merely wasted their breath. Another of John's confrères—

or disciples might be the better word—also took part in those public disputations at Avila, which coincided with the naming of St. Thomas Aquinas as a Doctor of the Church (April 11th, 1567) : this was Bartholomew Sanchez, afterwards Master of Theology and rector of Salamanca.

Among the *artistas* of 1567–1568 we may mention Rodrigo Nieto, a future Master of Theology and provincial of Castile : Luis de Ruiz, rector of Alcalá twelve years later, and Cristobal de Toledo, a future prior of Avila who took part in the General Chapter of 1580 as second *socius* of Castile.

Such men as these were, indeed, the " heart " of the Order, over whose intellects John had charge, under the supreme authority of Master Martin Garcia, then prior of St. Andrew's.[17]

Towards the summer of 1567 John was ordained priest by Don Pedro Gonzales de Mendoza, bishop of Salamanca, as Alonso relates. We have been unable to find any document, either in the archives of the cathedral or at Calatrava, that fixes the date and place of ordination. However, it is quite certain that at the beginning of the scholastic year 1567–1568 John was a priest, seeing that he was registered as *presbyter y teólogo*. It is probable that the ordination took place in the grave and massive Catedral Vieja, and in the next chapter I hope to show that it must have been before the summer.

· · · · · ·

At the beginning of September, 1567, John left Salamanca for Medina del Campo, accompanied by Pedro de Orozco. The rose-coloured city, with its forty parishes, thirty-eight convents, fifty-two printing houses, eighty-four libraries, its palaces resplendent with armorial bearings—faded away in the distance. The two travellers traversed the red plain of León set in its pale hills, and John left behind him the pleasant future that the University offered. He willingly surrendered the gold ring and doctor's cap to the Most Illustrious Lord Don Diego Lopez de Zuniga, the *Rector Magnificus*, He had eyes for nothing but a charterhouse.

CHAPTER VI

TWO ANSWERS FROM HEAVEN

John of St. Mathias and Pedro de Orozco, his fellow-student, cheerfully traversed the seventeen or eighteen leagues of plain lying between Salamanca and Medina del Campo. The feast of the Nativity of Our Lady, when the University vacation began, was at hand.[1] The August sun had scorched away all verdure ; there was nothing but stubble and white dust all along the flat plain, and, from point to point in the distance could be seen the yellow stone or red brick belfry of a village church pointing towards the sky.

The travellers reached the gate of St. Anne's, from which they had set out. Antonio de Heredia was prior, and had been so from the previous April ; he was, beyond question, one of the noblest figures of the province of Castile. He was a bachelor of Salamanca, an exemplary religious, fond of study and his cell. A remarkably fine-looking man (which certainly helps), Padre Antonio, in fact, was possessed of all the qualities necessary for the exercise of power. This was quickly recognised, for he had been appointed prior of St. Paul de la Moraleja when only twenty-six. He had accompanied Angel de Salazar to the Chapter of Rome in 1564 as first *socius*, and when the election for provincial was held at Avila in April he obtained five votes out of twenty.

As soon as the arrival of the young travellers was announced the worthy prior hastened to welcome them home. He was now fifty-seven, and his tall figure had grown slightly bent, but his countenance was always so gay and his exterior so neat and trim that he brought with him a feeling of youth and animation.[2] He warmly embraced the two young priests, and asked for their blessing.[3]

•   •   •   •   •   •

Father John, in deep emotion from the first moment of his arrival, asked Father Melchior Falcon, the sub-prior, for a few novices to help him, and the sacristan prepared the high altar of St. Anne's. He lit several candles, as recommended by Sibert de Beka for a young priest's first Mass. He also decked out the altar with white rose-scented linen and, after a final glance round, dismissed the novices and departed quite content. One morning, perhaps during the Octave of the Nativity, the Carmelite Church was filled with the faithful. In the front row was Catalina Alvarez, peaceful and recollected, surrounded by Francisco, Ana Isquierda and her grandchildren. Don Alvarez de Toledo was also present.

When the choir had chanted the *Gloria Patri* of the Introit, the procession entered the church. Two acolytes in albs carried tapers, the sub-deacon the book of the Gospels, the deacon the Missal ; and John of St. Mathias with his hands joined walked last, clad in golden vestments that glittered in the rays of the morning sun. Together with the ministers he recites the Psalm *Judica* as he draws nigh the altar of God who rejoiceth his youth. The linens are unfolded—the Mass begins. John was twenty-five years of age, fearful of human weakness, and his sole desire was to be pure enough to touch the Holy of Holies. This desire was a prayer that filled with its anguish all the depths of his heart—most of all after the Gradual, when the sub-deacon ascended the altar-steps to prepare the chalice, whilst the acolytes lit all the tapers. Never to offend God mortally. To bear the punishment due to sin, but never to commit it—that was his determination, that was the gift he implored of the God of Mercy, Who can do all things.

The great candle in the middle of the choir is lighted ; the acolytes bear their torches ; the incense rises in clouds ; the sacring bell is rung, and John holds in his hands the Body of Christ, the Blood of Christ ; he hears the answer : " I grant thee what thou dost ask " ; and now he extends both arms in the form of a cross, according to the rite.

Later, at the Incarnation of Avila, John of the Cross was to confess to Sister Anna Maria that he was confirmed in

grace during his first Mass.[4] This gift does not take away
the power to commit sin, for the apostles themselves could
sin, but the first impulse is checked.[5] John kissed the Pax—
still holding the Sacred Host between his tightened fingers—
and, whilst the acolytes were carrying it to Catalina,
Francisco, Don Alvarez and the congregation, he spoke to
Jesus, present in the Sacrament—" *Salve salus mundi, verbum
Patris, Hostia sacra, viva caro, Deitas integra, verus homo*—Hail !
Saviour of the world, Word of the Father, Sacred Host,
true God and true Man." He received Holy Communion
himself, and administered it to his mother and brother, thus
giving Christ to them, who had given him to Christ.

After the *Corpus tuum Domine* of the ablutions, the young
priest uttered the vibrant hymn of praise : " *Tibi laus, tibi
gloria, tibi gratiarum actio. O ! beata et benedicta et gloriosa
Trinitas, Pater et Filius et Spiritus Sanctus.*" [6]

.   .   .   .   .   .

Immediately after celebrating his first Mass John felt
strongly urged to a life of solitude. He deliberately made
up his mind to leave for Santa Maria del Paular and live alone
with Christ. He could easily do so, because the Carmelites,
like all other mendicant friars, had permission to enter the
Carthusian Order without any preliminary authorisation
from the Holy See.[7] All that was needed was an agreement
between the superiors of both Orders.

Obviously John could not keep secret his resolve to
exchange his black habit and scapular for the white hood
and gown of the sons of St. Bruno. He must have spoken
of his intention ; and it is probable that the Father Prior
of St. Anne's was even then aware of it. The silence of the
third chapter of the *Foundations* [8] is in no way opposed to this
conjecture. We do not know if Father de Heredia, in his
turn, confided his own decision to John of St. Mathias.
It is possible that he did not wish to reveal his own resolution
prematurely to a young religious on the point of leaving his
Order. For the grave prior, who was so highly esteemed
in the province of Castile, had already made up his mind to
become a Carthusian. He had asked for permission, and

the Fathers had promised to receive him. They must have been the Carthusians either of Paular or Sagrameña, for those of Valbuena, Palazuelos and Huerta were too far away.

Padre Antonio, then, intended to become a Carthusian . . . yet no. It should rather be said that he *had* intended to ; for an important event had occurred to change his mind. At midnight on the eve of the Assumption, Teresa of Avila descended from her cart at the gate of St. Anne's. The prior had already seen her at Arevalo and been deeply moved at the sight of her ugly black veil, thick serge habit, and the clumsy *alpargatas* in which her aristocratic feet were shod.

Ribera, her confessor and biographer, in the description he has left of Teresa, speaks of her beautiful face, " with its complexion of lilies and roses," of her kindly but subtle mouth, and especially of her keen dark eyes, that pierced men to the soul.[9] Padre Antonio was captured by a charm at once divine and human ; up till now he had been busily engaged in securing a house for her foundation ; later on he was to do much more, and was always to remain a loyal follower of St. Teresa ; though a man of fifty-seven years, accustomed to command, clings naturally to his own judgment.

Father Hernandez said of the foundress : " She is a man and one of the manliest men I ever met." She had not hesitated to write to Rubeo and ask for his authorisation to undertake the reform of the Carmelite Fathers, so that she might have directors, and, later on, visitors, for her daughters, who would preserve them in the primitive spirit.[10] On August 16th the Master-General sent from Barcelona, to her whom he tenderly called *la mia figlia*, a patent giving permission to establish two houses of " contemplative Carmelite Fathers." Teresa had no subject in view and, not knowing what to do, unfolded her plan to the prior of St. Anne's " to see what advice he would give." Father de Heredia read the patent ; he was delighted, and promised the Mother to be the first religious of the reform. That was more than she had asked for ! She thought he was laughing at her, and

openly told him so. He had, indeed, always been a good
religious, led a retired life, been fond of study and his cell,
for he was a scholar, but Teresa did not think he was of a
stature to inaugurate such a mode of life. She said to
herself that he had not the requisite interior spirit and that
he could not promote the necessary austerity, as he was
delicate and by no means fitted for such a life of mortification. Julian of Avila reminds us that it was a question of
an heroic enterprise.[11]   A man may be an excellent religious,
interior and mortified, without being capable of habitual
heroism. Padre Antonio endeavoured to reassure Teresa,
telling her that God had, for a long time, been calling him
to lead a more penitential life, and that he had, in fact, made
up his mind to join the Carthusians. She did not show that
she was fully satisfied, even by this declaration, and asked
for delay, advising her postulant to exercise himself in the
new mode of life.

All this occurred before John's arrival in Medina and
after the reception of Rubeo's patent, consequently, between
August 20th and, in all probability, the first days of
September, 1567.

" A short time afterwards the grave Carmelite Fathers,"
as Alonso [12] tells us, " who were wont to visit Teresa and her
daughters in the apartments on the first floor of Blas de
Medina's mansion, where they lived whilst waiting until the
house in the Calle de Santiago was ready for them, spoke
to her in the highest terms of John of St. Mathias. His
companion, Pedro de Orozco, who knew him so well, told
the Foundress ' many admirable things concerning his mode
of life ' : how he carried out the Primitive Rule, was a model
of penance and recollection, how, like St. Alexis, he retired
to live beneath a staircase, and how the elder Fathers grew
more circumspect at his approach, such was the veneration
he inspired." [13]

One day in September John visited the Mother in her
house close by San Antolín's, either by invitation transmitted
through Pedro de Orozco [14] or at Father de Heredia's
suggestion. Anyhow, John, with the prior of St. Anne's
permission, called on Teresa, for we know from herself that

she observed the enclosure, even in Blas de Medina's mansion. After praying in the great gilt drawing-room, transformed into a chapel, John of the Cross saw Teresa for the first time. They "understood each other from the first." [15] Who can doubt it? Their eyes, their gestures, spoke of doing greater and better things, and those two geniuses of sanctity, who were set apart for the same work, understood one another. John of St. Mathias spoke first and told her of his desire for " higher perfection and a life of solitude," [16] and that he was about to go to the Carthusians " to separate himself from the world and hide himself in God." [17]

To John, that son of her soul, determined to weave his crown of thorns in the shade (like the young man in Zurbaran's picture),[18] Teresa, strong in her mission, revealed in a lightning flash of genius, the work of glorious immolation for which he had been created. She told him of her project, that marvellous project which would leave intact his ideal of being alone with God alone, namely, the resurrection of the primitive life of the Order of the Blessed Virgin. For a man enamoured of solitude what more attractive ideal than the eremitical life of the Fathers of Mount Carmel, with the freedom to give of his fulness to his fellow-men, which even the Fathers of the Desert had never contested? The fulness of the interior life is not diminished when one gives of one's superabundance ; and action in the case of the saints in no way interrupts the harmony of their being, which is centred on God alone. Teresa's own life was a proof of this, and John saw quite clearly, and it made him confident, that love was the sole motive power of her existence. She was active, but only for God ; she had a hunger for solitude. " What a torment," she wrote in 1562, when founding San José of Avila, " what torment for the poor soul that has reached the stage of union to have to begin once again to deal with men and to be condemned to see that poor farce called life passing before its eyes ! " [19] When one loves one lavishes strength and talent, and that is what Christ demanded from Teresa and John for the renovation of the Order of His Mother.

Teresa of Jesus, speaking in the *Foundations* of this son of her soul, says : " I urgently entreated him to wait until the Lord should give us a monastery, and made him see that, if he wished to embrace a more perfect life it would be better to do so in his own Order, and that this would give greater glory to God. He promised to do so on condition of not having to wait too long." This shows us how near he was to Paular. He loved straight roads : the Ascent of Mount Carmel is a short cut, a steep, perpendicular path.

Teresa was delighted and, with her usual frankness, must have shown John, as she certainly showed Padre Antonio, the Master-General's patent, in which John at once recognised Rubeo's great soul, his grasp of the primitive ideal and his desire for a reform. The province of Castile was on the point of extinction, no life was in it.

" We are overwhelmed with grief," wrote the Father-General, " at not beholding abundant fruits in the vineyard of Carmel. . . . It is our desire that all religious belonging to this Order should be so many bright mirrors, burning lamps, glowing torches and resplendent stars, capable of enlightening those who are travellers in the midst of this world. To this end our dearest wish is that they should devote themselves to a continual and familiar intercourse with God, and that, by means of prayer, the practice of holy meditation and contemplation, they should strive to unite themselves to Him in such manner that their spirit, even whilst still in the flesh, may live henceforth in Heaven, and only serve the body from sheer necessity." And he gave her permission to establish " two houses of religious, where they could spend their days in the celebration of Masses, the recitation and chanting of the divine office, and, at suitable times, in meditation and other spiritual exercises, so that these houses may be called, and in reality be, houses and monasteries of contemplative Carmelites."

He said in conclusion : " They may also assist their neighbour, if opportunity offers, and the ancient constitutions shall be followed in the manner we prescribe, under obedience to the present and future Fathers Provincial." [20]

What Rubeo then sets forth, in the middle of the sixteenth

century, had already been begun three centuries previously by the sternest defender of the primitive life of Carmel, Nicholas the Frenchman, successor to St. Simon Stock. In his *Ignea Sagitta* he writes :

" Has not our Saviour graciously led us into solitude where, in special intimacy, He desires to speak to our heart— He who showed Himself to His friends in order to console them, and revealed hidden mysteries to them in the upper room, and not in public, not in the street or in the midst of tumult ? . . . (Our Fathers) conscious of their own imperfection, persevered for long in the solitude of the desert, but, desiring to be of such use to their neighbours as not to incur guilt in their regard, they descended, though rarely, from their hermitage. That which they had so delightfully harvested with the sickle of contemplation in solitude, they then proceeded to tread upon the threshing-floor of preaching, and sowed with a generous hand." [21]

That, indeed, is the ideal which John and Teresa looked forward to, and desired for their children. We shall see that, during the whole course of John's existence, and in so far as the duties he assumed would permit, he was faithful to the primitive conception sketched out in 1567. He told Teresa that, knowingly and willingly " he had determined to take the habit without delay," [22] and he now recalled to mind that God had chosen him " to re-establish an Order in a new perfection." [23] This Order was his own ; it was Carmel. He now received from Teresa the complement of his own light from heaven that made radiantly clear what he had already been told.

She was overjoyed, for she now had a friar and a half to begin her reform, big Padre Antonio and " little Seneca ". *Frayle y medio !* But if John was small in stature he was, like herself, the *mujer grande*, great in spirit.*

．　　．　　．　　．　　．　　．

* When Mother Teresa left the parlour and rejoined the community, who were at recreation, she said : " I would have you know, my daughters, that I have already a friar and a half to begin the reform, and I am quite content." Mary Evangelist continues, " the holy Mother regarded John of the Cross as a complete friar, for she was enchanted with him." She still wished to try Antonio, " ordering him to fast, take the discipline and meditate " (Andrés, 13,482, J. 41).

Mother Teresa did not leave Medina for Alcalá de Henares until the beginning of November, and John may have returned to Salamanca only for the feast day of St. Luke, but, as we have seen above, he certainly did return.

In October, thanks to Father de Heredia's efforts, the nuns were able to take up residence in their new house in the Calle Santiago. It was no longer necessary to go to confession or hear Mass from behind the slit of a door on the staircase, as on the morning of the Assumption, nor had the Mother to watch by moonlight, as she used to do in her fear lest Genevese or Dutch Lutherans might insult the Blessed Sacrament !

John went occasionally to the convent before the school re-opened, and, no doubt, said Mass there, as Julian of Avila had returned to San José at Avila. He was well acquainted with the high, warm, red-brick wall of the Calle Santiago, and felt quite at home as he passed beneath the heavy keystone of the arch to the Carmelite Convent. The little whitewashed court, with its large tile, has a friendly feeling, and, from behind the grille of the *locutorio*, he could hear the soft, maternal tones of Teresa's voice. One day he took his mother, good and poverty-stricken Catalina, along with him and introduced her to the Mother and her daughters, who adopted her as one of the family. They assisted her afterwards when age prevented her from working and Francisco was unable to assist her. In the account books for 1571 there is an entry, signed by the saint herself, who was then prioress, for the price of a pair of shoes purchased for Catalina Alvarez. And when, in the " year of influenza," 1580,[24] the widow of Gonzalo de Yepes rested for ever from her labours, the Carmelite nuns of Medina found a place for her remains beneath an arched vault in their cloister.

CHAPTER VII

EARLY in July, 1568, Teresa of Jesus and Sister Antoinette of the Holy Ghost stopped in Medina while Julian of Avila, her faithful chaplain, accompanied by Mgr. Alvaro de Mendoza's secretary, went up to Valladolid to solicit the goodwill of the ecclesiastical administrator on behalf of a foundation in that noble city, the residence of the kings of Castile.

Father John of St. Mathias had brought his first year's theology at the University of Salamanca to an abrupt conclusion. On May 10th the 253 students of the " Vesper " chair elected the Benedictine, Master Pedro de la Fuente [1] as substitute for Master Juan de Guevara, who went off on vacation. John hastened home, for, at this time, an attendance of only six months and a day during the scholastic year was required as a minimum by the University statutes.

As soon as the Foundress arrived Antonio de Heredia and John called at the Calle Santiago, and Teresa hastened to the grille to tell them that a gentleman in Avila, Don Rafael Mejia Velasquez, had given a house, " in a hamlet of some twenty hearths at most," to begin the reform of the Carmelite Fathers. After leaving Avila for Medina she had stopped there with her companion. Duruelo, about eight and a half leagues from Avila, was so unimportant that people did not even know where it was.

" I shall never forget," says Teresa, in the twelfth and thirteenth chapters of her *Foundations*, on which we now rely, " the weariness and the meanderings of this journey. Owing to them we did not arrive till nightfall. When we entered the house its condition was so unattractive, both on account of its extreme filthiness and the presence of harvesters, that we did not wish to take the risk of spending the night there.

" Our whole monastery consisted of a *portal*, suitable enough, a room with an alcove and loft, and a little kitchen. . . . My companion, though better than I and a great lover of penance, could not bear the thought of seeing me establish a convent there. ' I really do assure you, Mother,' she said, ' that the most fervent spirit in the world would find it intolerable. I beg you to give up the idea.' The priest who was with me thought likewise, but, when I had told him of my plan, he did not oppose it. So we went and passed the night in the Church. I must say that, tired out as we were, we much preferred not to watch that night."

Teresa appealed to Padre Antonio : " If he had the courage to spend a while there God would certainly arrange everything soon. . . ." Padre Antonio cried that " he was ready to dwell not only in this place but in a pigsty," and Father John " was of the same mind." One could understand this of " little " Father John who, even amongst the *los de paño*,* was leading " a perfect and most exemplary life " : but what about the delicate prior of St. Anne's ? Could he live in a cowshed ?

Padre Antonio had been tested by tribulation during the previous year, and had borne it admirably. Philip II, intent on the reform of the monastic orders in his kingdom, had written him that he wished to see him at work on the reform of his own Order. Unfortunately, the religious of St. Anne's heard the great news and all the Carmelite Fathers of Castile were annoyed. What did he mean by thus dishonouring his own Order in the sight of seculars ? To add to his troubles it was also learned that Padre Antonio had been communicating with the Carthusians in the idea of joining them ; and, in addition, planning with Mother Teresa to introduce novelties into the province ! " There is no need now to fear his failing," thought the Foundress, " for God has given more courage to Padre Antonio than to me."

---

* " Fathers of the Cloth," *i.e.*, the Observants, whose habits were not made of rough serge.

It was vital to establish the foundation as quickly as possible ; but they had to obtain the authorisation of the Provincial and his substitute, as required by the Master-General's patent. Teresa optimistically thought that the Superiors would consider that a beginning, in such a hamlet and such a dwelling-place, could give no offence to the regular monasteries, and, with this hope firmly planted in her strong heart the *tan baratona*,[2] the great " *business woman* " set to work. " *Obras, que no palabras* "—deeds, not words— was ever her motto ; and the great thing was to make a beginning. Padre Antonio was impatient, and as for little Father John, had he not given his promise the previous year " solely on condition that he should not have to wait long " ?

. . . . . .

Early in August, whilst Teresa was at prayer, Our Lord told her to hurry on the foundation at Valladolid, because its benefactor, Don Bernardin de Mendoza, was suffering greatly in Purgatory. She still needed much for the foundation but, as her sole thought was of her friend's dire necessity, she at once set off, accompanied by Antoinette of the Holy Ghost and Mary of the Cross—the third and fifth nuns professed at San José of Avila—and Mother Isabella Arias, formerly sub-prioress of the Incarnation. The inseparable Julian of Avila and Father John rode alongside the cart.

They entered Valladolid on August 10th, 1568, the feast of St. Lawrence, tired out naturally by their thirty-mile journey, but for all that, happy and recollected. With Teresa, religious observance was easy in spite of the joltings of the amazing vehicles whirled along in a cloud of yellow dust by jingling mules urged on by the oaths of the *mozos*. She carried a clock about with her to mark the hours for prayer and a little bell to end the time of silence and mark the beginning of recreation—invariably a cheerful time. Blessed Anne of St. Bartholomew, who knew her better than anyone, tells us " that she did not like melancholy people, that she herself was not gloomy, and did not wish others to be so in her company ; she used to say, ' *may God deliver me from surly saints.'* " [3] Gloomy people and affected prayers (as she called them) wearied her.[4] It is easy to understand the joy of the Discalced Franciscan nuns at Madrid at having amongst them " a saint so like anyone else."

They must have travelled by night—in order to save time, or, perhaps, merely to avoid sunstroke—for Teresa relates that, despite the fatigue of the journey, she had to go and hear Mass in a Carmelite church near the south-western gate of the city. " It was so far off," she confesses, " that I felt my sufferings redoubled." Although she does not say so, it was here, in all probability, that Father John said Mass that morning of St. Lawrence's day, with the authorisation of the prior, Ambrosio de Castro, and Miguel Maldonado, the sacristan.

It is a good twenty minutes' walk along the Simancas Road from the vast Carmelite Church (now a military hospital) to Rio de Olmos, Don Bernardin's property. It is an interesting fact that, before it was bequeathed to Teresa, it had been occupied by Franciscans and, before that, in 1551, by Carmelite Fathers newly arrived in Valladolid. All had abandoned it on account of the unhealthiness of the site. It is not known whether Teresa was aware of this, but, in any case, she wrote : " I was very much upset when I saw the house ; I saw it would be folly to establish nuns in such a place, save at enormous expense ; moreover, if the site was pleasant, on account of the *huerta*, which was really delightful, the neighbourhood of the river made it obviously unhealthy." The nuns remained there only from August 15th to October 31st.

Still we should pause on this spot, now marked only by a granite column broken off close to the ground, where the property called *Los Ingleses* ends. Everything round is peaceful, and the plain stretches away unbroken by any rising ground ; about 80 yards off is the River Pisuerga, hidden by a screen of foliage, and we are standing about 15 or 20 feet above it. Half-way down a little spring flows quietly through the grass. Beneath the elms, as we move down towards the river, lie paths made for contemplation. The whole countryside is silent. Formerly the *huerta* was surrounded by vines that rejoiced the sight with their golden clusters. John appreciated and loved this prospect, and he loved the company of the nuns.

Before leaving Medina Teresa had asked Padre Antonio "to do all he could about getting together a few little things" for Duruelo. But, with the prior's consent, she had carried off Father John, who had a better work before him ; for Teresa wished to reveal to him the secrets of her soul. Truly it needed a John of the Cross to understand this royal soul and thoroughly enter into its thoughts.

No one will deny that Teresa was a genius, and that, when she adopted the primitive rule of Carmel she literally renewed " all that Carmel means." For it had to be born anew.[5] Before she did so her heart had been pierced by the seraph's dart, and she lived henceforward with the torment and the rapture of the wound, " dying because she could not die." John of the Cross, remembering this, wrote in *The Living Flame* : " The soul may feel itself attacked by a seraph bearing a feathered dart, armed with a most ardent love. . . . Very few reach this state, but some [souls] have reached it, especially [the souls of] those whose spirit and power are destined to be conveyed to a succession of disciples, God giving richness and value to the leader, for the sake of the spiritual destiny of those who are to come after him."

> *¡ Oh cauterio suave !*
> *¡ Oh regalada llaga !* *

.   .   .   .   .   .

About August 15th Julian of Avila was able to celebrate the first Mass at Rio de Olmos, in the room marked out as the future chapel.[6] When he gave the saint Communion, he saw that she was in a profound ecstasy, for, at that very moment, Don Bernardin appeared to her " with a joyous,

---

* (O sweet cautery ! O delightful wound ! *Llama*, Cancion II–Ger. II, 409, 414, 415.)   Like Francis of Assisi, the Virgin of Avila and Juan de Yepes, poor and free, praised and sang of love, contemplative, consuming love, whose living flame breaks forth in burning zeal.

resplendent countenance. With his hands joined," writes
Teresa, " he thanked me for what I had done in freeing him
from Purgatory, and his soul mounted to Heaven." Rubens
has illustrated the scene in a picture now in the Antwerp
Gallery. This incident emphasises the dominant note of
Teresa's soul—the apostolate by contemplation.

The Carmelite nuns of Valladolid still possess the manuscript of *The Way of Perfection*, as retouched by the Mother ;
the first draft was completed in 1565, and we read in the
twelfth chapter : " Let us call to mind our holy Fathers,
the hermits of former days whose lives we strive to imitate." [7]
Teresa, it is clear, desired that the Rule of Our Lady of
Mount Carmel should be observed " in its entirety, without
mitigation ; that is to say, as it was drawn up by Father
Hugh, Cardinal of Santa Sabina, and given, in 1248, the
fifth year of the Pontificate of Pope Innocent IV." [8] But
why revive the sufferings and isolation of the solitaries of
Carmel ? No doubt because a free heart, emptied of all
created things, is needed for divine contemplation, but,
above all, because this life, " materially so severe," and as
poor, will save souls. Teresa, reflecting on the calamities
that were desolating France, and the ravages of the
Lutherans, wrote, at the beginning of the *Camino* : " It
seemed to me, I would have given a thousand lives to save
only one of those souls who were being lost in such numbers
in that country. . . . My heart breaks at the sight of so
many souls damning themselves. Ah ! if only I did not
see so many more being lost every day ! " [9]

" Oh ! my sisters in Jesus Christ ! Help me to ask this
grace from Our Lord. It is to this end that He has brought
you all here, this is your work, and to this all your desires
should tend. . . . If it should ever happen that your
prayers, desires, disciplines and fasts are no longer directed
towards this end that I have shown you, then tell yourselves
that you are no longer fulfilling the purpose for which Our
Lord brought you here." [10]

Teresa clearly, freshly and vigorously, emphasises the
apostolic character of the Carmelite contemplative life.
Hitherto it had never been expressed with such force. " I

feel certain that this apostolic aim gave birth to all the convents founded during her lifetime, and after her death " was the solemn deposition of the Venerable Anne of Jesus.[11] If her reform may, perhaps, have surpassed in its rigour what the Primitive Rule foresaw—if, from this time forth, men and women went to Carmel to make a complete sacrifice of their lives—it was to save France from Lutheranism, it was because one day—this we should never forget—the Franciscan Father Maldonado,* just arrived from the Indies, had spoken at the grille of San José at Avila " of the millions of souls who were being lost " in those far-off lands, and had exhorted the nuns to penance. On that occasion Teresa had retired in tears to a hermitage, and her apostolic zeal increased immeasurably, for, as she writes, " such is the attraction God has given me." [12] The enemies of God were depriving Him of souls ! Teresa was soon to take alarm at the austerities of her first sons : yet it was she who had sounded the note of danger and proclaimed a holy war against those powerful demons who are driven out only " by prayer and fasting." And John was her disciple.

.   .   .   .   .   .

On August 15th canonical possession was taken of Rio de Olmos, and Doña Arias, Mother Isabella of the Cross, was established prioress of this convent of Our Lady's Conception. From that time forward, whilst the workmen were building the enclosure, and Julian of Avila was going to and fro between the house and the city, organising all that was necessary for the fixing of the hatch and grilles, Teresa was initiating John " in our whole mode of life." She instructed him fully in each of the community exercises, both as regards mortifications and as regards the cordial internal relations of the Community, and the manner of spending recreations ; she cheerfully admitted that he was so virtuous that she had more to learn from him than he from her ; but, just now, that was not the point ; she was thinking only of instructing him " in all things observed by the sisters."

* Antonio Maldonado, not, as is commonly said, Alonso Maldonado, quite a different man. See *Book of Foundations*, London, 1913, p. 9 (Transl.).

In doing so she in no way transgressed the powers granted her by the Master-General ; she was not interfering. The constitutions drawn up for the contemplative Carmelite Fathers,[13] in conformity with the patent of August 16th, 1567, were modelled on those of the nuns. In the Spanish original, to which Rubeo's autograph signature is appended, mistakes occur, such as : " the Mother Prioress," " the nuns," instead of " the Father Prior," " the religious," and these phrases have been written over and corrected, so that it is clear the author had the constitutions of the Carmelite nuns before him. Not only the same spirit, but the same observance should, as far as possible, reign in the houses of both Brothers and Sisters, for such was the intention of the Master-General and the Mother Foundress. They were in perfect agreement, and if proof be needed we know that when the General stayed at Avila (April, 1567) Teresa presented him with the constitutions she had drawn up, both for the Brothers and the Sisters, and he gave them his approval. Father Angel de Salazar was present, as he testified at Valladolid in 1595, when an enquiry was being held with a view to Teresa's canonisation.[14]

. ·   .   .   .   .   .

Reading the *Vida* and the *Camino*, the two treatises already composed by Teresa, one is struck by her attraction to holy poverty.

One of the last joys of St. Peter of Alcantara, the old Franciscan ascetic who was " so emaciated that he might have been made of roots of trees," [15] was that he had aroused this feeling in her. He strongly supported Teresa against Father Ibañes, who had sent her " two sheets of paper crammed with arguments and theological principles " in order to dissuade her from founding convents without any revenues. For this once " she renounced " the benefit of theology, " and roundly begged the learned Dominican to spare her his science." [16]   " The great honour of the poor is in being really poor." [17]

Teresa of Jesus, who had made St. Joseph her banker—and with no small success—never hesitated at useful expenditure. She was too supernatural and too intelligent to do things by halves. She practised the theological virtue of hope : " Teresa and three ducats is nothing, but God, Teresa and three ducats is everything."

Julian of Avila points out that " the holy mother saw quite clearly that the convent at Rio de Olmos could not last, and yet, brief as the stay there must be, she was careful to arrange for all that was required for a regular convent." [18] Not indeed that she built for eternity, for all things will crumble away on the Day of General Judgment. " It is not fitting that a house for thirteen poor little women should make a great noise when it collapses on that day : really poor people must not make much noise . . . the smallest corner is large enough for thirteen poor women. Have an enclosure with a few hermitages where you can pray in solitude, but no fine buildings ! As St. Clare used to say, the walls of holy poverty are very high. There is one thing I beg of you for the love of Jesus. Our badge is holy poverty, and you know how it was treasured, and how loyally practised, by our holy Fathers at the foundation of our Order ; one in a position to know has told me that they kept nothing from one day to the next. If poverty is no longer observed by us with such external perfection, let us strive to have perfect interior poverty. Let it be seen in everything—in our houses, clothes, words, and, much more, in our thoughts." [19]

John of St. Mathias must have felt his heart swell within him at such an appeal, at such a command, which pointed out to him the road to deprivation and poverty of spirit.

Despite certain remarks in the *Camino* and *Fundaçiones*, Teresa, like St. Peter of Alcantara, did not insist so much on mortification of the flesh as on *desnudez*—the solitude and silence so necessary and fruitful for the spiritual life. She did not feel it necessary to enjoin on her daughters " a number of observances " that constrain the upward flight of the spirit. " May God grant," she wrote, " that we faithfully carry out those observances which our holy Fathers inaugurated and practised so well themselves," [20] and hence, at Rio de Olmos, they devoutly recited the hours, observed recollection, kept the enclosure, and practised manual labour, as laid down by the Primitive Rule and *The Institution of the first friars.* Happiness reigned in the " little spot belonging to our good God." Thus, " the mode of life introduced under divine inspiration by the holy mother for her daughters," wrote Quiroga, " resembled, in every respect, that led by our ancient Fathers." [21]

.   .   .   .   .   .

The Primitive Rule does not prescribe absolute silence, save from after Compline until Prime of the following day. Teresa, in order to put a stop to unnecessary conversation, settled on two hours for recreation, one at mid-day, the other in the evening, during which time " things are so combined that we learn to know our faults, at the same time enjoying relaxation which helps us the better to support the austerity of the Rule. But the slightest detraction is strictly forbidden." [22]

Teresa speaks, in the *Camino*, of mutual love, with a wisdom and breadth of view which reveal a profound knowledge of the human heart. These pages are for ever true. She determines accurately the limits of friendship, allowing neither too much nor too little. There is nothing cold or formal about those recreations she speaks of, which are so useful for acquiring self-knowledge. They have not the slightest appearance of prescribed duties. The sisters chat as they work—for Teresa did not intend them to be idle. In 1576 she asked Fathers Gracian and Mariano to make their religious weave osier baskets during recreation, for the important point is to insist " on the virtues and not on corporal austerities." [23] This does not prevent gaiety, even though there be no great desire for laughter.[24] One day, whilst she was still at Rio de Olmos, very tired and already feverish, she was going to her cell at recreation time when a young lay-sister—a novice—who saw her slipping away, said to her : " Are you not coming with us, Reverend Mother ? " Teresa smiled and said : " All right, Sister, I'm coming." [25] She had a tabor and castanets, and she sang and danced. " A queer sort of Mother Foundress ! "

¡ Oh Hermosura que excedéis,
A todas las hermosuras !
Sin herir dolor hacéis
Y sin dolor deshacéis
El amor de las criaturas.*

In her, the mystical impulse, poetry and childlike gaiety were all in harmony. She said to some peevish sisters who took scandal, " All this is needed to make life endurable." [27] Father John was not scandalised, and we shall see him, later on, acting in the same way more than once. He is a poet, the poet of the dark night, but also the poet of joy and of love.

Recreations, then, were never boring in Teresa's convents, and the nuns learned to live in peace and harmony. If, in 1577, Sister Mary of the Cross became neurasthenic, it was not Teresa's fault, nor the fault of her cousin, Sister Antoinette of the Holy Ghost, nor of Casilda de Padilla— whom Teresa mentions in the *Fundaciones*, telling how at twelve years old she eluded her governess and, after putting her " chapines " up her sleeves, tucked up her skirts and ran off to shut herself up in the Carmelite Convent of Valladolid.[28] Such were the postulants received in those days. There was Bela, Gracian's little sister, and Teresita, Lorenzo de Cepeda's daughter. " The cleverness of this little creature is extraordinary. Not a feast day passes but she invents some tableau in her hermitage or at recreation. She also makes her own little poems, which she sings with so much grace that we are all enchanted. She gives me only one cause of anxiety ; I cannot get her mouth right, for she had a very haughty pout, and laughs very coldly, and yet she is always smiling. . . . I have told you all this to make you laugh a little." [29]

. . . . . .

And yet, despite the general goodwill and the Mother Foundress's animation, life at Rio de Olmos was not without its anxieties.

* Oh Beauty, surpassing all beauty, thou makest us suffer without wounding, and, without suffering destroyest the love of creatures.[26]

" Gradually almost all the nuns fell seriously ill " [30]—
of a quartan fever, as Julian of Avila tells us [31]—and we have
already seen that Teresa did not escape. John had nursed
contagious diseases at the hospital in Medina. They
appreciated his experience—and his courage. Yet Teresa
did not hesitate, even in these trying circumstances, to put
him to the test and to speak harshly to him. She admits the
fact to Francisco de Salcedo, and is forced to conclude :
" We never discovered a solitary imperfection in him . . .
we shall certainly miss him here." [32] John helped the little
community during this trial, consoling and directing them
with a youthful authority that was very touching. One
morning the sister sacristan forgot to lay out the altar linen.
Mass was about to begin, and she was anxious to make up
for her forgetfulness, but, as she was afraid of the Mother's
noticing it, she did not leave her place, and asked Father
John, in a low voice, to take out the corporals without
seeming to do so. John, however, took the opportunity of
teaching her simplicity, and said : " *Come, Sister, get them
out yourself, and if the Mother Foundress asks what you are carrying,
tell her simply that you are repairing your forgetfulness.*" [33] The
incident is minute, but revealing. Teresa might well write :
" I find him full of wisdom. . . . I think we are beginning
well. This Father is far advanced in prayer, and has good
judgment. May the Lord prosper him : *Llévelo el Señor
adelante.*" [34]

These words, this desire, tell us a great deal. Teresa was
in need of religious who observed the Primitive Rule to
direct her daughters. She held it " necessary." The
Master-General, at her instigation, withdrew his previous
refusal and authorised her to found two convents of " Contemplative Carmelites, capable of enlightening and guiding
those who are travellers through this world." Unfortunate
misunderstandings were no doubt to arise, but the important
point is that, even then, John Baptist Rubeo remembered
Teresa's desires and gave orders to form and carefully select
from amongst the " Contemplatives " confessors for the nuns
of the primitive observance. [35]

Father Alonso Gonzalez, provincial of Castile, happened

just then to be in Valladolid : Teresa went to him to make
her request, and show him the Father-General's patents.
We are not quite sure what he thought of Padre Antonio,
but he had known John at Salamanca, and there was not
a single one of his brethren who did not speak well of John.
Teresa was an excellent advocate and brought forward so
many reasons—amongst others, she pointed out the account
he would have to render to God if he hindered such a good
work—that Father Alonso gave in.

In the meantime the brother and sister of the donor of
Rio de Olmos, Doña Maria de Mendoza and the bishop of
Avila, arrived.   The latter had always helped and protected
Teresa and was one of her greatest friends.   They arranged
about the foundation of Duruelo with Father Gonzalez
and, in particular, with Father Angel de Salazar, whom
she most feared—it is hard to tell why, for Gracian was later
to recognise that " the province (of Discalced Carmelites)
was under great obligations to this holy man." [36]

When the two were won over it was settled that Father
John of the Cross—as John of St. Mathias was to be called
henceforward—should go to Duruelo and put the house in
as habitable a state as possible.   Teresa was very anxious
that something should be done.   She took up her quill pen,
and in her firm handwriting began :

" To Don Francisco de Salcedo at Avila.

" May Jesus be with you ! Thanks be to God, after writing
seven or eight business letters, which I could not put off, I
have still a little leisure left to find rest in sending you these
few lines. . . . Pray, talk to this Father, and give him help.
He is indeed small in stature, but, in my opinion, he is very
great in the sight of God.   I find him most fitted for our
kind of life ; I really do believe that God is calling him to
this enterprise.   He is still young, but he has always practised the most austere penance.   The Lord visibly supports
him with His hand.   Nevertheless, he really needs all the
graces he has received, to begin the work all alone and in
such a generous spirit.   He will tell you himself how things
are going on at Valladolid."

Despite her weariness she jests with her faithful friend, the *Caballero Santo* :

" You would give six ducats to see me ? That seems a large sum to me.   I ought then to be even more generous if I am to pay you a visit ! It is true you are worth more than I, for what value has a poor little nun ? You, at any rate, can give cider, cakes, radishes and lettuce, for you have a garden, and I know that it is you who are doing the work of a servant, bringing us apples—so you deserve a little more esteem.   Talking about cider, they say there is a very good brand here, at Valladolid.   But, as we have not a Francisco de Salcedo here, we do not know the taste of it, and have not even a hope of doing so. . . .

" Your unworthy and true servant,

" TERESA OF JESUS, *Carmelita.*"

Always haunted by her project, and with Father John ever in mind, she writes eagerly : " Once again I ask you, as an alms, to talk with this Father. Tell him what you think is most suitable for his mode of life. I have been greatly encouraged at seeing the spirit with which God animates him, and the virtue he has shown on many occasions. It seems to me that we are beginning well . . . " [37]

CHAPTER VIII

" THE LITTLE STABLE OF BETHLEHEM "

ABOUT the end of September, or quite early in October,[1] Father John and the workman* lent him by Teresa arrived at Duruelo. They came from Avila, where John had been on a visit to Teresa's friends. The dark, snow-capped Sierra de Gredos lay far behind them, and the valley stretched out like two great wings in front : whilst, in the centre the Rio Almar whirled along its stones and yellow sands.

The village was hidden away in the midst of green oak trees, and close at hand rolled the shining river. It was open, fertile country ; a charming, gracious solitude. As soon as John and his companion arrived they began to set in order the dwelling-house which had been inhabited by Don Rafael's steward.[2] At nightfall the workman went off to look for some food. When John, towards the end of his life, was telling Father Jerome of the Cross about his first supper at Duruelo, he confessed : " I assure you that I enjoyed those bits of bread as much as if I had been eating pheasant." [3]

On the following morning, at daybreak, John, clothed in the short, narrow habit of rough serge which the Sisters at Medina del Campo had made for him,[4] put on the vestments given by Teresa and offered up the Holy Sacrifice.[5] The primitive observance had begun.

The saint's biographers have delighted to point out the resemblance of the life at Duruelo not only to that of the prophet Elias, " father and chief of all Carmelites," [6] but also to that of the Palestinian and Egyptian solitaries. A close study of the clothing, dwelling-places and customs of

---

* Perhaps this was the man, mentioned by Father Jerome of the Cross, who accompanied the saint with the intention of becoming a lay-brother (Jaén, I. O. fo. 8).

the monks of the East shows that John of St. Mathias, before beginning the reform, had made an attentive examination of the usages of the Fathers of the Desert. He did not dye the serge of the habit like the Syrian monks mentioned by St. John Chrysostom; the "primitives" were long accustomed to wear an untanned leather cincture; they used the anchorite's staff and, even in 1581, went barefooted, as the Gospel enjoins.[7]

After some weeks Father Antonio, accompanied by Brother Joseph and a religious from Medina, arrived at Duruelo. He had gladly surrendered the priorship of St. Anne's to Father Gonzalez and, although he had been advised to give the life a trial first, he had made a vow to observe the Primitive Rule. His joy was great at the sight of the little hamlet : it was a divine springtime, though, according to the calendar, it was mid-autumn. The old man unpacked a few things—including the five hour-glasses at which Teresa laughed so heartily—and then took formal possession of the convent.

Father John had made good use of his time : the little house was now habitable, and both Padre Antonio and himself regarded it as a delightful spot. The Foundress had seen what could be done : the former loft had now been turned into a choir ; one could only enter it by stooping very low but, towards the centre it was lofty enough, so that they were able to recite the divine office and also hear Mass, which was said in the *portal*, now turned into a chapel.

John had set up, according to St. Teresa's plan, a couple of little hermitages. He put them at the two corners of the choir, looking towards the chapel. They were so low that one's head touched the roof, and one could only remain in them sitting or lying. There was a view of the altar from two small windows. These hermitages served as cells for Father John and Father Antonio. The other religious slept in another room under the attics. The kitchen was divided into two parts, one of which served as a refectory. In face of such poverty and humility it was easy to remember " our true founders, the holy Fathers from whom we are descended." It was a " little stable of Bethlehem. I called it that," writes Teresa, " for, in my opinion, it was worthy of the name."

.   .   .   .   .   .

" In the year 1568, on November 28th, this monastery of Our Lady of Mount Carmel was founded in the village of Duruelo. In the said monastery, aided by the help and grace of the Holy Spirit, life was begun according to the strict observance of the primitive Rule as bequeathed to us by our first Fathers. When the Very Reverend Father Master Alonso Gonzalez was provincial, Brother Antonio of Jesus, Brother John of the Cross and Brother Joseph of Christ began to live, aided by the grace of God, according to all the rigour of the Rule." [8] The foundation was canonically established and, in a short time, Gonzalez appointed Father Antonio prior, Father John sub-prior and master of novices. The official documents were addressed to : " *R^{do} Patri Praesentato alias de Heredia nunc vero de Jesus cognominato . . . qui fuit et est illorum Discalceatorum director et Rector.*" *

It was Antonio who was charged by the superiors with the carrying out of the work for which Mother Teresa had petitioned. His age and distinction, and above all, the numerous official positions he had held, inspired the fullest confidence. John of the Cross was only a young father, twenty-six years of age, fresh from the college of St. Andrew.

But if we look at the divine origin of the Reform of St. Teresa, and not its earthly façade, it was John, the privileged son of Our Lady, who had the real mission of reforming the Order. He knew it himself : it was not the feverish ardours of youth that carried him along, mere imagination. It was a well-defined ideal, which his resolute judgment, enlightened by a faith transparent but austere, accepted and was determined to maintain. The ideal of Mount Carmel born again in the thought of Teresa of Jesus, took deep root in John of the Cross. He meant to bring it into being " even

* " To the Reverend Father Licenciate, formerly called de Heredia, but now of Jesus . . . who has been, and is, director and rector of the Discalced." (*Reg. Rubei*, fo. 371.)

were it to cost him his life." [9] "He was courageous," as Teresa well knew,[10] and Padre Antonio was not "of the stature to inaugurate such a mode of life." He had not the necessary "interior spirit," nor could he "foster the requisite austerity." It was a case of a return to the primitive life, to that true prayer which takes possession of the whole man, *die ac nocte in lege Domini meditantes et in orationibus vigilantes.*" [11] From his novitiate at Santa Ana de Medina, John had lived by prayer, and already he knew from experience that true prayer, which takes possession of the whole man, is not so much a matter of a solitary life amidst hills and forests, not even the Carthusian life—in spite of its attraction— but rather interior solitude, which creates deep places to be filled with the love of God. Who has sought solitude in Nature more eagerly, or more gladly discovered God behind "those things He has clothed with beauty" [12] than St. John of the Cross—save possibly St. Francis of Assisi? Now the Poverello, three years before his death, already bearing the marks of Christ, with a heart full to over- flowing with song, wrote this supreme command to Brother Elias : "I am going to tell you, as well as I can, what I think, and it is this—you must consider it a grace when the brethren, as well as other men, are against you. You should actually desire it. And you should love those who are opposed to you, and desire nothing but what the Lord wishes to give you. Look upon that as a better thing than a retreat in a hermitage." [13] This sense of the spiritual efficacy of being despised is deeply embedded in St. John's teaching. He makes a frontal attack on the desire for honour, to complete his teaching on the All and the Nothing. There are three degrees to be attained : to try and learn to despise ourselves and to wish that others should do so ; to speak always to our own disadvantage, and desire that others should do the same ; to try to have a low opinion of ourselves, and wish that others may have the same.[14]

John of the Cross had doubtless already experienced this interior tragedy when his brethren at Salamanca avoided him saying : "Let us be off before the devil comes," [15] and he could not forget now, at this moment of his life, that neglect and cruel abandonment are the great ascetical means whereby souls are emptied of every attachment, not only to creatures, but even to themselves. We can, must, have a resting place, says the primitive Rule,[16] but Mount Carmel was, for John of the Cross, not so much a resting place as a continual spiritual progress. Carmel is not to be contemplated or rested in, it is to be climbed laboriously, by the way of " *la nada* "—nothingness. John deliberately left the administration of the reform to others ; he was, in truth, without friends or influence at court,[17] and without the dignity of office. God intended him to work on the foundations, his share was the soul.

The former pupil of the Jesuits at Medina, and of the University of Salamanca, was a born logician. Supernatural means for a supernatural end : hence mystical contemplation and a humility that reaches to a joyful acceptance of contempt. Others did not succeed, for their means were not sufficiently pure, but he did, because he knew how to make a cross out of any wood that came to his hand—the cross of his redemption. Each new deprivation of poor human happiness became, for him, another and higher step on the ladder of love. " The last shall be first," [18] is perfectly true when the Kingdom of God is in question. Jerome Gracian and Nicholas Doria passed away, but John of the Cross abides. He was the master handing on sure knowledge ; and on August 24th, 1926, he was declared Doctor of the Universal Church.

Antonio of Jesus was also to pass away : he was conscious of a mission, and, in order to carry it out, he had wanted the first place in the new-born reform. Well, let him have it ! John of the Cross was not the one to dispute it ; " The soul enamoured of God is tender, gracious, humble and patient." [19] One day in 1588 Luis de San Angel, in presence of the superiors of his Order at Madrid, told of a discovery he had made at Mancera in the previous summer. " Whilst looking out of curiosity through the Book of Professions at Mancera and Duruelo, he saw that the first profession was that of our Father, John of the Cross. It was written in his own hand, which he knew quite well because he had often seen it." Hence he concluded that John was the first to begin the reform ; but the latter replied, with a smile : " *Be quiet, my son, don't say that.*" And it seemed to Luis that, when John of the Cross made this remark, " he took care that Padre Antonio, who was also present, should not hear " ; for even then Padre Antonio used to complain " that Father John of the Cross had become a discalced Carmelite, and begun the new life without waiting for him, as had been agreed on." [20]

If Teresa of Jesus had been in such haste to clothe " little Father John " with the primitive serge habit at the grille of the *locutorio* at Medina, and send him immediately to Duruelo, it was because she knew that Padre Antonio could not do what was to be done according to her intentions.[21] And in this she was not mistaken.

" Padre Antonio of Jesus, immediately after his arrival (at Duruelo) altered the mode of community life as it had been established in concert with our holy Mother, who had also established it amongst the nuns. Two reasons, amongst others, strongly moved him to do so. First : in order not to antagonise the Observant Fathers too much, in the beginning . . . by separating himself too obviously from them on points of community life in no way contrary to the Rule. Second : as our holy Mother's enlightened mind was not then too fully recognised, he was afraid lest the province might not approve of the idea that, in such an important matter as the establishing of a religious life, he should be governed by the opinion of a woman and not by what had been laid down by the general chapters of the Order." [22]

Here was the crux of the situation. In writing this, the first historian of St. John of the Cross had in mind a constitution of the Order, drawn up at the Chapter of Venice in 1524, presided over by the Father-General, Nicholas Audet, in which " it was ordained that, in each province, there should be some houses of reformed religious who should observe the primitive rule, and who, resembling the others in dress, should be different in their manner of living." [23] It was a question of the two convents anticipated by Blessed

John Soreth : but these " convents *pro totaliter reformatis* " (contrary to what Quiroga and Jerome of St. Joseph believed),[24] were not bound to live according to the primitive Rule, but only according to the strict observance of the Rule as mitigated by Eugenius IV.[25] We should not forget that Rubeo was delighted to find in San José at Avila " the observance of the primitive Rule in all its rigour, whereas, in the rest of the Order, all the monasteries were observing the mitigated Rule." [26]

Now the ancient constitutions of Soreth and Audet did not at all anticipate that the religious who should live in these convents should make a second profession.[27]

Hence, Padre Antonio, having resigned his priorship, and of his own motion made a vow to keep the primitive Rule, yet in his anxiety not to do anything that might cause a division, did not make a new religious profession—as Jeronimo de San José explains, in his valuable manuscript notes [28]—and, on his arrival at Duruelo, " introduced the same community exercises as those in which he had been brought up, accompanying and investing them, indeed, with a more reformed life, in conformity with the Rule." [29]

The constitutions of St. Teresa, according to which John of the Cross had begun to order his life—those constitutions which de Salazar had seen handed by Teresa to Rubeo, and of which there is a copy in Rome [30]—Padre Antonio proposed to replace by regulations in accordance with his own taste, and in harmony with current legislation.

What was John to do ? Was he to rebel against the fine old man, who was too nervous as to what might be said, and too respectful of the traditional letter ? Certainly not—for the spirit was safe. John of the Cross humbled himself : he would live his own ideal, notwithstanding the five hour-glasses. Moreover, the prudent Teresa was quick to persuade Padre Antonio, who was jealous of his authority. " On her advice the primitives at Duruelo drew up constitutions which were approved by the provincial, and inserted by Father Gracian amongst those he enacted, by apostolic authority "—in 1576.[31]

Angelus of the Presentation is not sufficiently explicit

when he summarises this most valuable piece of information
—supplied by Jeronimo and reported by Andrew of the
Incarnation—in the one line : Padre Antonio " drew up
the constitutions which we observed in the beginning." [32]
There can be no possible doubt—for Anne of Jesus tells us
that she learned it from Fathers Antonio and John themselves—that they had " received from Teresa of Jesus, in a
very complete fashion, both the order and form of their
mode of life." And Teresa herself was fond of telling Anne
" the questions the Fathers put to her." [33]

> *La paciencia,*
> *Todo lo alcanza.* *

A day was to come when John would establish complete
harmony between the life of prayer and the liturgical life
for the Discalced Carmelites. In 1576, at Almodovar the
man who had introduced evening meditation, *de prima
noche,*† succeeded in reducing the time allotted to choral
chant and certain community prayers, which were still
observed on account of Padre Antonio's scruples.‡

But the essentials were preserved : the ancient liturgy of
the Holy Sepulchre,[34] the cult of Our Blessed Lady, and
obedience to " The Father of the Order." §

.   .   .   .   .   .

All this took place in conformity with the ideas and the
wise advice of Rubeo himself. Compare the patent, dated
August 16th, 1567, for the foundation of the Discalced
Fathers, with those of April 27th and May 16th, 1567, for
the foundation of the Sisters.[35] The formulas employed in
the latter are far more categorical than in the former, where

---

* " Patience attaineth to all things " (St. Teresa's bookmark).
† " Y assi a la oracion de prima noche ꝗ el dicho siervo de Dios introdujo
en su religion . . . " (Luis de San Angel, Baeza P. A., fo. 50). We find
mental prayer, made in common and at a fixed hour, in the *Modus Meditandi*
of Louis Barbo, who reformed several Benedictine abbeys in the fifteenth
century. Cf. H. Watrigant, S.J., *Quelques promoteurs de la méditation méthodique
au quinzième siècle.* (Paris, 1919.)
‡ To understand the meaning of this restriction we should bear in mind
that they were then accustomed to chant the whole of the Divine Office every
day, as we shall see in the next chapter.
§ *Pater spiritualis hujus Ordinis,* as Rubeo liked to be called according to
ancient usage (*Reg. Rubei,* fo. 104).

Rubeo does not use even the term: Primitive Rule. The Sisters "shall live in conformity with the first rule. No Provincial, Vicar or Prior of this Province shall have power to command them. . . . They shall be obliged to live according to the first Rule and our constitutions." As for the Brothers: "They shall follow the ancient constitutions in the manner we prescribe, and in obedience to the present, or any future, Reverend Father Provincial." And the Master-General concludes: "We give to the Reverend Fathers and Masters, Brother Alonso Gonzalez, provincial of Castile, and Brother Angel de Salazar, prior of our convent of Avila, power and faculty to receive, in the name of the Order, two houses of our profession, obedience, and habit." Teresa herself declares that it was "in order to avoid difficulties that he (Rubeo) handed over the business to the actual provincial, and the one who had just laid down his office." [36] When Don Alvaro de Mendoza, before leaving Avila, asked Rubeo for "authorisation to establish in his diocese some monasteries of Discalced Fathers of the first Rule, the Father-General was disposed to grant it, but meeting with some opposition in the Order, he postponed the project so as not to cause trouble in the Province." [37]

This was the delicate situation in the light of which we may understand why Padre Antonio, on arriving at Duruelo, "altered the mode of common life as it had been established in concert with our holy Mother." [38]

.　　.　　.　　.　　.　　.

On January 8th, 1569, the Master-General was still ignorant of the foundation, and wished "to know if the two monasteries of contemplative Carmelite Fathers are established, so that," as he writes to the prioress of Medina, "I may be able to render to them—as to our convents of nuns—such services in the spiritual order as are in my power." [39] He may, perhaps, have heard of the constitutions of Duruelo from Antonio—or from Gonzalez, who approved them—and therefore abandoned the idea of imposing Teresa's, which he had adopted when passing through Avila.

After all these explanations we can fully appreciate what

Teresa meant, when, on looking back " to a time when she had frequently regretted that this Reform had ever taken place," she wrote in the *Fundaciones* : " The Discalced Fathers had not yet constitutions from our Most Reverend Father General. . . . If they had had to wait for them, or for a mode of government suited to them, many difficulties would have arisen, because some were of one opinion and some of another." [40]

.   .   .   .   .   .

Luis de San Angel learned from Padre Antonio himself that John of the Cross, who was then a priest, had returned from Salamanca with a longing for greater perfection. [41]

It would seem as though it was not so much solitude that Padre Antonio had sought amongst the Carthusians as a greater austerity of life. It has been well said that at all times the Charterhouse has had a particular attraction for Carmelites. Padre Antonio was an active man, and did not possess the Carthusian temperament. At the Chapter of Almodovar he wavered, and was rather inclined to Father Jerome Gracian's apostolic interpretation of the Rule. Quiroga supplies us with a revealing incident when he says that it was Antonio who urged those at Duruelo " to preach and hear confessions for the spiritual welfare of the whole neighbourhood, which was in a state of ignorance." [42] On the other hand, Teresa's constitutions for the primitives, and Rubeo's patent, prudently restricted external ministrations. [43]

There were many hermits in Spain during the sixteenth century living in the deserts of Castile and on the sierras of Andalusia, but they led an extremely active life. Emile Gebhart [44] has noted that if Don Quixote, the national hero, be closely regarded, he manifests " the most characteristic, the most *Spanish* traits of St. Ignatius and St. Teresa. He is, like them, devoted to a sublime ideal, and persuades himself that it is in man's power to become an angel." Like them, " he knew how to combine two apparently contradictory spiritual states : ecstasy and action." But when Don Quixote " attempts to realise his vision he is constrained to bend beneath the blows of fists and cudgels."

John had not the Foundress's remarkable genius for the active life. Not, of course, that it was a mere craving for action that drew her out of her solitude ! " The spirit that animated her was so fervent as to allow her no truce," and this, as Julian of Avila says, was the cause of " her spiritual activity." He goes on to explain that " God, having chosen her as an instrument . . . by a necessary consequence endowed her with all graces and qualities suitable for so noble an employment." [45]

John of the Cross had to carry out a mission other than Teresa's, a mission even more intimate, more hidden ; and, therefore, his spiritual temperament differs from hers. If, at one time he sought the austere and solitary life of a Carthusian, it was not because he was afraid of action ; no, what he feared was that he might not give enough to God and might, therefore, be less closely united to Him in mystical union. The Carmelite ideal, as he saw it during his first interview with Teresa at Medina del Campo, did not definitely exclude the apostolate. Rubeo's constitutions took account, at any rate, of " the preacher " * and his patent called for sons " capable of enlightening and guiding those who are still travellers through this world." [46]

John, then, was not surprised or disconcerted at being sent by Padre Antonio to preach and hear confessions in the surrounding villages. Ignorant peasants had to be taught the Catechism ; Christ must be given to the disinherited. John may have hungered for solitude, but his heart, like Padre Antonio's, burned with a zeal which by its vital action escaped all systemisation. And so, John of the Cross in his little " stable " at Duruelo practised contemplation with no other thought in his mind but love. It is the way in which a work is done that counts, and his apostolate at Duruelo was as profoundly Carmelite as the apostolate of his whole life.

* The office of " preacher," especially before Rubeo's time, was much sought after. It gave a right to certain privileges. Preaching was not, however, entirely reserved to " the preacher," who was appointed by the provincia chapter. Analecta O.C. *IV*, 114–*Silv. VI*, 402.

As there was no lay-brother, Francisco de Yepes set out with John very early in the morning in his apostolic journeys, and was thus able to hear many of the sermons of his beloved brother. Besides preaching, John heard the confessions of all who came to him.[47] The brothers, then, without delay, *muy a priesa*,[48] departed from church and hamlet and halted, on the road to the convent, by a wayside spring. John, worn out by his exertions, asked Francis for the bread and cheese the latter brought with him [49] ; he had no mind for the excellent presbytery meals. On one occasion he excused himself, as well as he could, to a peasant who had been sent by the parish priest to ask him to remain for dinner. He could not do so, he said, as he was unwilling to accept any human recompense for work done for God. When the poor, out of their poverty, brought him a few gifts as an alms, he would not accept them.[50] There are many other incidents that might be related, Francisco confided to Tomas Perez de Molina, only they would take too long.[51]

Would anyone dare to deduce from these eremetical and wholly supernatural methods that John preached and heard confessions reluctantly? The prudent, upright and spiritual [52] Eliseus of the Martyrs, who lived for many years at Granada with the saint, relates in his *Memoirs* that John made his own the wonderful saying of Dionysius the Areopagite : " *Of all divine things, the most divine is to co-operate with God in the salvation of souls. . . .* He used to say that compassion for one's neighbour increases in proportion as the soul is united to God by love." [53]

This incident, and this saying, lay bare the Carmelite soul of St. John of the Cross. Quiroga was right : John's life was, as St. Denys remarks in another connection, " not a mere empty story, but something vital, and hence we must consider it in its smallest details, and revere the secret of the divine plans that lies hidden beneath all its manifestations."[54]

The work of the Reform was immense, unrivalled and, above all, spiritual. It sought for the spirit of the Order where it might still be found, discovered and renewed it in the souls of those two great saints who were likewise geniuses. God never worked for the restoration of an Order with such generosity. The greater good of Christ's mystical body was in question, for the mission of Carmel, in which the eremitical and apostolic lives are harmoniously united, " is to preserve in the Church a lofty spirit of prayer." *

.   .   .   .   .   .

At the beginning of March, 1569, in the season of Lent, Teresa passed through Duruelo on her way to establish a convent at Toledo. She arrived in the morning, and Padre Antonio, looking as cheerful as usual, was sweeping the ground before the chapel door. " What are you doing, Father, and what has become of your dignity ? " asked Teresa. " Cursed be the time when I had any," replied the prior cheerfully. And the *buena madre* entered the *portal*. She was " filled with admiration on seeing the spirit of devotion which God diffused there." Two merchants from Medina, who were with her, were in tears. It is true that there were crosses, many death's heads ! But this was the fashion of the time, and we need not imagine that these objects were indicative of a gloomy or pessimistic type of piety. The Venerable Anne of Jesus tells us that Teresa herself occasionally ate very unsavoury food out of a skull.[55] But there was, in particular, a little wooden cross which Teresa never forgot. It was placed beside the holy water stoup. Father John—it must have been he—had pasted on to the cross a paper picture of Christ crucified which inspired the Mother with greater devotion than any work of art. John carved crucifixes, and made sketches of Christ in His agony that are heartrending. He was a Spaniard and lived in the days when *pietas* were the fashion : those who see him as a pure intellectual are wrong ; he was a mystic and a realist.

The Mother finished her inspection of the house, which had been uninhabitable so short a time before. And now everything " breathed devotion." She went up to the attic, where Father John, the Father of the Observance, Brother Joseph and the Father-prior recited Divine Office.

* This remark, quoted in *Le Carmel* by a Discalced Carmelite (Paris, *Art Cathol.*, 1922) p. 8, is taken from Father Garrigou-Lagrange.

Both the little hermitages, filled with hay on account of the extreme cold, had a stone pillow, little crucifix and skull.

A gentleman from the neighbouring village, an acquaintance of Teresa's, paid her a visit with his wife. They could not say enough about the sanctity of the friars, and the great good they were doing in all the countryside. Just imagine ! People from the neighbourhood were going to that poor chapel to take the discipline.[56] The Fathers did not leave the chapel after Matins, but remained on praying till Prime, and their mental prayer was so intense that, on rising to recite the Hours, their habits were covered with snow without their ever noticing it. " It is not perfect prayer," said St. Anthony the Hermit, " if the monk perceives he is praying." [57] The roof at Duruelo was, naturally and supernaturally, open to the skies.

This holy vigil followed a day of hard toil, for, as we have seen, they preached and heard confessions until late in the evening in villages that were a league and a half or two leagues distant from the monastery. They went barefooted through the snow and cold, and often returned home hungry, for the *cena* was only eaten after they had got back. They did not, indeed, lack the necessaries of life, because the villagers gladly supplied them with even more than they needed, and the cooking was not too badly done since the arrival of Catalina Alvarez from Medina to look after it. Ana Isquierda washed the hermits' clothes, and Francisco de Yepes swept out their cells.[58]

Teresa was delighted with this apostolic labour, which, in her compassion, she had so much desired. When she accepted Don Rafael's poor little house she realised that the people of the neighbourhood were without religious instruction because there were no monasteries in the district. She even declared that this was one of the reasons why she had been pleased to see a convent established there. The evangelisation of the idolators amongst whom they lived was a tradition dear to Egyptian monks, and Apollonios of Hermopolis converted to the faith ten pagan villages not far from his monastery.[59]

"These Fathers and I conversed," Teresa remarks in *The Foundations*, "on some special points." She advised prudence, as "it was her idea that men of talent should enter the Order, and they should not be repelled by too much severity." [60] Life was hard at Duruelo, and Teresa asked Padre Antonio and John "to moderate their austerities, which were extreme." It had cost her "so many wishes and so many prayers to obtain from the Lord suitable subjects to begin this mode of life" that "she feared to see the devil shortening their days before her hopes were fully realised." But the Fathers made light of these remarks and went on with their penances.

One evening Father John of the Cross, exhausted by fatigue and by some days of illness, asked the prior's permission to take his collation a little earlier. But as soon as he had eaten he was grieved at having given in to "Brother Ass," and, perhaps, disedified the brethren. He went to Padre Antonio and asked permission to accuse himself of his fault in presence of the community. When the hour for the meal arrived John entered the little refectory with bared shoulders and holding a discipline in his hand. He advanced to the centre of the room, knelt down on a heap of stones and broken tiles which he had spread on the floor, and scourged himself to blood. He then accused himself in a loud and moving voice ; the discipline whistled again and its blows fell like hail on his flesh. He fell exhausted and broken on the sharp potsherds. The floor ran red. The brethren were stricken with fear and wonder. After a long silence Padre Antonio, in the name of obedience, ordered John to retire and pray to God to pardon them all for their wretched unworthiness.

This incident, which is told by his first biographers,*

* Quiroga, 125, Cyp. 111, Jer., 135. All these historians love to point out that it was John of the Cross who introduced into the Reform the " extraordinary penances " still in vogue. When Francis visited John at Segovia shortly before the saint's death, he saw a skull in the refectory, a religious kissing the feet of the prior and the brethren during the meal, and before going to bed in the evening he heard the clappers (as during Holy Week) struck, and the words chanted, " My brethren, let us occupy ourselves with God, and He will occupy Himself with us." On another evening : " Let us watch, my brethren, that Death may not surprise us. My brethren, the yoke of the Lord

reveals the heroism of a soul alive with love. At such a
moment " interior joy renders all things easy " : life in a
hovel, open to the four winds of heaven, watchings, nakedness, scourgings unto blood. Teresa says : " There is more
real interior happiness when bodily comforts are lacking
than when we find ourselves comfortably housed. What
does it matter whether our cell is spacious and well-built ?—
we shall not live in it for ever. We shall not always be looking
at its walls. And in eternity the mansions of the blessed
will correspond with their love. All things, except those
necessary for the preservation of life, should be used spar-
ingly. In short, to Padre Antonio and Father John, it
seemed merely a matter of a few pleasant torments. As
soon as one has courage to undergo them, all the difficulty
disappears."

No doubt the measure of the eminence of a religious order
lies, not in the austerity it practises, but in the prudence with
which its observances are conformed to the end of the
institute.[61] Truth to the facts compels the statement that
Teresa of Jesus and John of the Cross set out to climb " a
trackless and waterless " mountain, right up to the topmost
peak, where the fruit of Wisdom is eaten in the freedom of
pure love. They did not intend to build halfway up the
Mount of Carmel. The Foundress asked for less austerity,
not from softness, but lest the work might perish. Nay,
has she not made an appeal, in the *Camino*, that sounds like
a military command ?[62] " The Lutherans are ravaging
France like wolves, their sect is increasing and, while
Christians grow tepid and poverty is despised, an immense
conflagration is devouring the earth, and Christ is yet again
condemned to death. . . . Let us make reparation and
follow out the maxims of the Gospel as perfectly as possible."
" Let us in some way resemble our King, whose only place
of rest was the stable of Bethlehem in which He was born,
and the cross on which He died."

.   .   .   .   .   .

is sweet ; why do we find it heavy ? " (B. N. M., MS. 8568, fo. 373. Dép.
of Francisco de Yepes). All these practices certainly go back to the time of
St. John of the Cross.

Whilst galleons, heavily laden with gold and spices, and flying the banners of Castile and Leon, were entering the harbour of Cadiz, the riches of America were sapping the vitality of the sons of the *Conquistadores*. There was need of Poverty.

Lutheranism was spreading, and not only in France ; it penetrated even the heart of Spain, the Court of Charles the Fifth. One of his secretaries, Alonso de Valdés, his preacher Vives, and his chaplain Casalla, joined the sect. The movement was crushed. In 1560 the Grand Inquisitor committed to the flames all works suspected of heresy, whilst at Valladolid and Seville, in the same year and previously in 1559, heretics were burned alive.[63]

Brother John also fought, but with love, not fire. The root of Martin Luther's error consists in an inordinate desire for sensible experiences of divine grace, a perversion of Tauler's mysticism—leading to a despair of ever being a *friend of God*, and to a search for salvation by a kind of faith —trust operating without good works and unvivified by charity.[64] To this corruption of Christianity John of the Cross opposes the supernatural life in all its integrity—its supreme work of transformation and loving union with God. He begs us, by word and example, not to rest in the senses, which may deceive, but to abandon ourselves, wholly and entirely, to a pure, living faith, informed by charity and working by charity, a faith that is the sole proportionate means to a living union with God. The heretical Illuminism of the *Alumbrados*, first condemned in 1568, had no more vigorous opponent than the Doctor *de los Martires*, that truly poor man who offered himself as a sacrifice and was obedient even unto the death of the cross.

Mother Teresa, in the first chapter of *The Foundations*, tells us : " I always envied those who could devote themselves to this work for souls, though they might suffer a thousand deaths."[65] Whilst she was still deeply afflicted at the fact that she was unable to do more, Our Lord appeared to her. It was evening, and she was at prayer in the convent of San José of Avila. He showed great love for her, and said to console her : " Wait a little, my daughter, and you will

see great things." [66]   The great things which she could not
then foresee were now being accomplished.   On leaving
Duruelo, at the beginning of March, 1569, " her soul over-
flowing with consolation," she, who so deeply loved and
esteemed her daughters, said to herself : " Our Lord has
now granted me a grace far greater than that of founding
monasteries for nuns."

CHAPTER IX

THE MODERATOR OF VIRTUES

On Saturday, May 28th, 1569, the eve of Pentecost, Mother Teresa was sitting in the refectory of her little monastery in the Plazuela del Barrio Nuevo at Toledo. A fortnight previously Fray Magdaleno (Juan Gutierrez de la Magdalena), the prior of the Mitigated Carmelites, had celebrated the foundation mass in the presence of Doña Luisa de la Cerda ; the grilles had then been fixed and they were at last able " to rejoice for a while in the company of Our Lord." [1] The poverty was so great that Teresa felt " enriched with many golden spiritual treasures," [2] and was experiencing such deep joy that she could scarcely eat. But her happiness was not destined to last long, for she was just then informed that a *criado*, from the Princess d'Eboli, was asking to see her. His business was to request her to leave for Pastrana at once to make a new foundation which had been determined on for some time. It would be unwise to go against the wishes of the wife of Don Ruy Gomez de Silva, councillor to Philip II, and yet she hesitated to leave Toledo so soon. She sent the messenger to have a meal, and went herself " to ask Our Lord to give her the grace of writing a letter to the Princess in such a way as not to displease her. . . . I was at this point," she goes on to say, " when it was said to me, on behalf of Our Lord, that I should not fail to go : it was not a question of this foundation alone, but of something more important : I was to bring the Rule and Constitutions with me.

" Despite the grave reasons which seemed to stand in the way of my departure, I believed that, after such words, I could not dispense myself from acting as I am accustomed to do in such circumstances, namely, to refer the whole matter to my confessor [Father Vincent Baron, O.P.]. I sent for him. But I did not tell him anything of what I had heard during my prayer. I am always more peaceful so. I beseech Our Lord to enlighten my confessors with natural light, and, when He wishes a thing done, He knows how to suggest it to their hearts. I have seen that many and many a time, and it was the case now. My confessor, having examined the whole matter, decided that I must go."

On Monday, May 30th, accompanied by Isabella of St. Paul, the first professed sister of San José of Avila, and Doña Antonia del Aguila of the Incarnation, Teresa left "the house of her repose." She went down towards the Vega between high ochre walls of rock with a ribbon of blue sky above. The mules nervously dug their hoofs into the loose stones, for Toledo is built on the ledges of a high hard rock, ringed almost completely round by the valley of the Tagus. The little company turned its back on the grim yellow gorge, leaving behind the rosy, Moorish tower of Santo Tomé, and, on the left, San Juan de los Reyes, which bears, suspended on its proud façade, the chains of Christians rescued from the vanquished Arabs. Toledo of the Moors ; turbulent, mysterious, had received its baptism. They passed through the Cambron gate, and came out on the plain of the Vega which stretched before them green and smiling beneath a wide and gracious expanse of sky. The Tagus, now at peace, glided along by little green islands. Teresa moved along the high plateaux that stretch in ridges right on to Madrid.

We know, from the account in *The Foundations*, that the Mother and her companions alighted again at the Convent of Our Lady of the Angels, where Doña Eleonora Mascareñas, formerly governess to Philip II, began to tell her of a hermit who wanted to meet her. Teresa reflected that, so far, she had " only two religious," so that it would be well to persuade this hermit to adopt their way of life. She at once requested Doña Eleonora to arrange a meeting ; this was easily done, for the hermit and his companion, Juan de la Miseria, were staying at her house, which adjoined the Convent of the Discalced Franciscan nuns.

Mariano de Azzaro was a Neapolitan nobleman who, when a fellow-student of the future Gregory XIII, had been passionately devoted to poetry, eloquence, law and, above all, mathematics. The Council of Trent had accredited the young diplomat with a mission to the Court of Poland, where the kindness of Catherine of Austria led to his settling for a brief period. Later Philip II, whom he had followed to Saint-Quentin as a Commander of the Order of St. John of Jerusalem, employed the geometrician in making the River Guadalquivir navigable from Cordova to Seville. The attempt was a failure, and Mariano, whose soul had been tried by two years spent in prison on a false charge, now heard his *veni sequere*. Feeling no attraction for a cenobite life, he took refuge with the hermits of Tardon, in the Sierra Morena. The prior, Matthew de la Fuente, the restorer of the Order of St. Basil in Spain, was one of John of Avila's disciples.

Mariano de Azzaro told Teresa something of the life he had led for eight years in the desert of Andalusia until summoned by Philip II to Aranjuez for the canalisation of the Tagus. Each hermit had his own cell ; they did not recite the divine office, and only met to hear Mass in an oratory. They had no revenues ; they did not beg, but lived in poverty, by manual labour. Teresa exclaimed that it seemed to her as if she were listening to a description of " the lives of our Fathers in olden days," and immediately showed him a copy of the primitive Rule, pointing out that it offered the same sort of observances, especially manual labour. " Covetousness is ruining the world," said Mariano, " and bringing contempt on religious " ; and Mother Teresa heartily agreed. The hermit withdrew, " with his mind almost made up," promising that he would think the whole night through on how these ideals agreed, whilst Teresa, overcome with joy at the thought of the glory this hermit would render to God by joining our Order, now understood the meaning of the interior locution she had heard in Toledo. Yes ; it was certainly " something far more important than a convent for nuns."

Mariano arrived on the following day, and told the Mother that she had won him over to her enterprise. " A woman : no ; God : yes," was Teresa's answer. In one of the frescoes that still adorn the cloister of the convent at Pastrana, devoutly occupied by the sons of St. Peter of Alcantara since 1855, we see Teresa handing the Carmelite Rule to a hermit pictured with a delicate oval face.

Mariano, like Teresa, was of an active temperament ; they at once discussed how to start. Don Ruy Gomez had given him a fine hermitage and plot of land at Pastrana for the purpose of establishing a community of hermits. He offered it to Teresa. There, it was agreed, he and his companion, Juan de la Miseria, would take the Carmelite habit. Juan was an Italian, and had led a romantic life, but was withal " a great servant of God, and most simple in the things of this world." This pupil of Coello was one day to paint a portrait of Teresa. It is said that it did not please her, but the portrait at Seville is so maternal, with such a tenderness of supernatural love, that we should be deeply grateful to Giovanni Narducci for what is almost a masterpiece. Our two hermits introduced to Teresa one of Princess Catalina's ladies of honour, Juana Pizaña, a woman of no great beauty, masculine looking, and with a countenance ravaged by fifteen years of bitter suffering. The soul of this Portuguese saint, the future Catherine of the Conception, had been tried in the furnace ; she was lovable, because she was also of a joyous disposition.[3]

Teresa lost no time in writing to the Father Provincial and to Father de Salazar, for their consent to the establishment of another convent of contemplative Carmelites, and then set off for Pastrana, " overwhelmed with joy."

Mariano was a true hermit, a really poor man, " pure and chaste," who had, moreover, the right of entry at Court. Who, then, could help forgiving him for his fiery disposition, which flared out in acts of impatience and indiscretion.[4] Teresa of Avila was not afraid of enlisting men who were, perhaps, only inclined to a solitary life because the intense social life of a community obliterates individuality. Teresa had the faculty of friendship ; but, above all, she had the supernatural love needful to bind together such precious souls as these, for in future it was not to be merely a matter of understanding and influencing, but also of uniting

mature men, each with his own way of looking at things, men of formed character, no longer malleable, who therefore must be united in a higher harmony. On the following day, Father Balthazar Nieto, who was residing in the Convent of St. Anne, brought the nuns from Medina del Campo to Pastrana, for he also meant to join the Reform. He was a southerner, had been a member of the Convent of Seville, whence he went to Castile, as the result of some unfortunate affairs, and, "without being very old, was no longer young." He was exactly forty-five years of age, an excellent preacher, but violent, suspicious, and with a taste for extravagant penances. Later on Teresa was to fear "for the salvation of his soul." This terrible Macarius [5] would have been far better off, she thought, in his own den : *a su guarida !* In the year 1577, in a fit of jealousy, which he almost immediately regretted and repaired, he was to bring false charges against Father Gracian, with the connivance of Miguel de la Columna, a travelling companion of the young visitor of Andalusia.[6] Meanwhile this same Miguel, who, the Mother said, was wanting in judgment,[7] was just then on his way to Pastrana, accompanied by Father Anthony of Jesus. When he denounced Gracian to Philip II he stated that he was " the third person who had adopted this mode of life."*

Mother Teresa, who had all the necessary permissions, urgently begged Father Anthony, " the first of our religious," to begin this second foundation. But as Father Balthazar had just arrived from Medina, Mariano de Azzaro did not want to delay further in taking the habit, and the Mother hastily made it for him with her own hands. The ceremony took place on July 10th, 1569, in the chapel of the Ducal palace, with its six-foot-thick walls, decorated in the Moorish style. Doña Ana de la Cerda, aunt of the Duchess of Eboli, had built this fortress, in the heart of the city, after first illegally imprisoning the Municipal Council of Pastrana to prevent their raising any objections.[8]

The Venerable Padre Antonio arrived on July 13th, and took solemn possession of the hill which had been presented

---

* " El tercero que tome manera de vivir." Arch. Carm. Des. Rome. *Acts of the Discalced,* cod. 1. no. 15. Cf. also B.N.M. 8020, f. 100.

by the dukes, and Mariano's imagination immediately set about building and organising. The first thing was to have a conduit between the fountain at Pastrana and the hermitage of San Pedro de Arriba, without which the kitchen garden could not possibly be irrigated. Then a subterranean corridor three hundred yards long, to connect the house, now transformed into a convent, with the hermitage where the divine office was to be celebrated. And above all, some fine, well-placed grottoes should be hollowed out of the rough soil. " Oh ! that Father Mariano," as Francis of St. Mary lamented at a later date, " who digs mines in mountains, and lives underground ! " But Padre Antonio was delighted with everything ; his joy was at its height when Father Francis Espinel arrived from Toledo accompanied by Isabella of St. Dominic and Catherine of the Conception, the Portuguese saint, who were destined for the new convent of Carmelite nuns.[9]

At Toledo Father Espinel saw Teresa, who had returned from Pastrana on July 21st, and told her of his desire to become a Discalced Carmelite. He belonged to the Observants, was sixty-five years of age, from the south of France, Perpignan, and an able man, but his austerities were of the same order as those of Mariano and Balthazar. In 1566 he had founded the Carmelite College at Alcalá. Grave charges were brought against him, and he was deprived of the rectorship, even after an appeal to the General. No doubt the reason for this punishment was the extravagant mortifications he had imposed on his subjects. Whilst prior of Mancera he had made himself so much disliked that the Apostolic Commissary was forced to send him to La Roda, and we know that the austerities he afterwards imposed on the Carmelite nuns of Malagon exasperated Teresa for years. We shall meet him again at Baeza.

After instituting, at the request of Don Ruy Gomez, mental prayer all day and all night (by relays) and leaving this heavy burden on his enthusiastic disciples, Padre Antonio appointed Father Balthazar of Jesus, who was still a novice, as the vicar of the Convent of St. Peter, and then returned to Duruelo. It was mid-November, and when

Father Balthazar, who was a great preacher, was away from home, Father Francis of the Conception, Espinel, was superior of "The Virgin's Dovecot." [10]

. . . . . .

When Father Anthony returned to his tranquil little spiritual Bethlehem, he found there two novices to whom Father John of the Cross had given the habit on October 4th. One of them, a native of Avila, was a choir brother named John Baptist ; the other, a simple lay-brother, Peter of the Angels, had been born at Lanzaita. John Baptist died in 1577 at the convent of the Socorro in Vallalid, and Peter died there also on July 17th, 1613. Father John of the Cross dearly loved Brother Peter, who was a lay-brother and had heard an interior voice saying to him, "*Entre los pobres me hallarás,*" "Thou shalt find me amongst the poor." [11] The *pobres*, however, were not the Alcantarins of Areñas, but the primitives of Duruelo. Father John initiated this beloved son into spiritual poverty—*la desnudez.* And love filled the soul of Brother Peter as he contemplated the sorrows of Jesus. This simple soul prayed to God that he might be spared extraordinary favours and receive only " the gift of tears."

John loved the little ones of this world, the really poor, and was severe in his treatment of others. We are told that a young doctor of Salamanca once came to ask for the habit, and his first inquiry was about the library. Father John, by way of reply, took away the few books he possessed and handed him a child's catechism [12] ; but John of the Cross did not hesitate to throw himself on his knees before a novice who, in a fit of temper, was insulting him. It was an act of humility, but also an act of subtle psychology. His disciples would certainly " have followed him to Turkey." [13]

Where souls were concerned John was a master of arts. Asceticism and meditation were, in his eyes, merely means to an end, which was the summit of Carmel, where the soul enjoys the fruit of love's wisdom. " Union with God is the end of the contemplative life, the last perfection of man. Begun in exile, it will be consummated in the fatherland." [14]

He took good care to set his disciples on the road to divine union. Hence, Quiroga goes on to say, " our holy father exercised them usefully and with full success in mental prayer, and not haphazard, like some spiritual masters. He divided it into three parts : an imaginative representation of the mysteries on which one is to meditate . . . an intellectual consideration of the mysteries so represented . . . a living and attentive repose in which the fruit is gathered and the understanding opened to the divine illumination. . . . One passes from natural to supernatural knowledge, when the soul settles down into this peaceful, loving and tranquil repose of faith." *

Next comes the three celebrated signs, already sketched out by previous spiritual writers, the author of the Taulerian *Institutiones* amongst others.[15] Meditation becomes impracticable, the imagination ceases to work ; the soul has no desire to fix the imagination or senses on any particular object external or internal ; it takes pleasure in finding itself alone with God in a state of loving attention and without any particular speculation.

The simultaneous presence of these three signs is essential. If the first sign exists by itself, then inability to imagine and meditate may arise from distraction and want of recollection, whence follows the necessity of the second sign. But the third is also essential, because the mere fact of being unable to meditate or discourse on matters not divine may spring from melancholia or some other natural disposition of the head or heart, which produces a certain suspension of

* *El don que tuvo S. Juan de la Cruz para guiar las almas a Dios.* (Ger. III, 517). Diego of Jesus says that the servant of God taught " *cinque modi di far orazione che sono lettioni et meditationi de libri sacri, et unione et contemplatione et rendimento de gratie.*" Jaén, P.A., f. 116. The P.A. of Jaén is in Italian and preserved in the Archives of the Congregation of Rites. Moreover, the Instruction for Novices, which was approved of by the Consulta on January 11th, 1590, at which John of the Cross took part, contains the following passage : (la oracion) " comunmente se suele dividir (en siete partes) : preparacion, leccion, meditacion, contemplacion, agimiento de grácias, peticion y epilogo." *Instrucción de Novicios Descalzos* . . . republished by Father Evaristo, C.D. (Toledo, 1925), pp. 106–107. These testimonies enable us to see how the teaching contained in the following lines of the *Llama* (Cancion III, § 5, Ger. II, 445) was carried out in practice : "And in order that we may the better understand this condition of beginners, it should be known that the needs and practice of beginners consists in meditation and discursive acts by means of the imagination. The soul in this state should have matter on which to meditate."

activity in the senses. Hence the peaceful and loving attention in which the third sign consists, is essential.* John of the Cross is at least as prudent as our modern psychiatrists. It should be carefully noted that he taught his novices " to spend but little time in imaginative representation ; they should rather attend to the intellectual examination of the mystery that they might go on to a still more enlightened consideration, proceeding from the moving power of God." [16]

Juan de Jesus Maria Araballes, Master of Novices at Pastrana, testified to the same effect, and John, as we have said, was later to approve this teaching—no subjection to a fixed method, and the avoidance of excessive speculation. There are some who, possessing some little brilliance of mind, spend the whole time of prayer in ingenious reflections and subtle disquisitions. Of what use is that ? " The important thing is that the soul should concentrate on what the understanding, in that divine silence and almost without any discourse, reveals to the will through a light, an illumination, infused into it by God." [17] And Quiroga also says : " The operation of the soul, in this contemplation of faith, is called passive, not because the soul is absolutely inert, but because God is the principal agent." [18]

We now see why we should learn " to prefer, during prayer, a few simple, artless, prudent words, to a multitude of elaborate phrases." And how we must avoid " going to prayer to seek ourselves." [19] " John," says Quiroga, " condemned all excitation of the senses, and long discourses during prayer, even if concerned with the usefulness of virtue, because such discourses hinder the divine influence by which the infused virtues are increased and perfected." [20] He taught his sons to walk " in the way of the true knowledge and love of God, by means of the light of faith, illumined by the gift of Wisdom." [21] This is the swift, safe way, the royal road.

" If perfection consists in charity, and not in ecstasies,

---

* Subida, Bk. II, Ch. XI ; Ger. 1, 150. These three signs will be found again, regarded from the angle of the passive night, in Ch. IX (sec. 10) of La Noche (Ger. II, 28, etc.).

joys and sweetnesses, which are sometimes caused by the
devil or human nature (because human love may be
accompanied by such manifestations), why should we be
disturbed when deprived of them ? "

" The end of prayer is to unite our will to God's, and to
love Him above all else, hence it is not right to abandon
prayer because of aridities ; on the contrary, it should be
proportionately increased, for Jesus ' being in agony,
prayed the longer.' "

" All foods are made up of substance and savour. The
latter, however, is not always indispensable. Spiritual joys,
far from being the perfection of prayer, are a mark of weakness, *indicio de flaqueza* ; beginners, in particular, receive such
sensible favours from Our Lord. Our Father, St. Elias,
after eating a piece of bread, cooked under the ashes, set
out by a steep ascent to go to Horeb." [22]

All John needed was one year of probation to turn his
novices into contemplatives. He points out in the *Llama* :
" [the passing over to contemplation] often takes place after
a short time, especially in the case of persons consecrated
to God, for, having renounced the world, their mind and
spirit agree better together and are more easily conformed
to God. Hence they pass on to exercises of the spirit
operated by Him." [23]

" The whole progress of the contemplative soul consists
in its being moved by God," John restricted his own part
to placing it " in a state to receive this motion." [24]   Human
effort left to itself, no matter how vigorously it may act, will
not sanctify : that is accomplished by the Spirit of Love,
and if mortification comes to be regarded as an end in itself
it may easily degenerate into fanaticism.

.   .   .   .   .   .

Padre Antonio was almost always away from Duruelo.
He used to visit Don Luis IV, Lord of Mancera and of the
Five Towns, and was an intimate friend of the family.
When Don Luis' daughter, Doña Isabel de Leyva, was
born, as the mother was in grave danger the good old man
was brought to see her. He placed his scapular upon her

and quickly withdrew. The child was born : Padre Antonio was recalled and, on seeing the *niña* he said smilingly " It is by the power of the holy scapular that you are here, is it not ? Well, one day you will wear it and be a nun of my Order." His prophecy was fulfilled.[25]

Don Luis offered the " primitives " a church which he had built to receive a splendid retable imported from Flanders. " I never saw anything more beautiful in my life," wrote Teresa, and Anthony " was so charmed with it that he consented to transfer the monastery from Duruelo." That Flemish Madonna must certainly have been beautiful !—a real " primitive," perhaps one of Van Eyck's or Memling's Virgins, with oval face, fair hair and downcast eyes looking at the Child Jesus. Early in 1570 Don Luis undertook to build a small convent near the church, and Padre Antonio preached a course of Lenten sermons to the villagers. In spite of an attack of quartan fever, he helped to lay the foundations and might have been seen mixing with his feet the clay to make the bricks for the partition walls ; carrying them to the masons ; bringing soil to the workmen who were building the rough earthen walls ; sifting lime and sand ; and carrying all sorts of materials on his back. On the morning of June 11th, the move was ceremoniously carried out.[26] Calced and Discalced Carmelites walked in brotherly procession from Duruelo to Mancera de Abajo. They traversed a wind-swept, sunlit plain, and of a sudden they saw, lying in a hollow, the rugged little village, so typical of old Castile. The brown, sombre, dimly-lighted, severe-looking church with its three naves is still standing to-day. From the outer court one can see, close at hand, upon a hillock, the site of the primitive monastery, with the dark and distant Sierra de Gredos in the background.

On this morning of June 11th, 1570, the procession made its way up the slope of this miniature Mount Carmel, among villagers dressed in their Sunday best—flexible gaiters, short breeches, wide sashes, tightly-fitting vests with silver buttons, large, pointed felt hats on their brown heads, filigree rings in their ears. The Fathers of the Mitigation, Alonso de Vilalba, and Martin Garcia, rector of St. Andrew of Salamanca, followed the *primitives*. The provincial, Alonso González, said the first Mass and reserved the Blessed Sacrament. Father Anthony preached the sermon.

In this fashion Duruelo, the Bethlehem of the Reform, came to an end, and the Monastery of Mancera de Abajo was inaugurated on the feast of St. Barnabas.

The Virgin of the retable, for love of whom they had abandoned Duruelo, though " there was no water to be had, and it seemed impossible ever to get any " near her church, this Flemish Virgin now performed an act of supernatural gratitude. She must have been a compassionate Virgin and said to her Son : " They have no water." St. Teresa tells the story : " One evening, after supper, Father Anthony, who was prior, happened to be in the cloister with the religious, and they were talking about the lack of water. The prior stood up and taking the staff he usually carried in his hand, traced with it, I believe, on a certain spot, the sign of the cross. At least he pointed out the spot with the staff and said : ' Look, dig there ! ' They had not dug far down when water gushed up in abundance. This water is excellent for drinking and the supply has never given out. There is thought to have been something miraculous about this."

On the following October 8th, Brother John Baptist and Brother Peter of the Angels made their profession to " Father Friar John of the Cross, sub-prior of this house, the Very Reverend Father Friar Anthony of Jesus, being prior." The witnesses for the first were Brother Peter of the Angels and Brother Joseph of Christ, who had come from St. Anne's, and of whom there is no further mention ; for the second, Brother John Baptist, "Brother Anthony of St. Paul, who did not sign, being absent when the document was drawn up." [27]

Towards the end of the same year, certainly after November 1st,[28] the Venerable Anne of Jesus, who was still a novice, stopped at Mancera. She mentions the fact in St. Teresa's process of canonisation, and adds the detail that Father Anthony of Jesus was prior and Father John of the Cross sub-prior, but this does not imply that both were there

at the time, nor that this was when confidences were exchanged. If the Spanish text [29] be closely examined, we see
that Mother Anne's deposition is padded with everything
that she had ever heard, both from Teresa and the first
Discalced Fathers, about the Reform. And this explains a
real difficulty, namely, how to reconcile Father John's presence at Mancera, when Anne was passing through in
November, and his departure, in mid-October, for Pastrana,
in company with Brother Peter of the Angels.[30]

.   .   .   .   .   .

On the previous July 10th Mother Teresa had been pre-
sent at Pastrana for the profession of Brother Mariano and
Brother Juan de la Miseria. It would seem as if it was
probably at her suggestion that Padre Antonio sent Father
John " to form and fashion the second monastery, in accord-
ance with the original Rule." [31] The Foundress of the
Reform simply meant " to have the rule of Our Lady and
Queen kept according to its primitive perfection." [32] Our
Lady was served with so much fervour at Pastrana that
Teresa left others, more capable than herself, the task of
describing it, if the Divine Master should think fit, because,
as she confesses, " it is beyond my powers."

In 1374 a Dominican, John Stokes, maintained that the
Carmelite Fathers had been established by St. Mary of
Egypt, and two decrees of the University of Cambridge were
needed before the controversy was settled in favour of " the
Brethren of the Virgin." Hence there was now no question
of the latter following in practice the rigorous austerities of
that illustrious penitent. The Mother, as we have seen,
much preferred virtues to austerities,[33] and rejected observances not in conformity with the Rule. To depart from the
path followed by our holy Fathers, " and to adopt another
of one's own, or at the suggestion of others, would be a grave
error." [34] Now, before John was sent to Pastrana, during
the frequent absences of Father Balthazar, the " Virgin's
dove-cot " was, as we have said, in the hands of Father
Francis of the Conception. There can be no doubt that this
Father went beyond the limits of the Primitive Rule. The

Reforma itself admits that " the first masters allowed them-selves to be carried too far," and that " prudence demands a balance that does not transgress the powers of nature." [35] The customs of Pastrana arose, in fact, from the community's excess of fervour.

" The Divine Office was always chanted in its entirety, as if each day had been a feast. The Little Office of the Blessed Virgin, the Penitential and Gradual Psalms, and the Office of the Dead were also recited, in accordance with the rites of the Carmelite breviary." [36] We should further remember that Padre Antonio had instituted perpetual prayer, by day and by night. And yet even that did not suffice for those pioneers in asceticism, buried in Mariano's subterranean vaults, with their rough pine-wood columns. [37] For eight years they underwent privations of an inhuman rigour. Seated on the ground—it was only after fourteen years that benches were provided [38]—they ate their wild cabbage or beetroot, and occasionally dried peas, the national *garbanzos*. Hunger supplied the sauce. They fasted " as much as at Tabenna," says the *Reforma*.* During recreation they wove linen, and at a later period, at Seville and Lisbon, they made rigging for the navy. In this respect Teresa fully agreed with Mariano, as we know. [39] In the midst of these " giants of the Reform," who fought at San Pedro, was Fray Juan de la Miseria, " simple as a child," who used to call the Virgin Mary " his dove." [40]

Father John of the Cross and his faithful Peter of the Angels had soon covered the twelve leagues that lie between Madrid and Pastrana. They went on foot, soliciting alms, helping the poor they chanced to meet, says Quiroga, who was told by Brother Peter of the edification he had received throughout the journey from his Father Master, " by his discourses on God and his rare virtues." [41]

They drew nigh the town and saw it merged into the grey hillside, its winding streets so narrow that the roofs met overhead. When one walks to-day through those break-

---

* L. II, Ch. XXXII, *passim.* Inocencio de S. Andrés, who had lived at Pastrana almost from the first, confirms, in his deposition what the *Reforma* tells us of the austerity of the Fathers of this convent (Baeza, I. O. fo. 111, v).

neck lanes one notices, here and there, the façade of some
old hidalgo's mansion, or some convent such as that of the
Conceptionistas, with their white serge habits and blue veils,
which, up to 1574, was occupied by Carmelite nuns, victims
of the Princess of Eboli's wretched intrigues. Father John
must often have visited this rising monastery. Was it in
Pastrana or Segovia, whither the community was eventually
transferred, that Sister Beatrice of the Blessed Sacrament
heard him predict that she would not experience the death
agony ? Beatrice was a mystic, " a rose of Lebanon," as
Our Lord called her in a revelation to Mother Isabella of
St. Dominic.[42] As for the " holy Portuguese "—Catherine
of the Conception—she " went to Heaven laughing," as St.
Teresa put it.

But it was the spiritual joy that John bore about with him,
a joy founded on peace in Christ that made the marvellous
atmosphere in which he dwelt. " Even if all things vanish
and crumble away, if events disappoint our expectations, it
is in vain to be disturbed." [43] What matter, after all, to have
left Duruelo and Mancera, the peaceful, quiet places he had
known, for this new land invaded by Flemings, Jews, Portuguese and Moorish craftsmen from the Albaicin, whom Don
Ruy Gomez had imported from Granada? [44] And why fear
this turbulent environment on which, willy nilly, John was
to set his mark ? John of the Cross creates his own atmosphere, and is no more influenced by a Father Mariano than
by a Father Balthazar, nay, even a Father Francis of the
Conception.

After following, for another quarter of a league, the white
road that winds like a ribbon along the flank of the mountain, Father John and his companion climbed the Carmelite
hillside clad in superb pine woods and luxuriant olive trees
that looks down graciously over three valleys. They left
behind them grey Pastrana planted amidst its verdure-clad
hills. They bore along with them a peace that no violence
could conquer, because, like joy, it is a fruit of the Spirit.
The soul is more elevated by mystical acts of love than by
the courageous practice of virtue, even the virtue of forti-
tude. Pascal wisely remarked : " I do not admit that an

excess of virtue is of any value unless I see at the same time
an excess of the opposite virtue. Greatness is not shown by
running to one extreme, but by attaining to both extremes
at once and filling in all the space between." [45]   Father
John knew this from experience, for he practised charity,
and it is charity that best fills what lies between extremes.
Love is the bond of perfection, and when a higher degree of
love is reached the whole moral life is elevated. Such,
according to Father Eliseus of the Martyrs, [46] was the
opinion of Father John of the Cross. *Desnudez*, spiritual
detachment, surrenders the whole soul to love. Corporal
macerations, which stir up the hidden depths of man's
natural activity, may lead to Illuminism, and we then reach
what John himself calls " an animal penitence, towards
which one is inclined by the satisfaction to be found therein,
and this is proper to beasts." [47]   Should anyone do more
than he must, Our Lord will reward him on the Day of
Judgment. But discretion, the mistress of the virtues, should
always be employed." Father John of the Cross undoubtedly
reflected on this ultimate counsel of the Primitive Rule, when
he came into contact with the " giants " of Pastrana. He
arrived as a " moderator of the virtues," amongst those
extravagantly generous spirits, who were more inclined, like
the Eastern monks of Sceté or Tabenna, to asceticism, than
to the truly spiritual life. " Now man's good," says St.
Thomas Aquinas, " his justice, consists especially in interior
acts, in faith, hope and charity, and not in exterior acts.
The former are an end to be sought for its own sake, whilst
the latter, for which we make an offering of our bodies to
God, are a means to the end. In that which is sought as an
end, one need not observe measure ; in that the more is
always the better. But, on the contrary, in that which is
sought as a means to the end, we should adopt measure proportionate to that end. Man should place no bounds to his
charity ; but, on the other hand, he should, in his exterior
acts, employ a discretion governed by charity." [48]

Father John, on his arrival, took over the government of
the house " with the double title of Master and Vicar." [49]
There were fourteen religious, four of whom were professed :

Ambrose Mariano, Juan de la Miseria, Gabriel of the Assumption and Bartholomew of St. Albert, who had come from the Observants. Amongst the ten novices, one Cyril, and three Peters, two of whom were Andalusians, had also left the Observants. Father Peter of St. Jerome, a native of Saragossa, had filled important offices amongst the latter, and Peter of the Apostles, a native of Viso, four leagues from Seville, was to die a martyr's death in the New World.

Amongst the others the learned Augustine of the Kings, of Ecija, holds a prominent place, a future provincial of Andalusia, whose body remained incorrupt after death. It may seem surprising that there is no mention of Father Francis, that redoubtable ascetic, among those who were professed ; he had gone to Alcalá to make preparations for a new establishment. This foundation was just then absorbing all the energies of the elders at Pastrana, so that there can be no doubt that John was a most welcome arrival.

What impression did he make on the novitiate ? We cannot doubt that a Gaspar of St. Mary, an Albert of St. Francis, already ripe for Heaven, gladly received his teachings. The pure and simple Brother Eliseus of St. Ildephonsus made the master's soul his mirror.*

John instructed the novices not only by his fervent words, but also by object lessons. He brought them to see Francisco de Yepes (who had followed him in his removals) at work, and said to his children, as he once did to the Duke of Pastrana : " He is my brother, a poor working man, who has to earn his own living." [50]

Francisco was faithful to the Lord as to an intimate friend. He may, perhaps, have told the novices of the five conditions which he regarded as necessary in order to preserve this faithfulness to a beloved friend :—

" To satisfy him in that which we know is agreeable to him.
" To rejoice at all his good fortune, prosperity and triumphs.

* He declared that Father John condemned particular devotions in community life, and that in his own time the plates, cups and bowls were yellow in colour, and not white (Andrés, 13482, J. 30).

" To reveal our secrets to him and tell him of what is
closest to our heart.

" To speak well of him on all occasions.

" To risk goods, life and honour for his sake." [51]

.   .   .   .   .   .

I have had the privilege of spending several hours in that
vast *cueva*, hollowed out of the friable, yellow-coloured clay,
which lies just beneath the *palomar*, the primitive dove-cot
that has been transformed into an oratory.[52]

> *Joannes a Cruce, Fontiveri*
> *Natus, vixit in hoc antro*
> *Ubedae vita cessit, Segobiae*
> *Corpus ejus. In pace requiescit.*

(John of the Cross, born at Fontiveros, lived in this cave.
He died at Ubeda. His body rests in peace at Segovia.)

It is a wide, deep, well-ventilated cavern ; in the morning the sun shines in on it, and it sparkles with a scattered
dust of red gold. If John gazed up from the place where he
slept, or the lower corner where he prayed, he could see
only a tiny patch of sky. One must stand close against the
rock-balustrade, at the opening of the grotto, from which a
narrow stairway ascends, before one can see the ground
beneath.   .

The green Vega lies ninety yards below. Opposite
stands a mountain with patches of olive trees, and a little
line of trees runs along the crest. Farther off is Bolarca, the
first solitude, which was founded on August 13th, 1592, and
where Father Bartholomew of St. Basil, in transports of love,
preached to the trees and birds.[53]

John's first stay at Pastrana was brief. When Balthazar
returned, early in 1571, John left for Alcalá.

CHAPTER X

THE UNIVERSITY OF ALCALÁ

WHEN Teresa arrived at Pastrana in July, 1570, for the profession of Mariano and Juan de la Miseria, there had been some talk of founding a college at Alcalá de Henares, " both on account of the ease with which study might be carried on there, and also because there was a better opportunity of obtaining distinguished members." [1]   Teresa had suffered so much from " suspicious semi-doctors " (and they had so often " cost [her] dearly "), [2] that she at once gave her support to an institution which would secure real masters for the Reform : did she not tell Mariano that she had always wished for " men of talent," even if, in order to draw them to the Reform, it were necessary to mitigate its rigours ? [3]   Carmelite contemplatives are called on to direct interior souls : if they are theologians, even though lacking in mystical experience, they will be able to enlighten others : on that point Teresa was certain.

A decision reached, some slight fear remained of approaching the Master-General for a licence to establish a third foundation. In his patent of August 16th, 1567, he had given permission for only two, and, on August 8th of this year 1570, he wrote to say that he did not wish to go beyond that number. [4]   In short, rather than risk a refusal, they turned to another authority which had been set up as the result of Philip II's intervention. On August 20th, the " holy Dominican provincial," Father Peter Fernandez, had been charged by Pope Pius V, at the king's request, to make an apostolic visitation of the Carmelite Fathers of Castile, whilst another friar preacher, Francis de Vargas, received a similar commission for Andalusia. The authorisation for an establishment in Alcalá was granted by the visitor, but needed confirmation from Rubeo, who was asked to give it by Don Ruy Gomez, the founder and benefactor of the convent, as we learn from Mary of St. Joseph.[5] The Master-General was hurt by the nomination of Apostolic visitors, and, on the following November 1st, he, in turn, appointed " defenders of the Order " for each of the Spanish provinces [6]. Amongst those of Castile was Father Anthony de Heredia, now " of Jesus," but they were never called on to take action.

Padre Antonio was at all times a favourite with the General, who, on June 21st, 1574, gave him permission to make a foundation at Almodovar.

No, John Baptist Rubeo was not a narrow-minded man ; he loved the primitive ideal of his Order, and had gladly given Teresa permission to establish two convents of contemplatives. If, on August 8th, he forbade her to found any more, and fixed the number of religious in each of these two communities at twenty, it was merely because he had learned that several Castilian, and even Andalusian, Carmelites had left their own convents to lead a new form of life at Pastrana and this had created a disturbance throughout the whole province. Again, amongst those who joined the primitives was Balthazar Nieto, whom Rubeo had been forced to punish for abetting the flight of his brother Melchior, who had been condemned to the galleys. The least that could be said of his later behaviour was that he showed a bad spirit, and the " Father of the Order " feared lest turbulent spirits like Melchior and Gaspar Nieto, as well as Ambrosio de Castro, Juan de Mora and their friends, " might corrupt the whole flock of contemplatives." [7]

When Father Francis of the Conception completed the purchase from the Observants of the very house he had himself procured for them in 1566, Father Balthazar took possession. This occurred, as we have said, on November 1st, 1570.[8] He took with him Father Peter of St. Jerome, a former dignitary in the Order, Brother Mariano and two aristocratic novices, Brother Gabriel of the Assumption, Don Ruy Gomez's standard-bearer, and Brother Augustine of the Kings.

Brother Gabriel was a man of sound common-sense ; he

was no metaphysician [9]; whilst Brother Augustine, who was so angelic that Mother Teresa, on seeing him serve Mass one day at San Pedro de Arriba, could not refrain from going to embrace him, was an intellectual, attracted by the *Summa* of Theology.[10]   Brother Gabriel was not to remain at Alcalá because, as the *Reforma* tells us, Father John of the Cross, who had, on Balthazar's return, been appointed rector of the college, selected the young professed cleric, "whose intelligence he recognised," as master of novices instead of himself.[11] Father Augustine of the Kings returned to the Dove-cot to make his profession on January 12th, 1571, but we shall meet him again at the University.[12]

Whilst Father Balthazar of Jesus was living in the house of " Our Lady of Mount Carmel," close to the Puerta de los Aguadöres, he used to preach frequently. His apostolic zeal and garb of poverty made conversions, which were needed in that crowd of gay students who were in danger of being corrupted by " the atmosphere of the Court." Madrid, alas, was only six leagues away !

When Father John took over the government of the college a reputation for fervour and austerity had already been acquired.

At Alcalá, in a wide plain open to all the winds, the weather is liable to great extremes. The winter of 1571 was so severe that people did not venture out of doors, even when well wrapped up.[13] Our students, for their part, went barefoot through the wide streets, over the ice, or, what was worse, the melting snow. They were a pleasanter sight than the half-naked penitents who went in procession, scourging themselves with whips tipped with glass beads. Comfortable people indoors, looked out through the windows, frightened, amazed, admiring. There were generous hearts that heard the call.

The question has been asked, what was the " hidden reason "[14] of John's change from Pastrana to Alcalá? As a matter of fact, there were very few religious at this epoch capable of directing others, and John enjoyed both a moral and intellectual authority in the eyes of all his brethren.

Not that he was a ruler : the Foundress only placed him third in that respect. If Gracian could not be elected provincial, then "Father Anthony of Jesus should be nominated, or Father John of the Cross." [15] But John was something better than an administrator ; he was a man of great mentality, and the Mother was well aware of the need of penetrating the Brethren with the same ideal from the very beginning, when each house was still going its own way.[16] Thanks to him, the work was accomplished at Alcalá, the great University town, even as it had been so humbly at Duruelo, Mancera and Pastrana itself. Had not Our Lord told Teresa in Salamanca, about the middle of February, 1571, that she should see her Order flourish ? [17]

.   .   .   .   .   .

To-day, when grass is growing in the University clòisters, let us, before following John of the Cross and his sons, recall the glorious work accomplished there by the Franciscan friar, Jimenes de Cisneros, Archbishop of Toledo and Chancellor of Castile, when he inaugurated the University in the very heart of the old Moorish city, *Al Kalah*,[18] on March 14th, 1498.

Knowledge was feverishly pursued and mud walls were rapidly rising : " I will leave enough gold to have them turned into marble," said Cisneros to Ferdinand the Catholic.

On July 26th, 1508, a lecture on Aristotle's Ethics opened the course of studies. In the following year the Archbishop, at the head of his fleet, captured Oran from the Moors, plundered the mosques and, in a short time, African camels were galloping through Spain, making straight for the crenellated citadel of peaceful and studious Alcalá, loaded with vessels of gold and silver, priceless manuscripts.[19]

Cisneros, who was nearly eighty, began drawing up the first constitutions ; these bear the date January 22nd, 1510.

While Salamanca had been democratic, Alcalá was to be avowedly aristocratic. At the head of the University was the College of St. Ildephonsus, which was governed by the rector and his ninety-three fellows, in their scarlet robes, draped with wide, flowing stoles. Twelve collegiate priests constituted the spiritual supports of the edifice.

Jimenes de Cisneros' sympathies were entirely with the teaching of the Sorbonne, and hence he laid it down that all things be done " according to the use and wont of Paris."

There were forty-two chairs altogether, six of theology, six of canon law, four of medicine, one of anatomy, another of surgery, eight of literature or arts, one of moral philosophy, one of mathematics, four of the Greek and Hebrew languages, four of rhetoric, and six of grammar. Scarcely had these chairs been created than they were filled by masters and learned men, who came not only from all the great universities of Spain, but also from those of France and Italy. They set to work at once in the " three-language cloister," which to-day lies deserted. In 1520 the Polyglot Bible appeared : it was a scientific work, conceived in accordance with Origen's plan, and Jimenes de Cisneros paid for manuscripts, copyists and type-founders. Ten folio volumes were printed. He planned, too, a monumental edition of Aristotle, in three columns, one giving the Greek text, another the old Latin translation, and the third a new version. Vergara immediately set about the translation of several treatises, but the death of the Archbishop put an end to the undertaking, and the materials were deposited in the library of the Cathedral of Toledo. No longer could Cisneros be heard keeping up a discussion, as he stood at a window open to the pure air of the plain, with the celebrated Anthony of Lebrija, on passages from the Bible or problems of government. But his work endured, and when the Carmelites of Pastrana arrived, in 1571, to follow out their courses of philosophy and theology with the *artistas* of Santa Balbina's or Santa Catalina's, the young philologists of St. Eugene's or St. Isidore's, the remark made by Francis I when visiting the cloisters and the Moorish paranymph with its galleries of tribunes, was still repeated : " Your Jimenes alone did more than a whole line of kings has accomplished in France." Alcalá was still " the eighth wonder of the world."

In 1565 important changes took place in the Faculty of Theology as the result of a visitation made by the licentiate, Juan de Orlando, the official nominee of the Chapter of SS. Justus and Pastor, whose canonries were reserved for doctors of the University cloister.

Henceforth the Faculty was to consist of six chairs : the " Prime " chair of St. Thomas, held by Juan Ruiz de Villaran in the years 1571–1572, the " Prime " Chair of Scotus, held by Juan Calderon, and a Chair of Scripture, of which the titular holder, at the moment, was Juan Cantero. All three " lectured " in turn, for one hour every morning, in the hall of Theology. In these years, 1571 and 1572, in the afternoon Juan Alonso, a professor in the " minor " chair of St. Thomas, began the courses, followed by the Dominican, Jeronimo de Almonacir, the titular holder of the Vesper Chair (in Nominalism) and finally, Pedro Irana closed the day with a lecture on Durandus.

Each professor was obliged to teach in conformity with the spirit of the chair he held. Juan Ruiz de Villaran, canon of Sigüenza, and Doctor Juan Alonso had to divide up the *Summa Theologica* between them, and follow a fixed course of lectures, that were to extend over four years. Hence, in January, 1575, when the former was lecturing on the treatise *De Angelis*, the latter was lecturing on the treatise *De Gratia*. Through lack of registers, we cannot settle what was being taught in 1571–1572.

It is impossible to state precisely to which of these lectures John of the Cross brought his pupils. Although, at the Chapter of Alcalá in 1581, when the Reform was definitely established as a separate province, a recommendation was made to read and follow the authors of the Order,[20] it seems probable that the forerunners of the celebrated *Complutenses* went, by preference, to the lectures on St. Thomas. The intellectual training of Father John of the Cross at Salamanca had been on Thomist lines, and we know, from the *Reforma*, that Brother Augustine of the Kings, one of the first and most illustrious students of Alcalá, loved the Angelic Doctor, whom he venerated as his Master.[21]

It is, therefore, most probable that the Carmelite students

attended the morning and evening lectures on the *Summa Theologica*, according to the University reforms of 1565, to which we have referred, and also, no doubt, assisted at the daily lecture on Scripture. A scholastic disputation was held every week, at which the theological students, and all those preparing for the baccalaureate or licentiate were bound to assist. It would seem as if the brethren were, at this period, free to take out degrees. The constitutions of 1576, drawn up by Gracian, when he became Apostolic Visitor, simply suppressed, from humility, the privileges and exemptions of masters, licenciates, and bachelors.[22] It was only in 1581, and by the Constitutions of Alcalá, when the intellectual life of the Order was better organised, that the reception of University degrees themselves was strictly forbidden in the Reform.[23]

A text from Echard,[24] confirmed by an allusion of Dominic Bañes himself, has led some to suggest that the famous Friar Preacher held a chair of Theology in the University of Alcalá, " in or about 1567," [25] but there is no mention of his name in the University records. It is, of course, possible that Bañes was teaching during that year in the Dominican College of St. Thomas, attached to the University. Possibly, too, he may have occasionally taken the place of Pedro Portocarrero, the University professor, who resided in that college. To suppose that Bañes remained at Alcalá long enough to have been still there in 1571 is no longer possible, owing to the discovery of the Vatican Codex Ottob. 1054, which states that Dominic Vanes (*sic*) was teaching the *Tertia Pars* of the *Summa* in that same year at St. Stephen's in Salamanca. Bañes had just been promoted Master of Theology by the General Chapter of Rome.[26] Hence it is not surprising that in his letter of April 23rd, 1572, to St. Teresa, from Salamanca, Bañes makes no reference to Father John of the Cross, as might be expected if he had met John in Alcalá. Bañes, who was a great friend of Teresa's, had evidently no doctrinal influence on the little Carmelite group or its thirty-year-old rector.

John spent a fruitful sixteen months at Alcalá. Apart from his intellectual life—did he, perhaps, coach his stu-

dents ?*—he heard the confessions and was the spiritual
guide of the nuns of the *Imagen*, a Carmelite convent established by Mary of Jesus, of Granada, in 1563. It was she who,
when passing through Toledo, told Teresa that the Primitive Rule implied a most rigorous vow of poverty. He was
also the director of his sons, and the young Carmelites,
thanks to his sound mystical doctrine and example, " tasted
in prayer the divine sweetnesses with which the Holy Spirit
favours souls who seek their sole consolation in God." [27]
" Almost all the religious of this college," Quiroga adds,
" were great contemplatives." They rivalled each other in
study as well as in prayer, but prayer came first.

> *Religioso y estudiante*
> *Religioso por delante.* [28]

The intellectual life and the spiritual life, as understood by
St. John of the Cross, are not opposed : in fact they help
each other ; by simple, obscure contemplation the soul is
refined, purified and elevated ; it turns from sensible things
and images to become a partaker of the nature of the
Wisdom of love. But, inferior to this experimental, mystical
Wisdom, there is a theological Wisdom, a science subordinate
to that of the Science of God and the Blessed. Theology aids
the soul in its task of detachment ; it tears it from itself,
fixing it upon its object and rooting it in faith, " the proximate and proportionate means of Union." [29]

The intellectual and spiritual life of the college were then
so keen as to rouse the admiration of the holy Dominican
Provincial, Father Fernandez, when he made his apostolic
visitation.[30] They lived intensely, and all their activity was
expended in the service of God of Whom they were learning
a fuller knowledge, a fuller enjoyment.

It is said that one student went so far as to think of
abstaining from sleep ! This Spanish Macarius gradually
reduced his allowance of sleep by degrees ; he had reached

---

* A valuable detail, mentioned by Alonso (B. 1, Ch. XXI) helps us to see
John's intellectual bent. As some devout persons in Alcalá had asked him to
write the lives of Justus and Pastor, saints and martyrs, and patrons of the city,
he excused himself from doing so " because it seemed to him that, if he made
the attempt he should write a devotional, and not an historical work."

a point at which he was able to do with an hour's repose, when Our Lord reminded him that his flesh was not yet glorified.

. . . . . .

In the *Peregrinations of Anastasius*, an old student of Alcalá, Jerome Gracian, of whom more later, describes the University students coming at nightfall to pray at Mount Carmel, and, whilst a religious chanted the *Miserere*, they gave themselves the discipline.[31] It is easy to understand how a life as perfect as that led by the Discalced was bound to attract chosen souls. Teresa says that the novitiate at Pastrana, whose caves were familar to the Court and University, " was enriched with numerous members, some of whom had taken their degrees." [32]

On January 1st, 1572, a young Catalan priest, Juan Roca, bachelor of Theology, who had gone to Alcalá to complete his studies, received the habit of the Order at Pastrana.[33] When Mother Teresa heard of this reception she appears to have exclaimed : " Now we have a man in the house." This was too much to say, for Father John of Jesus had neither the gift of governing nor a sense of proportion, as the Mother was soon to discover. He was one of those severe characters for whom the Rule has no liking.[34]

The novice, in his first fervour, wrote to his friend, Jerome Gracian, a young priest, twenty-six years of age, who had just been made Master of Arts, that is to say, a bachelor of the University of Alcalá, which was no small thing.[35] Roca made his boast of " the excellence and the antiquity of Carmel " ; shortly after, behold Gracian, who had not the least intention of becoming a Carmelite, on his way to Pastrana to arrange with Mother Isabella of St. Dominic the reception of Doña Barbara de Castillo.[36] The prioress, who was a great servant of God, was charmed with him, and got all the sisters to pray that Our Lord would not suffer Gracian to depart, but would give him the habit. They prayed, fasted and took the discipline. " For," said they, " at this time, there were very few men amongst our religious, and scarcely one who could be compared with this distinguished visitor, whose family had received royal favours." Gracian paid a visit to his friend John of Jesus Roca at San Pedro de Arriba. The surroundings impressed him. He overcame his repugnance, and, on March 25th, 1572, put on the serge habit of the Brothers of the Virgin, his *Well-beloved*. He was afterwards known as Brother Jerome of the Mother of God, or simply as Gracian.

"Father Gracian passed his year of probation like the humblest of young novices. His virtue was especially conspicuous on one occasion when the prior (Balthazar of Jesus) was absent, and authority had been entrusted to a young religious, who had not yet made his studies and had no talent or prudence in government. He could not have had any experience, for he had only recently joined . . . His manner of guiding his brethren was peculiar . . ."

This master of novices was Father Angelus of St. Gabriel. The Father Gabriel of the Assumption who was selected by John of the Cross during his passing stay at Pastrana had not long retained the office, for he was soon entrusted with more important functions. Such is the *Reforma's* explanation, but it is not very convincing.[37] There is no indication of the nature of these important offices. The former Calced Carmelite, Peter of the Apostles, then succeeded Gabriel, but he soon left for La Roda.[38] During all this time Balthazar was away, either in Madrid [39] or La Roda,[40] and "some imprudent professed members" raged furiously, to the great misfortune of about thirty novices. One day, Gracian relates, they took a novice, stripped his shoulders and beat him until he should, like Elias, by the sole virtue of his prayers, kindle a pile of damp wood. They actually dared to say that therein lay perfection ![41] The new novice master, Angelus of St. Gabriel, was probably one of those "eccentrics." The great fervour and penance then reigning in this house were not enough to satisfy[42] this "victim of melancholia" as St. Teresa calls him ; so he gave orders that striking demonstrations should be given in the public squares, which rendered the poor novices ridiculous. Having no beast of burden, they had to play the part now and again themselves ! "Why are you carrying your wood on your shoulders like that ? " Father Mariano was asked one day. " To warm me twice over," was the reply.[43] They were no longer so cheerful under the iron rod of Angelus. He treated his novices as if they were machines and not men. " The excessive mortifications which he imposed " ruined their health. Mother Teresa had good reason to ask herself afterwards how " such distinguished men " as Gracian, " her beloved son, *su hijo querido* " [44] and John of Jesus Roca " submitted to it."

Father John of the Cross returned to Pastrana to moderate this ill-regulated virtue, and laid down " laws which he and Father Anthony had made at Duruelo, and which were observed at Mancera and Alcalá." [45] He certainly did not return before April, 1572, since Gracian, who had had a taste of Angelus' iron rule, did not take the habit until March 25th of that year.

John of the Cross must have known Gracian in the novitiate at Pastrana : they were nearly of an age, John being thirty, and Jerome twenty-seven. But there was not much likeness between them. John was, at that time, pale and emaciated of face, and reserved in deportment—*Senequito*, Teresa called him—whilst Gracian was fascinating and very pleasing to converse with—" an enchanter." [46] And how he let himself go.[47] It was the marvellous element in the mystical life that appealed to him.[48] He was a splendid preacher and shone in the pulpits of Seville.[49] John of the Cross, on the other hand, was most prudent in regard to the sensible phenomena of the supernatural, and preaching only deepened his desire for a solitary life. He had been thinking seriously of the Charterhouse at El Paular, and Gracian had been in communication with Father Gil Gonzalez, with the idea of becoming a Jesuit.

" Seneca ", then, was at Pastrana in April, and he relieved Angelus of his duty as master of novices ; the latter at once appealed to Mother Teresa who, the better to support John's wise decision, backed up her own with that of the illustrious Dominican theologian, Bañes, who wrote to her from Salamanca on April 23rd, 1572 : [50]

" For a religious who has embraced such a complete retirement from the world as that prescribed by the Primitive Rule, it is not mortification in conformity with prudence to be seen much in public without necessity, nor is the practice of public mortifications a suitable manner of training novices, since it promotes a spirit of dissipation, whilst their vocation is to live apart from the world. To claim in that way to imitate the Fathers of the Society is to create a religious life quite different from that of Carmel. The Jesuit fathers have no special dress ; their profession does not oblige them to retreat, silence, fasting or perpetual attendance at Choir . . . When we are told of St. Francis, that he was looked on as a madman, that he stripped himself, and then dressed like the poorest of the poor : I love that, because it was due to the impulsive action of the Holy Spirit ; but a desire to imitate such unusual deeds, without that special grace, is mere burlesque."

The matter having been thus settled by Teresa of Jesus and Dominic Bañes, John left the Dove-cot at Pastrana in May, 1572, and, after handing over the charge of the college at Alcalá to Father Gabriel of the Assumption, set out for Avila, summoned by Teresa.[51]

CHAPTER XI

AT THE CONVENT OF THE INCARNATION

At the northern foot of the austere citadel of Avila, girt with reddish walls and eighty-six huge towers, lies a large, solitary, rosy-coloured group of buildings surmounted by slender spires. It stands in an unsightly valley, through which some rivulets meander, with here and there a few clumps of trees. This is the Monastery of the Incarnation, or, as we should call it, the Annunciation.

The *señoras* of the Incarnation had been " *beatas* " before they became nuns ; in 1479 Doña Elvira Gonzáles de Medina formed them into a community. It was only under Doña Beatrix Guiera that they adopted the Carmelite rule.[1] Henceforward the Carmelite Fathers of the old convent, which was built on the city walls, facing the monastery, had jurisdiction over the nuns, and, no doubt, supplied them with confessors. In 1503 the Master-General, Peter Terrasse, gave permission to the prioress to choose a confessor from the Order who would have power to absolve the community from all censures and reserved cases four times a year.[2]

Luis Perez de Castro, of the province of Castile, supplies us with information about the nuns in his *Status Ordinis* of 1531 :[3] some of them were pious and holy, and most of them were of noble birth, but they were very poor, so poor indeed that the Very Reverend Father Rubeo, after visiting them in 1567, forbade them to receive any more novices, " for they would be in danger of dying of hunger." [4] There were already a large number. It is stated that there were a hundred and eighty nuns when Doña Teresa de Ahumada, the young lady in the orange-coloured dress, with black velvet trimmings, took the habit, which was made of the same cloth as that used by the Observants.[5] Twenty-seven years later Teresa left " the poor sisters of the Incarnation "

for other poor sisters who were more fervent. The foundations had begun. Teresa frequently drew on her former
convent for helpers elsewhere. In the course of time she
selected as many as thirty. It was her joy to serve " those
ladies " who had so well helped her.[6]

On June 27th, 1571, the Dominican, Father Fernandez,
made a visitation of the Incarnation. He decided that this
community " needed, both in temporal and spiritual
matters, the government of Mother Teresa of Jesus. He
first consulted the definitors of the Chapter of the Carmelite
Fathers, and then, with their consent, and in virtue of his
own authority, appointed the holy Mother to the office of
prioress." [7] Teresa was just then at Medina, in her little
convent in the Calle Santiago. She was thunderstruck at
the idea of leaving her daughters for a year, and governing
a convent where she had formerly led a lukewarm life, not
to speak of reforming it. Our Lord said to her : " O my
daughter, my daughter ! the nuns of the Incarnation are my
sisters, and thou still dost delay. Come, take courage.
What thou thinkest harmful to thy monasteries will be of
profit on both sides. Resist no longer, for great is My
power." [8]

On October 6th, 1571, she came to Avila to take up office,
bearing in her arms the statue of " our glorious Father,
St. Joseph." Father Angel de Salazar demanded that
she should be admitted, but the nuns protested, claiming
their canonical rights. " So, ladies, you do not wish to
receive Mother Teresa of Jesus ? " said the Provincial.
Doña Catalina de Castro then rose and said, " We do wish
to have her, and we love her." The greater number
followed suit, although, adds Doña Maria Pinel y Monroy,
" Mgr. Yepes, who was ill-informed, says that it was only a
minority." On the following morning, Teresa of Jesus
placed a statue of Our Lady of Mercy, holding the keys
of office in her hands in the prioress's stall. She then sat
at her feet and rang the bell for Chapter. From that time
peace began to reign " in that Babylon," so much so that
on November 7th the Mother was able to write to Doña
Luisa de la Cerda : " The sisters are gradually giving up

their conversations and their liberties." [9] Let us not take a black view of these. There may, perhaps, have been too much lively and somewhat frivolous conversation in the *locutorio*, and they may have eaten too much candied fruit whilst drinking a few thimblefuls of *Vino del Santo*, which was regarded as the best in Castile. Nothing worse than that, so far as history knows. Still, they were attached to that much, and the nuns told Teresa that the change was " death to them," but the prioress held fast ; and nobles who were too officious discovered that the prioress was in earnest, for she would have complained of them to Philip II.

There were a hundred and thirty nuns to be reformed, and the same number of mouths to be fed. " Our glorious Father, St. Joseph," was a vigilant sub-prior, and he needed to be, for a little nun who had not enough to eat might well long for the sweetmeats she used to get in the parlour. All were most grateful when the Mother received fowls for the sick nuns, and something that would furnish a meal for the poorest of the religious. She, herself, took nothing but bread from the monastery, and was even anxious to spare it that much expense.[10] She was deeply grieved at seeing those around her suffer, and, in a short time those who were most opposed to her became quite friendly. The parlours were closed during Lent of 1572, and all peacefully submitted to this innovation. " It is my Prioress (the Blessed Virgin) who is working these wonders," Teresa wrote on March 7th to Doña Maria de Mendoza. The ground was being broken up and prepared for the sowing : " Some of them are great servants of God, and almost all are making notable progress in the way of perfection." Who was to come to the assistance of Our Lady and Teresa, who was overwhelmed with work, exhausted by fever, and so sick that she no longer left " her little corner except to go to Mass " ? Doña Isabella Arias, the sub-prioress, helped her, and they got on very well together. But, in spite of all, she was lonely because Doña Isabella was not a person in whom Teresa could confide, or who could comfort her. And God left her " without even a confessor." [11]

.   .   .   .   .   .

"During the octave of Pentecost, Our Lord granted me a special favour, and led me to hope that this house would make progress. I mean the souls who compose it," wrote Teresa in an account dated May, 1572.[12] We know that Julian of Avila returned just then from Salamanca, where he had been authorised by Father Fernandez to send Discalced Carmelites to the convent to act as confessors. Teresa had never ceased from entrusting such a delicate affair to the Spirit of Wisdom and Counsel. What would the nuns, and, above all, what would the Mitigated Fathers of Avila, the community's confessors, think of this? After all, the only thing of importance was the glory of God ; all would go well, for in future there would be directors capable of bringing up souls in the "ways of the highest perfection." The Holy Spirit assured her of this, and she had a small house built, quite close to the monastery, for Father John of the Cross had already left Alcalá,[13] and the delicate charge of hearing the nuns' confessions had been entrusted to him. Father Germain of St. Mathias was assigned as his companion.[14]

A well-beloved daughter of John of the Cross, Ana Maria Gutierrez, who was then twenty-two years of age, was a witness of his arrival at the Incarnation, where she was a nun.[15] Long afterwards she remembered that Teresa introduced the young priest of thirty in these terms : "Ladies,[16] I am bringing you as a confessor, *un padre que es santo*," for the holy Mother held him in the highest esteem [17]. When Catalina Alvarez heard of this appointment she was very proud. He was "very young ; *muy moço*," as she told Francisca de Jesus afterwards, when teaching her how to weave in the Carmelite convent at Medina.[18]

"The Discalced Carmelite father who hears confessions here, Father John of the Cross,[19] is doing much good : he is very holy : *harto santo*," wrote Teresa on February 13th, 1573, to Father Gaspar de Salazar,[20] in a letter which gives us a picture of a convent that had been totally transformed. Obedience and recollection were held in such honour that Father Fernandez found nothing to correct in the course of his visitation in mid-January. It was marvellous. He wrote to the Duchess of Alba (January 22nd) to say that the hundred and thirty nuns " are living in the same sanctity and peace as the ten or twelve Discalced nuns in the convent of Alba. It has afforded me extraordinary consolation and surprise," and he went on to say that " all this is due to the Mother's presence," which made itself felt everywhere. Fernandez had just appointed Father Anthony of Jesus head of the old convent of the Mitigated Friars. He was entrusted with its reform, and Discalced Fathers occupied the positions of procurator, porter and sacristan. " Now, the Mother's presence is needed to encourage these Fathers." [21] They, too, had need to warm themselves at the living flame with which she glowed. For the past two months St. Teresa had been raised to the state of Mystical Marriage, to the peace of the Seventh Mansion.

On the octave of St. Martin's Day, 1572, Father John of the Cross said the Conventual Mass.[22] After he had received Holy Communion he went down the altar steps, and, bearing the ciborium, walked down the whole length of the vast white and gold Romanesque Church of the Incarnation. On reaching the Communion guichet, he bent his pale, brown face and beheld Teresa's glowing countenance. He divided the sacred Host, and she remembered having told him that she greatly loved large particles. She believed that he intended to mortify her. Formerly, Father Balthazar Alvarez had forbidden her to receive Holy Communion, in order to calm her loving transports, and it is likely that John wished to detach her from this sensible devotion. In 1586 he deprived the Venerable Anne of Jesus of the Eucharist, though she was famishing for it, and although it was a day for receiving Communion according to the Rule. The nuns of Granada were greatly surprised at his action.*

* Autograph deposition of Maria de la Cruz, December 3rd, 1634. (Arch. C.R., Brussels).
On three different occasions the saint imposed the same deprivation on Catherine of St. Albert. Cf. *infra*, Ch. XIV. The whole community at Granada was deprived of Communion on one Ash Wednesday morning. Maria de la Cruz, Ubeda I.O., f. 50. May we not see a precaution against Illuminism in this apparently harsh conduct ? The *Alumbrados* maintained that a person became more perfect by receiving a larger Host, or several Hosts, at Holy Communion. Menendez y Pelayo. *Heterodoxos Españoles*, L.V., Ch. I. (t. II), p. 553.

The Mother quickly reflected that this mattered little, since " Jesus Christ is wholly present in the least particle," and His Majesty said to her : " Fear not, daughter, that this can separate thee from me." Teresa returned to her stall of " second prioress " and it was there, probably, that Jesus appeared to her in a vision, in the interior of her soul and, giving her His right hand, said : " Look at this nail, it is the sign that, from this day forward, thou shalt be my spouse ; hitherto thou hast not deserved it. Henceforward thou shalt take care of my honour, not only because I am thy Creator, King and God, but also because thou art my true spouse. My honour is thine and thy honour is mine." The day passed in " a sort of delirium."

Was John's influence on the Mother Prioress exclusively ascetic ? Did he merely choose, with a holy liberty, as a witness relates, to allow her to lie prostrate on the ground for a long time to humble her ? [23] Did he simply break " the golden chain " that still bound her to a supreme, but sensible, spiritual delight ? He did more than that, and the proof lies in her writings. It has been pointed out that *The Elevations on the Canticle of Canticles*, composed in 1574, clearly manifest not only a progress, which is due, no doubt, to the psychological experience of a soul that had arrived at full self-consciousness, but also a doctrinal power to which John undoubtedly contributed.[24] " I seek here and there for light," said Teresa, " and find all I need in my little Seneca." She remained before him as if " in prayer," and said of him, in his absence, " no one knows the riches and treasures which God has placed in that holy soul : they are very great." [25] In December, 1578, she told Anne of Jesus that Father John " is really the father of my soul, and one of those who have done me most good by their words," for, " he combines the widest experience with the deepest knowledge." [26]

On one occasion—it was the Feast of the Most Holy Trinity—John of the Cross happened to be in the parlour— a small parlour about six feet and a half high, five feet long by five broad, paved with red bricks, having grey stone walls and a roughly timbered brown ceiling. He was sitting in a chair and, on the other side of the grille, Teresa was

sitting on a stool. He was speaking to her of the mystery
of the Trinity, " his favourite mystery," and his soul was
plunged in that abyss of fire. The ardour of the Spirit
seized his body and, as he held tightly to his chair, he was
raised aloft until he touched the ceiling. Teresa of Jesus
had been ravished by the same impetuous love.[27] Doña
Beatrix de Cepeda y Ocampo, the future Beatrice of Jesus,
opening the door to give her relative a message, was a
witness of this rapture, which resembled that of Elias.[28]
" One cannot speak of God to Father John of the Cross,
because he at once goes into an ecstasy and causes others to
do the same," said Teresa happily, by way of apology.[29]

The feast itself and the subject of conversation were bound
to enrapture Teresa, for, at that time, she was enjoying an
habitual, intellectual vision of the three Divine Persons.
Our Lord told her that she was taking the place of St. Mary
Magdalen. Her whole duty was then to love.[30] But she
had to deal with other matters, and combine Martha and
Mary. Martha complained of her sister,[31] but did not
John of the Cross envisage Magdalen in such a state of love
that any external occupation would be prejudicial to it?
This, certainly, is a delicate question, and yet may rightly
be asked.[32] " May the Lord deliver me from people who
are so elevated in spirituality that they wish at all costs to
bring everyone to perfect contemplation," said the Foundress
in her slightly malicious *Vejamen*, when criticising John's
sublime considerations, " of which the only fault is that they
have nothing to do with the question proposed." [33] But
there is nothing in these open shafts to separate Mother
Teresa from " the father of her soul." John and Teresa
have the same spirit and the same heart.* " I have found
a man according to the heart of God and my own," she
remarked.[34] John was profoundly impressed by Teresa,
whose soul, as he was aware, had reached the luminous
centre of the castle. When he deals, in his *Cantico*, with
phases that are preliminary to the mystic espousals, such as

---

* Andres de la Encarnación combats, in a dissertation, the false idea,
" current " in his time, " that the spirit of Our Holy Mother was different
from that of St. John of the Cross," 13483, R, 459.

" raptures, ecstasies, and subtle flights of the spirit," he does not dwell on the subject, but remarks that the blessed Teresa of Jesus, our Mother, left admirable writings on these topics, which he hoped would soon be printed.[35]

The five years—1572 to 1577—which John spent at the Incarnation were years of study and recollection, and also, as we shall see, of spiritual direction. What books did he read at this period? The constitutions of the Discalced Carmelites, approved in 1565,[36] recommended : *Cartujanos*, that is to say, Ludolph of Saxony's *Vita Christi ;* the *Flos Sanctorum*, probably the collection of lives of the saints made by Pedro de la Vega, which was very popular throughout Spain at the beginning of the sixteenth century ; the *Contemptus Mundi, i.e., The Imitation of Christ*, the *Oratorio de Religiosos*, a very detailed and precise manual of monastic discipline by Antonio de Guevara ; the works of Luis de Granada and Pedro de Alcántara.[37]

John had an opportunity of reading all those books, for they were prescribed by rule for all Carmelite libraries. Who can doubt that he made constant use of the *Imitation ?* There is a clearer indication in regard to the *Flos Sanctorum*, because Juan Evangelista, who was an eye-witness of the second period of his career, deposed that, apart from this work, he had seen no other books in his cell except a treatise by St. Augustine, the Bible and a breviary.[38] The daily recital of the divine office would, we should notice, recall to his mind, in the course of the year, extracts from the Fathers, and these may have contributed to his intellectual formation. Here is an instance : he quotes from St. Gregory on four occasions, and the passages are taken from the homilies that are read at Easter and Pentecost.[39] Might it not be these quotations that make Quiroga assert that he studied St. Gregory ? [40] *

St. John of the Cross rarely indicated his sources. Are we then to conclude that he was not influenced by previous writers ? No. His genius is in no way diminished if we see, for example, traces of the teachings of " the Admirable

---

* The same historian speaks of his study of Dionysius the Areopagite. I shall deal with Dionysius and also Tauler and Ruysbroeck in Ch. XVII.

Ruysbroeck " in his doctrine.   Is the " little way " of St.
Teresa of the Infant Jesus any less admirable because she
was enlightened by the writings of St. John of the Cross ?
She herself states that, for two important years of her
spiritual formation, " she had no other food." [41]

.   .   .   .   .   .

According to the Constitutions then in force,[42] the nuns
of the Incarnation were bound to go to confession every
week, or, at least, every fortnight, to a confessor appointed
by the Visitor.   In addition to the liturgical offices, according to the Carmelite rite, the hearing of the confessions of a
hundred and thirty nuns in narrow confessional boxes built
into the walls of the conventual church, was no slight task,
especially as it involved real spiritual direction.   Moreover,
it was part of the confessor's office, according to the Constitutions, to give his approval to the nuns' reading, and to
advise them in their difficulties.[43]   Rapid progress was made
as soon as Mother Teresa was not alone in guiding the
monastery.   We have excellent contemporary testimony as
to the state of the sanest section of the community in the
collective reply of twenty-two nuns to the *Spiritual Challenge*,[44]
issued by the novices of Pastrana.   John probably received
it from Gracian in September, 1572, some months after his
arrival at the Incarnation.

" The Challenger " and his brethren had suffered at the
hands of Father Angelus of St. Gabriel, and one may ask if it
was not at Teresa's or John's instigation that " the right
valiant and courageous knights," shut up in Mariano's
grottos, had issued their challenge ?   In the nuns' reply,
mention is made of a " Knight-errant," who desires the
perfection of obedience in exchange for all his merits for
one year, and, in all probability, this was John of the
Cross.[45]

One day Maria Gutierrez who, during the brief period
which she spent in the Reform, was known by the name of
Anne of Jesus, went to confession to John of the Cross.
Whilst awaiting her turn she had a revelation.   John, during
his first Mass, had been re-established in the innocence of a

two-year-old child, without malice or duplicity, and, like the Apostles, had been confirmed in grace, so as never afterwards to sin gravely. " I beg you to answer the question I am about to ask," said the nun to her confessor, and, when the promise was given, she asked him for what favour he had begged during his first Mass. John replied that he had implored His Majesty to grant him the grace never to commit a mortal sin, and to suffer, during this life, the penance for all those faults which, in his weakness, he might have committed, if God were not sustaining him. Ana Maria then asked if he believed he had been heard, and the saint replied that he believed his prayer had been heard as firmly as he believed he was a Christian.

The young nun adds, in her deposition, that she herself had evidence of how fully John had been heard, for, during many years, she had had opportunities of admiring " his innocence, his guileless manner of acting, as if he were a child. . . . His glance, as gentle as his words, revealed a most pure soul." [46] Does not this portrait recall the grace and strength of a Teresa of Lisieux? And how far we are from the frozen outline to be admired but not loved, on which so many pious authors, who have not known how to see the living man, have spent their time. " Elias was a man like unto us." [47]

John of the Cross was then about thirty. It was at this period that a young and beautiful woman, of good lineage, conceived a passion for him. She visited him on several occasions, and strove by every means to infatuate him. Seeing that she was unsuccessful she made up her mind to get into his cottage one evening. And as she had resolved, so she did. John was alone, and having a meal. He was surprised to see her, but did not, like St. Thomas Aquinas at Monte S. Giovanni, seize a burning brand from the hearth. He spoke to her gently, and the young woman burst into tears and departed in peace.[48] " *The holier the confessors, the milder they are, and the less easily scandalised.*" In these gracious words John of the Cross depicted himself on one occasion when he was addressing a lady of the convent who was very beautiful, courteous and musical, but so hot-tempered that she smashed everything about her. She was called Robert the Devil.[49]

Victories such as these had to be paid for. One evening, after hearing confessions, John passed out beneath the massive stone archway of the conventual church, walked down the little pathway, and moved along by the wall with its high buttresses of grey granite. The *Angelus* had just been rung and people were going home. He was eighty yards or so from his little cottage, when suddenly a man's figure sprang up, and with all the rage of passion seeking its prey, beat the poor friar so severely with a stick that he was knocked down, and the ruffian then fled. When he related this incident afterwards, John added that never in his whole life had he enjoyed sweeter consolation : this time men had treated him as they had treated Jesus. Demons, too, leagued themselves with men, and persecuted him during the night with frightful apparitions, and severe blows—witnessed sometimes by " his companions," Father Germain and Brother Francis of the Apostles.[50] *

But Jesus consoled His friend. On one occasion when he was contemplating Christ's dolorous cross, the Crucified One appeared to him in a corporeal vision, covered with wounds and blood, His bones dislocated, in the utter disfigurement to which His executioners had reduced him. When John recovered from his ecstasy, he made a sketch, with a sort of Indian ink, which is now venerated in the Convent of the Incarnation. The paper, about five inches long, is quite yellow, and Christ's countenance is barely discernible. The *Reforma*, whose three hundred year old account possesses real interest, says : " It would seem that Our Lord appeared to him, not in full face, but in profile, showing a large portion of His shoulders, which had been torn by scourges. It is difficult to give a foreshortened effect in perspective. Hence people with a good knowledge of painting have praised the work, and think it was wonderful that the Venerable Father, who was ignorant of the rules of art, drew this figure so

* Francis lived with the saint for a year and eight months. He was made prisoner with him on the occasion of the first kidnapping and transference to Medina (Andres, 13482 D. 196 and J. 73).

skilfully." [51]   The historian was, no doubt, unaware that
Juan de Yepes when a lad had learned the arts of painting
and wood-carving.   The drawing is pathetically and sub-
limely realistic ; its anatomy may be at fault, but that is a
point which may be left to specialists to settle.   Little did
Father John care.   Though he found fault with an exaggerated attachment to images and the polychromatic
statuary of the *pasos*, he taught that " one should always
select those which are most accurately drawn, and most
strongly move the will, and pay more attention to this factor
than to the value or interest attaching to the workmanship
and ornamentation." [52]   What he sought for was the
Invisible, the Mystery of Christ, the God-made-Man, seen
through the dislocated skeleton and tortured flesh.

He gave this sketch to his dear spiritual daughter Ana
Maria of Jesus, when he confided his secret to her, and she
kept it until she died ; she bequeathed it to Doña Maria
Pinel y Monroy.   Copies have been made of the drawing.[53]

John, as we may see, was not for ever imposing privations
on souls, nor was his fatherly care confined to advice and
instruction.   He acted like a true champion, sent petty
doctrinaires and lovers of visions about their business, and
induced the Sisters to dismiss all such.   An unwearied
patience, rooted in love, led to generous ascents to the summits.   He guided such souls on the upward path to divine
union in faith and self-spoliation, *en fé y en desnudez*, and
passed far beyond the stage of mere discourse, in which those
misleading teachers would have imprisoned them for life.[54]
Sister Ana Maria was amazed, and one day asked him how
he dealt with his nuns so that he was able to induce them to
do immediately all that he desired.   " *It is God who does all
that*," was his reply.[55]

The nuns were won by his sensitive tenderness.   If anyone
brought him a tempting dish he had it given to the sick.[56]
One day, when he went to hear confessions in the convent
infirmary he noticed the miserable habit worn by the nun
who was sweeping the room, and, out of pity, went and
begged an alms to procure her another.[57]   Even in such
matters he was a Father, and hence the Father of Heaven

took pleasure in this human image of his bounty, and used him as an instrument of His omnipotence.

Doña Maria Yera, one of the principal nuns, fell ill, and they thought she was dead. When John and his companions arrived, all the sisters were in a state of distress. " Father," said Ana Maria, " how has this happened ? You take great care of your daughter, seeing that she has died without confession and the sacraments." John made no reply ; he went to the choir (perhaps at the spot now shown at the entrance to the chapel of the Transverberation) and began to pray. After some time the nun whom they thought dead was restored to life. They told John. " Are you satisfied now, daughter ? " said he to Ana Maria. He heard Doña Maria Yera's confession, gave her the last sacraments, and she was now ready to set out upon the journey to eternity.[58]

.　　.　　.　　.　　.　　.

We can well imagine how often the " turn " and the parlour grilles of the Incarnation must have heard such marvellous favours spoken of ! They were enough to make John of the Cross popular. Nuns of other Orders became anxious to share in such a treasure, and asked for his direction and advice ; [59] and the little Discalced Carmelite began to rival the influence exerted by the Dominicans at Santo Tomás and the Jesuits at San Gil. If anything would excite the attention of the Inquisitors, it was surely that quasi-resurrection of Doña Maria Yera, and the interest it aroused . . .

Setting aside those marvellous occurrences, which formed the staple of conversation in the *locutorios* of the Convents of Avila, what still remains ? A mystical doctrine which, admittedly, is not intended for " a carpenter's wife," a gift of banishing all evil spirits, and making visionaries die of disgust.

The Superiors of a convent of Augustinian nuns, who were perplexed as to the spiritual state of a nun who spoke several languages and was versed in every science, had recourse to John of the Cross. They had exhausted the resources of the learned. Mancio of Corpus Christi, Bartholomew of Medina and Luis de Leon had visited her,[60] and, struck with admiration at the clarity and exactitude with which she expounded Holy Writ and solved the most difficult scholastic problems, they declared that her knowledge was infused. John, in his turn, went to the convent, and when the nun saw him she began to sweat like a criminal. " The new Basil," before beginning the exorcisms, fasted and prayed, and Satan called to his aid three legions of devils. The exorcism was prolonged and severe ; the proud creature had been seduced when she was only six years of age. " And dwelt *amongst you*," replied the devil to the words " *Et verbum caro factum est.*" As the devil refused to depart, John called to his aid the Mother of God, St. Joseph, St. Augustine and St. Monica. In the end he commanded the prince of darkness to appear in person. " I, little monk ? Have I lost my slave ? " yelled the humiliated Lucifer. Some time afterwards the devil assumed human form, and announced the arrival of John of the Cross and a companion at the convent gate. When the possessed nun arrived at the *locutorio*, she thought they were confessors from the Incarnation Monastery, and the lying and hopeless advice which they gave drove her to tears. At this juncture, the real John of the Cross and his companion entered, and immediately the diabolical phantoms vanished ; Satan, at the end of his resources, now handed over the pact signed in the nun's own blood.[61]

Mother Teresa, on her return from the Duchess of Alba, wrote in March, 1573, to Inés of Jesus, the prioress of Medina : " My daughter, I am very much distressed at the illness of Sister Isabella of St. Jerome, and am sending you the holy Father John of the Cross. He has received from God the gift of delivering possessed persons from the power of the devil. Even here, in Avila, he has just cast out three legions of those wicked spirits from a certain person. He commanded each, in the name of God, to give its true name, and they immediately obeyed him." [62]

We may say, for the consolation of psychiatrists that, after examining Isabella of St. Jerome, he decided that she was suffering from " melancholia." [63]

As we may see, the Confessor of the Incarnation, far from urging people to perform extraordinary actions, cured those who were fond of marvels : and the Inquisitors of Santo Tomás had an abler coadjutor for the driving of Illuminism out of Spain than the executioners of Valladolid or Toledo. They must have rejoiced one evening, on the Feast of the Holy Trinity—a day on which, as we have said, something memorable always occurred in the life of John of the Cross. Whilst at recreation, either in the cloister of Silence or of the King, news was brought that in the course of solemn Vespers, a possessed nun had been transported into the middle of the choir by the devil, and delivered by John in the name of the Father, Son and Holy Ghost.[64]

If cases of possession seem rarer in these days of the subconscious, the reason, perhaps, may be that the devil has less need to seduce Christians, who obey him only too completely. One thing for which he will always exercise his trickery—" this cunning one very artfully takes up his position just where the senses make contact with the spiritual "—is to make the soul seize the bait of sensible phenomena, to " draw her away from the pure depths of the Holy Spirit in which she was plunged, swallowed up in God, without foothold or support. . . . And it is amazing how much importance the demon attaches to that ![65]"

.   .   .   .   .   .

Mother Teresa, after a stay of nearly six months in Salamanca with Doña Quiteria, who had accompanied her thither,[66] wrote, in a postscript of a letter dated February, 1574, to her friend the bishop of Avila asking him to let her know if the Father Visitor would authorise her to spend a few days at St. Joseph's. Shortly afterwards she arrived at the Incarnation, left Doña Quiteria there, and on the night of March 18th arrived at Segovia, accompanied by Father John of the Cross and the foundresses. On the following day, the feast of St. Joseph, Julian of Avila said Mass at a very early hour, and in the course of the morning reserved the Blessed Sacrament. The *provisor* arrived in a rage because he had not been previously informed and, (while Julian, seeing him so angry, hid behind a ladder which had been left in the hall), saw John, who was quite calm, "*como un hermitaño santo* " : [67] " Who arranged all this, Father ? " The reply was unheard, but the threat that followed was : " Remove it all.   And you may expect me to send you to prison." [68]

However, he was not to be cast into prison just then. That was to come afterwards, and on a far more grievous charge !

Although John had refused " the delights which God lets souls taste in contemplation," still we should remember that he had seen Christ Crucified and, as St. Teresa says, " that is a great help to practise the virtues most perfectly." [69] About this time she had a revelation.   She beheld " a great storm of trials—*una gran tempestad de trabajos.*" [70]

CHAPTER XII

THE GREAT STORM OF TRIALS

On October 15th, 1578, Teresa of Jesus wrote to Father Gracian : " I have been deeply grieved at the news of the death of our Father General : I am in the greatest distress. I did not stop crying the first day, and was not able to do anything else ; I abandoned myself to grief because we gave him so much annoyance, and he certainly did not deserve it. If we had had recourse to him, all the difficulties would now be smoothed away. May God forgive those who always prevented it ! At least, I should always have been able to come to an understanding with Your Paternity, despite the little credit I have had with you on this point." [1]

The Discalced Carmelite nuns of the Corpus Christi monastery at Alcalá are in possession of the autograph of this letter, and so we can be quite certain Teresa did pronounce this judgment. How clear and startling is the light it throws—a light which may well be used here towards a full understanding and, above all, a calm judgment on a delicate question : let it be our " lighthouse " in the tempest to be described.

·   ·   ·   ·   ·   ·

We have said that, in 1570, at the request of Philip II, whose autocracy was augmented by his zeal, St. Pius V nominated as Apostolic Visitors, the Dominican Father Fernandez for the Carmelites of Castile, and another Friar Preacher, Francis de Vargas, for those of Andalusia. This royal interference had been displeasing to the Most Reverend Father Rubeo, and, before the end of the year, he hastened to appoint " defenders of the Order " in each of the Spanish provinces.[2] Anthony de Heredia, the first of the Discalced Fathers, was one of these.

Father Fernandez was a holy religious, and all went well in Castile. He was able, without much difficulty, to appoint Discalced Fathers as heads of the Mitigated Friars of Toledo and Avila, and, as we may recall, he appointed Teresa of Avila prioress of the Incarnation, with the consent of the nuns. We have also seen that the Master General granted all the patents he was asked for up to those given on June 21st, 1574, for the foundation of the Almodovar del Campo. It was just at this moment that Rubeo received, to his great displeasure, complaints from the Mitigated Fathers of Andalusia. How was it that the Andalusians, who gave him such a bad reception in 1566, now had recourse to him? Had they not asked, in the following year, and with royal approbation, to be exempted from visitation by the Masters General, and had they not been satisfied when a Dominican was appointed? This change of front is easily explained. The Visitor Vargas, supported by the King and the Nuncio, had skilfully introduced Discalced Fathers into Peñuela, Granada and Seville, when all the decrees of the Master General expressly forbade their installation in Andalusia. Still worse, he had appointed as superior, Father Balthazar of Jesus Nieto, whom we have seen already at Pastrana and Alcalá, and this turbulent and hot-headed man was far from being *persona grata* with the Master General. Several grave decisions had been given against him by Rubeo, as also against his brothers, Gaspar and Melchior.[3] Balthazar, wisely enough, did not administer the office conferred on him by Vargas; but by his efforts, Father Gracian, who was just out of the novitiate, quietly arrived in Andalusia, accompanied by the excitable Mariano, in September, 1573; and the Visitor, delighted at meeting the former hermit of Tardon once more, and also at making Gracian's acquaintance, not only confirmed Balthazar's patent in favour of the latter, but granted him another, by which Gracian was made Visitor and Reformer of the Mitigated Andalusian Carmelites. In brief, Vargas conferred the widest apostolic powers together with the most thankless task on this young religious, who was only six months professed. Gracian demurred, but the fiery Mariano urged him so strongly that in the end he accepted. One may now imagine the feelings of the Mitigated Fathers on hearing of this proceeding, and why they wrote to the General. He was their only hope.

Teresa, ignorant of the difficulties that had already arisen in the south of Spain, delighted with the success of her work, and supporting it with all her courage,[4] wrote, on May 14th, 1574, to the prioress of Valladolid : " Oh ! if you saw how the movement in favour of our Discalced Carmelite Fathers is growing, though secretly ! It is something for which to bless God. The movement has been started by those who went to Andalusia, Gracian and Mariano. My joy is lessened at the thought of the annoyance it will give our General, whom I love so much. On the other hand, I see the ruin to which we were exposed." [5]

The letter from the Mitigated of Seville to Father Rubeo obviously reached San-Martino-dei-Monti after the patent authorising the double foundation at Almodovar had been despatched on June 21st, 1574.

In July the Master General heard of the unexpected development of Teresa's work in Andalusia, and believed that she was responsible for it. And yet, from 1572 she had been working with John of the Cross at the Incarnation for the welfare of the old Order. At Segovia, to which she had been sent by the Visitor, " she could do nothing but think, when not in a state of ecstasy, of the penury of the large, poverty-stricken monastery." [6] It would seem as if neither she, nor John, nor even Anthony, who was being utilised by Fernandez at Avila and Toledo, were kept fully informed of the activities of Balthazar and Mariano. The latter were the promoters of the movement in favour of independence, which was enthusiastically supported by Vargas.

On August 3rd, Rubeo had recourse to the Holy See, and obtained the recall of the Visitors. In order to avoid a schism in the Order he prudently kept the Brief secret, intending to publish it at the General Chapter to be held at Piacenza on May 21st, 1575. But the Apostolic Nuncio in Spain, who heard of what had happened in Rome, was urged by Philip II to exercise his powers as a legate *a latere*, and, on September 22nd, 1574, appointed Fernandez for

Castile and Vargas and Gracian, *in solidum*, for Andalusia, as "reformers," instead of the Visitors who had been recalled.[7]

We must not imagine that the Master General, whom Teresa, in a letter written on February 5th, 1571, described "as a wise man and a saint," [8] took up a sullen and spiteful attitude in these circumstances. Far from it. Rubeo had a high esteem and affection for Teresa, "*la mia figlia*" as he called her. He always remembered the visit he had paid to San José in 1567, and how pleased he had been with the Carmelites' mode of life. He regarded it as a mirror of the beginnings of the Order, approved of everything and gave ample faculties.[9] All that had not come to an end, and "this favourite of God" did not intend to act in Philip II's autocratic fashion.

He wrote two letters to Teresa, in October, 1574, and January, 1575, but, unfortunately, they are lost ; however, Teresa's reply indicates their contents.

The messages from the Father General, which should normally have reached their destination in November, 1574, and February, 1575, did not reach Teresa in Seville until June 17th, 1575. On October 6th, 1574, Teresa, who had just got back from Segovia, finished her term as prioress of the Incarnation, and Mother Isabella Arias was elected in her place.

After a short stay at St. Joseph's, where Father John could conveniently visit her, she had gone to Valladolid and, writing from there on January 6th, 1575, told Don Teutonio de Braganza [10] that she meant to go to Avila after the Epiphany, and would spend a day or two at Medina on the way ; she would then go on, without delay, to Toledo (Malagon) and Beas, in order to complete the foundation : "Beas, which is five leagues on this side of Andalusia," as she was careful to tell Mother Mary Baptist [11] in a letter written in the previous September. She fully intended, as far as herself was concerned, to obey Rubeo's commands.

At Beas she met Gracian for the first time. He spent from April 6th to April 30th in her company, and Teresa wrote to her niece that they were " the best days in my life." [12] And, without exaggeration : " In my eyes he is a most accomplished man. . . . I have never seen such a high degree of perfection combined with such graciousness." All she wished for was one thing ; that he might be the superior of the Carmelite nuns.

In fact Beas is fairly and squarely in the region of Andalusia. Gracian, making use of his apostolic powers, and in spite of the opposition of the elements and Teresa's perplexity, for she " knew quite well that the Most Reverend Father Rubeo of Ravenna would be displeased," [13] sent the poor sexagenarian to found a convent at Seville, in the very height of a torrid summer. At Ecija, moved by the Holy Ghost, she made a vow to obey this Father in all things, " provided they were not contrary to the obedience she had vowed." *

This took place on May 24th, 1575, during Pentecost, and, by a strange coincidence, the General Chapter had just opened in Italy " in the most opulent and noble city of Piacenza." [14]

.   .   .   .   .   .

The reader may remember that in 1532 it was decreed that the Spanish provinces, on account of their poverty, should send only three instead of nine delegates to the General Chapter. Now Martin Garcia, whom we have already seen in the convent of St. Andrew at Salamanca, did not arrive in time at Piacenza, because he had been delayed at sea. The *socius* from Andalusia, Augustine Suarez, was not able to take part in the proceedings until after Vespers on June 9th. [15] Nothing need be said of the Portuguese delegate, as he was not specially called on to interfere in the question to be decided. No documents had been forwarded by the Discalced Fathers : there were no letters from Teresa to Rubeo, for she only received his in Seville. What happened ? The members of the Chapter pronounced a verdict on incomplete evidence, the acts of the Master General and the report of the Andalusian friars. Still, in strict

* *Relaciones*, XL–XLI ; *Silv.*, II, 69–71 ; C. P., II, 254–257. It is well for the reader to bear in mind that Teresa, in her letters, from this time forward frequently calls Gracian *Paul* or *Eliseus*, as her letters were liable to fall into the hands of the Mitigated.

Carmelite justice, the evidence was quite sufficient for them to declare the Discalced " disobedient, rebellious and contumacious," and order them to leave within three days such houses as had been established without the Master General's permission, and even, if necessary, to employ the secular arm. Apart from this comprehensive double sentence, which also obliged recalcitrants to appear before the Master General, " within three months from the day in which they may attempt to withdraw from obedience," [16] the definitors ordered Mariano, the former hermit of Tardon, and Balthazar Nieto to be expelled if they persisted in disobeying the patents.[17] We now know who those were who " always prevented " recourse to the General.

On June 18th, Mother Teresa, who was in Seville, after having received the " impatiently expected " letters of October and January, wrote with the greatest affection to the Master General. Whilst defending her sons against the charge of insubordination, she could not avoid " directing a criticism against them." She writes to her Father and General that they now see " they would have done better by following a different course, so as not to displease your lordship." She goes on : " I have had several disputes with Father Mariano, for he is very excitable. As for Father Gracian, he is an angel ; if he had been here, things would have gone quite differently ; he only came to Seville by order of Father Balthazar, who was then prior at Pastrana. I may tell you that, if you only knew him, you would be delighted to count him amongst your sons. In my opinion, he certainly is one, and so too is Father Mariano. The latter is a virtuous, penitential man, who has won the esteem of all by his qualities. The demon, no doubt, as your lordship remarks, is causing all this trouble, and this father has said much the drift of which he does not see. As for myself, I take no account of it, and at times pass over a great deal that he says . . . For the love of Our Lord, rest assured that all the Discalced Carmelites taken together are nothing to me, should they go so far as merely to touch your robe. This is the absolute truth, and to cause you the slightest trouble would be touching the very apple of my eye." [18]

As for Father Anthony of Jesus, in spite of the powers given him by the Nuncio, he had never acted before asking the Father General's permission. "And if Teresa of Jesus had been present, perhaps matters would have been looked into yet more closely."

This mother's pleading arrived too late. At Madrid, Gracian, conscious of his office of reformer, did not submit to the decree of Piacenza, which ordered the evacuation of Peñuela, Granada and Seville. He was excommunicated by Father Angel de Salazar. What would he have done with the seventy odd Discalced Carmelite Friars who were living in the three disputed monasteries of Andalusia?

The Nuncio annulled the excommunication fulminated by Salazar, and on the following August 3rd, granted Gracian most ample patents as Apostolic Commissary over the Discalced Friars, setting aside any decrees of the Chapter of Piacenza to the contrary, *non obstantibus . . . diffinitionibus capituli generalis.*[19] Gracian now undertook the visitation of his Castilian convents. *Macarius, i.e.,* Father Balthazar Nieto, turned from him in a fit of jealousy. This passionate man had become such a terrifying figure that Teresa feared for the salvation of his soul. She said so to Gracian in a letter, written on September 27th, in which she also suggested that he should remedy matters in the Convent of the Incarnation.[20] She was anxious that the Nuncio himself should take charge of that house. After a week's work, he might be able to leave Father John there as vicar. It is clear that Mother Isabella Arias had not been able to keep the nuns up to the standard established by Teresa.

During the autumn, Gracian made a visitation of the Incarnation, and everything passed off well. Teresa, writing from Seville in October, tells him that "Seneca is quite content, and says that he has found more than he could have wished for in his superior. He offers up repeated thanksgivings to God." *

Gracian was back in Seville in the middle of November, and Teresa urged him to write to Rubeo. "It is quite bad

---

* Seneca. This was her name for John of the Cross. Silv., VII, 193, note and 195. Engl. I, 230, note.

enough that things are being carried out against his will ; why refuse him kind words, or seem to pay no attention to him ? Consider carefully, Father, that we have promised him obedience." [21]

On December 30th, Teresa wrote to the prioress of Valladolid that she had received a notification of Rubeo's command to choose a convent in which she should shut herself up for ever, and make no more foundations, because, according to the Council of Trent, she should no longer go abroad. But the Visitor (Gracian) had not allowed her to leave Seville, " and, just now, he has greater powers than our Most Reverend Father General." He did not wish her to leave until the following summer, and she thus finishes her long letter : " You may write to Isabella of the Cross that I can be a much greater help to her at Seville than in her Monastery of the Incarnation, and that is what I am doing. I trust that, if God gives another year's life to the Pope, the King, the Nuncio and our Father (Gracian), everything will be perfectly settled. But should one of them fail, we are lost, considering the dispositions of our Most Reverend Father General. It is true that God might remedy matters by some other means. At the moment, I am thinking of writing to our Father General, and showing him more respect than ever, because I love him very much and am deeply indebted to him. I am really troubled at seeing what he has done, as the result of the false information that was given him."

She was deeply grieved. Mary of St. Joseph wrote : " The feeling that she had incurred the indignation (of Father Rubeo) was the most keenly felt affliction which Mother Teresa had to endure at this epoch, because she had the love and veneration of a true daughter for him." [22]

In February, 1576, her letter to the Father of the entire Order was sent to Rome ; it is one of the noblest Teresa ever wrote. After loyally defending her sons, " because it would be a great treason and a black shame to deceive a Father whom she loved so much," she goes on to define her position. Father Angel de Salazar " wrote to me that I could remedy my situation by having recourse to the Pope's

Apostolic Chamber, as if that ought to have given me much comfort. But indeed, if it brought me no joy, but the deepest grief, I should never think of disobeying. May God preserve me from seeking my satisfaction by going against your wishes." [23]

At the end of June, as Gracian did not detain her any longer, she shut herself up for more than a year with the Carmelites of San José of Toledo "in her holiday home."

. . . . . .

Gracian's apostolic visitation of the Convent of the Incarnation had not produced peace of mind amongst the nuns—far from it. The Mitigated Friars continued to visit the nuns, and say Mass in the convent [24]—there were several foundation Masses to be celebrated every day. In Teresa's time, when the Friars were under the jurisdiction of Father Anthony, they did not visit or say Mass, or at least did so but rarely. Their presence now caused trouble. Towards the end of 1575, or the beginning of 1576, Father Valdemoro, the prior of Avila, expelled John of the Cross and Germain of St. Mathias from their cottage, "with many insults and to the great scandal of the whole city." [25] He so ill-treated the nuns that "it is pitiful to see the distress they are in." The poor nuns took the blame on themselves, so as to exonerate the terrible prior.

When the Nuncio heard the news, he immediately gave orders for the two Discalced Fathers, who were confined in St. Anne's at Medina, to be restored to their functions, [26] and also forbade, under pain of excommunication, any of the Mitigated to go to the Convent of the Incarnation to transact business, hear confessions, or say Mass. Only Discalced Carmelites and secular priests were allowed to do so. [27]

Matters seemed to rest there for the moment. On April 29th, Teresa wrote to Mary Baptist: "I only know what you tell me about Avila." [28] It is certain that the Nuncio's action caused the Mitigated to reflect, and when, on May 12th, the Provincial Chapter of Castile met at St. Paul de la Moraleja, it would seem that the election of a prior for Avila was a prolonged business. Father Valdemoro was removed, and as the former Provincial, the prudent Alonso González, declined the difficult post, the election was referred back to the community of Avila.[29]   The decrees of Piacenza were promulgated at the end of the Chapter.

The *Reforma*[30] tells us that the priors of Mancera, Pastrana and Alcalá, who were officially recognised by the Order, had been summoned to Saint Paul de la Moraleja, but arrived only in time to hear the reading of a decree regulating the relations between Discalced and Calced, against which John of Jesus Roca, the prior of Mancera uttered a strong protest.

We have the actual text of this decree, which was drawn up by Rubeo at Piacenza, when, on the conclusion of the Chapter,[31] the Castilian delegate arrived on June 30th. Martin Garcia freely and fully accepted the decision,[32] and, contrary to what the *Reforma* says, the Discalced and Calced Friars had not been fused.   On the contrary, the Provincial was expressly forbidden the appointment of *primitives* to any of the convents of the Mitigated in the province, and the Discalced were likewise forbidden to receive any Castilian Carmelites or religious from any other Order.   Hence there was no deadly fusion.   On the other hand, it is quite true that the Master General, dissatisfied with what had happened in Andalusia, was resolved on maintaining strictly the decisions of the Chapters allowing two or three reformed houses for each province.[33]   He had only carried out decisions taken by his predecessors when he gave patents to Teresa in 1567.   He anticipated the sanctions that should be applied, if ever, " under pretext of living in still greater perfection, any attempt were made at a separation from the province (of Castile), by favour of the secular authorities, by briefs or other concessions from Rome."[34]   Rubeo had no desire for a reform that would end in disruption, or one not grafted on the trunk of the Order.   He had suffered enough from his conflicts with the Congregation of Albi, and the attitude taken up by that of Mantua, which went so far as even to expunge the name of Blessed Soreth from its constitutions.[35]   Such an attitude of independence was only too contagious, and hence the Master General meant, at any cost, to confine the reform of St. Teresa within the limits dictated by his own prudence and the laws of his Order. There was no mention of bare feet, staves and the suppression of the liturgical chant, in the rule approved by Innocent IV. But it was on those very innovations, forbidden by Rubeo, that the " primitives " insisted, as also on the name " Discalced," because, according to them, the resumption of such observances was, in reality, a return to the mode of life carried out at the beginning of the Order. Here, again, it was the summit of Carmel they wished to reach, and, in order to do that, to walk barefoot, staff in hand, was not undertaking too much. Julian of Avila had at once seen that it was a " heroic " undertaking.[36] The Father General clearly perceived that the " primitives " were exalted by a new spirit and that their idea of moderation was to have none. Calling to mind the conciliatory spirit which Anthony de Heredia had shown from the very beginning, Rubeo authorised him, by name, to attend the Provincial Chapter, with the same powers as their lawfully acknowledged priors. The Discalced Friars decided that they could not accept these decrees, as the Reform could not exist if it were not allowed to spread. Teresa felt that, though it was " a mortal grief (to her) to go against the known will of her superior, she should not abandon an enterprise in which she clearly saw that the glory of Our Lord and the growth of the Order were concerned." [37]

On September 8th Gracian, employing his apostolic powers, which are " superior to those of the Most Reverend General," [38] assembled the principal Discalced Fathers at Almodovar. It was his reply to both the Chapters of Moraleja and Piacenza. John of the Cross was summoned from Avila. In the manuscript copy of the letter of Convocation, dated August 3rd, we see that Gracian commanded the Discalced priors " to meet in chapter and elect definitors and a provincial." This meant the establishment of " all the houses of Discalced men and women . . . as a province and congregation . . . *como desde agora las Hazemos,* as we do from this time forward." The " primitives " found themselves faced with an accomplished fact : Jerome

Gracian, in a decree dated September 1st, 1576, recalls
that he himself set up the separate province and now confirms its establishment. But, since the meeting on August
3rd he had been thinking, and had now reached the conclusion that it would not be reasonable to have a provincial elected at the head of the Reform whilst he was
Apostolic Commissary. He, therefore, put off the election
to some future date, after he had ceased to hold office ; in
other words, he appointed himself superior.*

Furthermore, at the meeting on August 3rd, Gracian—
with that independence which, if we look closely, we realise
caused Teresa some uneasiness—decided, in accordance
with Fernandez and Vargas, that they would obey only the
General of the Order, and that only the latter, in person, or
a Discalced Father delegated by him, can make a visitation
of Carmelite convents[39]. It is obvious that, when Gracian
speaks in such a fashion, he is taking the Congregation of
Mantua as his model.[40]

The Fathers assembled at Almodovar agreed to send two
religious to the Holy See, to settle this serious question.[41]

The earliest historians [42] are agreed that a divergence of
ideals between Gracian and Anthony of Jesus on the one

* The brief of the Nuncio Ormaneto, to which Gracian refers in his letter
of Convocation of August 3rd, does not aim at, authorise, or command the
erection of a separate province. It is no use for Gracian to declare, in his
ordinance of September 1st, that, by erecting a separate province he was
carrying out the express wish of Ormaneto, because Teresa's letter, of September 6th, to Gracian shows that the matter was still only in the state of a
project as far as the Nuncio was concerned. (*Silv.*, VII, 271. *Greg.*, I, 327.)
Gracian, by setting up a separate province and putting himself at the head of it,
was acting arbitrarily. With all due respect to the *Reforma* (L. III, Ch. L,
§§ 4 and 6) he was not the provincial of the Andalusian Mitigated ! Nor is
that all. In a letter of October 16th, 1578 (to Diego de Cardenas and Gutierrez
de la Magdalena, provincials of the Mitigation (Arch. Calc. Carm. Rome.
Acta. Desc. Cod. I, No. 17) which contains a copy of the ordinance of September 1st, the Nuncio Sega states that Gracian overstepped his powers in
1576 by formulating, at Almodovar a decree in which he commands, on the
expiration of his own office as Apostolic Commissary, Anthony of Jesus, first
definitor, to convoke a chapter with a view to the election of a provincial.
We shall see in Ch. XIV the tragic results of this flagrant illegality. We shall
only note that this decree remained secret up to then : " *et questo si è tenuto
celato.*" Letter from Sega to the Cardinal of St. Sixtus (Papal Secretary of
State) November 13th, 1578. Archives of Calced Carm. Rome. Acts of
Discalced, Cod. I, No. 26.

hand, and John of the Cross on the other, was manifested at this meeting. The former favoured the apostolic, and the latter, the hidden life.

Quiroga, indeed, delights in laying emphasis on the point that when John was at Duruelo and Mancera he used to go " preaching and hearing confessions in the neighbouring villages, by order of Father Anthony, the superior of those two houses." [43] Yet John spoke at Almodovar in favour of the contemplative life. He pointed out that even now the apostolate had gone too far, and that the number of community exercises " established by Father Anthony, in conformity with the manners and customs of the Fathers of the Observance," was excessive. We gather that the time spent in chanting the office in choir was to be reduced, and some prayers, recited in common, were suppressed because the constitutions of Duruelo, concerning solitude and retreat, were retained. [44]

It is probable that John stopped at Toledo on his way back to Avila. " The Fathers have gone back quite pleased [with the Chapter] " Teresa wrote to " The Father of her soul " on the 20th, and added : " And so am I when I see how perfectly it was carried out. . . . I have also been pleased to hear of a project which they have of setting up a separate province, through the mediation of our Father General : *por vía de nuestro Padre general*, and of working for it at all costs, for, to be in opposition with one's superior is an intolerable state of affairs." [45]

Teresa spoke words of gold, but she was clearly in ignorance of what we now know, namely, that Gracian had done neither more nor less than set up the Discalced into a separate province and congregation, using powers which anyhow she in all good faith believed were unlimited ; this explains the encouragement she gave him. [46] What was Rubeo to do, when faced with this situation, which now only needed papal sanction ? Was he to remain silent, and go on with the drawing up of a case against the *primitivi ?* That task was to be Tostado's. Subsequently Antonio de San José read, in some papers presented to the Royal Council, that the General was urging the Discalced to make foundations " because when they had five houses he would divide them into a province " [47] ; but the time for such a plan had gone by.

.   .   .   .   .   .

On February 28th, 1577, Teresa wrote to her brother, Don Lorenzo, from her little cell in Toledo " as remote as a hermitage and very cheerful " [48] : " Really, our rows are such as to give us an idea of what the world is like. The whole thing is like a comedy." [49]

Everything, indeed, was in a state of confusion since the meeting at Almodovar, both in Castile and Andalusia, to which Gracian had returned. Valdemoro, who had expelled Father John and Father Germain from the Incarnation, now struck up a strong friendship with Mariano, and the latter, with this unexpected ally, tried to establish a foundation in Madrid. " I think the friendship of the Reverend Father who has gone to solicit your Reverence's support is really charming," wrote Teresa with a touch of malice. [50]

From time to time a gracious vision passed before the Mother's eyes, such, for instance, as a procession of " those little friars " on their way from Peñuela to Alcalá. " They seemed saints to me [51]," she wrote, " and when the world sees those Discalced Carmelites it must surely realise that they are hermits devoted to contemplation." [52] Their aim, from the first, was, of course, the contemplative life, but she never lost sight of her desire that they should be spiritual guides to her daughters : " As for me, I am fully persuaded that no remedy will be found for our convents until we have a member of the family to direct them. Look at the Convent of the Incarnation, it is now something for which to thank God." [53]

External constraint, without interior expansion is bound to produce much suffering,[54] but John of the Cross had, thanks to God, the gift of setting souls at ease. He understood Lorenzo de Cepeda, and Teresa shows how happy this made her. [55]

In 1577 the opposition grew stronger. Father Jeronimo

Tostado, the Father General's delegate, who was to see that the decrees of Piacenza were carried out, was now in the Peninsula. But Teresa had also issued her orders to the energetic Mariano, who was busily engaged in negotiating for the foundation at Madrid.[56] "You are bound to submit to Father Tostado, and to obey him, but not if he goes against the acts of the apostolic [visitors] : that would ruin us completely." She spoke so decisively because she intended that "the work of the Reform, which was meant to do so much good" must go on, and she felt she was in complete agreement with Rubeo's original ideas. Four days later she sent another letter, referring to the designs of the prior of the Carmelite house in Toledo, Father Maldonado, who was the right-hand man of the Vicar-General, Tostado. As long as this Father "does not receive a letter from Our Most Reverend Father General he will neglect nothing to prevent a foundation in Madrid ; because, according to him, there is no reformer, and His Lordship the Nuncio can do nothing except through himself. This Father is absolutely certain on this point, and firmly believes that the Discalced Carmelites are going against obedience, and that the Mitigated Carmelites are in no way bound to obey the Visitors, but only the General." "One would think to hear them," she says, "that they have a new brief, and yet they have only the decree published a year and a half ago by the General Chapter." [57]

Both parties had a strong case, and who was to settle the dispute ? "Good Sr. Nicholas, when he was passing through, said, as I remember, that the Discalced Carmelites should secure a Cardinal protector." [58] This remark of Teresa's brings an important personage on the scene. This same Nicholas, who counselled so wisely, took the habit at Seville in the month of April, and was later to be known as Nicholas of Jesus Mary Doria.

Direct recourse to Rome would doubtless have settled all difficulties, but it is very probable that Philip II would not hear of it, as he was anxious to rule the Church in Spain through the Nuncio ; hence the two Discalced Fathers who had been appointed at Almodovar to go to Rome were not destined to go there for some time.

Through want of diplomatic skill things went from bad to worse with those children of light. " O Father, what a bad line the Discalced Carmelites are taking in these negotiations," Teresa wrote to Mariano on May 9th. "The foundation [at Salamanca] would have taken place before this if they had only known how to go about it, and now they have only made themselves ridiculous. Believe me, one never succeeds when one acts unseasonably. Yet I believe it is all Our Lord's will and that herein lies hidden some deep mystery. Some day it will be revealed." [59]

Trials increased. June 18th the Nuncio Ormaneto, the great protector of Teresa's undertaking, died, and Tostado, who was in Madrid, was ready for action.[60] On August 29th the new Nuncio, Sega, arrived. At Toledo Teresa had processions organised " that whatever might bring the greatest glory to God should take place." [61] And her powerful pen still travelled from room to room of the Castle of the Soul, each one more radiant with divine light. Old Father Antonio had gone into hiding in the suburb of Antequeruela, amidst the ruins of Cardinal Tavera's hospital.[62] But Maldonado, strong in his good faith, kept watch and ward from his convent overlooking the bridge of Alcántara. In this summer of 1577 Tostado imprisoned the old man " who was the first to embrace the reform," as he maintained that the latter was a rebel. In a letter dated August 26th, Gracian says that Tostado deeply regretted his action, and that Antonio was quickly released.[63]

At the end of July Teresa felt the storm rising, and set out for San José of Avila to put this convent under Gracian's jurisdiction. Poor little convent ! Francisco de Salcedo, always a friend, wanted to write these simple words to the bishop : " Lord, we have no bread," but Teresa would not allow it. All the same, an alms sent by Don Alvaro de Mendoza was exceedingly well timed.[64]

Trials, " the dry bread of the perfect," [65] were not wanting to Teresa. A calumnious pamphlet was circulated about Gracian, and the person responsible was Father Balthazar

Nieto, who employed for this abominable work poor Brother Miguel de la Columna, " who, before becoming a religious, had been a servant in our monasteries." [66] We have already met him at Pastrana with Father Anthony. Both repented their deed, which was so grievous to Teresa, and both did penance for it. On September 18th she wrote to the King : " Gracian is really, in my belief, a man sent by God and His Blessed Mother. For more than seventeen years I myself have had to suffer from the Mitigated Fathers, and I did not know how I could go on bearing such a trial which surpassed my feeble strength ; but he was my support." With true foresight the Reformer feared for the morrow. In a postscript to the King she states : " As long as Father Tostado remains as he now is, I fear lest the Visitation, far from being profitable, may, on the contrary, prove very harmful, especially as he is accompanied by this Friar Preacher who was once a Mitigated Carmelite." [67] She was quite right, for the Friar Preacher was none other than Father Balthazar Nieto.

. . . . . .

On September 6th Teresa, writing to the bishop of Avila, Don Alvaro de Mendoza, thus confides in him : " Father Gracian seems fully determined not to allow me to go to the Incarnation. As for myself, I fear only God, but just now there could be nothing worse for us than to send me there." [68]

The sisters had fully determined to elect Teresa as soon as Doña Isabella Arias's term of office had expired. Towards mid-October Father Gutierrez de la Maddalena, the provincial of the Calced, went to preside at the election at the command of the Vicar-General, Tostado. Teresa writes in a style worthy of Madame de Sévigné : " He was liberally equipped with censures and excommunications for all the sisters who should vote for me. Fifty-five nuns voted for me as if they had never been threatened. Each time that one of them gave me her suffrage the provincial excommunicated her and loaded her with maledictions ; he crushed the voting papers in his fist, struck them and burnt them. And so the sisters are excommunicated . . . ; there is no Mass, no admittance to choir, not even outside the time of divine office. Nobody is allowed to speak to them, not even their confessors or parents."

On the day after this election, "full of beatings," the provincial returned to begin all over again. He renewed the excommunications and, summoning those opposed to Teresa—there were forty-four of them—he made them appoint a new prioress (Doña Ana of Toledo) and sent for Tostado's confirmation of the election. The new prioress was confirmed in her office, but the opposition held out, and declared that they would obey her only as vicaress.[69]

The two parties : Tostado and Gutierrez on the one hand, and the fifty-five nuns backed up by the theologians on the other, refused to come to terms, so that matters were in the same state on November 10th. Doña Ana was obeyed, but only as vicaress. John of the Cross sent a letter to Teresa, and if Francisco de Yepes was in Avila then we may be sure that the letter was transmitted. Velasco states that he saw Teresa frequently, and that she would not suffer herself to be interrupted when conversing with him for hours in the parlour, or even in a confessional.[70] John's letter stated that if the excommunication was not removed the monastery was bound to fall into a state of confusion.[71] The Mother at once wrote to the licentiate, Padilla, who had been employed by the King in his projects for reforming the religious orders. It is quite clear then that John supported the fifty-five nuns in their opposition. "Oh ! nuns of the Incarnation ! how much you have cost me, and how greatly you are indebted to me,"[72] he said to the older sisters, after "the whale had vomited him out."[73]

The Carmelite Fathers of Avila went back to the convent,[74] and the Discalced were confined to the cottage built by Teresa four years previously. After the election the opposition could not hear Mass, or even speak to their confessors.[75]

Whilst the tide of troubles grew even greater, John of the Cross it seems would cross the stony valley, with its scattered tufts of grass, very secretly—*muy disimulado*,[76] and, mounting the steep slope where powdered granite grated under his feet, would pay a visit to his sisters at St. Joseph's. To his right lay the Cathedral—a fortress of a church—and to the left St. Vincent's. It was the month of November, the air was cold but crystal clear. John could see every detail of the countryside, even the black summits of the Sierra de Gredos bounding the horizon. The harsh Avilan landscape speaks of bitter strife and victory. "Death, yes ; surrender, never." [77] The Mitigated Carmelites were now far away on the other side of the city, and John was about to see " *la buena Madre* " once more, in peace and quietness, and for a brief, intimate moment which angels remember. Teresa must have realised the truth of Our Lord's words : " He can travel the same road as you." [78] His was the purity and innocence of a child of God ! That last good-bye before the great darkness of Toledo, must surely have been very beautiful. The Mother was finishing her book of the *Mansions*. When the grille closed he carried away the image of Teresa of Jesus in her sixty-second year, grown old and tired, but always "young in her desires." [79]

The letter she received from John before Martinmas revealed great confusion at the Incarnation.

Even after Tostado had delegated Maldonado, the Prior of Toledo, to remove the excommunication from the nuns, peace had not returned to the convent. He had caused the sisters much annoyance, and acted so contrary to justice and the laws of the Order, that the nuns were deeply distressed, and, as they told Teresa, not freed from their former troubles.[80] Maldonado was fully determined to see the decrees of Piacenza carried out, " even if he should have to employ the secular arm." He aimed at the head, and sounded John's dispositions, seeking to persuade him to go back to the Observants, and abandon the novelties that were scandalising the Order. John refused.[81] We know that he did not love half-measures, and that the primitive ideal alone had value in his eyes. The Discalced Fathers realised that John's position was growing more and more delicate, and appointed him Prior of Mancera, because that convent was officially recognised by the General and the decrees of Piacenza.[82] It was too late. When Maldonado's proposals were refused, he now saw only one means left, and that was to apply the decrees by force, and carry off Fathers John and Germain. His intention was well-known, and both the relations of the nuns and the friends of the confessors set up a vigilant watch on the hermitage to prevent their being carried off by force. The Mitigated did not stir, and the three days' grace, prescribed by rule, passed by quietly. John knew, by a divine light, all that was about to happen, and told Ana Maria, who cried out it was impossible, seeing how " worn, spent, and weakened by mortifications he had been." Nevertheless, he replied, it would be so.[83] The desire to suffer for the sake of Jesus, Whom he had seen bruised and mangled by divine love, gave him strength, and, from his cell, he saw the cross approaching. It stood aloft over the old convent of his Order that had been built on those rosy ramparts. From the " *Puerta del Carmen* " one looks over a sunlit plain that lies far below. John could see it from his miserable little cottage which a gust of wind could destroy. But the prospect that stretched before him was a sea of suffering.

On the night of 3rd–4th of December, when all fears of a forcible removal had passed, Maldonado, having appealed to " the secular arm," made a surprise attack, broke open the door,[84] and captured the two confessors. John allowed himself to be seized like a lamb : the hour had come for him to suffer yet more with Christ.

The two Fathers, " carried off like malefactors," were brought to the ancient Carmelite monastery, and, when they had been " scourged twice," were locked up in separate cells.[85] In the morning, the Prior ordered John to be led out of his prison for interrogation, and the latter, on finding that Maldonado was still making his thanksgiving, escaped through the conventual church, " in order to get rid of certain papers which, in the hurry of his capture, they had forgotten to seize." [86] He was scarcely more than a seven minutes' walk from the cottage. He locked the door, and had sufficient time to tear up some papers, and swallow the rest.[87] These papers, according to Jerome of St. Joseph, dealt with matters connected with the Reform,[88] and not with mysticism, as has been gratuitously conjectured. An attempt was being made to force the door from without, but John appeared and gave himself up. Rumours reached Teresa of the abduction, and she immediately took up her pen, and had recourse to Philip II : she demanded justice, and lodged a complaint against Maldonado.

" He has been appointed Vicar-General," she wrote, " and that must be because he is better qualified to make martyrs than any of the rest. The whole city is scandalised. Everyone is asking how he could have had such audacity. He is not a prelate, and has not revealed the powers in virtue of which he is acting, yet he has dared to rage against the Carmelites of the Reform, who are subject to the Apostolic Commissary, and that in a place close to Your Majesty's dwelling. He and his seem to fear neither justice nor God. As for myself, I am desolated to see our Fathers in the hands of those people. They have long been desirous of getting hold of them. But I would prefer to see them in the hands of the Moors ; they would probably meet with greater mercy. As for this Discalced Carmelite Father, this great servant of God (Father John), he is so enfeebled by all he has endured, that I fear for his life. For the love of God, I implore Your Majesty to have him set at liberty at once. The Mitigated are saying everywhere that they are going to destroy the Fathers of the Reform, because Father Tostado has given orders to that effect. If Your Majesty does not act, I know not what will happen, for we have no earthly helper but you." [89]

Whilst Teresa was writing this imploring letter, John's serge habit was being forcibly exchanged for the cloth of the Mitigation,[90] and he was on his way to Toledo in great secrecy and great suffering. A kind-hearted young muleteer, who accompanied the tragic group, suggested to John that he should escape. The saint refused. At night-fall the good fellow related to the innkeeper all that he had seen : the cruelty of the friar and the gentle patience of the saint. John of the Cross protested that he placed his whole confidence in God, and hoped for great mercy from Him on account of his sufferings.[91]   On December 10th, Teresa wrote to the Prioress of Seville :

" Father Maldonado has carried off Father John of the Cross in order to bring him before Father Tostado. As for the Prior of Avila, he has brought Father Germain to Saint Paul de la Moraleja ; and the poor priest went on the journey with blood pouring from his mouth. . . . The nuns —more afflicted at this than at their own trials, which, all the same, have been very great—say that the Fathers are saints ; and that, during all the years they spent near their monastery—by order of the Apostolic Commissary and the late Nuncio—no one has ever seen anything in them save what was worthy of the Apostles themselves." [92]

CHAPTER XIII

A CRY IN THE WILDERNESS

PHILIP II had a high regard for Tcresa, and yet the petition which she addressed to His Majesty had no result. It
certainly reached the sovereign, for he was informed of all
petitions addressed to him. From his palace in Madrid, as
from the Escurial, the impassive monarch, who could be
distracted only by the buffooneries of his duenna, no doubt
kept a watchful eye on the case of the Reform, as an item
in his schemes of policy.[1]

It seems clear from Teresa's correspondence that the
Royal Council was at once informed of the double abduction.[2] At first she exercised patience, because the Christmas
festivities were at hand, " and no legal matters may be dealt
with until after the Epiphany."[3] But by January 16th her
uneasiness began to increase. She feared some misfortune.
No one knew the whereabouts of Father John.[4] The provincial, Magdaleno, put about a report that he had been
sent to Rome by Tostado.[5] It was absolutely imperative
that Mariano should go and see the King. April was already
upon them. He must really point our how long the little
saint had been kept prisoner. Doña Guiomar, and all the
Sisters too, were weeping for Father John of the Cross.[6]
Philip II was well aware of it, for Teresa had written to him
on December 4th ; he was a saint not only in the eyes of
the nuns, but in the eyes of the whole of Avila as well. It
was no exaggeration. He was a saint, and had been one all
his life. He was a man of the greatest worth.[7] The King
summoned Mariano.[8] And the mysterious silence was unbroken. " I am astonished," Teresa wrote to Gracian, " at
the spell under which Father John of the Cross lies."[9] And
again, on August 14th, she wondered what could be done to
set him free.[10] On August 19th the news of his miraculous

escape had not yet reached her, and she urged Gracian, who was in Madrid, to see that some person of importance should plead John's case with the Nuncio. " One would have only to ask him to enquire into the virtues of this Father, and point out how unjust it is to keep him shut up . . . Mgr. Sega would give an order to have him set free immediately, and would send him to one of our monasteries. I cannot understand this unfortunate fact, but there seems nobody to be found who remembers our saint." [11]

The saint of Carmel was immured in the convent of Toledo, the chief monastery of the Castilian Carmelites.[12]   He was shut up in a closet [13] from that moment at the beginning of December, 1577, when, on his arrival from Avila, he traversed the strange streets of the suburb of Antequeruela, passed through the Moorish Puerta del Sol blindfolded,[14] and, after a few minutes' walk within the ramparts, crossed the threshold of the monastery.

The Carmel of the Mitigated friars is in the east of Toledo, looking down on the bridge of Alcantara.   Beneath its arches the Tagus, after running swift and unchecked through the plain, now enters a wild, reddish defile, and begins its journey round the gloomy rock on which the gold and violet cluster of palaces, mansions, minarets and campaniles glows and mellows.   The tawny river grumbles along as it turns in a semicircle from the bridge of Alcántara to the bridge of St. Martin.   Its sullen murmur rises up to the city on the heights ; the convent stands on the lower slope of the city's granite base.

Since the Peninsular War, there remain only a few strips of the walls of the Carmelite Church, built on the site of Santa Maria de Alficen, which went back to the Visigothic era.   The Moors had left it for the use of the Mozarabic Christians.

In the early days of the Reconquest, the Archbishop established his seat there.   In memory of this, the Calced Carmelites had the privilege of carrying in processions a cross, worked with cords and tassels, like that used in the cathedral.   But it was only in the sixteenth century that they took possession of this venerable corner of Toledo,

which, up to 1504, was still occupied by the Commanders of Santiago. They built a monastery on the spot and dedicated it to Our Lady of Mount Carmel. It was a large, solidly-built edifice. The Church was vast and built in the Græco-Roman style ; the entrance was through a notable Doric door of carved stonework, surmounted by a statue of Our Lady. The image of " Christ de las Aguas " was venerated in this monastery, and the meetings of the celebrated confraternity of " Santa Vera Cruz " were also held here.[15] The Very Reverend Father Rubeo was not mistaken when he declared that the Convent of Toledo was the finest in the province. This monastery, if we are to judge from some old walls that still look down from an angle on the bridge of Alcantara, must have been very much like the Carmelite Convent at Avila, now turned into a prison. There was a wing about one hundred and fifty to one hundred and eighty feet long, and about forty-six feet high. It was divided into three storeys, with square windows at regular intervals in the walls which were nearly three feet thick. But Toledan stone is not like the bluish granite of Avila. It is a red ochre-coloured stone with nothing of the warm hue of Salamanca. Still, despite its exquisite Jewish, Moorish and Christian art, its warm colour and burning sky, Toledo stands up bare and forbidding. Teresa, who dwelt in the Moorish place of Doña Luisa de la Cerda, felt this ; " I have never in all my life," she writes, " seen anything more barren of taste than this land." [16] The proud soul of this Saracen city outsoars, at a bound, all desire. Barrès spoke truly, " it is a cry in the wilderness." [17]

. . . . . .

According to Teresa,[18] Father John of the Cross was brought before the Very Reverend Father Tostado on the day after his arrival. Jeronimo Tostado, doctor of the University of Paris, provincial of Catalonia, consultor of the Inquisition, vicar-general and commissary for Spain and Portugal, after effecting the reformation of the Monastery at Naples, the most difficult to handle in the whole Order, was a religious of great authority.[19] We have seen how, on his arrival in the

M 2

Peninsula, he had been led to attack the Discalced Carmelites far more severely than Rubeo had envisaged. John of the Cross was appearing, for the second time in his monastic life, before the highest authority of his Order. Ten years previously, at Salamanca, he had attracted the attention of the Father General, who appointed him Master of Students ; he may then have confided to Rubeo his desire to lead the solitary primitive life. Now, when, with the General's authorisation, this life of the first days of the Order was, thanks to Teresa's genius, restored and he, more Teresian than any, had given all his substance, so that he was nothing but an emaciated skeleton, he was appearing again to be judged for the gigantic thing that had been done.

El Greco had been working in Toledo since 1575. " His canvases are the complement of St. Teresa's treatises and the poems of St. John of the Cross. They initiate us into the interior life of noble Castilians." [20] He had already painted, for the Cathedral Canons, his *Parting of Christ's Tunic*, that great figure of Jesus draped in red ; and, shortly after, he painted his *Saint Maurice* for the Escurial. In the former picture, the immutable Word, divinely free, allows Himself to be despoiled, like a lamb led to the slaughter ; in the second, His disciple, Maurice, strong in the faith, freely offers himself up to martyrdom. John was to become, in his own body and his own soul, the very theme that the genius of El Greco was now developing—a soldier ready to endure human justice for the cause of Divine Truth, a spirit like a burning flame.

Jeronimo Tostado notified him of the final decisions of the Chapter of Piacenza. [21] John, like Teresa, could not accept them. His position was clear : he would submit to Father Tostado and obey him, but not if he went against the decrees of the Apostolic visitors. According to Fernandez, " as long as Father Tostado had not obtained powers that overruled those of the visitors, the regulations of the latter remained valid." [22] This point was of the greatest importance, for both John and Germain were " carrying out the duties of office " (as confessors to the Incarnation) by order of the Apostolic visitor—Fernandez *—and the former Nuncio : and these, at the moment when John was captured, were dependent on yet another visitor—Gracian.[23] Was Tostado satisfied with receiving a formal act of refusal, or did he engage in a discussion ? The question at issue was involved in a legal tangle, where acts and decrees contradicted each other. Was the General Chapter right, or the visitor ? John might have pointed out that Gracian had been appointed *reformer* by the Nuncio Ormaneto, "*non obstantibus . . . diffinitionibus capituli generalis,*" and that Rome confirmed the decision of its Legate *a latere*.[24] Tostado, no doubt, replied that Ormaneto was dead, and John's answer must surely have been the same as Teresa's :

"When the former Nuncio died, we certainly thought that the powers of the visitor had expired. Nevertheless, the theologians and canonists, both of Alcalá and Madrid, and some of Toledo, having been consulted, answered in the negative, because the visitation had begun. . . . Some theologians, and in particular Romero (of Avila), have given the following decision : ' so long as the Nuncio (Sega) does not publish the powers in virtue of which he commands in the present case, Father Gracian is not obliged to terminate his visitation ' ; and they gave plenty of grounds for this decision. Now, the Nuncio has, so far, not published these powers." [25]

Granted : yet, in spite of the opinion of all those theologians, for three months Gracian had not made use of any of his powers, not even in signing anything. What did that mean save that the Nuncio had forbidden him to continue the visitation ? John protested, and said that it was the King who had suspended the visitation until the Pope,

---

* According to Alonso, St. John of the Cross, in the time of Fernandez, tried to leave his post at the Incarnation for a convent of Discalced because the office belonged to the Mitigated. But Fernandez would not allow him. When Gracian was elected, John, knowing that the Mitigated wanted, at any cost, to recover the position he held, tried again to resign his office, but could not do so, because the Convent of the Incarnation would not consent. . . . The saint in no way interfered with the rights of others ; he left everything to the Convent, including alms for the needs of poor nuns. The monastery only supplied him with abstinence diet, such as is given on Fridays. We can understand that the nuns used every means in their power with the Nuncio Ormaneto and the Apostolic Commissaries, past and present, to keep John of the Cross, and, in point of fact, they succeeded. L.I., c. XXVII.

informed of Sega's claims, should send word to the Nuncio
to refrain from dealing with the affairs of the Reform.[26]

These replies by way of justification, which Father John
could, and must, have made to Tostado—they are extant
in Teresa's correspondence—naturally call forth a stinging
retort : Did not the Father of the Order, in his patent of
August 16th, 1567, warn you against the temptation of
separating yourself from the province of Castile by the favour
of princes, and thanks to briefs and other concessions from
Rome, on the pretext of living in greater perfection ?[27]

Such a retort would not have affected John of the Cross.
His conscience was clear. He had never gone against the
orders of the Master General. He was incapable of doing
so. At a far later date, when one of his sons, blinded by
passion, tried to drive him out of the Reformed Order, he
calmly replied : " *The habit cannot be taken away from any save
those who refuse to amend or obey ; as for me, I am quite ready to
repair all my faults and to obey, no matter what penance may be
imposed on me.*"[28]

What actually happened was the work of Divine Providence. It is clear that the Reform of Carmel was a work
designed by God, and conducted by Him through human
difficulties. Therefore, John, without fear of going astray,
relied on the orders and the acts of God : the success of the
Reform, resulting from God's words, which produce what
they signify. The " great things " promised to Teresa were
coming to pass ; had he not heard, long ago, that he would
bring about a new perfection in his Order ?[29] On the day
he met Teresa it was a revelation ; the promise made so
long ago was now being fulfilled ; he understood what it
meant : its realisation was showing that it was divine, and
he clung to it with an act of that faith which belongs to the
order of gifts of the Holy Ghost.[30] His power of erring was,
as it were, hindered by his confirmation in grace.[31] and he
no more sinned against the Holy Ghost than he did against
the obedience which he venerated.[32] Like Maurice, of
whom El Greco, perhaps, was dreaming up yonder in the
lofty city, he would receive the punishment, prescribed by
the Constitutions of Soreth, against rebels[33] ; but, in the

inner chamber of his will—confident that he was not disobeying—he would not resist Our Lord.   God first.

There was a spiritual treasure, a mystical ideal, to be
preserved. From now onwards, this ideal must live its own
life—the separation in the Order must come or the ideal
would die in the stress of daily conflict. John, like Teresa,
would not yield on this.[34] Let them take away his serge
habit and force him to put on heavy shoes, a Discalced
Carmelite he would remain at heart. He was offered the
priorship of a convent if he would consent to an alliance,
which he knew would now, inevitably, bring about the
destruction of the heroic edifice reared by Teresa, Antony
and the friars of Mancera and Pastrana. God permitted it
to happen that neither Tostado, who was, after all, a just man,
nor the other Calced Carmelites, should understand John's
opposition and mental agony. " As they have the superiors
on their side, they do not think they are going against the
will of God." John was regarded as a rebel.[35] Maldonado
says so : " The Discalced Carmelites are acting against
obedience ; the Calced Carmelites are in no way bound to
submit to the visitors, but to the General." [36] There is no
occasion to take scandal ; humanly speaking, the conflict of
jurisdictions is explicable, and the passion that John was
about to undergo is luminous in the light of the Cross.

It is easier to understand what followed if we read the
legal codes that were then in force, and imagine what
Spanish life was like in the sixteenth century.

The *auto-da-fés* were not, indeed, as frequent as they had
been at the end of the fifteenth century when, from February 12th, 1486, to March 10th, 1487, the Inquisition of
Castile held six solemn courts at Toledo and tried five
thousand two hundred and fifty cases. However, from 1575
to 1610, the Inquisition of Toledo held twelve general courts,
tried three hundred and sixty-six cases, fourteen of which
ended with the stake, whilst eight hundred and seventy-six
cases were decided before the *autillos*, which had not power
to put to death.[37] In that very year, 1577–1578, when John
of the Cross was Maldonado's prisoner, a solemn *auto-da-fé*
may have been held. Not long before, Mother Teresa had,

by her prayers, converted a Turk who was being taken to Toledo to undergo the " questions " of the Inquisitors.[38]

The Carmelites certainly remembered the *auto-da-fé* held on Sunday, June 18th, 1570, when the Dominican Juan Ruiz preached on the lost sheep. The whole of the Plaza Zoco-dover, made famous by Cervantes, quite close to the convent, had been thronged from the previous evening, as if for a bull fight. And, on the following day, all the religious and clergy of the city were to be seen arriving on the platform behind the banner and green cross of the Inquisition, in the wake of thirty-nine prisoners, amongst whom were French-men from Paris and Lyons, and Flemings from Bruges and Antwerp, muffled up in the grey tunic and blue scapular adorned with a yellow cross : the *san benito*. Even better remembered was the famous *auto* on June 4th, 1571, at which the Sardinian, Sigismund Archel, who was found guilty of Lutheranism, had appeared after a legal process that dragged on for nine years.[39] People in those days were not soft-hearted as they are now. They had, moreover, a keen sense of the public good, as well as a passion for the faith. " It is better that some die," wrote Teresa to Gracian, at the end of 1575, " than that wrong should be done to all." [40] If John of the Cross had written anything suspect, he would certainly have been brought before the Inquisition, in accordance with Rubeo's decree.[41] Tostado would have seen to that : he was a consultor of the Inquisition. John was not denounced.[42] He was simply punished in the Carmelite Monastery in accordance with the Blessed Soreth's constitutions dealing with cases of rebellion.[43] He was both disobedient and rebellious in the eyes of the Calced, because he had no right to reside at the Incarnation without the General's written permission,[44] and, more-over, he had not submitted to the decrees of Piacenza and the commands of Tostado. This was, in their eyes, " a very great crime," hence " there should be no surprise at the harsh way in which he was treated, even though some vindictiveness was mingled with religious zeal." God per-mitted it to " purify and refine " still further the soul of John of the Cross,[45] which had, indeed, for years, been like Ezechiel's empty brazen cauldron, over burning coals.[46]

After his appearance before Tostado, John was very rigorously imprisoned in the monastery. The gaoler, John of St. Mary,[47] as well as Innocent of St. Andrew,[48] Alonso and Quiroga[49] saw this prison, and Mary of Jesus[50] of Toledo, and John of St. Anne [51] at the Calvario, heard John himself describe it, shortly after his miraculous escape.

It was a narrow cavity, in a wall, and was about six feet wide by ten long. " Small as he is, he found it hard to stay in it," wrote Teresa after his deliverance. The only opening in this hole for light and air, says his gaoler, was a small dormer window in one corner. This description agrees perfectly with that of Quiroga, another eye-witness. In fact, if the prisoner were to have any light at all, the sun had to be shining into a gallery out of which opened a large hall containing the closet that now served as a prison. The window was high up in the wall, and John had to stand on a stool in order to recite his office. Towards the end of his imprisonment, John of St. Mary gave him a light.

The door was locked, and the key entrusted to a reliable, conscientious gaoler. The Constitutions decree that all the Brethren are responsible for holding a prisoner.[52] When the news arrived, in March, 1578, that Germain of St. Mathias had escaped, not only was the cell locked, but also the hall. At first every evening, afterwards three times a week, and finally, when they had grown tired, occasionally on Fridays,[53] Father John of the Cross was brought down to the refectory, and had his meal on the floor. Bread and water : that was all. Soreth had prescribed this humiliating fast three times a week for incorrigible offenders.[54] He had also prescribed public disciplines in Chapter.[55] These were administered to Father John in the refectory. He knelt down, half naked, his chest heaving, his head bowed, like the Man of Sorrows, and the friars, each of them whip in hand, walked in a circle and scourged him.[56] John of the Cross, sovereignly free and resigned, endured it " all with patience and love." [57] " Insensible block ! " [58] they shouted at him, furious at the power of such silent endurance. He did not answer, unless silence might be taken for assent. He certainly did not intend to disown Mother Teresa. He suffered from the fact that she had no news of him.* When tempted to surrender by the offer of a priorship, he replied that he would not turn back, " even if it were to cost him his life." " He was as immovable as a rock," said one of the Calced lay-brothers.[59] The Fathers, exasperated by such incorrigible obstinacy, scowled at him with deep-set, brooding eyes, and John heard them mutter : " What folly ! a reform that exaggerates the Primitive rule and, still worse, refuses obedience to the Father of the Order ! And its leader !—a restless gad-about woman." [60] " And who else ? Just this little brother of no account." Such harsh words and deeds and John's silence and serenity drew tears of compassion from the young novices : " That man is a saint," they told themselves.[61]

John of the Cross pulled his tunic over shoulders that were to bear the marks of those blows for ever,[62] and the wool was soon clotted with blood. He then went back to his cell. When the warm weather arrived—in Toledo the heat of summer is infernal—this purple relic, which he wore for nine months,[63] was a torment such as Benedict Joseph Labre never knew.

" The devil is doing his darkest work," wrote Teresa on January 16th, to Don Teutonio de Braganza,[64] " you would think that God had given him permission to show his power over us." She had an intuition of John's martyrdom. On March 11th she wrote in her agony to Gracian : " God treats His friends terribly. He does not wrong them, for He treated His own Son in the same way." [65] This dereliction, which one can explain but never comprehend, recalls to mind the prologue of the Book of Job.

According to Soreth's regulations,[66] the most venerable Fathers came in turn to the dungeon to exhort the prisoner to abandon a reform that could not last, because God would not long tolerate disobedience. Was it not pride that urged

* The venerable Anne of St. Albert deposed that the saint, speaking of his prison, told her : " *I was, at times, saddened by the thought that people would say I had turned back on what I had begun, and I felt how the Holy Mother would be grieved.*" Andrés, 13,482, I, 53.

him to separate himself from his Order, resist the Master
General, who was such a wise and holy man, and Father
Tostado, famed throughout both Peninsulas for his prudence ? And they invoked Theology and Canon Law. John
was quite well aware that, when he was captured, he was a
subject of the Apostolic visitor : the whole point in dispute
was, did that authority still subsist ? The theologians consulted by Teresa said yes. But what answer had the Pope
given to the royal request for a decision ? What had
become of Gracian's powers ?

Prelates of the Order passing through Toledo were lodged
in the adjoining room, and conversed about the favours
which the Nuncio, Sega, had conferred on them. His Excel-
lency was trying to have Tostado appointed visitor. And
that would be the end of the Discalced. This piece of news
was quite true.[67] John turned giddy at the thought of such
a collapse of Teresa's lifework.[68] Suppose it were true ?
Suppose he were cherishing an illusion ? It was enough to
wreck one's soul ! He ate the bread and sardines which
they brought him,[69] in order to drive away his weakness,
and the " food was so seasoned that, from several indicat-
tions, it seemed to him that he could see death coming." [70]
We know from Teresa [71] that fresh sardines were very hard
to get in Toledo, even during the winter. But the demon
tormented the prisoner, urging him to think that men meant
to poison him. At every mouthful, he made an act of love,
that he might not yield to the temptation of calumny.[72]

.   .   .   .   .   .

Sufferings such as these are described in the *Sixth Mansion* : insults, slanders, calumnies, physical sufferings, agony
of soul and an inclination to accept the devil's suggestion.[73]
The psychology of St. Teresa anticipates the admirable
synthesis of that masterly work by John of the Cross, the
Dark Night.* " It is rare to experience this," he says.[74]
He actually lived it. Fifteen years had gone by since he
deliberately renounced the chaplaincy in the hospital of

---

* We shall describe his four great masterpieces when we come to the period
at which they were composed.

Medina, which Don Alvarez de Toledo had urged him to accept [75], and which meant in the future a happy priestly life in the company of his mother Catalina—and chosen the habit of the Brothers of Our Lady. To this " courageous conversion " [76] Our Lord must have responded " very early," [77] by infusing the grace of obscure and purifying contemplation.

In the verse of Psalm LXIII : " *In terra deserta, invia et inaquosa*," which has been mystically commented on in the *Institution*,[78] David leads us to understand—" and this," wrote John, " is wonderful,"—that it is not spiritual delights or the innumerable joys which the soul has already been granted, that are the real dispositions and means for knowing the divine glory, but rather aridity and the spoliation of the sensitive faculties, here represented by " the desert land where there is no water." And he does not say that the concepts and considerations concerning God, which have hitherto been so familiar, lead souls to an experience and vision of the Divine Power, but rather the inability to fix the mind on God, and to advance by means of meditation, here represented by " the desert land where there is no way." [79]

However short the passive night of the senses may be for those who are strong and fit to suffer, John endured it for a " long period," for he was " destined to pass on to the sublime and happy state of loving union." [80] " Many months and years " [81] were to elapse between his departure from *this* night, and his entry into the " night of horror " [82] of the spirit. During " this period of prosperity," [83] God granted him a " full and plenteous " taste of sweetness which He communicated more abundantly than of old.[84] It reacted on his senses, and there were " raptures, ecstasies and dislocation of the bones." [85] Later came the passive night of the spirit, which lasted " for years." [86] It is intense, but the resulting union is profound. The apex of John's soul had to " be softened, humbled, purified, and rendered so subtle, simple and delicate that it might become one with the spirit of God." [87] There were moments when obscure contemplation, instead of serving only for purification, became, by Divine dispensation, illuminative and loving. His soul, freed from this prison [88] and placed in a state of ease and liberty, felt and tasted an abundant, sweet peace and a loving familiarity with God. The soul of John felt that " her sufferings were at an end " [89] . . . But, in fact, the last months were to prove atrocious. To the mystical night were added the black plots of devils and of men, the darkness of the *cárcel* . . .

Suddenly, the little exhausted Brother, with his pale face darkened by suffering and the horrors of his dungeon, rose up, and a cry, made possible only by purification patiently endured, resounded in the desert of his soul, a cry by which Toledo, reaching up into the heavens, will remain famous for ever.

> *¿ A dónde te escondiste,*
> *Amado, y me dejaste con gemido ?*
> *Como el ciervo huiste,*
> *Habiéndome herido ;*

> " Where hiddest thou apart,
> Beloved, and left me with my anguish ?
> Thou fleddest like the hart ;
> Pierced with thy love, I languish." [90]

The Saint of Carmel, " come forth " [91] from the passive night of the spirit, endured the most exquisite sufferings : purifying yet joy-bringing, the pangs of impatient love. He complains lovingly to Christ that He has hidden Himself, after piercing his heart, and lo ! the prison now shone with a lovely welcome light. His soul delighted in it so greatly that it seemed to him he was in glory. And Jesus replied to his complaint : " I am here with thee to deliver thee from all evil." [92] Sure of his Well-Beloved, he will seek Him once more without pause or respite, no longer fearing " the harts," conquering " forts and frontiers." [93]

The soul that loves " would wish to be turned into tongues to praise the Lord." [94] To sing is the mark of a lover, and well they know it in Carmel. Without art or splendour, magnificently, like John of the Cross, all our mystics are poets, from Teresa of Jesus to Teresa of the Child Jesus. We can understand why John took down from the willow tree the harp he had carried in Zion,[95] and sang of his wounds in poetry that, as Menendez y Pelayo said, "surpasses all that has been written in Spanish." [96]

> ¿ Por qué, pues has llagado [97]
> A aqueste corazón, no le sanaste ?

> Wherefore, since thou hast wounded this heart,
> Didst thou not heal it ?

The pangs of impatient love, unlike his former sufferings in this respect, cannot last long : one must " receive or die." [98] " Dying for love of you, Beloved what shall I do ? —Just die," they sang below in the streets.   And John heard.[99]

A poetry " with more ardent passion than any secular poetry," [100] helps us to understand the pangs in all their intensity preparatory to the mystery of divine union.[101]

> Y dice el Pastorcico :   ¡ Ay desdichado
> De aquel que de mi amor ha hecho ausencia
> Y no quiere gozar la mi presencia
> ¡ Y el pecho por su amor muy lastimado !

> " Now, woe is me ! " cried the Shepherd Lad,
> " A loved one's absence is my torment here,
> Who taketh no delight to have me near,
> Wounded with love of whom, my heart is sad ! "

> Y a cabo de un gran rato se ha encumbrado
> Sobre un árbol do abrió sus brazos bellos,
> Y muerto se ha quedado, asido de ellos
> El pecho del amor muy lastimado.[102]

> Long waited he ; then, to a Tree above
> Mounted, his sweet and yearning arms he spread ;
> And from his outstretched arms he hangeth dead,
> His sad heart wounded mortally with love.

We may surmise then, that, in the intense seclusion of his prison, these pangs were soon followed by the state of spiritual betrothal.   It cannot be believed that, after this, a whole year elapsed during which he enjoyed only those lofty spiritual consolations which proximately dispose the soul for *la consumada unión de amor*.[103] The first thirty stanzas of the *Cántico*, which John took away with him from prison in August, 1578, celebrate not only the betrothal but the spiritual marriage.[104] Besides, " the year of Assuerus " is a mere metaphor, for John himself has taken care to tell us that " God takes a longer time with one soul than with another, because He takes account of the different needs of each." [105] Suffering and joy were so closely intermingled in the dungeon of Toledo that we can see how John's replies, at a later date, to the enquiries of Anne of St. Albert and Mary of Jesus Sandoval can be harmonised. " I asked him," says the latter, " if he received consolations from God ; he told me that this was a rare thing ; and I think he told me that he never had any and that he suffered both in body and soul." John had no consolations, because the wound of love left him inconsolable, the victim of impatient desire. And yet he also said : " *Anne, my daughter, one single grace of all those which God granted me there, could not be repaid by many years of imprisonment*." [106] Mary of Jesus of Toledo heard him make the same avowal on the day of his miraculous escape from prison.[107]

The Saint of Carmel experienced, in his prison, that sense of plenitude [108] which is a mark of consummate union. The *Cántico*, and also the poem in the *Noche*, composed in Toledo,[109] sing of that mystical marriage.

> ¡ *Oh noche, que guiaste,*
> *Oh noche amable más que la alborada !*
> *Oh noche, que juntaste*
> *Amado con amada,*
> *Amada en el Amado transformada.*

> Oh, night that led me,
> Oh, lovelier than dawn, that night of gloom,
> Oh, night that wed me,
> Bride to her groom,
> The Bride transmuted into her Bridegroom !

> *En mi pecho florido,*
> *Que entero para él sólo se guardaba,*
> *Allí quedó dormido,*
> *Y yo le regalaba*
> *Y el ventalle de cedros aire daba :*

> On my blossomed breast,
> My heart whose all for him alone is saved,
> My beloved did rest,
> Took love he craved,
> While over him refreshing cedars waved.[110]

Yes, those lines do indeed express spiritual enlightenment and loving union with God.[111]

Twice the dungeon was lit up by night as if it were day. The supernatural brightness shone through the cracks of the door. His first harsh gaoler saw the light and ran off to warn Maldonado, who arrived with two religious. " Whence comes this light ? " said the prior, " I forbade you to have any." He had scarcely finished when darkness returned. " He is a saint or a sorcerer," said the prior as he closed the door.[112] The door might be closed and darkness return, but John of the Cross had had a divine experience. He sang with a taste of Heaven on his lips :

> *Que bien sé yo la fuente que mana y corre*
> *Aunque es de noche.*

> How well I know the fount that springs and flows,
> Though it be night.[113]

In addition to the first thirty stanzas of the *Cántico* which were " inspired by love under the influence of a flood of mystical light," the poem of the *Noche* and the *Pastorcico era penado*, he also composed during his imprisonment the lines : *In principio erat Verbum*, in which he celebrates " the bond of love ineffable, of which no tongue may speak."* " What matter hatred and persecution, for they cannot touch the intimacy of the Divine Persons or separate them," said St. Hilary.

> The love that joins them is a love immense,
> A single and the self-same love,
> Their own essence ;
> For even as is the unity of love,
> So is that love's Omnipotence. [114] †

* " This Being is Each one, and alone makes them One, in a way ineffable, beyond the reach of words." (*Living Flame*, Ed. 1912, p. 278.)
† " And as that Love which makes them one is infinite Itself ; for one love makes one the Three, and is their Being as well, and that love, the more it makes them One, the more it is their Love." (*Op. cit.*)

Thus did the *frailecillo* console himself; " loaded by his brethren with ignominies and insults . . . he never uttered a murmur or complaint : he might have been an angel. It was surely one of the highest excellences Our Lord conferred on him." [115] Some think that John only composed these poems in his mind, and retained them in his memory.[116] But Innocent of St. Andrew deposed that John asked his gaoler one day " for the charity of a little paper and ink, because he needed them for certain purposes of devotion." [117] He probably made this request to Fray Juan de Santa Maria. This explains the fact that he carried away from his prison a note-book containing the poems enumerated by Magdalene of the Holy Ghost.[118]

Alonso tells us that this Juan de Santa Maria, who came from Valladolid, replaced from the beginning of May the harsh gaoler whom he had at the beginning. Did the Carmelites mitigate the punishment, seeing that Gracian, supported by Rome and Madrid, had resumed his apostolic visitation armed with " royal letters patent by which he was enabled to make use of the secular arm in all places " ? [119] The Nuncio Sega was now unable to render them any assistance because he could no longer interfere with the government of the religious.[120] The question cannot be settled, but, in any case, during the month of June the hole became " such a purgatory of heat and stench " [121] that Juan de Santa Maria, a youth of only twenty-eight, touched by the patience of his prisoner, who was suffering from acute dysentery and dreadful fever, let his heart be softened.[122]

" I sometimes opened the door of his prison that he might take a little air in the hall . . . and I left him there, shut in from the outside, whilst the religious were taking their mid-day siesta. And when they began to come out, or make a little noise, I hurried off at once to open the hall and tell him to get back to his prison. And the blessed Father at once did so, joining his hands and thanking me for the charity I had done him. And, although I had not known him previously, the mere sight of his virtuous behaviour led me to think that he was a holy soul who had reached sublime heights and, on that account I rejoiced to be able to give him some little refreshment." [123]

Summer was advancing, the torrid African summer of Toledo. Corpus Christi went by and John, who always celebrated this feast with great joy and solemnity, praying for long hours before the Blessed Sacrament in a rapture of loving admiration,[124] spent it alone, without Mass or Communion, in his dark dungeon. Still, who can doubt that for him it was a glorious feast?

> *Aquesta viva fuente, que deseo,*
> *En este pan de vida yo la veo*
> *Aunque de noche.*[125]

> Living fount of my desire that I
> In this Bread of Life can still descry,
> Though it be night.

Outside, the great cathedral bell was tolling. From out the bronze gate of the five Gothic naves passed the procession beneath the emerald, ruby and sapphire lights of the great stained-glass windows that glowed like molten copper. Along the steep, narrow streets hung with tapestry, over the pathways that sparkled with yellow sand, passed the great Monstrance made of gold from the New World. . . .

On August 14th the prior and two religious entered the dungeon. John was so weak that he could scarcely move. He remained motionless, thinking that it was his gaoler. When Maldonado saw this, he stirred him with his foot, and asked him why he did not stand up in his presence. The poor saint replied by begging pardon, and said he had not recognised the prior, and could not rise promptly on account of his infirmities.

"What were you thinking about," said Maldonado, "since you were so absorbed?"

"I was thinking," replied John, "that to-morrow is the feast of Our Lady, and that it would be a great consolation for me if I could say Mass."

"Not in my time," said the prior.

On the following night Our Lady appeared to the poor little Brother; she was resplendent with beauty and glory—

marvellously more lovely than the Byzantine Virgin of the *Sagrario* with her royal mantle embroidered with eighty thousand pearls. To the prisoner, himself the unexampled incarnation of the Carmelite vocation—" to live constantly in the service of the Lord God and His Mother the Virgin Mary "—[126] she said :

" Have patience, my son, for thy trials will soon cease, thou shalt leave this prison, say Mass, and be consoled." Brother Martin of the Assumption [127] heard this from John of the Cross himself on one occasion when he wished to excite his devotion to Our Lady. It is she who was later to bear him up as he crossed a turbulent river, all unknowing that he was about to reconcile a poor unfrocked friar with his God. It was she who would protect him with her mantle when the walls crashed down on his cell in Cordova. " A few years before his death," when he was telling Martin the story of his rescue from the pond, he said that the innumerable favours which the Mother of God had bestowed on him were such that the mere sight of her image gave him new life and brought love and brightness to his soul.[128]

Not only Martin, but John's other faithful companion, Juan Evangelista, said that they had learned from him that he was *Devotísimo de Nuestra Señora*. He spoke of her with the greatest tenderness. They always saw him reciting her office on his knees, and when on a journey, or above all, when he felt tired or sad, he refreshed his memory with thoughts of Mary, or chanted a hymn to the Virgin.[129]

.   .   .   .   .   .

Father Alonso de la Madre de Dios, in his valuable deposition at the Apostolic process of Segovia, then procurator for preliminary informations, voicing what was known from tradition, stated that Brother John of the Cross was frequently visited in his dungeon by Our Lord and the Most Blessed Virgin.[130]

One day, during the Octave of the Assumption, when John, worn out by privation, blows, sickness and the stifling heat, was asking himself how Heaven would ever get him out, Mary let him see, in spirit, a window, high up in the gallery overlooking the Tagus, and told him that he would descend from it, and that she would help him.[131] She also showed him how to unscrew the two locks of his prison, the lock of the dungeon and that of the hall.

John, now certain of his approaching delivery, thanked his kind gaoler, and made him a present of a crucifix which Mother Teresa had given him when he took the habit.[132]

"On one of the last days that the holy Father spent in prison," says Juan de Santa Maria, "he begged my forgiveness for all the annoyance and trouble he had given me, and, in gratitude and thanks for the charity I had shown him, asked me to accept a crucifix which had been given him, and which should be valued highly, not only on account of what it was in itself, but also on account of the person from whom it had come. The cross was of an exquisite wood, and all the instruments of the passion of Our Lord were in high relief; the figure of Christ was of bronze. The saint was accustomed to wear this cross beneath his scapular and next his heart. I have it still." [133]

On reading these reminiscences of Juan de Santa Maria we might be tempted to believe that this kind gaoler had some inkling of the projected escape, and helped in it as far as he discreetly could.[134] By Soreth's Constitutions, if, through the gaoler's negligence or malice, a prisoner escapes, the gaoler should take his place,[135] so that John's exquisite charity would scarcely have allowed him to say anything of his plans to Juan de Santa Maria, if the latter was to be saved from such a punishment. By keeping his secret to himself he could make greater use of the concessions which the Brother increasingly allowed him.

Juan de Santa Maria was now accustomed to allow his prisoner to leave the hall every evening whilst the community was at supper,[136] and John had thus a quarter of an hour's freedom to move about. He tried to recognise the window he had seen in the vision, and succeeded. To reach it he had to traverse the whole convent, because the prison was in front of the monastery, which faced the Plaza Zocodover, and the window was at the back, in a gallery overlooking the Tagus.[137]

It was the first time, since December, 1577, that John had set eyes on Toledo. From the window that looked down on the Tagus, nearly one hundred and fifty feet below, the prisoner could see opposite him the green and yellow fields of the Vega, part of the suburb of Antequeruela, down whose bleak slopes he had come the night of his arrival. Facing him was the hospital of Cardinal Tavera, in whose ruins Padre Antonio had been hiding a year ago.[138] To the right, far away in the distance, was the village of Yepes, where to-day the noble *casa* of his ancestors is still pointed out. It was still quite bright at six or seven o'clock of an evening in a late August. The setting sun heightened the bottle-green or grey-blue tones of the round enamelled tiles. The rampart and roads were all powdered with fine white dust. At this he merely glanced, because his whole attention was concentrated on his plan of escape. The window was very high up and there was nothing underneath it but the top of a wall, and beyond that the river. The danger was obvious. John went back to his cell, and Juan de Santa Maria appeared with his frugal supper : the brother went off to fetch some water. The prisoner, who every morning had been loosening the screws of the lock whilst his gaoler was absent,[139] now loosened the " bolts of the padlock " so that they remained just as he wanted them, without attracting any attention.[140]

Unfortunately two strange religious entered the hall. According to Alonso they were Jeronimo Tostado and his companion, who had just arrived.[141] The weather was hot, and they left the door leading out into the gallery open, placing their beds close beside it so as to get the benefit of the fresh air. They conversed for a great part of the night, whilst John, strong in the promise given him by Mary, kept praying.[142] He had already sewn together strips torn from two old coverlets, and this rope—lengthened by a tunic which the sub-prior had given him three days previously, accompanied by a severe scourging[143]—he tied to the hook of his lamp. John prayed : he could no longer resist the force within him.[144] When the two friars were asleep he pushed at the door of his prison sufficiently hard to open it.

The padlock remained hanging, but the staples fell to the
floor. The two Carmelites, frightened at the noise, shouted
out : " Who is there ? " John kept quite still and waited.
As nothing happened they fell asleep. Then, passing close
between the two beds, he made straight for the window,
following in every detail an interior command. The
window, which was a sort of small balcony, *miradorcillo*, was
supported by a piece of wood, like a joist, that rested on a
brick wall. To this John attached his lamp bracket and
the tunic and coverlets hung down. Invoking God and His
Holy Mother, he let himself down into the empty darkness.
The rope was about nine feet too short. It was about two
o'clock in the morning ; there was no moon ; only the
hollow rumble of the Tagus.

John knew that he was on the summit of the ramparts of
Toledo. The wall was not crenellated, but was covered with
stones that had been hewn to build the church of an adjacent
convent. Two feet further on, he fell from the whole height
of the rampart and rolled down the steep river bank. He
saw a dog close at hand devouring offal that had been thrown
out of the refectory.[145] He threatened the animal, that
in its flight it might show him some way of escape. The dog
leaped down into a lower courtyard, but John was, by now,
quite exhausted. However, his present danger and his confidence in the Blessed Virgin gave him courage ; he jumped.

He found himself in a confined space outside the enclosure
of the Royal Franciscan Convent of the Conception, with
its Arabic *cupolas* of glazed tiles. The daughters of Beatrice
de Silva publicly professed their belief in the Immaculate
Conception, and wore the white habit and blue mantle
in which the Queen of Heaven was clad whenever she
appeared to the Blessed Beatrice.[146] The sisters, therefore,
were on good terms with the Carmelites, and, in the month
of May a cross on the dividing wall was covered with flowers
and venerated by both monasteries.

The space in which John now found himself lay between
the enclosures of the two convents. It was irregular in
shape. The front of the convent faced the Carmelite
monastery, which lay along the Tagus, but, as the city wall

here formed a right angle and the ground widened in two directions, one sideways and the other towards the bridge of Alcantara, this enclosed spot faced the river. At its upper end, close to the apse of the Conceptionists' church, and not far from their porter's lodge, was a wall surrounded by a hedge, which separated the Carmelite enclosure from the narrow little street leading to the Plaza Zocodover.[147] It was towards this wall, which no longer exists, that John was moving, in agony of mind, when he saw a glorious nimbus of light and heard a voice saying to him : " Follow me." He thought the dog had run off in this direction, but he saw no one. The wall was very high. He leant against it, his courage gone, when he was suddenly taken up and lifted over the wall.[148] When he found himself in the little street the light had disappeared, leaving him in a dazzled condition which, he says, lasted for two or three days.[149]

At sunrise, Alonso relates, some of the Fathers going to the balcony for a breath of fresh air, saw the lamp-bracket and the improvised rope, and were suspicious. Meeting the gaoler, they asked where was the prisoner ? Juan de Santa Maria replied that he had locked him up the previous evening and that the guests had slept in front of his door. They were, in fact, still in bed when the news of John's escape was announced to them.

Jeronimo Tostado and the prior Maldonado, with some of their brethren, probably followed exactly in the prisoner's footsteps. They could scarcely believe their eyes when they saw the strips of the coverlet and tunic hanging from the lamp-bracket. The friars were greatly astonished that the beam which supported the window had held, because " the wall was very thin, only half a brick thick, with a piece of wood of the same width on top, in order that the religious might lean on it without spoiling their habits ; and this piece of wood was not fastened at the ends." They all thought that the mere weight of the coverlets would have been sufficient to displace it. As for the iron lamp-bracket, it seemed a miracle that it had not even bent. And the gaoler summed the matter up thus : " As I am certain that he could not escape by any other way, I regard his flight as miraculous, and ordained by Our Lord, in order that His servant should not suffer any longer, and that he might help the reform of the Discalced. And, although I was deprived of my rights and privileges for some days, still, in spite of all, I was glad that he had escaped, and so were some other religious, because we had compassion on him, seeing him suffer with so much courage." [150]

At that very moment, and only a short distance away, John, who had up to this taken refuge in the *zaguán* (a covered entrance) of a house in order to avoid the attentions of passers-by, [151] was now moving very slowly towards the porter's lodge [152] of the Carmelite nuns of San José, close to the little mosque dedicated to "Cristo de la Luz." It was barely five o'clock. The Angelus was ringing in all the convents. The portress, Leonor de Jesus, [153] was thunderstruck, and ran off to tell the prioress [154] that Father John of the Cross was asking her to " come to his aid and hide him, because, if the Carmelite friars caught him, they would lash him to ribands." Mother Anne of the Angels happened just then to be with Sister Anne of the Mother of God who was very ill, and the latter said to her : " Mother, I feel very ill, but I will not take physic till I have first gone to confession." Father John was immediately brought inside the enclosure. " He was so exhausted and disfigured that he looked like an image of death." [155] The Calced, accompanied by *alguazils*, were already at the turn and in the parlour, and were about to visit the church and sacristy. Sister San Jeronimo, a very circumspect lay-sister, had received them. [156]

All the sisters gathered round John of the Cross. The infirmarian, Teresa of the Conception, a lay-sister, brought him stewed pears and lemonade—all he could take, so exhausted, and also so overjoyed was he at finding himself at liberty in this little convent, which had been Mother Teresa's " prison." [157]

About ten o'clock, when all the Masses were over and the church closed, John went down to it by the inner door reserved for the sister sacristans. He had a meal there, after putting on the dress of a secular priest which, the sisters said, did not suit him too badly. When the Com-

munity had finished their dinner, they went to the choir
and spent the hour of recreation there. After Vespers, the
nuns returned with their work, and spent the whole evening
in the saint's company. It seemed very short to them on
account of what he said to them about God.

Constança de la Cruz deposed that John recited a poem
on the Most Blessed Trinity composed in prison, and another fellow-novice, Isabella of Jesus and Mary, adds that
he did so from memory, and that there were three poems
beginning with :

> En el principio moraba
> El Verbo . . .

Whilst the saint repeated the verses, one of the sisters took
them down.[158] He told the story of his imprisonment, his
escape, and the favours granted him by Our Lord and His
Blessed Mother. He confessed that never in his life had he
felt such contentment or enjoyed such an abundance of
supernatural light and sweetness as during his incarceration.
And he spoke of the Calced friars as great benefactors.[159]

The Venerable Mary of Jesus, who was to be professed
on September 8th, heard these avowals, and two autograph
letters of hers have been preserved, containing John's own
testimony of the sufferings and graces that God had showered
down on him so abundantly.[160] It is an acknowledged
historical fact : " Our Lady had set him free." [161] *

In the evening, the prioress sent a note to Don Pedro
Gonzales de Mendoza, canon and treasurer of the Church
of Toledo, begging him to come to the convent with a car-
riage and two trustworthy servants. He came, and immediately removed the fugitive to the hospital of *Santa Cruz*, of
which he was the steward for that year.[162]

The Carmelite nuns of San José long preserved the
habit and the wretched rags worn by the Saint of Carmel
in his dungeon at Toledo.[163]

---

* When he felt the nails sufficiently loose " in the middle of the night he
pushed open the door . . ." (Bar., 192). To leave the reader under the
impression of an escape without any miraculous intervention or recourse to
the supernatural, is an outrage on truth, since, in MS. 12738, in the very place
where Baruzi examined it (Bar., 194, note 1), the testimony of the Venerable
Mary of Jesus of Toledo may be found. It was said of old : *Suppressio veri,
enuntiatio falsi.*

CHAPTER XIV

ABOUT the end of October, Father John of the Cross, mounted on a little ass, on account of his weakness, set out from Almodovar del Campo for El Calvario, of which monastery he had just been appointed vicar. El Calvario is a hermitage on the northern side of Andalusia, close to the source of the Guadalquivir. He may, perhaps, have crossed the Sierra Morena by the Pass of the Dogs, that *Puerto del Despeñaperros*, through which the vanquished Moors had fled. Three years previously, Mother Teresa's carts had gone astray on the summit of those "prodigiously high" rocks, "where my Father, Saint Joseph," saved them.[1] Green oak trees clung desperately to those red marble rocks, with their huge, regular steps. Father John's outfit, led, no doubt, by a friar native of this hillside, had not much to endure. A grey and white speck, amidst all this blood-red splendour, he rode in short stages down the flanks of sierras, less steep, but still pretty broken. After the Pass of Guadalimar, he came to Beas de Segura and, in the heart of the city, knocked at the gate of " the monastery of blessed Saint Joseph."[2]

Beas, *muy deleitosa y de buen temple*,[3] was a charming town, with a delightful climate, a haven of peace and tender happiness, sunshine after storm. The prioress was Anne of Jesus, whom Teresa loved as if she were her own daughter. For more than a year she had shared her cell with Anne in Salamanca ; she liked to make the sign of the cross on Anne's forehead, and to watch her as she slept.[4]

Anne was the daughter of Don Diego Lobera of Placencia and his wife, Doña Francisca de Torres of Biscaya, and was born in Medina del Campo, on November 25th, 1545. She was now thirty-three years of age, tall and well built ; though very cheerful, she had " the grand manner." Her skin was very fair, and she had beautiful hands. When she carried stones, or any heavy weight, her face flushed and became resplendent.[5] "My daughter and crown," Teresa wrote to her in the following year [6]; and the great Masters of Salamanca, Luis de Leon, Bañes and Curiel, spoke of Anne as "if she had been already canonised." [7] Master Antolinez, the future Archbishop of Santiago, said that her knowledge was infused : [8] Master Curiel consulted her and, on leaving the grille, declared that she was "one of the wonders of the world." [9] At a later period, he re-read her letters from France, "like the epistles of St. Paul." [10] Luis de Leon who was, like the others, amazed at her knowledge of most difficult scriptural passages, was often heard to say that "she knew more about them, without study, than he did after many years' teaching." [11] Jerome of the Holy Ghost says that Bañes, when lecturing on Theology, quoted from Anne of Jesus in support of his own view in the *De Auxiliis* controversy.[12] This great friend of Teresa went so far as to say that Anne was her equal in sanctity and her superior in ability.[13]

John found, then, at Beas, another Mother Teresa, who was even then considered so holy, on account of the number of her miracles, revelations and ecstasies, that "he was almost annoyed about it," says Manrique.[14] But they were instantly united by one strong bond. Anne had a passion for their Order. There was nothing she would not do for her brethren. "See how she found a fine house for our Fathers of Peñuela," Teresa wrote to Mariano, "Your Reverences would certainly not have found it so quickly." [15] It was, indeed, thanks to Anne's efforts, that the transference of the Fathers from Peñuela to Calvario was carried out, after the first chapter at Almodovar, on September 8th, 1576.

John brought the very latest news to Beas. He had taken part in the assembly at Almodovar, on October 9th, and had previously been at Avila and Medina. This assembly at Almodovar was a most unfortunate one. In April, 1578, Teresa had already put Gracian on his guard : "My brother has brought you a letter in which I said what a dangerous thing it is, in the opinion of Doctor Rueda and

Master Daza, to proceed to the election of priors, without the Pope's or the General's permission, because it is a question of jurisdiction. As I have written to you at length on this point, I will now only beg you, for the love of Our Lord, to reflect seriously." [16] The Nuncio Sega, exasperated, withdrew Gracian's powers on July 23rd. Anthony of Jesus—elected first definitor in 1576—on the strength of the powers he had then received, after consulting theologians and canonists, came to the conclusion that he was bound in conscience, *so pena de pecar*, to summon a chapter.[17] John, after his escape from prison in Toledo, took part in the proceedings. "I am inclined to think," wrote Father Francis of St. Mary, "that there must have been a difference of opinion amongst the capitulars, and that our Father John of the Cross, doing violence to his habitual reserve and modesty, must have disapproved of the project." [18] To elect a provincial was, in the circumstances, to inflict a mortal wound on the Reform of St. Teresa. The Nuncio, more and more irritated, was about to annul Anthony's election as provincial, launch an excommunication against the members of the chapter, throw some into prison, and place the rest under the authority of the Calced friars.

John, who probably foresaw these unfortunate results, strongly urged that the King and Pope should be petitioned for a separate province, and that the documents should be signed by all the capitulars.[19] However, in order to determine John's position clearly, we should need some knowledge of the negotiations that preceded this unfortunate assembly of October 9th, and we only know that, during the two months of his residence in the Santa Cruz hospital, under the protection of Don Pedro Gonzales de Mendoza, he had gone to Medina to look for the Father Provincial of the Discalced who was staying with the Carmelite nuns. Germain of St. Mathias accompanied John, and both resided with the sisters, *como escondidos*, as if they were in hiding.[20]

Who is designated by the words : "the Father Provincial " ? Was it Father Anthony ? He, no doubt, was still in Andalusia, about to make a visitation, and ignorant, unfor-

tunately, of the fact that his powers had expired, thanks to
the revocation of Gracian's,[21] or was it Gracian himself?
But Teresa had just begged him to remain in Madrid, concealed in the house of Don Pedro de Peralta.[22] Moreover,
it may be gathered from the persuasive tone of Teresa's
correspondence that, as she had once again seen John in
Medina, and perhaps in Avila,[23] she was informing Gracian
on matters of which he had not seen or heard. The scraps of
her August and September letters are full of precise detail, of
keen emotion : " I never cease thinking, I do assure you, of
all the torments that Father John of the Cross was made to
endure. I do not know how God permits such things. . . .
And yet, your Paternity is far from knowing all. . . . I envy
him greatly. Blessed be God for having found sufficient
courage in him to be able to endure such a martyrdom ! "[24]
Her whole soul, the soul of the *niña* who had dragged off
Roderick, in far off days, *a tierra de Moros*, is to be found in
those lines. One may imagine her, tightly clasping the
inner grille of the *locutorio*, in Medina or Avila, her broad
face suffused with colour, fixing her dark eyes on John and
Germain, his companion, and the burning words that arose
to her lips, as the Saint of Carmel spoke of his sufferings
with so much cheerfulness that they might have had nothing
to do with himself.[25]

" ¡ *Como un Job pacientísimo ! ¡ como un apóstol !* "[26] she mur-
mured. He was, in truth, the son of her soul, and when she
had first met him, eleven years previously, she realised that
he was the man to undertake the " heroic "[27] enterprise of
which she was dreaming. He had, as she said, " courage."[28]
At the sight of the little saint, " so weak that he could not
stand upright," [29] still aching from blows, and with his legs
swollen by his prison fetters," [30] she could not help writing
to Gracian, " her beloved son " : " If, in spite of such an
easy life, you thus complain, what would you have done if
you had to live Father John's life ? "[31] And, in mid-Septem-
ber, when they were all going down to Almodovar : " I
have been deeply grieved that, ill as he is, he was allowed
to set out there immediately. God grant he may not die
now ! See that he is well looked after at Almodovar, and

that he does not go away ; if you wish to please me do not neglect to give orders to have this carried out. I assure you, Father, that you would have few such as he left to you if he chanced to die." [32] Yet, despite this urgent, motherly recommendation, John was selected to replace Peter of the Angels at Calvario,[33] far away on the confines of the Sierra Morena.

.   .   .   .   .   .

We may be sure that Anne of Jesus experienced the same emotion as Teresa at the sight of the Saint of Carmel. Was he not the very incarnation of the ideal which she was, later on, to sketch in a few lines for the Provincial of the Mitigated, who was threatening to make a visitation of Beas ? " Granted that Mother Teresa could not, like Elias, clothe herself in camel's hair, yet she exchanged your fine material and cloth for rough, coarse serge. And she imitates the prophet, as far as she can, by fasting, solitude, penance and prayer. Let me tell your Reverence once more, that, rather than cut ourselves off from the trunk, we would die a thousand deaths. In my opinion, it is your Paternity and all the Mitigated who have cut themselves off ; they certainly do not imitate their Father Saint Elias, since they seek for fine clothing, for society instead of solicitude, and for news instead of constant prayer ! " [34] Here is perfect agreement with Teresa who wrote : " It is alleged that this is a new Order, and that these are innovations ! But let them simply read the Primitive Rule, and they will see that we are doing nothing else than observing it, without mitigation, just as the Pope first granted it." [35] This same agreement as to the Order's object shed its light on the welcome given to John of the Cross by the Prioress of Beas.

The community assembled in the *locutorio*. John, seated on a Dagobert chair, which is still preserved, had just finished the tale of his own trials, those of the Reform, and even those of the Order—for he had just heard at Toledo, from Don Pedro Gonzales de Mendoza, that the Most Reverend Father Rubeo had died on September 5th, and this, says Alonso, caused him great distress.[36] Anne of Jesus, desiring to put an end to such sad reflections, had some Christmas carols sung. Frances of the Mother of God and Lucy of St. Joseph sang :

Quien no sabe de penas
En esta triste valle de dolores
No sabe de buenas
Ni ha gustado de amores
Pues penas es el traje de amadores.[37]

He who knows not the pains,
That, sighing in this vale of tears, we prove,
Knows not our richest gains,
Nor him love's raptures move,
For suffering is the badge of those who love.

John felt an ecstasy approaching, and made a sign for them to stop. They did not understand. It was in vain he clutched the grille with his hands ; his body was raised above the ground. He remained in ecstasy for an hour, and, when he returned to earth, he told them not to be surprised : he had received so much light in prison as to the value of suffering, and had suffered so very little for love ! [38]

The Sisters of Beas, young and ardent, clustered around Anne, were filled with admiration.

Each of them had a history. Beatrice of St. Michael was twenty-nine years of age. She was a Toledan. She had been a lovely, golden-haired child, but one day she cut off her tresses and, having packed them into a coffer with her little jewels, brought them to her mother and said that all was now over for her, and she would belong to God alone. On the day of her profession—August 14th, 1571—when intoning the *Deus in adjutorium* at Vespers, she was rapt in ecstasy.

St. Teresa had intended her to establish the convent at Beas. One day, when she was talking to Anne of Jesus in the sacristy of the new convent, Beatrice came in, and Teresa, at the sight of her, fell into a deep and prolonged state of absorption. " I saw, in such a marvellous manner, the greatness and glory of God in the soul of that angel that my own soul was enraptured by it," she afterwards told

Anne of Jesus. At Granada, where she was prioress four times, as well as at Beas, Beatrice of St. Michael revered John as " the Father of her soul, and one of the most admirable saints in God's Church." [39]

Catherine of St. Albert was a lay-sister with a beautiful tranquil countenance under her white veil. She was a native of Jaen, and had thought at first of joining the Discalced Franciscans, but afterwards entered the Carmelite convent at Beas. She used all her intelligence and energy without counting the cost in the service of her sisters and in dying to self. John appreciated her virile soul, responsive to the movings of the Holy Ghost. He said afterwards :

" If you only knew, my daughters, if you only knew the treasure you possess in Catherine of St. Albert, you would kiss her footprints. She is a garden of flowers, offering sweet perfumes at the feet of Our Lord ; she is a heaven, a paradise where He takes His repose and fixes His habitation. If I had never known her, I could never have believed that, in such calamitous times as ours, a soul could be found to serve Our Lord with such fidelity, to abandon itself to Him so perfectly, to live in such close union with His Majesty. I am not at all surprised that God communicates Himself so frequently to her."

He was speaking from experience, for he had tested Catherine, going so far as to refuse her Holy Communion three times on days when it was prescribed by rule. The little sister had said that she would surely receive Communion from his hands on that day ! [40]

Beside her was a delicate girl of eighteen, Magdalene of the Holy Ghost, a future prioress of Cordova and a witness of the utmost value, frequently quoted in these pages. She was not an Andalusian, having been born at Belmonte in the diocese of Cuenca. Her uncle, Father Rodriguez, an apostle of the Society of Jesus, brought her to Mother Anne, of whom he had been the spiritual director. The Mother thought of sending her away during her novitiate, on account of her delicacy, but Jesus said : " Leave Me to hew this stone for My own building, because I mean her to occupy a place of honour in it." Under John's guidance Magdalene was destined to become a great nun.[41]

On December 2nd, 1576, Frances of the Mother of God—then just seventeen—was miraculously set down in the poor Carmelite refectory of Beas during the nuns' collation. Our Lord stood beside her. Mother Anne, her aunts, Catherine and Mary of Jesus, hesitated at the sight of this unexpected postulant. But her explanations were most convincing. "Madam," she said to Anne of Jesus, "when children are still very small, they cling closely to their mother's breast, and if asked why, they cannot tell ; in the same way I cannot explain my love for the religious life." This "little Teresa" was at Beas, enjoying the vision of the Child Jesus and the countenance of her Saviour, when John arrived there. Like Magdalene of the Holy Ghost, she lived to a great age, after having suffered fifty years of physical martyrdom. We shall meet her again at Granada.[42]

The foundress of the convent, Catherine of Jesus, was thirty-eight, the daughter of Sancho Rodriguez de Sandoval. She was converted at fourteen years of age by the sight of the title on the Cross. Desiring no other spouse than Christ, she often after that withdrew to an inner courtyard, where she moistened her face and then exposed it to the sun in the hope of growing ugly. Catherine's crucified soul became a marvellous instrument of love. Before her death, on February 23rd, 1586, in her convent of Beas, which she ruled for four years after Anne's departure, she begged that John's Canticle, "Where hast thou hidden Thyself, O my Beloved?" should be sung to her.[43] She afterwards appeared to him, glorified, as also to the sub-prioress of Malaga, Mary of Jesus, whom she had drawn after her on the royal road of the Cross.

Mary of Jesus Sandoval tells us how deeply impressed she was by John of the Cross, and we may also divine the thoughts of Mary of the Visitation, Mary of St. Peter, Lucretia of the Incarnation, Isabella of Jesus, Lucy of St. Joseph, Mary of the Cross, Louise of the Saviour and Eleanor Baptist.

"The first time I saw him in our convent of Beas he had

just been appointed prior (vicar) of Calvario. He had
recently come out from the prison in which the Calced
Fathers had kept him for nine months. . . . The holy
Father's appearance showed clearly the extent of his
sufferings in prison ; his face could not have been thinner,
or more disfigured. The first sight of him attracted my
soul. I had been suffering from great spiritual trials for
many years without the slightest consolation, because
confessors were not able to understand them. Father John
of the Cross so completely won my confidence that I went
to his Reverence to confession, and opened out my soul to
him. He understood me immediately, set me on my way
assured, and heartened me to bear what I still have to
suffer. I acted according to his advice as long as he lived.
When he was absent I let him know of my spiritual necessities by letter. No sooner had I received his reply than
all my difficulties vanished. He called me : ' *My daughter
Mary*,' and I gloried in having such a father." [44]

Mary of Jesus confided in John of the Cross from the very
beginning : Magdalene of the Holy Ghost did so after a
short time.[45] Even if it appears probable that hitherto
Mother Anne had been rather tenacious of the spiritual
guidance of her daughters—" her nuns were, indeed, quite
content, and loved their prioress dearly " [46]—it is only just
to recognise that she allowed them to reveal their souls to
the Saint of Carmel.

How are we to reconcile this praiseworthy behaviour with
the strange complaint contained implicitly in a letter of
Teresa's, dated by her editors in the December of that
year [47] : " How fine of you, my daughter, to come to me
with your complaints with so little reason. Haven't you
got Father John of the Cross, who is a most heavenly and
divine man ? "

It is so easy to raise problems and create difficulties that
we should pause for a moment's reflection ; a little psychology will set us right ! In the first place, Anne of Jesus was
not a Carmelite nun who was anxious to find directors for
herself or her daughters. On March 2nd, 1577, Teresa
wrote to Mary of St. Joseph : " The prioress of Beas writes

to tell me that the sisters of her monastery have only one confessor, to whom they mention only their sins, and that they all make their confessions in half an hour ; she adds that one should act thus everywhere." [48]

Honestly, then, can we treat Teresa's note in such a deadly serious spirit ? Surely it is a very trivial matter that is in question, and we have no right to exaggerate the grievance simply because Teresa answered Anne that she and her daughters have " a great treasure in this saint," and that in all Castile there is not a director to take his place who is as " perfect and who communicates so much fervour to aid souls advancing on the road to Heaven." [49]

Let us not forget that Mother Teresa stoutly defended her friends, and, when writing, did so in a lively, impetuous, and slightly ironical style. Even her praise contains a little lesson, " a grain of pepper," as Fray Antonio used to say. [50] And, because she expected a great deal from Anne, she would never let anything pass. She sent a sharp reproach to her whole community in 1576 : " In my opinion you show little confidence in Our Lord, seeing that you fear you may lack necessities." [51] Again, on May 30th, 1582, she sent to Anne, then at Granada, one of her *cartas terribles*. [52] Why ? Because Anne of Jesus, on her own initiative, had taken some young nuns from Beas with her for a new foundation, and sent back to Villanueva de la Jara *dos monjas legas viejas*, two old lay-sisters who would have been a source of embarrassment for their hosts in those hard times. [53]

Teresa, relying on the glowing accounts she had received of the foundation at Granada, was waiting there for her daughter. Six months previously she had written to Gracian : " Anne of Jesus will be annoyed, because she would have liked to make all the arrangements herself. Are you satisfied with the choice made ? Then be firm, and see that it is carried out." [54] On the threshold of Anne's career *la buena Madre* had zealously expelled the spirit of independence and what she called " infernal customs " from Burgos. She ordered " this letter to be shown to the Mother sub-prioress and to . . . Father John of the Cross so that they may read it." [55] John cannot have been ignorant of

Teresa's fundamental view of Anne, for he had seen the Mother at Avila before the foundation at Granada, and they had conversed freely for a whole evening.[56] He was not surprised at the " terrible letter." He knew what it dealt with because he had, together with the Vicar Provincial, Diego of the Trinity,[57] made all the arrangements for the journey and approved of what had been done. He always preserved his affection for Anne of Jesus : Frances of the Mother of God recalls this fact when writing in her seventieth year, on May 3rd, 1635, to the prioress of Brussels. She says : " I do not remember, Mother, anything particular that the holy Father, Brother John of the Cross, ever said, but I do know that he had a great love and esteem for my saint : *sólo sé que tenía muy grande amor y estima a mi santa.*" [58]

Friendship discovers or produces an equality between friends. We have already referred to some of the causes that produced sympathy and love between Anne of Jesus and John of the Cross, and there were others, even more spiritual.

Anne of Lobera, invited to embrace poverty of spirit, on entering the Carmelite Convent of San José at Avila, felt a love of solitude and silence take possession of her soul.[59] She loved to read the acts of the martyrs and, like John of the Cross, in the community exercises she played seriously at suffering.[60] But the time had not yet arrived for her really to resemble the Crucified. After the trials at Madrid, to be described later, we may imagine Mother Anne, in Brussels, reading of Job and suffering his tortures.[61] On November 25th, 1615—she was then seventy years of age— she wrote to her friend the Augustinian Bishop, Diego de Guevara : " How impossible to understand the distance that lies between desire and action. . . . How well God knows how to make and unmake ! . . . I cannot express how God holds me. I used to call Him ' Him who covereth my sins,' but now He seems to manifest them by a chastening which has reduced me to such a disturbing and pitiable state that I shut my eyes to the sufferings that are yet to come. Day and night, I take myself to pieces, nor can I find a moment's repose. But I am still allowed to hear Mass daily, and Holy Communion is brought to me at the little window so that I may receive His Divine Majesty, and I then tear myself limb from limb with pain and trembling. . . . nothing is wanting to me but to be in hell."

We have here the state of spiritual destitution and destruction described by John of the Cross. So, from the days at Beas—apart from the slight difference noted by Manrique —we can tell that there was the deep sympathy between them of two souls who felt that they were both vowed to the most complete purification. The trials of Madrid and Brussels correspond to the sufferings of Toledo and Ubeda.

Beatrice of the Conception [62] who, after 1594, never left Anne of Jesus, and Father Hilary of St. Augustine,[63] who knew her at Salamanca and was her confessor at Brussels, reveal the secret of Anne's strange silence at the process of John's beatification. Our Lord had revealed to each the graces of the other, to speak of one was to speak of both.

.   .   .   .   .   .

After the visit at Beas, John set out for Calvario.

The hermitage stands in a fold of the mountain, which slopes away without a break ; it has a rectangular, white-washed façade, dazzlingly bright in the sunlight, and is surrounded by some orange, fig, almond and olive trees. On the other side of the " great valley " of the Guadalquivir, towards which the hermitage faces, is the glorious mountain range of the *Sincola y Sincoluella*, stretching along the entire horizon.[64]

The first person John met was Brother Hilarion of Jesus, the porter, an old man of seventy, with long hair and beard, such as the lay-brothers then wore.[65] White with age, he looked like St. Onuphrius amidst the mountains of Egypt.

Two years previously, about thirty religious had left a Peñuela for Calvario.[66] Hence, the farm which had been bought from the parish priest was too small, as was also his oratory, which was only seven yards long by four and a half wide, with a graceful cupola. We are told that for the first years after their arrival, all the hermits slept together in one room on hurdles made of rosemary boughs, as they had done at Peñuela.[67]   The lack of solitude does not help contemplation.

John of the Cross, the better to enjoy "mountains and solitary wooded valleys," [68] which at Toledo he could only do in his loving imagination, and also "to lead his religious to love solitude, was accustomed to bring them, from time to time, to a stream or pleasant rocky spot, and having spiritually entertained and recreated them . . . he divided them up and scattered them, one by one, over the mountain, to speak to God in solitude and dispose themselves to receive the spiritual nourishment of His divine influence. He hid himself that he might do the same." [69]   This took the place of evening meditation.

His historians say, with truth, that the solitude of Calvario was made for contemplatives. John's whole care, in this *beata solitudo*, was to lead his sons on to mystical union. Of what use had been the unbridled asceticism of the former prior, Peter of the Angels ? The God of Christians is not a tyrannical and bloodthirsty divinity. Their food consisted of raw herbs, confidently selected by an "expert." This was Brother Alonso, the cook, who led his mule along and looked at what it fed on, so that he might collect it.[70] A good many of them would have preferred that he should cease from troubling himself to prepare anything. On feast days they had a sort of stew made of bread-crumbs seasoned with oil, garlic and pepper, and many thought that this little relaxation was unnecessary. Father Peter of St. Hilarion says that the same *régime* was carried out under John of the Cross, but, at the same time, he insists especially on the purely spiritual influence that the saint exercised.[71]

Quiroga gives this detail : " When those who ate only raw herbs maintained that houses in solitudes should lead a more austere and rigorous life than those in cities . . . John replied that there was only one rule for all monasteries. . . . But that, in fact, as men's minds are more inclined to society than to solitude and withdrawal from creatures, it was necessary that in hermitages one should have a little more, well-regulated, corporeal solace than elsewhere." [72]

Courage may be broken by too many supererogatory exactions. " You are going to Rome a Discalced Carmelite, you will return a Calced one," [73] John had predicted to Peter of the Angels at Almodovar. The terrible ascetic did, in point of fact, allow himself to be seduced by the easy life of the Neapolitan Court, and joined the Mitigated Friars. On his return to Granada, he even sold his white serge mantle, and little cloaks for children were made out of it. [74] His austerities had not increased his supernatural love, and in that lies all. It is the one thing necessary.

Brocard of St. Peter, who was porter in John's time, relates that he used to carve wooden figures of Christ in his spare time. [75] He also made a first sketch of " the mount of perfection," a plan of his doctrine. [76] He loved Carmel not only *ratione loci*, by reason of its site, because it was the verdant cradle of his Order, and for the beauty of its mountain, but also for another reason : Carmel is the summit on which one eats the fruit of the Wisdom of Love. It was John's intention that men should climb its slopes in spirit, *en espíritu*, [77] walking in his footsteps. Let us follow this itinerary of the soul.

The hard, steep road of spiritual annihilation is indicated by a text in that strange, rhythmic, prose writing which has been called the Canticle of the Absolute :

> " To come to the enjoyment of all,
> Seek not to enjoy anything . . . "

At the peak of this ascent are the virtues, gifts and fruits of the Spirit, which bring about the reign " of the honour and glory of God." Then come those marvellous words as a crown : " Here, there is no longer any road, because, for the just man, there is no longer any law." It is the fulfilment of the text—" All those things shall be added," and of the promise made to the soul that has abandoned all for love, and dug deep in the supernatural in order to win " the Kingdom of God and His Justice."

The ascent of Carmel is guided by an invincible logic. It purifies without ceasing, and cuts to the quick that the soul may follow the straight line without any divergence. The logic is inhuman, if the logician be not, in addition, a subtle and loving psychologist. John of the Cross intervenes only to save Eternal Life. His vigorous asceticism is demanded by his lofty mysticism. *Todo y nada.* The Whole is the explanation of the Nothing. " It is clear from the very fact that the soul attaches itself to what is only a creature, that the more deeply such an appetite is rooted in it, the less capable is it of God, for two contraries cannot abide in the same subject. . . . What proportion can there be between the creature and the Creator, the sensual and the spiritual, the visible and the invisible, the passing and the eternal, between pure, spiritual, heavenly food and mere sensual food of the senses, between the nakedness of Christ and attachment to any thing ? " [78]

Yes, " according to the teachings of philosophy, two contraries cannot subsist in one and the same subject," [79] . . . and again : " the soul's affection for, and attachment to, the creature produce a likeness between them . . ., love establishes an equality between the lover and the beloved. . . . Furthermore, love not only creates an equality with, but a subjection to, the object. Hence a soul that loves anything apart from God, renders itself incapable of divine union and transformation. . . . All earthly and heavenly things are as nothing in comparison with God. [80] . . . All the being of creatures, when compared with God's infinite Being, is nothing . . . and all the beauty of creatures, when compared with God's infinite Beauty, is supreme ugliness . . . all the goodness of earthly creatures compared with the infinite goodness of God is supreme malice. . . . Nothing is good but God alone " [81] (Luke xviii. 19). " The soul is utterly ignorant if it thinks it can reach the high estate of divine union without first emptying itself of the appetite for whatever natural and supernatural things may belong to self-love. Christ Our Lord teaches us the way in St. Luke : ' Everyone of you that doth not renounce all that he possesseth cannot be my disciple.' [82] (Luke xiv. 33). Such is the ascent of Mount Carmel in the spirit of perfection. It is the road of Nothingness, of the negation of all earthly and heavenly good things, of the latter just as much as the former. [83]

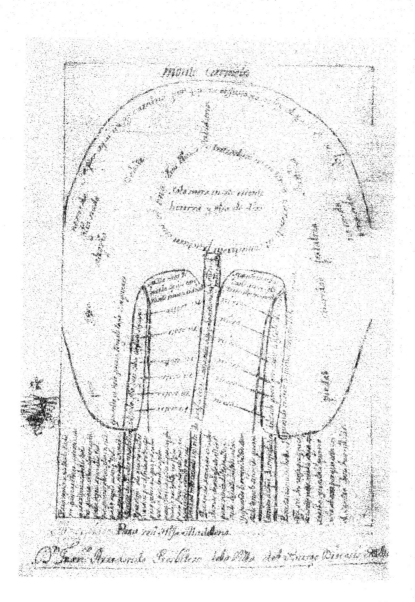

A oscuras y sin nada

In darkness and nothingness,

by which we are to understand " the extinction or, better, the mortification " of the appetites,[84] and not the mere non-possession of things.[85] For " the appetites weary and fatigue the soul, and they are restless, difficult little children, hard to satisfy [86] . . . they torment and afflict it like stinging bees [87] . . . they blind and obscure the reason.[88] . . . The eyes of a moth avail it but little because the attraction of the beauty of light leads it to be consumed in the flame." [89] The appetites, like the " women who mourned for Adonis, the god of their love [90] . . . weep and desire what the will is attached to." [91] The feeble soul always hears them crying out : Give, Give.[92] They may be compared to leeches,[93] or, even worse, to " the young of the viper which, whilst still growing within the womb, devour and kill their mother." [94]

" All the appetites are not equally harmful "—he is here speaking of those to which the will consents.[95] With still more reason, " natural appetites are of little or no hindrance to the soul's union with God, when they are not consented to, and do not proceed beyond the first movements. . . . Moreover, it is impossible to get rid of, or mortify them totally in this life.[96] . . . But all wilful appetites should be radically eliminated. And the soul should be purified from every imperfection, however small, if it wishes to attain complete union.[97] . . . Such habitual imperfections are, for example : talkativeness, a slight attachment which one cannot resolve to break, whether it be to a person, book, cell, dress or a dish that one fancies.[98] . . . It matters little if a bird is tied by a thin or thick piece of string, it cannot fly until it has broken the thread.[99] . . . If the soul is to enter on divine union, all that is living in it must die, no matter whether it be great or small, much or little : the soul should not covet any of these things, it must rid itself of them, as if such things did not exist for it, or it for them. This is St. Paul's teaching to the Corinthians ; ' and they that use the world ' must be ' as if they used it not.' [100] This renuncia-

tion of all one's tastes, the mortification of all one's appetites " is, in fact, the " Dark Night," [101] *the dark night of the
ascent of Mount Carmel.*[102]   And yet it is only a *twilight.*[103]

Let us now enter on " the way which the soul must follow
if it is to arrive at union : Faith, which for the understanding
is as dark as night." [104]   " Faith, the wonderful way for
attaining the goal :—God ! " [105]   Faith is *Midnight* and God
is the *Coming Day.*[106]

John of the Cross had learned, in the schools of Salamanca, that our nature is insufficient for attaining union
with the Divine ; and Quiroga says that it pained him to
see there many spiritual masters " introducing methods of
prayer based more on human artifice and industry than on
the operations of grace." [107]   Such means should be pro-
portioned to its end.[108]   Now the being of God " is not
accessible either to the understanding, the spirit, the
imagination or any of the senses." [109]   " Faith alone is the
proximate and proportionate means that can unite the soul
to God." [110]   John of the Cross regarded this statement as
self-evident, and his personal experience considerably enriched his knowledge.   He knew that " there are many
souls who think that they do not possess a spirit of prayer,
even though they have it in a high degree, as there are some
who firmly believe they enjoy it, and yet have scarcely
any." [111]   They allow themselves to be deceived by sensible
appearances.   John jealously safeguards Faith, which is
equivalent to saying that he rejects all other kinds of knowledge and perception, not only natural but supernatural,
such as visions, revelations and interior locutions.[112]   The
soul should progressively divest itself of everything.   Christ
is the word of God.   There is no other.   What would we
have more ? [113]

" How narrow is the gate and strait the way that leadeth
to life : and few there are that find it " (Matt. vii. 14).
When Our Lord teaches " this strait way " in St. Mark, He
teaches this admirable doctrine : If any man will come after
Me, let him deny himself, and take up his cross, and follow
Me.   For whosoever shall save his life, shall lose it ; and
whosoever shall lose his life for My sake and the gospel shall

save it (Mark viii. 34–35). Who can teach us fully to understand, practise and delight in the lofty doctrine here taught
by Our Saviour? The renunciation of self! [114] To seek
oneself in God is to seek God's caresses and delights. But
to seek God in oneself is not only to will to be deprived of
this or that for God, but to be inclined to choose, for
Christ's sake, whatsoever is most tasteless, whether in
things of God or the world. That really is the love of
God. [115]

Love demands this extreme purity and will not tolerate an
alloy. It is an act of the soul. It tends to take us out of
ourselves. It is by a divine " operation " that " the will
unites itself to God and finds its term in Him, who is Love,
and not by feelings and apprehensions coming from its own
appetite which take their repose in the soul as in their own
end and fulfilment." [116] Hence, on that narrow way that
leads straight to the summit of Carmel, there is room for
naught but abnegation and the cross, that staff on which
we are to lean. [117]

We must penetrate still farther into the *Mystery of the Gate
and the Way*—Christ. [118] The first two stanzas of the poem :
En una noche oscura, which have served in the *Subida* as a
theme to show the extent to which the royal soul should
exercise its activity, *lo activo*, in the spiritual life are again
dwelt upon by John in the *Noche*, his chief work. The time
has now come " to explain the second *aspect* of ' the night,'
of the senses and spirit, and not, as we should carefully note,
another period of this night. We are dealing here with
lo pasivo, that is to say, with God's action on the soul, without
any positive concurrence on its part, save free consent." [119]

We have seen how John of the Cross triumphantly
emerged from the dark night at Toledo, after a spiritual life
of courageous endurance for the space of fifteen years. He
took up his pen at Calvario because he knew how souls
suffer, and sympathised with those " who do not
advance," [120] " who are satisfied with dealing meanly with
God." [121] " Great is their necessity." [122] " If you have

decided to pass through nakedness of spirit," [123] consider this truth : you resolutely desire to serve God,[124] and yet you are only weak infants.[125] Poor beginners who fall into the *seven capital sins* of spiritual persons ! You experience much fervour, and do not omit any of your pious exercises [126] ; do not be too self-satisfied ! You show pride in your conversation—discoursing on mysticism.[127] Your confessors do not approve of your spirit and conduct, and you decide that they are not spiritual men.[128] To convince others of your spirit and devotion, you make yourself singular by signs, sighings, and other such actions [129] ; if you are blamed for this you grow sad beyond measure at your faults, you get enraged with yourselves because you are not yet saints.[130] See these covetous minds : they must possess and read a large number of spiritual treatises.[131] They load themselves down with images, rosaries, curious and costly crucifixes.[132] Others collect *Agnus Deis,* relics and amulets : they are children laden with toys.[133] They must get rid of these if they want to be perfect.[134] Here in Calvario, says John, " I have known a person who wore, for more than ten years, a cross roughly made from a blessed palm, fastened by a twisted pin, which he never left aside, and always wore on his person until I took it away. And he was a man of no small intelligence and judgment. Another employed the knobs of a fish's backbone to count his beads, and his devotion was no less valuable in the sight of God." * [135] The sensual are to be pitied. They cannot avoid suffering [136] from the sensibility of their nature,[137] and their ever restless minds.[138] The dark night will regulate such affections.[139] Some are angered because spiritual things no longer have any flavour.[140] Others are always hungry : these are gluttons, who think of nothing but corporal acts of penance,[141] and weary their confessors. The envious forgets that he should rejoice that another possesses virtues he has not.[142] Away in a corner you find those undermined by acedia. Many desire that God shall accomplish their wishes, and cannot bear to will what is pleasing to Him. . . .

---

* He seems to be referring here to himself. Cf. Dep. J. Juan Evangelista, as reported by Quiroga, 443, and Cyprian, 398.

They end by thinking that what is not to their liking is not the will of God.[143]

This sketch is famous. It shows how needful it is for poor beginners that God should lead them into the dark night. " In that night he will wean them from all sensible attractions, by utter dryness and interior darkness ; with God's help they will abandon their puerilities and acquire virtues in quite another way." [144]

The soul, after the sweetness enjoyed by beginners,[145] and now fully converted to God,[146] is abruptly plunged into passive dryness, which will correct the failings of its lower faculties by cutting off what nourishes them. The purification of the senses is not always the cause of this dryness—" frequently " —*muchas veces*—" it may accompany sin, imperfection, a want of energy, tepidity, or even an unbalanced character, or bodily indisposition." [147] How may such purifying dryness be recognised ? Three signs will help us to discover whether or not a person has been led " into the way of contemplation without images," and " without discourse." [148]

1. One no longer finds any taste or consolation in divine things, and still less in creatures.[149]
2. As a rule there is a sense of uneasiness, a harassing anxiety at the remembrance of God, and one is afraid that one is not serving Him.[150]
3. One cannot meditate or discourse by means of the imagination as one was accustomed to do.[151]

" Now especially is the time when spiritual persons, if they have not someone to understand them, fall back." [152] " They should be aided and reassured." In reality, " they are doing a great deal by remaining patient, and by persevering in prayer even though they achieve nothing by it . . . contenting themselves with a loving and restful look towards God." [153] One day the soul, having crossed the threshold of the *narrow Gate of the night of the senses*, will enter, after ecstatic years of *bonanza*,[154] on the *hard and steep Way of the night of the spirit*. The inferior powers are now strengthened and divine action has become possible. " As this is a rare experience," [155] John of the Cross here gives us a magnificent description of *aniquilación*, or spiritual distress.[156]

Divine Wisdom tortures the soul because of its very excellence.[157] The keener the natural light, the more is the owl blinded by it.[158] This ray of mystical Wisdom is " a ray of darkness."[159]

The divine and human are now face to face.[160] The " old man " must be put to death ; the soul feels its spiritual substance going to pieces, dissolving. . . . It is a cruel death of the spirit.[161] The soul is swallowed alive by a wild beast, and digested in its dark interior. One may say of such a soul that it goes down alive to hell. . . . But an hour of such suffering in the course of one's life is more efficacious than several hours of purification after death.[162] The most powerful texts in David, Job, or Jeremiah supply us with only the faintest glimpse of this dreadful suffering.[163]

When the roots [164] of imperfections have been torn up, and the stains of the " old man " washed out by " the soap and strong lye of the night of the spirit," [165] the soul is at length purified. A ray of Wisdom traverses the soul, which neither sees nor suffers from the ray, because now there is nothing to stop its passage, and the soul is bathed in a light that reaches to and penetrates all things, both earthly and heavenly. " It realises mystically and interiorly St. Paul's phrase : having nothing and possessing all things. This happiness is due to poverty of spirit." [166]

> *A oscuras y segura :*
>
> In darkness and security.

What greater security than no longer to trust in things of sense,[167] what surer than the way of suffering,[168] than the advance into darkness,[169] than that hidden love which is ever awake ? [170] " Mystical Wisdom has hidden the soul within Itself " [171] ; and the soul now " sees itself transported into a deep and vast solitude, to which no creature can have access, an immense illimitable desert, which is all the more delectable, lovely and enjoyable, in so far as it is profound, boundless and empty . . . the abyss of Wisdom then elevates and dilates the soul, quenching its thirst in the very fountains of love." [172]

The soul, despite certain fluctuations which precede complete pacification,[173] mounts up "without knowing how," [174] the steps of the staircase of secret love :

Por la secreta escala disfrazada.

It is saved by the fact that it is " disguised " in white, green and red, the three colours of the theological virtues which dispose the three powers of the soul for divine union. Faith darkens the understanding and empties it of all natural knowledge, thus disposing it to unite itself to the divine Wisdom. Hope empties and separates the memory from the possession of creatures. . . . Charity empties the affections and appetites of the will of all that is not God, and places them in Him alone. It is impossible to arrive at perfect love without travelling clad in those three colours.[175]

But, wonderful divine logic ! when all those conditions are fulfilled " let the soul at once make room . . . , *luego*— and it is wholly illuminated and transformed in God." [176] Immediately—*luego*—this word, pregnant with hope, is frequently employed by the Saint of Carmel.* But as in John's own case, courage and heroic patience, extending over many years, are needed to " reach this promised land of divine union." [177] †

John slowly and vividly elaborated these great outlines in his *pláticas*, " more admirable even than his writings." [178] The reader may remember that, before his prayer on the mountain he was wont to address " a little spiritual discourse " to his religious ; " his eyes shone like twin lights,

---

* Gabriel of St. Mary Magdalene, O.C.D. " The union of transformation in the doctrine of St. John of the Cross." (*Vie Spirituelle*, March, 1925, Supplement, pp. 127, etc.) St. Teresa teaches the same doctrine in *The Interior Castle*, VII. Mansion, Ch. II. (*Silv.* IV, 189 ; C.P., III, 289). However, we should not forget that " God does not raise all those to contemplation who exercise themselves in the way of the spirit, nor even half of them : Why ? He alone knows." (Ger. II, 32.) Nevertheless, the night of the senses is not unusual. But the night of the spirit is " the privilege of very few : *la espiritual es de muy pocos.*" (Ger., II, 26.)

† Cf. Ch. XIII. John, strong in his own experience, commanded masters of novices to teach " the beaten path of the virtues by which our forefathers attained perfection." (Alonso, II, Ch. X.)

and his cheeks like glowing brasiers." [179]   Mary of Jesus says
that " when it was a question of speaking about God he was
inexhaustible." [180]   At Beas they were well aware of this fact.
The hermits of Calvario, recognising the generous assistance
given them by Mother Anne and her daughters, were accustomed to celebrate certain feast days at their convent, and
John took charge of the community's spiritual direction.[181]

During the winter months of 1578 and the spring of 1579,
which John spent at Calvario, he used, every Saturday, to
take *la Majada de las Vacas* and climb up the reddish-coloured
hill.   He wandered away from the *río colorado* into a solitude
that echoed with the murmur of the pines, the Arab song
of a scarlet-vested labourer, and the crystal waters of the
Fonte Labrada which tasted so sweetly.   He sometimes
climbed the mountain range by way of *Los Nevazos* or
perhaps, by the *Pico Corincia*. . . . Here the whitish rock
lies all around one, bare even of bindweed and arnica.
Far below, the ground is speckled with olive-trees : thorough-
bred horses, with nostrils dilated, and long black manes and
tails, scour the meadows.   All round stands a noble range
of rocky mountains, whose summits are clad with snow
throughout winter.   Their slopes are flecked alternately
with sun and shade that reveal deep chasms, giving sharp
outlines to the landscape.   Suddenly Beas appears beneath
us clad in verdure, and spread out like a fan along a slope.
In the morning the village looks delightful, with the blue
smoke curling above its roofs.

Local tradition marks the spot where John used to rest
after his two or three leagues' climb.   A cross used to stand
there.   It is said that a landlord had it removed, and this
irreverent act made his land barren.   John used to rest and
look down at Beas. . . . Mother Anne's convent lay there
beneath his eyes, right in the heart of the town.   A *cavaleria*,
with brimming hampers, rides down the path in single file,
followed by an Andalusian in blue blouse and tobacco-
coloured felt hat, with a stick in his hand.   We can imagine
the holy hermit rising up and moving down towards the
clear and rapid River Beas.   He crosses it and in a few
minutes is in the Carmelite " hospice," standing before the

fireplace in a lofty room containing the historic table made of three pine planks, with its three rows of large nails.

At Beas he taught his "solid and substantial doctrine," and, as he gave spiritual nourishment to Anne of Jesus, Mary of Jesus and Frances of the Mother of God, his doctrine became more definite in outline. He had the art of placing himself at the level of his hearers, and Alonso tells us that he reminded the cook, Sister Catherine, "who was more holy than sharp," of how frogs behave. Like them, let her hide herself and plunge into the depths. By word, and later in writing, he gave each of them her appropriate spiritual message. He told them : " *Do what the little sheep does, ruminate over what I have told you until I come again.*" [182] On his return, he asked questions and commented on the replies.

It was a real pleasure, says Anne of the Mother of God, to see " how, at the time of the saint's lectures, Catherine of St. Albert spiritually and intellectually entered into all he said, and grew proportionally inflamed with a great interior fire. Moreover, she made such a point of taking notes whilst he was giving an instruction or conversing, that she succeeded in making up a little book, two fingers thick, from which she would never be parted. When she had anything to do, she used to place it before her so that she could read at the same time, and often fell into such profound prayer that she uttered great sighs mingled with expressions of love of Our Lord, and remained in trance." [183]

Magdalene of the Holy Ghost also took notes, so that she could read them when John was absent. She complained that she had been robbed of almost all the pages she had written. One of them contained a well-known passage from the first book of the *Subida* :

"Always seek, by preference, not the easiest, but the most
    difficult :
Not the most tasty, but the most insipid ;
Not what pleases, but what does not attract ;
Not what consoles, but what afflicts ;
Not what eases you, but what demands hard work ;
Not more, but less ;
Not the highest and most precious, but the lowliest and most
    despised ;

> Not the desire of anything, but the non-desire ;
> Not to seek the best in things, but the less good,
> And to place oneself, for Jesus Christ's sake, in nakedness,
>   emptiness and poverty of all that this world contains." [184]

This celebrated passage immediately precedes, in the thirteenth chapter of the *Subida*, " the Canticle of the Absolute," of which the verses—as we may remember— " are written on the picture of the Mount which is to be found in the beginning of this book." [185] We are now certain that John, whilst at Beas, developed the chief theme of the *Dark Night of the Ascent of Mount Carmel*, whilst the sisters followed " the road-map," the *monteçillo*, which he had given them, and which they all carried in their breviaries.[186] The one here given bears this dedication : *Para mi hija Madalena :* for my daughter Magdalene.

Beas, then, as well as Calvario " placed a pen in the hand " of Father John.[187]

The nuns questioned him on some stanzas of the Spiritual Canticle. When Magdalene of the Holy Ghost asked if God had inspired him with these words, he answered : " *My daughter, sometimes it was God who gave them to me, and sometimes it was myself who sought for them.*" [188] Certain *declaraciones* were the result of those conversations. But it was only at Granada, when Anne of Jesus begged him to write a commentary on the *Cántico*, that the *Doctor de los Mártires* consented to do so, knowing that the Lord had given Anne a special grace. She had been withdrawn " from the ranks of beginners, and led further into the bosom of God's love." [189]

All the Carmelite nuns of Beas would certainly have been ready to sign the eulogy which Mother Teresa bestowed on John of the Cross in a letter, dated December, 1578 by the editors. When we know that just at this time the Reform was on the point of being condemned, and that Gracian, rendered powerless, was obliged, by the Nuncio's order, to take up his residence in the College of Alcalá, we grasp the full meaning of her words, we reach a deeper comprehension of them :—

" I assure you that it would be a wonderful favour to have

Father John of the Cross here. He is, indeed, the Father of my soul, and one of those who have done me the greatest good by their words. Have recourse to him, my daughters, in all simplicity ; you may, I assure you, have the same confidence in him as you have in me, and you will be pleased with him. He is very high in the interior life, and what is more, joins the widest experience to the most profound knowledge. The sisters of Avila, who were accustomed to his doctrine, sorely miss him. Thank God, Whose will it is that you should have him so near you. I am writing to ask him to help you. I know how charitable he is ; he will go to you whenever you need him." [190]

This was true to the letter. "This heavenly and divine man," as Teresa called him, left Calvario in the spring of 1579. He subsequently returned to Beas from Baeza, and even from Granada, and remained for a month and more in close proximity to those whom he cherished above all,[191] and of whom he was most especially the " *maestro y padre— master and father.*" [192]

CHAPTER XV

THE RECTORSHIP OF BAEZA

On the evening of June 13th, 1579, four Discalced Carmelites, staff in hand, clad in serge habits and wide som-
breros, entered the town of Baeza in Andalusia.[1] They were
Peter of St. Hilarion, the future prior of Mexico,[2] the true-
hearted John of St. Anne,[3] the austere and pacific Innocent of St. Andrew, whose cheeks were furrowed by tears.[4]
In their midst walked John of the Cross, with the faculties
of the bishop of Jaen, and of Father Angel de Salazar in
his pocket, who had, by the Nuncio's order, been ruling
the Reform since April 1st, whilst awaiting a settlement at
Madrid, of the points in dispute between the Mitigated and
the Discalced.[5]

A mule went before them laden with a table and all the
requisites for the celebration of the Holy Sacrifice. Nothing
else, and even that was a gift from the sisters of Beas.
Mother Anne of Jesus had placed not only her influence but
her poor belongings at the disposal of her brothers.[6] In
this fashion they had travelled, fasting, six leagues from
Calvario, probably going along the banks of the Guadalquivir. The following day was the feast of the Most Blessed
Trinity.

Late in the evening, the mule halted opposite one of the
houses of " Señor Escos," towards the west of the town, near
the. *Puerta de Ubeda*.[7] They set to work at once to transform
a room on the ground floor into a chapel, and attached the
foundation bell to a window. It was all done " without
anyone in the neighbourhood noticing anything until the
bell rang for Mass in the morning." * A young girl, fifteen

---

* The bell to be rung to notify the neighbours that Mass was about to be
said. This was sufficient to render the foundation canonically legal. (B. Z.)

years of age, Juana de Ajona, ran up, and found, as she relates, Father John of the Cross knocking down a wall in the room where the Holy Sacrifice was to be celebrated. She immediately began, with another person from the neighbourhood, to clean up the room so that Mass might be said as soon as possible.[8]   Father Francis of the Conception, Espinel, whom we have seen at Pastrana, had come from the solitude of Jesus-Mary de la Peñuela, where he was prior.   The rugged old man of seventy-five had brought, as a gift for the young community, a Father twenty-six and a half years old, John of Jesus, whom John of the Cross had remarked on his first visit to Peñuela, and had wished for as vice-rector and Master of Novices.[9]   This made in all, as Juana de Ajona tells us, five " real " Discalced Carmelites with John of the Cross.[10]

John said the Mass of the Most Blessed Trinity with intense devotion.[11]   Everything was poor.   *La Reforma* says that, instead of pearls and emeralds, they had wild flowers and plants.[12]   John's affection for the mystery of the Trinity was, doubtless, his reason for selecting June 14th for the foundation of the College of Our Lady of Mount Carmel.   It was also the patronal feast of the University of Baeza, whose portal bears an imposing figure of the Trinity : God the Father wearing a mitre with the Dove on His heart, and the Son dead at His feet.

The earliest historians note amongst the visitors on this feast day : Doctor Carlebal, Doctor Diego Perez and Doctor Ojada.[13]   They were not strangers, and two of them had, certainly, been attracted to Calvario by the fame of the wisdom of Peter of the Holy Angel, " a fine mountaineer with a clear, ruddy complexion and snowy locks," a spiritual son of John of Avila, and the professor of Sacred Scripture had questioned the rustic author of *Brother Contrition* and *Brother Sheep* as to the meaning of an obscure passage in the *Apocalypse*.[14]   How far had these men brought about the foundation at Baeza ? [15]

It is difficult to say with certainty.   A friend of the prior of Peñuela, Father Nuñez Marcelo, touched at the sight of the poverty of the new establishment, hastened to send some

mattresses that evening, but John, whilst heartily thanking
him for his charity, would not accept them.[16] The community wanted to keep up the practices observed on the
mountain, and live rigorously according to the fashion of
Scete and Tabenna.[17] This refusal was, undoubtedly, a
matter of conversation for the whole town, and people said,
in hushed tones, that for eight nights running, devils had
tormented the holy penitents.[18] The Masters of the University came again : they grew enthusiastic at having in their
midst those hermits of Calvario and Peñuela of whom they
had heard such wonders. They at once began singing their
praises in their University lectures, and this, coupled with
the striking appearance and zeal of the hermits, induced,
during those first years, " a number of students to take the
habit in our monasteries." [19] This displeased other professors who were not quite so mystical.[20] The Rector withstood the opposition, and preached to the students of the
happiness of their companions who had joined the Carmelites.[21] When Luis de San Angel [22] was a student at Baeza,
he frequented the society of St. John of the Cross, saying " it
is wonderful to hear him dealing with the mysteries of faith."
And yet, the young and distinguished Luis de la Torre
" could boast of possessing all the knowledge acquired in the
schools by the children of the nobility ! " Father John
spoke of mysteries " as clearly as of something he could see
and on which his gaze was fixed." We can understand how
" the gravest persons, saints and scholars, masters and
University professors "—at that time both numerous and
learned—" flocked to John as a divine oracle, and departed
marvelling at his conversation." " What deep wisdom ! " [23]
said Doctors Ojada, Becerra and Sepulveda, with whom he
had discoursed on certain difficult texts of Scripture.[24]
" Doctor Ojada, prior of St. Andrew's, and padrone of the
University, and Doctor Molina, prior of St. Paul's, in particular, esteemed him highly." [25] If the austere Carmelite
surroundings attracted some, many more were captivated
by John's infused knowledge. His doctrine was compared
with that of John of Avila, the revered spiritual master to
whom Andalusia owed so much.

Infused knowledge works wonders with men of humility.
. . .

Juan de San Pablo had just taken the habit. He was a student in Canon Law and, in order to pass the time, asked for a book *de su facultad*. The Father Master went looking for the Rector, John of the Cross, who pointed to a piece of paper on which Juan was to write out the *Pater Noster*. The learned novice was to study this for half an hour or an hour every morning. The Father Master carried out the order, and Jerome of the Cross, who relates the incident,[26] saw his learned fellow novice long prostrate in prayer, carrying out this exercise. Juan de San Pablo held the paper in his hand, and a *puntero*, the little twig of wood used by children in reading and spelling out their letters : for several days he shed such abundant tears that they fell like two rivulets, *hilo a hilo*, from his eyes to the ground. Happy, O Lord ! is the soul whom Thou dost instruct.[27]

When the number of young Carmelites increased, and Sebastian of St. Hilary,[28] and Francisco Indigno [29] had taken the habit, the Father Rector organised scholastic studies in his college, and inaugurated academical exercises at which the Doctors assisted.[30] He attached much importance to treating theological questions, especially those dealing with morals, in this living fashion. John himself argued well, and " distinguished " and " resolved " in true scholastic style. The most experienced religious agreed that he might have presided over theses at Alcalá or Salamanca.[31] When he dealt with the science of God, he was uplifted by the Spirit, and exclaimed : " Up, little children, let us get on the road and stride forward to Life Eternal." [32]

The Carmelite students, however, also attended the theological lectures of the University, as they were accustomed to do at Alcalá.[33]

They had not to go far to arrive at the University buildings, with their graceful, beautiful and noble surroundings :

the charming Gothic palace of Benevento, the Phœnician fountain of *Los Leones*, and the triumphal arch of Charles the Fifth outlined against the blue sky. When we leave the busy white streets, we find ourselves amid a peaceful delightful labyrinth of shady walks surrounding the stone Cathedral with its Moorish porch. No dwelling can now be seen, and the soul, prepared for flight by tranquil recollection, expands suddenly before a scene of calm splendour bathed in light—the *Sierra Magina*, on the opposite bank of the Guadalquivir. The mountain is over six thousand feet high, crowned with snow in winter : in summer it stands out blue against fields of golden grain and the soft green of the olives.

John had a passionate love of Nature. At Calvario, he scattered his religious along the mountain side to make their meditation. He accepted a plot of land at Castellar de San Esteban, on the bank of the Guadalimar, about five leagues from Baeza, in order to promote a spirit of recollection in his students. He went, occasionally, to this solitude and " spent a whole week " there. Taking John of St. Anne as his companion, he used to wander through the fields and along the streams, passing the time in reciting hymns and psalms in praise of God. In the stillness of the night, after spending some time in solitary prayer, he would rise and seek his companion : they sat side by side in a verdant meadow on the bank of the flowing stream, and John would speak of the beauty of the heavens, the moon and stars, or of the sweet harmony of the movements of the spheres, and would thus ascend to the Heaven of the Blessed.

At times, when John's companion saw that night was advancing, that he needed rest and that the dew might bring on an illness, he would beg the saint to go in. " *Willingly*," John would answer, "*for I see Your Reverence is longing for some sleep.*"

Thus John had planned life at the *granja* of St. Anne's.[34]

And if, as some say, twenty or thirty days used to pass without the religious ever leaving their monastery in Baeza,[35] surely the students, under such a rector, must have gone on an occasional walk, if only to that spot in the south of the town which, as we have seen, rejoices both the soul and senses.

" Lift up thine eyes to contemplate the hills :

Gaze now on the plain." [36]

The soul is more profoundly educated when it studies God in the book of creation than in the books of men. A moment's wonder at the sight of the *Sierra Magina* completed the teaching they had received on the benches of the lofty University hall, and had pondered on beneath the Roman arcades of the *patio*.

On the wall of the *Aula Maxima* we may still read : " Remember, I have not laboured for myself alone, but for all those who seek Wisdom " [37] ; and there is an inscription over one of the four gates in the cloister :

Ubi humilitas, ibi Sapientia :
Where humility is, there is Wisdom. [38]

There was an air of solid grandeur and grave modesty in the little University of Andalusia. Don Rodrigo Lopez and his heirs had bled themselves white to erect the beautiful buildings (which were completed in 1548) and to obtain a University charter from Pius V for their work. They had scarcely a penny left to establish the eight indispensable chairs. [39]

．　　．　　．　　．　　．　　．

When the students returned to their monastery they must have recognised that their Fathers also had not selfishly made provision for themselves alone, but for all seekers of Wisdom. John of the Cross loved solitude and poverty and, in so far as these are aids to contemplation and Carmelite ideals, he fought on their behalf. " He was wont to speak in praise of the solitary life of the ancients, and the fruit which they gathered from seclusion, penance and prayer." [40] But we should be misinterpreting mystical contemplation, which is a higher activity, if we opposed it to apostolic labours. John would not have exalted action ; he was a son of the hermits of Mount Carmel, but he felt bound to impart to interior souls some of the living water of Wisdom, which he drank at its source, for such was his vocation as a disciple of Teresa. Read the "Prologue" to the *Dark Night* [41] (composed at this period) and you will understand what was the essential apostolate of John of the Cross. What induced him to write was the confidence he felt that Our Lord would enable him to help a number of souls who were in dire necessity. God had given them the talent and grace to advance, and he felt they were bargaining ignobly with Him. This was due to ignorance, to want of energy, and also to absence of advice to set them on the road. What can be more torturing for the soul than to have as a spiritual guide a Job's comforter or artisan from Babel, when God is leading it onward by the lofty road of obscure contemplation and aridity? And that for years and years! John knew that *his* doctrine [42] would never attract a large number. "We are not here dealing with moral questions arising from a pleasing form of spirituality which is enjoyed by souls who seek God by the way of sweetness; but of a solid and substantial doctrine, good for them indeed as for all, but only if they desire to take the road of the poor in spirit." [43]

There are royal souls in the world who are determined to ascend Mount Carmel. They understand that John's teaching will set them free, because it transcends every form of life. It is supremely exacting in what it asks, it reaches the very depths of the soul; and then its work is done. Love and do what you will. But love, with all the seriousness of love.*

Shortly afterwards, at Granada, such souls were found in Doña Ana de Peñalosa, Doña Juana de Pedraza and others. At Baeza a young girl of noble birth, Doña Bernardina de Robles, who had hitherto been directed by the Jesuits, revealed her soul to the Carmelite Rector. She was eighteen years of age, and distressed at the fact that she did not experience any sorrow for her sins. He said to her gently: "*My daughter, do not grieve at not feeling sorrow for your sins. Seek only to serve God blindly and in peace—be resigned to His*

---

* *Dilige et quod vis fac.* This saying of St. Augustine (In Ep. St. Johannis, Tr. VII, Ch. IV, 8), though frequently quoted in the above sense, in reality refers to something quite different. (B.Z.)

will.'' John made her a *beata* * of Mount Carmel, and she continued living with her own family for four years, like a St. Catherine of Sienna ; she then became a Carmelite nun—Sor Bernardina of Jesus. She was a mystic. The Blessed Trinity said to her : " I am thy heart.'' [44]

Maria de la Paz was scarcely more than twenty-six. She was a *beata*, not very intelligent, it seems, and rather restless. She hesitated as to whether she should take John for her confessor, because she did not think he was very learned, and was not sure if he would understand her. However, she did not breathe a word of these doubts to anyone. When she did go, full of hesitancy, to confession, John said to her : " *My daughter, I am learned, and am so for my sins.''* [45] And when, though she understood, she finally urged him to explain why he said that, he replied : " *My daughter, I said that because you needed it.''*

A little eleven-year-old girl, Doña Justa de Paz, wanted to know Father John of the Cross : she entered the Carmelite Church to hear Mass. A religious came out of the sacristy and ascended the altar. Certain that it was the Father Rector, she asked and found she was right. The very sight of him brought her peace, and she felt a sort of cheerfulness and a new spirit take possession of her, together with a desire to be very pleasing to God.[46]

He used to say Mass with so much recollection that he occasionally went into ecstasy. Martin de San José says that when John was at Baeza, in 1580, he became so rapt that he remained with the chalice in his hand after receiving Holy Communion. He was so completely lifted out of himself that he forgot to finish Mass and left the altar. A voice was heard from the congregation crying out : " Call the angels to come and finish the Mass which the Holy Father forgets he has not completed.'' It was from Mother Peñuela, a very holy nun who thus let her Andalusian fervour break out.[47]

Two of St. Teresa's letters, assigned by Fr. Silverio [48] to December, 1579, tell us that John, at this time used to visit,

* Leading a religious life in the world, though not bound by religious vows. (B.Z.)

from charity, the little Carmelite paradise of Caravaca.[49] Was it in December, 1579 or the end of June, 1581, when he had returned from presiding over the elections, that he was seen, during Mass, surrounded by rays that came from the Sacred Host?[50] He admitted to Anne of St. Albert: "*My daughter, I always carry my soul into the heart of the Most Blessed Trinity, and that is where my Lord Jesus Christ wishes me to carry it. . . . My daughter, so great is the consolation my soul receives there that I do not dare enter where I am very recollected because, it seems to me, my weak nature cannot support such extremes. And I abstain from saying Mass for some days, lest something should irresistibly happen to me that would be widely spoken of. I then ask Our Lord to enlarge my natural capacity or else snatch me from this life, and I pray that I may no longer have the care of souls.*[51] He had to endure, for many more years, those " cries and groanings "[52] which the impetuosity of the Divine Spirit wrung from him. At Segovia, as at Baeza, he would wound his hands by striking his fists against the wall to avoid interior absorption.[53] He was found in a state of rapture on his bed at Ubeda.[54] Nevertheless, who can doubt that the Divine communications which he had been receiving ever since Toledo, although accompanied by raptures, were " purely spiritual ? "[55]

I am not unaware that John of the Cross himself declares that " in the case of the perfect, who have undergone the purification of the second night (viz., that of the spirit) there is no longer any question of raptures or physical sufferings."[56] If, then, as I think I have shown,[57] John's purifying sufferings were terminated when he was in prison, and he was then raised to the state of spiritual marriage, a delicate problem confronts us, in analysing which it is important not to forget that God, for ends known to Himself, may have wished to make manifest certain great favours that, as St. Teresa remarks, are usually concealed.[58]

John of the Cross invokes her authority in the *Cántico*, when dealing with mystical betrothal ; he explains the meaning of the painless flight of the purified spirit, whose whole activity is absorbed in God, and then goes on to say :

"This would be the place to specify the characteristics of the various forms of raptures, ecstasies, elevations and flights of the spirit which may be observed in contemplatives ; but, in order to remain faithful to the plan I have drawn up . . . I leave this to persons more competent than myself. Our blessed Mother Teresa of Jesus has devoted some admirable pages to those spiritual states, and I hope, by God's goodness, that they will soon be published." [59]

Let us turn, then, to the Seventh Mansion of the *Interior Castle*, to which he alludes.[60] Teresa here deals with the frequency of what we should call ecstasies without enfeebling reactions. The original bears on the margin, in the saint's handwriting : "That is to say, the use of the senses is not lost." "Here the powers are not suspended, they simply do not act, and are, as it were, seized with astonishment."

If we consider only the descriptions left by witnesses, it certainly seems as if, in John's case, the powers of the soul were not merely "seized with astonishment." Would not his soul, then, on entering this Seventh Mansion, have lost, as Teresa says, "that great weakness which it finds so painful, and from which nothing can set it free ? " John of the Cross will himself answer this question. The soul has, indeed, lost this great weakness, "still, that alone does not suffice to enable it to escape all pain when it finds itself confronted with such greatness and glory." [61]

"The soul, under God's touch, enjoys, according to the measure of its substance and powers. Moreover, its super-abundant felicity reaches the body ; and the whole sensitive substance, the limbs, bones and marrow rejoice, and not lightly, but with an impression of great happiness and glory, which is felt even in the extremities of the feet and hands." [62]

John does not hesitate to call this ravishing transport of love *arrobamiento de amor*.[63] It is quite distinct from the ecstasy preceding spiritual marriage. Moreover, we should not forget that John was prematurely aged by suffering and privations, that his nervous system was extremely delicate and, accordingly, offered less resistance. Even when his soul was completely purified he did not dare venture where he would be wholly recollected. It seemed to him that his " natural weakness—*flaco natural*—could not support such extremes." [64] It certainly would never have occurred to him to consider " the weakness of ecstasy " [65] as " the most mysterious phenomenon of the physical and moral world ! " [66]

God did not " enlarge his natural capacity " in this respect, nor set him free from " the care of souls." [67]

.   .   .   .   .   .

The Carmelite Church at Baeza was thronged : the supernatural was irresistibly attractive. The Vice-Rector, the saintly John of Jesus, and Father Innocent of St. Andrew, the author of *Teología Mística y espejo de la Vida eterna* [68] were overwhelmed with work. The latter says : " When Father John of the Cross was Rector of the College of Baeza the confessors were in the confessional day and night, and they could not manage to confess everybody. . . . There was never such assiduity in hearing confessions as when the saint was superior, so zealous was he for the salvation of souls." [69] He never spared himself ; and it would be a very mistaken idea of true contemplation and perfect charity to imagine John of the Cross such a specialist in the spiritual life that only chosen souls had access to him. The saints, like Christ, make themselves all things to all men. They know how to leave the flock and go after the lost sheep. Brother Martin of the Assumption,[70] a noble character, whose Master at Peñuela had been John of Jesus the Holy, was appointed to act as porter at Baeza, his native town. One day a cousin of his, a free-thinking, evil-living captain, asked the brother to send him an " easy " confessor. Martin spoke to John, who told him to ask the captain to wait an instant, and he would hear his confession. He went down, heard the *caballero's* confession, and the man was converted. He conceived such a liking for the saint's doctrine that he used to come to the convent night and day—*de noche y de día*—and take part in the community exercises. John of the Cross, thanks to " his excellent doctrine," won many from a life of sin. . . .

So great were his zeal and love for the salvation of souls that he used instantly to hear the confessions of all who came to him, rich and poor, with great tenderness and charity.[71] He helped all sorts the *caballero*, the holy Sor Bernardina and Doña Justa de Paz, Mother Peñuela, to whom he made a present of his discipline to defend herself against the devil,[72] Teresa de Ybros, a shepherd's wife, whose prayer, ecstasies and visions were guided by Gracian, who thought them true and perfect,[73] the youthful Doña Isabel de Soria, who saw a ray of light issuing from the tabernacle and touching John on the breast.[74]

Inside the cloister his action was far-reaching. Did he not love supremely to deal with " members of our sacred Order of the Primitives of Mount Carmel ? "[75] He used to summon his religious in turn and ask them about their prayer.[76] Brother John of St. Anne was tormented by the problem of predestination : John assumed the firm tone of discipline and calmed the sufferer.[77]

John of the Cross discovered the absolute, which consists in the perfect love of God and of one's neighbour for God's sake. Charity is perfect when union cannot be lost. John gave himself, without thought of self, to others, as if it were their due, and for those who received the gift, how sweet it was !

The year of the influenza epidemic, 1580, was marked by great trials. Father Francis Espinel, not wanting to be a burden on the college, had gone to die of a tumour in the hospital of the Conception.[78] The decision of the old Prior of Peñuela to act thus grieved John, as was learned from his own action later. Jerome of the Cross relates that a lay-brother to whom he had given the habit, fell ill whilst John was away. As the house was very poor and there were many others ill, the religious who was acting as Superior had the brother taken to a hospital in which the hermits of Peñuela were usually nursed. John, on his return, asked how the brother was. The Superior told him what he had done. The Rector asked, without anger—he knew not how to be angry—but with severity[79] : " Why be wanting in charity towards a lay-brother ? " And he immediately ordered that the brother be brought back to the college. There, John with much tenderness nursed, petted and visited him, and acted in the same way with all who were sick.[80] John of Jesus the Holy—if it were he—might well be excused for this difficult decision.   There were seventeen or eighteen ill in the community, not to mention nine others who had been brought from Calvario.[81]   There were no beds, no bedding, nothing but planks ! [82]   What of it ? John, once infirmarian at Medina, demanded from his community the same care and devotion for the sick as Nature demands from blood relations.   He was inflexible on this point of charity, by which one can so easily recognise that God is truly loved, since the purely human element does not come in among religious ! One night John gave orders to Innocent of St. Andrew to sit up with a brother suffering from brain-fever. At three o'clock the infirmarian fell asleep, and whilst he was slumbering the patient put on his habit, got up, and knelt down.   The Rector arrived, and scolded Father Innocent, " *con mucho rigor*—very severely—though gently." [83]

In 1583, at the provincial chapter of Almodovar, John was reproved for not visiting the laity often enough.   The holy Prior prostrated himself and said : *Benedicite*.   The Superior gave him permission to speak.   "*Father, if the time I ought to spend in paying visits and asking for alms is spent by me in my cell begging Our Lord to inspire those persons to do what they ought and if, as far as I am concerned, I am persuaded that His Majesty will supply me in this world with what is necessary, then why should I pay visits, apart from those required by charity or necessity ?* "

Gracian had nothing to say in reply.[84]   When, then, his invalids needed beds and bedding, John was content with recommending them to God.   And, in fact, on the following day, no other steps having been taken, twenty-four or twenty-five mattresses arrived with a number of pillows, to the great delight of the infirmarian, who tells the tale.   To complete his joy, Teresa de Ybros, Mother Teresa, as she was called, brought thirty chickens to the porter's lodge.   "*You see*," said the Rector, "*how right it is to trust always to the mercy of God.*" [85]   His supernatural confidence and scrupulous sense of justice even led him to refuse generous stipends for Masses —three hundred *jules*—from people who wanted to insist on being favoured out of their turn. Jerome of the Cross saw that, and the porter, knowing that in three or four days time there would be no more Masses requiring to be offered for anyone, went off grumbling.[86]

Incidents such as these were frequent in the life of John of the Cross. Often and often they sat down to table in front of empty plates, which God was soon to fill.[87] Two lay-brothers, who begged for alms from door to door on Wednesdays and Saturdays, had doubtless brought back a poor harvest.[88] At such a blessed moment, without which the friars would never have been poor in the things which the poor lack, the Father Rector reminded them of the reason of their privation in such a fashion as to kindle love in their hearts. " *My children*," said he, " *what is it to be poor if not to be in want ? Have we not made a vow of poverty ? Then let us cherish it.*" [89]

It is a great thing to know how to raise the soul, when the stomach is crying aloud ; it is fine, too, to be able to silence its cries by speaking of God. The cook, Brother John of St. Euphemia, tells us that the Rector spoke so loftily and sweetly of Christ during recreation, that he himself and the other religious who were to have their meal at the second table, used to put it off in order to listen to him.[90] John sometimes recalled the sufferings of the martyrs, and selected judges, a procurator, an executioner. He played the part of the martyr himself.[91] And, as Anne of Jesus did with her daughters, he gave orders that he should be struck in good earnest.[92] Were these more painful scenes sweeter to the Father Rector than the simple representation of the mystery of Christmas, given on the evening of December 24th, in this year 1580 ? Old Brother Gabriel of the Mother of God shall tell us all about it, for he was the sacristan.

" The servant of God, when Rector of the College of Baeza, had a statue of Our Lady placed on a litter during this blessed night of the Nativity and, accompanied by all the community, it was borne in procession through the convent cloister. [The Father Rector] stationed a religious behind every door in the cloister, who was to answer from within, when hospitality was asked for. The procession advanced along the cloister with such devotion that it took almost an hour to go from one door to the next—there were four doors in the cloister. When they reached the Church, it was time for Matins. Near the high altar, on the Gospel side, was a little cabin, made of branches, to serve as a crib, of straw and clay, with the mule and the ox, and lastly the statue of the Lord St. Joseph. The Virgin and the new-born Divine Child were placed in it, and all adored Him with such great devotion that one cannot express the sentiments felt by the people on seeing the feast of the Nativity cele-brated in this way." [93]

It was a Christmas Day of the poor. The chasubles and altar furnishings were of cheap stuff, but clean and well-kept.[94] John, faithful to his principles, refused splendid vestments.[95] He helped the painter and sculptor, Juan de Vera, to decorate the church.[96] As a hanging for the pulpit, they long employed just a Carmelite's white mantle.[97] A Christmas of the poor, but a Christmas of burning love. During recreation St. John of the Cross was carried away with delight. He stood up, took the Infant Jesus in his arms, and began to dance and sing :

> *Mi dulce y tierno Jesús,*
> *Si amores me han de matar*
> *Agora tienen lugar.*[98]

> My sweet and tender Jesus,
> If Thy dear Love can slay,
> It is to-day

.   .   .   .   .   .

In 1580, his mother, Catalina Alvarez, died of influenza, *el catarro universal.* John must have been deeply grieved at her loss. Was he not thinking of her when he wrote in the *Dark Night* : " When a soul has determined to turn to God and serve Him alone, He usually caresses it . . . as a loving mother does her tender child, warming it at her breast, nourishing it with her milk, and with sweet and delicate foods, bearing it about in her arms, and covering it with caresses . . .[99] In a short time, there will be no more milk, the soft food of children ; bread with its crust instead . . . the food of the strong." [100]

Words chosen from among the sweetest in the Spanish language, tenderness for his mother, his eldest brother, pity for souls without a guide, for the sad, for the sick—where is the character so often attributed to this Pilgrim of the Absolute ? Like the son of Monica, John knew that " it is better to weep and lament than to lose one's grief and with it a true human heart." [101] We have never seen him " at the end of the road, bleeding and terrible, yet dry-eyed." [102] One of the two phrases which he gave to his daughter Magdalene at this time, for her soul's welfare, seems to reflect a struggle of his own :

" Strengthen your heart against all that might attract you towards anything other than God : then love suffering for Christ's sake." [103]

Strengthen your heart. . . . Each of the sisters at Beas had a commentary on that text.

" The first care must be to keep yourself in an equal love and forgetfulness towards everyone, whether our relations or others : detach your heart from all. You must, in a way, even detach yourself more from relations, fearing lest flesh and blood be revived through the natural love which always exists between members of the same family, and which must be mortified in order to arrive at spiritual perfection. Regard them all as strangers, and you will thus fulfil your duties better towards them than if you gave them an affection due to God alone. Have no more love for one than another, for you may be mistaken. What God loves best, deserves most love ; now, you do not know whom God loves best. By forgetting them all equally, as it behoves you to do, for the sake of holy recollection, you will set yourself free from the error of more or less, in what concerns them. Do not think of them ; neither well nor badly ; avoid them as you fittingly can." [104]

These words sound harsh, and does not John deserve the

reproach of his disciple, Teresa of Lisieux, for having written them : " I do not understand saints who do not love their own family " ? [105]

Jesus said : " If any man come to me, and hate not his father, and mother . . . he cannot be my disciple." [106] Yet to hate one's own is not a rule of Christian morality. St. Thomas gives the same explanation of this text as St. Gregory : " Those of our kindred who oppose our progress towards God should be hated and avoided." [107]   The Angelic Doctor expressly states that they should otherwise be loved more intensely than the holiest souls,[108] and the Carmelites of Salamanca say that, absolutely speaking, the love of our own kindred comes first.[109]   But here, John of the Cross is transcending the standard of ordinary conduct, when he declares that indifference and equality are necessary to reach the state of holy recollection.   The ascent of Mount Carmel is steep.   Those whom he guides must, at all costs, be led upwards : Catherine of Jesus, Mary of Jesus, Magdalene of the Holy Ghost, Frances of the Mother of God, were *almas reales*, royal souls, if ever there were such, and they were to be led to *desnudez*, spiritual destitution, the state in which souls enjoy the delights of the Holy Spirit, and they were to be led *en breve*, promptly, and very swiftly, *a mucha priesa*.   He did not wait for God to deign, by an extraordinary intervention, to ravish their souls, or give such a command as He had given Teresa : " I do not desire you to converse any more with men, but with angels." [110]   Such a road is slow, and the triumphant self-subsistent word is, undoubtedly, not always pronounced.   The steep way of nothingness is more certain and rapid.   " Take thy only son, whom thou dost love," was the command of a jealous God.[111]   Hence, all things should be courageously renounced.   But when once the golden cord is broken, and the heart detached and purified in " the strong lye of the night of the spirit," [112] it will then, having reached the stage of union that cannot be lost, begin to love with a tenderness hitherto unknown, for grace elevates, and does not destroy, nature.   The soul, then, loves without the least alloy of self-seeking.   It only desires for those it loves, their true good—

Almighty God. There is no danger in such love : the heart keeps its freedom.

John of the Cross often used to say that he loved none so much as his daughters of Beas.[113] It was in virtue of this loving tenderness, that he treated them with such supernatural severity.

"Father John used to say from experience, that nuns' confessors should treat them rather coldly, because gentleness towards women only serves to misplace their affection : *de trocar la afición*, and, as a result, there is no progress. He confessed that, for having dealt too kindly with a woman, God had punished him by not letting him see her grave fault." [114]

In a perfect soul the passions " no longer reign, or do so but slightly, *poco o nada*." [115] " Formerly, the waters of bitterness rose up within her." But now : " the virtuous soul has lost its weakness, and kept strength, constancy and perfection. The same is true of the soul as of the angels, who weigh and judge things that cause grief, without experiencing any themselves, and exercise the works of mercy and compassion without the feeling of compassion." *Poco o nada*, yes. But John of the Cross goes on, " sometimes, in certain circumstances, God acts in an exceptional manner. He allows the soul to feel and suffer, so that it may merit all the more, as He did in the case of the Virgin Mother, but the state it has reached does not, of itself, imply this." [116] *Poco o nada* is the ordinary rule.

To grasp the true meaning of the cautions addressed to the sisters at Beas, we must try to visualise the environment and atmosphere they were uttered in ; the gracious and heroic atmosphere of sanctity.

" I scarcely ever see you when you come," Teresa wrote to Gracian. " Your sister has less claim on your affection than I ; she has her husband and children to love, and poor Laurencia has no one in the world but this Father." [117] *La buena madre*, " who sometimes needed a little consolation," [118] could understand the sorrow of John of the Cross when he had crossed the Sierra Morena.[119] On the day after the chapter at Alcalá when the Reform had been erected into a separate province, she wrote to the young Provincial :

" I forgot to ask you for my Easter cake. May God grant that you will hear my request ! I must tell you that I had once to console Father John of the Cross at the grief he felt when he found himself in Andalusia : he cannot abide the people there.[120] I told him that, if it pleased God to give us a separate province, I would plead to have him brought back to Castile. Now, he begs me to keep my word : he is afraid of being elected Prior of Baeza, and warns me that he will beg you not to confirm the election. It would be only reasonable to give him this consolation, provided it is in your power, for he has filled up the measure of suffering : *que harto está de padecer.*" [121]

These words are startling and they soften even to sweetness the harsh and almost inhuman teaching of the *Cautelas*. We must, indeed, set side by side the doctrine and the life, and understand one in the light of the other. But what we, in our clumsy language might call the weakness of the saints, is like the Weakness of Christ in the Garden of Olives. Our Lord allows them to feel and fill up the measure of suffering so that they may merit all the more. They beg for mercy, yet their *Fiat* is graven in their heart and deepens its tenderness. How revealing are the lines that John, on his return from Caravaca, wrote to Catherine of Jesus, of Valladolid, on July 6th [122] : " Although I do not know where you are, I am writing you these lines, for I am sure that our Mother will send them to you if you are not travelling with her ; if, in fact, you are not with her, let us console one another, for I am even more solitary and exiled here. Since the whale swallowed me and vomited me out in this foreign port I have become fit as never before to see her, and the saints who are with her. This is God's loving action. Desolation cuts sharp, but behind the darkness of suffering a great light is growing. God grant that we walk not in darkness. Oh ! how much I have to say to you, but I write quite in the dark, and doubt if this letter will ever reach you. That is why I do not finish it. Recommend me to God. And now I will say no more, for I do not feel as if I could." [123]

Clearly he is in intense grief. It looks as if he felt cast aside. Yet *he* could not have suffered from that. He had been elected second definitor at the Chapter of Alcalá, and it was his own undoubted wish to remain in the background. Moreover, he had desired Gracian's election and the separation of the province. He had strongly supported the departure of the Fathers to Rome and " would have given his life if necessary " for Jerome of the Mother of God.*

The separation certainly caused him much pain. He was homesick for Castile, his native plains, fertile but open and rugged land of sacrifice. He would have been a solitary in Castile, but not isolated, as in Andalusia. The following lines were obviously written at this period :

> *En soledad vivía,*
> *En soledad ha puesto ya su nido*
> *Y en soledad la guia*
> *A solas su querido,*
> *También en soledad de amor herido.*

> All lonely her abode,
> Hid in a lonely nest her lonely bed.
> Then on a lonely road,
> By her Beloved led,
> Whose heart, love-wounded, too, had lonely bled.[124]

* Letter to Gracian, February, 1580 (*Silv.*, VIII, 415 ; *Greg.*, II, 519). Nothing is more certain than that John desired and had foreseen a separate province for the *Descalcez*, (Alonso, *Vida*, Bk. I, Chs. XXXVI and XLI, quoted by Silv., VIII, 415, note 2, Jer. 381), their situation and numbers required it. Alonso says there were ten monasteries of men and ten of women. There were 280 brothers and about 170 nuns. " My Lord," Philip II said to the Nuncio, " everybody says that you do not like the Discalced Friars, and you make them feel it too much." These severe words, reported by *La Reforma*, had opened a period of reconciliation. Sega, assisted by four assessors, undertook to settle the dispute. On July 15th, 1579, he submitted a report to the King in favour of the Discalced and, on November 11th, praised St. Teresa's work to the Cardinal of St. Sixtus, the protector of the Order. In this document he does justice to the austerity of the *primitivi*. The latter, whilst waiting for the brief that was to set them free, were governed by Angel de Salazar, who was not wanting in wisdom and kindness. Elections were held regularly, both for the Mitigated and the Discalced, at the same provincial chapter. At the one held at Moraleja on November 15th, 1579, Father Angelus, as we see, held the office of Vicar-General. When John of Jesus, Roca, and Diego of the Trinity had spent more than a year in Rome, doing everything that lay in their power, a brief, establishing the Discalced as an autonomous province, but under the jurisdiction of the Prior General, was obtained, not without difficulty, thanks to the King and the Nunciatura. On these matters, see Maria de San José, *Libro de las Recreaciones*, already quoted, p. 119, C.P. IV, doc. 44) and Jerónimo Gracian, *Peregrinación*, already referred

On November 28th, 1581, Teresa was "much consoled," [125] for she met John again in Avila, where she, too, felt "very much alone." [126]   "As it is natural to wish to have our love returned"—she wrote in the same month to Mary of St. Joseph [127]—"it cannot be wrong, because Our Lord also wants His love returned." This was their last interview. John, now restored to peace, bore for ever in his heart the living portrait of her whom he always called "our Mother"; she would answer gaily, "Father, why do you not call me 'my daughter'?" [128]   After her death, which occurred in the following year, he always carried about with him a speaking likeness of the *Santa*, "which greatly consoled and encouraged him." * [129]   It was the last thing he sacrificed.   One day, on arriving at Calvario from Baeza, he bravely destroyed a bundle of Teresa's letters so that he might be free, completely free to love. [130]

If it be well to call attention to what has been styled the "weaknesses" of the saints, to console us over our own, we should never allow this consideration to interfere with our appreciation of their heroism, nor of their glory.

.   .   .   .   .   .

John used to go from Baeza—and, later, from Granada—to spend a month or so in proximity to the sisters at Beas. When he was unable to visit them he wrote spiritual letters " Beginning with the prioress and ending with the youngest, he named them all, and to each he gave a maxim, telling them to practise it so that they might increase in virtue." [131]

On November 18th, 1586, he wrote to them from Malaga : " *I will most certainly come and let you see how far I am from forgetting you, and we shall see the wealth acquired in pure love.*" [132]

One day, as he was leaving the nuns' hospice on his way home to the monastery, a tile fell from the church, which was in course of construction, and broke on the head of his companion, Jerome of the Cross ; the latter did not feel it,

to, p. 44, C.P. IV, doc. 56) ; *Ref.*, Bk. IV, Ch. XXXIX ; Bk. V., Chs. I, II and VII—the documents on which we base our statements may be found in the archives of the Calced Carmelite Fathers at Rome. *Acta Discalc.*, cod. I.

* In the month of March, 1588, he predicted Teresa's beatification to Father Angelus of St. John : "You will see it before you die." Alonso, Bk. II, Ch. XVII ; Quiroga, 639 ; Cyprian, 579.

and, thanks to the saint's protection, had only to shake his white mantle.[133] We are not certain if this was the period at which John, whilst putting on his priest's vestments, knew, by revelation, that Sister Frances of the Mother of God was in choir, and most anxious to hear the Three Divine Persons speak. Our Lord told John to console Frances by celebrating the Mass of the Blessed Trinity. When the Holy Sacrifice was over, John called her and said : " *My daughter, how can I thank you, and how can I be sufficiently grateful to you, all my life, for being the cause of Our Lord's commanding me to celebrate the Mass of the Most Blessed Trinity. I have received an extra-ordinary grace : I saw, at the moment of the consecration, the Three Divine Persons, amidst a resplendent cloud.*" After he had said this he fell into a rapture, and his face glowed like a seraph's. The ecstasy lasted for half an hour.[134]

This young nun, who was twenty years of age, lived in a state of perpetual spiritual joy from the time of her profession. John once asked her what was the subject of her mental prayer. She replied : the contemplation of the beauty and greatness of God. Overjoyed [135] at such an answer, he brought her, after a few days, the five last strophes of the Spiritual Canticle :

Gocémonos Amado
Y vámonos a ver en tu hermosura
Al monte y al collado
Do mana el agua pura
Entremos más adentro en la espesura.[136]

With joy, Beloved, we
Will scale the hill, and where the mountain steepens,
And in Thy beauty see
Where the living waters lie,
Pressing in further where the darkness deepens.

Can we not read through this mystical experience a desire for the mountain of Calvario and the hillside of Beas, beneath which runs a transparent river ? And, in particular, the desire of his suffering heart to go there and mirror his soul in beauty ? But the final cry bravely affirms that he will enter, *en la espesura de la Cruz :* into the darkness of the Cross,[137] there to taste of " the inexhaustible depths of the Wisdom and knowledge of God." [138]

CHAPTER XVI

GRANADA IN THE SIXTEENTH CENTURY

TERESA had said : " Wherever Anne of Jesus is, I am not required, for I know that she will act with more intelligence than I." John of the Cross, a little annoyed at his inability to obtain on his journey money for the printing of the Alcalá Constitutions,[1] and much more at his inability to bring back—" with the care and attention most certainly befitting her person and age "—" our Most Reverend and most religious Mother Teresa of Jesus," [2] was returning to establish a foundation at Granada. On the carts that had come from Andalusia for Teresa,[3] were seated Sister Antoinette of the Holy Ghost (whom John had met at Valladolid in 1568)[4] and Mother Mary of Christ, ex-Prioress of Avila, delighted at the change.[5] Beatrice of Jesus, who had been present at the double rapture of John and Teresa in the Incarnation at Avila,[6] joined them at Malagon. The little caravan arrived at Beas on December 8th, 1581, after a journey of ten days.[7]

The sisters handed Mother Anne the patent appointing her Prioress of the new convent of Granada, and ordering her to take Beatrice of St. Michael, Eleanor Baptist and Lucy of St. Joseph along with her.[8] For more than a month they held themselves in readiness to start at the least sign from the Father Vicar-Provincial, Diego of the Trinity. " This had been settled with Father John of the Cross." At last, on January 13th, 1582, the messenger brought the order.[9] " Immediately," relates Anne of Jesus, " there arose such a dreadful storm that it seemed as if the world were about to melt away beneath hail and water. I had such a violent attack of illness that they thought I was going to die. The doctors, and all who saw me, decided my departure was impossible considering the grief and the supernatural torments I was enduring. As to myself, all this only increased my courage, and I was more energetic than ever in trying to procure mules for the journey. . . . We set out on a Monday at three o'clock in the morning. All those who were leaving were overjoyed, persuaded that Our Lord would gain much glory from their journey. The weather was fine, but, on account of recent storms, the roads were so bad that our mules had great difficulty in struggling through. The two religious who accompanied us—they were Father John of the Cross and Father Peter of the Angels— discussed how to obtain the Archbishop's authorisation, and how he might be made more disposed to bid us welcome.[10]

An unpublished deposition of Juan Evangelista's tells us of John's journey to Granada, and his request for the Archbishop's permission, but Don Juan Mendez de Salvatierra gave him a very unfavourable reply, as well as some insulting remarks, and John returned without having obtained anything.[11] It was the eve of the feast of St. Sebastian. The saint's peaceful gentleness and prudence were, however, to win a victory over His Grace the Archbishop, but not in the manner they expected. God, attentive to John's efforts, took the matter in hand.[12]

The first stage had brought our nuns " to the Torre de Perogil where they left Sister Catherine of the Angels who was to become a lay-sister . . . her virtues and pious desires were known to all. The third stage brought them to Dayfontes." [13] " When we reached it on that evening," says Anne of Jesus, " we heard a frightful thunderclap. At Granada, at that very instant, the lightning struck the Archbishop's own house, quite close to his bedroom . . . it burned part of his library and killed some of his mules. . . . This event, it is said, softened him towards us. It is quite certain that no one ever remembers having seen Granada struck by lightning at that season of the year." [14] But, on the other hand, the owner of the property went back on his promise. Don Luis de Mercado, auditor of the Chancery of Granada, chatting with his sister, Doña Ana de Peñalosa, said : " . . . Since these nuns are on their way, you might as well see if they could stay in our house.

We could give them a few rooms for themselves until they find some place or other to stay." This excellent woman, who, for several years had been constantly in her oratory, where she bewailed the deaths of her husband and only daughter, at once began to feel her courage revive. She hastened to prepare her house and to make all necessary arrangements to fit up a chapel and some rooms. Everything was very nice, but small, because the house was not large.

" We arrived," Mother Anne goes on, " on the feast of SS. Fabian and Sebastian, at three o'clock in the morning. We had selected this hour so as to have greater privacy. The holy lady awaited us at the street door, where she received us with much devotion and many tears. We also wept whilst chanting a *Laudate Dominium*." [15]

A message was sent to the Archbishop's palace, and the *provisor*, Antonio Barba, arrived at seven o'clock. A little bell in the tower was rung and Mass solemnly celebrated. " Our Father John of the Cross, the first Discalced Father of the Reform, sang the Gospel, and Father Peter of the Angels sang the Epistle." [16] Others then said Mass in succession. All Granada flocked to the house as if there were a jubilee. And, the Mother says finally, " the people unanimously proclaimed that we were saints, and that God had visited the country by sending us there." [17]

As the Archbishop did not give them a *maravédi*, Teresa's daughters at once began to enjoy a life of poverty. Señora Doña Ana gave them alms, but not much, and, moreover, nobody thought about them. They were seen staying at a house which was a centre for the poor and a source of help to nearly all the monasteries and hospitals of the district; hence people imagined the nuns needed nothing. Doña Ana, seeing her guests always content and happy, did not realise the insufficiency of her gifts. Happily the Discalced Fathers sent them a little bread and fish from their monastery of " *Los Mártires*." They were themselves in want, for this was a year of famine and sterility, and Andalusia had much to suffer.[18]

The Conventuals of the Carmelite monastery *Los Mártires*, close to the Alhambra, had elected John of the Cross Prior.[19] He arrived at a bad time because they had to build, and had not enough to live on. Scarcely had he taken up office than the creditors began to clamour. " *Very well,*" said he, " *let us pay, let us satisfy these debts, even though we have nothing to eat, and have to suffer want.*" [20] And, contrary to his inclination, he went out begging. He did not, it would seem, often do so because, later on, the Vicar-Provincial had to urge him, convinced as he was that if John did not visit the nobility he could not support his community. On this occasion John took his cloak and set out, accompanied by Jerome of the Cross.[21] In the palace of the *Audiencia*,[22] in the Plaza Nueva, the Prior asked Don Pedro de Castro's " forgiveness for not having paid a visit sooner," assuring him that, in the convent, " they never ceased from committing himself and his affairs to God." The President replied that to visit or not to visit mattered very little, because, by definition, monks were men who confined their lives to their monasteries.

After this John paid two more visits to members of the *Audiencia*, who made the same remark. On their return he said to Jerome : " *What is your opinion ? Since we commit no fault by not visiting, and since these people think more highly of our retired life, let us return to the convent, remain recollected, and God will provide what is needed.*" [23]

Going to God is actually such a simple matter. And that is what he always did.

The procurators of *Los Mártires* were taught in a hard school. " Shall we not be patient, my son, for one day in which we are in need ! " and Juan Evangelista returned to his office. When, after some reflection, he came back to the saint to point out that there were invalids in the house, John reproached him with his want of confidence, and told him that, even if there were, he should remain in his cell arranging the matter with God. But dinner-time came round and Juan Evangelista returned to the charge : " Father, this is tempting God, Who wishes us to do what lies in our power. Will Your Reverence give me leave to go and seek for what is necessary ? " The Prior smiled : " *All right, go down and you will see how God confounds your lack of faith.*" The poor procurator was scarcely outside the house when he met the zelator, Bravo, who gave him twelve pieces of gold from the members of the *Audiencia.* Juan Evangelista did not remember whether they were *doblones* or *escudos.*[24]

Yes, Juan Evangelista and Agostin de San José spent sleepless nights when, on whispering their little word of alarm in the Prior's ear, after Compline, the only reply they received was an invitation to pray. But how was a man to pray tranquilly in his cell when there was nothing to offer his brothers next day but herbs from the garden ? [25] Prayer is a torture when you are burning to *do* something.

Some procurator or other went to John three times whilst he was hearing the confession of his young penitent, Doña Juana de Pedraza. Once more John replied that the procurator of his convent should be a man who hoped in God and not in his own efforts. He told Doña Juana that an alms would soon be forthcoming. As she left the monastery, she met an unknown woman bringing four ducats.[26]

Such incidents were many. Here is another. The story is told by a painter, Francisco Ruiz, who lived close to the Alhambra. Whilst he was gilding a tabernacle for the Prior, he used to have his meals in the convent. One day, on entering the refectory at mid-day, he saw that there was nothing but bread and salt on the table. But John gave such a spiritual exhortation to his religious that they were all consoled and happy, and left the table as if they had eaten an excellent meal. They had scarcely gone from the refectory when the door-bell rang. John said to the porter : " *Go and see who is ringing, brother.*" Francisco went with the brother and saw a roan mule of Don Luis de Cordoba's.[27] In one hamper were some freshly-caught fish, in the other bread, and on top of that a leather bottle of wine. The porter led in the mule, and John ordered him to cook the fish so that they might have dinner immediately.[28]

In 1584, which was such a year of dearth that the aged said that they remembered nothing like it, and there was talk of famine on all sides, the poor Prior of *Los Mártires* was able, by a divine revenge, to supply abundant succour to the needy at the convent gates, and secretly, to the poor of the upper classes. In spite of such charitable folly, there was always a small supply of wheat in store. Luis de San Angel, the refectorian, often saw the community—thirty brethren, not to mention guests—fed from this supply. The saint took no greater trouble than to send out an old lay-brother, who was so decrepit that he went around on a beast of burden, every Wednesday and Saturday, begging for a little bread. He brought back so little that there was not enough to distribute to the poor at the gate.[29] And yet, John kept on building without a pause.

.   .   .   .   .   .

When we visit to-day the beautiful gardens of M. Hubert Meersmans,* where flowers from Angers bloom side by side with tropical palms, we forget that the hill of *Los Mártires* was very bare in the days of St. John of the Cross. Under the Sultans, this cavernous hill of Ahabul was used as a convict prison : *el corral de Cautivos*. When Christian prisoners were not working, they were shut up in the *Masmoras*, conical-shaped caverns which were hollowed out, prepared, some say, by peasants,[30] and others, by Aben Alahmar,[31] for the storage of grain. In 1564 the hill was bare. On the map in the *Civitates orbis terrarum*, the hermitage, built by Isabella the Catholic in memory of the martyrs and especially of Don Pedro Pasqual, is not surrounded by foliage.[32] It had been occupied, since 1573, by Discalced Carmelite Fathers,[33] who enjoyed the favour of the Count of Tendilla and his wife, *née* Mendoza, as well as that of Don Alonso de Granada Venegas. Hence Francis of Jesus, the first vicar, was able to build a large reservoir, which received from the high white *alcázar* of the Generalifa, the fresh sparkling water destined for the cisterns of the red fortress of the *Alhambra*.[34] Afterwards, the city granted a site for a garden, which was finished as late as 1600. The vine was planted under Gabriel of the Conception. In 1580, Augustine of the Kings

---

* I desire to thank the owner of *Los Mártires* for the readiness he showed in facilitating my researches at Granada.

set about a building—*un quarto*—which he linked up with the hermitage.[35] The community was, certainly, much too closely packed together in the chaplain's small room, where, at first, " three or four beds, made of mats woven from esparto, stood side by side, with stones all round to mark the different places, and other stones to serve as pillows." [36] Augustine began with one *real* and twelve *maravedis.*

In 1582, John of the Cross paid off the debt and, as he obtained as much as he had hoped for, he went on with the building.   In his first priorship, he built an aqueduct, by which water reaches a large reservoir, and that is all that now remains of his labour.[37] John did not disdain to work himself ; he mixed lime and sand with his own hands, and made bricks.[38] Francisco de Yepes came on from Castile and, as was known, helped at the mason-work. John used to introduce him to noble visitors with : " *Sir, this is my brother whom I love most of all in the world.*" [39] We read in the *Gazetilla Curiosa* that John added new buildings to the monastery, and laid the foundations of the existing church.[40] From another trustworthy source, we learn that it was only between 1614 and 1620 that the church was erected, and the hermitage turned into a chapter room—a *De Profundis,* as the people called it.[41] Moreover, the royal chaplains were admitted, up to 1595, to celebrate the feast of SS. Cosmas and Damian in the oratory, which they had handed over to the Carmelites in 1573. These statements are contradictory, but it is possible that John built some portion of this church, since Eliseus of the Martyrs, in 1591, " built the bell-tower and placed three bells in it." The great building looked out on the Vega ; it was begun by Gregory of the Holy Angel in 1594, in a time of peace and prosperity, and was finished only in 1600. It is, therefore, certain that John never saw the Carmelite Monastery, built of grey stone from the Sierra Elvira, and shown in the engraving in *Spanish Scenery.*[42] The monastery " of the martyrs " was, in his time, a much simpler structure. It was a severe, solitary locality, " with nothing to attract the senses." [43] " I believe, Father," a visiting Provincial said jokingly, " that you are a peasant's son, since you love the country so

much." "*Why, no*," replied John, "*I am the son of a poor weaver.*" [44]

As the solitude and silence of the fields raise up the mind, so does the lovely sight of simple things ; and it is an excellent thing to love them.[45] During John's second priorship (Pentecost, 1583, to Pentecost, 1585) he had the cloister built, *un hermoso claustro*.[46] "It is certainly the most beautiful and regular of any of our Spanish convents," wrote Francis of St. Mary. "It is built of stone. Elegance is combined with solidity. The arrangement of the apertures for light is joined with such marvellous art to a tone of devotion and simplicity . . . that you never grow tired of admiring it, and always find it equally pleasing. Our venerable Father was the first to lower the height of the cloisters, because he believed that, if they were too lofty, they would be less favourable to recollection." [47] In 1588, before leaving Granada, he had pictures painted in this model cloister.[48] "St. John of the Cross's cedar," now three hundred years old, then first raised its slender column. Behind the Martyr's hill lay the Alhambra and, still higher up, the white Generalifa, the summer residence of the Sultans.

John had no love for paying visits by which something was to be gained, but he always paid such as are demanded by charity and good manners.[49] During the seven years he spent in Granada, he used to visit the Alcade of the Alhambra, where Balthazar Nieto and Gabriel of the Conception had received hospitality on their arrival in that city.[50] Gratitude would have constrained even the most unsociable hermit to do that much. The Count of Tendilla had, on one occasion, pledged the gold buttons of his doublet for the Carmelite Fathers, and Doña Catalina of Mendoza, the pearls of her ear-rings.[51] From the days of Charles the Fifth, little care had been taken of the Moorish palace. John, perhaps, closed his eyes to its beauty, for it did not, like the beauties of nature, lead him to God. "*We do not travel to see, but not to see,*" he remarked one day to a companion who was interested in the marvellous buildings of the Marquis de Santa Cruz.[52] If he wished, John was quite free to examine the great Moorish castle at his leisure.

The Alhambra ! A fortress with massive towers, "faced with red and orange," [53] an enchanted palace in which the soul may repose at its pleasure. The vegetation of the Pyrenees mingles with that of Africa. Ice-cold water from the Sierras flashes in marble fountains. Ornamented with gilt or painted stucco, looking like lace, its ramparts are encrusted, breast-high, with brilliant tiles. Slender colonnades, light and graceful arcades. On the niches of the Hall of the Ambassadors, whose windows look down on the Albaicin * and the murmuring water of the Darro far below, you read : "Whosoever cometh to me, and thirsteth, will find in me pure water, limpid, sweet and undefiled : " [54] a promise of Paradise to those ignorant of the life with God.

" This is a picture of the Paradise promised to the devout : there will be streams of incorruptible water, and rivers of milk, whose taste will never change, and rivers of wine, the delight of those who drink ; streams of limpid honey ; there will be all sorts of fruits, and the pardon of the Lord." . . . " In the gardens of delight, those most advanced, and some of the others, will repose on beds artistically arranged, and facing each other ; round about stand ever-youthful atten-dants with goblets, ewers and glasses of limpid drink. They shall not suffer headache ; it shall not make them drunk. They shall also have choice fruits, and the flesh of such birds as they may desire ; houris with large, dark eyes, like pearls, will be the reward of their faith." [55]   Is that, then, Heaven, Oh ! Father John of the Cross, you who have just come from your beautiful, humble, tranquil cloister, into this riot of florid imagery, this paradise of the senses ? Wait ! . . . When the Carmelite nuns were still living with Don Luis de Mercado, one of them saw the saint, with Doña Ana de Peñalosa, like another Magdalen, in tears at his feet : his face was upraised and he was saying : " *Nothing, nothing, nothing,—even to leaving one's very skin and all else for Christ.*" [56]

.   .   .   .   .   .

John of the Cross composed his greatest mystical works amidst surroundings which spoke of a Moslem life that had

* A quarter of the city inhabited by Moors who had come from Baeza.

gone deep and had not yet been uprooted. What was the condition of Granada at the end of the sixteenth century? It would be well to form some idea of it before beginning a chapter devoted to the " *Doctor of Los Mártires.*"

On the second day of the First Rebi of 897, Abu Abdallah, *el rey Chico*, had fled by the *Torre de los Siete Suelos*, which opens out on the hill of *Los Mártires*. On January 2nd, 1492, the Arab Kingdom of Granada fell, and with it, Musulman dominion in Spain. It had lasted for seven hundred and eighty-one years.[57]

Ferdinand and Isabella drew up conditions of capitulation which were most honourable for the vanquished. They showed themselves good rulers. In fact, the Moors of Granada exchanged masters, and that was all. Their social and religious life did not suffer from the change.[58] But, after the intervention of the Cardinal of Toledo, Ximenes Cisneros, who came to Granada " to reconcile the Elches or renegades of Granada and their children . . . and to take cognisance of cases of heresy within certain prescribed limits, and according to the procedure of the Holy Office,"[59] in the year 1500, the Moors submitted officially, and accepted baptism, on condition of a " promise to allow them the use of their own language and customs, and that they should not be submitted to the Inquisition until after a period of forty years."[60] Don Fernando de Talavera, the prudent Archbishop of Granada, himself brought about their conversion. It is reckoned that he baptised seventy thousand Moslems. " Mahomet can be found no longer in Granada," was a popular saying. And yet his law lived on in all hearts.[61]

A Moorish manuscript in the Mejanes Library at Aix-en-Provence, written in Spanish, but in Arabic characters, contains a letter of advice addressed by the Mufti of Oran to the Musulmans of Andalusia; it is dated the end of December, 1503. This theological and casuistical document was provoked by an edict published in Granada, on July 20th, 1501, and confirmed by a pragmatic sanction, on February 12th, 1502, which pronounces sentence of banishment from the kingdom on all those who still refused to receive baptism. It deals, says M. J. Cantineau, with the means of reconciling the strict obligations of Musulman law and a profession of Christianity, so that the Moors could still remain in Spain.

The doctor of Oran wrote :

" I expressly request you to maintain the law of Islam amongst you, and to teach it to such of your children as are old enough to receive it. . . . If you are prevented from saying your *Prayer*, perform at night what you should have done during the day, and it will not be imputed to you as sin. . . . And, if they force you, at the hour of *Prayer*, to bow down before idols, and be present at their rites, then purify yourself with the intention of performing your Prayer, your prayer of obligation. Bow down, when they bow down before their idols, with the intention of serving Almighty God, even though it be not in the direction of Mecca, as in the prayer of Fear, when two armies meet on the field of battle. . . . If they force you to utter *a word of abjuration* do so, if it be possible, in a contrary sense, and with secret words ; if not, speak as they speak, and let your hearts be no less firm in the religion of Islam, rejecting and denying in your heart all that they may force you to say." [62]

This letter makes the situation obvious : the Moors of Granada were simply pretending to be Christians.

After the solemn visit of Charles the Fifth, on June 5th, 1526—" when languishing *zambras* and lively *leylas* " were danced in public before His Majesty [63]—a *Junta*, presided over at Madrid, by Don Alonso Manrique, the Grand Inquisitor, began to study how to reform the Moors in Granada. " In six sessions, it was decided that the Moors should be deprived of their family names, abandon their language, learn the Castilian idiom, adapt their dress to the Spanish model, and unveil the faces of their women." There was an amnesty for the past, but no appeal for the future.[64] This decree, the execution of which was suspended for financial reasons, was re-enacted in full by an edict of Philip II, on November 17th, 1566 ; its execution provoked a conspiracy and desperate resistance on the part of the Moors. On Christmas night, 1568, in the heart of the Alpuxarras, they elected a king. A guerilla warfare ensued. Philip II grew tired, and handed over the command to Don Juan. When, on November 1st, 1570, the rebels had laid the flag and scimitar of Aben Abu at his feet, the expulsion began of all the Moors of Granada who had revolted and submitted.[65] Granada was ruined and worn out. The Vega had become barren. But the fatal policy went on. " Special tribunals were erected to judge, without further appeal, on all matters of birth and race."[66] Philip II, to tranquillise his conscience, promulgated a law, on July 20th, 1572, " which exempted from slavery boys under ten and a half years of age, and girls under nine and a half, captured in the course of the revolt, but subjected them, up to twenty, to unpaid service in devout families. . . . As no one was charged with the enforcement of this law it was almost everywhere evaded."[67] The families of the victors retained their Moorish slaves.[68] In the very heart of Granada, then, there was a whole mass of young persons, free or slave, who grew up without ever becoming Spanish, and who were Christians only on the surface.

It would seem as if there were no Moorish adults in the Albaicin. From 1571 to 1598, the Holy Office (transferred in 1526 from Jaen to Granada [69]) discovered only one Musulman, most likely the person who figured in the *auto-da-fé* in Granada on May 27th, 1593, when five Judaisers were burnt in person, and five more in effigy.[70] This, no doubt, was due to fear, which sealed their consciences and prevented them from making the slightest sign that would reveal their religion. Remember the edict : no further pardon for Moors who had emigrated, and ventured to approach within ten leagues of the Kingdom of Granada ; slavery for children from ten and a half to seventeen.[71] " A hundred lashes, four years in the galleys and, in the case of a second offence, the galleys for life, for all who carried any arms save a blunt knife, who should speak, read, write or issue decrees in Arabic, who should take Turkish baths, dance the *Zambra*, or play on Moorish instruments."[72]

" It should not be forgotten that the Sovereign Pontiffs never ceased from protesting against the line of action pursued in Spain : they always kept the door open for repentance : they constantly demanded that the Inquisition should abandon its punishments ; and on every occasion that they were asked for edicts of pardon the Popes granted them." [73]   But the Inquisitors at Granada had no need to pardon, for no one ever pleaded guilty of infidelity, not even in confession. The Moors did not believe in edicts of pardon. Underneath a Spanish and Christian mask, the sons of the three or four thousand Moors [74] whom Jimenes had baptised by aspersion—at least such as had survived persecution—always practised in the greatest secrecy the ceremonies of the Moslem religion. They fasted during the Ramadan, and celebrated the *Pascua de los alaceres o alerces* all September, withdrawing to the mountains, on the pretext of a holiday, so as to do so with greater ease. Poor folk, who had to work for a living, were in danger of being denounced, as, for instance, one Miguel Callosa of Gandia, who had been noticed fasting in the Moorish manner.[75] They carried out the ritual ablutions behind closed doors, even though the muezzin was not chanting the praises of Allah in a neighbouring minaret. Bermudez de Pedraza, a contemporary historian,[76] describes the Moor as charitable, hard-working, skilful : he had his children baptised, only to wash away immediately the sacred chrism and give them Moorish names. After a marriage had been solemnised in church they went home and put on their Moorish dress ; the forbidden musical instruments were taken from a press and they danced the *Zambra antigua.* " Since you obstinately refuse to come to Christ, know that to-day there is born in Spain one who will drive you hence," the Dominican Vargas, Apostolic Visitor of the Carmelites in Andalusia,[77] cried out prophetically at Ricla, on April 14th, 1578, the day on which Philip III was born.[78]

We may well believe that John mingled with Moors during his sojourn (nearly seven years) at *Los Mártires.* We know that the Archbishop of Granada had offered Father Balthazar Nieto a house close to the parish church of St. Gregory the

Great, at the end of the Albaicin, so that the Discalced might administer the sacraments to the Moors. "But," says Francis of St. Mary haughtily, " the obstinacy of this race, more easily conquered than subdued, the slight assistance to be hoped for in that part of the city, the difficulty of going up to the convent and down to Granada, the repugnance experienced by the inhabitants for those Christians who were only so in appearance, and whose rebellion had caused so much recent trouble, determined our Fathers to refuse this offer." [79] The Prior of the Martyrs, without going down to the Albaicin, found, at his own door, at the *barrio de Antequeruela*, the descendants of those Moors who had formerly come from Antequera.[80] The former Prior, Augustine of the Kings—although *catedrático de Santo Tomás* in the University of Granada—had not disdained to hear the confessions of " the poor and rich, *blanco o negro*, Moors and whites." [81] We cannot identify the Moors, for they bore Spanish names. Perhaps " Francisco Ruiz pintor," close to the Alhambra, was a Morisco, for they were skilled craftsmen.[82]

· · · · · ·

On August 29th, 1582, the Carmelite nuns, accompanied by the Corregidor, a few assistants and the Discalced friars,[83] departed from Doña Ana de Peñalosa's house to take up their residence in one belonging to Don Alonso de Granada y Alarcon, close to the Pilar del Toro, in the *calle Elvira*, the street of the Holy Office. For more than two years the Prior of *Los Mártires* visited them there, bringing abundant alms to his daughters, which they needed, because the warlike families of the first novices meant to reduce their indomitable children by famine, as one of them, the daughter of a captain who had fought in the Moorish rebellion, tells us.[84] *Ordinariamente*, as a rule, John heard their confessions and gave them spiritual direction, says another contemporary nun, Catherine of the Holy Ghost.[85] Mother Anne of Jesus confided in him : " She told him in confession, and out of it, all that happened to her." [86] At Beas she had consulted him about the Granada foundation, and in

Granada she summoned him and Father J. B. de Ribera, to submit an interior locution to their decision. This Jesuit and his confrère, Juan Jerónimo, heard her confessions,[87] thoroughly in the spirit of Teresa.[88] They were not the only confessors, as Anne herself relates : " It is quite true that, almost without our doing anything to that end, we had Masses and sermons from the most famous priests and preachers of the city. They were glad to hear our confessions, and to receive information as to our mode of life." [89]

It was John of the Cross, however, who guided and shaped the soul of the Prioress. Dominic Bañes was perfectly right : Anne, whose humility, prudence and religious spirit had been recognised by Teresa of Jesus, had greatly advanced in those virtues since the latter's death.[90] This had occurred on October 4th, 1582, and the saint appeared almost at once to the Prioress of Granada. John was just then commenting on his own *Spiritual Canticle* in *pláticas* delivered at the grille in the Calle Elvira. He guided the Mother's soul so straight into the heart of suffering " [91] that she wished she could always enjoy its fruit : " the pomegranates which are the mysteries of Christ." [92] Is it possible that the consideration and intuition of Our Lord Jesus Christ, recommended by Anne in a letter to novices dated March 8th, 1605, can be fundamentally opposed to the *Sanjuanista* doctrine, traces of which were observed by St. Francis de Sales in the Carmelite Convent of Dijon, after Anne of Jesus had stayed there ? [93]

In response to a wish of the great Prioress, John of the Cross gave, in writing, not exactly his own experiences, but a general explanation, *alguna luz en general*, of those stanzas " composed in a state of love, under the influence of an abundant mystical illumination. Anne was, by divine grace, no longer a beginner, and the practice of mystical theology is never far from those who have come to a knowledge of it by love." [94] John, in his prologue to the *Living Flame*, composed at the same period,[95] did not give a like testimony to his spiritual daughter, Ana de Peñalosa, who had asked him to write that work. And yet, though Ana had been inconsolable until the arrival of the Carmelite nuns in her

house, " she had henceforth endured her sufferings joyously and easily, and even desired more." [96]

The teaching of St. John of the Cross, though primarily intended for the Carmelite friars and nuns of the Reform, is not esoteric. The Doctor of *Los Mártires* sowed the divine grain with such a lavish hand that he has been declared a doctor of the Universal Church by His Holiness Pius XI.[97] In the city of Granada, at the close of the sixteenth century, his influence was already undeniable. He was an apostle ; and it is only doctrines of exclusively intellectual interest that are not preached. " His doctrine," as Teresa had said,[98] " is life and charity." We are ignorant of the influence exercised by the Prior on the University life of Granada, in which the Carmelites had taken part ever since, by order of Angel de Salazar, Augustine of the Kings had taught theology there.[99] We are free to imagine Father John of the Cross and the celebrated negro scholar, Juan Latino, conversing together strolling along the Vega, the latter consoling himself in his declining years and bitter distress, by the company of the Doctor of Light.[100] We can be more confident about his apostolate in the numerous convents of the city, which weighed so heavily on the Archbishop's shoulders ! He directed the two " *beaterios* " close to *Los Mártires*, one of " *las Madres Potencianas*," and the other of " *Melchoras*," and the holy foundress, Potenciana of Jesus, had the benefit of his advice.[101]

" The charity of this servant of God for his neighbour was great. Some he withdrew from vice, correcting and inspiring respect in them by a mere glance. He enkindled divine love in those with whom he had to deal or meet, gently leading them on towards perfection : he helped them without ever growing tired, athirst as he was for the salvation of souls. . . Luis de San Angel often saw him beset by scrupulous and tormented persons who wearied others who would not listen to them ; but John heard and consoled them, never growing weary, and with such graciousness as to make one bless Our Lord for it. To conclude, he received, consoled, strengthened and rejoiced, without respect of persons, all who had recourse to him, both religious and seculars, and they were many, and of all sorts and conditions." [102]

His apostolate was universal, and all the more efficacious for its profundity. The wretched are far from being insensible to the living waters that flow from the heights, provided the charity of Christ be the canal. He who tenderly called Juana de Pedraza : *hija mía en el Señor*, and who sent her the magnificent letter dated October 12th, 1589,* which all spiritual persons should read in seasons of discouragement ; he whose words were imprinted on the

---

* " Jesus be in your soul ! and thanks be to Him for having confided it to me that, as you say, I may not forget the poor in taking my ease. I am very much annoyed to think that you believe such a thing is possible. It would be very wrong, after so many kindnesses received, when I least deserved them. There could be nothing more unlikely than that I should forget you.

" Consider what takes place in a soul in your present state. As you are walking in the darkness and emptiness of spiritual poverty, you think that all things and persons are failing you ; that is not surprising, since it also seems to you that God is failing you. Nevertheless, you want for nothing ; do not speak of anything ; do not say anything ;—you would not know what to say—all you feel is but a fear without a foundation. He who wishes for nothing but God walks not in darkness, even should he see himself still more obscure and poorer ; he who is no longer inspired with his own views, his own personal tastes, in regard to God or creatures, he who knows not his own will in this or that, has nothing to keep him back, and nothing to ask for. You are in an excellent way, abandon yourself, and rejoice. Who are you to dare take care of yourself? Dear soul, you would still be troubled. You could never be better than now, for you have never been so humble and submissive, you have never had so little esteem for self and all earthly things. You would never have known either how wretched you are, or how good God is ; you have never served God with so much purity and disinterestedness as you are doing to-day. You are not dragged back by imperfection of your own will and your self-interest, as you were, perhaps, of old.

" What do you desire ? What kind of life, what sort of earthly activity are you dreaming of ? What idea are you forming of the service of God, if not to abstain from evil, to keep His commandments, and carry out His wishes, as well as possible ? If you have that, what need have you of other ideas, of other lights, and other attractions, acquired here and there, a perpetual source of perils and dangers to the soul, which is deceived and fascinated by its own lights, and led astray by its own powers ? It is, therefore, a great favour from God when He so darkens and impoverishes the soul that it no longer deceives itself. And if there be no error, what, then, remains to be done, but walk in the sure way of God's faith, and His Church's, living in complete, obscure faith, in a firm hope, and in the fulness of charity, and then awaiting our good from on high, living here below like travellers, poor, banished, orphans, thirsty, gone astray, with all our hopes there on high ? Rejoice, and rest on God, for He has given you proofs that that is how you should act ; otherwise, one may foresee Him growing angry with you, because of your foolishness, since He is leading you by the best of all ways, and establishing you in a sure and certain place. Desire nothing but this way, calm your soul, because it is good ; go to communion as usual ; and to confession, when you have something definite to tell, and you need ask for nothing else. When you need anything, write to me,

heart of " maestro Juan Sanchez Mirano," a descendant of
the Conquistadores of Spain,[103] found, we may well suppose,
words of fire and love for the poor baptised Moors of the
Antiqueruela, when they met him on the slope of *Los
Mártires*. His faith was so ardent that it rekindled theirs.
Who shall tell us of the real conversions wrought by John of
the Cross amongst those nominal Spaniards, constantly
threatened by the Inquisition ? Balthazar of Jesus saw him
regularly hearing " the confession of a *mulata* named
Potentiana, and other poor persons. He made no distinction between them and the rich who came to seek his
advice." [104] One day after his death, Peter of the Mother of
God, who was staying in a *venta* at Alcalá la Real, summoned
a poor slave woman and, showing her a relic of the saint
which he wore round his neck, said to her : " Fatima, what
does this flesh tell you ? " And she answered, " Oh ! what
a lovely Lady, and what a sweet Child may be seen
there ! " [105] And she called another slave to see it.

The Arab, as a rule, cannot abide learned processes of
reasoning. What he needs, in order to believe, is to see
living images of Jesus Christ. In the case of the children
of Islam, even more perhaps than in that of the Chinese,
one should recognise the fact that they are inclined to solitude, prayer, and contemplation, as His Holiness Pope
Pius XI remarks in his Encyclical *Rerum Ecclesiae*.[106] Hence,
those who are continuing Father de Foucauld's work believe,
with the Pope, that Islam will only be converted by contemplatives. Here is the answer to the anxiety of St. Louis
who, when he lay dying, asked : " Whom shall we send
to Tunis ? " In the convert hulks of Tunis, Father Jerome
Gracian, promotor of Carmelite Missions, was branded with
red-hot iron, and suffered a fearful imprisonment.[107]

and write often and quickly, making use of Doña Ana, in default of the
nuns.
" I have been rather unwell, but am now better, but Brother John Evangelist
is sick. Recommend him to God, and also myself, my daughter in the Lord.
" BROTHER JOHN OF THE CROSS."
Segovia,
October 12th, 1589. (Letter XIV, p. 170.)

The sons of Elias descended one day from Mount Carmel, with the multi-coloured *morraqq' ah* on their shoulders,[108] hoping to win back the East from Mohammed. To that Biblical promontory where their fellow religious, in 1291, were struck down by the scimitar as they sang the *Salve Regina*, *[109] they brought back the faith in 1631. They also evangelised Persia (1607), Mesopotamia (1623) and, in 1731, encamped at Bagdad, the old intellectual capital of Mohammedan Asia where (the Mohammedan mystic) Al Hallaj had suffered—Bagdad, " the gift of God," [110] which has never since been abandoned by the Discalced Carmelite Fathers of France.[111]

* This incident occurs in none of the extant manuscripts, and appears to be an interpolation. (B.Z.)

CHAPTER XVII

THE DOCTOR OF " LOS MARTIRES "

AT the end of the street of the Holy Office and the Carmelites stands the superb, horseshoe-shaped Moorish arcade of the *Puerta Elvira* ; to the right, along the Arab wall, over which towers Santa Isabel la Real, is *la cuesta de Alacaba*. It is the district of El' Oqâb. About 1215, the Musulman philosopher, Ibn Sab'in, on his arrival in Granada, alighted there, and stayed with some religious who had made a vow of poverty, *al foqarâ*.[1]

Even under the Catholic Kings and the *régime* of the Inquisition, the place remained a centre of profound Musulman life. About the end of the sixteenth century, el Mancebo de Arevalo travelled through Spain, observing the wretched situation of his co-religionists and receiving from them the teachings of the ancients.[2] He arrived at Granada and, on the Prophet's birthday (the feast of Mulud), paid a visit to *La Mora de Ubeda*, close to the *Puerta Elvira*.[3]

" This Moorish woman was leading a retired life, overshadowed by poverty, bewailing the fall of Islam. . . . It was a period of decay for all Moslems. . . She no longer left her house, only prayed sitting, and did not fast at Ramadan. . . . She was very old, ninety-three years of age. She was so tall and large-limbed as to cause astonishment. I have never seen her equal, and "—el Mancebo goes on—" I have never met anyone who saw such an enormous woman, and I shall say nothing further about her strangeness except that her little finger is larger than my middle one. She was dressed in serge and wore *alpargates* of esparto-grass. . . . She never married, and no one ever remembers her to have known man. . . . She had no heirs, all having disappeared at the fall of Granada. She had one niece, a daughter of her sister's, to whom she had given a third of her fortune, and no more, because she maintained that a woman cannot dispossess herself, in her life-time, of more than a third of her possessions, if she is in good health and over eighty years old. The same holds true of a man over ninety. . . . But either may leave a fortune to those entrusted with the duty of teaching. And she suggested to me that, if I wished to remain with her, she would make me heir to her books and possessions—she had quite sufficient for herself. But, as my covetousness was not of the Spanish sort, I did not wish to accept."

The *Mora* of Ubeda did not "speak elegantly. Her phrases were harsh and her tone of voice common. But, for instructive ideas, her like could not be found amidst the whole world of scholars. . . . Doctors came to pay her compliments on great festivals, and at other stated times. But what enhanced her fame, above all, was the strong affection she manifested towards everyone, and this was not due to any natural gift but to divine providence." . . . If " she was unlettered, yet she reasoned with such good sense and judgment, that it is impossible to say how much light she threw upon our honoured Koran. . . . Great was her power of divination. . . . All Granada and its environs were ruled by what she said.[4] The people declared that she was highly esteemed above all those of her country for her knowledge of our law and customs. . . . She was well known to all nations, because she showed me," says El Mancebo, "letters from the four rites of our law, not to speak of others from great muftis and scholars."

El Mancebo de Arevalo remained with the Mooress until the day of the moon of *Rabia el ahar* (that is to say, for a month), and afterwards regretted that he had not stayed for a year.

The presence of this woman, who believed that it was her mission " to make her religion resplendent "[5] in Granada, to suffer, and even die in its defence, and, in any case, her undoubted influence over " the whole region " just when the prior of *Los Mártires* was still writing the *Ascent of Mount*

Carmel and the *Dark Night*,* is, certainly remarkably interesting, if we bear in mind that the two works of which an
analysis was given, when we were dealing with the period
when John had begun to write them, contain, as we shall
see, a criticism of Illuminism, and that Spanish Illuminism
is largely indebted to Musulman spiritual influence. Now,
says El Mancebo, " the Moorish woman of Ubeda closely
followed the doctrine of Mohammed Algazel." [6]

Al Gāzzāli—1059–1111—the *doctor communis* of Islam, is,
even to this day, a theological authority of the first rank in
Mecca, the University of Al Azhar at Cairo, and La Madraza
at Fez.

Avicenna, who had introduced Greek philosophical tradition to Islam, was twenty-two years dead. Algazel, who
held a chair in the Academy of Bagdad, interrupted his
teaching in order to practise solitude in the neighbourhood
of the mosques of Damascus and Jerusalem. He tells us
himself in his *Munqid* [7] that he found it hard to experience
ecstatic illumination ; and Ibn' Arabi, in the thirteenth
century, recalls a very curious passage, in which Algazel
attributes the imperfection of his mystical revelations to his
philosophical studies. [8] He explains this in the Ihyā', a
theological *Summa*, which he finished at Bagdad on his
return to that city : all knowledge acquired by the exercise

* Juan Evangelista, who states that he took the habit at Granada a year and
a half after the saint's election as prior (Andres, 13482, B. 26) bears witness to
the fact that he saw John compose, at Granada, the *Subida*, the *Noche*, the
Cántico and the *Llama*. Moreover, he states that the *Subida* and *Noche* were
composed gradually and with frequent interruptions. (Andres, 13482, B. 25.)
Later, in a letter from Granada to Jerome of St. Joseph (18 Feb. 1630), he says
definitely that, as far as the composition of the saint's work at Granada is
concerned, " what is certain, *lo que es sin duda*, is that the stanzas *Adónde* . . .
and the *Llama* were written here, because he began and finished them in my
time." " As for the *Subida*," he goes on, " I found that it was begun when I
came to take the habit. . . . But there is no doubt that he wrote the *Noche*
here, because I saw him compose part of it : *porque le vide escribir parte de ella*."
And he now adds that he took the habit at Christmas, 1582 (Andres, 13482,
B. 26)—Innocent of St. Andrew, the saint's companion at Calvario, Baeza
and Granada (Baeza P.A. f. 131) tells us that, whilst they were living together
John at his request, composed the *Noche* : *uno de ellos lo hizo estando el con el,
y viviendo juntos, y a peticion suya el qual comienza*—en una Noche Obcura [*sic*]
(Andres, 13482, B. 3).

of the inductive or deductive reason is an obstacle to the reception of infused knowledge ; a person ignorant of the profane sciences is better fitted to receive illumination than the philosopher or the *faqih*. And he then shows how pure ideas, engraven upon the eternal scroll of destiny, are unable to reflect themselves upon the mirror of the soul except its surface is perfectly clear, free from all stain and sin, and except the veil of sensations has been raised. " It is a theory of mystical illumination," according to Sr. Asín Palacios, " in which Plotinian elements [9] seem to be combined with ideas taken from the Gospel. These ideas were, in fact, quite well known to Al Gāzzāli : *Beati mundo corde, quoniam ipsi Deum videbunt* " (Ihyā', iii, 237).

But let us not be led astray : Christian ideas, such as these, which we also find in the mouth of the Moorish woman, were incorporated into Musulman theology, yet this did not suffice to make Algazel's mysticism a true one.

The *sufi** may excel in the practice of voluntary poverty, because Jesus, the prophet, has said : " Lay not up to your-selves treasures on earth : where the rust and moth con-sume " (Matt. vi. 19), and because He answered the rich young man : " If thou wilt be perfect, go sell what thou hast, and give to the poor " (Matt. xix. 21).[10] He may offer no resistance, because Jesus, the Son of Mary, has declared : " You have heard that it hath been said : a tooth for a tooth, a nose for a nose (*sic*). But I say to you not to resist evil with evil ; but if one strike thee on thy right cheek, turn to him also the left " (Ihyā iv. 52) [11] ; still, it is none the less true that the " infused science " which he expects from contemplation is obtained by psychological and physiological means, deriving from Syrian Gnostics or Hindu Yogis. No doubt, Algazel regarded ecstasy as a supernatural effect of divine grace ; but this is of no avail, since, contrary to the methods of prayer employed by Catholic mystics, the " exercises " which he suggests, ter-minate, not only in occasional abnormal and morbid states, but in the highest degree of *fana* : an absolute state of unconsciousness on the part of the subject.

* From *souf* (woven). The man clothed in wool, the religious, the hermit.

If the method of reciting the *Pater Noster*, in the *Exercises of St. Ignatius*, recalls at times a breathing exercise,[12] it has quite another object in view, and does not terminate in such excesses as the *hou ! hâ ! hâ !* of modern Islamic confraternities. Based as these are on a state of exaltation, they lead individuals only into actions belonging wholly to the natural order, precious material in the devil's hands !

In Carmel, the religious never for a moment imitates the *sufi* " seated on the ground and repeating the word ' Allah ' until his tongue ceases to move and the word issues from his lips without the motion of the tongue, the very lips are still, and the image of the word abides in the heart alone ; nay, more, . . . until the sensible image of the name is effaced from the heart, and all that remains alive is the idea of its signification, by means of such a powerful suggestion that the spirit can think of no other object " (Ihyā, iii, 15, 17). The word for this has been found, it is auto-suggestion. And if the " sons of the prophets," in the Old Testament, danced to the sound of instruments,[13] as did the monks whom Cassian saw in the monasteries of Egypt,[14] how far can that be likened to the *assāma*, in which the initiates, grouped round the singer (qawwāl), at first remain seated, with rigid limbs and heads bent towards the ground, until the violent excitement provoked by the music grips them and makes them applaud and dance till they lose consciousness ? [15] Such mysticism is either natural or diabolic : it is certainly not supernatural.

Even if the " mystical " states of sufis had certain apparent analogies with those of Catholic contemplatives, they would not be supernatural, because, in sound philosophy, the object is what gives the act its specification. Gāzzāli is not a pantheist, his prayer is not, like that of Plotinus, a magical pressure of the soul on the divine elements of a cosmic world in which all things are in sympathy [16] ; still, it leads us only to the confines of creation, because his God, the God of Mahomet, remains inaccessible to the faithful. It may, perhaps, be true that the latter " digs down into, and hollows out, the foundations of his heart, by sweeping away all earthly cares," and thus, " will see pouring in a know-

ledge that will completely fill it," [17] but will he discover the
hidden root that supports it? [18] I know not, but what I do
know is that God,—unless, indeed, touched by the child of
Ismail's good faith and purity, He should convert him,—
will not give the son of the bondswoman a share in His own
inner life.*

In Gāzzāli's case, the mystical problem depends on a
monotheistic theology, systematically ignoring the Trinitarian dogma.[19]

Before examining the diabolical results that a false
mysticism could produce in sixteenth-century Granada, and
the masterly practical fashion in which John countered it,
let us see how the *Spiritual Canticle* and the *Living Flame of
Love*, those two great Trinitarian works of the Doctor of Los
Mártires, written at Granada, are opposed to the pure
divine unity professed by Algazel. The higher sciences are
their own defence. To set out the theological doctrine of a
master is at once to teach and refute. It is the apologetic of
the Saints.

.   .   .   .   .   .

Father John had still kept his scanty,[20] torn and patched
habit of coarse serge.[21] After the discipline, which he took

---

* Granted a Mahommedan's good faith and conversion to the unchangeable
good, and also his recognition of a Divine Saviour—especially since he invokes
the God of Abraham in his daily prayers and burial and marriage ceremonies—
he might come to make an act of living faith and, thus justified, be enabled to
accomplish true mystical acts. Undoubtedly, there might come to such a
person a conversion to the unchangeable good, and an interior promise made
to God to sin no more, either against the natural law or that of his own conscience. Still, unfortunately, the saying of *Hadith* must be remembered : " I
place my happiness in women and perfumes, and my pleasure in prayer."
Mystical charismata, such as miracles and martyrdom, are proofs of the omnipotent sanctity of the Church. (L. de Grandmaison, *Recherches de Science religieuse*,
January–April, 1922.) Father Arintero saw this when he incorporated his
Evolución mística in his *Desenvolvimiento y Vitalidad de la Iglesia*. (Salamanca,
1908.) Hence, God will not permit miracles, or even charismatic manifestations in circumstances where error might gain credit from them. (Ami du
Clergé, 1900, pp. 117, etc. ; 1929, pp. 81, etc.) Moreover, true mystics quickly
fly from corrupt surroundings ; the authentic marks of the Spirit, therefore, do
not habitually run the risk of bearing witness to error. The case of *Al Hallaj,
mystical martyr of Islam, executed at Bagdad on March 26th*, 922 (L. Massignon,
Paris, 1922) is exceptional. The celebrated remark of St. Irenaeus may,
perhaps, be fittingly applied to him. May not Al Hallaj have been " an
addition to the glorious army of witnesses to Christ ? " *Velut adjectio quaedam
donata eis.* (Adv. Her. IV, 33, 9–10. P.G., VII, 1078.)

habitually, he resumed the worn tunic, which he only laid aside when it was in ribbons, but which was always free from vermin.[22] He rested " his little beast," [23] for two or three hours, on a plank bed, between two white coverlets.[24] He rose earlier than the others,[25] at once made himself neat and clean,[26] and went off to the corner of a staircase from which he could see a vast expanse of sky and countryside.[27] This corner meant more to him than the *mirador* of the Generalifa, surrounded by palm trees, and embowered in dense myrtles, where the soul is enchanted by the sound of murmuring waters.[28] This nook on a staircase was not so high, but more favourable to recollection.

Through the marvellously clear and rarefied air, he saw at his feet the Vega, whither he was wont to lead his religious for recreation.[29] . . . The oleanders bloomed there amid hedges of fig, pistachio and pomegranate trees.[30] One day, on reaching the bank of the Genil or Darro, he called his companions : " *Come, my brethren, and see how these little animals, God's creatures, praise Him. Lift up your minds ; and, since creatures without reason or intelligence do so, have we not a far greater obligation to praise Him ?* " On saying this, he fell into a rapture. His sons wandered away, scattering through the garden, and leaving him to his contemplation.[31]

Was this a cosmic ecstasy in which " God is not given me apart from things, in which God and things are given me simultaneously " ? *

Certainly not. John of the Cross is not a quasi-pantheist. Creatures simply recalled him to God because their Creator " had clothed them in beauty." [32]

Like those great contemplatives, the hermits of Mount Carmel, John believed that human things do not lead us to God as much as His own natural works. Luis de San Angel states expressly that it was John " who introduced the custom of going out to the *huerta* to make mental prayer amongst the trees." [33] " The servant of God, full of love of heaven, devoted himself with such great fervour to prayer that he might be seen diligently seeking secret spots, favourable to contemplation. And thus, at the hour for evening

* Baruzi, p. 668.

meditation, *de prima noche*, which he introduced into his Order, he used to go into the garden, and made his religious do likewise, amidst the trees in the great solitude around the Convent of Granada. There they remained with great devotion and tranquillity, and, at morning prayer he led them out into a little garden which was further within the enclosure." [34]

John of the Cross, up earlier than the rest, kept vigil, hidden away in his little corner. He was the *passer solitarius in tecto*. A sparrow of plain, drab plumage, alone on the highest peak of contemplation, singing in his soul, that is ever turned towards love ! [35] No longer through a dark night do you seek Him, " burning with anxious love." [36] Since Toledo your impatient love could no longer bear the babbling of creatures. [37]

> *La noche sosegada*
> *En par de los levantes de la aurora,*
> *La música callada,*
> *La soledad sonora . . .*

> The night's deep peaceful mood,
> And dim approaching dawn's first orient rays ;
> The singing solitude,
> A symphony of praise. [38]

Such is your Well-Beloved. To you " the clear morning light of knowledge " has already come. [39]

The great nocturnal language of the *Subida* and the *Noche* [40] were vanishing as " the *canciones*, that tell of the love between the soul and Christ her spouse," were being kindled in the fires of dawn. [41]

During those days of 1584, [42] when he had, as I imagine, celebrated the votive Mass *de Trinitate*, to which he had a great devotion, *devotísimo in extremo*, [43] the Prior of *Los Mártires* quickly retired to his cell. Completely absorbed, because " love lives where it loves," [44] he had not noticed those who kissed his scapular. [45] His brown face shone resplendently. [46] He admitted : " *God communicates the mystery of the Trinity to this sinner in such a way that if His Majesty did not strengthen my weakness by a special help, it would be impossible for me to live.*" [47] And he began to write on his knees,* having nothing else in his cell, which was "the humblest in the house," [48] but a crucifix, a picture of the Blessed Virgin, a table and stool and, for his books, only a breviary, the Bible, Saint Augustine *Contra Gentes* (*sic*) and a *Flos Sanctorum*.[49] In case he needed any other book, " he borrowed it from the library and returned it immediately." [50] He knew the Bible almost entirely by heart, and the copy which he used was no more his own than his note-book,[51] which, indeed, he gave away.[52] He studied his Bible " in the most solitary spots of *Los Mártires*," [53] and expounded the depths of a gospel or psalm in long and frequent *pláticas*.[54] Juan Evangelista heard him explaining texts of Scripture hundreds of times, and even more, *infinitas veces*.[55] During recreation his friars asked him : " ' Father, what does the Holy Ghost mean in this chapter, or in this passage of Holy Scripture ? ' And he answered in sublime fashion, as if he had been studying that very passage for several days." [56] As he was a scholastic, he was, no doubt, a good theologian, but all agreed in saying that he was aided by a special light from on high in his explanations of the Scriptures.[57]

We may say, in truth, that Jesus Christ was John's text-book.[58] His soul was enamoured of Christ, and desired to be united with Him in a clear and essential vision.[59] It had drunk, in that secret cellar, of the wine mingled with perfumes,[60] the wine that endureth, the wine that flows through, and penetrates all the veins and members ; the substance of his soul was athirst for God ; the understanding absorbed knowledge and wisdom ; the will a most gracious love, and the memory, pleasure, delightful remembrances and glory.[61]

How wonderful the glory of that transformation ! God and the soul are but one, like the crystal and the ray, the coal and the fire, the brightness of the sun and stars.[62] But mere words cannot express it, and the Holy Spirit is needed to grasp the hand and move the pen.[63] . . . Who, indeed, can write what God teaches those living souls, in

---

* The Venerable Anne of Jesus said that the saint wrote the Spiritual Canticle " entirely on his knees : *todo le escribió de rodillas*." Andrés, 13482, B. 22.)

whom He dwells ? Who can express in words what He causes them to experience and desire ? No one, assuredly, not even those souls themselves. Imagery, comparisons and symbols, express something of what they feel. Out of the abundance of their spirit they pour forth mystical secrets, rather than declare them by reasonings.[64] Who can still doubt that the Saint of Carmel first lived the life of transforming union, before giving expression to it ? His secretary and confidant, Juan Evangelista, saw John of the Cross " composing and writing " his works ; and Father John " did not employ books, but all he wrote was written from the experimental knowledge which he had lived." [65]

At the request of Anne of Jesus, John wrote a commentary on his *Spiritual Canticle*,[66]—surely not " an extraordinary impoverishment of the poem." *

In the *Subida* and *Noche* he celebrated the created, supernatural element in the theological virtues and gifts ; in the *Canticle*, as in the *Living Flame of Love*, he glorified the uncreated supernatural, " the Word together with the Father and the Holy Ghost . . . hidden in the inmost centre of the soul." " And yet (John warns us) he who wishes to find [Our Lord] should withdraw himself in desire from all created things, and enter into a most profound recollection in the depths of self, making no more account of all created things than if they had no existence. St. Augustine cried out in his soliloquies : ' O Lord, I sought Thee amiss, and deceived myself ; seeking Thee without, whilst Thou wast within me.' " [67]

This secret, restless, incessant search for the hidden God, daring to the point of possessing Him, is the theme of the *Canticle*, which, as far as love is concerned, may be placed on a level with Solomon's.[68] How can one know one loves ? The soul may easily recognise whether or not it loves God. If it loves it has no longer any heart for itself, but only for Him. . . . When the heart is truly ravished, it experiences agonies . . . ; it cannot be at peace or repose without possession.[69] " The hurt " is slight, the " wound " profound. O the light of His eyes ! [70] Then comes the first

* Baruzi, 360.

equality of love which sets itself free in ecstasy.[71] And the plaintive prayer : "Withdraw those divine eyes."[72] But He approaches swiftly, for He, too, is wounded with the same wound.[73] The ecstatic flight takes place in the very breath of love which operates within the bosom of the Trinity. This panting after fresh waters attracts Christ.[74] Here are the gifts of spiritual espousals : the Spirit teaches like a torrent of glory,[75] offers food that invigorates,[76] and communicates the strength of a lion.[77] The virtues blossom like flowers : mountain flowers, lilies of the valley, roses from far-off lands ; heroic virtues, flowers of early morning.[78]

De flores y esmeraldas
En las frescas mañanas escogidas
Haremos las guirnaldas
En tu amor florecidas
Y en un cabello mío entretejidas.

Fresh with the morning dew,
Sweet blossoms we cull, and emeraldry rare,
For in thy love they grew,
And weave a garland fair,
Bound with one strand of thy beloved's hair.[79]

This is the braid of charity. And "vehement" desire increases within an intimacy that knows no bounds. The soul desires, in the deepest solitude, to gather with Him "sheaves of roses."[80] The south wind, "that enkindles love," wafts the perfumes of the virtues, for which the Well-Beloved hungers.[81] This is the second equality of love,[82] consummated union.[83] It is the season of fruitfulness.[84] The soul lives no longer, but Christ lives in it. It acquires His own true beauty. "I shall be thyself in thy beauty, and thou wilt be myself in thy beauty."[85]

The adoption of the children of God is consummated. Now, in proportion as the soul is a child of God, God sends the Spirit of His Son into the heart. And the Spirit draws in the soul into the Father and the Son. . . . He renders the soul capable of breathing in God with the same breath of love that exists between the Father and the Son, and is none other than Himself, Love. The deiform soul, united to the Trinity, is God by participation. It is the accomplishment in men of the Gospel promise of the eternal *In Unum*. Souls, created for such greatness, and invited to it, what are you doing ? How do you occupy yourselves ? Your demands are abjectness, and your possessions destitution.[86]

The *Living Flame*, composed in a fortnight,[87] at the request of Doña Ana de Peñalosa, also treats of the highest degree of perfection that may be attained in this life, the transformation of the soul in God ; it thus describes " a love better qualified and more perfect." [88]   This love is like a billet of wood put into a furnace.   Already drained dry of its tears and shrivelled, it is first of all united to the fire and transformed into it ; but, in time, as the fire burns up, the wood also grows warmer, becomes incandescent, and throws out its own flames and sparks.   It is of this degree of love that the soul is here speaking.[89]   It suffers no longer : the *Llama de amor viva* is no longer to be dreaded, " it consumes, but does not torment." [90]   Henceforward the soul's acts are flames, which shoot up with all the greater force, for the fire of union is more intense, and the will more ravished and absorbed in the flame of the Holy Spirit.[91]   Under the special impulse of God these acts are divine.[92]   From them results an enjoyment of eternal life.   When the soul is absorbed in Wisdom the Spirit of Love sends forth His glowing flames.[93]   The whole Trinity is at work.   The burning is attributed to the Holy Ghost.   He, who could destroy a thousand worlds more easily than fire does a thread, does not annihilate the soul.   His fiery purgation is sweet.[94]   The wound, the Seraph's intoxicating wound,[95] is attributed to the Word.   Let there but be in the depths of this wound the minutest mustard seed that is inflammable to the circling flame and it will be living seas of fire.[96]   The making of actual contact is attributed to the Father : the touch of substance with substance : *toque de sustancia*, such as many saints have experienced in this life.   John did not care to speak of it, " for there are no words to explain and give names to divine things as lofty as these, which take place in these souls.   For them, the only appropriate language is personal hearing and tasting ; to be silent and enjoy, when one has the happiness of receiving them." [97]   These are

precious avowals of a personal experience. How could John's early historians place the date of " the spiritual marriage " so late? [98] But I have already said why I disagree with them. The indications discoverable in *The Living Flame* confirm the data of the *Canticle* discussed above. And John, strengthened by God, enters into a new stanza :

O lámparas de fuego

The lamps are the attributes of God.[99]

Las profundas cavernas del sentido.

The caverns are the soul's faculties : the memory, understanding and will.[100] Emptied and purified, they experience an intolerable hunger and thirst for God.[101] Abyss calleth to abyss. *Fiat lux.* And the caverns are marvellously and ravishingly immersed in the admirable splendours of the divine lamps. Illuminated and inflamed in God, and not content with an offering of themselves to Him, they reflect back, on and in God, the splendours they have received, glorifying Him in their love. They tend towards Him, all engulfed as they are within Him. They become, in their turn, burning lamps, amidst the splendours of those that are divine.[102]

The symbol of " the lamps and the cavern " may be found in outline in the Koran : " God is the light of the heavens and the earth, his light is like a niche in a wall." [103] The Moorish woman of Ubeda must have been familiar with it. She also knew that her master, Mohammed Algazel, entitled one of his treatises *Mishkat Al-Anwar* : the niche for lights.[104] The lights here symbolise, as they do for John, the divine attributes : " Power and Glory, both lights of Allah." [105] This is a curious and interesting fact, but one that should not unduly surprise us, when we reflect that the Moslem doctor, as well as the Doctor of Los Mártires, could find the imagery of the lamps in the *Canticle of Canticles* : *Lampades ejus, lampades ignis atque flammarum*,[106] and also that of the caverns : *in foraminibus petrae, in caverna maceriae.*[107] No doubt a search would reveal other points of similarity. It is possible that John may have had the

Mishkat in his hands ; and still more likely that he may have read some passages of Ramon Martin's *Pugio Fidei*. In addition, we may remember that the Arab tradition was still living in Granada. But what matters a similar vocabulary, if the content is, as we have seen, essentially different ? We employ, in ordinary conversation, formulas used by other persons with a quite different signification. The Doctor of Los Mártires has dealt, in the language of genius, with the Inner Life of God, of which Gāzzāli had not the faintest idea. We reach, with the saint, the heart of the mystery in our own inner selves.

> ¡ *Cuán manso y amoroso*
> *Recuerdas en mi seno*
> *Donde secretamente solo moras :*
> *Y en tu aspirar sabroso*
> *De bien y gloria lleno*
> *Cuán delicadamente me enamoras !*

How gently, tenderly,
In my heart dost Thou awake,
Where Thou alone has made Thy secret nest !
And in Thy breath's fragrancy,
Of gifts and glory make (so delicately !)
Love stir in my breast ! [108]

This " awakening " is a movement produced by the Word in the substance of the soul with such power, greatness and glory, with such an intimate sweetness, that it seems to the soul as if all the perfumes, aromas and flowers of this world mingle their scents together, as if kingdoms and empires, the powers and virtues of heaven were moved. All the virtues, substances, perfections and graces of all creatures shine out in all their splendour and unite together in one harmony. St. John said : " All things were made by Him : and without Him was made nothing that was made. In Him was life." And the Apostle added : " In Him we live and move and have our being." [109] What a joy to know creatures through God, and not the Cause through His effects ! And the saint believes that, at this moment of awakening, God draws aside some of the manifold intervening veils and curtains.[110]

John thus concludes *The Living Flame of Love* : " I would

rather not speak ; indeed I will be silent concerning it, for I see clearly that I am unable to talk of it, and what I could say would make it seem less than it is." [111] It is heaven on earth, and how can that be expressed ? . . .

Brother Albert of the Virgin, the porter of Los Mártires, was on his death-bed. " His countenance was inflamed, and sent forth, as it were, a ray of heavenly light, which made it so marvellously beautiful that all were enraptured at the sight, and shed silent tears of consolation . . ." Brother Albert suddenly cried aloud : " Ah ! I have seen it. Ah ! I have seen it. Ah ! I have seen it," and, lowering his arms, folded them upon his breast. As he was about to close his eyes, our Venerable Father John of the Cross hastened to ask him : " Brother Albert, what have you seen ? " And he answered : " Love, love," and remained in an ecstasy.[112]

.   .   .   .

Baruzi thinks that " a more vital synthesis has been accomplished (in St. John of the Cross) than, perhaps, in any other Catholic mystic, because, to an intense love of a God who is Father, Son and Holy Ghost, there is joined a pure adhesion to the essential divinity, to the ' deity ' and, even though the term is not found in his vocabulary, to the ' One.' "

What right has philosophy to meddle here ? * Are prayer, contemplation, the Christian life itself, mere functions of knowledge, and a knowledge loved for its own sake ? It would be a barren, a radically irreligious, and amoral idealism. The attitude of the saints is absolutely different. Love, the supernatural love of charity, is the cause of their contemplation.[113] Their object most undoubtedly is not the metaphysical *One*, at which monists and pantheists arrive. The saints are not interested in " the return towards a world substantially penetrated." † Their

---

* Baruzi, 698. The philosophical refutation of M. J. Baruzi's book does not come within our scope ; we refer the reader to the weighty study by M. Roland Dalbiez, professor of philosophy, entitled : *Une récente interprétation de saint Jean de la Croix.* (Editions de la *Vie spirituelle*.) Dom Philippe Chevallier, O.S.B., had already analysed and pointed out Baruzi's errors in his *Saint Jean de la Croix en Sorbonne.* (*Vie spirituelle*, Supp., May, 1925.)

† Baruzi, 288.

object is the one God in the three divine persons of theological faith.

Contemporaries and historians connect John's teaching with that of Denys the Areopagite, not so much, perhaps, to indicate a particularly close spiritual filiation, as to mark a relationship with the great mystical tradition, of which Denys was considered the best qualified interpreter.

"... And it is the common opinion of those who read (his writings) that the doctrine and spirit, which the Apostle St. Paul communicated to St. Denys, his disciple, for the whole Church, shines resplendent in them." [114]

".... Hence readers compare this doctrine with that of St. Denys the Areopagite: this is well known and true." [115]

Some critics, at the present day, and, even before John's time, authors like Nicholas of Cusa,[116] compare Denys with Proclus, or, at any rate, observe a marked neo-Platonist strain in his writings. The question then arises, did John also, through Denys, feel this neo-Platonist influence? If we regard the essential lines of his mystical doctrine, the answer will be in the negative.

Those who endeavour to show that John was dependent, through Denys, on Plotinus, are greatly mistaken. There is an infinite distance between them. Plotinus sought for a philosophical contemplation which is utterly foreign to faith. " Hence his illusion of preparing for divine unions by means of mathematics or dialectics. Hence, too, his description of the dark night and the cloud in a purely dialectical sense. ...

" There is no trace, in neo-Platonist contemplation, of that sacred terror and anguish, which overwhelmed the prophets. And, indeed, if mystical preparation only consists in such a stripping of self and dialectical ascension, it may be laborious, but not agonising; it does not attack, in the depths of the soul, those evil roots of which it is ignorant; with the Catholic mystic, on the other hand, faith, urged by charity, penetrates, like a sword, even unto the dividing of the soul and spirit; it wounds, it burns in those depths of the soul which God alone can reach, and this it is which renders the agony so painful and solitary.

" God answered the prayer of Moses : ' Show me thy face,' with, ' I will have pity on whom I will have pity,' and that is the last word of Christian mysticism. No man can force his way into the cloud wherein God hides Himself : no man can, by his own efforts, grasp those supernatural gifts of which God disposes as He pleases : *Non volentis neque currentis, sed miserentis est Dei.* Here, above all, the neo-Platonism of Plotinus is opposed to Christianity : the God of the philosophers, transcending thought as well as life, ignores all those who depend on Him, and are unconsciously attracted by His goodness. They are not awakened or elevated by grace ; but they feel the poverty of their own nature and the sovereign fulness of the Supreme Good ; they strive to raise themselves up to it :—some succeed, in a brief state of trance : Plotinus, according to Porphyry, did so on three occasions ; the greater number fail, and fall back grievously upon themselves : thus, Porphyry himself was haunted by the thought of suicide, and only escaped it by abandoning the School and flying to Sicily. The rare individuals who are so privileged, and succeed in this giddy ascent, do not discover in it the principle of a new life, of an abiding union with God, but only a barren and transient state of intoxication." [117] If we take Clement of Alexandria literally, we may, perhaps, discover, even in the case of a Christian, ambitions after a contemplation understood in the neo-Platonist sense, but they do not lead us beyond the confines of natural theology.[118] With John of the Cross we plunge, as we have seen, into the pure supernatural, the complete Trinitarian theology.

Living faith is " the one, only, proximate, and proportionate means by which the soul unites itself with God ; for, so great is the resemblance between the soul and God, that no other difference remains than that which distinguishes God seen from God believed in. God is infinite, and faith proposes Him to us as infinite ; God is three and one, and faith proposes Him to us as three and one. God is darkness to our understanding, and faith, in point of fact, blinds and darkens our understanding. Hence, it is by this means alone that God manifests Himself to the soul in the divine light that surpasseth all understanding. And on that account, the more faith the soul has, the more closely is it united to God." [119]

This capital principle was ever before John's mind and dominates his mystical synthesis in which everything tends to develop the life of faith. We are far removed from a type of contemplation sought after for the delight of the intellect alone. He states that a soul may have a most elevated knowledge of God, and enjoy sublime contemplation, but " all that, as St. Paul teaches, will be of no avail to unite it to God, if it is not inflamed with charity." [120]

Hence he does not put contemplation before us as an end in itself. For him, it is an attitude of the soul. The end is union by love, with all that love demands. That is what distinguishes " his doctrine," [121] like all Catholic mysticism, from natural or diabolical counterfeits, as was pointed out in connection with Algazel.

A new opinion has been advanced of late that Spanish Illuminism owes far more to Musulman influence than to that of the Northern mystics. It would seem that, in the case of the *alumbrados*, there exist " far more marked resemblances, as far as spiritual doctrines and practices are concerned, to the *iluminados* of Andalusian Islam, in the twelfth century, than to the German mystics, with whom they are usually compared, and of whom they are believed to be disciples." [122] This opinion will be readily accepted by those who bear in mind the " exercises " which were taught by Algazel, to induce a state of ecstasy.

The names of Tauler and Herp are, indeed, on the Indexes of the Spanish Inquisition, but that does not imply that their doctrine was the cause of Illuminism. Menendez y Pelayo is too severe on them.[123] Besides, even the best teaching may be abused. We have already noted that, through Tauler's *Institutions*,[124] John is indebted to tradition for his scheme of the three signs, whereby to recognise that the soul may enter upon contemplation.

The eighth chapter deals with the sole means of salvation for those who advance " stripped of consolation," namely, " firmly to attach themselves to an utterly simple and naked faith." The twenty-second chapter deals with " nakedness of spirit," and the thirty-second with the " three degrees of poverty." These are, obviously, themes familiar to the author of the *Subida* and the *Noche*. Nay more, an outline of Tauler's thought, expressed in his own way, may be found in the first sermon for the fifth Sunday after Trinity. On the other hand, the comparative study of the great mystics is still in its infancy and, when we meet with coincidences, we are but too much inclined to conclude that we have reciprocal influences. For my part, I may at once say that I believe in the fundamental independence of St. John of the Cross. His point of view is not Tauler's, nor even Ruysbroeck's ; and yet they would seem to have been his precursors.[125] John speaks of God, and is not concerned with any particular philosophical theory. He treats, especially, of that supernatural work of purification which he had lived himself. The German mystics, who were of a more speculative bent, were far more interested in the natural depths of the soul. Consider Ruysbroeck in the *Mirror of Eternal Salvation* which, according to his Benedictine translators, " is, as it were, a synopsis of his whole doctrine." [126]

" The superior part of our soul . . . is like unto an eternal, living mirror of God, ever uninterruptedly receiving the eternal generation of the Son, and the image of the Holy Trinity in which God knows Himself. We all possess this image, as a life eternal, apart from ourselves, before being created ; and, in our created nature, it is the superessence of our essence and eternal life. And hence the substance of our soul possesses three properties which constitute only one in nature . . . an essential nakedness, without images, by which we resemble and are united to the Father and His divine nature . . . ; the brightness of a mirror in which we receive the Son of God, Eternal Truth. By this brightness, we are like unto Him, but in the act of receiving we are one with Him. . . . The spark of the soul : this is an inner and natural tendency of the soul towards its source, and here we receive the Holy Ghost, the love of God. By this inmost tendency we are like unto the Holy Ghost ; but in the act of receiving we become one spirit and one love with God.

" These three properties constitute one single, undivided substance of the soul, a living substratum and domain of the higher powers. There is a likeness and union in us all by nature ; but, as for sinners, they remain hidden in their own depth, beneath the thick covering of their sins." [127]

According to this theory, divine grace is still needed, and Ruysbroeck remains orthodox, because, if grace and the divine gifts enable us to remove the rust of sin and eliminate all that hinders the image of God from appearing, they also confer " on our soul *another sort of resemblance to God,* which Ruysbroeck calls *resemblance by love and the virtues.*" [128] However, it is also quite true that Ruysbroeck did not distinguish the merely natural from the supernatural order as clearly as St. Thomas.[129] John's theology is quite different, and far more faithful to that of Aquinas. He has not felt, through the Augustinian theory of the image of the Trinity in man's soul, the neo-Platonist influences which may be observed in Ruysbroeck. According to him, if the soul is to be united to God, nature must not only be *purified* by grace, but radically *super-elevated,* and the process of union depends entirely on the essentially supernatural energies of a living faith. Contemplation has its birth in faith, and this doctrine was so dear to John that he did not hesitate to write that " in some way . . . faith serves in this life for divine union, as the light of glory serves in the next, as a means for the clear vision of God." [130]

Without attempting a comparative study of those two great masters, John of the Cross and Ruysbroeck, it may be said that what first strikes us, in the case of the latter, is not so much his " sanjuanist " expressions [such as " without mode and without manner," [131] " the not-knowing and obscurity," [132] " the nakedness of the three powers of the soul and their transformation," [133] " the hurt, the wound of love," [134] and " the divine touch " [135]]—as the vehemence of desire, which is so characteristic of John.[136] Both are hurrying towards God—towards God by Christ—and both practise the stripping of self, even unto nakedness, to attain that end.[137] We are at the very antipodes of a passivity ill-understood. Hence both had a divine mission to write against spurious mystics. In Chapter LXXVI of Ruysbroeck's *Ornament of Spiritual Espousals* are, already, condemnations launched against Quietism[138]; and a rapid collation of John's writings enables us to discern the elements of a masterly refutation of the errors of Illuminism, which were condemned in 1568 and 1574, and finally, on May 9th, 1623, by Cardinal Andres Pacheco, the Inquisitor General.[139]

John of the Cross certainly did not believe that " ardours, tendernesses, and swoonings, which are sometimes experienced at prayer, are signs that the soul is in the state of grace and in possession of the Holy Ghost." He never failed in the observance of his rule, on the pretext that " mental prayer is of divine precept and that, by the fulfilment of this precept, all other duties are accomplished." On the contrary, both at Granada and Segovia, when these monasteries were in course of erection, he took part in manual labours which, according to the Illuminists, " should not be carried out by the servants of God." If he recommended only a reasonable use of " images," he did not exclude them. He had pictures painted for the cloister of *Los Mártires*, and made a present of a gilt figure of the Child Jesus, which is still venerated, to the Carmelite nuns residing in the house of " The Great Captain." At the Incarnation in Avila, Christ appeared to him on the Cross, and John made a sketch of the vision. He used to celebrate Mass, with a passionate love for the Blessed Eucharist, which enraptured him and irradiated his countenance, as happened once at Malaga on the feast of St. Martin, whom he used to call *mi Señor*.[140] He knew that the Blessed Trinity, " the greatest saint in Heaven," as he said to Maria de la Cruz,[141] is not seen in this life, where contemplation, however ecstatic, is always within the order of faith. His works, like his life, are a eulogy of the infused moral and theological virtues. He is certainly not the man to teach that " the perfect have no need to perform acts of virtue."

The *Alumbrados* maintained that " servants of God should not obey superiors in matters that might interfere with contemplation." But John, far from practising a Lutheran independence, [142] humbly submitted even to disgrace, and, in the prologues to the *Cántico* and *Llama*, declares that not only does he base himself on the Divine Scriptures, but submits to the censure of those who are more enlightened and, above all, " to the judgment of Our Holy Mother, the Roman Catholic Church, under whose direction no one goes astray." [143] Furthermore, he told Mother Anne of Jesus that he would employ scholastic theology, which was detested by the *Alumbrados*, in order to explain the highest mystical states. His attempt was successful : Melchior Cano was not moved to cry out from his grave, as he had once cried out at Carranza's propositions, " Let us close our books, let our Universities perish, let studies die out, and let us all give ourselves up to prayer ! " [144]

Yet it must never be forgotten that if John of the Cross is indeed a critic, he is also " a touchstone for the problems raised by Spanish Illuminism in the sixteenth century " (Baruzi, 265). No spiritual writer was ever more on his guard against error than he. But no one ever more vigorously defended the liberty of souls on whom God is pleased to work. In a parenthesis in the *Llama*, he is carried away at great length by his indignation. " Illuminism and deception " say the master-blacksmiths, [145] as they hammer away at souls who are inclined to solitude and repose in God. And he, whose whole existence, since his studies at Salamanca, had suffered from seeing souls entrusted to directors who mingled the vulgar unguents of their own exercises with divine perfumes, [146] shattered in his turn, and pulverised by his writings, those wretched teachers who smite like black-smiths. [147] He did so because God's interests were at stake. He will not admit that the *Alumbrados* are mystics. Those are Illuminists who quench their thirst with a demoniacal or naturalist mysticism. There are minds to-day led astray by the symbolism of " the dark night," desiring to be dissolved with the dissolution of pantheism. *Cupio dissolvi*, but not *et esse cum Christo !* [148] It is a modern peril, as it was a peril in Granada, and one to be exorcised by the example of John's wisdom, his heroism and mysticism, based on absolute detachment.

The Conquest, as we have seen, did not liberate Granada from the power of Mahomet. The younger generations in that city, from 1582 to 1588, still breathed a Musulman atmosphere ; the Moorish woman of Ubeda had fostered Algazel's doctrine ; the devil was very busy, and many embraced a false mysticism almost innocently.

St. John of the Cross denounced, at the very beginning of the *Noche oscura*, " demonstrations, movements, strange attitudes, and ecstasies in the presence of witnesses," [149] which were distinguishing features of the *Alumbrados*.[150] In the *Subida*,[151] he urgently warned people against interior locutions, visions, revelations, and spiritual feelings. We cannot be certain but that some natural or diabolical element may be mingled with such manifestations. The wisest course is not to be attached to them. As for desiring and demanding them, such conduct is not merely foolish, but is also offensive to God. By giving us His Son, His eternal Word, He has said everything, once and for all, and nothing more remains to be uttered.[152] Let us not tempt the Lord. Let us fear " the spirit of madness." [153] John knew, and he saw round him,[154] shocking abominations into which many had fallen through not having curbed their spiritual gluttony.[155] He uttered a warning : nature and the devil abet each other ; people glide from the sensible to the sensual, without being aware of the fact. Sensitive souls are so easily intoxicated that they become engulfed in the attractions and enjoyment of vice.[156] Moreover, the passion to enjoy . . . the preternatural is, in the case of some, so powerful, that they end by not merely concluding a definite and formal pact with the devil, but by procuring, for their witchcrafts and abominations, sacred objects, and, what cannot be mentioned without horror, the Body of Our Lord Jesus Christ.[157]

When John wrote these lines, he had definite cases in mind. There was the notorious possessed woman of Avila, who defeated all the efforts of Mancio of Corpus Christi, Bartho-lomew de Medina and Luis de León.[158]   There were the two possessed women of Manchuela at Jaen,[159] the devil, who was only to be cast out by prayer and fasting,[160] and the case of Isnorafé, a village mysteriously hidden away on the summit of a conical mountain.[161]   Somebody brought him Doña Juana de Pedraza, who, for thirteen years, had the devil by her side.   John set her free after four readings from the Gospel of the sick.   There was also another case of a woman persecuted by apparitions from the age of seven,[162] and lastly, the woman who had such a great fear of " little Seneca." [163]

It is certainly true that the devil feared John.   At the Carmelite Convent of " The Great Captain," as soon as the evil one saw the saint he cried out, by the mouth of Sister Asuncion, who had been possessed for eight or nine months :
" Curse you, who torment me so, you are my greatest enemy."   John told Isabel de la Encarnacion, who tells the story, to keep Sister Asuncion in her own cell, and one night the possessed nun got under the bed and lifted it with amazing strength.[164]

Possessed people were brought to him from all quarters.[165] The devil was furious and at the same time fearful.

Before confessionals were installed at *Los Mártires*, Alonso tells us, " a very spiritual person " who confided in Father John of the Cross saw, in a corner of the church, a multitude of toads, bears and monkeys wandering about, tempting the faithful, and when the Father looked at them she saw them creep back in terror to their corner.[166]

" I cannot conquer this little Brother, and know not how to bring about his fall.   Why cannot he leave me here ? He has persecuted me for many years in different places." And the demoniac muttered the names of the places.   Juan Evangelista, who had accompanied the saint, heard this confession by bringing his ear close to the mouth of the demoniac.   " *Stop, stop*," replied John, " *do not believe this liar*." [167]   Juan also told Luis de San Angel that the evil spirits regarded John as another Basil.   And he confessed that one day, on his wishing to exorcise in the presence of

John, the demoniac replied : "What more? Is it not enough, fool, that thy Father torments me." This was in 1586, in the church of "The Great Captain." [168] It may, perhaps, be suggested that John, after all, cured only a few neurotics from whom a skilful modern alienist would soon remove those delusions of diabolical possession. This is not the case. John of the Cross had no idea of competing against psychiatrists. And yet "he was skilled in diagnosis." * After having seen, at St. Teresa's request, Isabella of St. Jerome at Medina, he gave his opinion : " *This is not due to the devil, but to want of judgment and very great foolishness.*" [169]

The devil was made furious by John's diagnosis. He would have preferred the punishment prescribed by the Inquisition : a hundred blows with a stick, and a walk through the streets holding a black candle. [170] He avenged himself by sending women to tempt the saint, as, for instance, in the *hospitium* of the Incarnation of Avila, when he was thirty years of age. [171] But John triumphed in the serenest fashion. " His conversation and behaviour were of a heavenly purity." [172] " When people drew near to kiss his hands and scapular, they perceived a most sweet odour." [173] The devil, disgusted, set about efforts on a grander scale.

One day, on the Plaza de la Encarnacion, not far from the Cathedral, which was opened a few months later (September 8th, 1583), a woman approached John with a child in her arms, and said that as it belonged to him, he must support it. John rebuffed her, but as the woman kept following him, and aroused the curiosity of the crowd, he asked : " *Who is the mother of this child ?* "

" A young girl belonging to one of the best families."

" *Where did the girl live before she came to Granada ?* "

" She was born here and never went half a league outside its walls."

" *How old is the child ?* "

" Almost a year."

" *Well,*" said John calmly and quietly, " *its birth must then*

* The phrase is one of Professor Laignel-Lavastine's. Cf. *La Méthode concentrique dans l'étude des psychonévroses.* (Paris, 1928), p. 125.

be a miracle, and a miracle of a high order, for I have not been a year in Granada yet, and I never was here before." [174]

About this time the pure-hearted saint went through a short but severe trial. An epidemic of bubonic plague,[175] of which Father Peter Diego died at Seville in the month of May, 1582, attacked him whilst celebrating Mass in the Convent of Anne of Jesus. As he was unable to walk, he had to be carried away, burning with fever. But, at the end of three days' prayers, God cured him, and he was spared the necessity of submitting to nursing painful to his instinctive modesty.

The whole atmosphere of diabolism and passion that existed in Granada, still so Musulman, was inevitably bound either to excite or terrify souls who were still young.[176]

On June 15th, 1584, Gracian arrived at the Carmelite Convent in the *Calle Elvira* to give the habit to Isabel de la Encarnacion. Father Peter of Carmel availed himself of the opportunity to have a very troublesome penitent, called by the old chronicler, " the Sibyl of Carmel," [177] examined in the parlour of *Los Mártires*, by the young Provincial who had been made illustrious by the friendship of Teresa of Jesus.

Doña Maria Machuca de Alfaro was a young girl of intellectual gifts, about twenty years of age, of more rank than wealth, who lived close to the Alhambra. Her father was a lawyer, pleading in the Chancery. Being intelligent, and living in a studious society of brothers and cousins, she first took up the study of philosophy and law. But, as her confessor allowed her to have a Bible, she presently went in for mysticism.[178] She was tormented by a host of temptations and scruples for the space of four years, and the blasphemies which she uttered against her will deeply distressed her. She intended to denounce herself to the Holy Office. Once Father Peter, an " extremely spiritual and very well-educated man," began to direct her, he induced her to practise mental prayer. The young girl then wanted to withdraw to a hermitage. Gracian also strongly encouraged her to read the Sacred Scriptures, " that treasure of light, hope and patience," [179] and as she could not become a Carmelite, he authorised her to put on the habit of the *beatas* of the Order. She still underwent the same sufferings. She sang beautifully, *en una preciosa tonada castellana* ; to an old Castilian air : *Vide humilitatem meam et laborem meum, et dimitte universa delicta mea.* (See my abjection and my labour, and forgive me all my sins. Ps. xxiv. 18.)

Gracian does not seem to have inspired Doña Maria Machuca with any " excessive desires for the extraordinary. He was intelligent as far as prayer was concerned, and yet he did not esteem or admire anything else," says Father Dositheus,[180] who was himself a lecturer in philosophy and theology, as well as a good historian. If we are to believe Dositheus, John aimed his writings at counteracting " the harmful doctrine " of the young Provincial, which was causing " an infinity of abuses in monasteries." Long before Dositheus, Quiroga had certainly written : " Our Blessed Father exhorted . . . the Father Provincial in secret, to correct some failings he had noticed in his method of governing and directing nuns, and in particular, not to believe in visions and revelations, or to be too sympathetic with the nuns in such matters, and he pointed out the harm he was causing by so acting." [181] The Carmelite nuns " were racking their brains and tiring their minds by their efforts at producing beautiful ideas and seeing visions," and Dositheus [182] goes on to say that " many of them began to compose mystical treatises in order to appear spiritual."

No special study has yet been issued of Jeronimo Gracian's *Spiritual Works*, published at Madrid in 1616.[183] The minor works that I have been able to obtain do not allow of a definite judgment. However, several singularities may be noted : there is a fine flow of words rather more suited to a popular preacher than a prudent theologian ; there is also a very marked taste for odd, imaginative constructions. For instance, in his famous vision at Tunis, Gracian beheld five worlds. In each of these there were twenty spheres which are, in the natural world : hell, purgatory, limbo, the bosom of Abraham, the four elements, the seven planets, the four great heavens, and lastly, God.[184] The least that can be said of this is that it is somewhat complicated. Yet it is less so than his armorial bearings, which I shall not attempt to describe.[185]

His vocabulary is disconcerting. However little one may have studied the teaching of St. John of the Cross, one is surprised, and even disturbed, at reading the following from the pen of a man who was St. Teresa's friend : " In this kind of (intellectual) vision, I have received great mercies from Our Lord, and almost my whole mind is set on them. I have much for which to be grateful to God for having led me by this way, because such visions are more sure and fruitful than external ones, and here the demon can do less harm." [186] In another work, he states that he uses the word " vision " generically, and to express any form of knowledge whatsoever.[187] This is a little more reassuring, but are we dealing here with mystical matters or not ? It is a question which must be asked frequently. Gracian wrote an *Apologia contra los que ponen la perfección en la aniquilación total*.[188] It can scarcely be maintained that this work fulfils our reasonable expectations. In his *Los caminos de la perfección* he explains that *aniquilación total* simply means abandoning one's will to God.[189] Certain passages, which are clearer, might make us more indulgent,[190] but it must candidly be confessed that we are only too often confronted by an extravagant imagination, which takes pleasure in transposing, dividing and subdividing. It would be necessary, after a critical study of all his works, to arrive at some agreement as to the meaning of his terminology. But, even at this stage, one may say without imprudence that he has not the spiritual mentality of John of the Cross. Did he really appreciate the latter at his true value ? He was not, as we shall see, influenced by John when it would have been most advantageous for himself.[191] They both suffered for the same cause, but in a different way, and they led different lives. Later on, Gracian makes " Cyril " thus address him : " How do you know but that it (Gracian's disgrace) was a means which God made use of to prevent your talents from being concealed in such narrow limits (encogimiento) as some of the Discalced, on a pretext of recollection and perfection, affect ; for God does not give talents in vain, nor does He mean them to be hidden away in a cell or a desert. Although such a life may be good for some, there are others whom God wishes to lead by another way ; vocations are of many kinds." [192]

Although Gracian here had Doria and the " fervents " in his mind, as we shall see later,[193] this anxiety to defend *his talents*, and, afterwards, to defend *his honour*,[194] prevents us from ranking him amongst those who consider all such things as " dung," [195] and who are willing to lose themselves in Christ.[196] I am not judging ; I am noting a difference between the method of St. John of the Cross and that of Jerome Gracian of the Mother of God.* We must not forget the assurances which Teresa, always skilful in producing happy relations, gave Gracian in 1575 and in 1580, of John's satisfaction [197] and loyalty [198] towards his then superior, but it does not seem that Gracian fully responded. Teresa, on two occasions, asked him, whilst in office, for favours on behalf of John of the Cross—in September, 1578, that he might not leave Almodovar,[199] and in March, 1581, that he might be brought back to Castile [200]—and on neither occasion was she listened to. She had some justification for writing to Gracian : " I cannot understand this unfortunate business ; but no one is ever found to remember this saint." [201] " And yet, if he were to die, you would have few like him." [202] One notes, not without uneasiness, Gracian's silence in regard to John. Even in the thirteenth dialogue of the *Peregrinación de Anastasio*, where he recounts the foundation of some monasteries, amongst others Mancera, Pastrana and Alcalá, he speaks of Anthony, Mariano and the others, but makes no allusion whatever to St. John of the Cross.[203]

.   .   .   .   .   .

One day, in 1585,[204] Doña Maria Machuca's cousin, the future Mary of the Assumption, said to her :

" Do you know where we are going ? "

---

* It is only just to refer here to the almost heroic close of Gracian's experiences and life. See St. Teresa's *Book of Foundations*. (London, 1913, Ch. XXIII, note 2, p. 205). B.Z.

"To *Los Mártires*, as before."

"No," replied the cousin, "because we shall find the Father Prior in the convent of the Carmelite nuns."

Curiously enough Doña Maria had not yet met St. John of the Cross.

When they arrived at "The Great Captain"—where Anne of Jesus and her companions had been living since the end of 1584—they found John on his knees, preparing to say Mass. Urged by her friend, Doña Maria approached, and asked him to hear her confession. He consented, and sat down on a bench in the church. Kneeling at his feet, she began to give him an account of her soul, her religious practices, her desires. She also told him that she was too poor to be able to pay the rather high dowry required by the Carmelites. The saint at once recognised the precious pearl set by God in the heart of Doña Maria. He encouraged her, told her to assist at his Mass, to go to Communion, and that he would pray God to accomplish her desires, if such were His will. He placed her opposite the choir grille, so that the nuns might see her. It was a sound psychological stroke, because Doña Maria was very charming. As soon as Mass was over, he presented the young girl to the community. He expatiated on her talents: she had a good voice, knew how to recite the office and to make mental prayer, and, above all, she had great desires. As the postulant made satisfactory replies to all the questions, she very quickly made a good impression. It was only at this stage —as the chronicler quietly remarks—that John mentioned the fact that she would have a very slender dowry. Mother Anne of Jesus, who was well aware of the convent's pitiable resources, expressed her regret. Then the saint broke out: "Is it possible, Mother, to lose a girl of good will,[205] and try to keep this spouse from God for four or five reals more or less?" Judgment was delivered, and Doña Maria Machuca became the celebrated Maria de la Cruz.

We can now appreciate Mother Anne's whimsical remark to Isabel de la Encarnacion: "I am afraid to deal with Father John of the Cross about the temporal affairs of the convent, because I do not know if he understands me or pays attention to what I say, he is always so completely absorbed and inflamed with the love of God." [206] Even before this, whilst at Baeza, he used to go through the cloisters, striking his knuckles against the wall so as to avoid falling into an ecstasy. [207]

Yet John was not deficient in practical intelligence. He knew how to deal with business matters when necessary. A valuable document, the original of which was in the archives of Duruelo, and of which there is a copy in the National Library of Madrid, [208] may be quoted. He was writing to Anne of St. Albert, the Prioress of Caravaca :

" It vexed me that you did not sign and seal a written deed with those Fathers . . . since, as far as I can see, they are not people who will keep their word. Hence I believe that not only will they avoid the complete fulfilment of their promises, but if you delay in the least they will make it an excuse to do nothing at all if it suits them better. Pay close attention, therefore, to my advice. Say nothing at all, either to them or anyone else, and deal with M. Gonzales Muñoz about the purchase of the house which is on the other side, and have the deed signed and sealed : as they see they have the upper hand they are acting haughtily. It matters very little if people afterwards hear that we bought this house simply to extricate ourselves from an awkward position. In this way, and without breaking our heads over it, we can force those Fathers to come to an agreement with us, and consent to what is most important, as far as we are concerned. Sometimes one ruse can only be foiled by another."

John of the Cross was not equipped with Gracian's irresistible charm or Doria's indomitable will so as to make him a successful man of affairs, but he had what was far greater and better—the holy independence of those who are no longer attached to this world.

CHAPTER XVIII

NICHOLAS OF JESUS-MARY DORIA

THERE are two portraits hanging side by side in the hermitage of St. Teresa at Pastrana : one is of Father Jerome Gracian of the Mother of God, and the other of Father Nicholas of Jesus-Mary Doria. Gracian's open countenance allows us to conjecture that he was a man with whom it was easy to get on. Doria's head is striking. The profile is angular, the aspect commanding : no trace of feeling, merely a cold determination to succeed. Under the habit of Father Mariano's former disciple [1] was a skilful diplomatist. The son of a noble Genoese house established at Seville, he had rendered assistance to the King of Spain in a delicate matter of international finance [2] ; to the Archbishop, Don Christopher de Rojas y Sandoval,[3] who was head over ears in debt ; and even to Teresa of Jesus, whose sole earthly wealth was three ducats.* Teresa was overjoyed when " Don Nicholas " entered the novitiate.[4] She saw him and blessed God for having given the Order " a subject of such value and great virtue." [5]

He was only two months professed when, on May 22nd, 1578—in the midst of a crisis—she asked herself " why he should not go to Rome," [6] because he was " *tan discreto*," remarkably prudent. At Madrid, from the very convent of the Mitigated Carmelites, did he not *con tanta disimulación*, defend the interests of the Reform, that no one ever found it out. One may understand, then, why Teresa " loved him greatly in the Lord," and held him " in high esteem." [7]

---

* Letter to Mary of St. Joseph (September 7th, 1576) : " I know what happened to me when I was in need ; it is very hard to obtain money in Seville. And hence, I did not dare, for the moment, offend Don Nicholas." *Silv.*, VII, 279 ; *Greg.*, I, 338, etc. ; *English*, II, 32. He had sent St. Teresa a postulant who was unsuited for the Carmelite life, but the saint had to give her a trial to humour Don Nicholas. (B.Z.)

Three years later there was question of electing him Provincial at Alcalá ; and as the " fervents " had seen him find fault, in the name of poverty, with the Flemish tapestries in the chapter-room,[8] they easily obtained him for the post of *socius*. He would, they believed, support Gracian, whom they did not regard as sufficiently firm.[9] " Oh ! how delighted I am to hear that Your Paternity has such a good companion," wrote Teresa to Gracian.[10] She, even better than the " fervents," realised the defects of her " Paul " and, long before his nomination she had gladly seen the coming together of the two.

" Father Nicholas stayed three or four days with me in Avila. I was very well pleased when I saw that Your Paternity had someone with whom you could manage the affairs of the Order, capable of helping you, and who corresponded with my own desires ; I have suffered severely from the fact that you were, from that point of view, so isolated in the Order. This Father, most certainly, seemed to me to be wise, judicious and, moreover, a servant of God. He has not the great graciousness and affability that God has given Paul. He grants to few so many gifts at once. However, he is a man of judgment, very humble, very penitential, and knows how to win people's goodwill. He will fully realise Paul's worth, and is firmly resolved to follow him in all things ; that has afforded me much joy. May Paul come to an understanding with him ! He will, I believe, if it were only to please me. May they always agree ! We shall derive much advantage from it, and that would be a great consolation for me. . . . Yes, Father, may Your Paternity not fail to come to an understanding with him ; either I am greatly deceived, or he will be a precious resource for a host of things. We have talked together at great length, and formed many plans. May the Lord be pleased to hasten the day when we can carry them out, and perfectly arrange everything in this flock of the Virgin, which costs Paul so much ! " [11]

It must have been a great " trial " for her to discover, in December, 1581, that Doria " insists that everything should be carried out according to his own way of looking at

things." [12]   Nevertheless, she begged him not to be
" fearful ; *mogigato*," and not to fail to write to Gracian
" all that he thinks suitable." [13]   And it may have grieved
her even more to see " her dear son " falling out with Doria,
than to see him leaving her—she who was to die before the
end of that year 1582—and leaving her, too, that he might
return to Andalusia, where God knew what perils beset
him ! The long letter dated September 1st, her last, must
be read if we are fully to understand our Mother's anguish.
Her last message was for Father John : " *Al padre Fray Juan
de la Cruz mis encomiendas.*" [14]

The men whom Teresa wished to unite, for the good of
the Reform, were of utterly incompatible natures.   Gracian,
exasperated, soon sent Doria to Italy in order to have elbow-
room.   The pretext was obvious.   He was to render
obedience to the Most Reverend Father Caffardo, and ask
for the confirmation of all that had been done at Alcalá.[15]
Even before that Chapter, Teresa had asked her sons to send
a humble letter to the Prior General, declaring that they
were his faithful subjects.[16]   It was a mere matter of justice.

Doria arrived, dressed in a white mantle, at the house of
his brother—John Baptist Doria—in Genoa.   He was accompanied by a lay-brother, Juan de Santiago.   All Doria's
baggage was " a breviary rolled up in his night-scapular,
fastened by a discipline to his cincture on the right side." [17]
At the end of July he met and made an impression on
Caffardo.   The Prior General recalled the most humble
letter of submission, which had been forwarded, in December,
1578, by Doria, who was then a young professed friar of
thirty-eight, and which bore, amongst other signatures, that
of John of the Cross.[18]   He at once appointed Gracian's
incompatible *socius* his own " delegate in Spain." [19]   The
descendant of the Dorias willingly accepted this office, but
the humble friar refused the purple and the Archbishopric
of Genoa. [20]

.   .   .   .   .   .

On Doria's return from Italy, at the end of April, 1583,
he proceeded to the Chapter of Almodovar.   He had a little

ass which carried a pack-saddle for his mantle, and which he used as a mount. He put up at an inn in Toledo. Shortly afterwards, the Father Provincial, accompanied by Father Gregory of the Holy Angel, arrived. Both of them were mounted on mules, which were saddled and bridled.

"Well, now, Father," said Doria jestingly, "it was only yesterday Your Paternity imposed on us a law [21] forbidding us to travel with saddle-animals ; how comes it that Your Reverence and your companion are violating it so soon ? "

Gracian began to laugh, and gave orders to have the saddle-bows removed, so as to have the saddles lower. But that was not enough to placate " the lion of Carmel," and messengers were despatched for pack-saddles. They set out for Malagon. The Carmelites had prepared a great dinner, at which, unfortunately, some chickens figured on the bill of fare. The sight of them enraged Doria :

" Is this the way, Fathers, that we are travelling to the Chapter of the Reform ? Whoever likes may eat meat ; if there are any eggs, that will do for me." [22]

At Almodovar, he denounced, with great fervour, all that he considered reprehensible. But, when he gave an account of his mission to Caffardo, and showed his powers as " the General's delegate in Spain," the Chapter was divided. " Our great Doria," confronted with the attitude of a number of the Fathers, was forced publicly to resign his delegation.[23] And the subject " missions " was discussed.

On March 20th, 1582, a group of five religious had left Lisbon for the Congo, and all had perished by shipwreck. Gracian, feeling that he was supported by Philip II, intended to renew the attempt.

There seems some disagreement among the early historians as to John's attitude. According to the *Reforma* : " Some members of the Chapter, and especially our Venerable Father John of the Cross, saw, with great displeasure, that the Order, which had scarcely emerged from its swaddling clothes, was taking such a heavy burden on its shoulders and scattering its subjects, who were needed for the many foundations which were already being established, and which were asked for. Nevertheless, the majority, bearing in mind the King's express command, and the entreaties of the Provincial, decided in favour of missions, and it was decreed that we should continue to carry them on."

When " missions had thus been accepted, the Father Provincial went further, and suggested missions in Italy and other Catholic countries. . . . Father John of the Cross, in particular, opposed the suggestion with so much zeal that, forgetting his habitual modesty on this occasion, he advanced two or three paces whilst presenting his view. Amongst the objections which he added to those already put forward, the most important was that the new reformers of Carmel were obliged, by the Rule, to retirement, both by day and by night, in their cells. He said that if the service of one's neighbour is not in conformity with the rules of each institution, it will bring about the ruin of the institution and lead to trouble and confusion ; moreover, that as charity is the mother of observance, or rather one and the same thing with it and not something different, to violate the laws of an institution, is in fact to injure charity by putting it in opposition with itself. Hence, he concluded that as our rule obliges us so particularly to solitude, retirement and meditation on the law of the Lord, both by day and night, this was the form of charity recommended to us by God, and not that, which has for its object to labour for the salvation of souls, for that has been confided by God to other Orders." [24]

The *Chronica* of Portugal [25] makes no mention of John's attitude ; and, if he had, by any chance, made himself the champion of the missionary party, it would certainly not have failed to note the fact, seeing that it gives a long account of Ambrose Mariano's plea in favour of missions. Speaking of Mariano, it says : " His opinion was strongly contested, by some of those present, who maintained that this work is little in conformity with the rules of our institution." Was John of the Cross one of those in opposition, as the *Reforma* asserts ? Quiroga thus analyses John's position in this assembly of fiery hermits and enthusiastic " missionaries."

" Our Blessed Father, taking up a middle position between these two extremes, said he did not believe it was God's will that the Order of His Mother should be confined and restricted within the limits of Spain ; but that it should spread and extend through all those provinces of the Church in which it could preserve its character. This must be done as in the days of the Apostles, when our Fathers of old followed the preaching of the Gospel throughout all the provinces of the East, and then at once withdrew to the deserts, where they led a solitary and monastic life, in order to win by divine contemplation God's graces on behalf of those who were preaching to infidels." [26]

It sounds like a commentary on the Encyclical *Rerum Ecclesiae*, delivered three centuries in advance.[27]

John, then, according to Quiroga, was quite willing that foundations should be made outside Spain and over the whole world, provided apostolic work should not interfere with contemplation, any more than at Baeza or Granada. The saint's life confirms the accuracy of the historian's interpretation. If the mission to Guinea is not " directed to this end, and is only for the instruction of barbarians in matters of faith," it is the concern of other Orders.[28] When later on Thomas of Jesus and John of Jesus-Mary, eminent mystical theologians, became zealous promoters of Carmelite missions, they constantly took care to remind the missioners of the demands of the contemplative ideal, according to the reform of St. Teresa.[29]

It is obvious that Gracian has not John of the Cross in mind when he writes : " It was imputed to me as a very bad deed, that I sent these religious [to Italy, the Indies, the Congo, and Ethiopia]. There are some who think that the whole of Carmelite perfection consists in never leaving one's cell, in never missing an item of choir observance, even if the whole world were on fire. They believe that it is all for the good of the Order if convents are multiplied in little Spanish villages, whilst other places are neglected." [30]

John made foundations at Baeza, and he was to make others at Cordova and Segovia, and these were not " little villages." On October 9th, 1585, at the Chapter of Pas-

trana, he signed the document authorising Jean de Quinta-
doine de Brétigny to establish convents of Discalced Carmelite nuns in France.[31] He rejoiced to see the reform in
Mexico proceeding as prosperously and regularly as that in
Spain,[32] and he agreed at a later period to go there.

In 1618, Father Eliseus of the Martyrs, who knew John
quite intimately at Granada, put together some recollections
of him : and this first Provincial of the Indies bears witness
to the apostolic spirit of Carmel's saint.

" [John of the Cross], interpreting those words of Christ :
Did you not know that I must be about my Father's business
(Luke ii. 49), said that, in this context, the Father's business
should not be otherwise interpreted than the redemption of
the world and the good of souls, Christ Our Lord having
employed the means preordained by the Eternal Father.
And he said that Denys the Areopagite, in confirmation of
this truth, wrote the marvellous saying : ' *Of all divine things
the most divine is to co-operate with God in the salvation of souls.*'
. . . The operations proper to God Himself shine out in
this, and it is a great glory to imitate Him. And he also
said that it is an evident truth that compassion for one's
neighbour increases in proportion as the soul is united to
God by love. For the more the soul loves, the more does it
desire that this same God should be loved and honoured by
all men ; and the more this desire increases, the more does
it work to that end, both in prayer and in all other necessary
exercises which it can undertake.

" And there is so much fervour and strength in the charity
of such a soul that those who have been thus seized upon
by God cannot confine themselves to their own personal
advantage, and thereby be contented ; it seems to them a
very little thing that they should go to Heaven alone, and
they endeavour, with a heavenly solicitude and affection,
and an exquisite diligence, to lead many others with them.
Such is the effect of their great love of God, and it has its
source in perfect prayer and contemplation."

An invaluable incident related by Alonso illustrates and

confirms these recollections.   One day, at Granada during recreation, John was seen piling up a little heap of gravel. He divided it into several parts and having put a very small pebble apart, stood gazing at it, wrapped in wonder.

Noticing that the religious were watching him attentively, he said : " My mind is drawn to the thought that in all those parts of the world, our true Lord and God is not known, and that He is only known in this little corner.   And even here, His Majesty has said : *Pauci vero electi !* " [33]

There is no hiatus between John's life and his teaching. We may see this when he goes on to tell us that " the desire of one's neighbour's good springs from the spiritual and contemplative life ;   and as the latter is ours according to the Rule, this zeal for our neighbour's advancement and welfare is commanded and enjoined on us by the Rule.   The Rule, in fact, bids us observe the mixed life. . . . It is the life which Our Saviour chose for Himself, as being the most perfect. . . . Orders which embrace this life . . . are, in themselves, the most perfect.   But though [John of the Cross] thus spoke and taught, it was not well to broadcast it while the religious were so few . . . it might cause them uneasiness ; . . . it would even be better to let them think otherwise, until there was a large number of Brethren." [34]

This passage—valuable, whatever literary graces it lacks —and this incident, enable us to reconcile the data supplied by Francis of St. Mary, Belchior of St. Anne, and Quiroga. The testimony of Eliseus of the Martyrs shows the full importance of Quiroga's words : " taking up a middle position between these two extremes." . . . This " happy mean " between the eremitical and missionary currents marks the highest point of the wisdom of the Reform.

Here the Saint of Carmel always stood, and hence he dominated the two extremes : Doria and Gracian.   Energy is needed to stand so high above contending passions.   But, as Teresa said, he had courage.   We must not, however, suppose that John stood aloof from the battle of life.   He had a keen sense of responsibility.   The few steps forward which

he took at the Chapter of Almodovar, when maintaining
his opinion, should not surprise us. When he found fault he
did so, indeed, " with a gracious severity ; when he exhorted, it was with paternal love, never departing from an
admirable serenity and gravity." He embraced those whom
he had just punished, when, having carried out their penance, they kissed his scapular.[35] But the lamb could grow
wrath because he never compromised with either evil or
baseness.

" Never in his life did he speak artfully or with duplicity.
He held such conduct in horror." Eliseus of the Martyrs
heard him say : " Double dealing is ruining the purity and
sincerity of our Order ; and, from this point of view,
nothing is more unfortunate than to profess the doctrine of
human prudence which only weakens souls."

And he also said that " the vice of ambition amongst the
reformed is practically incurable, for it is the most insidious
vice of all. It alters and influences government and affects
proceedings which appear so virtuous and perfect that it
seems wrong to oppose them, so the spiritual evil goes
unremedied." [36]

At Almodovar he denounced " ambition and greed for
command and office." [37] He thought it important not to
wait until such an evil had gained dominion over men's
hearts. He insisted that " Superiors should not grow old in
their posts, and should not be re-elected when their term of
office had expired." [38] And when it was objected that this
would result in the election of Superiors of little experience,
he replied that no religious order had ever grown lax on
account of a Superior's want of experience, seeing how
easily that could be remedied. Moreover, it was well to put
subjects in charge, in order to try them, since the members
of chapters did not always look for the most worthy, but for
such as they might find more adaptable to their own
wishes.[39] When he was Vicar Provincial of Andalusia, loyal
to his own principles, he gave an order, at Baeza, that
election should be by secret ballot : *vote for whomsoever you
believe worthy of being Superior of this house*, he said.[40] The
majority of the chapter of Almodovar were not of his way

of thinking. He was confirmed, against his will, in his office as Prior, and returned to Granada.[41]

.   .   .   .   .   .

On November 8th, 1584, the Carmelite nuns, Anne of Jesus being Prioress, moved from the *Calle Elvira* to the house of "The Great Captain," Gonzalvo of Cordova, who had driven out the Moors in 1492. "It was most suitable for us, and the best situated in Granada," according to Anne.[42] This splendid mansion is large, central and healthful. The *patio* is surrounded by arcades, supported on tall shafts, about sixty feet long and forty-eight wide. Was there a "view over the whole countryside," [43] such as Teresa loved? To-day *Los Mártires* can be discerned from a terrace. For three months, whilst the church and choir were being prepared, "Mass was said in an inner room," [44] doubtless the little oratory on the top floor, venerated to-day because the saint said Mass there. The little convent bell tinkled, and "John celebrated Mass with grace, reverence and feeling, neither slowly nor rapidly, observing wise measure yet full of ardour." [45]

There was a fine statue of the Child Jesus in the convent— it was the saint's and was made of gilded wood—and the tiny fingers of the right hand, raised in a gesture of benediction, seem to be asking for something.* Whenever John saw it, he said to the Sisters [46] : "*Do you know that He is saying to you with His tiny fingers : ' O ! soul, give me thy heart' ?*" It may have been from the breast of this statue that rays of light were seen streaming towards the saint and his hearers one day when he was delivering a *plática*.[47]

The Sisters of Granada felt their hearts inflamed by his words full of depth.[48] These were the calm and fervent years when he finished the *Cántico* and, perhaps, wrote the *Llama*, 1583–84. The nuns were magnetised by his spirit which was "concentrated" on God,[49] and in which "the Holy Spirit brought the glorious vibrations of His fire." [50] They all longed to hear him speak, but he was "chary of speech." [51] They often said : "Father, give me permission

* It may now be seen in the middle of the altar in the oratory.

to take a drink." He used to smile and the expected answer was always the same : " *Drink with the desire of drinking for God.*"[52] He used to smile, but was neither too joyful nor sorrowful : he laughed but little and with great moderation.[53] Passing near the washing-place one day, with its great red and green jars, beneath the citron-tree which reaches up to the wooden gallery and seems to support the house with its lovely foliage, he entered into an ecstasy, in which he said that if anyone in that monastery were to fall away, it would be from breaking the vow of poverty.[54] Did he fear such a lordly setting for his daughters ? Teresa had written : " May God preserve us from mansions, and from large and ornate houses."[55] But, in the house of " The Great Captain," the love for *desnudez* was not wanting. The five great beams supporting the refectory roof, decorated with arabesques painted in distemper, certainly do not suggest futility. There is little likelihood that the soul of a " primitive " would grow weak in such a noble yet home-like setting. Mother Isabella of the Incarnation (on whom John once worked a miracle [56]) relates that, on the feast of St. Hilarion, they built, close to Mother Anne's bed, a replica of a blessed anchorite's cell—it must have been a very small one !—and a novice, dressed as a hermit, with a great hempen wig, received a procession of solitaries in the cell.[57] This was typical in one of Teresa's convents.

In the month of December, 1584, Gracian set out for Lisbon, and appointed John, by simple nomination, Vicar Provincial of Andalusia. In this capacity, the saint made a foundation of Carmelite nuns at Malaga on February 17th, 1585.[58] He appointed Mary of Christ Prioress : she had been professed at Avila, and was sub-Prioress at Granada.

On her way over the Sierra, she fell from her mount, and her companions thought that she was dead, but John placed his hands on the wound, stanched the blood with a cloth, and, without any other remedy, she arose healed. She was a strong-minded woman, and spoke so seldom, that it was said she ruled by her silence and actions. John was loyal to her to the end.[59] Nevertheless, on one occasion he did not go to her assistance, but the reason of this will never be known.

In the month of May, 1585, he was present at the Chapter of Lisbon. Mother Anne of Jesus seemed sad, as Frances of the Mother of God tells us. " She said to me : ' Frances, my daughter, pray for the house of Malaga, for you will see misfortune come upon it. . . . If Father John were here, I would send him there ; and, perhaps, as he is so holy, he would prevent the devil from operating.' " When he returned from Lisbon, Anne asked him to go to Malaga. He did not consent, and, on the vigil of SS. Peter and Paul, Catherine Evangelist threw herself out of a window.[60] Manrique tells us that they were able to give her the last sacraments.[61]

John of the Cross enjoyed the sovereign independence of the perfect. Apart from religious obedience, he had no other master than the Spirit of God.

At Lisbon, " all the capitulars " [62]—they were twenty-seven in number—visited the Prioress of the Monastery of the Annunciation, the celebrated Dominican stigmatic.[63] John alone took no interest in her. When he left the convent of St. Philip, it was to go down to the sea. One day the learned Augustine of the Kings saw John standing with his back against the wall of the Arsenal, Bible in hand,[64] and suggested to him to get his mantle and accompany him to la monja de las llagas, the nun with the wounds. John declined. He had no need to see those marked with stigmata, for he believed it was better to abide in faith in the wounds of Jesus Christ. Some blamed him for this [65] ; what followed ? The Prior of St. Philip, the excitable Mariano, brought some linen cloths, bearing a bloodstained cross on them, to Seville, to show them to Mary of St. Joseph.[66] The worthy Bartholomew of St. Basil returned from his visit to the convent with a small phial of water which had flowed from the stigmata.[67] John still said that it was trickery. At length Philip II grew uneasy and ordered Gracian to see if there were any grounds for referring this disquieting nun to the Holy Office. It was discovered that she was in favour of

allowing Lutherans to enter the Kingdom. With some soap
and hot water the Inquisitors made short work of the wounds
of this adventuress.[68]

Historians and eye-witnesses alike relate this incident,
which serves to show John's sturdy independence. It
occurred whilst the provincial Chapter was being held in
Lisbon. " He was never a party man," is Alonso's testimony. " He had none of the human respect or weakness to
be seen in others. This apostolic man was devoid of servile
fear and interest when it came to voting at elections ! " [69]
But, after all, that is only an act of natural uprightness.

Gracian told John in confidence that he wished to have
Doria, who was still in Genoa, as his successor in the office
of Provincial. John told him not to do so, because, if Doria
became Provincial, he would deprive Gracian of his habit.[70]
The latter paid no attention to this ; and, out of twenty-
eight votes, twenty-six were cast for " the lion of Carmel." *
Ambrose Mariano and Alphonsus of the Angels each received
one vote.[71] Alphonsus, who had been a novice in Pastrana,
was a prudent Superior, well-versed both in mysticism and
scholastic theology, and was also an apostle.[72] We do not
know for whom John voted, but he was not a man to be
influenced by others. Mariano, who was irrepressible, once
said in his graceful Italian way—" Ah ! Father John, when
will this pumpkin be ripe ? " " *It will be ripe when God ripens
it, and no sooner, even if it were to remain green to the end.*" [73]

He listened to Jerome Gracian defending himself before
the assembled Chapter,[74] and answering, to the best of his
ability, the charges which Doria had brought against him
at Almodovar in 1583, charges that had almost led the
definitors to forbid Gracian to preach.[75] Teresa, with her
jealous watchfulness and loving foresight, was far more alive
than any of the " fervents " to the weak spot in her *Paul*.
On September 1st, 1582, she had uttered a cry of alarm :

" The time for the Chapter is approaching, and I should
not like any fault to be found with you. See to it, for the love
of God, and take care how you preach in Andalusia. I
never wanted you to stay there long. . . . Anyhow, do not

* The old chronicler, in his admiration for Doria, gives him this title.

think of becoming an Andalusian ; you are not made to live in that country. When you preach, even though you do so rarely, I beg you again to watch carefully over what you say. . . . I implore you, for the love of God, carefully to watch everything you do. Do not trust the nuns ; when they want anything, they will represent it to you in a thousand ways in order to attain their end. . . . May Our Lord be pleased to guard you, as I beg Him to do, and preserve you from all danger." [76]

At Lisbon, Gracian, his heart heavy at the " calumnies " of which he knew he stood accused, spoke, advanced arguments, and quoted texts.[77] He had persuaded himself again that it would not be right to allow himself to " be condemned without any fault of his own, remain infamous for the rest of his life and lose the fruit of talents useful to the Church, knowing, as he did, that it is a mortal sin to accept defamation when one is in a public position, and that one is bound to defend one's honour."[78] John's view remains unknown : doubtless he thought that Teresa was not there to help her son " to bear misfortune with the cheerfulness of a Saint Jerome."[79]

In August, John of the Cross gave the habit to his spiritual daughter, Maria de la Cruz.[80] The Carmelite nuns led the young sister into their principal parlour to receive the saint's blessing. They asked : " Does Your Reverence love her greatly, because she is called ' of the Cross ' ? " He answered that he would, indeed, love her greatly if she were a true friend of the Cross.[81] In October he was at Pastrana, where the Chapter of Lisbon was to be reopened, under the presidency of the new Provincial, who had arrived from Genoa.[82]

In this novitiate, which had known such fiery heroism, Doria made such a speech, that " not only the flock, but the shepherds themselves were frozen with terror."

" Rigorous observance, Fathers, because, with the relaxation which Your Reverences see for yourselves, we are rapidly marching to ruin. Yesterday we rivalled the

Thebaid and Sceté ; to-day their very names affright us. What many were formerly wont to do has now become a dream. . . . If we desire the progress of our Reform— observance ; if the salvation of souls—observance. Fathers, I would not think I was true to my conscience if I did not repeat these things without ceasing. . . . Even after my death my bones, clashing together in the tomb, will cry out : ' observance of the Rule, observance of the Rule.' But, as it is morally impossible for superiors perfectly to establish observance if they do not bear the weight of the Rule and constitutions like their subjects, my motto henceforth shall be : the common life. The superior, the preacher, the lector, the great, the favourite now eat meat without obvious necessity, and often by way of needless precaution, or absent themselves from choir ; even, what is not without danger, leave the monastery : in such circumstances, what energy can be expected from a poor subject who nibbles a morsel of codfish, goes to matins, is naked or badly clad, and is neglected when he is ill ? " [83]

Many a time had " good Mother Teresa " constrained Gracian to have his meals in the nuns' parlour at Seville,[84] and even " to eat a little meat from time to time." [85] Exceptions were made for this *Santa Santorum*.[86] " He seriously needs them. There is a vast difference between a superior and a simple religious. Moreover, we are deeply interested in his health," she wrote to Mary of St. Joseph.[87] But Doria was not up to Teresa's standard ; she always took the big, broad view in everything, whilst he made use of his ability as a banker to see that two hundred ducats should be repaid suddenly to his brother Horace, who was a canon of Toledo. And meanwhile, the poor Mother, who had given her orders, was left impatiently awaiting the sum at San José of Avila. The prebendary of Toledo could not have been in such a hurry to have his money returned.[88]

Gracian, now Vicar Provincial and Prior of Lisbon, was " deeply wounded," [89] and left Pastrana, where as a novice he had borne humiliation bravely. Angelus of St. Gabriel's iron rod was a mild staff when compared with " our great " Doria's. Shortly afterwards, Gracian, exasperated, published his "*Apology for charity, against some who, under the pretext of observance of rules, weaken and disturb it in religious orders.*" [90]

John of the Cross, now Vicar Provincial of Andalusia, returned quietly to Granada, accompanied by Louis of St. Jerome.[91] They had been away for two months. Scarcely had he got back than, on Christmas night, the daughters of Anne of Jesus sent for him to *Los Mártires*, for their Mother was very ill. John hastened off, and whilst on his way, hearing the bell for the *Te Deum* being rung, believed with those who were with him, that Anne was dead, and that the bell was being tolled "twice" for the repose of her soul. All the nuns were gathered round Anne who, to cheer them up, showed them a little poem she had composed for the Nativity.[92] They pointed out to John a charming statue of the Child Jesus, lying on a cushion. He cried out : "*Lord, if love is to slay me, the hour has now come !*" [93]

His heart was on fire with love for the Divine Babe. He may, perhaps, have danced again with the statue in his arms, as he had formerly done at Baeza.[94] Maria de la Cruz does not tell us. John of the Cross, half-way between what the "fervents" called Gracian's "lax discipline," and what the latter called "Doria's pharisaism," [95] had become a little child, and entered into the Kingdom of Heaven.[96] *Ni otro, ni esotro*—neither one or the other [97]—he had climbed the Mount of Carmel, all alone, by the way of the Spirit. Without weakness or rigorism, he was the incarnation of the primitive ideal, "the Evangelical counsels lived with all perfection" [98]—in a word, the very spirit of Teresa. *He* would not have taken to Lisbon a memorandum containing "more than thirty alterations to be made in the Carmelite nuns' constitutions." [99] "*Mirad !*" Teresa would have cried, "merely reading these statutes exhausted me ; what would it be if I had to observe them ? Believe me, our Rule does not need such severe people ; it is enough in itself." [100] John had no attraction for *recios*, harsh creatures, as Blessed Anne of St. Bartholomew once called them.[101] We may reasonably ask, was he not more inclined to Gracian's "discretion and extreme graciousness" ? [102] Let us remember that when "Seneca" first met Gracian, "he found in him all that could be desired in a superior." [103]   It is true that " Paul is a magician." [104]   John of the Cross, most assuredly, did not regard material perfection as an end. His mysticism is not that of " the regular observance," of which Doria might be styled, without exaggeration, a fanatic.

Towards the end of his life, when General of the Order, Doria paid a visit to the holy solitude of Bolarque. Whilst there, he heard read in the refectory a book which counselled prudence in the practice of works of penance, and it made him so angry that he wanted to have the pernicious work burned. It was pointed out to him that the book contained excellent matter, but Doria would not hear of it. " How can it be good, when it contains such a chapter as that ? Let Your Reverences remove it from this holy solitude, and let it no longer be read here . . . souls are being lost through such prudent discretion." [105]   That is a type of holiness which St. Teresa would not have believed in.[106] Nicholas Doria, however " perfect " [107] he may have been, could never have understood the soul of John of the Cross. He saw the saint arrive for the solemn opening of the Chapter of Alcalá, " dressed more poorly than the fifty capitulars," and was edified.[108] He considered that the words he spoke " were warming like little grains of pepper." [109] He once entrusted John with the examination of a deluded nun, " who was always saying to God, and to whom God was always saying, extravagant things." [110]   Doria was right : small as he was, John was worth more than his weight in gold.[111]   Unfortunately, the former banker of Seville, who had written a " treatise on exchange," [112] was an administrator, who undertook to manage the Reform of St. Teresa.

* * * * * *

Es muy amigable al hombre
Y pacífico a las bestias
Provechoso a la ciudad
Y aclimado en las aldeas.
Este animal es el asno,
¡ Perdonen sus reverencias ! *

* From a late eighteenth century manuscript of the Carmelite Fathers of Pastrana or Bolarque.

The very kindly friend of man,
And well-disposed towards all beasts.
Serviceable to the town
And knowing well the village,
Such a creature is the ass,
With all respect to your Reverences !

In the course of the year 1586, " this little beast of burden " [113] went, with sure and tranquil pace, up hill and down dale, carrying John of the Cross who was " weak, thin and pale, but always courageous," [114] along the roads of Andalusia. He often changed places with the Brother who accompanied him on foot.[115]

After presiding, on January 13th, at Anne's re-election,[116] he had preached at Linares on several occasions during Lent, whilst residing in Peñuela and even in Granada.[117] We shall see him later at Cordova, the Moslem city, in its yellowing walls looking up at the blue Sierra peopled with hermitages.[118] Mariano had lived in a hermitage at Tardon.[119] Don Luis de Cordova, who venerated John, entertained the saint in his palace until the Sunday after the Ascension.[120] On May 18th, " all the clergy and confraternities " accompanied the Carmelite Fathers from the *Iglesia Mayor*—the central nave within the Mosque with its hundreds of slender columns —to their convent of St. Roch. The Blessed Sacrament was borne along through decorated streets and *patios*, where pinks exhaled their fragrant perfume. " *All the gates were hung with beautiful tapestries, and the people came out, just as on Corpus Christi*," wrote John to Anne of St. Albert,[121] in a letter dated from Seville. Here, across the Guadalquivir, the white and well-proportioned mass of *Los Remedios* obliquely faces the rosy, gracious Giralda. " *I am now in Seville*," writes the zealous Vicar Provincial, " *busy with the transference of our Sisters. I have great hopes of establishing another convent of the Brethren here. So there will be two. Before the feast of S. John, I shall set out for Ecija, where, with God's grace, we shall found another convent, and then on at once to Malaga, and from there to the assembly*." [122]

Before the end of 1586, Doria twice summoned his council to meet at Madrid, in August and December. John fell sick

at Toledo, and was unable to assist at the first meeting [123]
at which Doria, pursuing his policy of a complete separation
from the trunk of the Order, and contrary to the wishes of
those who had always recited the Carmelite breviary, succeeded in abolishing our old and precious liturgy of the
Holy Sepulchre.[124] It would be a mistake to regard John's
forced stay in Toledo as a feint, a sort of protest, such as
Gracian had made. In December, though the snow lay
deep and he was weighed down with infirmities, he went
from Bujalance to Madrid, almost immediately after
receiving Doria's summons.[125] In August he had received
an order to return to Granada, and bring back at once
Anne of Jesus and the Sisters who were intended for the
Madrid foundation.[126] Malaga, Toledo, Granada, Madrid,
Granada—four hundred leagues in the midst of a torrid
summer. And John never laid aside his heavy serge habit or
woollen tunic : he wore them winter and summer.[127]

His little beast of burden—supposing that he made use of
it on this expedition—trod the burning roads of Andalusia.
John reflected on Doria's undertakings and the absence of
Gracian which, no reason being given, only encouraged the
opposition party. One may imagine John absorbed to such
an extent that they had to stand on each side of him to prevent him falling off at the stumbling of his ass,[128] while he
recited in a low voice according to his custom, the seventeenth chapter of St. John.[129] " I pray for them . . . Holy
Father, keep them in Thy Name whom Thou hast given
Me, that they may be one as We . . ."

Would that he could have thrown his hat between those
divided Superiors as he had done with the duellists of Manchuela de Jaen, crying : " *In the name of Our Lord Jesus
Christ, I command you to quarrel no more.*" [130] The combatants
kissed his feet, but it is easier to parry the blows of a *navaja*
than reconcile radically opposed tendencies. What more
could John have done to conquer Doria's harsh, authorita-
tive egoism and Gracian's melancholy and exasperated
selfishness?

Brother Martin of the Assumption, the saint's travelling
companion, was so much moved at hearing the cruel

scourgings which he gave himself, that he went with a light to the martyr's side, whereat John complained that he was old enough to look after himself.[131] The faithful Martin did not believe it. At Guadalcazar, whilst attending to John, who was violently ill, he removed a chain from his body and would not let him replace it ; the saint had worn it for seven years, and blood flowed forth when it was removed.[132] Juan Evangelista who, for nearly ten years, followed John in all his journeyings, tried to persuade the saint, before setting out on the road, to take off his penitential trunk-drawers, woven from esparto grass and full of knots. John would not consent : it was enough, he said, that " *the little beast should travel on an ass*." [133]

Very rarely would he agree to dine at a *venta*, as he had with Martin at the inn of Pedrera on his way from Malaga to Seville.[134] He took his meal in a corner, and woe to Juan Evangelista who brought him two trout, although they had cost but little.[135] Martin had to travel from Cordova to Seville with seven novices, and rely only on Lady Poverty.[136]

On summer nights John slept out in the open in order to be alone and thus avoid the shouts, oaths and yells of the muleteers and *picaros*.[137] In winter he slept as well as he could on the ground, far from the fire, round which the travellers used to sing, on a poor coverlet which he used to carry on the pack-saddle, taking great precautions because of the experience he had, against the effrontery of certain women.[138] Once at the inn of Alcolea, on the way from Cordova to Bujalance, he reproved one of these poor painted creatures in such a supernatural way that it overwhelmed her. She fainted away and only came to her senses after her hair and wrists had been well pulled, and plenty of water thrown on her by the *gente infernal* who frequented those inns. John then spoke to her of God, and the woman, quite converted, went to confession at St. Roch in Cordova, armed with a note from Father John. She was later married, Martin tells us, and wore the habit of St. Francis as well as a girdle of sea-rushes.[139]

It was not in *ventas* alone that morals were in danger. At the dead of night, in a private house, a young woman who had fallen in love with him entered John's room. She threatened to defame him should he utter a cry. But John's pure glance [140] pierced the depths of her heart as Christ's had pierced that of the woman taken in adultery.

In the monasteries he endured other forms of suffering. At Baeza and Cordova he took scarcely two or three hours' sleep : for the rest of the night he prayed on the altar steps, wrapped in his white cape. And at times, he even stretched himself upon a step with his cloak folded beneath his head. [141] Nor was he satisfied with such constant martyrdom : to purchase peace for others, he sank deeper down into the Nada.

When he arrived at a convent bearing a spiritual flame which at once enkindled all about him, [142] he first worshipped God and then went to visit the sick. [143] They were his little ones. For them he had a boundless, inventive, maternal charity. He exhorted them lovingly. It was a joy for the former infirmarian of Medina to make their beds, and even clean their utensils, *los servicios*. [144] He spared no expense. A lay-brother in Granada who had fractured a limb was treated like a prince's son. [145] This is how the man spoke whom Huysmans described as " dry-eyed." " *My son, I am going to prepare your food myself, and give it to you with my own hands. You will have a fine appetite.*" He roasted a fowl, brought it to the invalid, took a little salt, put it on a plate, cooled it with a little water and said : " *Now you shall see how nice it is.*" And he gave it to the patient in spoonfuls. [146] The austerest saints are ever the most gracious. We are reminded of Macarius running from Scété to Alexandria, thirty leagues away, to procure a little cake for a sick hermit. A " fervent " found fault with John for allowing too many of his religious to eat meat. [147] He did not eat much himself, but he never attempted to go without food altogether, or worked any miracles on those lines. On the contrary, he was convinced that eating in moderation was a duty, so as to support life without any miracle. [148]

Satisfied with what was supplied at the community table ; he ate quickly, " *con brevedad*," [149] so as to take the place of the reader, or whoever was washing up the dishes, and thus help others. Hence his little table napkin was as clean at the end of eight days as it had been after four. Whilst Prior, he was the first to practise mortifications in the refectory, such as kissing the feet of the religious, stretching himself out in the form of a cross, or lying prostrate on the threshold.[150]

His brethren reverenced him, and the more fervent asked their Provincials for permission to live under his direction.[151] But Brother Martin of the Assumption was annoyed : " Your Reverence should take care. You are a Superior, you should be esteemed and revered, and you should not humble yourself so much." [152]

" *Brother Martin*," said John, " *Imagine that enemies are coming to ill-treat us, and beat us severely with sticks, how would Your Charity put up with that ?* "

" With the grace of God Our Lord, I should bear it patiently."

And John of the Cross cried out, with fervour and indignation, " *What ! Brother Martin, why do you answer so coldly ? Have you not an immense desire to suffer martyrdom for Our Lord Jesus Christ ? We should urge them to strike us harder, and to make us martyrs for Christ, Our Redeemer.*" [153]

This great Spanish dream of a violent death *a tierra de moros* [154]—which, conjoined with an ardent love for Christ, urged John to play at martyrdom during recreation (standing half naked against an orange tree with Cristobal de San Alberto beating him until the blood flowed) [155]—was, to the profound and absorbing life of Carmel's saint, as flame is to fire.* It was the expansion of the abounding love, which interiorly consumed him, and sometimes brought about an ecstasy. There was an instance of this when he was going from Toledo to Cuerva. The attraction was irresistible : he halted and withdrew into the depths of a wood. As he delayed, and time was pressing, his companion went to look for John, and found him raised above the ground.[156]

---

* To arouse courage, he used, says Alonso, sometimes to consecrate a little brother a " knight of Christ." (Seg., P.A., f. 50.)

It was a great trial for the saint to be forced, for so many years, to deal with external affairs, when his whole soul was bent on fleeing to God in the depths of his spirit. He sighed for solitude, whilst dying of love for his brethren. "*If you wish me to know your sufferings,*" he wrote from Granada to the Prioress of Caravaca, "*go to that mirror of the Eternal Father, the Son, for in Him I see your soul every day, and you will, no doubt, depart consoled, and have no further need to beg at the gate of the poor.*" [157]

At the great Chapter of Valladolid, in April, 1587, which our Father, Saint Elias, covered with his mantle,[158] after John had been forced, full of confusion, to admit that he kept nothing for his private use, he knelt down, in the presence of all, accused himself of being unable to rule, and begged to be relieved of the priorship of *Los Mártires*, which had been entrusted to him for the third time.[159] No attention was paid to his request. "All recognised in him a special kind of authority, due to his union with God. . . ." [160] When he had a meal in convents, either of men or women, scraps of bread and drops of water that remained over were collected ; and it was a real mortification for those for whom there was nothing left.[161] Nobles and peasants were equally alive to his sanctity. The licentiate, Miguel de Valverde, said at Seville : "He is a seraph in the flesh, a flaming torch." [162]

"Who is that religious ? " an innkeeper asked George of St. Joseph, " surely he is a saint." [163]

Teresa of Jesus once said, " He is a saint, and has been one all his life." And she went on to add, " that he had reached as great a degree of sanctity as a creature can reach in this life." [164] His dark eyes saw the things of this world in the light of Eternal Wisdom. His government was just, " neither too mild, nor too severe " ; [165] for he weighed all things in God's balance.

"I have sometimes heard him say," Eliseus of the Martyrs remarks, " that no lie, however well concealed and skilfully constructed, when closely observed, fails to show, somehow or other, that it is a lie." [166] At St. Roch in

Cordova, a Carmelite friar, too fond of sweet things, had to admit to the clear-sighted Prior that he had pilfered some pots of jam that had been set apart for Christmas ! [167] " There is no devil, transformed into an angel of light, who, if attentively watched, does not end by showing himself for what he actually is. It is no use for a hypocrite to be clever, knavish and double-faced : you will find him out, by having to deal with him occasionally, and by observing him." [168] Martin of the Assumption also says that the Prior and conventuals at Granada wanted to receive a postulant on account of his good qualities. John thought he should be refused. When asked for his reasons, he said, " *You will see why.*" The man received the habit, and, shortly afterwards, the novice's wife appeared, with her two children, loudly demanding the restoration of her husband.[169]

Though he was only a Prior (and not the Provincial), he founded the Carmelite Monastery of Bujalance, on June 24th, 1587. Then, for a year, he laid aside his pilgrim's staff, which has been preserved by the Carmelite nuns of Granada. It is a slight hazel stick, about four feet long, from the top of which a gourd could be hung.

John used to hear the confessions of his daughters in " The Convent of the Great Captain," and say to each a few words of fire which came from his soul, inflamed with love of God.[170] " *Courage, look on high, towards Life Eternal.*[171] *Let us love to realise our own nothingness !* [172] *O hope of Heaven ! that obtaineth as much as is hoped for !* " [173] He consoled little Sister Augustine, and kept them all in peace.[174]

On one occasion John had a meal in the convent, and afterwards, during recreation, the Sisters listened to him as they worked. Mary Evangelist of Jesus and Mary of St. John, provided with their skein-winders, were striving to see which should finish first. Mary Evangelist was in a hurry, because she was much behind her companion. John said to her : " *Go quietly, do not lose peace and tranquillity of soul, you will finish first.*" This seemed impossible to the community, for Mary of St. John had a great start. Nevertheless, she stopped suddenly, and was unable to finish.[175]

John never worried. "Worry is always useless." [176] George of St. Joseph's pot of rice might boil over and burn just at meal time : "*Do not be worried, my son,*" said John kindly, "*let us have whatever else you've got. Our Lord does not mean us to eat rice.*" "That was the convent's golden age," the former cook pathetically concludes. [177]

He devoted his evenings to the spiritual formation of the friars, [178] and when he delivered his *pláticas*, raised their hearts to God. [179] They loved him as dearly as if he were the father of each one, so that, when he returned after a few hours' absence in the city, those who saw him ran to ask for his blessing, and kissed his hand or scapular. And John caressed them. [180] Not a single novice abandoned the habit in Luis de San Angel's time, though there were twelve of them. If John saw any of his sons " sad and lonely, he called him and led him aside, sometimes to the *huerta*, sometimes to the country : and, however great the friar's troubles, he returned happy and strengthened, filled with the desire to bear great afflictions for the love of Our Lord Jesus Christ." [181]

" All the novices had, in their breviaries, little slips on which were drawn and painted Mount Carmel and the Ascent . . . almost all the religious knew by heart the poem of the *Dark Night*. They used often to sing it during recreation after meals, or at any other periods of relaxation," [182] which the Father Prior excelled in providing, for he well knew how an intense community life may become burdensome to young hermits. On one occasion, he took a band of his sons, and walked with them as far as the Sierra Nevada. He said : "*We must be solitaries to-day, so let each of you go wherever he pleases on the mountain, quite alone, weeping, singing, or praying, as God moves him.*" [183] A religious asked him, in the presence of Juan Evangelista, why he took them into the country so frequently, *tan de ordinario :* He answered : "*So that when one is in the convent, one may have less desire to leave it.*" [184] Freedom, based on such wise motives, cannot be regarded as an extravagance, not to be imitated. John was a man of intelligence, enlightened by faith. He was never wanting in " Christian and monastic politeness."

His manners were " wonderfully gracious." He treated his friars as men, and not as machines. " When treated with unreasonable severity, they end by growing cowardly. . . . And he said that one might suspect the devil's interference when religious were ruled in such a fashion. If fear thus reigns, superiors no longer have anyone who will dare warn or contradict them, when they make a mistake." [185]

.   .   .   .   .   .

On June 19th, 1588, the first General Chapter of the Reform opened at Madrid. During the month of May, Gracian was deprived, by judgment of the definitory, " of active and passive voice, of all office in the province and in the Order." [186] This was in punishment of his criticism of superiors. It was believed that he had his superiors in mind, when he said that those men were " *visible demons and enemies of the Cross of Christ*, who, refusing to work on the missions, and expose themselves to the dangers of a sea voyage, turn others aside from this vocation." [187] Gracian's partisans denounced this proceeding as lacking humanity, and declared it was from " obvious motives of ambition that he had been refused a voice at the next Chapter, and declared ineligible for the office of Vicar General." [188] A brief of Sixtus the Fifth, obtained by the exertions of Doria and John of Jesus Roca in Rome and Madrid, was to be promulgated by the Apostolic notary.[189] This brief, *Cum de Statu*, erected the Reform into a Congregation, subject to " the General as the universal head of the whole Order," but governed by a Vicar General to be elected every six years by the Discalced. The Vicar was entrusted with " full, free and absolute power to make such statutes and ordinances as he should think fit . . . as also to change, partly or entirely, whatever he might find necessary to abrogate." To this was added, " power to retrench all manner of abuses, to command all prelates, superiors, provincials and others, whatsoever office they may hold, and all religious of the said congregation, and to enjoin them to observe inviolably whatever shall be generally ordained." [190]

It was now nine years since Teresa had first met Doria at

Avila—early in July, 1579—and in the meantime he had been ruminating " many projects." The day had at length come for him " to order all things perfectly in this dear flock of the Virgin." [191] The Lord had chosen Gracian,[192] " to sustain the beginnings of the Reform." His day was over.

Doria was elected Vicar General, as Anne of Jesus had foretold.[193] He was allotted six consultors, as specified in the brief, to assist in the government of the congregation : John of the Cross, Anthony of Jesus, Ambrose Mariano and three others. The *Consulta* was established.[194]

Sebastian of St. Hilary, who was present at the Chapter, as *Socius* from Cordova, says that John " spoke like an apostle, without human respect. He was guided by justice in all things." The Chapter " was very calm and peaceful." Sebastian adds that " he had not noticed any cabal. . . ." [195] What exactly does he mean by those ambiguous words ? What lies concealed behind this half-raised veil ? Was John of the Cross opposed to the establishment of the *Consulta ?* Mary of the Incarnation (Yoland de Salazar) tells us that John was no more in favour of its being set up than Gracian.[196] If so, did Doria merely tolerate his First Consultor ? This seems almost unbelievable, yet, however deferential John may have been, he was not a man who feared to speak his mind.

Between the sessions, John retired to the house of Matallana at the end of the second garden of St. Hermenegild's, far from the bustle of the convent ; and there, though God was constantly present to his spirit, he sank still deeper into the depths of prayer.[197] No doubt he recalled the presentiment he had had at Granada of sufferings to come, even more terrible than those of Toledo.[198] " *To suffer, to act, to be silent.*" [199] " *The apostolic life is a life of contempt.*" [200] Such were the phrases that were henceforward to fall from his pen.

He visited Anne of Jesus and heard the confessions of the Sisters [201] in the monastery which had been founded by Anne and himself in September, 1586, after a difficult and supernatural journey from Granada to Beas, Malagon, Toledo, and Illescas. Their arrival at Madrid had been signalised by a marvellous blaze of light, which certainly

did not proceed from the royal palace.[202] *Nuestra madre,*
John used to call Anne,[203] who was the consolation of those
who had lost their mother Teresa.   Doria, Anthony and
Mariano also felt this.[204] *Nuestra madre* was Teresa's equal
supernaturally, and surpassed her in natural gifts.[205]

The ardour of her charity was the cause of her illnesses.
" *What can be done, the Mother is sick with love, ?* " John would
say.[206]   He knew Anne's inner life, and often received the
same heavenly lights as she had been granted.[207]   During
Mass at Granada both had a terribly prophetic vision.[208]
The misfortunes which they had foreseen soon befell them.
The quasi-absolute concentration of power, intended to safeguard the Reform completely, became the common topic
of conversation for both Carmelite Fathers and nuns.   Thus
speaks the *Reforma* :

" In colleges . . . in the humblest buildings, nothing was
heard but cries, complaints and murmurs."   Such autocracy had never been seen in any religious Order.   And the
old chronicler lets himself go : " For Genoese and Venetians,
who rule bears, tigers, lions and wolves, the rod of iron may
be tolerated, and the arm upraised over their blood-stained
necks, in order that they may be reduced to reason, and
prevented from disturbing the republic.   But in religion, and
especially in a reformed religious order, in which all are like
simple, obedient and submissive sheep ! "   The priors complained bitterly at seeing themselves deprived, at a blow, of
the vote which they had exercised in former Chapters, and
that, too, contrary to a recent decree of the Sacred Congregation. . . .   The provincials lamented at seeing their authority reduced to a sort of mere administrative power.   And
what of the nuns?   " They will be grievously affected,
obliged as henceforward, to reveal minute personal details
and ordinary little failings to seven different persons . . .
as well as to answer juridical enquiries on many occasions.
. . . There will be tears, groans and lamentations because,
in many cases, the power of electing their superiors will be
withdrawn, and they will be restricted in their choice of
confessors." [209]

Had not Teresa said, twelve years previously, before John of Roca's regulations : " That is exactly what my daughters dread. They fear the coming of severe prelates who may overburthen them, imposing too heavy a load " ? [210]   But Doria considered " this new method of government which was employed at Genoa, his native city, *celestial*." [211]   And, according to his, Gracian's, own words, if Jerome Gracian of the Mother of God was elected at Valladolid to be Vicar Provincial of Mexico,[212] that was because his presence would have made it impossible to set up what Mary of the Incarnation characteristically called *la máquina de la Consulta*.[213]

It was a time for saints to remain tranquil and recollected ; later on they would be forced to act.

" When I saw my two saints," writes this same nun, who had abandoned the Court to follow Anne of Jesus, " together at the grille of the *locutorio* in our convent at Madrid, speaking of heaven, they seemed to me nothing but two seraphim, all on fire with the love of God's Majesty." [214]

CHAPTER XIX

THE PROOF OF MYSTICAL LOVE

It was decided that the seat of the new government should be established at Segovia, in order to avoid influences coming from Madrid,[1] and John was appointed Prior, with the duty, in the absence of the Vicar General, of governing the Consulta and the house, *como cosa propia*, as if it were his own.[2]

The Discalced Carmelite Fathers were recent arrivals in this old Castilian city. Father John had advised his spiritual daughter, Doña Ana de Peñalosa, to establish a college of the Reform there, seeing that her husband had left her, in his will, the choice of endowing either a hospital or a monastery in their native city.[3] On March 19th, 1574, John had brought the Sisters to Segovia,[4] and now the time had come to introduce the Brethren. The Vicar Provincial of Castile made the arrangements. On May 3rd, 1586, after a stay in the Archdeacon's house, the Discalced founders alighted at a convent which had been abandoned by the Trinitarians, quite close to the hermitage of *Nuestra Señora de Fuencisla*, outside the walls, to the west of the city, in the gorge of St. Mark.[5] As soon as the little church had been restored, it was dedicated to Our Lady of Mount Carmel, on July 13th. When John arrived on August 10th, 1588,[6] to take up his duties, two saints—John of Matha and John of God—had already honoured (we are told) the poor, narrow, insanitary buildings with their presence.

·   ·   ·   ·   ·   ·

On September 16th, the Consulta decided that the Vicar should make a visitation of the congregation,[7] and John took over full charge, even to the smallest details, until February, 1589.[8] He confirmed the election of the Prioress of Valencia,[9] and informed Mariano, and even Doria, of his

decisions.[10]   Administration devoured his time.   He slept
only two hours at night.[11]   The foundation of the Carmelite
nuns at Cordova was now imminent, and he watched over
it closely.[12]   Moreover, he had to see after the choir-books,
ceremonial, offices of the saints of the Order, the preliminary
instruction of novices,[13] and, in fact, to organise the whole
life of the congregation.   He could only answer letters
" briefly," [14] and had no opportunity of developing his
ideas.[15]   Once more, all were delighted with his government.
The discontented element had nothing new to advance in
the "memoranda" which they forwarded to Philip II, and
the King himself praised the Consulta on February 24th,
1589.[16]   On his general visitation Doria was not quite so
successful.   Wherever he went, the brethren were constrained,
afraid of the " machine " of which he was the inventor.[17]

In the *Libro de los Perlados* of Segovia, we read that Father
John of the Cross, *difinidor mayor*, ruled from August, 1588,
until the end of February, 1589, and then from October till
May, 1591.[18]   Why this break of eight months ?   It is
obvious that he was not away from home, as several letters,
dated April, June, July and September, 1589, were written
at Segovia.   The reason, perhaps, may have been that the
Vicar General resided only from February to October,
1589, at the seat of government of the Consulta, and
that John acted as president for the remainder of the
triennate.

It is certain that, in the same year, with a view to building
higher up and on drier soil, John, thanks to the generosity
of Doña Ana who may, perhaps, have already arrived in
Segovia, purchased part of the slope of a hill which looks
on the Alcazar.[19]   The Alcazar towers over the ravine
formed by the Eresma and the Clamorès, which are here
divided by its rocky prow.   Segovia is built on a lofty promontory between hills which rise from a dusty golden-
coloured soil.   The walls of the new Carmelite convent
began to rise.   John, at the end of his priorship, left two
buildings completely finished, and also a great part of the
church, a solid and sober construction, whose harmonious
plan we may admire to-day.   Exhausted as he was, he used

to labour with his hands, helping the masons, looking for stones amidst the rocks of the *huerta*, with his head bare winter and summer, and his feet shod only in *alpargatas*.[20] The winter is severe in Segovia, especially for a man with only a poor serge habit, and a cape so rough that it seemed as if it were made of goatskin, *de pelos de cabras*.[21] Mediocrities who aspire after a life of ideal tranquillity, who are frightened at the smallest effort, might well say that such " a contemplative life " does not help contemplation. But the true mystic, though fretted by the burden of matter, is never afraid of work. The weight of Love which he bears in his soul is as heavy as the Cross, and whenever he falls, there resounds in his royal spirit a call for the total annihilation of self. To the natural man this is folly, for he knows only the works of the flesh, and knows not how to savour those sublime extravagances which draw their reason from the Spirit of Wisdom and Knowledge. The soul penetrates the depths of mysteries, and judges all things according to the Supreme Cause. When it beholds the annihilation of the Word Incarnate, and the fund of misery subsisting in self, it desires to be naught, or even less, dust and refuse, in order that the glory of God may shine more resplendently amidst such humiliation.

John of the Cross, lost on the summit of Carmel, in the most ravishing contemplation he had yet experienced,[22] was now about to move forward, in full psychological liberty, and with all the strength of divine love, towards the *Exinanivit* of Jesus Christ.

After three hundred years, we climb, in silence or in tears, that high wall of reddish tufa, now clad in verdure, and mauve and yellow flowers, which stands at the end of the garden in Segovia. We look up, and see a few cypresses, and the great hermitage where " a grotto, scarcely longer than a recumbent man " is now venerated. " Nature had hollowed it out of the rock. . . . From it can be seen a wide expanse of sky, the city and its alcazars, temples and towers, the lofty sierras, and fields, stretching away from Segovia to Alba." [23]

To this grotto, *el Jilguero de Dios*—God's linnet, as Anne of Jesus and her daughters used to call John [24]—was wont to retire for the sake of solitude. Bernard of Jesus says that " from that grotto, a great stretch of sky, river and landscape may be seen." [25] There is nothing to break the calm of that wide stretch of countryside. The cry of *choucas*, the song of nightingales, the grave murmur of the river and whispering of the saint's fountain at the foot of the rock, only serve to accentuate the silence. As for storms and noisy tempests, John dispelled them with the sign of the cross.[26] Nature obeys the man who has won back his primitive kingship. Lions hollowed out a grave for Paul the Hermit, and Francis of Assisi preached to the birds.

John loved his silent grotto where he spent " all the time he could spare," and used to say, occasionally, to the religious who came looking for him : " *Leave me, Father, for the love of God, I am not made for dealing with the world.*" [27] Nevertheless, he did himself violence, and came down. " Eating, drinking, talking, transacting business—after all, what does it matter—if we never cease to think of God, by a desire of the heart? Nothing is of more importance for interior solitude." [28]

" Frequently " it was Doña Ana de Peñalosa and her niece, Ines de Mercado, who were waiting for him. Doña Ana, abandoning her palace in Segovia and her brother's house in Madrid, had a house built for herself near the convent, so that she might be close to her spiritual father. And his religious used to say : " Jerome, Paula and Eustochium are now speaking of God." [29]

He converted the elegant worldling, Angela de Aleman, and she laid aside her jewels, cut off her hair, wore a linen coif, a thick serge dress, cape and clogs. Bernarda and Geronima de Carrien remembered with delight that, when they were quite small, the Father Prior " very often " might be found in their parents' house or in that of Doña Angela del Espinosa, their aunt.[30]

It was not always in the grotto that just fitted him and was the smallest nook in which he could rest,[31] that John of the Cross would pray after the fashion of the anchorites.[32]

Juan Evangelista, who loved him so tenderly as to wish to be always in his company,[33] followed the saint and saw him at prayer during whole nights, his arms in the form of a cross, stretched beneath the trees. Juan also saw him " for several nights on end, *muchas noches enteras*, at the window of his cell, from whence the heavens and all the countryside were visible." " John knelt there in prayer, so inflamed and ravished in God that although Juan shook him, he could not bring him back to himself." Juan Evangelista " remained with him until morning, or until he had come to himself, and then the Venerable Father used to say : *What are you doing here, and why do you come ?* " [34] John would then say Mass, which was served by Bernard of Jesus, " almost every day during the three years the saint resided in Segovia." He used to pray for long hours before the Blessed Sacrament, and Bernard as he left, felt the heat of the furnace of love which inflamed the Father. John would sometimes sit for a long time close beside the good Brother whilst the latter was at work. The saint was lost in prayer all the time, no matter what the Brother was doing. Even during recreation his conversation was of God. He used to do violence to himself so as to be able to attend to ordinary affairs, and when walking in the company of others, John shut his hand and secretly struck the wall lest he might lose the thread of conversation. The result of this was that the backs of his hands became skinned.[35]

We should not be disconcerted at such absorption. The Holy Spirit enabled him to be more watchful than any other prior. One day, he told Bernard of Jesus to remove a ladder, and the latter just arrived as somebody was about to climb it in order to commit a grave sin.[36]

Mary of the Incarnation, the Carmelite Prioress, reports that, when John was at the grille, he might be seen making efforts to attend to the conversation, and was occasionally so absorbed as scarcely to know what was being said to him. " *Tell me, where are we ?* " he used to say, on recovering himself. He admitted to her that, " he did great violence to himself in order to speak of earthly things." It was clear that he had not full possession of himself, " elevated in God as he was." The Prioress, probably anxious about her spiritual father's health, once asked him what he had eaten. *" Do you think I remember ? "* was his reply.[37]

In fact, at this period, he ate very little, *muy poco*, says Bernard of Jesus, and when " anything was sent in to him from outside he did not eat it, but gave it to the religious." [38] Despite the absorbing business of the Consulta, his penances (which were such that Luis de San Angel wrote, asking him not to be so hard on himself, as he was not very strong,*), his frequent ecstasies, which were so hard to resist, the holy Prior always assisted at midnight matins.[39] What nervous system, however admirably balanced, could stand such a strain ? God sustains the organism of His saints lest they fail, and His reply to scientific naturalism is to leave in the hands of the medical faculty the wearied and exhausted bones of a St. Teresa of Lisieux, as proof of His omnipotence. That little Sister was a true daughter of St. John of the Cross. Contemplatives most certainly are not idlers. By day and by night they make themselves like to the suffering Christ Who saves the world. Men and women go to Carmel not to speculate and dream, but to " live and die of love."

On July 18th, 1589, John wrote to Mary of Jesus, the Prioress of Cordova : *" It is God's will that you should be in this state in your houses, which are so poor and so intolerable from the heat . . . that you may be able to experience what you have professed, which is the naked Christ :* que es a Cristo desnudamente ; *in this way, souls who may feel called will know in what spirit they should come."* [40]

He slept very little in the poor little cell which, *difinidor mayor* though he was, he had selected, underneath the staircase. It was so small as scarcely to be able to contain the planks on which he stretched himself and a shelf fixed to the wall by hinges. A wooden cross, a paper picture : that was all. But this poor cell was close to the choir,[41] and John of the Cross was the disciple whom Jesus loved.

Raising himself above all knowledge,[42] John lost himself with Christ in God. God cannot be found apart from Christ.

* Alcaudete, P.A., fo. 120. The saint replied that all that was nothing and scolded Luis de San Angel affectionately.

Once, whilst he was prior, during Holy Week—which he always celebrated " with great tenderness and feeling" [43]— he suffered so intensely from the sufferings and Passion of Christ Our Lord, that he was unable to leave the house and visit the Carmelite nuns.   Juan Evangelista mentioned the fact to Maria de la Encarnacion, and it was well known to all the Brethren.[44]

Nevertheless, he was faithful—even during periods of intense cold and snowstorms—in going every week to the Calle Canongia Nueva, and also at any other time he was required, to hear the nuns' confessions.[45]   Anne of St. Joseph, a Toledan, twenty-one years of age and a cousin of Gracian's, was directed by him.   She says : " He spoke of his former sufferings as of something extremely dear to him, and often recalled the graces which Our Lord had then bestowed on him . . . he used frequently to say : ' *My child, seek for nothing but the naked Cross, for that is a precious thing.*' " [46]   He said to Isabella of Christ, when she told him of her difficulties : " *Daughter, swallow those bitter morsels because, the more bitter you find them, the sweeter they are to God.*" [47] One day, in 1588, he was on his way to hear the confession of a sick nun, and whilst walking towards the staircase in the *patio*, he saw a picture of Our Lord, falling beneath the cross, crushed like grapes in the winepress.   He was rapt in wonder, his face became glowing.   Unable to resist the ecstasy, he ran to a wooden cross suspended from the cloister wall.   He embraced it most tenderly, and said some words in Latin, which the sisters could not understand.[48]

Love has its secrets, but John did not conceal them from his brother.   Francisco de Yepes knew from experience that true contemplation is marked by a two-fold, extreme tendency :

Subirse hasta no poder más.	To raise oneself to the uttermost.
Bajarse hasta no poder más.	To abase oneself to the uttermost.[49]

" When Father John of the Cross was in Segovia," relates Francisco,[50] " and whilst he was Superior there, he sent for me.   And I went to see him.   When I had spent two or three days in his company, I asked him to let me go.   He

told me to remain for two or three days longer, that he did
not know when we should meet again.[51]   It was the last
time I saw him.   One evening after supper, he took me by
the hand and led me into the garden.   When we were alone,
he said to me : " *I wish to tell you something that happened to
me with Our Lord.   We had a crucifix in the convent, and, one day,
when I was standing in front of it, it occurred to me that it would be
more suitable to have it in the church.*[52]   *I was anxious to have this
crucifix honoured, not only by the religious, but also by the people.
I carried out my idea.   After I had placed it in the church, as
fittingly as I could, and whilst in prayer before it one day, Christ
said to me : ' Brother John, ask me for what you wish, and I will
give it you, for the service you have done me.'   And I said to Him :
' Lord, what I wish you to give me are sufferings to be borne for
your sake, and that I may be despised and regarded as worthless.' "* [53]

" To be despised and regarded as worthless " was the
reply Jesus expected from John of the Cross.   Love demands
a striking resemblance, and Christ is above all the Man of
Sorrows, Whose countenance is disfigured by blood and
spittle.   Teresa of the Child Jesus wished to be called
" Teresa of the Holy Face," and in the end this was added
to her name.   Nothing but " sufferings to be borne " would
have sufficed for John of the Cross.   What distinguishes the
true mystic from all others is the way he is attracted, not
merely by penance and sufferings, but, with an increasing
thirst, by humiliation that ends in a demand for opprobrium
out of love for Christ.   Tomás Perez remembered that he
had written : " *Lord, may all men despise me and make me of no
account for love of Thee,*" when Francisco, who did not know
how to write, was dictating his deposition by order of his
confessor.[54]   Teaching such as this surpasses all heroism,
and eradicates all pride : it destroys the " appetite for
honour from which so many other appetites spring." [55]   The
ethic of human dignity does not attain such heights.   We
have here the test of true mystical love : Carmel's saint
united in himself the ecstatic light of Divine Wisdom and the
shattering folly of Christ despised.

He that has ears to hear, let him hear !

This incident in the saint's life, as contained in Francisco's deposition, enables us to see the moral sanity, the admirable equilibrium to be found in all the saints. With John of the Cross the most exacting love of God is in closest harmony with the most tender, brotherly love. It is the height of psychological liberty, or, better still, the triumph of grace over nature and it brings joy to heaven.

Catalina Alvarez appeared to her sons in the Carmelite Monastery of Segovia. Francisco's charming little daughter, who died when she was five, accompanied her grandmother. As is usual in the Alcazar of Heaven,[56] angelic music accompanied the vision.

.   .   .   .   .   .

On the occasion of a great jubilee, Alonso del Espiritu Santo heard John's general confession. He declared on oath that the saint's soul was more angelic than human and that he had never committed a grave sin in all his life.[57] Long before this, Teresa of Jesus said that " she tenderly loved John of the Cross, *amaba tiernamente*, because he had a most pure and candid soul, was a man without malice, no intriguer, and had reached a great height of contemplation and peace." [58]

> *La blanca palomica*
> *Al arca con el ramo se ha tornado.*
> *Y ya la tortolica*
> *Al socio deseado*
> *En las riberas verdes ha hallado.*[59]

> The pure white dove, returning,
> Her olive branch brings to the ark serene,
> The companion of her yearning
> The turtle-dove hath seen
> Where the river flows its verdant banks between.

Francisco Ureña, barber-surgeon to the monastery, on leaving John's cell, saw at the window *una paloma blanca*, a white dove ; and this spiritual man, who led a holy life, understood that the Holy Ghost, or an angel, had assumed this shape.[60] It was, perhaps, from the causeway that runs beside the monastery separating it from the mediaeval church of the Templars, *la Vera Cruz*, that he saw this symbolic messenger of peace and chaste affection. Bernard of Jesus also noticed a most beautiful white dove, *una paloma blanca muy hermosa*, on a beam over the door in John's cell, when the saint was not present, and on other occasions, when he was there : this dove made no sound, neither did it eat anything, or go with the other doves.[61]

What marvels love works ! Luca de San José carried off his Prior's miserable coverlet, wrapped it around him, and was no longer assailed by temptations against purity.[62] Virtue went out from John : he purified, for he himself was pure. His answer to Christ was not the answer of overbold love. He could be a victim, because he was a saint.

Whilst John was still in Granada, he pointed out that St. Paul, in the second epistle to the Corinthians, puts patience before miracles. " And I, too, can bear witness," wrote Eliseus of the Martyrs, " that Father John of the Cross, by the practice of this virtue, was a true apostle. He bore sufferings, grievous enough to beat down the cedars of Lebanon, with incomparable patience and endurance." [63] John knew by experience that sacrifice is no laughing matter. The sufferings he was now about to endure were not, like those of Toledo, simply purifying ; they were to be, what was far more to be dreaded, a copy of Christ's.[64] " I fill up those things that are wanting of the sufferings of Christ, in my flesh, for his body, which is the church." [65] John alone, with Anne of Jesus, was to guard the spirit of Carmel. Teresa had now been six years dead, and Gracian had lost all influence with his brethren.

On November 9th, 1588, John wrote to Ambrose Mariano, the third definitor, and Prior of Madrid : " *There is no news about Father Gracian, except that Father Anthony has already arrived.*" [66] The Consulta, then, had not ceased to take an active interest, even in Doria's absence, in Teresa of Jesus' poor friend. It is quite true that John " venerated the person of Jerome of the Mother of God for the gifts which God had granted him, and the incomparable services he had rendered the Order," but it is likewise true that he did not

" approve of his methods of action." [67]   At the Chapter of
Lisbon, he had warned Gracian not to have Doria elected,
because the latter would strip him of his habit,[68] but, now
that John was *difinidor mayor*, he seems to have felt bound
not to defend Gracian openly.   Bound by what ?   Certainly
not by fear of *the lion of Carmel*.   It was the result of Gracian's
own attitude ; and, indeed, the latter was quite safe, for the
Cardinal Archduke Albert had appointed him apostolic
commissary of the Mitigated Carmelite Fathers in Portugal.[69]   The friendship of a John of the Cross could not be
mere blind sympathy.   Teresa herself was well aware of
Gracian's deficiencies.   They had become accentuated under
Doria's exasperating *régime*, and we have no evidence that
John could have exercised at such a distance a pacifying
influence on his rather obstinate friend.   Moreover, the
failure at Lisbon did not encourage John to continue giving
good advice.

One day Juan Evangelista went to the Prior's cell to speak
to him.   He entered, and approached, thinking that John
was asleep on a bench.   He states that the saint was in an
ecstasy, raised and suspended above the ground.   He went
back to the bursar's office and, coming back later, found that
John had returned to himself.   Seeing the latter " not at
all like his usual self," [70] he asked what had happened,
because when he had previously entered, in order to speak
to John, he had seen him in an ecstasy : " *Do not say that, my
son, I was asleep.*"   But Juan was not satisfied, and insisted : " No, Father, I came in here, and saw you raised
above the ground."   John, thus driven into a corner,
revealed the following facts to his confessor.   " *Remember, I
command you not to mention what I am about to say to anyone, as
long as I live.   I was recommending Father Gracian's affairs to
God, and I beheld a sea, and our Father Vicar General and the
definitors went into it, and I cried out to them to come out, because
they were exposing themselves to the danger of being drowned, and
in the end, I saw they were all drowned.*" [71]   Juan Evangelista
(obviously at a much later date) attributed this to the fact
that they had done wrong in placing Gracian's cause in the
hands of seculars.

God blessed the attitude which John was to assume when confronted with Doria's frankly inexcusable, underhand dealings. Seeing that the superiors wished to drive Gracian out of the Order, Alonso says, " He was always at hand to advise them not to cast themselves into such a deep sea of scandal, adding that the Order had other chastisements for the punishment of any religious. Whilst he was definitor general, he prevented Gracian's expulsion by such arguments." [72]

Si lo es, sin duda alguna
Y amigo de perfección
Y es sola su pretensión
Colocarnos en la luna. *

Indeed he is without a doubt
Perfection's greatest friend as well,
And this he aims to bring about :
That in the moon we all should dwell !

This amusing and not malicious portrait of " our great Doria " was written by Mary of St. Joseph, " the best member of the Order," to whom Teresa once wrote " If they ask my advice they will select you as foundress when I die." [73] It is not poets alone who have fine dreams ; the kingdom of finance and business has its own idealists, and they are dangerous men whose plans must be carried out.

It was, perhaps, John of the Cross who warned Anne of Jesus, probably in June, 1588, that the Consultors intended at their first meeting to change several points in the Carmelite nuns' constitutions. [74] Anne acted cleverly. She twice managed to get out of Doria a reply which would protect her.

It was an ultimatum. Anne and her daughters were at the grille, in the presence of the Vicar General. Doria was presiding at the Consulta.

" Father," said Anne, " I am afraid the Fathers of the

* This quatrain is taken from *Redondillas exhortando a las Carmelitas Descalzas a conservar las Constituciones de Santa Teresa.* " Hermoso retrato del Padre Doria a quien acusa tan sólo de exagerado celo, salvando sus intenciones," wrote Don Vicente de la Fuente in a note (*Escritos de Santa Teresa,* Tomo segundo (1862). Apéndices. Sección quinta, número 4, p. 448).

Consulta may make many changes in the laws and constitutions which our Mother Foundress has left us."

" Not at all, Mother, Your Reverence need fear nothing. If anything is changed, it will only be some trifle."

" Our Constitutions are already authorised by the Nuncio of His Holiness ; would Your Reverence consent that, in order that the Constitutions may be still stronger, a brief of confirmation should be asked for from the Sovereign Pontiff ? "

" Certainly, Mother."

Mary of the Incarnation does not remember if anything else was said ; but what she did know was that, before Doria left, Anne, wishing to receive an even more definite assurance, said finally :

" Father, did Your Reverence not say it would be well to get a brief from Rome concerning our Constitutions ? " He answered " Yes," and that " if there were no one else to go to Rome for it he himself would go on his bare feet." He gave still more assurances and, after he had gone, Anne said :

" My daughters, you are witnesses to what our Father Vicar General has just said." [75]

Doria practised mental reservation.[76]   He would certainly go to Rome barefooted in order to have the rules of St. Teresa approved, but not yet ; he would go when, thanks to the brief *Cum de Statu,* he had made use " of the free and full faculty of changing the Constitutions, or making others, according to the needs of the new *régime.*" [77]   Anne had read him aright. As her superior, had he not expressly told her that she, Anne of Jesus, might have recourse to the Pope ? " For the greater security of her conscience, she took the advice of the wisest and greatest servants of God who were then to be found in Madrid (Don Teutonio de Braganza, and Fathers Luis de Leon and Dominic Bañes) [78] ; they all assured her that she might act with a safe conscience, and that, her superior having spoken as he had, she was not sinning against obedience. She therefore determined to take measures to apply for a brief by a letter written to His Holiness Sixtus the Fifth." [79]

Anne of Jesus managed with great secrecy to get the King's sister, the Empress Maria, interested in her cause, and "communicated in the same manner with Mother Mary of St. Joseph, the Prioress of Lisbon, who, influenced by Father Gracian, then residing in that city, entered into her views." [80]   In 1589, Doctor Marmol, a distinguished priest and a relative of Gracian's, supplied with money and letters, set out for the Eternal City.   He was a clever negotiator, and a fine speaker.   He spent more than ten months in Rome, without the superiors knowing anything of the matter.   During this time, Peter of the Purification went about Spain, in a borrowed habit, from one Carmelite convent to another, endeavouring to enlist supporters, and collect funds. [81]

However, in the end, the whole thing came out.   Doria took up his pen, and his letters elicited three replies, obviously drawn up by Anne's theological friends. [82]   As the nuns did not desist, Doria decided to summon an extra-ordinary Chapter, which opened in Madrid on June 10th, 1590. [83]   It was decreed that "in all matters, great and small, in questions of law as well as in those that concern paternal authority, in elections and observances, the nuns should depend upon the Consulta. . . ."   "The Chapter took another measure.   In view of the expected brief, it decreed that, in case the nuns should obtain a commissary, the Order would abandon their direction, and hand them over to the Sovereign Pontiff, so that he might confide their government to whomsoever he wished. . . . All this was due to the holy desire of maintaining the *Descalcez* (Reform) in its primitive rigour, the sole daughter of the zeal of our Father Doria."   It was decided, moreover, to recall Gracian from Portugal, in order to put a stop to his efforts on behalf of the nuns, and against the Consulta. [84]

Alonso and Jeronimo tell us that John protested against the fixed determination of "the whole Chapter," thus to abandon the daughters of Teresa of Jesus. [85]   Doria remembered this fact, when he learned from Luis de Leon himself, on the occasion of the reception of the brief *Salvatoris*, that Anne of Jesus and her daughters had asked for either

Gracian or John of the Cross as their superior.[86]   It was clear that both were accomplices in this feminine movement for independence. John of the Cross was fully informed of all that was going on. When the Prioress of Segovia had been urged " to protest against the government of superiors, and do her utmost to have the brief carried out . . . he told her certain things which she afterwards saw fulfilled, as she herself relates in her declaration on oath, wherein she specially comments on our blessed Father's certainty of the success (*i.e.* the outcome) of this innovation, and how little he was disturbed by such manifestations of domestic warfare and extravagant solicitude." [87]

.   .   .   .   .   .

John, according to his custom, halted, after passing the bridge. He was half-way to the Carmelite nunnery. He sat, with his back to the city, on a grey rock,[88] in the shade of the poplars of the Alcazar. It was the end of May. He raised his eyes. On the far side of the rapid and abundant waters of the Eresma, high up, dominating the pines, elms and Indian chestnuts, stood the rosy-walled Parral ; on his left, close to a cypress, was the hermitage which he had built amidst the convent crags. . . . In the distance lay the snowy range of the Guadarrama. . . . After a few moments' rest, the saint stood up, moved along by the high crenellated wall, passed under the horseshoe arch of the *Puerta Santiago*, and at length reached the Carmelite convent. He mounted the steep staircase that leads to the parlour. Madre Maria de la Encarnacion was already there with all her daughters around her. Quite close to the grille was Isabella of Jesus—she was then barely thirteen years of age, and she was watching the saint of Carmel as he entered. He smiled on her for he loved her *ternísimamente*, most tenderly, and knew that she was a predestined soul.[89]

He was about to leave Segovia to take part in the General Chapter of Madrid, which was to open on June 1st of this year 1591, at Saint Hermenegild's.[90] "Father, who knows but that Your Reverence may come back Provincial of this province ! " cried the fragile Maria de la Encarnacion, trembling with excitement. "*I shall be thrown into a corner,*[91] *like an old rag,*[92] *an old kitchen cloth,*"[93] was his answer, for he had been interiorly forewarned by God.

At Madrid, Nicholas Doria swept aside all obstacles to the advancement of his schemes. Luis de Leon[94] and Dominic Bañes had been, in turn, disgraced. "Why is Bañes meddling?" cried Philip II to his former banker, as Doria explained the state of affairs.[95] When Philip had read the memoranda of both friars and nuns, he praised the zeal of both parties, and ordered the definitory that the plan to abandon the direction of the Carmelite nuns should not be carried out, and that he himself would see that the nuns' brief should be revoked and that they should submit to the Order.[96]

The Chapter opened on the eve of Pentecost and, on the following Tuesday, June 4th, the elections were held : John was not re-elected to any post. "*Do not be disturbed at my having no office,*" he said to Gregory of the Holy Angel, "*it is a great mercy from God.*"[97] On June 5th, the Vicar General and definitors made an official note of John's offer to lead to Mexico an expedition of twelve Carmelites, who had been asked for by the Fathers in that country, and his proposal was accepted.[98] Quiroga adds another detail : on June 25th, this decision was definitely conveyed to John at Peñuela.[99] This is an error, for John was still in Madrid. He wrote from there, on July 6th, to Anne of Jesus, the foundress of Segovia :

"*As for myself . . . , set free from the charge of souls, and in possession of liberty, I may, if I wish, enjoy, with God's grace, peace, solitude and the delicious fruits of forgetfulness of self and all things. . . . What I ask of you, my daughter, is to pray to Our Lord that whatever happens He may continue this favour to me in future. For I am really afraid that they may send me back to Segovia, and not leave me with the full liberty that I now enjoy. Still I will do all in my power to escape from this office.*[100]

Assuming that the dates given are correct, what occurred between June 25th and July 6th? It seems clear that by July 6th John was no longer assigned to the Mexican expedition. There is only one explanation possible. John, by his offer to go to the American Indies, had forestalled, in the manner of the Saints, the inevitable course of events. Doria would, at all costs, take care that John should not be the superior of the Carmelite nuns. Now that Doria was aware of the fact that the brief *Non Ignoramus*, which had been asked for by the King, made no mention of the nomination of a commissary for the government of the nuns, such as had been obtained by Anne of Jesus in the previous year, there was no need to send into honourable exile a poor, worn-out creature like John of the Cross.[101] Something more effective could be done. John was to have a different experience of the cold rage of the *lion of Carmel*. Jerome Gracian of the Mother of God, Anne of Jesus, Mary of St. Joseph were also to suffer from his implacability.

Elias of Cortona, offended by Franciscan poverty, desired with all his mighty energy to impose laws that were only too human on his own Order.[102] Nicholas Doria also intended to be *the living rule* [103] of the Reform, now that " good Mother Teresa," as he called her, was no more. For three years John of the Cross had seconded Doria in his attempts at organisation ; obediently, but without passion, he had supported the machinery of the Consulta. But now that Doria, with his obsession for issuing decrees—he promulgated more than three hundred whilst in office [104]—intended to consecrate his work of destruction by a master stroke, the last finishing touch to the Teresian constitutions of Alcalá,* John protested. He felt, as Baruzi rightly observes, that the Carmel of Teresa of Jesus was threatened " to its foundations " (Baruzi, 215). The new force that was invading the organism was, little by little, killing charity. Another spirit —that of servile fear—was now creeping into all hearts. " What can be more dangerous than when no one says anything at Chapters, when everything is conceded and adopted ? "

" If at Chapters," John goes on, " assemblies and meetings, men no longer have the courage to say what the laws

---

* The text of the Constitutions of Discalced Carmelite nuns, which were approved in 1926, is in close conformity with the Alcalá edition of 1581. We are, of course, leaving out of account the inevitable modifications demanded by the new code of Canon Law.

of justice and charity oblige them to say, from weakness, cowardice or fear of annoying the superior and consequently not obtaining an office (which is ambition showing itself) the Order is lost and utterly relaxed." [105]

St. John of the Cross made a stand at Madrid. He undertook a firm and dignified defence of the oppressed—Jerome Gracian and the Carmelite nuns. He stood alone : not one of the elders dared raise a voice.[106] As Teresa had foreseen, he gave his life for Gracian.[107] There comes a moment for the kingly soul, sovereignly free with a liberty, not only moral but psychological, to turn instinctively to the Good, and face, without a second thought, contempt and martyrdom. Nicholas Doria sent John of the Cross in disgrace to the solitude of Peñuela.[108]

.   .   .   .   .   .

The Saint of Carmel himself begs readers of this drama not to be scandalised. This is what he wrote in the midst of his afflictions :

" Do not be sad for me. . . . I am not sad. What does greatly distress me is to see a fault imputed to one who has none. It is not men who do these things, but God, Who knows what we need, and ordains it for our good. Think nothing else, save that God ordains all. Where there is no love put in love, and you will draw love out. *Y a donde no hay amor, ponga amor y sacará amor . . .*" [109]

This letter is dated July 6th, 1591. Yet some days later, his human heart heavy from so much injustice, John of the Cross arrived one morning in Toledo, with Elias of St. Martin, Doria's future successor in the Generalship. It was four o'clock ; both said Mass. They then shut themselves up in a room to converse, and console each other. Father Julian of the Visitation frequently asked them to have a meal, but they asked to be left alone ; they did not want to eat. They remained together, far into the night : *hasta muy de noche.* Then John, just before leaving for Peñuela, declared, in the presence of all, that he was departing, completely consoled, and ready to bear any suffering whatsoever, with the grace which God had given him that day.[110]

CHAPTER XX

THE SECOND PEACE

At Granada, Isabel de la Encarnacion arranged with an artist to paint John's portrait, without his knowledge. They made use of an opportunity afforded them by his being rapt in ecstasy one day whilst giving an instruction to the nuns at the grille of the *Grán Capitán*.[1] Isabel was much pleased with the picture, and had some words inscribed on it which the saint had constantly on his lips : *Deus, vitam meam annuntiavi tibi : posuisti lacrimas meas in conspectu tuo.* O God, I have declared to thee my life : thou hast set my tears in thy sight (Psalm lv. 9). Copies of this portrait were made.[2] Juana de Pedraza obtained one, and another was taken by Anne of Jesus [3] to France, and afterwards to Flanders, where we shall hear of it again.[4]

We should be on our guard against imagining John of the Cross, even in ecstasy, as anything like one of El Greco's contorted saints. The "true portrait belonging to the Carmel of Troyes" is much more like one of Zurbaran's Carthusians.[5] John of the Cross, says Eliseus of the Martyrs, was " a man of medium build, his countenance was grave and venerable, rather brown in colour, his look was kindly, his society and conversation peaceable." Alonso says, " his aspect and visage corresponded with the Church's liturgy. At Passiontide, the compassion of his soul was revealed ; at Christmas, his tender affection for Jesus ; at Ascension, it was as if he mounted up to Heaven with Our Lord ; on feasts of the Blessed Virgin his love for the Mother of God was revealed." [6] But, even when the flame of ecstasy gilded that "rather swarthy countenance, *un poco moreno*, and nobly embellished it," [7] his features were not disturbed. It was the peace of the heights. No longer " the first peace of

331

the soul," but the peace after the night, transcending all things of sense.[8]

AT THE CONVENT OF THE DESERT OF PEÑUELA [9]

" Duruelo, Pastrana, Altomira, with their blazing splendours, present us with nothing to surpass Peñuela." [10] Gracian, in 1575, had noticed the fact. He wrote : " Silence, recollection, austerity and prayer were practised here in such fashion that it was the prototype of all the solitudes established later." [11]

After a year's abandonment following on the move to Calvario, the Fathers, at the urgent request of the inhabitants of Baeza,[12] resumed occupation of this " desert of Jesus and Mary of the Mountain of Peñuela " on August 11th, 1577. But as the town made a grant of some more land, they no longer lived in a marshy, airless spot. Whilst Francisco Espinel was Prior, " a more spacious church and a healthier house " were erected, and the religious began anew to cultivate the ground.[13] From the graves where lay the bones of the ancient Fathers there rose, in December, a perfume of roses and orange blossom.[14] Those who had been used to a common dormitory or huts of broom and cytisus, with a rush mat to lie on, and a goatskin coverlet, [15] blessed these more humane conditions. Not, indeed, that life was easy in the monastery. If we are to believe the old brother, John of St. Euphemia, who knew the Saint of Carmel, " at Peñuela, bread and a dish of cabbage was the usual food, fish a rarity." [16]

The religious gladly welcomed the arrival of the Father of the Reform. The Prior, Diego de la Concepcion, even asked him to undertake the spiritual direction of the whole community.[17] So, when the hour for recreation came round, John called the Brethren together. He gave them fragments of tile, and each tried who should throw nearest a paper mark which symbolised holy obedience. His eager cries stimulated the less successful. Diego of Jesus adds : " This teaches us what continual mental prayer he practised, even during recreation." [18] At

Peñuela, indeed, as at Segovia, he cultivated solitude in a marvellous way.

Even before daybreak, he went out to the *huerta*. There, by the banks of a stream, amidst the reeds, he often remained at prayer, until the heat of an August sun forced him home. He then returned, and said Mass. Afterwards, he withdrew to his cell, and gave himself up to prayer for as long as community exercises permitted. At other times, he went out into this solitude of Jesus and Mary and walked as if absorbed in God. Francis of St. Hilarion, who gives these valuable details, also tells us that John " spent some time in writing spiritual books." Some say that he passed the whole night in prayer in the garden and that, on one occasion, early in the morning, he was seen raised above the ground.[19]

How could John of St. Samson have said that there was a still higher life than that experienced here by John of the Cross ? [20]

He sometimes hid himself in the grottoes,[21] burying himself amidst the rocks. " *My son, do not be surprised at my spending time there, because I then have less matter for confession than when I converse with men,*" he used to say.[22] Man would never lose peace if he not only forgot his knowledge and laid aside his own ideas, but also refrained as much as possible from hearing, seeing and conversing. We are so light-minded and fragile that we can scarcely do this, despite our good habits, if only because our memory brings up matters that trouble and agitate the mind, even when the mind is in peace and tranquillity and recalling nothing. . . . " Indeed, it is always vain to disturb oneself, for it profiteth nothing. It is in vain to distress oneself even if everything is perishing, decaying and going wrong, for such distress brings more harm than good. But, to bear all things with peaceful and tranquil equanimity, not only brings much good to the soul, but also enables it in such adversities to judge with greater clearness and apply a suitable remedy." [23]

At this time John received distressing news in his letters

of spiritual direction, for he still kept up his correspondence.[24] Inquiries were being made into his conduct and some scandalised religious begged him " to protest against such an abuse of power by the Vicar General and his definitors, and to defend himself." He answered that he was a miserable worm, and that no one could do him wrong. Whatever his Creator assigned to him, and that alone, he ought to welcome for love of Him.[25]

More definite news arrived. The faithful Juan Evangelista wrote from Malaga [26] . . . In Andalusia, a certain Diego Evangelista was going from one Carmelite nunnery to another. What precisely were his powers ? It seemed that they were unlimited. He was making out a case against Gracian and John of the Cross. No one dared oppose him ; he was a member of the Consulta.[27] Isabel de la Encarnacion had been interrogated at the *Grán Capitán* in Granada. Feeling that hate was behind it, she grew angry : " Really," she said, " Father John should never have had anything to do with the Sisters if, thanks to them, he was to be treated so badly." But the secretary wrote it down : " This religious is clearly unworthy to live amongst the Discalced." It was only later that she discovered this false rendering of her words, because she was forced to sign her deposition on the spot, without reading it over.[28] It was a reign of terror : Diego offered presents to the Carmelite nuns ; he disturbed them by his commands and excommunications [29] ; panic caused the best of them to act foolishly. Agostina de San José, Isabel's sister, writing early in the seventeenth century, tells us how during this visit, " she was made guardian and custodian of several letters, which the nuns looked on as so many epistles of St. Paul, and sublime spiritual note-books," *una talega llena*, a bag full. She was ultimately told to burn them all, lest they might fall into Diego's hands.[30] Copies of John's portrait, which had been painted whilst he was in an ecstasy, were also destroyed.[31]

In Malaga—Juan Evangelista relates the incident—the interrogation even passed the bounds of decency, and Catherine of Jesus went in dismay to look for Father Balthazar, the confessor of the convent, who was luckily on the spot.

She had been made to say that, when she was in Granada,
Father John of the Cross had given her a kiss through the
grille ! It was utterly stupid ! He forbade persons even to
kiss his hands when he entered the enclosure.[32] Sebastian
of St. Hilary [33] says that his modesty was *excesiva*, and Sebastian had seen him conversing with the Sisters in Granada.
This is what had actually happened : Catherine was suffering from a sore beneath her ear. In the course of conversation in the *locutorio*, John, in the presence of all the nuns,
asked how it was. She raised the dressing quite simply, and
said : " Let Your Reverence see for yourself ! " The saint,
touching the sore with his finger, said : " *It is suppurating a
good deal.*" [34] That was all : it was just such a paternal
gesture as the former infirmarian of Medina might naturally
make. But the evil-minded see sin everywhere. Wisdom
alone gives eyes of discernment. And those who do not love
are never wise. Father Balthazar of Jesus heard Lucy of
St. Joseph complain, shortly after Catherine's remonstrance,
that the Visitor had not written down her statement accurately ; he told her to write to the Vicar General.[35] What
happened to the protest, and many others ? It is hard to
have to admit the fact, but it is the simple truth, Doria did
not punish Diego. When he saw the depositions which had
been taken in the convents of Granada, Malaga and Sanlúcar,[36] he disapproved of them, and said : " The Visitor had
no mandate to act thus,[37] and the charges he brings do not
affect Father John of the Cross." But he carefully preserved
the documents.[38] According to Quiroga, the next Chapter
was to examine into Diego's conduct.[39] I should like to
believe this. But, with Father Gregory of St. Joseph, I note
the fact that Doria, in 1587 and 1588, was able to punish
Gracian, by deprivation of active and passive voice in the
next two general Chapters, and that, in 1592, he felt himself
strong enough to drive Gracian from the Order.[40] There is
another point. Diego Evangelista was Doria's closest friend,
the man to whom he gave all his confidence.[41] Friendship
finds friends equal, or makes them so.[42] Moreover, after the
deplorable events related above, Doria did not break off his
friendship with the contemptible commissary. In 1593, he

brought Diego with him to the General Chapter of the whole Order in Cremona in order to give him an opportunity of showing off his ability as a preacher.[43] And after Doria's death, Diego was appointed Provincial of Andalusia. But he was not to enjoy the post. As his crime had been too lightly punished by men, he was struck down by God in the house of a secular at Alcalá la Real [44]—" this new saint," who " had fished for his provincialship in the blood of another." [45]

John, in the solitude of Peñuela, reflected that he had severely reprimanded Diego Evangelista at Seville, for having spent whole months away from his convent, preaching in only too human a fashion. He had also punished Father Chrysostom, the Prior of Ubeda, for the same fault.[46] He took up his pen : " *My soul does not suffer at all from what you tell me : it draws therefrom a lesson of the love of God and of one's neighbour.* As you see, the sons of my Mother have fought against me ! *Filii matris meae pugnaverunt contra me.*" [47] These words were written to the faithful Juan Evangelista in Malaga.

Intelligent observers believed that an effort was being made to discredit John of the Cross, so as to have him expelled.[48] It is only too true. A few months later, Diego Evangelista said : " If he were not dead, the habit would have been taken off his back, and he would have been driven out of the Order." [49] There were some gentle sons of the Virgin who were trembling at this moment lest, indeed, that very habit, which had been given to confound the devil, *qui datus est ad confusionem Sathane,*[50] should be dragged from the lacerated shoulders of their Father. John at once wrote to Juan de Santa Ana : " *Jesus !* . . . *my son, do not distress yourself on that account, the habit can be taken away only from those who refuse to amend or obey : now, as far as I am concerned, I am fully prepared to repair all my faults, and to obey, no matter what penance may be imposed on me.*" [51] " To die and perish rather than sin. These words, resolutely spoken, purify, elevate and enable us to grow in divine charity." *

It would seem as if, at this supreme moment when all the sons of St. Teresa were being handed over, bound hand and foot, to injustice, that John was weighing their souls. Were they loaded down by love ? Were they heavy enough " to sink so low that they could go no further,"—down to the very lowest depths of contempt ? Grace is a heavy weight ;—they, too, must suffer, as Christ had suffered, the depths of opprobrium. It would be terrible, but they, too, must be prepared to die and perish rather than sin.

The testing of the Reform of St. Teresa was too severe for ordinary strength. In Lisbon, Mary of St. Joseph, for having had recourse to the Pope, was confined for nine months in prison with a lock on the door. She was allowed to hear Mass only on days of obligation and to receive Holy Communion once a month, and even that was due to the tears of the nuns.[52]

Blasius of St. Albert, the delegate of the Consulta, carried out a visitation in Madrid. The Sisters " were overwhelmed with chapters, penances and reprimands." And this " doomsday," as Mary of the Incarnation called it, lasted from July 26th to the end of August. Anne of Jesus was to be regarded as a *huéspeda*, a stranger. Henceforth, she was not to have an active or passive voice in the affairs of the community. This lasted for three years. The sentence ran that she was to receive Holy Communion only at Easter, but thanks to the Empress, it was brought to her every month.[53]

It is here that Doria shows what manner of man he was. He could have been noble ; he behaved like a petty despot. Remember that he had been forced to admit to Mary of the Incarnation, that, in her petition for the brief, there had not been a great venial sin, and that it was only the manner and form in which the negotiations had been carried out that were blameworthy.[54] Anne of Jesus, on her death-bed, also solemnly declared to Father Hilary of St. Augus-

* *Antes morir y reventar, que pecar. . . .* Eliseus of the Martyrs, Ger., III, 60.

tine, who questioned her, with the object of inducing her to accuse herself, bidding her ask God's pardon for whatever guilt she had incurred by not submitting to her superiors, . . . that her conscience had nothing to reproach her with in this respect, and that she did not think she had ever been wanting in obedience.[55] Anne, from whose eyes, one day in Lent, two tears of blood had fallen : *le saltaron dos lágrimas de sangre viva,*[56] had a royal appreciation of humiliation. " Ah, Mother," said Mary of the Incarnation to her, " when will all this end ? When will they cease from accusing and mortifying you ? " She replied : " Silence, daughter, it is nothing to what I desire to suffer for the love of God ; because, were I to see myself led in disgrace through every street in Madrid, seated on an ass, and with a *caroça* on my head, it would afford me a sovereign content." [57] For the rest of her life she sighed after the years she had spent in Madrid. " All that I have learned since is nothing," she wrote to Diego de Guevara on June 1st, 1608. " It is only too true that were we shown the treasure to be found in insults and contempt, we should love those who are the occasions of them, if only we have not sinned. We shall see that on high, Father, and how little it matters either to be or not to be esteemed on earth." [58]

John knew that Mother Anne had Teresa's heroic courage. But what of Gracian ? Poor Gracian, whom Nicholas Doria and his definitors were anxious to see appear before them " humbly and adopting a becoming attitude." [59] He was in Madrid—summoned thither by the Chapter—imprisoned in a cell. Doria, haunted by the thought of him, was resolved to make him, as well as the whole Order, understand that an authority existed " capable of imposing a check on all those who might need it." [60] Poor Gracian ! Ten years previously, Teresa had written to him : " After enduring other characters, as you have with so much patience, you can only be pleased with a man who will not make you suffer." [61] No, Doria did not make Gracian suffer, he merely destroyed him. . . . On February 17th, 1592, Gregory of the Holy Angel, secretary to the Consulta, stripped Gracian of his habit and removed the monachal tonsure in the presence of the whole community in Madrid,[62] for his alleged crimes and acts of disobedience.* " He who had been chosen by the Blessed Virgin to raise up her Order,"[63] went out, clad in pilgrim's weeds, on his way to Rome, to go a-begging for the charity of a little justice.†

Poor Gracian ! John took up his pen, says Juan Evangelista, and in fine, close handwriting, despatched several letters demanding[64] that the man whom Teresa of Jesus had called " her first helper,"[65] should not be driven out of the Order.

The elements were more obedient to Love than was the Consulta. We know that John dispersed tempests by blessing the four corners of the heavens with his white cape.[66] Here is another miracle. One afternoon, Cristobal de Santa Maria went to ask his prior's permission to burn some stubble. He got a brand from the kitchen and set fire to the briars and bushes. The flames quickly drove through the stubble. The wind suddenly veered and the fire began to spread towards the monastery. It blazed nine feet high and could be heard crackling. The religious ran out and so did John. There was no human means of extinguishing a fire which stretched for a quarter of a league. The saint saw this, and went to kneel amongst the flames : *entre las llamas*, says Diego the prior, close to the olive orchard and the vineyard. He faced the fire, peaceful and splendid,

---

* We refer the reader for an account of Gracian's trial to Father Gregory of St. Joseph's work, already referred to : Le Père Jérôme Gratien . . . et ses juges (Pustet, 1904).

† Father Francis of the Holy Ghost, Conventual of Pamplona, and formerly a prelate of the Order, states, in a long account, that when he was Prior of Tortosa, Gracian, on his way to Rome, passed through that town without the habit. And that he (Gracian) told him that scarcely had he gone from the porter's lodge into the streets of Madrid, than God opened his eyes and let him see how badly he had behaved by not humbling himself and submitting to obedience and the correction of his superiors ; and that he realised he had been blinded as a punishment for his sins ; that those were the secret judgments of God ; that he knew well he was unworthy of being a religious, but that he would try and arrange to die in the Order, even if only in a " lay-brother's " habit. (Alm. 11, Cod. I, p. 395. Quoted by Andres, 13483, P.A. 75.)

Clement VIII, by a brief dated March 6th, 1596, annulled the sentence pronounced against Gracian. St. Teresa's poor friend, after wandering from country to country and spending two years in the hulks at Tunis, died at last, in 1614, with the Mitigated Carmelites of Brussels. (Bibl. Carm., I, cols. 645 to 650.)

besought the Lord, and the flames immediately died down before him.[67]

AT THE CONVENT OF " EL SEÑOR SAN MIGUEL " OF UBEDA.[68]

In June, at Madrid, the saint had told Juan de Santa Ana to go to Granada and collect the twelve religious whom he was to lead to the Indies. Ignorant, no doubt, of the depth of his disgrace, they now sent word to John that they were ready to follow him.[69] He replied that he had the joy to be out of office, and that he was making preparations and packing his baggage for other Indies,—for Heaven.[70] His health had become really bad. He fell ill on September 12th.[71] He wrote cautiously, on the 21st, to Doña Ana de Peñalosa : " *I am leaving for Ubeda to-morrow in order to get attention for a slight fever ; as it has been attacking me every day for over a week and I cannot get rid of it, I think I need medical care. But I go with the intention of returning soon ; for I certainly feel at peace in this holy solitude ; and, as for what you say about refraining from seeing too much of Father Brother Antonio, you may be sure that in this, as in everything else he may ask of me, I shall be as careful as possible.*" [72]

The reference is to Father Anthony of Jesus, whose restlessness and jealous disposition sometimes made it difficult for others to deal with him.[73] As soon as John had arrived in the province, he wrote to Father Anthony to ask where he was to live. The old man was touched and wrote back to say that he might select any convent he pleased. The saint protested that his only desire was to carry out the wishes of his superiors, and merely indicated a desire for solitude and retirement.[74] Anthony told him to remain at Peñuela.

Now that fever had taken a grip of John, obedience tore him, in his own despite, from his bed of rushes and heather,[75] for there was neither medicine nor doctor at Peñuela, and both were required.[76] Baeza and Ubeda were suggested to him. He decided against Baeza : the college he had founded, where the prior, Angelus of the Presentation, loved him and wanted him.[77] As he had to choose, he selected Ubeda, a recent foundation governed by Padre Francisco Crysos-tomo.[78] " *It is obedience*," he said, " *let us go.*" He mounted the little mule which had been procured for him by his friend Juan de Cuellar. It was led by a *mozo*.[79]

The journey was most painful and his leg caused him so much suffering that it seemed as if it were being cut off. For several days he could not swallow a morsel ; and he could scarcely remain on his mule. He spoke of God to the brother in order to deaden the pain.[80] They proceeded very, very slowly. Range after range of high, clumsy-shaped hills lay all around them ; a leprous-looking vegetation plastered the earth, the colour of wine-lees, on which the sun beat down. It was past the middle of September. When they were drawing near the Guadalimar, the brother suggested a halt. They had covered three leagues.[81] "Your Reverence can rest in the shadow of the bridge, and the joy of seeing the water will give you an appetite for a mouthful." John consented : " *I shall gladly take a rest, for I need one ; but as for eating, I cannot, because I have no appetite for any of the things which God has created, except asparagus, and that is out of season.*" [82] We are reminded of St. Thomas Aquinas and the " herrings he had eaten in France." [83] Saints have such exquisite little weaknesses, thanks to which they still remain human.

When they reached the bank, the brother helped the sick man to dismount and sit down near the bridge, which was built of the yellow stone of the district. A breath of freshness mounted up from the yellow waters of the stream, impregnated with mineral substances, and comforted the poor, exhausted body of the saint. " The stag seeks the shade ; and the hireling rests after his day's labour," [84] but not so John of the Cross.

The two travellers spoke of God. They suddenly saw, on a stone, a bundle of asparagus, bound with an osier twig, as in the market. The brother was astonished, because there is no asparagus to be obtained in that district towards the end of September. He was about to cry out that it was a miracle, when John hastened to say : " *Somebody must have left it there out of forgetfulness, and he will come looking for it ;*

*go back, and see if the owner is in the neighbourhood, so that we may
ask him to take away his property.*" The brother went to look,
but could find nobody. The saint then said : "*Brother,
put two cuartos on the stone for the poor man that gathered it. He
will come for his asparagus which he has certainly forgotten.*" [85]
Only then would he accept the bundle of asparagus thus
purchased from God, with the money of the poor. Bartholomew of St. Basil, at Ubeda, saw it with his own eyes and
touched it with his own hands.[86]

Four leagues—a journey of some hours—now lay between
our travellers and Ubeda. They climbed by steep paths
towards the Andalusian city in which John was to die.
Ubeda is one of those " poor and precious towns, iron-set
jewels, that appeal so strongly to the soul and charm it." [87]
It was getting late. Brown-faced *gitanos* swept by in coloured
carts drawn by mules. Sunburnt *muchachas*, wearing white
mantillas or having their hair tightly knotted, were coming
out of the Church of San Salvador. Our travellers were
gradually approaching the monastery through the narrow
little streets which are veritable beds of mountain torrents,
strewn with sharp stones hard on the feet, and in which
dazzling whitewashed houses look down on the traveller with
their narrow iron-barred windows. The Carmelite Monastery was built on the reddish city walls.

The sub-prior tells us that John of the Cross, sick unto
death, received from Padre Francisco Crysostomo " the
poorest and smallest cell in the convent ; there was nothing
in it but a wretched bed and a crucifix : *una pobre cama y
un Christo.*" [88] I see every reason to doubt that it looked out
over the gipsies' quarter, on to the mountains of Beas, on
whose slopes the eastern light moves in great masses, and
makes the thistles glow. That would have been too
charming.

The licentiate, Ambrosio de Villareal, came to see the sick
man, who was devoured with erysipelas. The disease had
been neglected, and many collections of pus had formed.
" He had five abscesses, in the form of a cross in his foot
. . . ; the largest in the middle,[89] just where the nail was
driven in when Our Lord was crucified, right at the junction

of the nerves and bones," as the physician told Ines de Salazar.[90] Her father, Fernando Diaz, as soon as he heard that John was in Ubeda, hastened to visit his holy friend. Ever since he had seen John chanting the Gospel with so much recollection at the foundation of La Mancha,[91] he had been accustomed to consult the saint on spiritual matters, travelling to Peñuela to do so ; and so intimate had they become, that Fernando used to take the altar linen home to have it washed. Diaz visited the convent every day during John's illness, and sometimes he went three or four times a day.[92] Did these attentions vex the prior ? or was it, perhaps, John's reprimands of his indiscreet zeal ? There was no peace in Ubeda, says Bartholomew of St. Basil.[93] One day the sick man asked Brother Francisco Garcia to do him the kindness of carrying the linen dressings to Doña Clara de Benavides to be washed, and as the brother was going out he met Padre Crysostomo, who stopped him and told him not to do so, as he himself would have the linen washed. The brother returned to John, who said : " *Do not be sad ; recommend me to God ; be patient ; and Our Lord will reward us.*" [94] The pious women who were the saint's friends felt the privation ; this linen, all stained with pus, gave out an exquisite perfume.[95] " It was just as if we had been handling flowers," said Catharine de Salazar.[96] On one occasion, when the dressings of Matthew of the Blessed Sacrament, who also had a sore, were mixed with the saint's, they quickly recognised the difference.[97]

Crysostomo's frankly hostile attitude intensely exasperated Diego de la Concepcion. Seeing that the prior was complaining of John's food and what he cost, Diego insulted him by sending six bushels of wheat from Peñuela for the religious, and six chickens for the invalid.[98]

Bernard of the Virgin noted, day by day, " the very great aversion " which the prior had for the saint. " He did everything he possibly could to annoy John, and forbade anyone going to see him without his own express permission. He often went in to the patient, and reminded him, as if from revenge, that when he, John of the Cross, was Vicar Provincial of Andalusia, he had humiliated him."

Francisco Crysostomo was one of the two preachers in
Seville whose zeal was much too human and who had been
reprimanded by John.   Finally, the prior, thinking that
Bernard was paying too much attention to the patient,
forbade him, under obedience, to give him any further help.
" Moved by compassion," says Bernard, " I wrote at once
to old Father Anthony of Jesus, who was then provincial,
telling him of all that had happened.   He came immediately
to Ubeda, and sharply reprimanded the prior for his want
of charity.   He remained about six days, and gave orders
that the invalid should be well treated ; he asked all the
religious to visit him, and help him in every possible way.
He then restored me to my office of infirmarian. . . . And
in case the prior should not provide what was necessary, he
told me to borrow, and let him know, so that he might send
me the money, as soon as possible."   John did not utter a
word of complaint.   He bore all these outrages," adds
Bernard, " with the patience of a saint." [99]

May I be forgiven for leaving nothing out ! Like José
de Jesus Maria Quiroga, I do not want " to deny the sufferings of our blessed Father, and thus obscure his lustre and
the brilliant splendour of his crown or lessen our ambition
to imitate him." [100]

John of the Cross had a piercing sense of human wretched-
ness which, here, almost verged on the diabolical.[101]   He
had shown this already in his *Cautelas* and *Avisos* : " Even
though you were surrounded by angels, many things would
not seem good to you, because you could not penetrate their
substance. . . . Should you live in the midst of demons,
God asks you to behave yourself amongst them, without
attending to their affairs.   Leave them entirely to themselves ; and, as for you, have no other care than to keep
your soul pure and wholly in God, and be not troubled by
any reflection on this or that.   Look upon it as certain and
advantageous that there will always be difficulties in convents and communities, for the devil never ceases from
trying to bring about the fall of saints, and God allows them

to be exercised and put to the proof. And, if you are not on
the watch, ever living as one not in the house, you cannot
become a true religious, despite all your efforts, or reach a
holy nakedness of spirit and state of recollection, or provide
against the dangers to which you will be exposed. The
second warning is : never regard your superior as anything
lower than God, be he what he may, since it is God who
keeps him in his place." [102] Yes, even though Padre
Crysostomo has just told you that you are a relaxed, imper-
fect religious ; that friends have certainly sent you delicate
viands, but that they have been sent back, for a little mutton
is quite good enough for you.[103] Never forget : " You are
not come to the convent save that others may exercise and
try you ; some by words, some by deeds, and others again
by adverse comments. In all these things, do you be like a
statue which one models, another paints, and a third gilds.
If you do not so act, you cannot conquer sensuality, and
sensitiveness, and you will not be able to deal rightly with
the other religious. And you will not attain holy peace or
be delivered from many falls and evils." [104] " Live in a
monastery as if no one else lived there . . . be not disturbed
if the whole world crumbles away . . . and preserve peace
of soul." [105]

To carry out this advice, as John did, to bear all things
with rare patience and in profound silence,[106] was to obtain,
in community life, the advantages of solitude and, at the
same time, " to find true humility, interior quietude and the
joy of the Holy Spirit." [107]

Padre Antonio was still in the monastery, making all
arrangements, with the greatest kindness, when Villareal
decided that what he had done for the patient up to the
present was not sufficient. The inflammation of the perios-
teum demanded a surgical operation. Pus was flowing abundantly from the five abscesses ; part of the foot and leg had
to be opened in order to discover the full extent of the
trouble, and apply appropriate treatment. The doctor,*

* According to some accounts, Ambrosio de Villareal was assisted by surgeons.

foreseeing extreme pain, told John that he would operate only
on the next day. He then probed the wounds, and, without
waiting, drove in a bistoury. "What have you done,
señor ? " said the patient.[108] He looked at the wound : the
nerves and bones were exposed,[109] from the heel to the top
of the calf of the leg : [110] "*Jesús ! eso ha hecho* : Jesus, this
is what Thou hast done." [111] Antonio was about to speak.
"*Excuse me, Father, I cannot answer*," said John of the Cross,
"*I am devoured by pain*." [112] It was only too true : Villareal
told Juan Evangelista : " He has endured the most amazing
pain with unrivalled patience." [113] The pus, the blood and
the mortified flesh [114] were on a porcelain plate. Diego of
Jesus took it up, smelled it and said : " That is not pus,"
and then, without a qualm, swallowed two mouthfuls, and
his headache vanished.[115]

But the other disease spread to such a degree that, as Isaias
says, from the sole of the foot unto the top of the head, there
was no soundness in him.[116] "*Look at me*," said John, "*it
seems to me that I am suffering*." And Luke relates that, having
turned John over, " I saw that he had two abscesses on the
hips which seemed to contain purulent matter. When the
surgeon came to see the leg, I told him about it. Another
operation was necessary. As Villareal apologised, "*no
matter*," John said, "*if it is the right thing to do*." He urged
the doctor to operate at once. No man, says Villareal,
could have stood it were he not most pleasing to God.[117]
One day, Bartholomew of St. Basil lifted the patient in order
to place him on a mattress whilst making the bed. When
he wished to put John back, the latter asked to be allowed
to get back to bed himself as well as he could. He dragged
himself along the floor to the bed. The young infirmarian
—he was twenty years of age—asked John why he had done
so, because it made him ashamed. The saint replied that
his shoulders were sore and that it pained him to be carried.
They then discovered another abscess, as large as a man's
hand, yet he had never complained.[118] On the next day
a great deal of pus was taken away from it. Alonso de la
Madre de Dios was quite justified in saying : *el parecía el
santo Job*, he is another Job [119] ; " he only needed the pot-

sherd to scrape the corrupt matter from his ulcers." [120]
John of the Cross might well say that he was a *gusano*, a
miserable worm.[121] He could, in all truth, apply to himself the words of the Psalmist : " I am a worm, and no
man : the reproach of men, and the outcast of the
people." [122]

The sight of this superhuman, continual immolation
moved good and simple folk to try and do something to
soothe the martyr's pains. Pedro de San José, who was
then a layman, seeing John " so racked with suffering."
thought that he might be soothed by hearing a little music.*
Let us listen to his naïve account of his kind action.

"... All the religious had gone to a funeral, for, at this
time, they used to go out to funerals † ; the witness, though
a layman, had been placed in charge of the house by the
prior. So, being alone with the venerable Father, Brother
John of the Cross, he went up to his cell and said to him :
' Father, would you like me to bring in some musicians to
soothe your pain, to distract and cheer you ? ' (This witness believed that the saint was afflicted by his long and
cruel sufferings.) And the saint said that, if they were
near at hand, and if it was no trouble to go and find them,
they might come in. The witness, delighted to see that he
had an opportunity of doing a service to the saint—which
he greatly desired to do—went out of the convent, and
brought in three musicians, who began to get ready and tune
their guitars, when the saint called Pedro de San José and
said to him : *Brother, I am most grateful for the kindness you
wished to do me ; I appreciate it very highly ; but, if God has
given me the great sufferings I am enduring, why wish to soothe and
lessen them by music ? For the love of Our Lord, thank those
gentlemen for the kindness they had wished to do me ; I look upon*

* In a deposition given by Quiroga (416 Cyp., 372) Pedro de San José
states : " . . . all the more so, because I knew well that he had a great love
for music."
† According to Jerome of the Cross, the saint had made an effort to prevent
the religious from going to funerals, and also to make them do all their travelling
on foot. (Andrés, 13482, J. 68.)

*it as having been done. Pay them, and send them away, for I wish
to endure without any relief the gracious gifts which God sends me
in order that, thanks to them, I may the better merit.* And Pedro
sent away the musicians." [123]

John of the Cross needed no guitars to sustain his courageous spirit. Was he thinking only of himself? Luke of the
Holy Ghost, his usual secretary, says that he used to dictate
from his bed spiritual letters to several people, amongst
others to Doña Ana de Peñalosa, with whom he kept up a
special correspondence. He told her of the great joy which
he experienced in suffering for Our Lord.[124] Love such as
this brings on ecstasy.[125] Luke tells us that John's love was
very plain to see. When he was attending to household
affairs, Luke saw his patient given up wholly to love, and
raised in ecstasy. John frequently asked to be left alone,
" and," says the young infirmarian, " it was not in order
that he might sleep, but to give himself more ardently to
the contemplation of heavenly things, so much so, indeed,
that, having recognised his desires, I used to send away the
religious and other visitors. And when I myself went in to
speak to him about his needs, he either made no reply at
all, being in a rapture, or answered amiss. Sometimes too,
when I entered, I saw him with his countenance glowing,
certainly not inflamed by his illness, which, on the contrary,
rendered him very thin and pale, but because he was speaking to God." [126] Ambrosio de la Villareal said to Fernando
de la Madre de Dios : " Let us leave the saint to pray.
When he has finished and come back to himself, we will
tend him. It would seem as if he was in a lofty state of
ecstasy, *arrobado a un alta contemplación.*" [127]

This mature doctor—he was then fifty-seven—was no
materialist. Frequent contact with John of the Cross had
transformed him into a new man.[128] He may, perhaps,
have already read, as he certainly did later on, " some
papers from the book of the *Llama* . . . four stanzas explained . . . written in his own hand," which John had
given him.[129] His range of vision was widened and deepened
and by spiritual indications he knew that his patient was
about to die. What the mystic had written of mystics

he could now observe in himself: " The death of such souls is always calm and gentle, more so even than their lives, because they die from an impetuous, yet pleasing encounter with love, like the swan which sings more melodiously on the approach of death. Hence David said that the death of the just is precious (Ps. lxv. 15). The floods of love in the soul are now prepared to cast themselves into the divine ocean, and are so vast and tranquil as already to seem like seas." [130]

CHAPTER XXI

ON THE SUMMIT OF THE LADDER OF LOVE

WHEN Villareal told John that he was soon to die, the saint cried out joyfully : *Laetatus sum in his quae dicta sunt mihi : in domum Domini ibimus* (Ps. cxxii. 1. I rejoiced in the things that were said to me : we shall go into the house of the Lord). The Fathers wished to give him Viaticum, but he said that he would tell them when he was ready.

Ever since December 7th, the Vigil of the Immaculate Conception, John had been aware of the date of his death.[1] He recalled, in order to console his friends, " how the Mother of God of Carmel comes on Saturdays, with grace and help, to Purgatory, and withdraws from it the souls of pious people, who have worn her holy scapular." And it seemed to Bartholomew of St. Basil that the remembrance of this favour rejoiced the saint. They quickly replied : " Father, Our Lord should take Your Reverence away on Saturday, and you will thus quickly escape from Purgatory, thanks to Our Lady." But, realising that a reference to his own sanctity was intended, John would not listen.[2] But he was once heard to say : " Blessed be the Lady who intends me to quit this life on a Saturday." [3] When they said to him that Our Lord " wished to take him on the vigil of the day on which the office of the Blessed Virgin is recited," he allowed the following more definite statement to escape his lips : " *I well know that God, our Lord, is about to do me the mercy and favour of allowing me to recite matins in Heaven.*" [4]

Two days before he died he made a bonfire. He burned, in the flame of a candle which Bartholomew brought him, all the letters which he kept in a little bag, *fardelillo*, under his pillow ; and there was a large number of them, *que eran en cantidad.*[5] He did so, " because it was a sin to be a friend of his." [6]

On Thursday evening he asked for the Viaticum, and received it with great devotion. To those seculars and religious who, for their consolation, begged for his habit, breviary, scapular, some asking for one thing, and some for another, he answered that he was a poor man who had nothing, and that they should have recourse to his superior.[7] Diego of Jesus, who usually assisted John, knelt down in front of him and asked for his blessing ; John refused, as he also refused to bless Luke of the Holy Ghost.[8] But at last, Diego continues, as I insisted, kissing his hand, he blessed me and, looking at me with special tenderness, on account of the affection I bore him, he said : " *Brother Diego, do you think I am going to die ?* " I said " Yes," but that I was resigned to the will of God, and that I always desired His will should be done. John then returned thanks and praised God.

Shortly afterwards he asked for the prior. Francisco Crysostomo returned with the brother. The saint, with great humility, asked pardon for the faults he might have committed, and for the trouble he had given those who had attended him during his illness. He then said : " *Father, the Virgin's habit that I have worn and made use of—I am poor and a beggar, having nothing in which to be buried—for the love of God, I beseech Your Reverence to give it me out of charity.*" The prior blessed him, and went out.[9]

It was not till later that the prior was turned to more humane feelings. Bartholomew of St. Basil says that he persevered in his natural disposition,[10] and does not state the exact time when " he thrice saw the prior on his knees at the foot of the saint's bed, shedding tears." [11] It was before John died, for Pedro de San José saw the wretched superior " making excuses to the invalid because, as the convent was so poor, he could not do more for him in his illness." John replied : " *Father Prior, I am quite satisfied ; I have had more than I deserve. Have confidence in Our Lord, a time will come when this house will have all it needs.*" And, in fact, at a later period, very fine buildings were erected.[12] Quiroga adds that the hardened superior " was so much troubled by those words, and the humble affection of our Blessed Father, that he went out of the cell weeping bitterly, and as if coming out of a lethargic and mortal slumber." [13]   Francisco Crysostomo was to expiate his offences and was not forgiven for having made a martyr of one of God's saints. " He died shortly afterwards," says Luis de San Angel, " deprived of his office, outside his convent and amongst seculars at Algaba, near Seville." [14]

On the morning of St. Lucy's Day, John of the Cross, whilst awaiting the end asked, as usual, what day it was, and, when told it was Friday, frequently asked what o'clock it was.   Later on, when told it was one o'clock and asked why he was so anxious to know, he replied : " *Glory to God, I am to chant matins in Heaven.*"

During his illness he was always recollected, but was especially so during this last day : he was also more silent and peaceful.   His eyes were closed, but from time to time he opened them and let them rest lovingly on a copper crucifix. [15]

About three o'clock, it was already dark—the sky was greatly overcast—he said : " *I should very much like Father Sebastian to be brought here before I die.*"   Sebastian of St. Hilary, to whom he had given the habit at Baeza and later his remissorial letters, [16] was ill of a malignant fever three cells away.   The young priest arrived with the help of the person who had given the message.   He remained with the saint for rather more than half an hour.   John gave him advice, and told him how to act in a matter which he entrusted to his care :

" *Father Sebastian, Your Reverence will be elected a prior of the Order.   Pay attention to what I tell you, and try to bring it to the notice of superiors, telling them that I mentioned it to you, on the point of death.*"   It was a matter that concerned the growth of the province.   Sebastian did not pay very much attention just then to what John told him.   But at a later period, when he spoke of the matter to his superiors, and saw the happy results, he regarded the saint's intervention as miraculous. [17]

At five o'clock, John said exultingly : " *I am happy, very happy, for without meriting it, I shall be in Heaven to-night.*" [18]

A short time afterwards, turning to the prior and Fernando Diaz : " *Father,*" said John, " *would Your Paternity let Señor Fernando's family know that they are not to expect him home, because he must stay here to-night.*" [19] A Brother went off at once. John then asked for Extreme Unction. He received it very devoutly, and answered the prayers said by the priest. He again asked the forgiveness of all.[20] Although he had received Viaticum two days previously, it is most likely that it was on this occasion that he affectionately begged the Father Prior to bring the Sacred Host that he might adore it. Brother Diego says : " He pronounced many most tender words to the Most Blessed Sacrament in my own presence, so that he moved everyone to devotion. Then taking leave, he said : " *I shall see you no more, my Lord, with eyes of flesh.*" [21]

Father Anthony of Jesus, and some of the older religious, wanted to stay by his side, but he begged them to go and rest. There was still plenty of time, and, besides, he would send for them.[22]

The clock struck nine, and John said : " Three hours more. *Incolatus meus prolongatus est.*" * Sebastian heard him say that he was happy to leave this world, for God had granted him three things : " Not to die a superior, to die where he was not even known, and to die after having suffered much." This happened three hours before his death. Those present were the sub-prior Fernando de la Madre de Dios, Bartholomew of St. Basil, Brother Diego, and some others, who kept coming in and going out.[23]

John had resumed his prayer. He was so quiet that they thought he was dead. When he became conscious again, he kissed the feet of a crucifix. They could not detect his breathing.

At ten o'clock, a bell was rung ; he asked the reason. He was told that the religious were going to Matins. " *And I,*" he said, " *by the mercy of my God, am going to recite them with the Virgin, Our Lady, in Heaven.*" [24]

Between nine and ten, Francisco Garcia, in his lay-

* My sojourning is prolonged. (Ps. cxix. 5. Alonso, Seg. P.A., fo. 63.)

A A

brother's habit, took up his position between the wall and the head of the bed, facing Fernando Diaz, the saint's true friend. The Brother, who was then thirty-four, composed himself to carry out his devotions and recite the Rosary, which he did every day, because he had a great devotion to Our Lady. As he was praying, memories began to throng into his mind. . . . " Is it possible, most holy Virgin, that I shall not have the joy of seeing something of what this saint beholds ? " He leaned on John's bed, beside the pillow, and gave himself up to contemplation.[25]

Eleven o'clock. A Father came and said to John : *Deo gratias.* He answered : " *Por siempre, rest yourself, Father, for I am not asleep.*"

Between eleven and half-past—the sick man had sent Pedro de San José to seek them [26]—about fourteen or fifteen religious, who were getting ready to go to Matins, arrived in his cell. They hung their lamps on the wall as they came in. They asked the saint how he was. John, grasping a rope that hung from a beam in the ceiling, raised himself up in bed. " *Fathers, shall we recite the De Profundis, I feel quite well.*" [27] He was, in fact, *muy sereno, hermoso y alegre* : very calm, beautiful and happy, as the sub-prior attests.[28] The friars consented. He began the Psalm, and the community responded. In this way they recited alternately *no se cuantos salmos* : " a number of psalms," says Francisco Garcia.[29] They were the Penitential Psalms which precede the commendation of a departing soul.[30]

The Brother was still in contemplation. Suddenly, " a globe of light (as large as a sieve) began to shine between the ceiling of the cell and the foot of the bed. Francisco Garcia saw it. It was so brilliant that it dimmed the lamps of the fourteen or fifteen friars, and the five altar-candles." [31]

John had not recited all the Psalms. He lay down again, saying that he thought he was tired. Again he asked : " What o'clock is it ? " He was told that it had not yet struck midnight. " *At midnight I shall be with God to recite Matins.*" The Brothers protested. They had confidence in the Divine Majesty, Who would restore him to health.[32]   Old Padre Antonio, bending under the weight of his eighty-one years, reminded him that he had supported the Reform, both in the beginning and at the time of the first foundations, as well as when he had been superior.   " *God knows what took place in those days*," was the saint's reply.[33]   And, then, immediately :   " *Father, this is not the time to be thinking of that ; it is by the merits of the blood of Our Lord Jesus Christ that I hope to be saved.*" [34]   The Brothers asked for his blessing and, at the Provincial's command, he gave it.[35]   He recommended them to be truly obedient, and to be perfect religious.[36]

Whilst they were reciting the Commendation of the Soul John made a sign for them to stop.   He wanted to have something read to him from *los Cantares*, the Canticle of Canticles.   The prior did so, and the saint, after repeating some of those ardent verses, exclaimed :   " What precious gems ! "

Shortly before midnight, he said to someone, probably Francisco Diaz :   *Hold the Crucifix.*   He then passed his arms underneath his tunic, and laid out his body with his own hands.   He then took back *el santo Christo*, and began to speak to it tenderly.[37]

Twelve o'clock rang out from the tower that flanks the Church of San Salvador.   " *Brother Diego*," said the dying man, " *tell them to ring the bell for Matins, for it is now time.*" Diego turned to Luke of the Holy Ghost and Francisco Garcia.   The latter went out immediately, because he was on duty that week.   When John heard the bell, holding the crucifix in his hands, he pronounced the words :   *In manus tuas, Domine, commendo spiritum meum.*[38]   He then looked round on all those present, as if to bid them good-bye, and kissed the crucifix.[39]

" At this moment," Diego goes on, " I was holding him up in my arms, without seeing that he had expired, and I suddenly saw a great brightness over the bed, in the shape of a globe. It shone like the sun and moon ; the lights on the altar, and the two wax-candles in the cell, were surrounded as if by a cloud, and seemed no longer to shine." *

Seeing the saint inert and lifeless, Diego said : " Our Father went to Heaven with that light." Then, with the help of Father Francis and Brother Matthew, he began to prepare the saint's body for burial. A most sweet perfume emanated from it.[40]

Somebody went off to where the bell-rope hung and said to Francisco Garcia : " Brother, when you have finished ringing for Matins, ring a double peal for Father John of the Cross ; he has just died." [41]

" A rapture, a more immeasurable union of love than of old, of more strength, of more power also, has burst the delicate veil that fluttered loose, slight and spiritualised— and has carried away the jewel of the soul." [42]

About one o'clock the community returned and recited some prayers. Each of them kissed affectionately the hands and feet of the servant of God.[43] It was raining heavily outside,[44] and yet so many people were arriving that the prior gave orders, despite the time of silence, to open all the doors.[45]

The news of his death was quickly spread by angels. Doña Clara de Benavides was aware of it even before the death knell was tolled. The child, for whose coming the

* " And at that moment, many of those present saw a very bright light, in the form of a globe, descending and resting on the body, and, so bright was it, that it dazzled them and they could no longer see the twenty-three lights in the cell. And, in the midst of this light they beheld the servant of God transported with love. The convent bell rang for Matins." (Alonso, Seg. P.A., fo. 63.) This account is not correct. It holds true for the moment when Francisco Garcia saw the globe of fire. The Brother, taking everything into account, speaks of a score of lights. Here, as we may see, there is mention of only seven. (The Community, no doubt, had gone off to Matins, after John's death.) Moreover, what does Alonso mean by " many of those present " ? In the *Vida*, after letting it be understood that all had seen the light, he mentions : Father Francisco Indigno, Father Brother Matthew of the Blessed Sacrament, Father Balthazar de la Concepción, Father Diego de Jesus and Francisco Garcia, the sole survivors of those who had witnessed John's death, all of whom deposed to having seen the light. (Bk. II, Ch. XXXI.) But, again, we know from the sub-prior that Matthew of the Blessed Sacrament, Brother Diego of Jesus, and the *donado*, Brother Francisco García, were those who saw the light. (Fernando de la Madre de Dios, Ubeda I.O., fo. 76.) Quiroga says, indeed, that three religious deposed to having seen it. According to him not all of them did. (Quir., 883, Cyp. III, 162.)

saint had prayed, struck her frequently within the womb.
and she understood what it meant to tell.[46] Up in the
Convent of *el Señor San Miguel,* within the poor, narrow cell,
men were contending as to who should cut off a lock of
hair, who should have a piece of the habit. Luke of the
Holy Ghost bit a morsel of flesh from the ulcerated leg.[47]

When, early on the morning of this Saturday, December 14th, 1591, the body was brought into the Church, Iñes
de Salazar saw a crowd struggling and a Father distributing
all John's possessions as if they were relics : his habit,
cincture, hair-shirt, breviary and the rest.[48] That did not
suffice : a Minim tore off a nail of the foot with his teeth ;
Domingo de Sotomayor, a Dominican, wanted to cut off a
finger.[49] From a window overlooking the cloister, Sebastian of St. Hilary, still an invalid, saw all the clergy and
nobility of Ubeda arrive for the funeral.[50] The prior of the
parish of San Isidoro of his own initiative prepared a funeral
oration.[51]

John died without a struggle and his face was peaceful
and most happy,[52] " white, but with a special whiteness
not to be seen in a corpse, though his countenance was
usually very pale and brown." [53] Though not seen with
earthly eyes, the triple crown of Christ the Spouse, of whom
he had sung in the *Cántico,*[54] lay like a halo on his brow.
The lovely white flowers of the Virgins, the dazzling flowers
of the Doctors, and the red carnations of the Martyrs, were
all blossoming gloriously on the dunghill of contempt.

Francisco de Yepes, bent beneath the weight of his sixty-
one years, was walking along the Plaza Mayor of Medina
del Campo, when he met a man who said, " What is the
meaning of this ? Here are you walking along without a
care and the whole world has set out for Segovia, to see
your brother, and you have not gone ! " [55]
Ever since John had gone to Andalusia, poor Francisco
had never heard a word of his beloved brother, and now,
without a word of notice, he was informed of his posthumous
glory.[56]

At the request of Doña Ana de Peñalosa and Don Luis de

Mercado, auditor of the Royal Council,[57] Doria had given orders for the saint's body to be conveyed secretly from Ubeda to Segovia. They were carried out most mysteriously, about two years after his happy death.[58]

" So God has broken the delicate web of our intercourse," [59] thought the weaver, as he went home to tell his wife, Ana Isquierda. They agreed that he must go, but it was Father Cristobal Caro who decided the matter.[60] Francisco went to the residence of the Jesuits, the Church of Santiago, which John had been accustomed to visit, in the days of Padre Bonifacio, and the journey was soon decided on. Francisco departed.

He was told, in Segovia, that the body was enclosed in a chest, the key of which was in Madrid. As a matter of fact, " the casket was lined, within and without, with crimson red velvet ; it had gold fringes and trimmings, was ornamented with a multitude of gilt nails, and closed by three locks," [61] of which the foundress kept the keys.

Francisco went off to Madrid. Doña Ana de Peñalosa was not at home. Whilst awaiting her arrival he was told that John, before leaving Segovia in 1591, had told Doña Ana, on her asking him : " When shall we see you again ? " " *Be silent, daughter, do not cry, you will send for, and will see me.*" [62] It had come to pass in a way she had never foreseen.

Ana came back. On learning that the saint's own brother was there, she welcomed him cordially. Francisco returned, happier by a hundred reals for his expenses,[63] and above all, " bearing the keys, with a letter for the Father Prior, and one of the saint's arms, to be replaced with the body." [64]

As he was walking along, towards those blue-black mountains, that grow greener as one moves towards them along the white road, he raised to his lips a small fragment of the sacred flesh which Doña Ana had given him for himself, and which he was to keep on an altar or, on great feast-days, carry about him, in a little bag slung round his neck. He put his whole heart and soul into that kiss : " *O hermano* : O my brother," said he, " how is it that you have gone and left me ! " And immediately a sweet perfume—even sweeter than that emanating from the relics of Mother Teresa at Medina [65]—was diffused, which consoled him to such a degree as he could not express—marvellously. [66]

But clouds were piling up, the heavens grew dark. A whirlwind arose—and they are terrible in these districts. " *Hermano*," cried Francisco, [67] " I believe you are in Heaven. Save me from this danger ; I do not know where I am." The hurricane still raged. He then called on the Virgin of Carmel : " Mother of God, I recommend myself to you. By the great services my brother rendered you, save me ! " Suddenly the tempest ceased, and the sun shone out. [68]

Clement X beatified John of the Cross on January 25th, 1675. Benedict XIII canonised him on December 26th, 1726. Pius XI declared him Doctor of the Universal Church on August 24th, 1926.

POSTSCRIPT

By Father Benedict Zimmerman, O.D.C.

St. John of the Cross at the time of his last illness and death was under a cloud. He himself had asked God as a favour that he might die, being despised and accounted for little (*Life*, Chap. XIX.). His request was granted. Had it not been for the loving solicitude of a faithful infirmarian and the fraternal kindness of his fellow-founder of the Reform, Anthony de Heredia, he would have been neglected and abandoned by all even at his last moment. A significant silence leaves us wondering what impression, if any, his death made upon the Vicar-General, Father Nicholas Doria. Those among his brethren who had revered him as a saint during his life, and the Carmelite nuns generally, did not dare to manifest their sentiments. No wonder, then, that for a quarter of a century no steps were taken towards the compilation of a biography. Fortunately the generation of friars and nuns who had personally known the saint was not yet extinct when the process of Beatification was begun in 1614, and though this was, of course, never published, it led to the publication of the biographies by Joseph of Jesus-Mary (Quiroga), Gregory of St. Joseph and Jerome of St. Joseph, which will be found frequently quoted in the Life of St. John of the Cross now before the reader. Several important phases of the life of the saint, especially the treatment he received at the hands of the Carmelites of the Old Observance, and the not less harsh treatment at the hands of Nicholas Doria, are quite unintelligible without a detailed knowledge of the general history of the Reform. The historiographer of the Discalced Carmelites, Francis of St. Mary—whose first volume (1644), under the conventional title of *Reforma*, brings the story down to the death of St. Teresa (1582), while the second (1655) deals at

considerable length with the life of St. John—found himself
in a most unenviable position. Nothing could be more
edifying than the first beginnings of the Reform ; then,
suddenly, without any apparent cause, a storm breaks out
which not only threatens the very existence of St. Teresa's
work, but which bursts over the head of St. John, the most
inoffensive of men, who is now subjected to tortures of
unexampled brutality. Likewise, towards the end of his
life, the saint becomes the victim, no one knows why or
wherefore, of the most acrimonious persecution. The fact
is, the author of the *Reforma*, writing as he did for the edification of his readers, the friars and nuns of his Order, in the
first instance left the story floating in the air, without
disclosing its base, and in the second instance, as a friend and
admirer of " our great Doria," failed to see the autocratical,
not to say tyrannical, disposition of his idol. Thus, not
only is the life story of St. John falsified, but the odium of his
martyrdom at Toledo is thrown without a word of explanation on the Calced Carmelites, and the final persecution is
represented as a kindly visitation from God in answer to
the prayer of a heroic soul.

This view of the life of St. John of the Cross has prevailed
until recently. In the middle of the last century the
Oratorian Fathers, under the leadership of Father Faber,
published a number of Lives of Modern Saints. St. John
of the Cross was to find a place among them, but the
ecclesiastical authorities considered the story too disconcerting, especially in view of the then prevailing circumstances, and the publication did not take place. Later on,
in 1888, David Lewis, M.A., the translator of the Works
of St. John of the Cross, and, I suppose, the author of that
Life, published it in the first volume of the second edition
of the Works (London, Thomas Baker). In the Preface he
gives a list of his authorities. Father Gerard of St. John
of the Cross, in the first volume of his critical edition of
the Works of the Saint (Toledo, 1912–1914) reprints the
Sketch of the Life of the Saint by Jerome of St. Joseph, with the
addition of some details from the Process of Beatification,
and the result of certain researches of his (Gerard's) own.

Some twenty years ago when the present writer was working in the Vatican and other Roman archives, notably those of the Calced Carmelites, a volume of *Letters of the General, John Baptist Rubeo* (1563–1578) was put in his hand. Among more than 800 official documents he found there the original patent granted by the General to St. Teresa for the establishment of two houses of Discalced Friars (N. 154, fol. 104^r, dated Barcelona, August 16th, 1567). This had been printed by the author of the *Reforma* and others, but an all-important clause had been omitted which in the original before me was thickly underlined, a sign that this identical paper had been submitted to the General Chapter at Piacenza, 1575, and that on the strength of this the sweeping condemnation of the Andalusian friaries had been pronounced by the Chapter. The clause in question forbids any attempt at a separatist movement on the part of the Discalced friars, and, in the event of such a thing happening, pronounces the severest penalties on them. (See my edition of the *Book of Foundations by St. Teresa*, London, Thomas Baker, 1913, p. 449.)

It was one of those thrilling moments, all too rare in human life, when an unexpected discovery places the key to a difficult problem in one's hand. For here lay the solution to the riddle of the " persecution " of the Discalced Friars by their Calced Brethren. Later on the whole collection of official documents concerning the four years of strife which had lain undisturbed in the archives for three hundred years was also placed at my disposal, and I was fortunate enough to find further evidence elsewhere. I made use of these sources in the edition of the *Book of Foundations* already mentioned, in the annotations to the *Acts of the General Chapters* (Rome, 1912), and in other publications, but the text of the documents has not yet been published.

The author of the present *Life of St. John of the Cross*, Father Bruno à Jesu-Maria, who on several occasions spent a good deal of time with me, both before and since he entered the Order, has seen, and, as the reader will notice, fully utilised these documents.

Another, hitherto unknown source for the *Life* was found

in the archives of the Sacred Congregation of Rites, namely, the original Apostolic process of Beatification, which was examined, excerpted and to a large extent photographed by Father Louis of the Blessed Trinity. Father Bruno himself, during a long journey in Spain was enabled not only to follow the footsteps of the saint, but also to collect a vast amount of material. Although there is never any real finality in human undertakings, the documentation of every portion of this *Life* is now so abundant and thorough-going that future discoveries can only affect details.

Soon after his profession in the Carmelite Order the author published, on the occasion of the Tercentenary of the Canonisation of St. Teresa, a small work, *Le Carmel, par un Carme déchaussé* (Paris, 1922), a kind of conspectus of the life and activities of the Order, which evidenced his exceptionally wide reading. The opportunity for undertaking a work of greater importance arose almost immediately, inasmuch as the Bicentenary of the Canonisation of St. John of the Cross (1926) was approaching. The first plan was to publish a symposium, the author himself and several of his brethren contributing papers on the various aspects of the life and works of St. John of the Cross. Preliminary studies by the future collaborators appeared in the publications of the Order and in various other reviews, and have been utilised in the work before us. But it was soon discovered that a symposium was not the best means for producing a work of lasting value, and the various collaborators divided among themselves the task of preparing the materials for a monumental *Life*, Father Bruno reserving to himself the lion's share of the work. Three times the whole book was written and re-written, until it was finished and perfected in every detail, and, it should be added, until every single statement had been fully scrutinised and documented. Although this caused a delay of three years in the publication, the result was so satisfactory that the French Academy awarded it the coveted distinction of " crowning " it.

Among the numerous figures which appear frequently in these pages there are two about which a word is not out of place in this short note : Father Jerome Gracian and

Father Nicholas Doria. Of the latter it has been said with truth that his Life has not been written, nor can it be written ; the same holds good with regard to the former. He looms large in the life of St. Teresa, of St. John of the Cross, and in the story of the Reform generally ; his biography would have to include all these subjects, and even then would be incomplete, because one important aspect, Gracian the Mystic, would still be wanting. To what an extent St. Teresa confided in him may be gathered from her innumerable letters to and about him. He was unquestionably the most promising man in the ranks of the Discalced Carmelites, his rich talents, perfect education, charming manners, high connection, tender piety and profound spirituality singling him out for the highest posts. Yet it was he who, unwittingly, brought the nascent Reform to the brink of ruin.

Philip II was an autocrat and bent upon uniting in his own hand the entire administration of his kingdom, ecclesiastical as well as political. Though a devout Catholic, he did not see eye to eye with the Pope in political matters, and took a much larger share in the government of the Church than is compatible with canonical rules. One of his pet plans was the reform of Religious Orders. Had this only extended to the enforcement of the laws laid down by the Council of Trent, the abolition of abuses or the correction of notorious faults, he would have deserved the highest encomium, and, indeed, many persons, for instance, St. Teresa, who only saw this side of him, paid him unstinted praise, calling him " our holy King " (*Book of Foundations*, XXIX, 25). But his intentions went much farther. He would have the Religious Orders exclusively under Spanish superiors, practically severed from the central authority, and under the supervision of the Royal counsel or some other department of the State. Probably the scheme grew by degrees and only gradually assumed large proportions, so that it is not to be wondered at if the Roman Court did not see through it from the first. On the contrary, the " holy design " of his Catholic Majesty was repeatedly praised in despatches to the Nuncio which were certainly meant to come to the knowledge of the king. Even when at length the interference passed all reasonable limits and Rome had to check his plans, this was done only in matters of absolute necessity, and the Nuncio was instructed to abstain as far as he possibly could from thwarting the king. The explanation of this attitude of the Holy See is not far to seek. Spain was the only reliable Catholic power, and the king's co-operation was indispensable for the protection of Catholic interests in England and the Low Countries, and especially for the preparation of naval warfare against the Turks. Compared with these weighty matters the position of the Religious Orders in Spain was quite an insignificant affair, being merely a point of practical policy, not a question of essential principles. It affected all religious Orders (with the sole exception of the Jesuits who were held in the highest favour at court), namely, the Franciscans (whose General was strictly forbidden by the king to come to Spain and make a visitation in person, 1576), Dominicans, Augustinians, Cistercians, Benedictines, Premonstratensians (whom the king wished to suppress altogether, 1572), Trinitarians, Minims and Mercedarians (the visitation of whose houses led to riots at Barcelona, 1577). Few Orders gave more trouble than the Carthusians. *Carthusia numquam reformata quia numquam deformata.* But the object of the reform was not to correct abuses which in their case were non-existent, but to bring the Order into subjection to the Crown, and for this purpose the splendid Carthusian monasteries were severed from the Grande Chartreuse, and after prolonged and painful negotiations in which the Nuncio had to recommend to the king gentleness, patience and prudence, were established as an independent Spanish congregation. This fact alone proves more than anything else the trend of Philip's policy.

All these painful events are long since forgotten, and so would have been the steps taken against the Carmelites, even those of Andalusia, who certainly did stand in need of reform. But the story has been immortalised by St. Teresa, on whose life and work these troubles cast a profound shadow. The complaint against the Andalusians, apart from some scandals which could and should have been dealt with by the Superiors, concerned the intrigues of parties and factions among them. " There are in this province," writes the Nuncio (Nicholas Ormaneto) in 1572, " some friars of a bad character, inveterate mischief makers, fomenting enmity and party strife among the rest. There are four of these whom I am endeavouring to disperse, sending them to other provinces, not an easy matter on account of the large following they have ; nevertheless I have every hope of success." One would think that, however difficult the matter was, it might have been accomplished in something less than six years ; but the measures taken were clearly not the most conducive to the desired end.

At his visitation of Andalusia in 1566–1567 the General, John-Baptist Rubeo, found " some masters in divinity and other fathers who have done well by the Order, great lovers of holy Obedience " ; but there were others of a different stamp of whom he sent some to the galleys, some he exiled from the province, and others he condemned to prison. He was a just but severe judge, and the Andalusians resented his austerity. Without waiting for his return to Italy they applied to the Holy See, probably through the king, for exemption from the supervision of the Italians, and the appointment of Apostolic visitors of Spanish nationality, mostly Dominicans, and actually obtained a Brief to that effect, of which the General remained in ignorance for five years. When at length it came to his knowledge, together with the reforming designs of the king, he obtained its revocation and nominated in each province a certain number of friars who were to meet the Apostolic visitors in order to safeguard the rights of the Order.

The visitor appointed for Castile met with no difficulty, and the visitation passed off without incident. Not so in Andalusia. Francis de Vargas, prior of the Dominicans at Cordova, evidently did not relish his duties. He visited the various friaries and obtained full insight into the state of the province, but having in the meantime been elected Provincial of his Order, made this an excuse for relinquishing his office and handing over his patents to a Discalced Carmelite of Pastrana whom he happened to know. This was one of the former Calced Carmelites of Andalusia who had gone over to the Discalced, some through a desire of a more perfect life, and others in order to escape punishments. As the friar chosen by Vargas belonged to this latter class and therefore could not have counted on much success as a visitor of his former *confrères*, the patent ultimately passed into the hands of Jerome Gracian, who at that time had only been professed three months. On some pretext he went to Andalusia where he met Vargas and concerted with him further proceedings. By an almost incredible error of judgment he neither then nor at any later moment informed the General of the position offered to, and accepted by him, nor of the measures he intended to adopt ; he entirely ignored the General. Had he restricted himself to the visitation of the province he might, perhaps, have been successful, but he combined with it an entirely different purpose, namely, the establishment of the Discalced friars in Andalusia, notwithstanding the explicit and repeated prohibition by the General.

The General learned the news in July, 1574, and it came like a thunderbolt ; the two things he had done his utmost to avoid had come to pass : the Discalced friars were establishing themselves independently of his authority and were drifting towards separation from the body of the Order, and several foundations, not authorised by him, had been made in Andalusia. Not only had Gracian kept him entirely in the dark, but several letters from Rubeo to St. Teresa demanding an account of what had happened, had failed to reach her, and therefore remained unanswered. A General Chapter assembled at Piacenza on Pentecost, 1575, at which the new separatist movement in Spain was discussed and in the absence of any account, official or private, from the Discalced fathers, Rubeo laid on the table the various patents conceded by him, in which the restrictive clauses already alluded to are underlined. The Chapter naturally ratified the penalties pronounced eight years previously by the General in the event of a contingency which now had become an accomplished fact. Gracian was declared excommunicated, the friars living in unauthorised friaries were ordered under penalty of rebellion to return to the friaries licensed by the General, and St. Teresa was relegated to one of her convents, to be chosen by herself. The acts of the Chapter soon became known in the provinces of Castile and Andalusia.

If Gracian's visitation of Andalusia during the three years 1572 to 1575 had been desultory, it now became positively a farce, since the Andalusians knew perfectly well that Gracian was in opposition to the General and the General Chapter, and that his powers were, to say the least, most doubtful.

From 1575 onward St. Teresa frequently advised Gracian to give up his fruitless " visitation," but he pleaded that the king wished it to continue ; yet the only thing he appears to have done was to renew the deposition of the Provincial, Augustine Suarez, who having been canonically elected (1572) and confirmed by the General (1573) had been confirmed in his office by the General Chapter till the middle of October, 1576. The reason for his deposition by the Visitor Francis Vargas was that the latter wished Gracian to be both Visitor and Provincial of the Calced Carmelites of Andalusia (document of August 3rd, 1575), though the Nuncio twice protested in Rome that it was not he who had nominated Gracian Provincial. Suarez evidently was not too sure of his own position, for, whenever Gracian came to Andalusia he withdrew to the friary of Ossuna, and when Gracian returned to Castile he reappeared and resumed the government of his province.

In May, 1576, the Calced Carmelites of Castile held their triennial Chapter at which the decrees of the General Chapter were promulgated. The delegates of the Discalced friars arrived only in time to lodge a protest as suggested by the Nuncio.

In the month of August following, Gracian summoned a Chapter of the Discalced friars both of Castile and Andalusia to Almodovar where, by an even greater error of judgment than the former, he established them as a separate province, independent of the already existing Spanish provinces. The establishment of provinces has always been the exclusive right of the General Chapters, neither the General in person nor in conjunction with his advisers having the requisite power. Although Gracian believed his powers as Apostolic Visitor or reformer to be superior to those of the General, the only excuse he could offer for such an unprecedented step was that he had heard the Nuncio say that such a separation ought to be made. But if the Nuncio had had the power to make it he would surely have done so himself. Gracian went even farther than that. Availing himself of the concessions the Congregation of Mantua (from the beginning of the fifteenth century) had gradually wrested from the Order, he allowed the General in person and accompanied by a Discalced Carmelite, to make the official visitation of the Discalced, but forbade him to make such a visitation through the instrumentality of any Calced friar. On November 11th St. Teresa writes to Gracian : " You mention that you have written to Rome : please God that the attempt may be successful " (Letters, II, 123). It was the first and last letter Gracian ever wrote to Rubeo, although St. Teresa had besought him time after time to write a nice, submissive letter. This letter is not extant, but can it have contained anything more conciliatory than the communication of the various false steps taken by Gracian at the Chapter of Almodovar ?

In the meantime the Calced Carmelites of Andalusia had sent delegates to Rome to lodge a complaint against Gracian. The Cardinal Secretary of State (Cardinal Philip Buoncompagni, nephew of Pope Gregory XIII) demanded an account of the happenings from the Nuncio, who, being seriously ill from the end of September to the end of November, replied through his secretary, Antonio Clementino : " With reference to the complaint of the Carmelites against Father Friar Jerome Gracian who calls himself Provincial of that Order, Mgr. the Nuncio has never made or nominated him Provincial,* but only Commissary for the

* The Nuncio Ormaneto's patent of III Nonas (3rd) August, 1575, for Gracian begins as follows : " Nicolaus Dei et Apostolicae Sedis gratia &c.

visitation and reform. He calls himself, as far as I know, Provincial because he was nominated Provincial two and a half years ago by a certain Father Francisco de Vargas, of the Order of St. Dominic, who being Commissary Apostolic in virtue of a Brief of Pius V of holy memory, had power to depose and to institute provincials in the Carmelite Order, and it appears that he deposed of the provincialship of Andalusia a certain friar Suarez, and put in his place this Father Jerome Gracian, and for this reason the latter calls himself Provincial " (October 29th, 1576). On his recovery the Nuncio himself wrote to the Cardinal Secretary (February 5th, 1577) : " At present these Calced friars have published here the report that the Discalced are excommunicated by their General for having founded friaries against his prohibition, and as I wanted to see how the matter stood I found nothing of the kind, for they founded the said houses under the obedience of the late Commissary Apostolic, nominated for the reform (of the Order) by Pius V of holy memory, who held most ample faculties. It was he who nominated Gracian Provincial, not I, and those who say it was I are not well informed ; but it is quite true that, as I wrote to your most illustrious Lordship, I made him Commissary for the visitation of that province, and so, things being as I have said, it is quite possible that he may call himself Provincial though not nominated by myself."

On September 20th, 1576, St. Teresa wrote to Gracian : " I was very glad that the project was discussed (at the Chapter of Almodovar) of our striving in every way for constitution as a separate province through the instrumentality of our Father General, for it is an intolerable conflict to contend with one's superior " (*Letters*, II, 50). It was,

Rev. do in Christo magistro fratri Hieronymo Gratiano de Matre Dei primitivi Ordinis Carmelitarum professori, provinciali et reformatori in provincia Bethica [Andalusia] pro reformatione omnium fratrum Ordinis Carmelitarum in eadem provincia Bethica, necnon in provincia Castellae fratrum Carmelitarum qui sequuntur regulam primitivam, commissario apostolico. Salutem &c. Cum tu alias ad nostrum et Sedis apostolicae beneplacitum visitator dicti Ordinis Carmelitarum in provincia Bethica deputatus fueris, ac visitationis et commissionis hujusmodi vigore visitationis munus inceperis &c." (From an authenticated copy.) Although Ormaneto had not bestowed on Gracian the Provincialship for Andalusia, he certainly countenanced Gracian's title to it.

however, too late, for Gracian had already adopted the fatal measure and could not now retrace his steps. It is incomprehensible that he, the son and brother of men who spent their whole life in the diplomatic service, should have so entirely neglected the most elementary rules of statesmanship and thereby stultified his lofty aspirations, and called down upon himself, and St. Teresa and her great undertaking, the just anger of the General, and the open enmity of the bulk of the Order.

This is one aspect of the matter, but there is another. " These Discalced fathers are leading a very holy life," writes the Nuncio to the Cardinal Secretary of State, " and are giving the greatest edification and are enjoying great credit with the people ; would that it pleased God that the others (the Calced) were like them and had as good a reputation. It thus happens that the former are favoured and protected both by the authorities and by all good people, which is not the case with the latter " (February 5th, 1577). And again : " In reply to what your illustrious Lordship writes about the Carmelite fathers, those who have given a wrong information to you about Father Gracian have acted very wickedly, for he is a man of great holiness, leading a very good life, and is endowed with a good understanding concerning all points of the Religious life " (March 4th, 1577). And so on. No one was in a better position to judge between the parties than the Nuncio. Why did he not exert himself to bring about a satisfactory settlement of the outstanding questions between the authorities of the Order and the nascent reform ? He, and he alone, was in a position to do this, and if extraordinary powers were required, he could easily have obtained them from the Pope through the Cardinal Secretary of State. The chief reason why that was not done was undoubtedly that there was no time for it. The term of his office as Nuncio was rapidly drawing to its end. A successor had already been nominated, and he could hardly have begun a long and intricate negotiation which he knew he could not carry through. Moreover, his health was seriously impaired. Though he had recovered from his illness of the previous year, he was again laid up, this time with a sharp attack of gout, towards the end of March, 1577. At the end of April he was well enough to write personally to Rome. On May 12th he conferred the First tonsure as well as a cardinal's biretta on the Archduke Albert of Austria,* the king's nephew, then in his eighteenth year ; on Whitsun Eve, May 25th, he invested him with the red hat and handed the Queen the golden rose, blessed by the Pope on *Laetare* Sunday. On June 8th he is reported seriously ill, on the 12th he is a little better and there is some hope of his recovery, but it did not last long, for on the 18th he died.

It has been stated that when the General J.-B. Rubeo first heard of the developments in Spain he wrote to St. Teresa for an account as to what had really happened, and why. He wanted to hear both sides, and no doubt wanted to justify in the eyes of the future Chapter the support he had given to the Discalced Carmelites. Unfortunately, owing to her displacements and to the wretched roads, these letters did not reach Teresa until the Chapter was over. St. Teresa's answers, dated June 18th, 1575 and beginning of February, 1576 (*Letters*, I, 199 and 254) have been described as a masterpiece, and so they are, but the very questions put by Rubeo received no answer. She says that Gracian and Mariano (who was also implicated) are very

---

* The Cardinal of Austria, or of the Holy Cross, as he was named, was the son of the Emperor Maximilian II and Mary, the sister of Philip II, and the brother of the Emperor Rudolf II. He had been created Cardinal deacon on March 3rd, 1577, without title, and later on, February 12th, 1580, in view of a possible ordination to the priesthood (which never took place), was promoted Cardinal priest of the Holy Cross in Jerusalem. He was almost always employed in the diplomatic service in various embassies, and for several years was Viceroy of Portugal, with which dignity he combined for two years (1583–1585) that of *legatus de latere*, thus uniting in his hand full political, military and ecclesiastical power. On November 7th, 1594, he was nominated titular Archbishop of Philippi in Macedonia and Coadjutor with right of succession to Cardinal Quiroga, Archbishop of Toledo and Primate of Spain. He actually succeeded, five days later, and on April 10th, 1595, received the pallium. In 1598 he resigned both the Archbishopric and the Cardinalate, and a fortnight later married his cousin, the Infanta Isabella Clara Eugenia ; they became joint governors of the Low Countries. He died July 13th, 1621. He had never had any Orders, only the First Tonsure. He was a man of most profound piety and led the life of a saint. While Viceroy of Portugal he befriended Father Jerome Gracian, then Provincial, and later on, after the latter's disgrace and rehabilitation, called him to Brussels. The Archduke, as well as the Infanta, his wife, proved the staunchest friends and protectors of the Discalced Carmelites, both friars and nuns.

good and holy, and have acted with the best intention, and if they have offended the General they are sorry, and will write letters of submission (which Mariano did about eight months later, and Gracian not at all). Putting oneself in the position of Rubeo, who had never been favoured with a single line from the Discalced friars, and therefore could not know what had happened, these letters proved her attachment to him, but gave no intelligent account of the events of the last four or five years ; and the good impression they might have produced was nullified by the ill-advised letter of Gracian of October or November, 1576

The Calced Carmelites of Andalusia had sent two men, the priors of Cordova and Utrera respectively, to lodge their complaints in Rome. " If the friars of Andalusia come here," writes the Cardinal Secretary of State at the beginning of 1576, " they will meet with such a reception that they will want to return to Spain with greater speed than brought them to Rome." Later in the year the Chapter of Almodovar of the Discalced friars decided also on sending delegates to Rome, but the measure was not pushed, and finally was allowed to drop, to the alarm and amazement of St. Teresa.

Rubeo took the proper step of sending a visitor to Spain, Master Jerome Tostado. What his instructions were we do not know, for they are neither among Rubeo's papers nor in the acts of the process. The choice of the visitor was most judicious. He was not an Italian, but, although a Portuguese by birth, had been many years prior at Barcelona, and had successfully introduced the laws of Trent into the province of Catalonia ; for three years he had been Rubeo's assistant in the visitation of Upper Italy, and also at Rome ; he was visitor and reformer of the monastery at Naples (under the Spanish Crown), the most troublesome house of the Order ; he was, further, visitor of Lombardy, and finally of Catalonia, presiding at a Chapter at Perpignan where he was elected Provincial. From this it will be seen that he was a man of great experience, trusted by his superior and by his subjects who otherwise would not have elected him Provincial. Yet he is one of those unfortunate men to whom an entirely undeserved odium attaches, and will remain attached to the end of time.

No sooner was it known that he was coming to inquire into the state of affairs than the Calced Carmelites spread the report that he was commissioned to " destroy " the Reform. The Discalced Carmelites took fright ; St. Teresa thoroughly believed it, as is proved by numerous passages in her letters. Tostado arrived at Barcelona in March, 1576, but as he had to make the visitation of Catalonia, he did not reach Madrid before August. He never was given a chance. The only person who received him with kindness was the Nuncio. " The Vicar-General (*i.e.*, Visitor-General) of the Carmelites has arrived here," writes the Nuncio to the Cardinal Secretary of State " and according to rumours disseminated here, he has come for no other purpose than to pull down the Discalced friars of his Order, especially in Andalusia ; he referred to the difficulties of the General of the Minims [of whom there is a good deal in the earlier part of the letter], and I, in order to gain a little time for the smoothing of these differences, persuaded him that, since he had to go also to Portugal for a visitation, he should go there first, and I did not fail to recommend him to the Most Serene Cardinal Infante * and to the Apostolic College in these kingdoms ; now he is probably back, and I shall not omit to help and favour him in every way I can, as I do with regard to all who come here from Rome. I should like to see those who are called Calced Carmelites not to display ill-will towards the Discalced who are strictly keeping their primitive rule " (February 5th, 1577).

Tostado, however, was not allowed to carry out his commission. The Counsel of State demanded to inspect his credentials, and finding them without the Royal *exequatur* compelled him to apply to Rome for fresh papers.

Meanwhile the new Nuncio, Mgr. Philip Sega, Bishop of Piacenza, arrived at Madrid, August 30th, 1577. He is

---

* Henry, son of King Emmanuel the Happy, Archbishop of Lisbon, Coimbra and Braga, since 1542 Cardinal Priest of *Quattro Coronati*, during the minority of King Sebastian (his grand-nephew) Regent of Portugal, succeeded the latter on the throne, being the last of the House of Aviz. On his death Portugal came under the Spanish Crown.

stated to have been prejudiced against the Discalced friars. How could it have been otherwise, considering that the latter had never presented their case in Rome, and that Tostado was prevented from making inquiries? The Nuncio, notwithstanding his prejudice, acted correctly, though he did not show favour to the Discalced friars, but the Calced seized the opportunity to carry out a most blameworthy design by forcibly removing St. John of the Cross and his assistant from the convent of the Incarnation at Avila where they were acting as confessors to the nuns, and conveying the former, a prisoner, to Toledo. St. John had taken no active part in any of the previous transactions. He filled, moreover, his place as it seems with the consent of the new Nuncio. The treatment he received at Toledo was brutal beyond expression; Father Bruno tells the story on unimpeachable evidence. He shows that one word of the saint would have released him from his sufferings, but that one word he would never say, because it would have been tantamount to a repudiation of the principles of the Reform. Nevertheless, the question presents itself: could he not have appealed to the Nuncio for protection and justice? At the very first moment he could certainly have done so, and in all probability even afterwards, for Tostado and the other leading men of the Calced friars would have been obliged to forward his protest. But he did nothing but suffer in silence, in imitation of his Lord and Master. He chose the highest line of conduct, and had his reward in the marvellous mystical experience granted him during the months of his martyrdom. Father Bruno shows that the friars of Toledo, judging him guilty of rebellion and disobedience, applied in the most literal sense the penalties detailed in the Constitutions of Blessed John Soreth. Other points in the same Constitutions, it would seem, were not quite as literally observed by them. It does not appear that the Nuncio knew anything, either at that time or later, of the treatment meted out to the saint. He did not understand the genesis of the quarrel, which evidently had never been explained to him, and therefore he was bewildered at the violence of passion displayed, but in his despatches to Rome he is perfectly fair, and clearly wished to be just to both sides. Unfortunately, soon after St. John's marvellous (not to say miraculous) escape from prison there occurred another deplorable mistake on the part of the Discalced friars, in spite of the prudent advice of both Gracian and St. John of the Cross, and now the Nuncio turned decidedly against the Reform. How, through the intervention of the Count de Tendilla at long last the whole question from its very root was sifted, and an amicable settlement brought about, has been told by Father Bruno. When the first preliminaries of peace had been agreed upon, St. Teresa had occasion to write to Father Gracian : " I am amazed at hearing that you wish for more crosses ; for God's sake leave us without them, for you do not bear them alone. Let us rest for a few days " (*Letters*, III, 214, dated April 21st, 1579). It was, indeed, St. John of the Cross and not Gracian, who had to bear the brunt of the day, and the marks of the stripes he received at Toledo remained visible until his death.

The second " martyrdom " of St. John of the Cross is even more puzzling than the first. When at length the quarrel with the Calced friars had been finally settled by the canonical establishment of a " Discalced " province, March, 1581, Father Jerome Gracian was elected Provincial with a majority of one vote, the minority voting for Anthony de Heredia, the founder, with St. John of the Cross, of the Reform among the friars. The latter was made prior of Granada, very much against his will, and remained there during the whole of the four years of Gracian's term of office. He was therefore far removed from the two Castiles, the centre of the activity of the Order, nor can he be described as an onlooker since he took no interest in anything external unless the most urgent duty compelled him thereto. He may have noticed in some general way that two contrary currents had set in, and that a crisis was unavoidable. As long as St. Teresa lived it did not break out, this last mortification being graciously spared her. But the cause of the trouble was there. It centred round the names of Gracian and Doria, two men as unlike each other as they possibly could be. St. Teresa had fondly hoped to bring them together, so that the gifts of the one might make up for the defects in the other, and *vice versâ*. Why did not this come to pass, as it did in other instances in history, both sacred and profane ? It cannot have been for lack of humility for they were both profoundly humble ; St. Teresa says so, and she was no mean judge. Perhaps, and this is the only charitable explanation that presents itself, each of them having his own large following, may have been forced onward by the crowd behind him. Leaders are not always free in the choice of their route march.

Gracian was an idealist, his ideals being of the loftiest. Doria was intensely practical, cold and calculating. Both were born leaders of men and could no more help having, each, a following, than a magnet can help attracting iron. Like Cæsar, either might have been first in a village, but neither could have been second in Rome. Gracian, with his idealism made numerous fatal mistakes, as he had done during his quarrel with the Calced Carmelites, when he nearly wrecked St. Teresa's work, imagining all the time he was doing wonders ; it was exactly the same while he was Provincial of the Discalced. Doria made no mistakes. Gracian was loved, but not trusted by his subjects, for with his inconsistencies they never knew where they were. Doria was trusted but not loved, on the contrary he was feared. But who would not rather live under a weak and vacillating government, than under a reign of terror ? And that is what happened when Doria succeeded Gracian in 1585 ; it was a swing of the pendulum from one extreme to the other. Gracian was inordinately fond of preaching, and spent whole seasons in this apostolic work when it was his manifest duty to attend to business ; he wrote an incredible number of books, but nothing commensurate with his talents, nothing that survived him. Doria wrote nothing, but he was ever at his post, no detail escaped him, no individualistic initiative was allowed to side-track his clear line of action. While Gracian was Provincial great projects and high aims were resolved upon, but were pursued with something less than the required energy ; during Doria's nine years of office all enterprise was stifled. They were both great men, but both just fell short of being among the greatest.

It was during Doria's term of office that St. John of the Cross was called to take a part in the government of the Reform, first as Provincial of Andalusia, then as Definitor, and finally as member, and during the absence of Doria as chairman, of the Consulta. Doria had just achieved one of the objects he had had in mind from the beginning, namely, the total separation of the Discalced friars and nuns from the trunk of the Order, not merely as a separate province, but as an independent congregation, only nominally subject to the General (1587). The position of St. John of the Cross as member, and occasionally chairman, of the Consulta is not quite clear. He intensely disliked any kind of superiority, but when put in such a position he exercised his duties with the utmost conscientiousness, though without enthusiasm, and probably without initiative. He was perhaps the only man Doria feared, because St. John himself knew no fear ; having come to a decision about the rights and wrongs of a question, no power on earth could make him change his view ; he would have faced the worst tyrant, for, being ever in search of occasions for suffering, he could but have earned his heart's desire.

The question which brought about the final breach between St. John and Doria concerned the Constitutions given by the Chapter of Alcalá in 1581 to the Carmelite nuns, which they proudly cherished as the chief legacy of St. Teresa, and which Ven. Anne of Jesus had got approved by the Apostolic See, but which, for Doria, were as yet too elastic. St. John certainly knew the mind of St. Teresa much better than did Doria, and he also knew that the soul is a living thing and not a machine. However, Doria had his own view as to what was profitable for the nuns, and any other view must be crushed out of existence. And so St. John was crushed. He was not vanquished in an unequal contest, for contest there was none, he was relegated to Andalusia and suffered silently as he had suffered at Toledo. Doria, whose vigilance never failed, cannot have remained in ignorance of the saint's illness at La Peñuela, of his removal to Ubeda, of his agonising disease, of his death, and of the glorious manifestations after his death. As far as we know none of these things elicited a single word from the great Doria. On his deathbed he felt qualms of conscience about his treatment of Gracian, still alive, but apparently none about St. John of the Cross. Inexplicable as it is, it is a fact. In one sense St. John's death left a mark on Doria's work, for it put a limit to his interference with the Constitutions of St. Teresa. In another sense it left him free to deal with Gracian as he thought fit, for St. John of the Cross had been Gracian's last prop. Why all this? We can only say with the Apostle : " How incomprehensible are His judgments, and how unsearchable His ways ! "

BENEDICT ZIMMERMAN, O.D.C.

CARMELITE CHURCH, KENSINGTON,
LONDON,
January 23rd, 1931.

NOTES

INTRODUCTION

1. The first two volumes—which have just now come to hand—of the edition of the saint's works, prepared by Father Silverio de Santa Teresa, C.D., the scholarly editor of St. Teresa's writings, published at Burgos. See, at the end of this volume, the Appendix to the Notes on the last chapter, p. 485.

2. He clearly indicates this himself in the *Prologue* of the Commentary dedicated to Anne of Jesus.

3. Lamentations of Jeremias, iii. 17–18.

4. *Ibid.*, 24.

5. 2 Cor. xii. 30.

6. Ezechiel i. 12.

7. *Canticle*, Stanza 28 (Ger. II, p. 312).

8. *Ibid.*, S. 28 (Ger. II, p. 313).

9. *Ibid.*, S. 27 (Ger. II, p. 308).

10. *Ibid.*, S. 13 (Ger. II, p. 231).

11. *Ascent*, Bk. II, Ch. VII and VIII.

12. See my article, *Expérience Mystique et Philosophie*, *Rev. de Phil.* (November—December, 1926, p. 22).

13. It is that " pure adhesion to the essential Divinity, to the Deity " Which, knowing Itself, and in Its own proper and absolute intimate life, is, precisely, the Trinity, whilst the One of the philosophers is only God known, from without, and by His effects. To congratulate John of the Cross, united to the Trinity, for having reached the One, is perfect nonsense. It is as if one congratulated Vergil for having added a knowledge of the alphabet to his poetry.

14. See p. 267.

15. *Canticle*, S. 27 (Ger. II, p. 307).

16. *The Living Flame*, S. III, verse 3, § 9 (Ger. II, p. 453).

17. *Ibid.*, S. II, verse 5 (Ger. II, p. 423).

18. As far as philosophy is concerned, John soars high above it, and makes the best use of what he had gathered from a teaching that, taking it all together, was not, perhaps, very homogeneous, but was certainly very solid ; one cannot see, from his writings, that he ever intended to make a purely personal, profound study of any strictly philosophical problem. Hence, it is useless to seek for original, philosophical theories in his works, and still more futile to congratulate him on a philosophical

eclecticism which, had he possessed it, would certainly not have constituted an element of any great strength. The truth is, he received a good, ordinary philosophical training, such as was then given at Salamanca, but he never desired to produce a philosophical work. His own special work and genius dealt with mystical theology, and the practical science of union with God.

19. The Carmelites of Salamanca refer to John of St. Thomas as the author who deals most satisfactorily with the gifts of the Holy Ghost : " Desiderantem vero luculentiorem horum et aliorum donorum notitiam remittimus ad Mag. Joan. a. St. Thom. I–II, q. 68, disp. 18, ubi de hac re profunde et sapientissime agit." Salmanticenses, *Curs. Theol.* tract. XVII *de Fide, disp.* IX, in princ. (ed. Palmé, p. 408).

20. *Canticle*, Prologue (Ger. II, pp. 161–162).

21. Father Garrigou-Lagrange, *L'Amour de Dieu et la Croix de Jésus.* Introduction. (Paris, 1929.) Cf. *The Letter of Postulation* addressed, on June 14th, 1926, in the name of the Collegio Angelico, by Fathers Hugon and Garrigou-Lagrange, to the Sovereign Pontiff, with a view to obtaining the title of Doctor of the Universal Church for St. John of the Cross, *Analecta O.C.D.* (October—December, 1926.)

22. Theology, of course, is *eminenter practical*, but even when it is dealing with human acts and man's journey to his last end, it still does so *modo speculativo*, by its speculative use of concepts. This " eminently practical " character of theology enables it to link up with the practical science, dealt with by John of the Cross, not only by its object, but also by its mode ; it is founded on faith, and, presupposing the experience of divine things, employs theological principles to guide souls in the interior ways.

23. Thus, for instance, the Augustinian division of the higher faculties into understanding, memory and will, which, from the point of view of *speculative* and ontological analysis, should give place to a twofold division (intelligence and will), is more in conformity with reality, and responds, better than the latter, to the needs of *practical* analysis, where we seek to distinguish the powers, not only according to their essential ontological articulations, but also according to the most important modes of activity in regard to human ends. From this point of view there is plenty of room for distinguishing between the function of a knowledge of objects, taken in themselves, for which the name of understanding is reserved, the function of appreciation of objects in their relation to the personal experience and interests of the subject, which is called memory, and the function of intense longing and love, which is the will. Hence, most mystical authors, and St. John of the Cross in particular, adopt this

division, which is traditional with them, and enables the Doctor of the *Dark Night* to put forward the most profound views on the relation of the virtue of hope with Memory, and on the purification of the latter by the former.

24. *Ascent*, Prologue (Ger. I, p. 30).

25. *Dark Night*, Bk. I, § 8 (Ger. II, p. 25).

26. J. and R. Maritain, *Prayer and Intelligence*, note 3 (Sheed and Ward).

27. Luke xiv. 26. " Si quis venit ad me, et non odit patrem suum et matrem, et uxorem et filios, et fratres, et sorores, adhuc autem et animam suam, non potest meus esse discipulus."

28. Gallonio had permission to visit his family, who were living in Rome, only once a year. Baronius never returned to Sora. Consolini, the well-beloved disciple, had two brothers and sisters, and " never wrote a line to any of them, or opened his mouth to ask if they were alive or dead." G. Rabeau, *La Fantaiie comique et la grace de Dieu, St. Philippe Neri*, in *La Vie Spirituelle*, Jul.—Aug., 1929, p. 215. The author rightly calls attention to the fact that the *rôle* of the family in social life has completely altered since St. Philip's time. It was powerful and oppressive in the sixteenth century ; to-day it is socially very much weakened, and is more and more threatened. It may be a legitimate inference, from such considerations, to say that if " Philip were living to-day," he would have recourse to much less rigorous means, but not that " he would have thought exactly the opposite " (*Ibid.*). The laws of interior detachment and spiritual progress do not change.

29. *Sum. Theol.*, II–II, q. 26 (*sed contra*). Cf. 26, 7 ad. 1.

30. " Si quis venit ad me, et non odit . . . adhuc et animam suam," Luke xiv. 26.

31. Cf. St. Thomas Aquinas, *Sum. Theol.*, II–II, 19, 6 ; 19, 8, ad. 2.

32. Father Louis of the Trinity, C.D., *Précautions spirituelles, Avis et Maximes de Saint Jean de la Croix*, Le Carmel, September 15th, 1925, p. 218. " The saint's own method of acting," the author adds, " should be sufficient to put us on our guard against general charges of excessive rigorism : when the convent was being founded at Duruelo, he brought his mother, his brother Francisco de Yepes, and his sister-in-law there, and employed them in humble tasks connected with the building ; he loved the Carmelite nuns of Beas with an affection which, from the very fact that it was absolutely spiritual, did not prevent him from having legitimate preferences ; as prior of Segovia, and, consequently, at the close of his heroic career, it gave him pleasure to send for, and keep, his well-beloved brother near him." All these exquisitely natural traits are mentioned by Father Bruno. It is curious to note that St. John of the Cross (who, indeed,

found himself in very different conditions, and had not, like St. Philip Neri, to work in the midst of the world) was, in this matter of family relationships, much less rigorous and severe than the tenderest and most humorous of saints.

33. We are not here referring to the divergencies in philosophy which, on some secondary points (perhaps, owing to the influence of Baconthorp and Michael of Bologna), may exist between St. John of the Cross and St. Thomas Aquinas. Moreover, it would be very foolish to exaggerate the importance of such divergencies, and, in any case, they do not affect the essential principles, or theological teaching of St. John of the Cross.

34. Cf., upon this point, the decisive text in *The Ascent of Carmel*, Bk. II, Ch. IV, " And, in the first place, to avoid all confusion, it behoves us to know that, in every soul, even in that of the greatest sinner on earth, God substantially abides and dwells. This sort of union always exists between God and His creatures. It preserves them in the being they possess in such-wise that, if this union were wanting they would be immediately annihilated, and cease to exist. When we speak of the union of the soul with God, we leave aside the substantial union, common to all created things, and are thinking of the soul's union of transformation in God by love. This latter type of union is not general; it exists only when a likeness in love is set up, hence the name ' union of likeness,' whilst the other is called essential or substantial union. The one is natural, the other supernatural. . . . As we have said, God is always present in the soul, by the gift and conservation of its natural being, but, for all that, He does not always communicate super-natural being to the soul. Such communication is the fruit of grace and love, and all souls do not enjoy it; and even those who do, do not enjoy it in the same degree, since there may be a higher or lower degree of love in those souls."

" . . . This doctrine at once enables us to see that, if the soul yields to creatures, or has a taste for them, either through attachment or habitual dispositions, it is, by that very fact, not even ready for such union; and the reason is that the soul does not wholly offer itself to God, that He may supernaturally transform it. The soul, therefore, should have no greater anxiety than to get rid of such obstacles and natural dissimili-tudes, so that God, who has already communicated Himself to it according to nature, may communicate Himself supernaturally by grace " (Ger. I, pp. 112–113).

The following passage in Chap. XIII has raised a difficulty: " As soon as the soul has succeeded in carefully purifying itself from such forms and images as may be grasped, it will bathe in this pure and simple light, and, whilst transforming itself therein, will attain the state of perfection. Indeed, *this light is never absent from the soul ;* the obstacle to its infusion arises from the forms and veils of created things, which envelop and embarrass the soul. On the other hand, take away these hindrances and veils . . . let the soul be established in a pure nakedness of poverty of spirit, and, having become pure and simple, it will immediately be transformed in the pure and simple divine wisdom, that is the Son of God. Since the natural element is now excluded from the soul, which is entrusted to love, the Divine will at once expand there, *naturally* and supernaturally, so that there may be no vacuum in nature " (*Ascent,* Bk. II, Ch. XIII, Ger. I, 165). This passage (from which previous editors omitted the word *naturally*) obviously should be interpreted according to the saint's general teaching, and finds its natural commentary in the explanations already given in the fourth chapter. As we have just seen, he there explains that, if the divine light is *never absent from the soul* (Ch. IV : " it dwells in it by nature "), since God is present, by His creative immensity in the soul, " the transformation of the soul in God by love " can only be effected when grace renders God present to the soul, by the union of likeness (or, as St. Thomas says, I, 8, 3 : " as the known and loved is in Him who knows and loves "), and it is only because the soul has " received from God this re-birth and sonship, which surpasses all understanding " (Ch. IV), that it can remove the veils and hindrances arising from creatures, and establish itself in nakedness of spirit. This condition is presupposed by all the saint says in Chapter XIII, and hence it is that, in a soul supernaturalised by grace, and " already handed over to love," the Divine, provided the soul has emptied itself of " the natural," at once pours itself forth *naturally* (according to " the substantial union common to all created things " by which it has already occupied the soul) *and supernaturally,* according to the union of grace and love.

35. St. John of the Cross attributes an essential *rôle,* in the mystical life, to the spiritual impulse of the Holy Ghost ; it is this impulse which for him marks the passage from the natural to the supernatural mode. Cf. especially, *The Ascent,* III, 1 ; *The Canticle,* Sta. 17 (" breathe through my garden . . . "), Sta. 24 and 31 ; *The Living Flame,* Sta. 3, verse 3. There is no mystical life without charity, according to St. John of the Cross : " *Nunca da Dios sabiduría mística sin amor* " (*Noche L.,* II, Ch. XII ; Ger. II, p. 88). His thought is, on this point, in direct opposition to that of the Franciscan School, represented in his own day by Osuna, who admitted the existence of the gifts without charity, and the possibility of contemplation for a sinner. (Cf. F. Crisógono de Jesús Sacramentado, C.D., *San Juan de la Cruz, Su obra científica,* Avila, 1929, p. 121).

36. Father Silverio, who has made a close study of the text

of St. John of the Cross, has made some very just observations on the fundamental agreement between these two Doctors. See *Obras de San Juan de la Cruz*, editadas y anotadas por el P. Silverio de S. Teresa, C.D., Burgos, 1929, v. 1, Preliminares, pp. 32, 33, 147. F. Marcelo del Niño Jesús, C.D., author of a *Cursus Philosophiae Scholasticae*, which has had a wide circulation in Spain, also recognises the conformity of doctrine between the two saints. Cf. Fué filósofo San Juan de la Cruz ?—*El Monte Carmelo*, Burgos, December, 1927.

37.   *The Ascent*, Prologue (Ger. I, p. 33).

38.   C. H., *Abrégé de toute la doctrine mystique de Saint Jean de la Croix*, préface, p. vi. (*La Vie Spirituelle*).

39.   *Op. cit.*

AUTHOR'S PREFACE

1.   The italics are ours.

2.   *Mensajero de Santa Teresa y de San Juan de la Cruz* (Madrid). April 15th, 1925, p. 70.

3.   It was here Father Gregory of St. Joseph discovered those details which, in the opinion of the author (Mgr. Demimuid) gave " some touch of novelty " to his *Saint Jean de la Croix* in the " Les Saints " collection. I feel bound to add that Father José de Jesus Maria (Quiroga) introduced into his *Historia de la Vida y Virtudes del Venerable P. Fray Juan de la Cruz*, surreptitiously published at Brussels in 1628, a number of testimonies which I have often come across in the Process, and still others which I shall borrow from him. M. Baruzi (p. 731) seems to me to be too hard on this historian, who, despite breaks in continuity (cf. Maria de la Encarnacion, dep. 1635, Arch. C. R. Brux.) shows a real fidelity to the most trustworthy sources.

4.   *Revue des Sciences philosophiques et théologiques*, t. XVI, 1927, pp. 39–50 and 165–177.

5.   Letter to Cardinals Luca, Pitra and Hergenroether, on the defence of historic truth, August 18th, 1883—The passage is borrowed from Cicero : *De Oratore*, II, § 62.

CHAPTER I

1.   As the parish registers were destroyed by a fire on July 27th, 1546, the date June 24th is attested only by an inscription in the baptistery : " En esta pila se bautizó el mistico dor. San Juan de la Cruz, primer Carmelita Descalzo, lustre y honra de esta nobilisíma villa de Fontíveros por haber sido natural de ella. Nació el año de 1542 a 24 de Junio. Murió el de 1591 a 14 de X.

Hízose siendo cura el ldo. Joseph Velado año de 1689." According to Alonso, L. I, Ch. I, he was born "fin del año mill y quinientos y quarenta y dos."

Some documents state : " Fray Juan de la Cruz, natural de Medina del Campo," but this is certainly wrong because Francisco de Yepes himself states that it was Fontiveros (B.N.M. MS. 12738, fo. 613) and so does Velasco.

Was the name John chosen simply because it was the feast of the Baptist, June 24th, or was it out of devotion? St. John the Baptist had long been honoured at Fontiveros. A chapel was erected in his honour in the parochial Church of St. Cyprian in 1571.

2. Quir. 369 ; Cyp. 329 ; Jer. 495.

3. ". . . demas de ser esta señora hermossa . . ." Alonso, Seg. P.A., fo. 43. ". . . tal disposicion hermosura y modestia como las que mas de su tiempo." Alonso, L. I, Ch. I.

4. ". . . de gente mui noble y principal y rica. . . ." Tomas Perez de Molina, Med. I. O., fo. 23.

5. The genealogy was established by the Father-General, John of the Holy Ghost, in a journey to Yepes and is preserved in the convent of Segovia in *El libro de las cosas*.

6. ". . . aunque el avorrecido de ellos. . . ." Alonso, Seg. P.A., fo. 43. Id. L. I, Ch. I. Father José de Velasco, B.N.M. MS. 19404, fo. 177.

7. ". . . ablando con tres personas biejas . . . que avian conocido a los dhos Alonso de Yepes y Catalina Alvarez supo que . . . su mesura onestitad retiro y apacibilidad con las de su calidad en que era imbidiada y amada de ellas su termino nobleça mostrava ser bien nacida. . . ." Alonso, Seg. P.A., fo. 43.

8. ". . . comian pan de cevada . . . tenia un tio Arcediano de torrijo. . . ." Tomas Perez de Molina, Med. I. O., fo. 23.

9. These events, and the following, are related by Velasco, L. I, Ch. I and II.

10. ". . . los hacia que fuesen devotos de la Madre de Dios. . . ." Catalina related it herself to Maria de S. Francisco, Med. I. O., fo. 20.

11. The saint's mother said that " desde niño avia sido como un Angel." Maria Evangelista, Med. I. O., fo. 31. Francisca de Jesús, *Ib.*, fo. 28.

12. Regestum Rubei, fo. 81.

13. ". . . Le oyo decir al dicho Siervo de Dios que siendo niño jugando con otros niños junto a una laguna muy cenagosa junto a la villa de Medina del Campo, o de ontiveros, aunque mas cierto esta que era en Medina del Campo, cayo en ella . . . y que en esta ocasion acudió a pasar por alli un labrador que venia del campo con una agujada en la mano. . . . Lo qual

este testigo le oyo decir muchas veces al dicho siervo de Dios . . . y que esto lo avia sucedido siendo de hedad de quatro o cinco años. . . ." Luis de S. Angel, Baeza. P.A., fo. 45.

14. *Gal.* vi. 14. Text of the Introit of the Mass of St. John of the Cross in the Carmelite Proper.

CHAPTER II

1. Vel., L. I, Ch. II.
2. " por la sterilidad y carestia destos años, paso el niño Juan con su madre y con su hermano Francisco a la villa de Arevalo . . ." Alonso, L. I, Ch. I.
3. " La madre después de viuda pasó muchos trabajos ; probó a poner a su hijo menor a oficio y probando el de carpintero, sastre, entallador y pintor, a ninguno de ellos asentó, aunque era muy amigo de trabagar." Francisco de Yepes, B.N.M. MS. 12738, fo. 613.
4. " El niño Juan siendo de nueve años levantandose de la cama se acostava sobre unos sarmientos por penitencia." Alonso, Seg. P.A., fo. 44.
5. Vel., L. I, Ch. II.
6. " para que alli le sustentasen y deprendiese letras." Alonso, Seg. P.A., fo. 44.
7. Tomas Perez de Molina, Med. I. O., fo. 23.
8. Francisco de Yepes, B.N.M. MS. 8568, fo. 371 *sq.*
9. Maria de S. Francisco, Med. I. O., fo. 20.
10. Vel., L. I, Ch. V.
11. Vel., L. IV, Ch. V.
12. Bar., 78 *sq.*
13. Constança Rodriguez, Med. P.A., fo. 72. Alonso, L. I, Ch. II.
14. " . . . de allí le enviaban al monasterio de la Penitencia porque serviese la iglesia y ayudase a misa. . . ." Gabriel de S. José, Med. P.A., fo. 53. Vel. (*ibid.*), fo. 50. Alonso, L. I, Ch. II.
15. Francisco de Yepes, B.N.M. MS. 12738, fo. 613.
16. In particular, those of the Miracle of St. Hugh (Provincial Museum of Seville).
17. " . . . entró de su voluntad en el Hospital " states Pedro Fernandez de Bustillo, who also says : " Conoci, hablé, traté al dicho siervo de Dios . . . muchacho estudiante y después que tomo el havito. . . ." Med. P.A., fo. 62 ; Maria Velasquez, *ibid.*, fo. 60.
18. " . . . Y pedia para los niños de la doctrina y las monjas le tenia mucho amor, por ser muy agudo y abil. En este tiempo le llevaron al hospital de las bubas con un señor que tenia quenta

con los enfermos y dieronle quydado que pidiese pᵃ los pobres
. . . " Francisco de Yepes, B.N.M. MS. 8568, fo. 371.

19. *En route*, pp. 110, 111.

20. Med. P.A., fo. 62. Maria Velasquez (*ibid.*), fo. 60.

21. Bar., 78.

22. *Ibid.*, 82 *sq.*

23. Vel., L. I, Ch. II.

24. Francisco de Yepes, B.N.M. MS. 12738, fo. 613.

25. Astraín, *Historia de la Compañía de Jesús en la Asistencia de España*, t. I, pp. 309 *sq.*

26. Francisco de Yepes, B.N.M. MS. 12738, fo. 613.

27. Astraín, *op. cit.*, Vol. IV, p. 105.

28. B.N.M. MS. 12738, fo. 613 *sq.*

29. Alonso, L. I., Ch. II.

30. *Summarium Segobien. Beat. et Canoniz. S.D. Joannis a Cruce*, Arch. Cong. Rit., p. 5, No. 2.

31. " . . . y tenia lugar que estudiase un poço por la mañana y otro rato por la tarde, y tenia tanto cuidado que en brebe tiempo supo mucho en la compañia de Jesús. . . . " B.N.M. MSS., 8568, fo. 371. Tomas Perez de Molina, Med. I. O., fo. 23.

32. " Juan Gomez del Espinosa . . . mayor de sesenta años y cerca de setenta . . . siendo este testigo vecino del hospital de la concepción desta dha villa que al presente llaman el general conoció en el dicho hospital a un cavallero llamado alonso alvarez de toledo que hera el que tenia a su cargo todo el dho hospital y entrava y salia este testigo diversas veces en el dho hospital . . . conocio muy bien en el dho hospital al dho alonso alvarez y tambien conocio un muchacho que estava con el y servia en el dho hospital . . . fue ansi que un dia viniendo este testigo a comer a su cassa oyo descir entre mucha gente de la vecindad del dho hospital que el dho niño de la doctrina avia caido en un poço del y yendole a sacar porque se pensava se avia ahogado porque el dicho poço hera muy hondo y este testigo le a visto le hallaron al dho niño de la doctrina vivo dentro del dho poço y que descia que una señora le avia tenido para que no se ahogasse y ansi le sacaron sin lesion ni daño alguno y se publicó que la Virgen Nra Sa. hera la que le avia sustentado y tenido para que no se ahogasse y este testigo vió despues de pasado este casso muchas y diversas veces al dho niño. . . ." Med. I. O., fo. 22. This account, which can scarcely be confused with Luis de San Angelo's, given in Ch. I, seems to be equally true. Juan Evangelista, the saint's companion, also says, " Se le oyo decir al mismo padre fray Juan de la Cruz por su propria boca como avia caido en el poço en la villa de Medina del Campo . . . no le dijo a este testigo lo aviese ayudado la madre de Dios ne tuviese otro favor del cielo porque estas

mercedes las guardava el para si. . . ." Jaen, I. O., fo. 5.
For the second fall, see, Elvira de Quevedo, Med. I. O., fo. 34.
Jeronimo de la Cruz, Jaen, P.A., fo. 124. Alonso, L. I, Ch. II,
and see also, Demimuid, *Saint Jean de la Croix*, p. 4 *sq.* (Paris,
Gabalda).

33. ". . . diose tan buena maña a su estudio, ayudandole
en el Nuestro Señor, que aprovecho muchó en poco tiempo. . . ."
Francisco de Yepes, B.N.M. MS. 12738, fo. 613 *sq.*

34. Vel., L. I, Ch. IV.

35. ". . . y contaban en el hospital que andandole a buscar
de noche no lo podian hallar y al cabo venian a verle entre las
tenadas de los manojos estudiando." Francisco de Yepes,
B.N.M. MS. 12738, fo. 613 *sq.* Cf. also Tomas Perez de
Molina, Med. I. O., fo. 23.

36. Astraín, *op. cit.*, t. II, p. 581.

37. Astraín, *op. cit.*, t. IV, p. 196.

38. Bar., 90 *sq.*

CHAPTER III

1. The sources of this chapter are : (*a*) *Constitutiones Ordinis
B. V. Mariae de Monte Carmelo*, 1462, copy of the Discalced
Carmelites of Bruges.

(*b*) The Constitutions of the Blessed John Soreth, *Correctae
ac emendatae per Rm. Mag. Nicolaum Audet, Ordinis Priorem Generalem
et Diffinitores Cap. gen. celebrati Venetiis. A.D. MDXXIV (Hispali,
1573)*.

(*c*) The articles of the Most Reverend Father John Baptist de
Rubeo of Ravenna's Reform, which are contained substantially
in the Constitutions, published at Venice after his visit, on the
frontispiece of which we may read : " *Constitutionum Compendium,
summam ultra antiquas constitutiones ordinis a S. Sorecto editas . . .
Venetiis, MDLXVIII.*

(*d*) *Regestum Joannis Baptiste de Rubbeis Generalis ab anno 1563–
1578*, by Father Benedict Zimmerman.

(*e*) *Acta Captitulorum Generalium Ordinis Fratrum B.V. Mariae de
Monte Carmelo, Vol. I, ab anno 1318 usque ad annum 1593, cum notis
praecipue a R.P. Benedicto Zimmerman O.C.D. mutuatis . . . edidit
ex libro ordinis officiali Fr. Gabriel Wessels* (Romae, 1912).

(*f*) *Ordinal* of Sibert de Beka, published by Father Benedict
Zimmerman (Paris, Picard, 1910) ; also the same B. Z.'s article
in the *Dict. d'Archéologie : Liturgie de l'ordre des Carmes*, t. II, col.
2166 *sq.*, and in the *Chroniques du Carmel :* Le Cérémonial de
Sibert de Beka, January, 1903, to May, 1905.

(*g*) *Ritus ordinis B.V. Mariae de Monte Carmelo*, articles published
in the *Analecta Ord. Carmelitarum*, Vols. I, II.

2. According to a tradition only to be found in the conscien-

tious historian Dositheé de St. Alexis, *Vie de Saint Jean de la Croix*, Vol. I, p. 2 (Paris, 1727). Neither Quiroga nor Jeronimo specify the month and the day.

3. Const., 1462. De induitione Novitiorum. (Incunable des Carmes de Bruges, c. 74).

4. *Ibid. Id.* Up to 1586 novices were distinguished from the professed by wearing a hood that was separated from the scapular. *Analecta, O. C.*, Vol. III, p. 209.

5. "Aquel caballero que tenia cuidado del hospital . . . le rogaba que cantase alli misa y se quedase por capellan del hospital. . . ." Francisco de Yepes, B.N.M. MS. 12738, fo. 613 *sq.*

6. "El dho siñor del dicho ospital le queria mucho y deseaba que se quedase alli para que fuese capellan y confesor de los pobres, mas el no gusto deste exerçiçio porque deseaba apartarse mas y apretarse mas. . . ." Tomas Perez de Molina, Med. I. O., fo. 23.

7. Alonso, Seg. P.A., fo. 45.

8. "Encendiendo se de dia en dia mas el amor ardiente de la immaculada Virgen Maria Madre de Dios se salió del dicho Hospital. . . ." Fernandez de Bustillo. Med. P.A., fo. 62. "Con la devoción tan grande que tenia de la Virgen nuestra Señora tomó el Habito de Carmelita. . . ." Juan Lopez Osoño, *ibid.*, fo. 58.

9. "Y asi se fué muy secretamente al convento de Santa Ana . . . donde pidió el habito. . . ." Francisco de Yepes, B.N.M. MS. 12738, fo. 613 *sq.*

10. "In cujus obsequio et honore fundata est nostra Religio de monte Carmeli," Acta Cap. Gen. apud Monspelium celebrati. Cf. Acta Cap. Gen., p. 7, and Antoine de la Présentation, appendix to Constitutions of 1357 (Marche, 1915), p. 149.

11. Jeronimo de la Cruz, Jaen, P.A., p. 125. As there was no postulancy, this fact is not surprising.

12. Vel., L. II, Ch. I.

13. Memorial histórico de Medina del Campo, Ch. XL, quoted by Silv., t. V, p. 21, note 2. Bibl. Carm., Vol. II, col. 87.

14. Ghent, 1894.

15. Brit. Mus. MSS. Harley, 3838, quoted by Zimmerman in his *Monumenta historica Carmelitana* (Lerins, 1907), and in his study *La Provincia de Castilla* (*El monte Carmelo*, Burgos, 1910), p. 370.

16. *Chronica Guglielmi de Sanvico*, in *Speculum Carmelitanum*, p. 211, Antwerp edition of 1680 ; French translation by R.F. Eliseus of the Nativity in *Carmel* (October—December, 1928).

17. Benedict Zimmerman, *Les Saints déserts des Carmes déchaussés*, p. 3 *et seq.* (Paris, 1927).

18. Vita S. Petri Thomae auct. Philippo Mazerio. Acta SS. Januar III, 612.

19. Fernandez de Bustillo, Med. P.A., fo. 62. Quir., p. 27 ; also Juan Gomez del Espinosa, Med. I. O., fo. 22 et Elvira de Quevedo, *ibid.*, fo. 34.

20. Alonso, Seg. P. A., fo. 45. Astrain, *op. cit.*, L. II, p. 576.

21. *Const. of Audet*, already quoted, Ch. I, § 36.

22. Ex codice Lud. Perez de Castro, Arch. O.C.C. Rome. On this Castilian Carmelite, cf. *Bibl. Carm.*, vol. II, col. 294 *sq.*

23. *La provincia de Castilla*, mentioned above.

24. *Fund.*, c. II, Silv., IV, 16 ; C. P., III, 66.

25. " Y le oyo decir este testigo a un Religioso muy biego q la dicha religion de Carmelitas estuvo en Castilla y Andalusia para acabarse y lo mismo oyo a otras personas y que era tanta la relajacion, q no avia quien quisiese estudiar en la dha religion y q solo procuraban ordenarse y con eso se contentaban." Luis de S. Angel, Baeza, P.A., fo. 50.

26. Alonso, Seg. P.A., fo. 45.

27. Cf. *Speculum Carmelitanum*, I, p. 9 *sq.* (Ed. 1680).

28. Cf. Jérôme De La Mère De Dieu. *La Tradition mystique du Carmel* in *La Vie Spirituelle* (January, March, 1924).

29. Alonso, Seg. P. A., fo. 45.

30. Antonio de Sagrameña, Med. I. O., fo. 8, and Jeronimo de Olmos, *id.*, fo. 35, and P.A., fo. 82.

31. Benedict Zimmerman, *Los Provinciales de Castilla* in *El Monte Carmelo*, 1910, p. 449 *sq.*

32. *Const.*, 1462. De modo professandi (c. 75). Alonso (L. I, Ch. III) maintains that John must have made his profession in the summer, because—he says—the text of the profession bears the name of " Rubeo of Ravenna, prior general." Rubeo from being vicar general, had become prior general at the chapter in May. It would be dangerous to follow Alonso, because the two copies of the profession, given by him, in his deposition (Seg. P.A., fo. 45) and in the *Vida* (L. I, Ch. III) are not quite alike, and that is a disturbing factor. We are encouraged in our reserve by a note of Mgr. Demimuid in his *Saint Jean de la Croix*, p. 25, already referred to.

CHAPTER IV

1. The convent at Cambridge had been burnt in 1513 and was now being rebuilt. From 1505 until its suppression in 1538 very few degrees were conferred at the Oxford convent : 24 Carmelites as against 57 Franciscans, 40 Dominicans, 23 Augustinians, 169 Benedictines and 44 Cistercians. Whilst from 1449 to 1463 there were 12 Carmelites as against 10 Franciscans, 13 Domi-

nicans, 9 Augustinians, 44 Benedictines and 8 Cistercians. In France, the *Studium Parisiense* " *quod inter coetera tenet principatum* " (*Const.*, 1324, rubr. 16, No. 26, *Mon.*, *Hist. Carm.*, p. 57) declined after the Wars of Religion and the ostracism of the Congregation of Albi. The Italian, Belgian and German provinces contributed scarcely anything.

2. " Sunt hodie plures quasi graduati quam fratres simplices," *Acta Cap.*, *Gen.*, p. 321.

3. Rev. Fr. Crisógono de Jesús, O.C.D., in his book, *San Juan de la Cruz : su obra científica* (Avila, 1929) strongly insists on the Baconian influences in the holy Doctor's works. On the ancient doctors of Carmel, consult the learned works of Father Xiberta, O.C., in the *Analecta O. Carm.* and the Barcelona *Criterion*. De Mag. Guidone Terreni (Guy of Perpignan), *Anal. O.C.*, Vol. V, pp. 113 and 233. *De Summa Theologiae Gerardi Bononiensis*, *ibid.*, p. 3, etc. *De Mag. Johanne Baconthorpe*, *O. Carm.*, *ibid.*, Vol. VI, p. 3, etc. See also, Wessels, O.C., *Joannes de Bachone*, *O.C.*, *et ejus schola* in the *Anal. O.C.*, Vol. III, pp. 84, 109, 168. Anastase de St. Paul, O.C.D., *De Michaele Anguani de Bononia* in the *Analecta O.C.D.*, Vol. IV, p. 41, etc., and the article *Michel de Bologne* in the *Dict. Theol. Cath.*, Vol. X, col. 1674, etc. Marcelo del Niño Jesús, *Apuntes históricos sobre la filosofía en la Orden Carmelitana* (Burgos, 1928). G. Michalski, Professor in the University of Cracow, *Le Criticisme et le scepticisime dans la philosophie*, containing information on Gerard of Bologna and Bacon (Cracow, 1926). *Bibl. Carm.*, under, *Gerardus de Bononia* (Vol. I, cols. 548 to 550) ; *Guido Terrena* (vol. I, cols. 581 to 588) ; *Joannes de Bachone* (Vol. I, cols. 743 to 753). *Michael Angrianus de Bononia* (Vol. II, cols. 433 to 446). Xiberta, *Analecta O.C.* VI, 338—379.

4. " De sustentar y alegar la doctrina de los doctores de nuestra Orden," C. XVI, Silv., VI, 482.

5. *Bibl. Carm.*, Vol. I, cols. 780 to 787.

6. *Reg Rubei*, fo. 106.

7. *Fund.*, Silv., V, 105 ; C. P., III, 183.

8. *Acta Cap. Gen.*, p. 428.

9. The Chapter of Venice decreed that student priests were only bound to celebrate twice a week, *Acta Cap. Gen.*, p. 429. But Soreth's Constitutions, P.I., Rub. XVII *in fine*, oblige students to assist at High Mass and Vespers.

10. Chapter of 1564. *Acta Cap Gen.*, p. 453. Rules for the Salamancan College.

11. Beltrán de Heredia, *La Fiesta de Santo Tomás en la Univ. de Salamanca.—Ciencia Tomista*, March, April, 1926, p. 204.

12. *Theologiae Sacrae.* Qua rerum divinarum cognitione hominum mentes imbutae terrena despiciant, coelum votis petant, beatamque jam nunc incipiant videre vitam.

13. Estatutos de 1561, tit. L, §§ 1 and 2. B. de Heredia, see p. 203.

14. *Acta Cap. Gen.*, p. 453.

15. Gustave Reynier, *La Vie universitaire dans l'ancienne Espagne*, p. 20 *et passim* (Paris, Picard, 1902).

16. Beltrán de Heredia, *Los Manuscritos del M. F. Francisco de Vitoria. El dictado en las aulas, Ciencia Tomista*, 1927, p. 315 *sq.*

17. Bar., 124, note 2.

18. Gr. de Santiago Vela, *Ensayo de una Biblioteca Ibero-Americana de la Orden de San Agustin.* Art. *Guevara* (Fray Juan de) v. III, 471. We learn at p. 468 that the Rector, alone or accompanied by the Dean, made a visitation every two months.

19. " Archivo Universitario " of the University of Salamanca ; Registro de matriculas año de 1564 to 1565, fo. 17 ; Registro de matriculas año de 1565 to 1566, fo. 12 ; Registro de matriculas año de 1566 to 1567, fo. 17 ; Registro de matriculas año de 1567 to 1568, fo. 16.

20. Beltrán de Heredia, *Actuación del M. Dom Báñez en la Universidad de Salamanca, Ciencia Tomista*, 1922, p. 64 *sq.*

21. Silv., VI, 481.

22. Quir., 47.

23. Arch. Univ. Salm. Procesos de Catedras, Collections 68 and 71.

24. Esperabé Arteaga, *Historia interna y documentada de la Universidad de Salamanca* (Salamanca, 1914–1917), Vol. I, p. 262.

25. *Spec. Carm.*, already quoted, Vol. II, p. 567.

26. The salary of a doctor in Canon Law was 272 florins, of a professor of Logic or Moral Theology 100. Reynier, *op. cit.*, p. 20.

27. Bañes, in II—II, q. 1, art. 7.

28. Cuervo, O. P., *Historiadores del Convento de San Esteban* (Salamanca, 1914–1916), Vol. I, p. 262. There is a MS. of Mancio's in the Vatican Library, *In codice Ottob*, No. 1058. It is a commentary on the *Pars Prima.* (Cf. Ehrle, *Der Katholik*, February, 1885). There should be a treatise *De Fide* in the B.N.M. A theological study on Mancio's teaching would require much time, and, moreover, we have no full biography of him. Jerome Lanoussa wrote a work on this theologian but it cannot be found. We trust that the learned Father Beltrán de Heredia or one of his Dominican confrères will soon devote a study to this Salamancan master.

Without wishing to go into the problem, we may remark that if Bañes, as M. Mahieu seems to say in his book, *François Suarez*, p. 43 (Lille, 1921), could not induce Mancio to accept physical predetermination, the first discussion on the *De Auxiliis* affair dates only from January, 1582. Molina's *Concordia* was published in 1588. There was no need then for John of St. Mathias to take an interest in, or decide on, either of the views. In this matter we may note that Michael of Bologna had a tendency towards predestination. We are using the word, of course, in its orthodox signification.

Bibl. Carm., Vol. II, col. 441, etc.

29. " Desde el principio de la tercera parte en adelante." Archives of the University of Salamanca, " Cuaderno de visitas de Catedras."

30. *Cántico*, Canción XXXVI (Ger., II, 598).

31. " Desde el principio de la Secunda Secundae en adelante," *Ibid.*, and Santiago Vela, already quoted, p. 472.

32. Dom Phil. Chevallier, *Le Cant. Spir. interpolé* (*Vie Spir.*, I, 1927, Suppl., p. 85).

33. Santiago Vela, *op. cit.*, pp. 415 and 482.

34. Silv., II, 20 ; Greg., III, 402.

35. Santiago Vela, *op. cit.*, p. 393.

36. " Desde la cuestion 76 de la Primera en adelante hasta el fin de lo de Anima, mas la cuestion 100 de la II—II··· y las cuestiones 183 hasta el fin." *Ibid.*, pp. 429 *sq.*, and 472.

37. C.P., III, 217. The Provincial Library of Burgos possesses a copy of Juan Gallo's *Commentarii in Cant. Cant.* (MS. 41). The MSS. Commentaries in No. 1135 of the B.N.M. may also be by him. We cannot definitely say so because the beginning is missing ; still, in the same codex a commentary on the first chapter of the Ep. to Timothy is attributed to Master Gallo. His theological commentaries are very probably in the Vatican Library. Father Beltrán will give an account of his life and—let us hope—his doctrines in the *Ciencia Tomista*.

38. " Cuaderno de visitas de Catedras."

39. Ger., II, 494.

40. *Acta Cap. Gen.*, p. 428.

41. Ger., II, 494.

CHAPTER V

1. Ref., L. II, Ch. II, § 3.

2. Apart from the works already mentioned in Ch. II and Ch. III, we are availing ourselves of the biography of John Baptist Rubeo, published by Father B. Zimmerman in the *Chroniques du Carmel*, in 1908, and his previous study, *Le Cérémonial de Sibert de Beka* (1903).

3. *Bibl. Carm.*, Vol. I, col. 639.

4. Beltrán de Heredia, *La Fiesta de S. Tomás*, already quoted.

5. Alonso de Villalobos wrote on January 22nd, 1606 : " . . . Yo vi, y tuve en mis manos unos como zaraguellos hechos de ésparto agudo, al modo de las redes que ponen en gallineros,

4396 ST. JOHN OF THE CROSS

y de lo mismo un jubon, y todo esto traia à raiz de las carnes, Y vi disciplinas bien asperas, y usadas, y gastadas llenas de sangre. Y vi en su celda una cama en que dormia a manera de cuezo (sin colchon) largo que tenia en un huero un madero por cabecera." Jer., 41, 42.

6. Iste vir Eliae par Baptistaeque Joanni. Tit. 55. Eccl. Remensis.

7. *Const. Rubei*, " De praecipuo gradu observantiae regularis."

8. *Fund.*, Ch. II ; Silv., V, 16 ; C. P., III, 65.

9. Alonso, L. I, Ch. IV.

10. Chap. XVII ; Silv., VI, 481.

11. "A la sexta pregunta : dijo este testigo que volviendo de Salamanca theologo pasante el dicho siervo de Dios del dicho convento de sancta Ana donde canto missa estando con muchos desseos de vida mas estrecha. . . . llego a esta villa nuestra madre sancta Theresia. . . ." Med. P.A., fo. 51.

12. *Const.*, 1462 ; P.I., Rubr. XV (versus finem).

13. " Y como leya en los autores antiguos que tratan de la vida perfecta, y alentada de nuestros Monges solitarios, que su continuo exercicio era la contemplacion divina, y por eso los llamavan por excelencia contemplativos, y que a esto mismo se ordenava el fin principal de la regla primitiva, mezclava entre las materias escolasticas que estudiava particular leccion de Autores mysticos ; particularmente de san Dionisio y de san Gregorio, para sacar dellos la sustancia de la contemplacion, en que por blanco de su instituto debia exercitarse, y hallava tan encontradas la doctrina antigua destos y de otros Santos, que la Iglesia de Christo tiene como per lumbreras clarisimas de sus verdades, y las opiniones nuevas, que en materia de oracion mental corrian en este tiempo, que gasto mucho en averiguarlas para sacar en limpio la esencia verdadera de la contemplacion provechosa, que era como fundamento de la vida que profesava. Y hallava poca resolucion desto en las personas espirituales que comunicava, por estar ya muy desusada la verdadera contemplacion, que enseñaron los Santos, por otros modos nuevos de orar que maestros modernos avian introduçido fundados mas en artificio humano, que en los recivos de la operacione divina, sobre lo qual y quanto le lastimava, hizo el venerable Padre un excelente discurso." Quir., pp. 35-36 ; Cyp., pp. 31-32 ; Ger., Vol. I, p. xxviii.

14. De Scoraille, *François Suarez* (Paris, 1914), p. 51.

15. *Const. Rubei*, De Studio et studentibus, § 13.

16. Alonso, Seg. P.A., fo. 46.

17. Martin Garcia was bound to teach Scripture every day by Audet's prescriptions. Cosme de Villiers states that one of his MSS. was to be found in the Valladolid Library : *De Sacrae Scripturae similitudinibus.*

CHAPTER VI

1. The scholastic year, at this period, was from St. Luke's Day, October 18th, to September 7th of the following year. It was in fact the *poco después* of St. Teresa (*Fund.*, Ch. III ; Silv., V, 29 ; C.P., III, 85), for, as we shall see, the Carmelite nuns arrived at Medina on August 15th. We hasten to add that there were a number of feast days on which there were no lectures, a month's vacation dating from December 8th, and another from Easter Sunday. Furthermore the students were bound to attend only for six months and a day. Beltrán de Heredia : *La Fiesta de S. Tomás en la universidad de Salamanca. Ciencia Tomista*, March, April, 1926, p. 208.

(2) *Fund.*, Ch. XIV ; Silv., V, 110 ; C.P. III, 189.

(3) It seems clear from what Velasco says (Med. P.A., fo. 50), and also Alonso (Seg. P.A., fo. 45) that it was when John of St. Mathias went to Medina to sing his first Mass that he first saw St. Teresa. There were not two separate journeys as some have contended. If one wishes for confirmation, we may add that the students of St. Andrew's did not return every year to their own convents. The Father Procurator of St. Anne's, for instance, sent Brother John cloth to make a habit in the middle of the University vacation, October 1st, 1566 (Alonso, L. I, Ch. III). It cost 52 reals. And a further interesting point is that we know from Jeronimo de Olmos, who was a Carmelite of St. Anne's, that, according to the bursar's accounts, this stuff was bought from a parish priest because, says Jeronimo, " we then wore black cloth." Med. P.A., fo. 82.

Pedro de Orozco, who accompanied John, was by no means the elderly religious that some biographers believe : the Teresian text does not say so : " Y el fué con otro por compañero " (*Fund.*, Ch. III). No doubt he went with John to celebrate his first Mass, for he was matriculated in 1567–1568 as " presbyter y teólogo " (Arch. Univ. Reg. de Matriculas, año 1567–1568, fo. 16 ; Fr. Pº Orozco n. de Medina del Campo, dioc. de Sal. pº y tº.).

4. Ana Maria de Jesus. Seg. P.A., fo. 109 ; Alonso, *ib.*, fo. 46 ; Quir., 390 ; Jer., 55 ; Vel. Med. I. O., fo. 10.

5. Salmanticenses *De necessitate gratiae*, Disp. III, dub. XI, n. 250.

6. This reconstitution has been made according to Father Zimmerman's " *Ceremonial*," *Ch. du Carmel*, already quoted.

7. An apostolic constitution of Martin V's, dated July 29th, 1418 (*Bull. Carm.*, I, 170, 1) inserted in the Bull of Eugene IV, dated March 28th, 1432 (*l.c.* 184), and of Nicholas V's, July 30th, 1454, granted at the request of Paul of Sicily, Procurator-General of the Carmelites (*l.c.* 240).

8. This Chapter is the chief source of the facts we are now relating, and reference to it should be made if not otherwise indicated.

9. *Vie de S. Thérèse* by Ribera, S.J. (translated by Bouix, Paris, 1868), p. 350. Anthony may have known Teresa when he was Prior at Avila. On March 2nd, 1565, Angel de Salazar commissioned Anthony and Garcia of Toledo to release her from her vow of perfection.

10. Letter to the Bishop of Avila, August, 1577 (Silv., VIII, 108 ; Greg., II, 128 ; Engl., II, 304.

11. Deposition of Julian of Avila, C.P., VI, 485.

12. Seg. P.A., fo. 47.

13. Jeronimo de la Cruz, Jaen, P.A., fo. 123 ; Velasco, Med. P.A., fo. 50.

14. Quir., 51 ; Cyp., 45.

15. Julian of Avila, *loc. cit.*

16. Luis de S. Angel, Baeza, P.A., fo. 46.

17. Tomas Perez de Molina, Med. P.A., fo. 23.

18. In the Provincial Museum of Seville.

19. *Vida*, Ch. XXI ; Silv., I, 161 ; C.P., I, 267.

20. *Reg. Rubei*, fo. 104 ; *Analecta O.C.*, IV, 196 *sq.* ; C.P., III, 515.

21. *Ignea sagitta*, MS. in the O.C.C. Arch., Rome, Ch. VI, fos. 597 and 599.

22. Julian of Avila, *loc. cit.*

23. Alonso, Seg. P.A., fo. 45.

24. Vel., L. I, Ch. VIII.

CHAPTER VII

1. Santiago Vela, *Ensayo*, quoted above, p. 472.

2. Silv., VII, 52 ; Greg., I, 67 ; Engl., I, 62 "such a bargainer."

3. B. Anne of St. Bartholomew's account, C.P., IV, 466.

4. "Cansabanla personas encapotadas oraciones estujadas que asi las llamaba ella." Dep. of Ven. Anne of Jesus, Arch. C. R. Brux.

5. Teresa always denied that she had done anything but resume St. Albert's rule in all its vigour. If the practice of going bare-footed was objected to, she answered, "that what has been done was necessary to distinguish you from the Mitigated," in a letter to Mariano of December 1st, 1576. Silv., VII, 396 ; Greg., I, 487 ; Engl., II, 174. On the question of bare feet, see Dom. L. Gougaud : *Anciennes traditions ascétiques.* Sec. II, *La Gymnopodie (Rev. d'Ascet. et de Myst.*, Toulouse, 1923), p. 140, etc.

6. Silv., V, 402. 7. Silv., III, 56 ; C.P., V, 100.

8. *Vida*, Ch. XXXVI ; Silv., I, 317 ; C.P., II, 86.

9. Silv., III, 9 ; C.P., V, 34.

10. Silv., III, 24 ; C.P., V, 52.

11. Arch. C. R. Brussels.

12. *Fund.*, Ch. I ; Silv., V, 11 ; C.P., VII, 59. Antonio Maldonado, different from Alonso Maldonado, who is generally, but wrongly, identified with the missioner mentioned in the *Book of Foundations*. See English edition, London, 1913, p. 9, note 1 [Editor].

13. Cf. Rev. B. Zimmerman, *Les saints déserts des Carmes Déchaussés*, Ch. IV. *Le plan du R. P. Rubeo* (Paris, Art. Cathol., 1927), p. 36 etc.

14. Silv., VI, p. viii.

15. *Vida*, Ch. XXVII ; Silv., I, 205 ; C. P., I, 293, and II, 420.

16. *Ibid.*, Ch. XXXV ; Silv., I, 297 ; C. P., II, 55.

17. *Camino*, Ch. II ; Silv., III, 15 ; C. P., V, 40.

18. C. P., III, 150, note 4. Deposition of Julian of Avila, C.P., VI, 473.

19. *Camino*, Ch. II ; Silv., III, 16 *et seq.* ; C.P., V, 41 *sq.*

20. *Ibid.*, Silv., III, 26 ; C.P., V, 54.

21. Quir., 60 ; Cyp., 53.

22. Constitutions primit., Silv., VI, 3 *sq. Fund.* XIII ; Silv. V, 104 ; C. P. 183.

23. Silv., VIII, 291 and 397 ; Greg., I, 351 and 488 ; Engl., II, 49 and 175.

24. *Camino*, Ch. VII ; Silv., III, 41 ; C.P., V, 82.

25. Ref., L. II, Ch. XVI, § 3.

26. Silv., VII, 12 ; Greg., II, 11 ; Engl., II, 199.

27. Quoted by Hoornaert : Sainte Térèse, ecrivain (Bruges, 1922), p. 177.

28. *Fund.*, Ch. XI ; Silv., V, 87 ; C.P., III, 162.

29. To Mary of Saint-Joseph, January, 1577 ; Silv., VIII, 24 ; Engl., II, 210.

30. *Fund.*, Ch. X ; Silv., V, 78 ; C.P., III, 152.

31. Silv., V, 403.

32. Silv., VII, 30 ; Greg., I, 38 ; Engl., I, 36. The Carmelites went to stay with Doña Maria de Mendoza only after October 31st, long after John's departure. Hence it is owing to an awkward anachronism that the *Histoire de Sainte Thérèse d'après les Bollandistes* (Paris, Lethellieux), p. 388, can speak of a " separate room where (the Father) could receive lessons from the saint at his leisure."

33. From a MS. preserved at the Carm. Convent of Segovia.

34. Letter to Salcedo, at the end of September, 1568. Silv., VII, 29 ; Engl., I, 38.

35. *Analecta O. C.*, III, p. 457.

36. Jeronimo Gracian : *Peregrinación de Anastasio.* Dial. III
(Burgos, 1905), p. 45.

37. Silv., VII, 30 ; Greg., I, 38 ; Engl., I, 38.

CHAPTER VIII

1. The date of September 30th, which is sometimes given,
rests merely on the vague data in Ch. XIV of the *Foundations.*
La Reforma is less categorical (Bk. VI, Ch. V, sec. 2) ; it speaks
of the end of September or early in October.

2. What remains are there now of the primitive hovel in the
modern farmhouse that has been built in the midst of the ruins
of our old convent ? It is difficult and dangerous to determine
on any. The village has also disappeared.

3. Jaen, P. A., fo. 126.

4. Catalina of Jesus, who was a novice at Medina when St.
John of the Cross and St. Teresa met there, relates that they
then made the woollen or serge habits that were worn
by the first Discalced, and that it was in the parlour that
John of the Cross put on the new habit and discarded his shoes,
whilst the holy Mother remained on the other side of the grille
(Med. P.A., fo. 70). According to the Paris Carmelites (III,
p. 186, note 2) one may read in the register of professions in the
monastery of Valladolid, that Sister Frances of Jesus left Medina,
still a secular, for Rio de Olmos and that she there received " the
serge and thin stuff intended for the habit and tunics." She says
that " these stuffs " were used to make the habit St. John of the
Cross needed to embrace the Reform. To reconcile these two
statements we should conclude that the materials sent to Rio de
Olmos were the same as those used by John of the Cross, in this
sense that they had been cut from the same pieces. Father
Silverio also believes that the saint put on the habit of the Reform
at Medina and, to strengthen this view, recalls the fact that,
according to Andres de la Encarnacion (13482, J. 9–13483, R.
285) it was common talk amongst the first Discalced that Father
Anthony used to rally (zumbaba) Father John for having
received the habit at the hands of a woman (Silv., V, 117.
Cf. Ger., I, 41, note 1). Mother Anne of Jesus tells us in her
deposition for the Canonisation of St. Teresa that the *xerga o*
sayal muy grossero y del color natural de la misma lana (Jer., 110) in
use amongst the friars and sisters " was a stuff of coarse wool
from which horse cloths and saddles of beasts of burthen were
made." Arch. C. R. Brus.

5. Was it in the " portal " or was it in the village church
where Teresa had spent the night on her former visit to Duruelo

in the preceding year ? It is difficult to know. Jerónimo says (p. 109) : " Aviendo dicho Missa en su Oratorio, o Iglesia." The *Reforma* did not venture to state anything definitely, no doubt on account of the text of the *Foundations* : " It was the first or second Sunday in Advent that Mass was said for the first time in that little stable," Ch. XIV; Silv., V, 109; C.P., III, 189.

The XIII and XIV Chapters of the *Foundations* are the chief source of this chapter.

6. Dux et Pater Carmelitarum (the saint's office in the Carmelite Liturgy). Luis de San Angel testifies that John reminded his friars that they belonged " to the religious order of Elias . . . which God has placed in the Church to be, both in the Old and New Testaments, a school of a penitential and mortified life." Andres, 13482, I, 58. And Jerome of the Cross says he sometimes spoke of the solitary life led by our ancient monks. Jaen, I. O., fo. 8 ; Andres, 13482, J. 28.

7. Dom Besse, *Les moines d'Orient* (Paris, Oudin, 1900), Ch. XI, p. 246 *sq.* Silv., VI, 407. Dom Gougaud, *La Gymnopodie* (R. A. M., 1923), p. 140, quoted above.

8. B.N.M. MS. 8020, fo. 96. The tense used (*començaron a vivir*) as the context shows (the transference from Duruelo to Mancera in 1570) proves that this act is to be placed after the foundation. The complete Spanish text is given by Silverio (V, 404). Luis de San Angel read, in the book of Professions, and also on an inscription placed on the wall at the chief entrance to the convent, how the Blessed Sacrament was placed in this little house of the monastery of Duruelo on the first Sunday in Advent, which fell on St. Andrew's Day, 1568 (Alcaudete, I. O., fo. 118). Alonso says that it was Saturday, November 28th (Seg. P.A., fo. 47).

9. Inocencio de San Andres, Baeza P.A., fo. 137. *Ibid.*, I. O., fo. 113.

10. Letter to Francis de Salcedo, end of September, 1568. Silv., VII, 30 ; Greg., I, 38 ; Engl., I, 37.

11. *Regula primitiva.*

12. *Cántico.* Canción V ; Ger., II, 513.

13. Joergensen, *Saint François d'Assise*, translated by Teodor de Wyzewa, 79th ed. (Paris, 1926), p. 373.

14. *Subida*, L. I, Ch. XIII ; Ed. Barcelona, 1619, pp. 84–85. Translated by Cyprian of the Nat. (Paris, 1665), p. 25.

15. Alonso, Seg. P.A., fo. 46.

16. Juxta situm loci quem inhabitare proposueritis.

17. Velasco mentions only a niece of Francisco de Yepes, Doña Maria de Otañez, " wife of Pedro de Prada, servitor of Queen Margaret of Austria, and actually of Philip III. One of her two children, Doña Ana, was in the palace in the service of

the Infantas, and the other, Doña Maria de Prada, was a lady in-waiting to the Queen who is now in France." B.N.M., L. III, p. 251.

18. Matth. xix. 30.

19. Autograph of Andujar, fo. 5. Baruzi, *Aphorismes*, p. 17. *Avis et Maximes*, translated by Greg., p. 201.

20. Alcaudete, I. O., fo. 118 ; Alonso, L. I, Ch. IX.

21. Quir., 71 ; Cyp., 74.

22. Quir., 78 ; Cyp., 69.

23. Quir., 476 ; Cyp., 430.

24. Jer., 242.

25. *Acta Cap. Gen.*, p. 371.

26. *Fund.*, Ch. II ; Silv., V, 15 ; C.P., III, 64.

According to Rubeo himself, there were at least two convents in which the Primitive Rule was observed, at Monte-Oliveto, near Genoa (*Const. Rub.*, p. 38, No. 68) and at Onda, near Valencia in Spain (*Reg. Rub.*, fo. 55). Patent of November 13th, 1565, published in the *Analecta O. C.*, Vol. IV, pp. 183–184.

27. *Acta Cap. Gen.*, *loc. cit.*, and text of constitutions.

28. Father Jeronimo de San José was commissioned by Father Esteban to write a history of the Reform and began to collect his materials. In 1628 he made a copy at Mancera of the Book of Professions at Duruelo. This scrupulously correct copy, written in his own hand, is contained in MS. 8020 of the B.N.M., beginning at folio 96. But, at the top of folio 99, there is no further trace of John's profession than this : " Yo frai Juan de la Cruz, natural de Medina del Campo hijo de." This *erased* text is disconcerting at first sight especially when confronted with the testimony of Luis de San Angel. What are we to think ? At a distance of thirty years the latter may have forgotten the tenor of the profession and it may, perhaps, not have been erased in 1587. He is satisfied with telling us that it is the first and is in the saint's handwriting. It is, in fact, the first, and the saint might have began to write it. He says he is a native of Medina but the Matriculation registers of Salamanca which were inspired by him, contain similar errors. Still, are we not going too far ?

" It should be noted," says Jeronimo at the 99th folio of MS. 8020, " that the written profession of none of the three first, O.V. Father Brother John of the Cross, Brother Anthony and Brother Joseph of Christ, can be found. A blank has been left as if for two professions. No. 2 is written in the margin opposite the erased line. Hence the first to appear is our Brother Anthony's. There is no place for the third, because Brother John Baptist's follows immediately. This enables us to suppose that Brother Joseph of Christ went back to the Observants or died very soon."

" The question has been asked, and some are doubtful as to whether our first Fathers, Fray Antonio and Fray Juan, made their profession in the Reform which they were beginning. Some say that, at the end of the first year, Father Antonio did not wish to make it, saying that it was not necessary and that our venerable Father John did make it but to whom and when remains unknown. It should have been either to the Father Provincial, Alonso Gonzalez or the Prior, Father Anthony, after one year at Duruelo. The other Observants who embraced the Reform, certainly made their profession after a year, renouncing the Mitigated Rule and promising to live according to the Primitive, as may be seen from some professions in this book, although they did not call it a profession but a renunciation. This is of no great importance because Pope Gregory XII, in the Brief of Separation (1581) says that they shall profess the Primitive Rule after one year's probation. And speaking of the first founders he also declares that : these same rules and observances were accepted after one year's probation by the said founders and by those of the Mitigation who were admitted, who made a new profession that consisted in their renouncing the mitigation and dispensations granted by our predecessor, Eugene IV. Others, who came from the world, took the same engagements." (This is reproduced in the *Reforma*, L. II, Ch. XXXIX, sec. 11. but the author deduces more from it than the testimony authorised by Jeronimo will admit). " Hence it follows that the first founders made their profession, if not Father Anthony, then, at least Father John, and it is for that reason that the profession of the latter was begun. Why did he not write it ? I answer that the diversity between the two might not be seen, since our venerated Father Anthony did not make his profession. And also because some doubt existed as to whom the title of first was due ; and consequently to allow no place for divergent views." We have a photo-typed copy of this document.

29. Quir., 78 ; Cyp., 69.

30. Arch. of the O.C.C., Rome. Document quoted in preceding chapter.

31. Andres, 13482, N. 87. In the General Archives (Alm. 5, cod. 2), " there is a paper with this title : the first Constitutions that we the Discalced Carmelites have had and that were drawn up in the Convent of Duruelo in 1568." *Ibid.*, B. 47.

32. *Id., ib.*, R., 217. Father Silverio, who quotes the documents of which we have photo-types (VI, 27) maintains the view we have just set out.

33. Deposition of Arch. C.R., Bruss.

34. " Digan el officio divino segun lo uso de la Iglesia Hierosolymitana." Const. de 1581, Cap. III De Officio Divino, I (Silv., VI, 468).

35. Silv., V, 333 and 335. The *Analecta O.C.* (IV, 198) gave August 10th as the date of the patent for the foundation of the Fathers, and Silverio copies them (V, 338). It is, no doubt, due to a misprint ; the *Regestum* gives August 16th. It should also be noted that this patent, as given by the *Reforma* (L. II, Ch. IV) and by the Carmelites of Paris (III, 515) is incomplete, and that, moreover, where the General speaks of the Carmelite Rule they took care to add the word *Primitive.*

36. *Fund.*, Ch. II. Silv., V, 16 ; C.P., III, 67.

37. *Id., ibid.*

38. Quir., 78 ; Cyp., 69.

39. C.P., III, 526.

40. *Fund.*, Ch. XXIII. Silv., V, 202 ; C.P., IV, 33.

41. Baeza, P.A., fo. 46.

42. Quir., 87, 126, 306 ; Cyp., 77, 112, 270.

43. *Analecta O.C.*, IV, 114 ; Silv., VI, 402.

44. *De Panurge à Sancho Pança* (Paris, 1915), p. 213 *sq.*

45. Julian of Avila's deposition for the Canonisation of St. Teresa, C.P., VI, 454, 455, 453.

46. *Analecta O.C.*, IV, 198. Silv., V, 336.

47. Francisco told Tomas Perez de Molina that John " fue predicador " and that " le oyo muchos sermones " and that at Duruelo " se occupava en confesar muchos que le venian a buscar para ello." Med., I. O., fo. 24.

48. Dep. of Francisco de Yepes, B.N.M. MS. 12738, fo. 613.

49. Med., I. O., fo. 24, and another deposition of Francisco's, B.N.M. MS. 8568, fo. 372.

50. B.N.M., *ibid.*

51. Med., *ibid.*

52. *Peregrinaçion de Anastasio*, quoted above, p. 212.

53. Ger., III, 64 ; see Ch. XVIII.

54. Quir., 97 ; Cyp., 86.

55. Arch. C.R., Brus.

56. Maria de S. Francisco, Med., I. O., fo. 20.

57. Cassian, Coll. IX, Ch. XXXI.

58. B.N.M. MS. 8568, fo. 371. Tomas Perez de Molina. Med. I. O., fo. 24.

59. Dom Besse : *Les Moines d'Orient*, quoted above, p. 437.

60. Letter of December 12th, 1576. Silv., VII, 396 ; Greg., I, 487 ; Engl., II, 174. " Era mi intento desear que entrasen buenos talentos, que con mucha aspereza se habian de espantar."

61. Summa II-II., q. 188, art. 6, ad. 3.

62. Ch. I and II. Silv., III ; C.P., V, *passim.*

63. Menendez y Pelayo : *Los Heterodoxos Españoles* (Madrid, 1887), Vol. II, p. 96 *sq.*

64. Cf. Jacques Maritain : *Trois Réformateurs* (Le Roseau d'Or, Plon, 1925).

65. *Fund.*, Ch. I. Silv., V, 12 ; C.P., III, p. 59.
66. *Ibid.*

CHAPTER IX

1. *Fund.*, Ch. XVII. Silv., V, 131 ; C.P., III, 219. Except where otherwise stated we shall draw from this source.

2. Silv., V, 123 ; C.P., III, 209.

3. C.P., III, 444.

4. See, in particular, in the *Epistolario*, the beginning of the letter of February 16th, 1577. Silv., VIII, 54 ; Greg., II, 67 ; Engl., II, 249 ; and that of March 15th, 1577. Silv., VIII, 72 ; Greg., II, 88 ; Engl., II, 266.

5. L. to Gracian, September 27th, 1575. Silv., VII, 189 ; Greg., I, 228 ; Engl., I, 218.

6. The text of this calumnious charge will be found in the Arch. of the O.C.C., Rome. Actes des Déchaussés, Cod. I, No. 15.

7. L. to the King, September 18th, 1577. Silv., VIII, 115 ; Greg., II, 135 ; Engl., II, 311.

8. We owe these details to R. F. Lorenzo Perez, archivist of the Franciscans of Alcantara, who kindly acted as our guide during our stay at Pastrana, his native place.

9. *Ref.*, L. IV, Ch. XLIV, § 2.

10. *Ref.*, L. IV, Ch. XLIV, § 3.

11. *Ref.*, L. XIII, Ch. XXXV, § 7.

12. Quir., 136 ; Cyp., 122.

13. Jeronimo de la Cruz. *Jaen*, P.A., fo. 131.

14. José de Jesus-Maria (Quiroga) : *El don que tuvo S. Juan de la Cruz para guiar las almas a Dios.* Published by Father Gerardo, III, 511, etc. ; C. II, p. 513. See also *La Vie Spirituelle* October, 1922, p. 155, etc.

15. *Instit.*, Ch. XXXV.

16. *El don que tuvo* . . ., p. 517.

17. *Instrucción de Novicios Descalzos* . . . re-edited by Father Evaristus, C.D. (Toledo, 1925), pp. 108–109.

18. *El don que tuvo* . . ., p. 558.

19. *Instrucción* . . ., p. 110.

20. *El don que tuvo* . . ., p. 520.

21. *Ibid.*, p. 553.

22. *Instrucción* . . ., pp. 112, 113.

23. Canción tercera, § 5. Ger., II, 445.

24. *El don que tuvo* . . ., p. 553.

25. *Ref.*, L. XI, Ch. VIII, § 4.

26. *Ibid.*, L. II, Ch. XXXIX.

27. B.N.M. MS. 8020, fo. 100 and 101. Silv., V, 405.

28. *Fund.*, Ch. XIX. Silv., V, 153 *sq.* ; C.P., III, 240.

29. "A la tercera pregunta . . . se cierto de que fué
fundadora de frailes, porque el mismo año que tomé el hábito en
Avila, antes que profesase, me trajó nuestra Madre a la fundación
de esta casa de Salamanca, y en Mancera . . . estuvimos, los
que veniamos, en el convento de los frailes descalzos, y nos
mostraron y dijeron lo que nuestra Madre Teresa y su compañera
Antonia del Espiritu Santo le habian tratado y enseñado a
componer en la fundación de aquel convento en el cual estaban
entonces los primeros dos descalzos que habia habido, que era
el padre fray Antonio de Jesus, prior, y por suprior el padre fray
Juan de la Cruz, los cuales habian recibido todo el orden y
modo de proceder que tenian de nuestra Madre. Y ella nos
contaba con gran gusto las menudencias que ellos le preguntaban
. . . y ellos en particular me dijeron a mi misma muchas cosas
de las que en esto pensaban con que se cierto fué tan fundadora
de ellos como de nosostros, y en ese lugar lo tienen todos ellos y
tendrán siempre." Deposition of Arch. C.R., Brussels. C.P.,
III, 194.

30. *Ref.*, L. II, Ch. XLII, § 2.
31. Quir., 139 ; Cyp., 123.
32. *Camino*, Ch. III. Silv., III, 21 ; C.P., V, 49.
33. Letter of 13 December, 1576. Silv., VII, 397 ; Greg., I,
488 ; Engl., II, 175.
34. *Camino*, Ch. IV. Silv., III, 26 ; C. P., V, 54.
35. *Ref.*, L. II, Ch. XLII, § 1.
36. *Ibid.*, L. II, Ch. XXXI, § 2.
37. *Ibid.*, Ch. XXX, § 3.
38. *Ibid.*, Ch. XXXII, § 5.
39. Letter of December 12th, 1576. Silv., VII, 397 ;
Greg., I, 488 ; Engl., II, 175.
40. *Ref.*, L. II, Ch. XXXVII, § 16.
41. Quir., 138 ; Cyp., 123.
42. C.P., III, 441.
43. *Subida*, L. III, Ch. V. Ger., I, 288.
44. C.P., III, 220, note 2. The archivist of the Convent of
Pastrana provided us with fuller information. It should also be
noted that Pastrana had been a centre of Illuminism. See Bar,
pp. 255, 256, 262.
45. *Pensées*, n. 358.
46. Ger., III, 62. The anagogical act of love that Thomas
of Jesus calls " aspiration " (*De contemplatione divina*, Ch. VIII)
is held in equal honour by John of St. Samson. Cf. Jerome of
the Mother of God, O.C.D., *La doctrine du V.F. Jean de Saint
Samson. La Vie Spirituelle* edition, 2nd Part, Ch. VI, p. 162, etc.
47. *Noche*, canción primera, § 7. Ger., II, 21.
48. *In Epistolam ad Romanos*, XII, 12.
49. *Ref.*, L. II, Ch. XLII, § 2, and L. III, Ch. I, § 3.

50. Quir., 370 ; Cyp., 329.

51. *Vel.*, L. I, Ch. V, and I, IV, Ch. V.

52. The sons of St. Peter of Alcantara who own these sacred places have collected in the restored chapel, the sacristy and another hermitage, a number of portraits of the former Fathers. These canvases measure about twenty-four inches.

53. Benedict Zimmerman, *Les Saints déserts*, *op. cit.*, p. 46 *sq.* *Ref.*, L. II, Ch. XXXVII, § 10.

CHAPTER X

1. *Ref.*, L. II, Ch. XLIII, § 2.

2. *Moradas*, 5th⁄e Mansion, Ch. I, Silv. IV, 173. C.P., VI, 133.

3. December 12th, 1576. Silv., VII, 396 ; Greg., I, 487 ; Engl., II, 175.

4. *Analecta O.C.*, Vol. IV, p. 211.

5. *Ref.*, L. II, Ch. XLIII, § 2. *Libro de las Recreaciones* por la Madre Maria de S. José (Burgos, 1913) : " En estos dos monasterios se ocuparon las dos licencias que el general habia dado a nuestra Madre, y para el colegio de Alcalá que fué el tercero, la alcanzó del mismo padre General, Ruy Gómez " (Recr., IX, p. 110).

6. *Analecta O.C.*, Vol. IV, p. 208, 209.

7. *Ibid.*, pp. 200, 201, 210 : " Ne totum ovile contemplativorum ab eis corrumpatur."

8. *Ref.*, L. VI, Ch. XXXIII, §§ 4 and 5.

9. *Ibid.*, L. VI, Ch. XXXIV, §§ 2 and 7.

10. *Ref.*, L. IX, Ch. XXI, §§ 1, 2, 3 : " Entrando en la iglesia vio a Fray Agustin ayudando a Missa, con tan gran modestia, que le pareció Angel baxado de el Cielo ; la Santa con la licencia de Madre, viendole tan modesto y devoto, se llego dessimuladamente a el y le abraçó." " Compuso el cielo en su persona un hermoso espectaculo . . . porque adornandole de hermosura el exterior, y el animo de honestas," etc.

11. The body of Father Gabriel rests to-day in the Church of San Pedro de Arriba together with those of Juan de Jesus-Maria Araballes and Nicholas Doria. *Ref.*, L. VI, Ch. XXXIV, § 8 ; Quir., 139 ; Cyp., 124.

12. *Ref.*, L. IX, Ch. XXI, § 5.

13. *Ibid.*

14. Bar., 175.

15. L. to Roque de Huerta, October, 1578. Silv., VIII, 262 ; Greg., II, 289 ; Engl., III, 130, where it is addressed " to an unknown person."

16. *Fund.*, Ch. XXIII. Silv., V, 202 ; C.P., IV, 33.

17. *Relaciones*, Silv., II, 47 ; C.P., II, 227.

18. We have used the following works : Hefele, *Le Cardinal Ximénès et l'Église d'Espagne à la fin du quinzième et au commencement du seizième siècles* (Trans. Sisson-Crampon, Paris, 1860), Ch. XI. G. Reynier, *La Vie universitaire dans l'ancienne Espagne*, already quoted. Beltrán de Heredia, *La enseñanza de S. Tomás en la Universidad de Alcalá* (*Ciencia Tomista*, 1916, pp. 245, 392 *sq*). and *Catedráticos de S. Escritura en la Universidad de Alcalá durante el siglo XVI°* (*Ciencia Tomista*, 1918, p. 140 ; 1919, pp. 49, 144).

19. About this time Jimenes had 80,000 Moslem books burnt at Granada, but took care to preserve 300 volumes dealing with medicine for his University of Alcalá. De Circourt, *Histoire des Mores Mudejares et des Morisques ou des Arabes d'Espagne sous la domination des Chrétiens* (Paris, 1848, Vol. II, p. 43).

20. Silv., VI, 482.

21. *Ref.*, L. IX, Ch. XXXI, § 1.

22. " . . . Ordenamos acerca de la humildad que manda la regla al prior y a todos los religiosos, que de aqui adelante, por ningunas exceptiones o privilegios que haya, ninguno de los graduados, presentados o maestros, se eximan del coro, refetorio ni de las demás obligaciones de la Regla." Cap. XV. Silv., VI, 408.

23. " Prohibimos . . . que ningun frayle de nuestra Provincia se pueda graduar de maestro, licenciado, bachiller, presentado, ni gozar de los tales grados . . . ninguno goza de preragativos de graduados sino que todos sigan vida Commun." Ch. XVII. Silv., VI, 481.

24. Quétif-Echard, *Scriptores Ordinis Praedicatorum*, Vol. II, p. 352.

25. *Dict. Théol. cath.*, art. Bañes, Vol. II, col. 140. *The Catholic Encyclopedia*, Vol. II, 247.

26. Beltrán de Heredia, *Actuación del maestro D. Bañes en la Universidad de Salamanca* (*Ciencia Tomista*, 1922, p. 69 *et* 71). Father Mandonnet has also given us information on details.

27. *Ref.*, L. II, Ch. XLIII, § 8.

28. Quir., 155 ; Cyp., 138 ; Ger., III, 196.

29. Cf. R.F. Garrigou-Lagrange on the relations between speculative and mystical theology in *Perfection chrétienne et contemplation*, according to St. Thomas Aquinas and St. John of the Cross, Ch. VI, art. 3. *L'Union de la vie intérieure et de la vie intellectuelle*, p. 628, and R.P. Gardeil, *La Structure de l'âme et l'expérience mystique*, p. 197.

30. Quir., 152 ; Cyp., 136.

31. *Peregrinación, op. cit.*, dial. XIII, p. 211.

32. *Ref.*, L. II, Ch. XXX, § 4, *et* Ch. XLIII, § 5 ; Quir., 138 ; Cyp., 123.

33. *Fund.*, Ch. XXIII. Silv., V, 196 ; C.P., IV, 25.

34. February, 1581. Silv., IX, 24 ; Greg., III, 120 ; and

November, 19th, 1576. Silv., VII, 357 ; Greg., I, 440 ; Engl., IV, 141 and II, 133.

35. *Master* does not signify *Doctor* as in the old religious Orders. The doctorate of theology was so rare that in the scholastic year 1511–1512, when Diego Valdadares was elected Rector of the college of the University of Alcalá, he was only a bachelor. Beltrán de Heredia, *La enseñanza de Santo Tomás*, already quoted (*Ciencia Tomista*, 1916, p. 249).

36. *Fund.*, Ch. XXIII *passim.* Silv., V, 195 *sq* ; C.P., IV, 22 *sq.*

37. L. VI, Ch. XXXIV, § 8.

38. *Jer.*, 158 ; *Bibl. Carm.*, Vol. II, 548.

39. *Peregrinación de Anastasio, op. cit.*, p. 22.

40. *Ref.*, L. II, Ch. LIV, § 3.

41. *Peregrinación, op. cit.*, p. 23.

42. *Ref.*, L. II, Ch. XLII, § 2.

43. *Ref.*, L. II, Ch. XXXIV, § 3. Inocencio de St. Andres, Baeza, I. O., fo. 111.

44. December, 1576, to Gracian. Silv., VII, 389 ; Greg., I, 478 ; Engl., II, 171.

45. Alonso, L. I, Ch. XXI.

46. *Fund.*, Ch. XXIII. Silv., V, 199 ; C.P., IV, 28, and letter of December 7th, 1576, to Gracian. Silv., VII, 385 ; Greg., I, 474 ; Engl., II, 163, " is wrought as though by magic," Spanish : encantador.

47. November, 1576. Silv., VII, 359 ; Greg., I, 432 ; Engl., II, 126.

48. See Ch. XVII.

49. May 12th, 1575, to Ines de Jesus. Silv., VII, 169 ; Greg., I, 204 ; Engl., I, 196.

50. Silv., VI, 131 ; *Ref.*, L. II, Ch. I.

51. *Ref.*, L. VI, Ch. XXXIV, § 8 ; Jer., Ch. 168.

CHAPTER XI

1. She was prioress from 1486 to 1528. D. Maria Pinel y Monroy. *Historia manuscrita del Convento de la Encarnación.* C.P., III, 572.

2. Benedict Zimmerman, *El convento de la Encarnación de Avila. El Monte Carmelo*, Burgos, 1910, pp. 259–265.

3. Arch. of O.C.C., Rome. MS. already referred to.

4. *Reg. Rub.*, fo. 98.

5. Account of Doña Maria Espinel to a religious of the Order. C.P. III., 575. 6. C.P., III, 292.

7. Pinel y Monroy, *op. cit.* C.P., III, 546.

8. *Relaciones*, Silv., II, 53 ; C.P., II, 240. Pinel y Monroy, *op. cit.* C.P., III, 547.

9. November 7th, 1571. Silv., VII, 80 ; Greg., I, 92 ; Engl., I, 89.

10. March 7th, 1572. Silv., VII, 87 ; Greg., I, 103 ; Engl., I, 98.

11. It is surprising that there should be any question of St. John of the Cross being already a confessor at the Incarnation when Teresa has said that she was "without a confessor" (Bar., 179, note 7). It was not the editors who dated Maria de Mendoza's letter, as has been gratuitously asserted. The saint herself says : *Son hoy siete de Marzo*. We may see it in the autograph letter at the Carmelite convent of Valladolid. On the other hand, St. John of the Cross was just then at Alcalá and there is no proof that Teresa knew when she wrote this letter that John would be appointed her confessor. Lastly, according to Julian of Avila (C.P., VI, 477) was it not Teresa herself who took steps to have John appointed ? " She endeavoured to have two Discalced religious, great servants of God, appointed as confessors to the convent."

12. *Relaciones*, Silv., II, 60 ; C.P., II, 245.

13. Dep. already referred to. C.P., II, 477.

14. It is commonly said that John was accompanied by Germain of St. Mathias. But was that possible ? By Fray Germain's admission that he had been a priest before entering the Order, it is clear that he should be making his novitiate just then at Pastrana, since, if we are to believe an account of the Convent of Mancera, where Germain died, he only made his profession on February 25th, 1573 (Silv., VIII, 142, note 1). It would seem as if Germain only came to Avila at a later date.

15. Ana Maria Gutierrez (of Jesus) deposed in 1616 that she was sixty-six years old. Seg. P.A., fo. 109. See C.P., III, 302, on Ana Maria.

16. Alonso, Seg. P.A., fo. 50.

17. Ana Maria, *ibid.*, fo. 109.

18. " Estando esta testigo en el dho convento (Medina), la dha madre entrava a enseñarla a tejer (decia) . . . que siendo muy moço le avian llevado por confesor y vicario de las monjas de la Encarnacion." Med. I. O., fo. 28.

19. September 27th, 1572, to Juana de Ahumada. Silv., VII, 97 ; Greg., I, 116 ; Engl., I, 112.

20. Silv., VII, 101, previously unpublished.

21. C.P., III, 557 ; Andres, 13482, D. 196.

22. *Relaciones*, November, 1572. Silv., II, 63 ; C.P., II, 246.

23. " La tuvo buen rato postrada, mostrando ella una alegre humildad, y el la libertad santa con que exercitava en la mortificacion las almas que governava." Quir., 181 ; Cyp., 162.

24. R. Hoornaert, *Le progrés de la pensée de sainte Térèse entre la Vie et le Château*, in *Revue des Sciences phil. et théol.*, 1924, p. 20 *sq.*

25. Quir., 251 ; Cyp., 227 ; Andres, 13482, D. 17.

26. Silv., VIII, 283 ; Greg., II, 333 ; Engl., III, 179.

27. Alonso, Seg. P.A., fo. 49 ; *Ref.*, L. VI, Ch. IX, § 2.

28. C.P., III, 310.

29. Baeza, P.A., fo. 49.

30. *Relaciones*, Silv., II, 61 ; *Ref.*, L. II, Ch. LIII, § 8. "Que ya solo en amar es mi ejercicio." *Cantico*, canción XIX. Ger., II, 497.

31. *Moradas* (setimas), Ch. I. Silv., IV, 184 ; C.P., VI, 282.

32. "Cuando alguna alma tuviese algo de este grado de solitario amor, grande agravio se le haria á ella y á la Iglesia si aunque fuese por poco espacio la quisiesen ocupar en cosas exteriores ó activas, aunque fuesen de mucho caudal. . . ." *Cantico*, canción XXVIII. Ger. II, 313. This important passage though not given in the Sanlucar MS., which we usually quote from on account of its incontestable authority, contains a daring thought. We are far from that doctrinal diminution with which the Jaen text has been reproached.

33. In a letter dated January 2nd, 1577, to her brother Lawrence, Teresa speaks of Francisco de Salcedo's reply (Silv., VIII, 9 ; Greg., II, 8 ; Engl., II, 197). This indication enables us to assign a date to the *Vejamen*.

34. Andres, 13482, B. 27.

35. *Cant.*, canción XII. Ger., II, 530.

36. Silv., VI, 5.

37. See Morel-Fatio, *Les lectures de S. Thérèse* (*Bulletin hispanique*, 1908), p. 17 *sq.*, and *Nouvelles études sur S. Thérèse* (Paris, Champion, 1911). Hoornaert, *S. Térèse écrivain*, pp. 340 to 344, 306 to 311, 345 and 346, 338 and 339, 374 to 381. Gaston Etchegoyen, *L'Amour divin, Essai sur les sources thérésiennes* (*Bibliothéque de l'École des Hautes Études hispaniques*, Fasc. IV, Bordeaux, 1923), pp. 36, 37, 38, 43, and *passim*.

38. "No le conocio al dho siervo de Dios en su celda sino fue el brebiario blibia (*sic.*), San Augustin contra gentes y un flos sanctorum y una cruz. . . ." Malaga, P.A., fo. 37. The same witness, according to B.N.M. MS. 12738, fo. 559, deposes : "Nunca jamas le uide leer otro libro sino la biblia . . . y en un P. Augustin contra hereses (*sic.*) y en el flos sanctor. . . ." Cf. Bar., 148, note 3. In the *Instruction for Novices* approved by St. John of the Cross on January 11th, 1590, there is a recommendation to read as a preparation for prayer the "glorioso doctor San Buenaventura y de nuestra madre Teresa de Jesus, y del muy devoto Padre Fray Luis de Granada, en el libro que de ella hace," *op. cit.*, p. 107.

39. *Subida*, Bk. III, Ch. XXX. Ger., I, 365 ; text taken from XXVIth homily on the Gospel of Low Sunday, second lesson in the Carm. breviary : " Nec fides habet meritum cui humana ratio praebet experimentum. *Noche*, Ch. II. Ger., II, 118 : text from XXXth homily read on Pentecost Sunday . . . Mentesque carnalium in sui amorem permutarit . . . intus facta sunt corda inflammantia. . . . " The same text is found in the *Llama*, C. II. Ger., II, p. 411. *Llama*, C. III. Ger., II, p. 441 : Text taken from the same homily on the Gospel, read on Pentecost Sunday : " Qui ergo mente integra Deum desiderat profecto jam habet quem amat."

40. " Particularmente de San Dionisio y de San Gregorio." Quir., 36, 38, 58 ; Cyp., 31, 33, 52.

41. *Histoire d'une Âme*, p. 146.

42. *Constituciones del Convento de la Encarnación de Avila que se observaban viviendo alli Santa Teresa de Jesús.* Silv., IX, 485.

43. *Ibid.*, pp. 485 and 488.

44. Silv., VI, 57 *sq.* ; Greg., I, 108.

45. Silv., VI, p. 69, note 1.

46. Seg. P.A., fo. 109 : " . . . Confirmandole en gracia como a los apostoles para que no pecase ni le ofendiese jamas gravemente . . . le concediese que no cometiese pecado mortal alguno. . . . "

47. *Jac.*, V, 17.

48. Juan Evangelista, Jaen I. O., fo. 7.

49. Ana Maria, Seg., fo. 109 ; Alonso, L. I, Ch. XXIII.

50. Jeronimo de la Cruz. Jaen P.A., fo. 138 ; Quir., 177 ; Cyp., 159.

51. L. VI, Ch. IX, § 3 ; Jer., 186.

52. *Subida*, Ch. XXXIV ; Ger., I, 372.

53. Alonso, Seg. P.A., fo. 61.

54. Jer., 174.

55. Seg. P.A., fo. 109.

56. *Ibid.*, fo. 109.

57. Quir., 172 ; Cyp., 154.

58. Ana Maria. *Ibid.*, fo. 110. On January 2nd, 1563, Maria Yera signed a contract of sale ; her name is last.

59. *Id., Ibid.*, fo. 109. Alonso, L. I, Ch. 24.

60. B.N.M. MS. 12738, fo. 29 : " . . . Llamaron a personas dotas i espirituales entre las cuales eran Mancio, frai Bartolome de Medina . . . i. fr. Luis de León. . . ." Deposition quoted by Baruzi, of which Alonso speaks. Seg. P.A., fo. 52 ; Bar., 133, note 3.

61. Alonso, *Ibid.* Jeronimo de la Cruz, Jaen P.A., 132 ; Quir., 688 *sq.* ; Cyp., 627 *sq.*

62. Silv., VII, 103 ; Greg., I, 117 and 516 ; Engl., I, 112. Silverio places it in March, 1573.

63. Maria de S. Francisco, Med. I. O., fo. 20.
64. Alonso, Seg. P.A., fo. 52.
65. *Llama*, Ch. III. Ger., II, 463.
66. C.P., III, 311 and 559.
67. Maria de la Encarnación. Seg. P.A., fo. 99.
68. C. P., III, 565. Told by Julian of Avila.
69. *Moradas* (sextas), Ch. IX. Silv., IV, 167 ; C.P., VI, 259.
70. *Relaciones*. Silv., II, 66 ; C.P., II, 249.

CHAPTER XII

1. Silv., VIII, 268–269 ; Greg., II, 315 ; Engl., III, 161.
2. *Analecta O.C.*, Vol. IV, pp. 208–209 (*Regestum Rubei*).
3. *Analecta O.C.*, Vol. IV, p. 200 *et passim* (*Regestum Rubei*).
4. She wrote to Philip II on June 11th, 1573 : " I venture to beg you to befriend us in certain affairs of which the licentiate John of Padilla will speak. . . . The matter cannot be divulged without doing harm to the very end we pursue and that is to procure God's honour and glory." Silv., VII, 106 ; Greg., I, 122 ; Engl., I, 120.
5. Silv., VII, 124 ; Engl., I, 145.
6. Matthew de las Penuelas. Silv., VII, 143 ; Greg., I, 177 ; Engl., I, 171.
7. *Acta Cap. Gen.*, p. 515, note.
8. " Es sabio y santo." Silv., VII, 65 ; Greg., I, 83 ; Engl., I, 76.
9. *Fund.*, Ch. II. C.P., III, 64 ; Silv., V, 15.
10. Silv., VII, 165 ; Greg., I, 197 ; Engl., I, 188.
11. Silv., VII, 150 ; Greg., I, 180 ; Engl., I, 174.
12. May 12th, 1575. Silv., VII, 169 ; Greg., I, 204 ; Engl., I, 195.
13. Maria de San José, *Libro de las Recreaciones*. Recreae. IX, p. 99 ; C.P., IV, 379. It is to be noted that, in the patents granted by Rubeo, the passages forbidding foundations in Andalusia are underlined.
14. *Acta Cap. Gen.*, p. 482.
15. *Acta Cap. Gen.*, p. 531.
16. " Et quia nonnulli inobedientes, rebelles atque contumaces, qui Discalciati vulgo vocantur contra Patentes et statuta Prioris generalis habitarunt et habitant extra Provinciam Castellae, quam veterem dicunt, nempe apud Granatam Hispalim et prope oppidum vulgo nuncupatum La Pegnola, nec voluerunt humiliter, adductis fallaciis et cavillis et tergiversationibus, mandata ejusdem Prioris Generalis et litteras accep-

tare : significabunt eisdem Carmelitis Discalciatis, sub poenis et censuris apostolicis, invocato etiam, si opus fuerit auxilio brachii saecularis, ut infra tres dies inde omnino abscedant : et quosvis contradicentes compescant, graviter puniant, et a nobis citatos esse, ut personaliter appareant, intiment et praesentibus testibus innotescere faciant, nisi ab eorum pervicacia resipuerint. " Implorabitur item favor R. Archiespiscoporum, Nuntiorum ejusdem Sanctissimi Dni. nostri : imo ejus legatorum a latere ; ut opportune illum exhibeant ; sicut idem summus Pontifex mandat in Litteris datis Romae apud sanctum Petrum sub annulo Piscatoris, die XV Aprilis 1575. Pontificatus sui anno 3° " (*Bull. Carm.*, II, p. 183 ; *Acta Cap. Gen.*, p. 509 *sq.*). The reference is to a counter-brief read at the opening of the Chapter. " Item Patres Primarii seu Diffinitores Judicarunt etiam auctoritate Apostolica, amovendos esse Carmelitas primae Regulae, qui vulgo Discalciati nuncupantur, a Conventibus obtentis extra Provinciam Castellae ; et etiam si quos in Castella accepissent contra Patentes et institutiones R^mi Patris Generalis, ab eis excludi et rejici. Item quod visitentur, et debitis institutis juxta priorem Regulam constringantur. Si vero aliqui ex illis obedire recusaverint ; citamus eos ut coram nobis compareant, infra spatium trium mensium, a die quo obedire recusaverint " (*Acta . . .* p. 527 ; *Ref.*, L. III, Ch. XL, §§ 1, 2, 3).

17. " Item sanxerunt F^rem Marianum alias Heremita del Tardo, et Fratrem Balthasarem Nieto alias Ordinis Minimorum (Father Balthazar had belonged to the ' Minimes ') si non resipuerint ab eorum inobedientia et rebellione adversus Patentes Prioris Generalis, tanquam incorrigibiles expulsos esse ab ordine Carmelitarum ; et reliquerunt eidem Generali ut eos remittat ad primam eorum professionem " (*Acta . . .*, pp. 533-534).

18. Silv., VII, 172 *sq.* ; Greg., II, 208 *sq.* ; Engl., I, 201.

19. *Acta Cap. Gen.*, p. 557, note.

20. Letter to Gracian. Silv., VII, 188 *sq.* ; Greg., I, 228 *sq.* ; Engl., I, 218.

21. Silv., VII, 203 ; Greg., I, 234 ; Engl., I, 223.

22. *Acta Cap. Gen.*, p. 557, note ; Silv., VII, 205 ; Greg., I, 249 *sq.* Gabriel Wessels, O.C., *S. Teresia et Capitulum generale Placentiae*, 1575 (*Analecta O.C.*, Vol. IV, p. 175 *sq.*). *Libro de las Recreaciones . . .*, loc. cit., C.P., IV, p. 379.

23. Silv., VII, 221 ; Greg., I, 265 ; Engl., I, 249.

24. Silv., VIII, 132 ; Greg., II, 150-151 ; Engl., III, 4.

25. Silv., VII, 222, VIII, 221 ; Greg., I, 267, II, 150 ; Engl., I, 251.

26. Silv., VII, 222, note 3 ; Engl., I, 251, note.

27. Silv., VIII, 132 ; Greg., II, 151 ; Engl., III, 4.

28. Silv., VII, 230 ; Greg., I, 276 ; Engl., I, 261.

29. MS. O.C.C., Rome.

30. L. III, Ch. L, § 3.
31. *Analecta O.C.*, Vol. III, p. 454 *sq.*
32. *Acta Cap. Gen.*, p. 538.
33. *Roque de Huerta*, August, 1578. Silv., VIII, 237 ; Greg., II, 280 ; Engl., III, 125.
34. *Analecta O.C.*, Vol. IV, p. 198.
35. *Const. Rubei*, No. 69.
36. Judicial deposition of Julian of Avila, published by the Carmelite nuns of Paris, Vol. VI, p. 485.
37. *Fund.*, XXVIII. Silv., V, 245 ; C.P., IV, p. 95.
38. . . . " Pues que las facultades de los visitatores appostolicos son superiores a las del Rem° general." This is how Gracian expresses himself in his letter of convocation, dated at the convent of Pastrana, August 3rd, 1576 (Arch. Carm. Cal., Rome. *Acts of the Discalced*, Cod. I, No. 10. Bula y licencias de los visitadores y mandamiento del p° fray Gerónimo Gracian de la Madre de Dios frayle descalzo. On August 3rd, 1575, as we have seen, the Nuncio, Ormaneto had granted Gracian the title of " provincial and reformer of the mitigated of Andalusia and Apostolic commissary of the Discalced, *non obstantibus diffinitionibus* capituli generalis." But there is a certain confusion here, because the authority of the general chapter is, like that of the General, *a jure*, universal and perpetual, whilst Gracian's authority was *ab homine* and regional (of no value outside Spain and hence incapable of constraining the General). It was also revocable. Gracian was not, in fact, immediately nominated by the Pope, but by the Nuncio (with the King's consent). *Acta Cap. Gen.*, pp. 557–558, note.
39. Gracian, in order to regulate the General's dealings with the separated province, relied on the official acts of the visitors, Vargas and Fernandez, who set aside the intervention of any inferior (Vargas, except Mariano or his partner should ask for it ; Fernandez—however for the Carmelite nuns of Castile alone— on condition that there was a Discalced capable of visiting them). Still, Gracian's intervention went beyond the mark here again, going beyond the regulations on which, he alleged, he based his action, and Andrew of the Incarnation himself testifies to this fact ; for Andrew had the decrees of Fernandez in his hands (Silv., VI, pp. xix to xxi) ; 1° he generalised and applied to all the Discalced friars and nuns, in Castile and Andalusia, what either one or other of the visitors had granted within the limits of his mission ; 2° he exaggerated the exceptional nature of the visitation. In fact, (*a*) if the General himself made the visitation he should be accompanied by some Discalced ; now, neither Vargas nor Fernandez had said anything about that ; (*b*) in case of delegation by the General it was necessary that the Discalced person selected should not be from those who had ever

been mitigated, and be accompanied by the Discalced Provincial. (Consequently, neither Anthony or John of the Cross would have been eligible as visitors.) But neither Vargas nor Fernandez went as far as that.

40. On the Carmelite reform of Mantua, see Wessels, *Anal. O.C.*, I, 196, IV, 105.

41. Quir., 463 ; Cyp., 414 ; Jer., 221.

42. Quir., 465 ; Cyp., 414–415 ; Jer., 223 ; *Ref.*, L. III, Ch. XLI.

43. Quir., 126 and 306 ; Cyp., 112 and 270.

44. Quir., 467, etc. ; Cyp., 421, etc. We may repeat, in order to make the meaning of this restriction clearer, that it should be remembered that the whole of the divine office was chanted.

45. Silv., VII, 291 ; Greg., I, 351 ; Engl., II, 49.

46. L. to Mary Baptist, December 30th, 1575. Silv., VII, 207 ; Greg., I, 250 ; Engl., I, 235.

47. Silv., VIII, 269, note 1. The note is not in the English translation.

48. Silv., VII, 301 ; Greg., I, 364 ; Engl., II, 61.

49. Silv., VIII, 61 ; Greg., II, 76 ; Engl., II, 257.

50. L. October, 1576. Silv., VII, 313 ; Greg., I, 382 ; Engl., II, 78.

51. L. to Mariano, November 3rd, 1576. Silv., VII, 342 ; Greg., I, 414 ; Engl., II, 111.

52. L. to Mariano, October 21st, 1576. Silv., VII, 322 ; Greg., I, 394 ; Engl., II, 89.

53. L. to Gracian, December, 1576. Silv., VII, 392 ; Greg., I, 482 ; Engl., II, 170.

54. L. to Gracian, January 9th, 1577. Silv., VIII, 17 ; Greg., II, 16 ; Engl., II, 204.

55. L. to L. de Cepeda, January 17th, 1577. Silv., VIII, 28 ; Greg., II, 28 ; Engl., II, 215.

56. L., February 6th, 1577. Silv., VIII, 45 ; Greg., II, 56 ; Engl., II, 239.

57. L. to Mariano, February 11th, 1577. Silv., VIII, 52 ; Greg., 65 ; Engl., II, 248.

58. L. to Mariano, February 16th, 1577, and to Maria de S. José, April 9th, 1577. Silv., VIII, 55, 75 ; Greg., II, 68, 92 ; Engl., II, 250, 270.

59. Silv., VIII, 82 ; Greg., II, 104 ; Engl., II, 281 (dated 19th).

60. L. to M. de S. José. Silv., VIII, 86 ; Greg., II, 107 ; Engl., II, 284.

61. L. to the Prioress of Caravaca, July 2nd, 1577. Silv., VIII, 94 ; Greg., II, 114 ; Engl., II, 291.

62. *Peregrinación de Anastasio*, Dial. II, p. 37.

63. L. of Gracian dated from Alcalá, August 23rd, 1577. Arch. Carm. Cal., Rome. *Acts of Discalced*, No. 16.

64. L. to Don Alvaro de Mendoza, September 6th, 1577. Silv., VIII, 113 ; Greg., II, 134 ; Engl., II, 309.

65. *Subida*, L. III, Ch. XXVII. Ger., I, 355.

66. L. to Philip II, September 18th, 1577. Silv., VIII, 115, etc. ; Greg., II, 135 ; Engl., II, 312.

67. *Ibid.*

68. Silv., VIII, 112 ; Greg., II, 134 ; Engl., II, 309.

69. L. to Maria de San José, October, 1577. Silv., VIII, 120 *sq.* ; Engl., II, 319. R. Hoornaert, *Sainte Térèse écrivain*, pp. 588–589.

70. Vel., L. V.

71. L. to Alonso de Aranda, November 10th, 1577. Silv., VIII, 125 ; Greg., II, 144 ; Engl., II, 321.

72. Relation of Doña Maria Espinel. C.P., III, p. 577 ; Greg., III, 515.

73. L., July 6th, 1581, to Catherine of Jesus. Ger., III, 79, *St. John of the Cross, Living Flame, and Minor Works* (London, 1912). Letter I, p. 145.

74. L. to Alonso de Aranda, already quoted.

75. L. to Gaspar de Salazar, December 7th, 1577. Silv., VIII, 135 ; Greg., II, 154 ; Engl., III, 7.

76. " Q para venir los dhos frailes descalzos a tratar con la dha sancta madre Theresa de Jesus . . . venian muy disimulados. . . ." says Mary of St. Francis, who states that she was in Avila when John was imprisoned. Med. I. O., fo. 21.

77. *Camino*, III. Silv., III, 20 ; C.P., V, 46.

78. Quir., 395 ; Cyp., 352.

79. L. to Gracian, May 14th, 1578. Silv., VIII, 213 ; Greg., II, 249 ; Engl., III, 95.

80. L. to Philip II, December 4th, 1577. Silv., VIII, 132 ; Greg., II, 151 ; Engl., III, 4 *sq.*

81. " . . . Porque el dho frai Juan de la Cruz no queria gardar sus hordenes y mandatos . . . le mandaron prender y encarzelar. . . ." Maria de S. Francisco. Med. I. O., fo. 21. *Ref.*, L. IV, Ch. XXVII, § 3.

82. Quir., 472 ; Cyp., 426.

83. " Acavado, gastado y flaco por la penitencia." Seg. P.A., fo. 109 ; Quir., 472 ; Cyp., 426.

84. Jer., 229. L., December 4th, to the King. Silv., VIII, 133 ; Greg., II, 151 ; Engl., III, 4–5.

85. L., December 10th, 1577, to Maria de San José. Silv., VIII, 141 ; Greg., 161 ; Engl., III, 13.

86. Jer., 230 ; *Ref.*, B. IV, Ch. XXVII, § 3. Teresa must not have known this when she wrote to the King on December 4th:

" Y tomaronles, en lo que tenian, los papeles." Silv., VIII, 133 ; Engl., III, 5.

87. *Ref., ibid.* Fray Juan Bautista Paveredo. B.N.M. MS. 12738, fo. 1215.

88. Bar., 187, note 3, and 192, note 2. The secret papers mentioned in both documents (MS. 12738, fo. 1215, and Serrano y Sanz : *Apuntes* . . ., Vol. I, Madrid, 1903, pp. 562–563) from the very fact that they were of such interest to the Observants, were clearly connected with the Reform, " eran de mayor secreto en orden a los negocios de la Reforma." Jer., 231.

89. Silv., VIII, 133 ; Greg., II, 151 ; Engl., III, 6.

90. Quir., 474 ; Cyp., 428.

91. Alonso, Seg. P.A., fo. 56. Jer., 238.

92. Silv., VIII, 141, etc. ; Greg., II, 161 ; Engl., III, 14. The historians do not state definitely that Maldonado in person brought John to Toledo.

CHAPTER XIII

1. Ed. Gachard, *Lettres de Philippe II à ses filles* (1581–1583), pp. 137 to 182 (Paris, 1884).

2. L., January 16th, 1578, to Don Teutonio de Braganza. Silv., VIII, 147 *sq.* ; Greg., II, 173 *sq.* ; Engl., III, 27 *sq.*

3. L., December 19th, 1577, to Mary of St. Joseph, prioress of Seville. Silv., VIII, 144 ; Greg., II, 164 ; Engl., III, 18.

4. L. of January 16th. Engl., III, 32.

5. L. to Roque de Huerta, March 9th, 1578. Silv., VIII, 179 ; Greg., II, 208 ; Engl., III, 58.

6. L. to Gracian, April 15th, 1578. Silv., VIII, 190 *sq.* ; Greg., II, 221 *sq.* ; Engl., III, 75.

7. L. of Jan. 16th and L. to the King, December 4th, 1577. Silv., VIII, 132 ; Greg., II, 150 ; Engl., III, 31, 4.

8. L. to Gracian, April 17th, 1578. Silv., VIII, 198 ; Greg., II, 229 ; Engl., III, 76.

9. L. to Gracian, May 22nd, 1578. Silv., VIII, 215 ; Greg., II, 253 ; Engl., III, 98.

10. L. to Gracian, Silv., VIII, 242 ; Greg., II, 292 ; Engl., III, 134.

11. L. to Gracian. Silv., VIII, 245, etc. ; Greg., II, 299 (August 19th, 1578) ; Engl., III, 141.

12. *Regestum Rubei*, 103, fo. 77 : " Conventum toletanum . . . hujus provinciae praecipuum."

13. Quir., 481 ; Cyp., 434 : " . . . porque como se avia hecho esta celda para retrete desta sala en que poner un servicio quando aposentava en ella algun prelado grave."

14. Dep. of Ana of St. Albert, B.N.M. MS. 12738, fo. 997, and of Fray Juan Bautista Paveredo, fo. 1215. Jer., 241.

15. *Toledo en la mano* por Don Sisto Ramon Parro, Vol. II, pp. 91 to 93 (Toledo, 1857).

16. " . . . y en mi vida he visto cosa más seca que esta tierra en cosa que sea de gusto." L. to Mary of St. Joseph, May 15th, 1577. Silv., VIII, 84–85 ; Greg., II, 101 ; Engl., II, 279.

17. *Du Sang, de la Volupté, de la Mort* (Paris, 1894).

18. L. to Mary of St. Joseph, December 10th, 1577 : " Fr. Maldonado, the prior of Toledo, has carried off St. John of the Cross with him to be presented to Fr. Tostado." Silv., VIII, 141 ; Greg., II, 161 ; Engl., III, 14 ; Alonso, Bk. I, Ch. XXXIII ; Quir., 476 ; Cyp., 429 ; and Jer., 242, are not of this opinion. According to them John was brought before a representative of the Vicar-General. There is nothing to prove that Tostado was not in Toledo. Teresa's correspondence shows that he was in Madrid on the preceding July 2nd (Silv., VIII, 94 ; Greg., II, 124 ; Engl., II, 290), and he seems afterwards to have directed the whole affair at close quarters. Letters to the King, September 18th, 1577, to Mary of St. Joseph, October, 1577, and to the King on December 4th. Engl., II, 313, 319 ; III, 5.

19. *Bibl. Carm.*, Vol. I, cols. 656–657 ; *Acta Cap. Gen.*, p. 486, note 3.

20. Maurice Barrès, *Greco, ou le Secret de Tolède*, p. 136 (Plon, 1924).

21. The legality of this notification for which Quiroga (476), Cyprian (429) and Jeronimo (242) make Tostado responsible : " the mitigated fathers spreading the report that it is he who is settling everything " (L. of January 16th, 1578. Silv., VIII, 152 ; Greg., II, 180 ; Engl., III, 135) is weakened by a statement of the Reforma (Bk. IV, Ch. XXVIII, sec. 1) : the King's *placet* was needed in Spain to carry out the Pope's commands. Now, according to " a royal provision preserved in the archives of the Order," of November 5th, 1577, a verdict obtained from the fiscal procurator, Chumazero, had deprived the Vicar-General of his powers (Silv., VIII, 154, note 1 ; Greg., II, 182. *Ramillete de mirra.* Acc. of Mary of St. Joseph. Burgos, 1913. C.P., IV, Doc. 44, 437).

22. L. to Mariano at Madrid, February 6th, 1577 (Silv., VIII, 45 ; Greg., II, 56 ; Engl., II, 239) and February 16th, 1577 (Silv., VIII, 56 ; Greg., II, 69 ; Engl., II, 251).

23. L. to Don Teutonio de Braganza. Silv., VIII, 151 ; Greg., II, 178 ; Engl., III, 31. According to the *Reforma* (L. IV, Ch. XXVII, sec. 2), the Nuncio Sega himself, by the King's express order, had, though with regret, confirmed

Ormaneto's decree appointing John and German as confessors of the Incarnation monastery.

24. *Acta Cap. Gen.*, p. 515, note : " quae auctoritas 27 Dec. (1574) a summo Pontifice confirmata fuit." P. 557, note. *Ref.*, L. III, Ch. XXXIX, § 4.

25. L. to Roque de Huerta, August, 1578. Silv., VIII, 237 *sq.* ; Greg., II, 280 *sq.* ; Engl., III, 122.

26. *Ibid.*, and Gracian : *Peregrinación de Anastasio*, Dialogo II, *op. cit.*, pp. 39 and 40. Quir., 476 ; Cyp., 429.

27. Patent of August 16th, 1567 ; *Regestum Rubei*, fo. 104. *Analecta O.C.*, Vol. IV, p. 198.

28. Cf. Ch. XX, Juan de Santa Ana. Malaga P.A., fo. 27. Alonso, Seg. P.A., fo. 58. Ger., III, 108.

29. Alonso, Seg. P.A., fo. 45. The saint related this supernatural occurrence to the venerable Anne of Jesus ; it was a well-attested fact in the eyes of the fathers and nuns at that time. Jeronimo de S. José, Seg. P.A., fo. 74. The texts have been given in Ch. III.

30. Salmant. *Cursus theologicus*, tract. XVII, de Fide. Disp. I, Dub. IV, § 2, No. 113. 1 Cor. xii, 9.

31. Salmant. *Cursus theologicus* : " De necessitate gratiae." Disp. III, dub. XI, No. 250. Cf. *supra*, Ch. V.

32. *Cautelas*. Cautela segunda. Ger., III, 5.

33. Quir., 479–480 ; Cyp., 432–433 : " The same fathers of the Observance began at once to treat him as a disobedient person and carried out the rigorous punishments prescribed for rebels." Jer., 248.

34. " The mitigated are saying everywhere that they will destroy the Reform because Father Tostado has ordered it." L. of December 4th, 1577, to the King (Silv., VIII, 133 ; Greg., II, 152 ; Engl., III, 5). " I believe we shall never see the end of these troubles until we have a separate province. Alas ! the devil opposes this plan with all his might " (L. of December 7th, 1577, to Gaspar de Salazar (Silv., VIII, 135 ; Greg., II, 154 ; Engl., III, 6). " I really cannot neglect to make use of all possible means to prevent the ruin of this Reform which has begun so well ; not one of the theologians who are my confessors gives any other advice " (L. of January 16th, 1578, to Don Teutonio de Braganza (Silv., VIII, 152 ; Greg., II, 180 ; Engl., III, 33).

35. L. of April 17th, 1578, to Gracian (Silv., VIII, 198 ; Greg., II, 228 ; Engl., III, 26). " These good fathers think that it is quite just to punish and torment those whom they look upon as disobedient to their general chapter, admitting none of the defences that he alleged in his own justification, which he founded on another, higher obedience that commanded him to do none of those things ordained by that chapter, which obedience

was well known and most manifest." Quir., 509 ; Cyp., 460 ; Alonso, Bk. I, Ch. XXXIII. See also Vel. Med. P.A., fo. 51.

36. L. to Mariano, February 11th, 1577. Silv., VIII, 53 ; Greg., II, 65 ; Engl., II, 248.

37. Lea, *History of the Inquisition of Spain* (New York, 1906), Vol. III, p. 210. Ch. Moeller : *Les Bûchers et les Autodafé* (*Revue d'Histoire ecclésiastique de Louvain*, p. 743 *sq.*).

38. Dep. of Ven. Anne of Jesus (Archives C.R., Brussels).

39. Conde de Cedillo : *Toledo en el siglo XVI*, después del vencimiento de las comunidades (Discursos leidos ante la Real Academia de la Historia en la recepción publica del Ilmo Señor D. Jerónimo Lopez de Ayala y Alvarez de Toledo, Conde de Cedillo, Vizconde de Palazuelos, el dia 23 de Junio de 1901). Madrid, 1901. Document X : *Autos de Inquisición en Toledo en* 1570 *y* 1571, p. 207 *sq.* and p. 53.

40. . . . " Es mejor se mueran unas, que no dañar a todas." L. to Gracian, October, 1575. Silv., VII, 195 ; Greg., I, 242 ; Engl., I, 229.

41. " Si aliquis fuerit suspectus de fide, vel male locutus de Ecclesia, vel libros suspectos habuerit qui hoc certo sciverint statim illum denuntiabunt sanctae Inquisitionis officio. Et secus facientes gladio excommunicationis confossos esse volumus et in carceribus detinendos ad annum, quo elapso, inde non extrahantur sine assensu prioris generalis." *Const. Rubei : De Moribus et conversatione mutua fratrum*, § 11. (Ed. Venice, 1568, p. 59.)

42. Cf. *supra*, Ch. XI. Menendez y Pelayo, without bringing forward the least proof, writes, in his *Historia de los heterodoxes españoles*, that St. John of the Cross was delated three or four times to the Inquisitions of Toledo, Valladolid and Seville. But neither Father Gerardo nor Father Silverio has found any trace of it in the Spanish archives. It is most probable that none will ever be discovered, for if Menendez's assertion had any foundation, his biographers would have said a few discreet words in defence of their hero, and all the witnesses at the process of beatification could not have kept silence on such a matter, as they actually did. Moreover, how is it that no antagonist of his lofty theology referred to such delations, when, after his death, his writings were twice denounced to the Spanish Inquisition (1622–1633) and once to the Roman (1668) ?

43. *Const.*, 1462, III, pars. R. II. *De Contumacibus et rebellibus et se erigentibus contra majores et officia*, Ch. 33. " Et qui speciali mandato a suo superiore sibi facto singulariter : vel sibi et aliis pluraliter non obedierit seu in contrarium iverit : pena rebellium que statim declarabitur puniatur. Et quicumque in hujusmodi praeceptis in presentia sui superioris pertinaciter non obedierit : aut inobedientiam suam maliciose et pertinaciter defenderit :

ipsum inobedientem contumacem et rebellem judicamus et carceri mancipandum quamdiu priori generali videbitur expedire."

44. *Acta Cap. Gen.*, p. 508 (Chapter of Piacenza, 1575). Cf. *supra*.

45. Quir., 479 ; Cyp., 432–433.

46. *Noche*, Ger., II, 64.

47. Seg. P.A., fo. 108. Dep. of Juan de Santa Maria, reproduced in the *Vida* . . . d'Alonso, L. I, Ch. XXXIII. Quir., 488 *sq.* ; Cyp., 440.

48. Baeza P.A., fo. 137, and I. O., fo. 113.

49. Alonso, L. I, Ch. XXXIII. " They put him in a very narrow dungeon which I can well describe because I saw it, not without great veneration." Quir., 480 ; Cyp., 453.

50. B.N.M. MS. 12738, fos. 809 and 817. These two letters of the venerable Mary of Jesus are reproduced by Father Joaquin de la Sagrada Familia, C.D., *Epistolario de la Sierva de Dios Sor Maria de Jesus* (Toledo, 1919), p. 255, etc.

51. Málaga P. A., fo. 26.

52. *Const.*, 1462, *loc. cit.*, " Injungentes omnibus fratribus per obedientiam salutarem quod praelatis sint in adjutorium contra inobedientes et contumaces et rebelles ad eos capiendum, ligandum, incarcerandum . . . si non fecerint voce et loco sint privati eoipso."

53. In the month of May the gaoler was replaced by Juan de Santa Maria, who received an order not to bring the saint down every Friday as had been done previously. John asked him : " Father, why have you deprived me of what I deserved ? " Alonso, Bk. I, Ch. XXXIII ; Jer., 250.

54. *Const.*, 1462. *De gravissima poena*, §§ 3–50. " Quicumque autem incarceratus fuerit, feriis secundis, quartis et sextis ad minus jejunet in pane et aqua nisi de venia prioris aliquid sibi misericorditer ministretur."

55. *Op. cit. De poena gravioris culpae*, § 2, Ch. 49. " In capitulo coram presidente denudatus dignam suis demeritis accipiet disciplinam ; qua accepta ad cellam sibi a priore assignatam vadat : in ea maneat usque ad horam comedendi et cum tempus comestionis advenerit intret refectorium et sedens infra in medio cum cappa : pane et aqua super asserem nudum humiliter vescat."

56. " Una disciplina, que llamen de rueda en que todos tienen parte." Quir., 482 ; Cyp., 435.

57. Juan de Santa Maria, *loc. cit.*

58. Ana de S. Alberto. B.N.M. MS. 12738, fo. 997.

59. " . . . aunque le costase la vida." Inocencio de S. Andres. Baeza P.A., 136 ; I. O. 113. " . . . tan inmobil como una piedra." Gabriel de S. José. Med. P.A., fo. 53.

60. L. of October 4th, 1578, to Father Paul Hernandez. Silv., VIII, 265 ; Greg., II, 311 ; Engl., III, 154. " Seeing her going from village to village and city to city, people said she had a *wandering spirit*." Julian of Avila, C.P., VI, 482.

61. Alonso, L. I, Ch. XXXIII.

62. *Ibid*., Quir., 482 ; Cyp., 435.

63. L. to Gracian, August, 1578. Silv., VIII, 252 ; Greg., II, 304 ; Engl., III, 147.

64. Silv., VIII, 149 ; Greg., II, 176 ; Engl., III, 29.

65. Silv., VIII, 181 ; Greg., II, 210 ; Engl., III, 60.

66. *Const*., 1462. *De poena gravioris culpae*, § 2, Ch. 49. " Prior tamen ne in desperationem labi possit ; quantum sibi videbitur expedire mittat ad eum fratres (*sic*) vel fratres discretos et devotos ; qui ipsum moneant et exhortent ad suas penitencias faciendas humiliter et devote . . .''

67. L. to Roque de Huerta, August, 1578. Silv., VIII, 239 ; Greg., II, 283 ; Engl., III, 125 ; Quir., 648 ; Cyp., 438–439.

68. Quir., 491 ; Cyp., 444 ; Jer., 258.

69. Quir., 481 ; Cyp., 434 ; Jer., 251.

70. Inocencio de S. Andres. Baeza P.A., fo. 137 : " Su comida era poca e de tal suerte adereçada q le oyo decir este que muchas veces, entendia que en ella venia muerte por muchos indicios que para ello tenia. . . ." *Id*., I. O., fo. 113.

71. L. to Laurence de Cepeda, January 2nd, 1577. " Try to get some more russet pears or some fresh sardines. Toledo is a queer place for persons obliged to fast because one cannot get even a fresh egg there." Silv., VIII, 11 ; Greg., II, 10 ; Engl., II, 198.

72. Quir., 482 ; Cyp., 435–436.

73. *Moradas* (Sextas) Cap. I. Silv., IV, 99 *sq*. ; C.P., VI, 167 ff.

74. *Noche*, Ger., II, 26.

75. Cf. Ch. II.

76. Ger., II, 6.

77. " . . . lo cual suele ser muy en breve, mayormente en gente religiosa." *Llama*, Ger., II, 445 ; *Noche, ibid*., 27.

78. Cf. *La Tradition mystique du Carmel*.

79. *Noche*, Ger., II, 42.

80. " Pero las almas que han de pasar á tan dichoso y alto estado como es la unión de amor, por muy aprisa que Dios las lleve, *horto tiempo* suelen durar en estas sequedades y tentaciones ordinariamente, como está visto por experiencia." Ger., II, 49, 50. (Italics ours.)

81. " Al alma que Dios ha de llevar adelante, no luego que sale de las sequedades y trabajos de la primera purgación y noche del sentido, pone Su Majestad en esta noche del espiritu, antes suele pasar *harto tiempo y años*, en que salida el alma del

estado de principiantes se ejercita en el de los aprovechados."
Ger., II, 51.

82. Ger., II, 52.
83. Ger., II, 56.
84. Ger., II, 52.
85. Ger., II, 52.
86. " Mas si ha de ser algo de veras, por fuerte que sea, *dura algunos años.*" Ger., II, 69.
87. Ger., II, 69.
88. " de tal mazmorra." The choice of this phrase leads one to think of the monastery of Los Mártires at Granada. Cf., *infra,* Ch. XVI.
89. Ger., II, 69.
90. Ger., II, 495.
91. Sali tras ti clamando, y eras ido. *Id.*
92. The saint later on said so to Francisca de la Madre de Dios. Andres, 13482, B. 11 ; Quir., 507 ; Cyp., 458.
93. Buscando mis amores,
    Iré por esos montes y riberas,
    Ni cogeré las flores.
    Ni temeré las fieras,
    Y pasaré los fuertes y fronteras.
                                                        Ger., II, 495.
94. *Vida,* XVI ; Silv., I, 119 ; C.P., I, 240.
95. *Sobre el Salmo, Super flumina Babylonis.* Ger., III, 184 and 142. Anne of St. Albert stated that the saint composed the poems *Cántico* and the *Super flumina* in prison. Andrés, 13482, B. 23.
96. " de fijo superiores a todos los que hay en castellano." Menendez y Pelayo : *Historia de los heterodoxos españoles* (Madrid, 1887, Vol. II, p. 583). Huysmans is incomprehensible : " to be a scholar and a saint, but not to have any artistic feeling, like St. John of the Cross, is really hard." *La Cathédrale,* p. 344.
97. Ger., II, 496.
98. *Noche,* Ger., II, 94 ; *Cántico,* II, 518 ; *Llama,* II, 441.
99. Jer., 308. " Did they know at that time where the worldly finished and the divine began ? Everything was turned *a lo divino.*" R. Hoornaert, *L'âme ardente de S. Jean de la Croix* (Bruges–Paris, 1929), p. 31. It was not the only occasion on which John was inspired by hearing a love song. Maria de la Cruz declares that it also happened at Granada. P. A., Ubeda, fo. 392. Cf. Louis de la Trinité, *Le Directeur d'âmes* (*Vie Spir.,* Vol. XVI., p. 178).
100. Menendez y Pelayo : *Discurso leído ante la Real Academia,* 6 de Mayo, 1881. Ger., I, XV.
101. *Noche,* Ger., II, 84–96.
102. *Un pastorcico solo está penado.* Ger., III, 173–174 and 140.

103. Ger., II, 577 and 578.

104. " Saco el Santo Padre cuando salio de la Carcel un cuaderno que estando en ella habia escrito de unos romances sobre el Evangelio : *In principio erat verbum ;* y unas coplas que dicen que *bien se yo la fuente que mana y corre aunque es de noche* y las canciones o liras que dicen ; *adonde te escondiste ?* hasta lo que dice ; *O Ninfas de Judea !* lo demás . . . Este cuaderno que el Santo escribio en la carcel, lo dejo en el convento de Beas, Y a mi me mandaran trasladarle algunas veces. . . ." Magdalena del E.S—B.N.M. MS. P.V.T. XVI. 12944, 132, fo. 2. The stanza *O Ninfas* is the thirty-first of the Canticle composed at Toledo. (Cf. *Cántico Espiritual y Poesias de San Juan de la Cruz, segun el Códice de Sanlúcar de Barrameda.* Reproducción fototipográfica. Edición y notas del P. Silverio de S. Teresa, C.D. (Burgos, 1928), Vol. I, p. 18; Ger., II, 499.) The betrothal takes place in the twelfth stanza : *Apártalos, Amado ;* and the marriage in the twenty-seventh : *Entrado se ha la Esposa.* There is no doubt that St. John gave expression to his own experiences in his poetry. He says so in the prologue to the *Cántico* (Gerardo, II, 493) and in the argument of the *Noche* (*ibid.*, p. 1). He wrote " these songs (those in the *Cántico* and the *Llama*) when his mind was elevated above itself and participated in those things there signified : *En participación de aquello que en ellas significava.*" Quir., 709 ; Cyp., 644 ; Jer., 304. How is it then that his first biographer, after having stated and recognised this fact, has dated, however tentatively, the saint's spiritual betrothal in 1578 or 1579 at Calvario (Quir., 562 ; Cyp., 510), and his elevation to the spiritual marriage at Segovia between 1588 and 1591 ? (Quir., 767 ; Cyp., III, 54). Jerónimo places the betrothal at Toledo (303) and the marriage in Andalusia before the *Llama* was written (598). Why these late and different datings which, consequently, make St. John just a writer on mysticism : " sicut scribae eorum," when he speaks in his Commentaries of his own personal experience : " tanquam potestatem habens " ? The biographers were impressed by certain testimonies : " según muchos indicios que refieren los testigos en sus informaciones. . . ." (Quir., 759). Those indications were, for Quiroga, special knowledge regarding the mysteries of the Incarnation and Redemption which are referred to in the *declaración* to stanza XXIX. It seems that there is no possible reason for placing these experiences before his priorship at Segovia. One could more easily understand the objection drawn from the abundance of raptures or certain sufferings later than his escape from prison in order to put back the date of the spiritual marriage—but to what year ? These raptures and sufferings, even if one confines oneself to a rapid examination of the saint's teaching, should disappear when the union has been

consummated (Ger., II, 53 and 588). We shall answer this last objection in Chapter XV.

105. *Llama.* Ger., II, 442.

106. B.N.M. MS. 12738, fo. 725 and fo. 1003. C.P., IV, 297.

107. "Y el dijo . . . que le hacia Nuestro Señor muchas mercedes en esta carcel de comunicarsele con grandes consuelos." B.N.M. MS. 12738, fos. 817–818.

108. "Y a su sabor reposa." :

> At her ease she rests
> Her head against
> The upholding arms of the Beloved.
>
> Ger., II, 579.

109. Mary of St. Joseph : "Y dize esta tº que ella mismo oyo deçir al benerale p. frai Juan de la Cruz que las dhas canciones de la noche oscura las habia escrito en el tiempo que le tubieren presso en toledo. . . ." Seg. P.A., fo. 29 ; Andrés, 13482, B. 53. Maria de la Encarnacion of Consuegra, to whom the saint was to give the habit at Madrid, says the same thing. Andrés, 13482, B. 17.

110. *Noche,* Ger., III, 157–158.

111. Ger., II, 1. Argumento.

112. Quir., 505 ; Cyp., 456–457 ; Jer., 305 *sq.*

113. Ger., III, 172. Cf. Magdalene of the Holy Ghost.

114. Este ser es cada una,
> Y éste sólo las unia
> En un inefable nudo
> Que decir no se sabia
> Por lo cual era infinito
> El amor que las unia,
> Porque un solo amor tres tienen,
> Que su esencia se decia ;
> Quel el amor, cuanto más uno
> Tanto más amor hacia.
>
> Ger., III, 174. Magdalene of the Holy Ghost.

115. Mary of Jesus Sandoval. B.N.M. MS. 12738, fo. 725 ; C.P., IV, 297.

116. Anne of St. Albert. B.N.M. MS. 12738, fo. 1003 ; Quir., 516 ; Cyp., 466.

117. "Un dia le pidió el P. Fr. Juan (a su carcelero) que hiciese caridad de un poco de papel y tinta porque queria hacer algunas cosas de devocien para entretenerse, y se lo trajo." Inocencio de San Andrés, B.N.M. MS. 8568, fo. 545.

118. Cf., *supra.*

119. L. to Roque de Huerta, August, 1578. Silv., VIII, 239 ; Greg., II, 282 ; Engl., III, 124.

120. "Vino de el Papa que el Nuncio ne se entremetiese

con frayles sino en los casos que el Rey le pidiese." *Peregrinación de Anastasio*, p. 40. Greg., II, 282, note 1.

121. Quir., 485 ; Cyp., 438.

122. ". . . camaras de sangre y terribles calenturas. . . ." Maria de San Francisco, I. O. Med., fo. 25 ; C.P., III, 354–355.

123. Juan de Santa Maria. Seg. P.A., fo. 108 ; Alonso, L. I., Ch. XXXIII ; Quir., 490 ; Cyp., 443.

124. Quir., 230 ; Cyp., 292.

125. Ger., III, 172.

126. "Domino Deo Virginique Matri Mariae jugiter deservire." *Chronique de Guillaume de Sanvico*. See Ch. III.

127. Martin de la Asuncion. Ubeda I. O., fo. 71 ; Quir., 507, 508 ; Cyp., 459–460 ; Jer., 357.

128. Francisca de la Madre de Dios reports this fact. Andrés, 13482, F. 4.

129. Juan Evangelista, Malaga P.A., fo. 34. Andrés, 13482, F. 55 ; Quir., 335 ; Cyp., 298.

130. Seg. P.A., fo. 57.

131. " Dijo que vino a estar tan malo y flaco, que le parecia se iba muriendo, y que estando en esto una octava de Nuestra Señora de la Asunción, se le apareció y mandó se fuese de la carcel, que ya se la dejaban abierta a las noches por el grande calor, y el temia el irse por estar tan malo, y no poder salir, sino con grandisima dificultad. Con todo esto, dice que muchas veces le torno a mandar se fuese y que Ella le ayudaria." Ven. Mary of Jesus, B.N.M. MS. 12738, fos. 817–818.

132. Jeronimo de Olmos. Med. P.A., fo. 82.

133. Juan de Santa Maria, Seg. P.A., fo. 108. According to Alonso the saint himself carved the instruments of the Passion by means of a small lancet. L. I., Ch. XXXIV.

134. Bar., 192 ; Demimuid, *op. cit.*, p. 83.

135. *Const.*, 1462. *De gravissima paena*, § 3, Ch. 50.

136. Up to this the prisoner had not had the same facilities. Blessed Anne of St. Bartholomew states, according to Jeronimo (p. 341) : " Tenia dêtro deste aposento un siervo (esto es un vaso para necessidades) y de tantos á tantos dias se le hazian ir a limpiar ; iva un Fraile con el y bolvia á encerrarle."

137. Quir., 520 ; Cyp., 470 ; Jer., 323.

138. *Peregrinación*, pp. 36, 37. Cf. P. Bruno de J. M. : *Notre Vénérable Père Antoine de Jesus*, in *Le Carmel*, No. 7, p. 119 (1925).

139. Fray Juan Bautista Paveredo. B.N.M. MS. 12738, fo. 1215.

140. Quir., 521 ; Cyp., 470 ; Jer., 324.

141. Quir., 521 *sq.* ; Cyp., 471 *sq.* ; Jer., 326 *sq* ; Alonso, L. I, Ch. XXXIV.

142. Sebastian of Saint Hilary. Jaén, P.A., fo. 94.

143. "An old tunic which the gaoler had given him out of compassion." Quir., 521 ; Cyp., 471 ; Alonso, Bk. I, Ch. XXXIII. This is the tunic, very probably, which Teresa says he got from the sub-prior in her letter to Gracian in August, 1578 (Silv., VIII, 252 ; Greg., II, 304 ; Engl., III, 147).

144. ". . . Nuestra Señora le consolaba en ella, y le visitaba y que le mando algunas veces se fuese de la carcel, y que en la ultima ya no lo pudo resistir porque le dijo se fuese, y que Ella le ayudaria : y ansi lo hizo segun el nos dijo. . . ." Ven. Mary of Jesus. B.N.M. MS. 12738, fos. 809 and 810.

145. We are following Quiroga in all this matter (522, etc.). Cyp., 472, etc. ; Jer., 527, etc. Juan de Santa Ana says that John found himself in a fowl pen, "un corral de conejos o gallinas." Malaga P.A., J. 26.

146. P. Ignace Beaufays, *Béatrice de Silva*, p. 23 (Bruxelles, 1927).

147. "This enclosure was behind their Church (the Conceptionists) though it was outside their cloister. He looked about in all directions to see if he could find some way out ; he found the whole place carefully bolted and barred, because this enclosure on the two sides overlooking the River Tagus is surrounded by the city wall which is built upon great rocks ; on the other side it adjoined the convent from which he had just escaped, and by the side overlooking the city, by which he thought the dog had run off, it was surrounded by such a high wall that, even though the wall had fallen down when I went to see it in order to describe this place : ' quando yo le fuy a reconocer para escrivir esto '—one could only enter it with difficulty." This description of Quiroga's (p. 526), Cyprian (p. 476), is reproduced by Jerónimo (p. 330). Thanks to the plans kindly supplied by Rev. Father Evaristo de la Virgen del Carmen, Discalced Carmelite of Toledo, we have been able to complete and control an attempt to reconstitute the place, which we tried to do on the spot itself.

148. "Y que estando en esto se encomendo a Dios, y me parece dijo tambien a Nuestra Señora ; que empezo a subir por una pared muy alta y que se hallo de la otra parte sin saber él como." Mary of Jesus, B.N.M., fos. 809–810.

". . . el corral esta sercado con la muralla de la ciudad y por otras partes con tapias muy altas de a seis o ocho tapias en alto y que viendose ymposiblitado de poder salir y junto con su mucha flaqueza quiso bolverse a la prission por donde avia benido y tan poco pudo subir y con la grande augustia que con esto tenia se avia encomendado deberas a Nuestra Sra y se avia arrimado a un rincon de la muralla y que no supo como se avia hallado en lo alto de alla por donde avia comensado a andar a oscuras y que aviendo passos muy dificultosisimos de pasar todos los hallo faciles hasta que llego a un derrunbadero de la muralla, y se dejo caer por el y se hallo a la voca de una calle. . . ." Juan of Santa Ana. Malaga P.A., fo. 26.

149. Quir., 527 ; Cyp., 477.

150. Dep. of Juan de Santa-Maria. Seg. P.A., fo. 108 ; Quir., 528–534 ; Cyp., 478–479.

151. " Y esto nos dijo él que, aquella noche pobre, se habia recogido en casa de una persona honrada pidio de limosna le dejasen alli hasta la mañana, dijo de Nuestra Señora en el zaguán de la casa." Ven. Mary of Jesus, B.N.M. MS. 12738, fos. 809–810. " . . . de fuerça avia de passar por la placa (Zocodover) donde las vendederas estavan con sus luzes, y le acosaron con palabras feas, y baldones, hasta que le perdieron de vista." Relation of the Blessed Anne of St. Bartholomew, quoted by Jeronimo, pp. 340 to 344.

152. " Muy passo a passo." Maria de San Francisco. Med. I. O., fo. 21.

153. C.P., III, 425.

154. " . . . le harian migajas. . . ." Ven. Maria of Jesus. B.N.M. MS. 12738, fos. 809–810.

155. " . . . tan consumido y desfigurado que parecia un retrato de la muerte." Maria of San Francisco. Med. I. O., fo. 21.

156. Alonso, L. I. Ch. XXXIII. ; C. P., III, 419.

157. C.P., III, 427 *sq.* ; Alonso, *ibid.*

158. Andres, 13482, B. 16 and 19. Cf. Magdalene of the Holy Ghost, note 104, *supra.*

159. Alonso, *ibid.*

160. Quoted, *supra* and *infra.*

161. Sebastian of St. Hilary. Jaén P.A., fo. 94.

162. Ven. Mary of Jesus. B.N.M. MS. 12738, fos. 810 and 818. Alonso, *ibid.* ; Quir., 532 ; Cyp., 482 ; Jer., 344 (relation of the Blessed Anne of St. Bartholomew).

163. R.P. Evaristo de la Virgen del Carmen, C.D., *San Juan de la Cruz* (Toledo, 1927), p. 103.

CHAPTER XIV

1. Account of Anne of Jesus. C.P., IV, 36.

2. Magdalene of the Holy Ghost. B.N.M. MS. 12944[132] ; Quiroga states expressly (p. 535 ; Cyp., 485) that the saint passed by the Carmelite Convent of Beas on his way to Calvario. Jerónimo (p. 349), and Silverio (VIII, 282) follow him here.

3. *Fund.*, Ch. XXII ; Silv., V, 182 ; C.P., IV, 1.

4. *Vie de la Vénérable Anne de Jésus,* by Rev. Angelus Manrique,

General of the Order of St. Bernard in Spain (Lyons, 1870), Vol. I, p. 91.

5. Magdalene of the Holy Ghost, Arch. C.R. Brussels. The paper is not dated.

6. Silv., VIII, 305 ; Greg., II, 336 ; Engl., III, 182.

7. Deposition of Beatrice of the Conception. Arch. C.R. Brussels.

8. Deposition of Hilary of St. Augustine, March 4th, 1627. Arch. C.R. Brussels.

9. Dep. of Joanna of the Holy Ghost. Arch. C.R. Brussels. We read in one of Magdalene's depositions (Arch. C.R. Brussels) that when Anne of Jesus was a conventual of Salamanca, Master Curiel won over to his own opinion, in theological matters, *otros muchos letrados de los más graves*, when he told them that the Mother shared it. Magdalene learned this from Jerome of the Cross, " one of the closest and dearest spiritual sons of the Holy Father, John of the Cross."

10. *Que parecian epistolas de San Pablo.* Dep. of Hilary of St. Augustine, March 4th, 1627. Arch. C.R. Brussels.

11. Dep. of Beatrice of the Conception. Arch. C.R. Brussels.

12. L. to Mary of the Incarnation at Consuegra, dated from Toledo, January 5th, 1624. Arch. C.R. Brussels.

13. *Bañes solía decir : la madre Ana de Jesús es tan santa como la madre Teresa de Jesús y de más talento.* Dep. of Joanna of the Holy Ghost, Salamanca. Arch. C.R. Brussels.

14. *Vie de la vén. Anne de Jesus. Op. cit.*, Vol. I, p. 196.

15. L. of October 21st, 1576. Silv., VII, 323–324 ; Greg., I, 396 ; Engl., II, 91.

16. L. of April 17th and April 15th, 1578. Silv., VIII, 200 and 190–191 ; Greg., II, 231 and 220 ; Engl., III, 78 and 69.

17. L. to Gracian, October 15th, 1578. Silv., VIII, 271 ; Greg., II, 319. Cf. *supra*, Ch. XII ; Engl., III, 165.

18. *Ref.*, L. IV, Ch. XXXI, § 3.

19. Alonso, L. I, Ch. XXXVI and XLI, quoted by Silv., VIII, 415, note 2.

20. " A buscar al padre provincial de los descalzos questava en este dicho convento." Francisca de Jesus. Med. I. O., fo. 29. Elvira de S. Angel. Med. I. O., fo. 16 ; Alonso, L. I, Ch. XXXVI.

21. L. to Gracian, September, 1578. Silv., VIII, 257, note 2 ; Greg., II, 308 ; Engl., III, 150, note 3.

22. L. to Gracian, August, 1578. Silv., VIII, 251 ; Greg., II, 303 ; Engl., III, 146.

23. Mother Mary Evangelist (Med. I. O., fo. 32) states that Teresa and the Father Provincial were in Medina. This valuable testimony of a nun of the *Calle Santiago* cannot be weakened by a letter of July 6th, 1581 (*Letters*, p. 145), in which

John says to Catalina of Jesus : " Since this whale swallowed me and vomited me into this strange port, I have never deserved to see her or the saints from there." This means that from his arrival in Andalusia he had never again seen Teresa and the religious of Castile. Since we know from reliable sources that, from August to October, 1578, he visited *los santos de por allá* (cf. his visit to the Incarnation at Avila, Greg., II, 306, already quoted, Ch. XII), and that he found them again at Almódovar, one must logically conclude that he might have seen Teresa at Avila or, at least, at Medina del Campo.

24. L. to Gracian, August, 1578. Silv., VIII, 252–253 ; Greg., II, 304–305 ; Engl., III, 147.

25. Francisca de Jesús. Med. I. O., fo. 29.

26. Maria de S. Francisco. Med. I. O., fo. 21.

27. Dep. of Julian of Avila.

28. L. to F. de Salcedo, towards the end of September, 1568. Silv., VII, 30 ; Greg., I, 38 ; Engl., I, 37.

29. Maria Evangelista. Med. I. O., fo. 32.

30. " . . . hinchadas las piernas de los hierros en que avia estado aprisionado." Francisca de Jesús. Med. I. O., fo. 29.

31. L. to Gracian, August, 1578. Silv., VIII, 251 ; Engl., III, 146.

32. L. to Gracian, September, 1578. Silv., VIII, 253 ; Greg., II, 306 ; Engl., III, 148.

33. *Ref.*, L. IV, Ch. XXXI, § 3.

34. Account of Frances of the Mother of God to Magdalene of the Holy Ghost at Cordova, September 1st, 1625. Arch. C.R. Brussels.

35. L. to P. Paul Hernandez, October 4th, 1578. Silv., VIII, 266 ; Greg., II, 313 ; Engl., III, 155.

36. L. I, Ch. XXXVI.

37. These names are supplied by Alonso (Bk. I, Ch. XXXVII). He raises a difficulty by adding that the two sisters went to confession on that very morning to John. It is true that he adds a little later on that the first visit took place on All Saints' Day, 1578, with which we agree.
It is absolutely impossible for Anne of the Mother of God to have sung this song (C. P., IV, 310, 311). She was only about twelve years of age in 1586 ! (Ubeda, I. O., fo. 48).

38. Alonso, L. I, Ch. LVI.

39. Arch. C.R. Brussels, *passim* ; C.P., III, 419 *sq.*

40. Ubeda P.A., fo. 409. Dep. of Ana de la Madre de Dios. B.N.M. P.V., Vol. XVI, MS. 12944^{132} and B.N.M. MS 8568 ; C.P., IV, 301 *sq.*

41. B.N.M. MS., P.V., Vol. XVI, 12944^{132}, fo. 2. Arch. C.R. Brussels. C.P., IV, 304 *sq.*

42. Arch. C.R. Brussels. C.P., IV, 306 *sq.*

43. B.N.M. MS. 12738, fo. 1375. *Fund.*, Ch. XXII. Silv., V, 181 *sq.* ; C.P., IV, 1 *sq.*, and 20–21.

44. B.N.M. MS. 12738, fo. 723. *Compendio historico de la vida . . . de la venerable Maria de Jesús* (Cordova, 1905). C.P., 295 *sq.*

45. Jer., 376.

46. L. to Mary of St. Joseph, March 2nd, 1577. Silv., VIII, 66 ; Greg., II, 83 ; Engl., II, 263.

47. Silv., VIII, 282–283 ; Greg., II, 333–334 ; Engl., III, 180. According to Magdalene of the Holy Ghost (B.N.M. M.S. 12944[132]), Anne's fears may have been due to the saint's youth. Anne was rather surprised that, *muy mozo*, John, when speaking of Teresa, referred to her as " *muy su hija*," my own daughter.

48. Silv., VIII, 66 ; Greg., II, 83 ; Engl., II, 263.

49. Silv., VIII, 282–283 ; Greg., II, 333–334 ; Engl., III, 180.

50. Quoted by Vicente de la Fuente : *Obras, carta*, C. XXXVI, p. 123[h]. R. Hoornaert, *Sainte Térèse, écrivain*, p. 579.

51. L. of July. Silv., VII, 262 ; Greg., I, 317 ; Engl., II, 16.

52. L. to Gracian, October 4th, 1579. Silv., VIII, 357 ; Greg., II, 440 ; Engl., III, 272.

53. L. from Magdalene of the Holy Ghost to Beatrice of the Conception, September 13th, 1623. Arch. C.R. Brussels.

54. L. November 29th, 1581, to Gracian. Silv., IX, 133 ; Greg., III, 247 ; Engl., IV, 258.

55. Silv., IX, 187 *sq.* ; Greg., III, 310 *sq.* ; Engl., IV, 326.

56. L. November 28th, 1581, to Don Pedro Castro y Nero. Silv., IX, 127 ; Greg., III, 239 ; Engl., IV, 251.

57. Greg., III, 311.

58. Arch. C.R. Brussels.

59. Dep. of Louis of the Assumption and of Magdalene of the Holy Ghost, undated. Arch. C.R. Brussels.

60. *Vie de la vénérable Anne de Jésus, op. cit.*, Vol. I, p. 171.

61. Anne of Jesus sent 200 ducats to Diego de Guevara, on January 21st, 1612, for the printing of *The Book of Job*. On November 25th, 1615, she told him " of what her devotion to that holy man Job had ended in." Quoted in the text. Arch. C.R. Brussels.

62. February 8th, 1623. Arch. C.R. Brussels.

63. " He knew by experience and several signs and indications that (Anne) possessed humility in an eminent degree. When Mother Anne was presented with the interrogatories so that she might bear witness to the sanctity and revelations of our venerable Father (John) of the Cross, although it was evident to us that she might have known many things worthy of admira-

tion, she refused to divulge them and acted as if she were ignorant. I asked her why she had not said all that she knew. . . . She answered that she had not dared to reveal them as she feared she might thereby exalt and reveal her own favours. The said Mother Anne, indeed, explained to the witness that when she made her confession to the venerable Father John of the Cross, the Lord had often reciprocally revealed to them in prayer secrets which they interchanged. . . ." *Processus servae Dei S. Annae de Jesus*, Vol. I. Dep. R.P. Hilarii a St. Augustino, Vic. Prov., Antwerpiae, 30 Julii, 1635, fo. 18, q. 20, *De humilitate*, Arch. C.R. Brussels ; Jeronimo, p. 498, etc.

64. The vegetation must have been much more abundant in the sixteenth century than it is now. I have ventured to say that the pine forests have been replaced by olive trees in Quincunxes which to-day are dotted on the mountain. We read, in fact, in *La Reforma*, L. III, Ch. LII, sec. 2, that " thick forests " existed, alternating here and there with " level spaces covered with trees laden with delicious fruit."

65. *Ref.*, L. III, Ch. LV, sec. 1. Gracian commanded that clerics should be distinguished from the brothers by the tonsure as in other communities. *Ref.*, L. III, Ch. XVII, secs. 1 and 2.

66. Innocent of St. Andrew. Baeza I. O., fo. 131 ; P.A., fo. 111 ; *Ref.*, L. III, Ch. LII, § 3.

67. *Ref.*, L. III, Ch. LV, § 7.

68. *Cánt.*, C. XIII ; Ger., II, 497.

69. Alonso, L. I, Ch. XXXVII ; Quir., 546 *sq.* ; Cyp., 495 *sq.*

70. Luis de S. Angel. Alcaudete I. O., fo. 120.

71. *Ref.*, L. III, Ch. LII, §§ 1 and 2.

72. Quir., 539 ; Cyp., 488 ; *Ref.*, L. III, Ch. LIII, § 3.

73. Luis de S. Angel. Alcaudete I. O., fo. 119.

74. Frances of the Mother of God to Magdalene of the Holy Ghost at Cordova, November 10th, 1624. Arch. C.R. Brussels.

75. Andres, 13482, F. 57.

76. An authentic copy of an autograph drawing formerly preserved in the Holy Desert of *Las Nieves*, which belonged to Magdalene of the Holy Ghost is supplied as an illustration. This copy may be found in MS. 6296 of the B.N.M., where we had it photographed.

We read on the next page : *Primer monte que nuestro V. Padre Fray Juan de la Cruz hizo de su mano para sus libros estando en el Calvario.* Magdelene of the Holy Ghost says that he afterwards altered this plan. Ger., I, 26.

77. *Noche.* Ger., II, 6.

78. *Subida.* Ger., I, 57.

79. *Ibid.*, 44.

80. *Ibid.*, 45.

81. *Ibid.*, 46.

82. *Ibid.*, 51.
83. Cf. reproduction of MS. 6296, B.N.M.
84. *Subida,* Ger., I, 41–42.
85. *Ibid.*, 43.
86. *Ibid.*, 59.
87. *Ibid.*, 62.
88. *Ibid.*, 65.
89. *Subida.* Ger., II, 66.
90. *Ibid.*, 73.
91. *Ibid.*, 73.
92. *Ibid.*, 76.
93. *Ibid.*, 76.
94. *Ibid.*, 76.
95. *Ibid.*, 78.
96. *Ibid.*, 78.
97. *Ibid.*, 79.
98. *Ibid.*, 80.
99. *Ibid.*, 80.
100. *Ibid.*, 82 and 83.
101. *Ibid.*, 94, 41, 38.
102. *Llama.* Ger., II, 401 and 629.
103. *Subida.* Ger. I, 40.
104. *Ibid.*, 38.
105. *Ibid.*, 100.
106. *Ibid.*, 100.
107. Quir., 36 ; Cyp., 32.
108. *Subida.* Ger., I, 127.
109. *Ibid.*, 107.
110. *Ibid.*, 132.
111. *Ibid.*, 32. *Prólogo.*
112. *Subida.* Ger., 135–136, and, in general, all the rest of the *Subida.*
113. *Ibid.*, 211.
114. *Ibid.*, 121–122.
115. *Ibid.*, 122.
116. *Ibid.*, 405, and Ger. III, 93. L. to a religious (*Letter* X, p. 160).
117. *Ibid.*, 123.
118. *Ibid.*, 125.
119. *Dict. Theol. Cath. Jean de la Croix* (Saint), by the Rev. P. Pascal du Saint-Sacrement, O.C.D., VIII, col. 779.
120. *Subida.* Ger., I, 29. *Prólogo. Noche,* II, 124.
121. *Subida.* Ger., I, 30.
122. *Ibid.*, 30.
123. *Ibid.*, 33.
124. *Noche.* Ger., II, 6.
125. *Ibid.*, 7.

126. *Ibid.*, 8.
127. *Ibid.*, 8.
128. *Ibid.*, 9.
129. *Ibid.*, 9.
130. *Ibid.*, 9.
131. *Ibid.*, 12.
132. *Ibid.*, 12.
133. *Ibid.*, 12.
134. *Ibid.*, 12.
135. *Ibid.*, 12.
136. *Noche.* Ger., II, 14.
137. *Ibid.*, 14.
138. *Ibid.*, 17. After having quoted Gerardo, II, 14 to 17, Prof. Laignel-Lavastine states in his work, *La Méthode Concentrique dans l'étude des psychonévrosés* (p. 134) : " You see how St. John of the Cross had rightly remarked that different emotions were capable, by reason of the small number of reflexes which our poor body has at its disposal, of arriving at analogous reactions.
" St. John of the Cross could not have been aware of the reactional similarities of the pneumogastric and the erector on the excitability of vagotonics.   His clinical remarks are no longer of any value.   They illustrate the theory I have put forward to explain the relations between pleasure and anxiety and even of every lively emotion, which reacts on the vagal system."
139. *Noche.* Ger., II, 18.
140. *Ibid.*, 19.
141. *Ibid.*, 21.
142. *Ibid.*, 24.
143. *Ibid.*, 24.
144. *Ibid.*, 25.
145. *Ibid.*, 7.
146. *Ibid.*, 6.
147. *Ibid.*, 28.
148. *Ibid.*, 33.
149. *Ibid.*, 28.
150. *Ibid.*, 28.
151. *Ibid.*, 31. The progress of modern psychology and psychiatry leave the value of these three signs intact.
152. Ger., II, 33.
153. *Ibid.*, 34.
154. *Ibid.*, 56.
155. *Ibid.*, 26.
156. *Ibid.*, 113.
157. *Ibid.*, 59.
158. *Ibid.*, 59.
159. *Ibid.*, 59.
160. *Ibid.*, 61.

161. *Ibid.*, 62.
162. *Ibid.*, 65.
163. *Ibid.*, 66.
164. *Ibid.*, 53.
165. *Ibid.*, 53.
166. *Ibid.*, 71 to 75.
167. *Ibid.*, 99.
168. *Ibid.*, 102.
169. *Ibid.*
170. *Ibid.*, 105.
171. Ger., II, 107.
172. *Ibid.*, 108.
173. *Ibid.*, 111.
174. *Ibid.*, 110.
175. *Ibid.*, 123.
176. *Ibid.*, 114.
177. *Ibid.*, 82.
178. *Ref.*, L. VI, Ch. XII, § 5.
179. Andres, 13482, J. 42.
180. B.N.M. MS. 12738 ; C.P., IV, 297.
181. *Ref.*, L. III, Ch. LIV, § 5 ; Alonso, L. I, Ch. XXXVII.
182. Alonso, L. I, Ch. XXXVII.
183. Ana de la Madre de Dios. Ubeda P.A., fo. 409 ; I. O., fo. 48. R.P. Louis de la Trinité : *Le Directeur d'âmes*, p. 177.
184. B.N.M. *Papeles varios*, Vol. XVI, MS. 12944[132], fo. 3, and fo. 4.
185. Ger., I, 90.
186. " Como le dice en el monte de la perfecion que hiço y le escrivio en el mismo convento de beas dando de su letra a cada religiosa una para el brebiario." Ana de la Me de Dios. Ubeda P.A., fo. 407.
187. Andres, 13482, 31.
188. B.N.M. P.V., Vol. XVI, MS. 12944[132], fo. 3. Dep. of Magdalene of the Holy Ghost.
189. *Cántico, Prólogo.* Ger., II, 49.
190. L. of December, 1578, to Anne de Jesus. Silv., VIII, 283 ; Greg., II, 333 ; Engl., III, 179.
191. B.N.M. MS. 12738, fo. 1461, quoted by Bar., p. 200, No. 1.
192. Ana de la Me de Dios. Ubeda P.A., fo. 408 ; I. O., fo. 49.

CHAPTER XV

1. Quir., 585 ; Cyp., 530 ; Jer., 414.
2. Jer., 359 and 444 ; *Ref.*, L. III, Ch. XVIII, § 9 ; L. VII, Ch. IV, § 4.

3. Malaga P.A., fo. 26 *sq.* Ger., III, 108 ; Jer., 447.

4. Baeza P.A., fo. 129 *sq.* ; I. O., fo. 111 *sq.* ; *Ref.*, L. XV, Ch. XX, § 8.

5. *Acta Cap. Gen.*, p. 562, note.

6. Dep. of Magdalene of the Holy Ghost, July 3rd, 1621. Arch. C.R. Brussels, and B.N.M. P.V., Vol. XVI, MS. 12944[132], fo. 4 *in fine*.

7. The house was purchased for 1,800 ducats, the greater part of which sum was supplied by the prior of the Church of Isnorafé. A notary in Baeza has the deed signed by John of the Cross. *Ref.*, Bk. IV, Ch. I, sec. 3.

8. Baeza P.A., fo. 108.

9. Quir., 586 ; Cyp., 531 ; *Ref.*, Bk. VII, Ch. LIII. The remains of Father Francis, as well as those of Father John of Jesus, repose in our convent at Ubeda.

10. Baeza P.A., fo. 108.

11. Jer., 415.

12. *Ref.*, L. IV, Ch. LI, § 3.

13. Quir., 513 ; Cyp., 531 ; *Ref.*, L. IV, Ch. XLI, § 4.

14. *Ref.*, L. IV, Ch. XLVII and Ch. L, § 2.

15. Alonso, L. I, Ch. XLII.

16. Quir., 588 ; Cyp., 532 ; *Ref.*, L. IV, Ch. XLI, § 5.

17. Quir., 591 ; Cyp., 536.

18. Jer., 415 and 416.

19. " Que se movieron a tomar el habito gran numero de estudiantes de la universitad estos primeros años, y probaron muy bien en la religion." Deposition of Peter of St. Hilarion. Quir., 594 ; Cyp., 538 ; *Ref.*, L. II, Ch. II, § 1 ; and also Quir., 587, and Cyp., 532.

20. Quir., 259 ; Cyp., 235.

21. *Ref.*, L. III, Ch. II, § 1.

22. Baeza P.A., fo. 45, 48[r] and 48[v].

23. Inocencio de San Andres. Baeza P.A., fo. 135, and I. O., fo. 112.

24. Alonso. Seg. P. A., fo. 62.

25. Sebastian of St. Hilary. Jaén P.A., fo. 97.

26. Jaen I. O., fo. 9 ; Jer., 436.

27. Ps. xciv. 12.

28. Jaen P.A., fo. 90.

29. Jer., 450.

30. Alonso, L. I, Ch. XLII.

31. . . . " Y no solo fue docto en teologia mistica mas tambien lo fué en teologia escolastica por que tenia lindo y agudo ingenio y en la moral y ansi vio hallarse a algunos exercicios de letras en Baeza y dava en el discurso de los argumentos tales disticiones y soluciones que oyo admirar a hombres doctos. . . ." Jeronimo de la Cruz. Jaen I. O., fos. 9 and

10, and B.N.M. MS. 12738, fo. 645. This was the origin of the cases of conscience ordained by the Constitutions. Andres, 12482, D. 24.

32. " Hijos caminemos y endeceremos a la Vida eterna." Dep. of Luis de San Angel. Baeza P.A., fo. 48.

33. " Acudiá nuestros estudiãtes a la universidad a oyr Teologia. . . ." Pedro de San Hilarion. Quir., 593 ; Cyp., 538.

34. Alonso, L. I., Ch. XLIII ; Jer., 420.

35. Inocencio de San Andres. Baeza I. O., fos. 111–112 ; Quir., 306 and 594 ; Cyp., 270 and 538.

36. Y mira con tu haz a las montañas.

.   .   .   .

Mas mira las campañas.
　　　　　Cántico, C. XXXIII ; Ger., II, 499.

37. Eccli. xxiv. 47.

38. Prov. xi. 2.

39. D. Miguel Lafuente Alcántara. *Historia de Granada comprendiendo las de sus cuatro provincias Almería. Jaén, Granada y Málaga desde remotos tiempos hasta nuestros días* (Granada, Imprenta y librería de Sanz, 1846), Vol. IV, p. 229 *sq.* ; B. N. Paris Oe., 1067. Reynier, *La vie universitaire dans l'ancienne Espagne*, Ch. III, p. 125 (Paris, 1912).

40. Jeronimo de la Cruz. Jaen I. O., fo. 8.

41. Ger., I, 30, 31 and 33.

42. Silv., VIII, 283 ; Greg., II, 333 ; Engl., III, 180.

43. *Prólogo.* Ger., I, 33.

44. " Yo soy tu corazón." *Ref.*, L. XVII, Ch. XXXI ; Jer., 452.

45. " Hija, letrado soy por mis pecados." Maria de la Paz. Baeza I. O., fo. 108 ; Jer., 458.

46. Doña Justa de Paz. Baeza P.A., fo. 103.

47. Martin de San José. Baeza I. O., fo. 101 ; Jer., 426 and 459.

48. Silv., VIII, 378–379 ; Greg., II, 355–356 ; Jer., 464 ; Engl., III, 181.

49. C.P., IV, 82.

50. Quir., 327–328 ; Cyp., 290–291.

51. B.N.M. MS. 12738, fos. 1003 and 37. " Our Lord is dealing with me in such a fashion that this weak disposition cannot endure it and so the little ass is very jaded." Andres, 13482, I, 10. Alonso, Bk. I, Ch. XLIII ; Quir., 317 ; Cyp., 280.

52. B.N.M. MS. 12738, fo. 997.

53. Cf. note 207, Ch. XVII. Quir., 219 ; Cyp., 198–199. Cf. *infra*, Ch. XIX.

54. " Arrobado en alta contemplación. . . ." Fernando de la Madre de Dios. Ubeda, P.A., fo. 203.

55. *Noche*, Ger., II, 52.

56. *Ibid.*, p. 53.

57. See *supra*, Ch. XIII.

58. *Moradas* (Setimas), Ch. III. Silv., IV, 197–198 ; C.P., VI, 300–301.

59. *Cántico*, canción XIII. Ger., II, 530.

60. Silv., IV, 197 ; C.P., VI, 300, note 1.

61. " Aunque no basta esto para dejar de recibir detrimento delante de tanta grandeza y gloria." *Llama*, canción IV. Ger., II, 480.

62. *Llama*, canción II. Ger., II, 420.

63. *Llama*, canción III. Ger., II, 432.

64. Ana de San Alberto. B.N.M. MS. 12738, fo. 37.

65. St. Hildegarde.

66. " To regard a nervous disturbance, a pathological attack, a trifling delirium as the most mysterious phenomena of the physical and moral world strikes me as very odd. If anyone wishes to establish religion on the unconscious, on the residuum left unexplained by science and philosophy, let him take as his starting point, some definite fact of life and thought, birth, death, progress, all that depends on time. But why build metaphysical constructions on the gradual fainting of an ecstastic when facts of the same nature may be observed in any normal sleep." Pierre Janet, *De l'angoisse à l'extase*, p. 467 (Alcan, 1926). Dr. Marcel Nathan, in a review of this work in *La Revue de Synthèse historique* (Vol. XLVI, pp. 102, 39), has given a judicious presentation of the Catholic view, and especially St. John's, in regard to ecstasy.

67. Ana de San Alberto. B.N.M. MS. 12738, fo. 37.

68. This title is given by Father Evaristo de la Virgen del Carmen, *San Juan de la Cruz*, op. cit., p. 114. Cosme de Villiers says that he wrote : " *Tres tratados de la Oración mental ; De la mortificación ; Del hombre interior* qui sub alio nomine sunt editi, anno 1617 " (*Bibl. Carm.*, Vol. I, col. 713). The author of *La Reforma* states : " Imprimio un Libro de Teologia mistica, que yo he visto, y leido muchas veces aunque salió en nombre de un Sacerdote amigo suyo porque su humildad siempre huyo las alabanças " (*Ref.*, Bk. XV, Ch. XX, sec. 8).

69. Inocencio de S. Andres. Baeza P.A., fo. 134 ; I. O., fo. 112 ; Quir., 306–307 ; Cyp., 270–271.

70. *Ref.*, L. XVI, Ch. V, § 4 *sq.*

71. Martin de la Asunción. Baeza I. O., fo. 70. Alonso, L. I, Ch. XLIII ; Quir., 269 ; Cyp., 235.

72. Martin de San José. Baeza I. O., fo. 102 ; Alonso, L. I, Ch. XLIII.

73. *Peregrinación de Anastasio, op. cit.,* p. 211.

74. Alonso. Seg. P.A., fo. 48 ; Jer., 457.

75. *Prólogo.* Ger., I, 33.

76. Quir., 252 ; Cyp., 229.

77. " . . . Y a este t° le sucedió teniendo una gran tentación de si era predestinado o no que sin aver dho nada al dho padre llego à este t° y le dijo que piensa, si dios le tiene para el ynfierno no dude sino que a de yr alla y le reprehendio diciendo que todo era amor propio, que amase a dios sin ynterés y asi le quito la tentacion." Juan de S. Ana, Granada P.A., fo. 27.

78. *Ref.,* L. IV, Ch. XLVI, § 3.

79. Inocencio de S. Andres. B.N.M. MS. 12738, fo. 229.

80. Jeronimo de la Cruz. Jaen P.A. fo. 131 ; I. O., fo. 9 ; Quir., 304 ; Cyp., 268-269.

81. Martin de la Asuncion. Ubeda, I. O., fo. 69.

82. Jer., 421 and 441.

83. Inocencio de S. Andres. Baeza P.A., fo. 133 ; B.N.M. MS. 12738, fo. 225.

84. Inocencio de S. Andres. Baeza P.A., fo. 13 ; I. O., fo. 113 ; Alonso, L. II, Ch. VII.

85. Martin de la Asuncion. Ubeda I. O., fo. 68.

86. Jeronimo de la Cruz. Jaen P.A., fo. 131 ; Quir., 589-590 ; Cyp., 534.

87. Martin de la Asuncion. Ubeda I. O., fo. 69 ; Jer., 422-423.

88. Quir., 211 ; Cyp., 191.

89. Inocencio de S. Andres. Baeza P.A., fo. 135.

90. Martin de San José. Baeza I. O., fo. 101, and Juan of S. Eufemia. *Ibid.,* fo. 103.

91. Sebastian of St. Hilary. Jaen P.A., fo. 90 ; B.N.M. MS. 8568, fo. 207. Cf. Ch. XVIII.

92. *Vie de la vénérable Anne de Jésus,* by the Rev. Father Angelo Manrique, Vol. I, p. 171.

93. Granada P.A., vol. not numbered, fo. 14. Dep. of Jerome of the Cross. Jaen P.A., fo. 124 ; I. O., fo. 8 ; Quir., 320-321 ; Cyp., 283 ; Jer., 426 *sq.*

94. Granada P.A., fo. 14.

95. Quir., 599 ; Cyp., 543.

96. " Juan de Vera, sculptor," deposes to having done " some works of carving and painting *algunas obras de scultura e pintura,"* in the convent of Baeza. He adds : " *y assistía con este testigo el dicho padre muchos ratos."* We may interpret this to mean that he " helped " the saint and was not merely present. Baeza I. O., fo. 105.

97. Quir., 445 (Dep. of Jeronimo de la Cruz) and 599-600 ; Cyp., 400 and 543.

98. Quir., 322 ; Cyp., 285 ; Jer., 429.

99. *Noche,* Ch. I ; Ger., II, 7.

100. ". . . le haga comer pan con corteza." Ger., II, 38.

101. ". . . melius . . . dolet et sanatur cor humanum quam non dolendo fit inhumanum." St. Augustine. (*Serm.* XXXIII, de Verbis Apostol.)

102. Huysmans. *En route,* pp. 110–111.

103. " tenga fortaleça en el coraçón contra todas las cosas que le mobieren a lo que no es Dios y sea amiga de las pasiones por Cristo." Dep. of Magdalene of the Holy Ghost. B.N.M., P.V., Vol. XVI, MS. 12944^{132} fo. 4.

104. *Cautelas* que ha menester traer siempre delante de si el que quisiere ser verdadero religioso y llegar en breve a la perfección dirigidas a las Carmelitas Descalzas de Béas. Ger., III, 2, and Introduction, pp. x. to xiii. A nun, Anne of Jesus of the Convent at Beas, states that when the saint departed he left some *cantelas* against the enemies of the soul. Andres, 13482, B. 12.

105. *Histoire d'une âme,* Ch. XII.

106. St. Luke xiv. 26.

107. *Catena aurea :* in Lucae Evang. xiv. 5.

108. *Sum Theol.,* II–II, q. 26, art. 7 : Utrum magis debeamus diligere meliores quam nobis conjunctiores ?

109. ". . . Personae . . . Deo magis conjunctae diligantur majori amore objectivo : quae vero magis ipsi diligenti amentur strictiori amore intensivo. . . . Si autem petas quaenam ex his dilectionibus sit simpliciter et absolute loquendo major, objectiva an intensiva ? Respondetur intensivam esse absolute perfectiorem objectiva." Tract XIX. De Charitate, Disp. III, § 2, No. 10.

110. The following consoling remark was addressed to Teresa in 1558 when she was living in the Convent of the Incarnation. She was then forty-three. " Ya no quiero que tengas conversación con hombres, sino con ángeles." *Vida,* Ch. XXIV ; Silv., I, 188 ; C. P., I, 309.

111. Gen. xxii. 2.

112. *Noche.* Ger., II, 53.

113. Frances of the Mother of God. B.N.M. MS. 12738, fo. 1461. See Ch. XIV.

114. Eliseus of the Martyrs. Ger., III, 64–65.

115. *Cántico,* C. XXXI. Ger., II, 588. It is of interest to note that this stanza : *O ninfas de Judea,* and the following ones were composed at Baeza. ". . . *Lo demas* (after the thirtieth) *compuso el Santo estando despues por Rector del Colegio de Baeza.*" Dep. of Magdalene of the Holy Ghost. B.N.M., P.V., Vol. XVI, MS. 12944^{132}, fo. 2, already referred to in Ch. XIII.

116. *Cántico,* C. XXX. Ger., II, 584.

117. L. to Gracian, September 20th, 1576. Silv., VII, 290 ; Greg., I, 350 ; Engl., II, 49.

118. L. of November 7th, 1571, to Doña Luisa de la Cerda. Silv., I, 79 ; Greg., I, 92 ; Engl., I, 89.

119. ". . . the saint herself, in the Seventh Mansion, could sketch only a rather too simple scheme for a reader unacquainted with her spiritual state. For instance, she states that in this last Mansion which leads to beatitude, ecstasies, aridities and interior trials cease ; now, if we study the history of her life, we see that she was still subject, during this very period, to irresistible raptures and exterior and interior trials of the most crucifying nature in her whole career. . . ." *Les Ascensions du cœur de Sainte Thérèse*, R.P. Petitot (*Vie Spirituelle*, October, 1922, p. 71).

120. Teresa did not like Andalusians. Silv., VII, 204, 227, 282, 374 ; VIII, 388 ; Greg., I, 247, 272, 342, 458 ; II, 486 ; Engl., I, 233, 257 ; II, 42, 149 ; III, 311.

121. L. to Gracian, March 23rd and 24th, 1581. Silv., IX, 46–47 ; Greg., III, 136 ; Engl., IV, 154.

122. *Acto de elección de Priora y demás officios en Caravaca.* Ger., III, 122 *sq.* ; C.P., IV, 431 and 432.

123. Ger., III, 79. *Letter* I, p. 145.

124. *Cántico*, C. XXXIV. Dep. of Magdalene of the Holy Ghost, B.N.M. MS., P.V., Vol. XVI, 12944[132], fo. 2.

125. L. to Don Pedro de Castro y Nero, November 28th, 1581. Silv., IX, 127 ; Greg., III, 239 ; Engl., IV, 251.

126. L. to Don Jeronimo Reinoso, September 9th, 1581. Silv., IX, 89 ; Greg., III, 195 ; Engl., IV, 213.

127. L. November 8th, 1581. Silv., IX, III ; Greg., III, 218 ; Engl., IV, 233.

128. ". . . confiando se los enviará nuestra Madre." L. a Catalina de Jesus, July 6th, 1581. Ger., III, 79 (*Letter* I, p. 145). Testimony of Mother Mary of the Blessed Sacrament of Caravaca. Andres, 13482, D. 66.

129. Quir., 447 ; Cyp., 401, 2.

130. "Estando recién profeso con nuestro santo Padre en Veas (habian ido a un negocio), traia consigo una taleguilla de Cartas de la Santa, y era al tiempo queo hacia el *Monte*. Dijome : para qué ando yo cargado de ésto ? Y no será bueno quemarlas ? Yo, que no sabia lo que era, le dije : como pareciere a Vuestra Reverencia y dijo : pues traiga una luz; con que se hizo el sacrificio ; y yo lo hago siempre que me acuerdo de no haberle dicho que me las diera a mi." From a letter of Jeronimo de la Cruz to Jerome of St. Joseph. Jerome took the habit at Baeza in 1579. Andres 13482, B. 59 ; Jer., 462. Cf. dep. of Gabriel de Cristo, Bar., p. 51, note 1.

131. "En la Inform. de Veas del año de 18, Dixo la M. francisca de la Mᵉ de Dios que preguntandola un Dia el Sᵗᵒ en que trahia la oracion ella dixo que en mirar la hermosura de Dios, y gozarse el . . . hizo unas cinco canciones a este tiempo

sobre esto, que comienzan : Gozemonos amado." Andres, 13482 B. 10. In the deposition quoted by Baruzi (214, note 5) Frances only says : " Otra bez q bino me trajo las coplas de gozemonos amado." B.N.M. MS. 12738, fo. 1461, already quoted. Alonso, Bk. I, Ch. XXXVII.

132. Ger., III, 83. *Letter* II, 146.

133. Jeronimo de la Cruz. Jaen P.A., fo. 140 ; Jer., 461.

134. Jer., 379. *Vide supra*, note 131.

135. Dep. of Frances of the Mother of God. B.N.M. MS, 12738, fo. 1461.

136. *Cántico*, C. XXXV. Ger., II, 500.

137. Ger., II, 597.

138. Rom. xi. 33. Note on the margin of the MS. of Sanlúcar (Ed. Silv., Vol. II, p. 139).

CHAPTER XVI

1. L. to Gracian, November 29th, 1581. Silv., IX, 132 ; Greg., III, 244 ; Engl., IV, 256.

2. *Foundation of Granada.* Account of Anne of Jesus. C.P., IV, 231.

3. *Foundation of Burgos.* Anne of St. Bartholomew's account. C.P., IV, 503.

4. Cf. *supra*, Ch. VII.

5. L. to Gracian, November 29th, 1581. Silv., IX, 131 ; Greg., III, 244 ; Engl., IV, 256.

6. Cf. Ch. XI.

7. *Origins of the Convent of Granada.* An account given by the first nuns. C.P., IV, 543.

8. *Ibid.*

9. C.P., IV, 234.

10. *Ibid.*

11. Arch. C.R. Brussels.

12. Isabel de la Encarnacion. Jaen, P.A., fo. 164.

13. C.P., IV, 235 and 544.

14. C.P., IV, 236. Juana Evangelista. Arch. C.R. Brussels ; C.P., IV, 544.

15. C.P., IV, 236.

16. C.P., IV, 545.

17. C.P., 238.

18. *Ibid.*, 239.

19. " En el mes de Marzo siguiente los religiosos del convento de Granada le elegieron en Prior de aquel convento conq el santo dexando a Baeza. . . ." Alonso, I, II, Ch. III ; *Ref.*, L. III, Ch. IX, § 4.

20. Jeronimo de la Cruz. Jaen P.A., fo. 132.

21. *Ibid.*, fo. 136.

22. This palace was built between 1584 and 1587. Don Miguel Lafuente y Alcantara. *Historia de Granada*, comprendiendo las de sus cuatro provincias Almería, Jaén, Granada y Málaga (Granada, 1846), IV, 261.

23. Jeronimo de la Cruz. *Ibid.*, fo. 136.

24. Alonso. Seg. P.A., fo. 5.

25. " . . . no avia para comer entonzes sino tan solamte una comida de garbanzos y ortigas quizadas. . . ." Juan Sanchez Mirano. Granada P.A., fo. 12.

26. Juana de Pedraza. Granada P.A., fo. 16.

27. It was this Don Luis de Cordova who afterwards favoured the foundation of St. Roch at Cordova. Cf. Ch. XVIII.

28. Father Ruiz Incola. Granada P.A., fo. 21.

29. Luis de S. Angel. Alcaudete I. O., fo. 119 ; Baeza P.A., fo. 49.

30. *Descripción del Reino de Granada* bajo la dominación de los Naseritas, sacada de los autores árabes . . . por Don Francisco Javier Simonet (Madrid, 1860), p. 197.

31. *Guía de Granada*, by M. Gomez Moreno (Granada, 1892), p. 178.

32. Brüm and Hogenberg, Cologne, 1567.

33. *Ref.*, Bk. III, Ch. IV, sec. 7. The following information is taken from *Protócolo y registro de la Fundación hacienda y obligaciones de este convento real de los santos Mártyres ordenados de año de 1617 sq.* B.N.M., Arch. Hist. Nacion. Granada, Leg. 49. Carm. Descalzos. On page 215 we find a *Cronologia de los Prelados* que a tenido este convento real de los santos martyres sacada de los Archivos deste convento y de los de la religion que estan en poder de nro. P. Fray Francisco de S. Maria, Historiador General de nro. Orden y prior deste casa, por cuyo mandato se escribió. Año de 1640.

34. Fr. J. Simonet. *Memoria presentada a la Comisión de Monumentos Históricos y Artisticos de la provincia de Granada acerca del campo de los Mártires*, February 24th, 1868. *Ref.*, L. III, Ch. V, § 5 *sq.*

35. *Ref.*, L. IX, Ch. XXII, § 2.

36. *Ref.*, L. III, Ch. IX, § 1.

37. *Ibid.*, § 8. In the *Cronologio de los Prelados*, already referred to, we read that this work was done during his second priorship.

38. Luis de S. Angel. Baeza P.A., fo. 54.

39. Quir., 369 ; Cyp., 329 ; Jer., 495.

40. " . . . que hoy tiene." *Gazetilla Curiosa. Papel* XXVIII, Lunes, October 15th, 1764.

41. *Guia de Granada*, p. 178. *Ref.*, L. III, Ch. VIII *in fine.* P. J. de Echeverria, *Paseos par Granada y sus contornos* . . . 1786, Vol. II, Paseo, No. XII.

42. Vivian (London, 1838). *Vista del convento de los Mártyres antes de su destrucción.* Reproduced in *S. Giovanni della Croce,* Rome, 1926 (No. unico). This picture of the convent of *Los Mártires,* destroyed in 1848 (La Fuente, *Guía,* 1849) conforms to the plan published by R. Garcia Lopez in *Ilustración Española y Americana* (XXX, p. 103, August 15th, 1877). Only a few portions of the wall of the convent now remain and they form part of M. Meersmans' house.

43. *Subida,* III, Ch. XXXVIII. Ger. I, 385.

44. Alonso. Seg. P.A., fo. 55 ; Quir., 368 ; Cyp., 328 ; Jer., 588.

45. *Subida,* III, Ch. XXIII. Ger., I, 340.

46. *Gazetilla curiosa.*

47. *Ref.,* L. IX, Ch. IX, § 8.

48. *Cronología de los Prelados.*

49. Inocencio de S. Andres. Baeza I. O., fo. 113.

50. *Ref.,* L. III, Ch. IV, § 3.

51. *Ibid.,* Ch. V, § 5.

52. Andres, 13482, I, 7. *Ref.,* L. VII, Ch. III, § 2.

53. Théophile Gautier. *Voyage en Espagne.*

54. The Arabic text was first published by Lafuente y Alcantara, *Inscripciones árabes de Granada* (Madrid, 1859, p. 108).

55. Sourates, 47, v. 16 and 17 and 56 v. 12 to 23. *Le Coran,* trans. E. Montet, Paris, 1929, pp. 678 and 726.

56. " Nada, nada nada hasta dar un pellejo y otro por Cristo." Andres 13482, J. 7 ; Jer., 596.

57. Fr. J. Simonet. *Descripción del Reino de Granada . . .* quoted above. Cuadro cronológico de las cinco dinastias.

58. Cf. A. de Circourt, *Histoire des Mores Mudejares et des Morisques on des Arabes d'Espagne sous la domination des chrétiens* (Paris, Dentu, 1848), pp. 424 to 444. This is one of the chief sources employed by Menendez y Pelayo in his *Heterodoxos Españoles.* Pedro Longas, *Vida religiosa de los Moriscos* (Madrid, 1915, p. 34). D. Fl. Janer, *Condición social de los Moriscos de España* (Madrid, 1857), and Fr. Fernandez y Gonzales, *Estado social y politico de los mudejares de Castilla* (Madrid, 1866).

59. Circourt, *op. cit.,* II, 36.

60. *Id. Ibid.,* II, 75.

61. *Id. Ibid.,* II, 81.

62. Letter of the Mufti of Oran to the Musulmans of Andalusia, published by J. Cantineau. *Journal Asiatique,* 1927, pp. 1 to 17.

63. Circourt, *op. cit.,* II, 222.

64. Circourt, *op. cit.,* II, 231 *sq.*

65. *Id. Ibid.,* III, 136.

66. *Id. Ibid.,* III, 149.

67. Marmol y Carvajal. *Rebelión y Castigos de los Moriscos de Granada*, I, p. 495. See Circourt, III, 149.

68. St. Teresa mentions the fact, in her *Life*, that there was a Moorish slave in her father's house.

69. Don Miguel Lafuente-Alcantara. *Historia de Granada . . .*, IV, 224.

70. *Id. Ibid.*, II, 225. The Inquisition at Toledo was more successful ; they discovered one hundred and ninety Moriscos, between 1575 and 1610, of whom only eleven were burned. Lea, *The Moriscos of Spain*, London, 1901, p. 105.

71. Circourt, *op. cit.*, III, 152.

72. *Id. Ibid.*, III, 150.

73. Bull of September 6th, 1567. Grand Inquisitor's Instruction of January 30th, 1571. Bulls of August 6th, 1574, and February 28th, 1597. Circourt, III, 159.

74. Circourt, *op. cit.*, II, 39, gives 4,000. Longas, *op. cit.*, p. 37, mentions only 3,000.

75. Longas, *op. cit.*, p. 224, note 1, and p. 50.

76. Quoted by Longas, p. 51 *sq.* Cf. Cantineau, *Letter*, already referred to, p. 11.

77. Cf. *supra*, Ch. XII.

78. Circourt, *op. cit.*, III, 157.

79. *Ref.*, III, Ch. IV, § 5.

80. Fr. J. Simonet. *Descripción del reino de Granada*, p. 197. *Ref.*, L. III, Ch. V, § 3.

81. *Ref.*, L. IX, Ch. XXII, §§ 4 and 5.

82. Granada P.A., fo. 21.

83. C.P., IV, 546.

84. Isabel de la Encarnacion. Jaen P.A., fos. 162, 164.

85. Granada P.A., fo. 18.

86. C.P., IV, 241.

87. *Ibid.*, 243.

88. " She (Teresa) told us that we should be grateful to God for having more than one confessor . . . ; she knew that we would preserve this privilege, if we did not ourselves renounce it in order to please those of our own Order. . . . Our superiors are pleased that we sometimes go to confession to religious of other Orders." Dep. jur. of Anne of Jesus. Arch. C.R. Brussels.

89. *Foundation of Granada*, already referred to. C.P., 241.

90. Arch. Nat. Paris, Series M, cart. 216.

91. *Cántico*, C. XXXVI. Ger., II, 599.

92. *Id. Ibid.*, p. 600.

93. Bar., 735.

94. *Cántico, Prólogo.* Ger., II, 493.

95. Ger., II, 383.

96. C. P., IV, 545.

97. The Discalced Carmelites have devoted a special number of the *Analecta Ordinis Carm. Disc.* (Rome, October–December, 1926) to the doctorate of St. John of the Cross. In it will be found copies of a score of petitions to the Holy See, one of which is signed by four hundred and fifty-seven cardinals, archbishops and bishops. The substance of the apostolic letter of August 24th, 1926, in which His Holiness Pius XI responded to the desires of the Universal Church, will also be found there.

98. L. to Anne de Jesus, December, 1578. Silv., VIII, 283 ; Greg., II, 333 ; Engl., III, 180.

99. *Ref.*, L. IX, Ch. XXII, § 5.

100. Antonio Marin-Ocete. *El negro Juan Latino* (Granada, 1925), p. 35.

101. *Gazetilla curiosa.* Lunes 20 de agosto, 1764.

102. Luis de San Angel. Baeza P.A., fo. 50. "He was skilful in calming souls and in quieting scruples by his great gentleness." Agostina de San José, B.N.M., 8568, fo. 411.

103. Granada P.A., fo. 12.

104. Ubeda I. O., fo. 66.

105. Alonso. Seg. P.A., fo. 45. "Factima, que le pareçe desta carne. . . ."

106. Encycl. of February 28th, 1926. *Acta Ap. Sed.* of March 1st, 1926.

107. *Peregrinación, op. cit.* Dial., VI, p. 90 *sq.*

108. "The Islamic tradition, thanks, no doubt, to some Christian ascetics of Syria, affirmed that the moraqqa'ah (a garment of material formed of multi-coloured patches worn over the shoulders) was the mantle worn by Jesus during his public life ; whilst the hair-cloth (*moson'h*) had been that of John the Baptist, and the white frock (*soúf*) that of Mahomet." L. Massignon, *La Passion d'Al-Hosayn Ibn-Mansour-al-Hallaj, martyr mystique de l'Islam*, executed at Bagdad on March 26th, 922 (Paris, Geuthner, 1922), p. 50. The Carmelites discarded the striped mantle in favour of the white cape at the General Chapter of Montpellier in 1287. *Acta Cap. Gen.*, p. 7.

109. *Chronica*, by Guillaume de Sanvico, already referred to in Ch. VIII. [The "singing of the Salve regina" is an interpolation ; it is not in the oldest MSS. ; there were no witnesses. Editor.]

110. In Persian. In Arabic, Bagdad signifies "house of peace."

111. Cf. *The Settlement of the Order of Carmelites in Mesopotamia.* A chronicle of the Mission from 1623 to 1733, English and Latin text. Sir Hermann Gollancz's edition (Oxford, 1927).

CHAPTER XVII

1. Bibl. Nat. Paris MS. 3347, fo. 174.
2. Menendez y Pelayo. *Heterodoxos Españoles*, II, 636.
3. El Mancebo de Arevalo, *Tafçira* (MS. in Spanish written in Arabic letters). MS. 62 published by J. Ribera and M. Asin in *Manuscritos arabes y aljamiados de la Biblioteca de la Junta* (Madrid, 1912).
4. " Por dicho dexta Mora xe gobernaba Granada y toda xu comarca. . . ."
5. " . . . no habia max alto alchihed que explandir nuextro aladin en tierra de gribecax. . . ."
6. " Xiguio exta Mora mucho a Mohammed Algazel. . . . " *La mystique d'Al-Ḡazzālī*, by Miguel Asin-Palácios. *Mélanges de la Faculté Orientale* (University of Beyrouth), Vol. VII, p. 67. Cf. *Gazali*, by Baron Carra de Vaux (Alcan, 1912).
7. It would seem as if Carra de Vaux were mistaken when he states that not only did he experience ecstastic states, but that he had " revelations such as it was impossible for him to describe." The Syrian experience was not so satisfactory. Carra, p. 202.
8. Al Futúhāt, III, 104.
9. In the third century after the Hegira, there was an Arabic translation of the *Enneades* of Plotinus, published by a Christian of Emesus under the inaccurate title *The Theology of Aristotle*.
10. *Ihẏa*, IV, 136.
11. Matt. v. 38–40.
12. Massignon. *Essai sur les origines du Lexique technique de la mystique musulmane* (Paris, Geuthner, 1922), p. 49.
13. IV Reg., III, 15.
14. *Inst.*, II, 23.
15. *Ihya*, II, 207.
16. *Enneades*. Bréhier, Vol. IV, p. 53.
17. *Merveilles du Cœur*, quoted by Carra de Vaux, p. 205.
18. Rom. ix. 18.
19. " Christianity is hateful only on account of the dogma of the Trinity and because it denies the mission of Mahomet ; all its other dogmas are truth itself." Asin, *op. cit.*, p. 100. It has been pointed out to me that this passage from Quistas 60 should be translated : " The Christian is hateful . . . only or two words alone ; the first : God is the third of three," etc. It is a question here of a quotation from the Koran which distorts that dogma of the Trinity and not by any means an attempt to refute this doctrine on the part of Ḡazzālī. The Musulman theologians of his day defined it much less inexactly. There is no explicit attack by Ḡazzālī on any Christian dogma ; he seems to ignore them of set purpose in his mysticism, and that is the gravest feature in it.

20. Sebastian of St. Hilary. Jaen P.A., fo. 91. Isabel de la Encarnacion, *ibid.*, fo. 166.

21. " Avito roto y hecho pedaços. . . ." Baltazar de Jesu. Ubeda, I. O., fo. 66, when he was Vicar-Provincial, " when he went to inspect the linen-rooms, if he had a good habit on, he put it aside, and put on the most torn." Martin de la Asuncion. Ubeda, I. O., fo. 70.

22. Andres 13482, B. 20 ; Quir., 345 ; Cyp., 307.

23. " . . . Bastele a la besteçuela . . . que asi llamava su carne. . . ." Quir., 347 ; Cyp., 309.

24. Seb. de S. Hil. Jaen P.A., fo. 93.

25. Luis de S. Angel. Baeza P.A., fo. 50.

26. Isabel de la Encarnacion. Jaen P.A., fo. 166 ; *Ref.* L. III, Ch. IX, § 10.

27. Luis de S. Angel. Baeza P.A., fo. 50.

28. *Descripición del Reino de Granada* . . . already referred to above. Fr. J. Simonet quotes an Italian, Andrea Navagero, who was on a mission to Charles V.

29. Quir., 253 ; Cyp., 229.

30. *Descripción, op. cit.*, p. 200.

31. Agostin de la Concepcion. Baeza P.A., fo. 69.

32. *Cántico*, C. V. Ger. II, 513.

33. Baeza P.A., fo. 50.

34. *Ibid.*

35. *Cántico*, C. XIV. Ger., II, 541.

36. *Noche*, C. I. Ger., II, 1.

37. *Cántico*, C. VII. Ger., II, 519.

38. *Cántico*, C. XIV. Ger., II, 532.

39. *Cántico*, C. XXXV. Ger., II, 595.

40. Bar., 321.

41. *Cántico*, sub-title. Ger., II, 491.

42. This date is settled by the Sanlucar de Barrameda MS. of which Father Silverio de Santa Teresa has published a photo-type copy (Burgos, 1928). Already quoted.

43. Maria de la Cruz. Ubeda P.A., fo. 387.

44. *Cántico*, C. VIII. Ger., II, 521.

45. Jeronimo de la Cruz. Jaen P.A., fo. 130.

46. Luis de S. Angel. Baeza P.A., fo. 50.

47. Quir., 357 and 739. Cyp., 280, and III, 28.

48. Juan Evangelista. Malaga P.A., fo. 37.

49. Ana de la Encarnacion. Malaga P.A., fo. 692. Baltazar de Jesús. Ubeda P.A., fo. 280 ; Alonso. Seg. P.A., fo. 62.

50. B.N.M. MS. 8568, fo. 119. Bar., p. 148, note 4.

51. Juan Evangelista. Jaén I. O., fo. 7.

52. " Casi savia de memoria." *Ibid.*, fo. 5.

53. Alonso de la Madre de Dios. B.N.M. MS. 12738, fo. 571.

54. Alonso, L. II, Ch. III. Sebast. of St. Hil. Jaén P.A., fo. 90.

55. Juan Evangelista. Jaen I. O., fo. 7.

56. Seb. of St. Hil. Jaen P.A., fo. 91.

57. " . . . en lo que fue mas aventajado fue en theologia positiva porque mostrava tener ymprontu la bribia . . . y los esposiciones que dava sobre . . . lugares della . . . se vio no podia ser . . . sino luz del cielo." Jerónimo de la Cruz. Jaén I. O., fo. 10. Cf. Baruzi, *Bulletin Hispanique*, Vol. XXIV, No. 1.

58. St. Ignatius of Antioch, *Letter to the Philadelphians* VIII, 2.

59. *Cántico*, Ger., II, 501.

60. *Ibid.*, 550.

61. *Ibid.*, 551.

62. *Ibid. Id.*

63. *Ibid.*, 550.

64. *Cántico*, 493.

65. " . . . de ciencia experimental que pasava por el." Juan Evangelista. Jaén I. O., fo. 7.

66. *Cántico*. Ger., II, 494.

67. *Ibid.*, 502.

68. *Ibid.*, 501.

69. *Ibid.*, 523.

70. *Ibid.*, 517, 518.

71. *Ibid.*, 544, 579.

72. *Ibid.*, 528.

73. *Ibid.*, 530.

74. *Ibid.*, 531.

75. *Ibid.*, 535.

76. *Ibid.*, 542.

77. *Ibid.*, 544.

78. *Ibid.*, 545.

79. *Ibid.*, 561 (Canción XXI).

80. *Ibid.*, 571.

81. *Ibid.*, 574-575.

82. *Ibid.*, 602-608.

83. *Ibid.*, 577.

84. *Ibid.*, 578.

85. *Ibid.*, 595.

86. *Ibid.*, 607-608.

87. "La llama de amor viva escriuiola siendo vicario provincial tambien en esta casa a peticion de Doña Ana de Peñalosa y lo escrivio en quince dias. . . ." Juan Evangelista. Andrés, 13482, B. 25. As we shall see in the next chapter, Gracian nominated John of the Cross Vicar-Provincial of Andalusia by simple commission before setting out for Lisbon in December, 1584. Nevertheless, it was at the Chapter of Pastrana, in October, 1585, that John's appointment was

confirmed and he ceased to be Prior of Granada. He still
resided at Los Mártires.

88. *Llama. Prólogo.* Ger., II, 385.

89. *Ibid.,* 399. *Noche.* Ger., II, 81 *sq.*

90. *Llama,* II, 397. *Cántico.* Ger., II, 327.

91. *Llama.* Ger., II, 389–390.

92. Garrigou-Lagrange. *Perfection chrétienne et contemplation,*
I, 365 *sq.*

93. *Llama.* Ger., II, 496.

94. *Ibid.,* 480–481.

95. *Ibid.,* 412–413.

96. *Ibid.,* 414.

97. *Ibid.,* 419.

98. Cf. Chs. XIII and XV.

99. *Llama.* Ger., II, 439.

100. *Ibid.,* 439.

101. *Ibid.,* 468.

102. *Ibid.,* 471.

103. *Qor.,* XXIV, 35.

104. Al-Gazzālī. *Mishkat Al-Anwar. The niche for lights,*
translated with introduction by Gairdner (London, 1924).
Asiatic Society Monographs. The niche in the wall of the
mosque where the lamp is placed.

105. *Mishkat, op. cit.,* p. 92.

106. Cant., Can., VIII, 6.

107. *Ibid.,* II, 14.

108. *Llama.* Ger., II, 475 (Canción IV).

109. *Ibid.,* 476. There is a remarkable passage here :
" todas a una parezcan moverse, al modo que al movimiento de
la tierra se mueven todas las cosas naturales que hay en ella
como si no fuesen nada."

110. " Quítale de delante algunos de los muchos velos y
cortinas que ella tiene antepuestos." *Ibid.,* p. 478. " Allah,"
it is written in the *Hadith,* " has seventy thousand veils of light
and darkness, and if he should remove the curtain that conceals
them, then the splendour of his aspect would certainly consume
all those who should approach his sight." *Mishkat Al-Anwar,* p. 44.

111. *Llama.* Ger., II, 483.

112. *Ref.,* L. III, Ch. XVII, § 5.

113. *Sum. Theol.,* II-II, q. CLXXXI, art. 1.

114. Thirty-fifth question in the questionnaire at the Informa-
ture Process. (*Información de Medina del Campo,* 1614, fo. 5ᵛ.)

115. Twenty-first question in the questionnaire of the Apostolic
Process. (*Proces. apostol de Segovia,* S. 49, fo. 4.)

116. Nicholas of Cusa was influenced by his surroundings,
but he thought it well to compare Dionysius with Proclus and
to show the harmony between the two doctrines. E. Vansteen-

berghe, *Le Cardinal Nicolas de Cuse* (Paris, 1920), pp. 409 to 441. The same author's : Autour de la Docte Ignorance, *Une controverse sur la théologie mystique au quinzième siècle.* Beitraege, XIV, 2–4 (Munster, 1915).

117. J. Lebreton, *La nuit obscure d'après S. Jean de la Croix.* R.A.M., 1928, pp. 18–19. A criticism will be found in this essay of the alleged influence of Plotinus on St. John of the Cross which has been maintained by Baruzi (602 *seq.*).

118. J. Lebreton, *La Théorie de la connaissance religieuse chez Clément d'Alexandrie.* Recherches science Rel., XVIII, pp. 457, 488.

119. *Subida*, L. II, Ch. VIII. Ger., I, 132–133.

120. *Cántico*, C. XII. Ger., II, 531.

121. L. to Anne of Jesus, December, 1578. Silv., VIII, 283 ; Greg., II, 333 ; Engl., III, 180.

122. Sr. Asin Palacios. *El místico Abenarabi, II. Noticias autobiográficas de su " Risalat Al-Cods "* (Madrid, *Revista de Archivos*, 1926), p. 10. " (La secta) de los *Alumbrados* que desde principios del S. XVI comenzó a extenderse por Andalucía con caracteres más análogos en sus doctrinas y prácticas espirituales a estos *iluminados* del islam andaluz del S. XII, que no a los místicos alemanes con quienes ordinariamente se les compara y de los cuales se les cree discípulos." This view has been adopted by the judicious defender of the mystics of the Low Countries, Pierre Groult in his *Mystiques des Pays Bas et la littérature espagnole du seizième siècle* (Louvain, 1927), p. 276.

123. *Heterodoxos, op. cit.,* Vol. II, L. V, Ch. I.

124. Cf. *supra*, Ch. IX. St. John of the Cross could have read Tauler in the Latin translation by Surius (1548) and even the *Institutions* in Spanish, at the end of the treatises of Serafin de Fermo in the Coimbra edition of 1551 (P. Groult, *op. cit.,* p. 67).

125. Whilst bearing in mind Groult's reserves (*op. cit.,* p. 74, etc.), which his researches permit him to make, we may put forward the idea that John might have read Ruysbroeck in the Latin edition of Surius, published in 1552, and have been influenced by him through Harphius, who was certainly well known in Spain at the end of the sixteenth century. Herp was in fact translated into Latin in 1560. This Franciscan had copied almost the whole of the *Ornament of Spiritual Marriage* . . . Louis of Blois also reflects Ruysbroeck's influence, and both Charles V and Philip II used to read his *Spiritual Institution.* We may thus see by what channels the lofty mysticism of the solitary of Groenendael may have reached St. John of the Cross. Quiroga states clearly in his *Don que tuvo S. Juan de la Cruz para guiar las almas a Dios* (published as an appendix to the works of St. John by Gerardo, III, 505–570) that John had a special gift for guiding souls not only " por experiencia en la oración, mas

también por la frecuente lección de las letras Sagradas y *escritos de los Santos*, particularmente de San Dionisio." May not Ruysbrocck be placed amongst these saints, whom Quiroga mentions (p. 538) and whom he calls " *maestro muy experimentado* " ? May not Tauler also be added ? Quiroga, speaking of " los grandes maestros de sabiduría mística," says that " uno de estos maestros docto y de grande experiencia en estas materias de espíritu . . . es el Reverendo Padre Fray Juan Taulerio " (p. 523). He also mentions Hugh of St. Victor (pp. 533, 535, 565) who employs an image, dear to John, of fire which attacks green wood and transforms it into its own element of fire. Cf. Patr. Migne, CLXXV, 117.

126. General Introduction to the Works of Ruysbroeck. (We quote after the 1917–1920 edition, published by the Benedictines of St. Paul of Wisques, Vol. I, p. 17.)

127. *Ibid.*, 1, p. 95 *sq.*

128. *Ibid.*, Vol. I, p. 45 (Introduction to the *Mirror of Eternal Salvation*). " Whatever resemblance they may show, or however great may be their works, they cannot attain a perfect resemblance without the grace of God. Even then if, by a sort of emptiness and detachment from earthly things, by means of the brightness of their natural intelligence and the return of their powers to their own proper foundation, they should succeed in recognising the natural tendency of their soul towards its principle, there would be nothing else there but this law, common to every created object, of resting on its cause to find there its repose. If, again, they had reached this penetration of their own essence which causes one to lose oneself and to act no longer externally, or internally under the form of love or knowledge, it would be time lost, because they do not possess the resemblance. The Spirit of God, indeed, no more than His love, does not remain inactive either in grace or in glory ; hence those men do not raise themselves above themselves ; what they feel is the natural inclination that they have for their principle, who is God." *The Kingdom of God's Lovers. Ibid.*, Vol. II, p. 144. We can understand how the famous Discalced Carmelite, Thomas of Jesus (cf. R.P. Jean Marie de l'E. J. : *Le Vénérable Père Thomas de Jésus*, a series of articles in *Le Carmel* in 1925–1926) made a formal defence of the orthodoxy of the lofty theology of the solitary of Groenendael. " Vir Dei in suis operibus doctrinam non solum non docuit orthodoxae contrariam, sed potius adeo coelestem et divinam ut per illam divinae et arcanae unionis animae cum Deo et totius mysticae Theologiae profundi sensus innotescant. . . ." *Relatio fide digna de Sanctitate vitae et miraculis . . . Joannis Rusbrockii*, Antwerpiae, Ex officina Plantiniana. MDCXXIII (B. Nat. Paris, Canonis. Inv. I, 394, p. 19.)

129. *Œuvres de Ruysbroeck*, II, p. 16 (Introduction).

130. *Subida*, L. II, Ch. XXII. Ger., I, 229.

131. *Ornement des Noces spirituelles*, III, pp. 109, 139, 189, 190. *Le Livre de la plus Haute Vérité*, II, p. 220.

132. *L'Anneau ou la Pierre brillante*, III, p. 253, and *Les sept degrés de l'échelle d'amour spirituel*, I, p. 284.

133. "There their naked intelligence is penetrated by eternal brightness, as the air is penetrated by the sun's light. The will, stripped and elevated, undergoes the transformation and penetration of boundless love, as the iron is penetrated by fire. And the memory, liberated and elevated, feels itself seized and established in a total absence of images." *The Book of Highest Truth*, II, p. 219.

134. *Ornement*, III, pp. 108 and 158.

135. *Miroir du salut éternel*, I, p. 144. *Livre de la plus Haute Vérité*, II, p. 214. *Ornement*, III, pp. 154, 158, 159.

136. *Les sept degrés* . . . I, p. 235 *sq. Ornement*, III, p. 209 *sq.* "Ruysbroeck . . . closely resembles John of the Cross in his lofty aspirations after the mystical absolute." Bar., 324.

137. Cf. Groult, *op. cit.*, pp. 34 to 36.

138. Ed. cit., III, 138 *sq.*

139. Menendez y Pelayo. *Heterodoxos*, L. V, Ch. I, *op. cit.*, Vol. II, pp. 553–554.

140. Juan Evangelista. Jaen I. O., fo. 6. Ana de la Encarnacion. Malaga P.A., fo. 69. Maria de la Cruz. Ubeda, I. O., fo. 49 ; Alonso, L. III, Ch. VIII.

141. Maria de la Cruz. Ubeda P.A., fo. 387. "En gracia tengole por el mayor santo del cielo."

142. "The errors of those who call themselves Alumbrados coincide closely with the said Lutheran errors." The Vergara Trial, fo. 134. Archivo Hist. Nat. de Madrid, quoted by Baruzi in : *Un moment de la lutte contre le Protestantisme et l'Illuminisme en Espagne au seizième siècle.* Revue d'Histoire et de Philosophie religieuses publiée par la Faculté de Théologie protestante de l'Université de Strasbourg, November–December, 1927, p. 548.

143. *Cánt.* Ger., II, 494 and *Llama. Ibid.*, 384.

144. "Cerremos los libros . . . perezcan las universidades, mueran los estudios e démonos a la oración." Fermín Caballero. *Conquenses ilustres*, II. *Vida del Il. Melchior Cano* (Madrid, 1871), App. No. 58, p. 599 ; Baruzi, *op. cit.*, p. 552.

145. "Alumbramientos y cosas de bausanes." *Llama.* Ger., II, 451.

146. *Llama.* Ger., II, 444.

147. ". . . martillar y macear con las potencias como herrero." *Ibid.*, 451.

148. Phil. i. 23.

149. *Noche.* Ger., II, 9.

150. Bar., 256.

151. *Subida*, L. II, Ch. XVIII *sq.* Ger., I, 196 *sq.*
152. *Subida.* Ger., I, 212.
153. *Ibid.*, 207.
154. ". . . de que tenemos experiencia." *Noche.* Ger., II, 44.
155. *Ibid.*
156. *Ibid.*, 17.
157. *Subida.* Ger., I, 364.
158. See Ch. XI.
159. Alonso, L. II, Ch. XIV ; Quir., 680 ; Cyp., 619 ; *Ref.*, L. VI, Ch. XXVI, § 3.
160. Quir., 680 ; Cyp., 619 ; Jer., 511 ; *Ref.*, L. VI, Ch. XXVI, § 8.
161. Alonso, L. I, Ch. XXXIX ; Quir., 687 ; Cyp., 626.
162. Quir., 683 *sq.* ; Cyp., 622 *sq.* ; Jer., 511 *sq.* ; *Ref.*, L. VI, Ch. XXII, § 6.
163. Quir., 687 ; Cyp., 625 ; Jer., 513 ; *Ref.*, L. VI, Ch. XXII, § 7.
164. Isabel de la Encarnacion. Jaen P.A., fo. 165.
165. Alonso, L. II, Ch. IX ; Quir., 687 ; Cyp., 626.
166. Alonso. Seg. P.A., fo. 53 ; Quir., 685 ; Cyp., 624 ; Jer., 515.
167. Quir., 686 ; Cyp., 625 ; Jer., 514 ; *Ref.*, L. VI, Ch. XXII, § 7.
168. Luis de S. Angel. Baeza P.A., fo. 52.
169. María de S. Francisco. Med. I. O., fo. 20.
170. *Peregrinación, op. cit.*, p. 213.
171. See Ch. XI.
172. Maria de la Cruz. Ubeda I. O., fo. 50.
173. Agostina de San José. B.N.M. MS. 8568, fo. 411.
174. Jeronimo de la Cruz. Jaen I. O., fo. 9.
175. Miguel M. de Pareja. *San Juan de la Cruz en Granada.* "La Alhambra," October 30th, 1904.
176. Quir., 434 ; Cyp., 389 ; Jer., 487.
177. *Ref.*, L. XXI, Ch. VII, § 1.
178. *Ibid.*, § 9.
179. *Ibid.*, Ch. VIII, § 1.
180. Dositheus of Saint-Alexis. *Vie de Saint Jean de la Croix*, ed. 1727, II, 433.
181. Quir., 718 ; Cyp., III, p. 7 ; Jer., 533.
182. Dositheus of Saint-Alexis, *op. cit., loc. cit.*
183. A list of his works will be found in *Bibl. Carm.*, Vol. I, col. 647.
184. *Peregrinación, op. cit.*, p. 283.
185. *Ibid.*, p. 169.
186. *Ibid.*, p. 280.
187. *Diálogos sobre la muerte de N. M. Teresa de Jesús* (Burgos, 1913), p. 49.

188. Brussels, 1609 ; Lyons, 1618, in French.

189. La España Editorial. Madrid, p. 81.

190. " Lastly, this infused spirit, a gift of the Lord, an excellent and perfect grace (James i. 17), which comes down from on high from the Father of lights, is of two sorts : one, ordinary, and obtained by many who practise mental prayer ; the other, rare, extraordinary, miraculous, and obtained by very few.   By the ordinary is meant the gifts of the Holy Spirit ; indeed, whoever perseveres in holy prayer with a pure mind, an inner light and fire of divine love, God gives very usually (inspirations of) the gifts of wisdom and counsel ; we see, besides, many souls, enriched with those heavenly graces and replenished with those abundant, spiritual riches." *Dilucidario del verdadero espíritu en que se declara la doctrina de la Santa Madre Teresa* (Madrid, 1604). The Carmelite nuns of Paris, following Don Vicente de la Fuente, severely judge Gracian's intentions, who " in his simplicity believed himself capable of retouching the saint's writings. . . . Furthermore, the *Dilucidario*, it must be recognised, throws no light whatever on the luminous writings of the incomparable mistress of mystical science." C.P., I, p. xlii, note 4.

191. See Ch. XVIII.

192. *Peregrinación*, p. 34.

193. See Ch. XVIII.

194. *Peregrinación*, p. 41.

195. Phil. iii. 8.

196. Garrigou-Lagrange. *Le Sens commun* (Beauchesne, 1919), p. 166.

197. L. to Gracian, October, 1575. Silv., VII, 195 ; Greg., I, 243 ; Engl., I, 230.

198. L. to Gracian, February, 1580. Silv., VIII, 415 ; Greg., II, 519 ; Engl., IV, 13.

199. L. to Gracian, September, 1578. Silv., VIII, 253 ; Greg., II, 306 ; Engl., III, 148.

200. L. to Gracian, March 23rd–24th, 1581. Silv., IX, 46 ; Greg., III, 136 ; Engl., IV, 154.

201. L. to Gracian, August 19th, 1578. Silv., VIII, 247 ; Greg., II, 299 ; Engl., III, 141.

202. L. to Gracian, September, 1578. Silv., VIII, 253 ; Greg., II, 306 ; Engl., III, 148.

203. *Peregrinación*, p. 193 *sq.*

204. *Ref.*, L. XXI, Ch. VIII, § 4 *sq.*

205. Maria de la Cruz. Ubeda I. O., fo. 50.

206. Isabel de la Encarnacion. Jaen P.A., fo. 164.

207. " . . . acordar este testigo . . . que el dho siervo de Dios fray Juan de la Cruz una o dos vezes en el dho collegio de Baeza andar por los claustros del con una compostura de un Angel dando con los artejos de las manos en las paredes . . .

aquel pasear y dar aquellos golpes era para divertirse un poco de la grandeza de los fervores ynteriores de su alma. . . ." José de la Madre de Dios. Granada P.A., fo. 13.

208. Andres states that he saw the original of this letter at Duruelo and that he had copied it himself authentically (*sic*) (13482, I, 60). The tenor of the letter is confirmed by a licence to proceed given by John of the Cross on March 2nd, 1587. According to Andres (13483, R, 440) the original of this authorisation was "in the possession of the religious of Caravaca and it was extracted from a Protocolo cod. 28, fo. 172."

CHAPTER XVIII

1. *Ref.*, L. II, Ch. XXVII, § 9 ; L. IV, Ch. XXIX, § 3.
2. *Peregrinación, op. cit.*, pp. 71 and 203.
3. *Ibid.*, p. 202.
4. L. to Mary of St. Joseph, April 9th, 1577. Silv., VIII, 75 ; Greg., II, 92 ; Engl., II, 270.
5. To the same, June 24th, 1579. Silv., VIII, 333 ; Greg., II, 408 ; Engl., III, 244.
6. L. to Gracian, May 22nd, 1578. Silv., VIII, 216 ; Greg., II, 253 ; Engl., III, 99.
7. *Fund.*, Ch. XXX. Silv., V, 287 ; C.P., IV, 160 *sq.* Maria de S. José. *Ramillete de Mirra* (Burgos, 1913), p. 147. C.P., IV, 438 ; *Ref.*, L. IV, Ch. XXIX, § 7.
8. *Ref.*, L. VIII, Ch. LXXVII, § 5.
9. L. to Gracian, September 1st, 1582. Silv., IX, 227 ; Greg., III, 357 ; Engl., IV, 358 ; *Ref.*, L. V, Ch. XXVII, § 6 ; Quir., 620 ; Cyp., 561.
10. L. to Gracian, March 23rd–24th, 1581. Silv., IX, 45 ; Greg., III, 137 ; Engl., IV, 154.
11. To the same, July 7th, 1579. Silv., VIII, 337 ; Greg., II, 413 ; Engl., III, 249.
12. To the same, December, 1581. Silv., IX, 140 ; Greg., III, 255 ; Engl., IV, 265.
13. L. to Doria, March, 1582. Silv., IX, 166 ; Greg., III, 301 ; Engl., IV, 310.
14. L. to Gracian, September 1st, 1582. Silv., III, 225 ; Greg., III, 356 ; Engl., IV, 359 follg.
15. *Ref.*, L. V, Ch. XXVII, §§ 4 and 5.
16. L. of September 5th, 1581. Silv., IX, 88 ; Greg., III, 194 ; Engl., IV, 212.
17. Arch. of Discalced Carmelites, Rome 221, J. 2 MS. leaves.
18. L. to Mary of St. Joseph, July 14th, 1582. Silv., IX, 207 ; Greg., III, 334 ; Engl., IV, 339. Arch. of Calced Carm.,

Rome. We do not agree with the *Acta Cap. Gen.*, p. 562, note, where it is said that the saint is referred to here. At this time he was not in Seville but at Calvario, and his signature would not appear as one of the last of about twenty. Moreover, when the document is examined, it can be seen that the signature is quite different from those of the saint that may be found elsewhere.

19. *Ref.*, L. VI, Ch. XVIII, § 8.

20. *Ref.*, L. VIII, Ch. LXXVII, § 7.

21. "... Ordenamos que nuestros frayles caminen a pie ... ni el Prior ni el Provincial pueda dispensar sino es con enfermedad o necessidad urgente ... el caminar sea en algun asnillo ... pero si fuere camino largo y urgente necessidad, puedan yr en mulos, con albarda y sin silla, y ya que lleven freno, no sean las guarniciones de cuero, sino de cañamo. Y esto entendemos ansi de los Priores como Provinciales y Visitadores." *Constitutions of Alcalá*, L. I, Ch. IX, No. 14 ; Silv., VI, 475.

22. *Ref.*, L. VI, Ch. XVIII, §§ 1 and 2.

23. *Ibid.*, §§ 8 and 9.

24. *Ibid.*, §§ 10 and 11.

25. Belchior de S. Anna, C.D. *Chrónica de Carmelitas Descalços Particular do Reyno de Portugal e Provincia de San Felippe.* Liboa, Henrique Valente de Oliviera, 1657, Vol. I, L. I, Ch. XXII, p. 112 *sq.*

26. "Pero nuestro Venerable Padre Fray Juan de la Cruz siguiendo el sentimiento medio entre estos dos estremos dezia, que no tenia por gusto de Dios q esta reformaciô de la orden de su Madre se quedase en solos los terminos de España, sino que se estendiese por todas las provicias de la Iglesia, que fuesen acomodadas para guardar su instituto. Pero que esta extension se hiziese como en tiempo de los Apostoles quâdo los monges nuestros mayores seguian la predicacion del Evangelio por todas las provincias Orientales, y luego se retiravan a los desiertos adonde asentavan la vida monastica y retirada, para solicitar desde alli en la contemplación divina los auxilios de Dios para los que predicavan a los infieles." Quir., 714 ; Cyp., III, 4.

27. Encyclical already referred to in Ch. XVI.

28. "Como aquella region de Guinea no era acomodada para esto y el intento desta mision no se ordenava a este fin, sino solamente a instruyr aquellos barbaros en las cosas de la fe tocava aora esto mas a otras religiones que a la nuestra, pues no avia venido aun el tiempo en que acompañando a nuestro Padre Elias aviamos de hazer este oficio en los tiempos postreros." Quir., 715 ; Cyp., III, 4.

29. "Ex his inferendum nostro Carmelitarum instituto quod in contemplativae potissimum vitam dirigitur, et in actionem

prout ex contemplatione derivatur, illas congruere missiones in quibus contemplativae vitae exercitia illaesa servantur ; quare vitandae sunt missiones illae vagae, et quae oppidatim sine certis sedibus excurrunt maxime si id fiat per diuturnum tempus. Nam brevi aliquo temporis spatio oppidatim missionum studio vacare, ac postea domum, sive ad Conventum redire ad reficienda retia, spiritumque renovandum nullatenus sunt damnandae : cum in Europa tempore quadragesimae, pro habendis ad populum concionibus, aut aestatis, pro re temporali a mendicantibus (allusion to collection of alms) quantumvis reformatis idem fieri soleat.

" Deinde etiam existimo illas missiones in quibus praecipuae nostrae regulae capita aut regularis observantia servari nequeunt statui nostro non omnino expedire : quare nullatenus sunt propria electione a praelatis assumendae nisi vel extrema aut gravi urgente necessitate aut summo Pontifice mandante, qui scienter praecipiens justissime dispensat ut minora bona propter majora omittantur, et tunc sine haesitatione parendum erit. Quare illae missiones consentanae nobis censentur, quae ad eas infidelium regiones instituuntur, ubi sine detrimento principalium austeritatis nostrae capitum coenobia condantur, ubi exercitia observantiae frequentari possint, quantum fert tempus et loci occasio et quod reliquum est proximorum saluti erogatur." Thomas de Jesus. *Expositio in Regulum Carmelit.* Prol. Dub., V, § 7 (Ed., Cologne, 1684), I, 472.

John of Jesus and Mary teaches that missioners should practise the evangelical counsels before teaching them : " . . . ea tamen consilia, quoe ad proprium Institutum pertinent, potissimum colere studeant. Sic enim ad infidelium salutem destinantur ut non sine certa sede vagari, sed ubi potuerint. Instituti nostri coenobia, de superiorum venia, condere vitantur ; ut quaedam velut Christianae Religionis arces construant, ubi vires quandoque resumant, ut alacrius ad praelia progrediantur." Joannes a Jesu-Maria. *Instructio Missionum,* Ch. IX. Opera omnia, (Florentiae, 1774), Vol. III, p. 284.

30. *Peregrinación,* p. 51.

31. Champagnot. *Vie de M. de Brétigny,* L. I, Ch. V.

32. " Siguieron observando la vida regular de los conventos de España y formaron bien pronto la floreciente Provincia de S. Alberto de Mejico. . . ." Florencio del Niño Jesus. *La Orden de Santa Teresa, la Fundación de la Propaganda Fide y las Misiones Carmelitanas* (Madrid, 1923), p. 11.

33. Ger., III, 63 and 64, and Alonso, L. II, Ch. VI.

34. Quir., 714 ; Cyp., III, 4.

35. Eliseus of the Martyrs. Ger., III, 60 ; Alonso, L. I, Ch. XLIII.

36. *Id. Ibid.*

37. Quir., 718 ; Cyp., III, 5.

38. *Ibid.*

39. Quir., 717 ; Cyp., III, 6.

40. Luis de S. Angel. Baeza P.A., fo. 51.

41. *Ref.*, L. V, Ch. XVIII, § 8.

42. *Foundation of Granada.* Mother Anne's account, already quoted, C.P., IV, 243.

43. Letter of Anne of Jesus to Don Christopher de Lobera, Brussels, February 25th, 1621. Arch. C.R., Brussels.

44. *Origin of the Granada Convent.* Account of the first nuns, already quoted. C.P., IV, 547.

45. "Dezia missa con grande espiritu y reberenzia no larga ni breve, sino con una medida prudentisima y debota. . . ." Maria de la Cruz. Ubeda P.A., fo. 391.

46. Maria de la Cruz. *Ibid.*, fo. 390.

47. Alonso. Seg. P.A., fo. 49.

48. Quir., 248 ; Cyp., 225.

49. *Llama.* Ger., II, 394.

50. *Ibid.*, 396.

51. Eliseus of the Martyrs. Ger., III, 59.

52. "Padre nro deme vuesa reberenzia licenzia para vever. El respondia beba con deseo de vever a dios." Maria de la Cruz. Ubeda P.A., 390 ; Alonso, L. II, Ch. VI.

53. Luis de S. Angel. Alcaudete I. O., fo. 119 ; Alonso, Seg. P.A., fo. 61. Eliseus of the Martyrs. Ger., III, 59.

54. Convent tradition.

55. *Camino*, Ch. II.   Silv., III, 16 ; C.P., V. 43 ; Quir., 670 ; Cyp., 610.

56. Quir., 670 ; Cyp., 610.

57. Arch. C.R., Brussels.

58. *Ref.*, L. VI, Ch. XLIV.

59. *Ibid.*, Ch. XLV, §§ 2 and 3.

60. L. to Beatrice of the Conception, September 13th, 1625. Arch. C.R., Brussels. Francisca de la Madre de Dios had just come from Beas.

61. *Vie de la Vénérable Anne de Jesus*, Lyons, 1870, Vol. I, p. 287.

62. "Todos los padres del capitulo. . . ." Juan Evangelista. Jaen I. O., fo. 5.

63. Luis de San Angel. Alcaudete I. O., fo. 118. Cf. Mortier, *Histoire des Maîtres Généraux de l'Ordre des Frères Prêcheurs*, Vol. V, p. 635 *sq.* (Paris, 1911).

64. Quir., 287 ; Cyp., 252.

65. Juan Evangelista, fo. 5.

66. *Ref.*, L. VI, Ch. XLI, § 5.

67. Juan Evangelista. Quir., 288 ; Cyp., 253.

68. *Peregr. de Anastasio*, pp. 52–53.

69. Seg. P. A., fo. 51.

70. " Oyo decir a Religiosos fidedignos que se hallaron en el Capitulo Provincial que se hiço en Lisboa año de quin ochenta y seis que tratando el padre Gracián (q era provincial entonces de toda la Congr^{on} de los descalços carmelitas) con el siervo de Dios fray Ju^o de la Cruz que queria hacer provincial y succcssor suyo al padre fray Nicolas de Jhs. Maria, alias oria, que a la saçon estaba en Genova fundando un convento, le respondió el dicho siervo de Dios fray Juan de la Cruz al dicho Padre Gracián q no lo hiciese porque si el dicho P^e fray Nicolas de Jhs. M. salia por provincial avia de quitar el avito al dicho Padre Gracián, y assi le sucedió q no aviendo creydo el dho Padre Gracián al dicho siervo de Dios lo que le dijo y aconsejaba, a poco tiempo el dicho fray Nicolas de Jhs. Mⁿ quito el avito al dicho padre Gracián con gran sentimiento de los religiosos de la orden. . . ." Luis de S. Angel. Baeza P.A., fo. 56.

It is strange when one comes across another account by Luis de San Angel, made at Alcaudete ten years before this one. In this case it is just a simple idea that John conveyed to Gracian : " Your Reverence is electing a provincial who will take away your habit " (I. O., fo. 119). This contrast is certainly not without importance. A witness forgets in the course of time. Here, he remembers. The same thing was to happen to Juan Evangelista of Segovia, and precisely concerning another precious trait in the Gracian affair. It seems clear that the witnesses were still afraid, in 1618, of publishing their recollections.

Gracian's elegant explanation of this election at Lisbon may be read with interest in his *Peregrinación de Anastasio*. " At this chapter Father Nicolas de Oria, a man of great holiness and prudence, was elected provincial, in his absence : I myself wished to have some little rest from the fatigue of government, but I could not, because shortly afterwards (October 17th, 1585) I was sent as Vicar-Provincial to Portugal " (pp. 50–51).

71. *Ref.*, L. VI, Ch. XVI, § 3.

72. *Ref.*, L. XI, Ch. XXIII, §§ 1, 2, 3.

73. " . . . y por esta entereza solia dezirle el Padre Fray Mariano de San Benito con la gracia con que desia otras cosas a su modo Italiano ; Padre Fray Joan esta tu calavaça quando se a de madurar ? Llamando calavaça a la caveça calva del venerable Padre. Y respondiole el santo no a la gracia sino a lo que significava en ella diziendo ; madurara quando Dios la madurare y no antes, aunque esta verde hasta la muerte." Quir., 401 ; Cyp., 358.

74. *Ref.*, L. VI, Ch. XVI, §§ 4, 5, 6.

75. *Ibid.*, Ch. XVIII, §§ 15 *sq.*

76. L. to Gracian. Silv., IX, 225 ; Greg., III, 358 ; Engl., IV, 359.

77. *Ref.*, L. VI, Ch. XLVI, § 5.

78. *Peregrinación de Anastasio*, p. 41. *Ref.*, *ibid.*, § 6.
79. L. to Don Teutonio de Braganza, January 16th, 1578. Silv., VIII, 150 ; Greg, II, 176 ; Engl., III, 30.
80. See Ch. XVII.
81. Maria de la Cruz. Ubeda I. O., fo. 50.
82. *Ref.*, L. VII, Ch. I.
83. *Ibid.*, § 5.
84. Silv., VII, 243, 279, 295, 330, 363 and 381 ; Greg., I, 291, 337, 358, 381, 447 and 469 ; Engl., I, 279 ; II, 38, 46 [?], 77, 138 and 165.
85. L. to Maria de San José, October 31st, 1576. Silv., VII, 336 ; Greg., I, 409 ; Engl., II, 104.
86. Silv., IX, 60 ; Greg., III, 154 ; Engl., IV, 171.
87. L. to Maria de San José, June 15th, 1576. Silv., VII, 245 ; Greg., I, 293 ; Engl., I, 279.
88. L. to Maria de San José, November 8th, 1581. Silv., IX, 113 *sq.* ; Greg., III, 222 *sq.* ; Engl., IV, 238.
89. *Ref.*, L. VII, Ch. I, § 7.
90. *Ibid.*
91. Luis de San Jeronimo. Baeza P.A., fo. 63.
92. An autograph account by Maria de la Cruz, December 3rd, 1634. Arch. C.R., Brussels.
93. Maria de la Cruz. Ubeda P.A., fo. 390.
94. See *supra*, Ch. XV.
95. *Ref.*, L. VII, Ch. I, § 8.
96. Matt. xviii. 3.
97. See the *Montecillo*.
98. *Camino*, Ch. I. Silv., III, 10 ; C.P., V, 34.
99. Maria de San José. *Ramillete de Mirra*, p. 152.
100. " Crea que no sufre nuestra Regla personas pesadas, que ella lo es harto." L. to Gracian, November 19th, 1576. Silv., VII, 358 ; Greg., I, 441 ; Engl., II, 133.
101. Autograph MS. (in the archives of the Carmelite Convent of the Rosary at Antwerp).
102. L. to Maria Bautista, November 2nd, 1576. Silv., VII, 338 ; Greg., I, 410 ; Engl., II, 106.
103. L. to Gracian, October, 1575. Silv., VII, 195 ; Greg., I, 243 ; Engl., I, 230.
104. L. to Gracian, December 7th, 1576. Silv., VII, 385 ; Greg., I, 474 ; Engl., II, 163.
105. *Ref.*, L. VIII, Ch. LXXIX, § 2.
106. L. to Gracian, December, 1581. Silv., IX, 140 ; Greg., III, 255 ; Engl., IV, 265.
107. *Fund.*, Ch. XXX. Silv., V, 187 ; C.P., IV, 160.
108. Alonso. Seg. P.A., fo. 55.
109. Quir., 388 ; Cyp., 346.
110. *Censura.* Ger., III, 110 . Engl. ed. 1912, Vol. IV, 181.

111. " . . . un granito de oro ansi chiquito como le veyan."
Luis de S. Angel. Baeza P.A., fo. 53.

112. *Bibl. Carm.*, II, col. 497.

113. Jeronimo de la Cruz. Jacn P.A., fo. 137.

114. Sebastian of St. Hilary. Jaen P.A., fo. 93.

115. Gabriel de la Madre de Dios. Granada P.A., fo. 14.

116. Arch. of the Carmelite Nuns at Granada.

117. " Este testigo le vio muchas beces yr por tiempo de quaresma desde la penuela a la billa de linares . . . a predicar y solia acavado de predicar bolverse a la penuela sin comer . . . " Martin de la Asuncion. Ubeda I. O., fo. 70. On March 29th, 1586, John of the Cross signed at Granada a permission for a Carmelite nun at Seville to make her profession. Andres, 13483 R, 440 ; Ger., III, 124.

118. We have visited some that still exist. Cf. *Memorias que se conservan de algunos ermitaños que han existido en la sierra de Córdoba desde los tiempos más remotos hasta nuestros dias e Historia de la actual congregación de Nuestra Señora de Belén*, por Don Manuel Gutierrez de los Rios (Cordova, 1911).

119. *Fund.*, Ch. XVII. Silv., V, 136 ; C.P., III, 227.

120. Don Luis Fernandez de Córdoba, Obispo de Málaga. Granada P.A., fo. 27. The witness was then dean of the cathedral church. Cf., *supra*, Ch. XVI. On May 22nd, 1586, John of the Cross granted dimissorial letters, at Cordova, for two friars, natives of Consuegra. Andrés 13483 R, 440.

121. L. to Ana de San Alberto. June, 1586. Ger., III, 80. Letter VII, p. 155.

122. *Ibid.*

123. Nevertheless, there is a letter extant in the archives of the Calced Carmelites in Rome from the Council to Caffardo, dated at Madrid, August xiiij, 1586, signed by Doria, Mariano, Gregory Nazianzen, John Baptist (of Ronda) and John of the Cross. We have a photograph of this document ; the : *fr. Jo*[es] *a Cruce diff*[or] seems to be in John's handwriting, though the script looks as if he were rather feverish. It will be easily seen that Doria had strong reasons for insisting that John, who was ill in Toledo, should go to Madrid to sign this document. It was a matter of obtaining the General's permission to have a special procurator in Rome to look after the " affairs of the Discalced." These " affairs " were not the Missions, as the petition suggests, since Doria took no interest in these. What John of Jesus Roca, the bearer of the letter, was really to see to was the transformation of the province into a separate congregation and also, perhaps, the establishment of the Consulta. What was St. John's attitude ? All that can be said is that, even if he were opposed to Doria's scheme, he was bound to sign a decision arrived at by the majority.

124. " En el tercero (punto) que era dexar el Breviario antiguo Carmelitano i recibir el Romano, se dividieron algo : el Provincial, i el padre Fray Gregorio Nazianzeno, que siendo Clerigos seglares se avian criado con el Romano ; fueron de su parte. Los que siempre avian rezado el Carmelitano, lo defendian. I alfin vencio la autoridad de los primeros. . . . ." *Ref.*, L. VII, C. XLVI, § 3.

125. *Ibid.*, Ch. II, § 5.

126. Maria de la Encarnacion. June 30th, 1633. Arch. C.R., Brussels. *Ref.*, L. VII, Ch. XLVII.

127. Sebast. of S. Hil. Jaen P.A., fo. 91.

128. *Ref.*, L. VII, Ch. III, § 1.

129. Jeronimo de la Cruz. Jaen P.A., fo. 137. We quote verses 9 to 11.

130. Martin de la Asuncion. Ubeda I. O., fo. 70.

131. *Ibid.*, fo. 70.

132. *Ibid.*, fo. 70.

133. " Bastele a la besteçuela (que asi llamava a su carne) el regalo de yr a cavallo." Quir., 347 ; Cyp., 309.

134. Martin. *Ibid.*, fo. 68.

135. Juan Evangelista. Jaen I. O., fo. 5.

136. Martin. *Ibid.*, fo. 69.

137. Cf. the picturesque accounts of the journeys in the *Foundations*. C.P., III and IV, Documents 6, 9, 13, 17, 21, 22, 26, 27, 31, 32.

138. *Ref.*, L. VII, Ch. III, § 3.

139. Martin. *Ibid.*, fo. 70.

140. Maria de la Cruz. Ubeda I. O., fo. 50.

141. Martin. *Ibid.*, fo. 70.

142. Jeronimo de la Cruz. Jaen P.A., fo. 130.

143. Luis de San Angel. Baeza P.A., fo. 50.

144. Alonso. Seg. P.A., fo. 51.

145. Jeronimo de la Cruz. *Ibid.*, fo. 130.

146. *Ibid.*, 130.

147. Jorge de San José. Jaen I. O., fo. 7.

148. Quir., 353 ; Cyp., 314 ; B.N.M. MS. 12738, fo. 885 ; Bar., 221.

149. Martin. Ubeda I. O., fo. 70.

150. Sebast. of S. Hil. Jaen P.A., fo. 92 ; Jeronimo de la Cruz, *Ibid.*, fo. 136.

151. Alonso. Seg. P.A., fo. 51.

152. Martin. *Ibid.*, fo. 70.

153. Martin. *Ibid.*, fo. 69.

154. *Vida*, Cap. I. Silv., I, 6 ; C.P., I, 46.

155. Martin. *Ibid.*, fo. 69. Alonso, L. II, Ch. XIV. Cf., *supra*, Ch. XV.

56. *Ibid.*, fo. 61.

157. L. to Ana de San Alberto. Ger., III, 81. *Letter* V, p. 153.

158. Alonso, L. II, Ch. XVI ; *Ref.*, L. VII, Ch. L, § 10.

159. Jeronimo de la Cruz. Jaen P.A., fos. 135 and 137.

160. Alonso. Seg. P.A., fo. 50.

161. Maria de la Cruz. Ubeda I. O., fo. 50 ; Alonso, Seg. P.A., fo. 54.

162. Alonso. Seg. P.A., fo. 50.

163. Jorge de San José. Jaen I. O., fo. 8.

164. L. to Philip II, December 4th, 1577 (Silv., VIII, 132 ; Greg., II, 150 ; Engl., III, 4). " His Majesty will remember that after Father John's death. . . . . . . y en particular a oydo decir esta tº que el rey felipe segundo con la noticia que tenia de la santidad del dho siervo de Dios aviendo savido que un religioso de la orden llamado frai Juan Evangelista segun le parece a esta tº llevava un dedo del dicho siervo de Dios a la corte y aviendole visto y tenido en su mano Su Mgᵈ paresiendole ser reliquia de mucha estimacion se quedo con ella sin quererse la bolver al dicho religioso. . . ." M. Ana de la Encarnacion. Malaga P.A., fo. 70. " . . . tanta quanta (santidad) una pura criatura podia tener en esta vida. . . ." Andres, 13482, D. 47.

165. *Ref.*, L. VII, Ch. II, § 2.

166. Eliseus of the Martyrs (G. III, 66).

167. Martin. Ubeda I. O., fo. 69.

168. Eliseus of the Martyrs. *Ibid.*

169. Martin. *Ibid.*

170. Maria de la Madre de Dios. Baeza I. O., fo. 105.

171. " Alto de aqui a vida eterna." Maria de la Madre de Dios. Baeza I. O., fo. 106. M. Sanchez Mirano. Granada P.A., fo. 12. Juana de Pedraza. Granada P.A., fo. 11. Luis de San Angel. Baeza P.A., fo. 47. Isabel de la Encarnacion. Jaen I. O., fo. 21. Agostina de San José. B.N.M. MS., 8560, fo. 411.

172. " Amemos en ponernos en nuestra nada." Maria de la Cruz. Ubeda I. O., fo. 49.

173. " O esperança del Cielo que tanto alcanças quanto esperas." Luis de San Angel, Baeza P.A., fo. 47. Sebastian of St. Hilary, Jaen P.A., fo. 90.

174. Agostina de San José. Baeza I. O., fo. 107, and B.N.M. MS., 8568, fo. 411.

175. Isabel de la Encarnacion. Jaen I. O., fo. 22. Maria de la Madre de Dios. Baeza I. O., fo. 106.

176. *Subida*, L. III, Ch. V. Ger., I, 288.

177. Jorge de San José. Jaen I. O., fo. 7.

178. *Summarium.* Seg., 75.

179. " Levantava el corazon a Dios." Juan Evangelista. Jaen, I. O., fo. 5.

180. Baeza I. O. Cues. 10, fo. 133. After the *Summarium.*
181. Luis de San Angel. Baeza P.A., fo. 50.
182. José de la Madre de Dios. Granada P.A., fo. 13.
183. Alonso. Seg. P.A., fo. 51.
184. Jaen I. O., fo. 6.
185. Eliseus of the Martyrs. Ger., III, 65–66.
186. *Ref.*, L. II, Ch. II, § 7.
187. *Estimulo de la Propagación de la Fé.* . . . Lisbon, 1586, fo. 28. P. Grégoire de Saint-Joseph. *Jérôme Gracien et ses Juges*, p. 47, note 3.
188. *Ref.*, L. II, Ch. II, § 8.
189. *Ibid.*, Ch. I, § 4.
190. *Bull. Carm.*, Vol. II, 237 ; *Ref., ibid.*, § 5.
191. L. to Gracian, July 7th, 1579. Silv., VIII, 337 ; Greg., II, 413 ; Engl., III, 250.
192. L. to Maria de San José, December 7th, 1576. Silv., VII, 381 ; Greg., I, 469 ; Engl., II, 158.
193. Maria de la Encarnacion, 1633. Arch. C.R., Brussels.
194. *Ref.*, L. VIII, Ch. VIII, § 3.
195. Jaen P.A., fo. 92.
196. Dep. Jur., April 20th, 1634. Arch. C.R., Brussels.
197. B.N.M. MS., 12738, fo. 885.
198. *Ref.*, L. VIII, Ch. IX, § 2.
199. To the Carmelite nuns of Beas, November 22nd, 1587. Ger., III, 84–85. *Letter* III, p. 150.
200. To Leonor Bautista, February 8th, 1588. Ger., III, 86. Letter IV, p. 151.
201. " I heard a number of the facts here reported from the mouth of our blessed Father brother John of the Cross himself, with whom I conversed and to whom I often went to confession, in our house in Madrid during the two sojourns he made there." Deposition of Maria de la Encarnacion, March 2nd, 1622. Arch. C.R., Brussels.
202. Voyage from Granada to Madrid. Juana Evangelista. Arch. C.R., Brussels.
203. L. of Maria de la Encarnacion to Marguerite of Jesus, September 23rd, 1634. Arch. C.R., Brussels.
204. Declaration made on January 27th, 1622, by Juan de la Ciguela, sacristan of the Carmelite nuns in Madrid, at its foundation. Arch. C.R., Brussels.
205. " Con quien mas familiarmente trato y comunico la V[ble] Me Ana de Jesus su espiritu fue con nro S[o] p[e] fray Juan de la Cruz y el la tuvo en gran veneracion y respeto, y alli en Madrid confessandome yo con esto n[o] santo me decia grandes alabanças de nra V[ble] Me Ana de Jesus y entre cosas me decia q en las partes y valor natural aun le parecia la avia Dios dado algo mas que nra gloriosa M[e] Sta Teresa y que en lo sobrenatural no era menos."

Maria de la Encarnacion. L. to Marguerite of Jesus, September 23rd, 1634. Arch. C.R., Brussels.

206. Reported by Maria de la Encarnacion. Arch. C.R., Brussels.

207. Dep. of Hilary of St. Augustine and Beatrix de la Concepcion, already given. Arch. C.R., Brussels.

208. *Ref.*, L. VIII, Ch. IX, § 2.

209. *Ref.*, L. VIII, Ch. IX *passim.*

210. L. to Gracian, November 19th, 1576. Silv., VII, 357 ; Greg., I, 440 ; Engl., II, 133.

211. Maria de la Encarnacion, 1633. Arch. C.R., Brussels.

212. *Peregr. de Anastasio,* p. 63.

213. Maria de la Encarnacion. *Ibid.,*

214. L. to Marguerite of Jesus, September 23rd, 1634. Arch. C.R., Brussels.

CHAPTER XIX

1. *Ref.*, L. VIII, Ch. XI, § 3.

2. *Ibid.*, § 4. According to Alonso (Bk. II, Ch. XVII), John acted as Superior only when Doria was away.

3. *Ibid.*, L. VII, Ch. XXXV, § 2.

4. See, *supra,* Ch. XI. It was at this time that Mother Isabella of St. Dominic " had a special communication with him. . . . The Father was to call this daughter, as a rule, ' the interior man.' " *Vie de la Bienheureuse Isabelle de Saint Dominique,* by Jean Michel Baptiste de la Nuce. Folio MS., p. 91, etc. Arch. C.R., Brussels.

5. *Ref.*, L. VII, Ch. XXXV, § 3. Libro principal llamado *Becerro.* Arch. of Carmelites of Segovia.

6. MS. Arch. of the Carmelite Nuns of Segovia. Jer., 612.

7. Ger., III, 100 ; Jer., 612–613.

8. *Ref.*, L. VIII, Ch. XI, §§ 4 and 5.

9. Ger., III, 133.

10. L., November 9th, 1588 (Ger., III, 87. Letter VIII, p. 156) and L. to Doria, September 21st, 1588 (*Ibid.*, 100).

11. Andres, 13482, B. 20.

12. L. to Leonor de San Gabriel (July 8th, and also during this month, 1589) to Maria de Jesus (July 18th, 1589), Letter XI, p. 165, and to Magdalena del Espiritu Santo (July 28th, 1589), Letter XIII, p. 169. Ger., III, 95 to 99 ; Jer., 618.

13. Jer., 615. See *supra,* Ch. IX, some extracts from the *Instrucción de Novicios* approved by the Consulta on January 11th, 1590.

14. L. of February, 1589. Ger., III, 90. Letter IX, p. 158.

15. L. of June 7th, 1589, preserved in the C.R., Brussels, and first published in *Le Carmel,* May–June, August, 1927.

16. Jer., 614.

17. *Ref.*, L. VIII, Ch. XI, § 5.

18. Arch. of Disc. Carm. of Segovia.

19. The contract was signed and sealed on January 18th, 1589. Arch. of Disc. Carm. of Segovia.

20. Jer., 628. Martin de la Asuncion. Ubeda, I. O., fo. 70.

21. Bernard de Jesus. Seg. I. O., fo. 108.

22. Quir., 755 ; Cyp., III, 42.

23. *Libro de las Cosas.* Arch. Carm. at Segovia.

24. Ines of St. Augustine says that he was so called because he was never heard to say a word that did not refer to God. Andres, 13482, D. 30.

25. Seg. I. O., fo. 107, and Alonso, Seg. P.A., fo. 49.

26. Quir., 695–696 ; Cyp., 633. It was the same in Granada B.N.M. MS., 12738, fos. 571 and 865, quoted by Baruzi, 212. Quir., 642 ; Cyp., 582.

27. "Todo el tiempo que podia . . . queno estoy para tratar con gente. . . ." Elvira de San Angel. Med., I. O., fo. 15.

28. *Avisos.* Ger., III, 12.

29. Alonso, L. II, Ch. XVIII.

30. Maria de la Encarnacion. Seg. P.A., fo. 101. ". . . muy de ordinario. . . ." D. Bernarda and Jeronima de Carrien. Med. P.A., fos. 79 and 80.

31. Bernardo de Jesus. Seg. I. O., fo. 108.

32. *Subida*, L. III, Ch. XLI ; Ger., I, 390.

33. Elvira de San Angel. Med. I. O., fo. 15.

34. Maria de la Concepcion. Seg. P.A., 36. B.N.M. MS. 19404, fo. 146. Maria de la Encarnacion. Seg., I. O., fo. 99.

35. Bernardo de Jesus. Seg. I. O., fos. 108 and 107.

36. *Ibid.*, fo. 108.

37. Seg. I. O., fo. 99.

38. Seg. I. O., fo. 108.

39. Bernardo de Jesus. Seg. I. O., fo. 108.

40. Ger., III, 98. Letter XII, p. 167.

41. Bernardo de Jesus. Seg. I. O., fo. 108. Luca de San José. *Ibid.*, fo. 106. Alonso. Seg. P.A., fo. 55.

42. The poem :
> " Entréme donde no supe
> Y quedéme no sabiendo
> Toda ciencia trascendiendo "

according to the MS. of Alba de Tormes, was composed at Segovia in an ecstasy (Bar., 221–222). Note, however, that it is also to be found in the Sanlucar MS. (Ed. Silv., Vol. II, p. 185).

43. "Con grande ternura y sentimiento. . . ." Jeronimo de la Cruz. Jaen I. O., fo. 8.

44. Maria de la Encarnacion. Seg. I. O., fo. 99.

45. Arch. MS. of the Carmelites of Segovia.

46. Relation of Ana de San José, *Ibid.*, and B.N.M. MS. 8₅68, fo. 424. Andres, 13₁82, 1, 44.

47. Seg. P.A., fo. 30.

48. Arch. MS. of the Carmelites of Segovia. Quir., 761 ; Cyp., III, 48 ; Jer., 639.

49. Vel., L. IV, Ch. V.

50. " Estando el P. Fr. Juan de la Cruz en Segovia, siendo alli prelado, envio a llamarme aqui, yo fui a verle, y después de haber estado alli dos o tres dias le pedi licencia para venirme, dijome que me detuviese algunos dias más, que no sabia cuando nos volveriamos a ver ; fué esta la ultima vez que le vi ; acabando de cenar una noche tomóme por la mano y llevóme a la huerta y estando alli solos me dijo quiero contaros una cosa que me sucedió con nuestro señor : teniamos un crucifijo en el convento, y estandó yo un dia delante de el, pareciame estaria más decente-mente en la iglesia, y con deseo de que no solo los religiosos le reverenciasen sino tambien los de fuera, hicelo como me habia parecido, despues de tenerle en la iglesia puesto lo más decente-mente que pude, estando un dia en oración delante de él, me dijo : ' Fr. Juan pideme lo que quisieres que yo te lo concederé, por este servicio que me has hecho,' yo le dije : ' Señor, lo que quiero que me deis es trabajos que padecer por Vos. y que sea yo menospreciado y tenido en poco.' " Francisco de Yepes. B.N.M. MS., 12738, fo. 613 *sq.*

51. *No tengais tanta priesa que no sabeis quando nos veremos . . .* another deposition of Francisco de Yepes. B.N.M. MS. 8568, fo. 371. According to Alonso (Bk. II, Ch. XVII) Francisco had already been once to Segovia, to console himself for the loss of his five children. The saint saw his nephews in great glory and told Francisco so.

52. Francisco, in another deposition says that John had this image in his cell : " . . . Que tenia nuestro señor en la celda y que no le vian (*sic*) sino es los que alli entraban, y le dije señor no estays aqui bien, por que no vs ven todos los que entran en la yglesia yo quiero haceros poner en el cuerpo de la yglesia para que todos vs adoren, y vs vendigan, y asi lo hiçe. . . ." B.N.M. MS. 8568, fo. 371. John's cell looked out on the choir of the church.

53. Two specially qualified witnesses : Tomas Perez de Molina, who remembered what Francisco de Yepes had dictated to him, by order of his confessor (Med. I. O., fo. 24) and Maria de la Encarnacion, prioress of the convent of Segovia when John lived in that city (Seg. I. O., fo. 101) both definitely state that our Lord asked : " What do you want for this service,—este servicio ? "

Alonso states that, in his own time, the miraculous image was placed in the monks' choir, above the prior, between two candles. The bishop, Don Melchior de Sandoval, had granted forty days' indulgence (Alonso, Seg. P.A., fo. 61). The picture is now in the Church. We have examined it. It is painted on leather.

54. " Que todos me desonren y no hagan casso de mi por vro Amor." Med. I. O., fo. 24. These words are given in Francisco's second deposition, contained in MS. 8568, fo. 373, in the B.N.M. : " Y ansi estando en oracion delante del señor entendi una palabra de gran consuelo que me dijo el señor pideme mercedes por eso que as hecho todo quanto pidiereste dare y entonces respondi yo pues señor lo que yo vs pido es que todos me deshonrren y no hagan caso de mi por vuestro amor. . . ."

55. *Subida.* Ed Barcelona, 1619. Translated by Cyp. of the Nat., Paris, 1645, p. 25.

56. *Vel.*, L. I, Ch. VIII.

57. Quir., 394 ; Cyp., 350. Luis de S. Angel heard the same thing at Segovia from Antonio del Espiritu Santo, speaking on oath. Baeza P.A., fo. 51. Perhaps there is some confusion here.

58. Mary of the Incarnation of Consuegra heard Ven. Anne of Jesus and Mary of the Nativity report this. Andres, 13482, D. 30.

59. *Cántico*, cancion XXXIII. Ger., II, 499.

60. Maria de la Concepción. Seg. P.A., fo. 36.

61. Seg. I. O., fo. 108.

62. Luca de San José. Seg. I. O., fo. 106. Quir., 439 ; Cyp., 393.

63. Eliseus of the Martyrs. Ger., III, 64.

64. *Cántico*, canción XXX. Ger., II, 584.

65. Col. i. 24.

66. Ger., III, 87. Letter VIII, p. 157.

67. *Ref.*, L. VIII, Ch. VIII, § 8.

68. See preceding chapter.

69. *Peregr. de Anastasio*, p. 55.

70. " Muy de otra manera que solia. . . ." Juan Ev. Malaga P.A., fo. 36.

71. " Yo estava encomendando a nuestro S⁰ʳ este negocio del padre Gracian y representaseme una mar y nuestro Padre Vicario General y los difinidores entravan en ella y que les dava boces que se saliesen porque se yuan anegando y al fin vi de que se avian ahogado todos. . . ." Juan Ev. Malaga P.A., fo. 36.

It is most remarkable that when Juan Evangelista made his deposition at the preliminary process at Jaen, ten years previously, he was—like Luis de San Angel (cf. prec. ch.)—much less explicit. He contented himself with saying that John of the Cross confided to him—as his confessor—what had been revealed

to him concerning the affairs of the Order. Jaen I. O., fo. 5.
The *Reforma* alludes to this " view " confided to Evangelista :
" The whole body of definitors threw themselves, of their own
accord, into this abyss, if not of sins, at least of confusion,
diversity of judgment, doubts and contradictions, as O.V.F.
John of the Cross had foreseen." Bk. VIII, Ch. XXXV, sec. 1.

72. " Visitando al pᵉ Gracian los perlados, viendo el santo,
que se tirana aecharle de orden siempre les fue alamano dicien-
doles ; nosemétiesen enpielago tam pfundo iescandaloso,
añadiendo ; queotros castigos tenia laorde paracastigar aqual-
quiera religioso ; estorvolo consus razones el tiempo que fue
Difinidor general. . . ." Alonso, L. II, Ch. XX.

73. L. to Gracian, June 15th, 1576. Silv., VII, 239 ; Greg.,
I, 287 ; Engl., I, 272. L. to Maria de San José, March 17th,
1582. Silv., IX, 169 ; Greg., III, 290 ; Engl., IV, 298.

74. " Junto con esto un santo religioso de ñros padres
desçalcos que a la saçon nos confesaba dio abiso a ñra venerable
mᵉ de que el sabia por muy cierto que a la primera junta que
abian de tener los padres consultores trataban y querian mudar
algunas cosas de ñras constituciones." Maria de la Encarnacion, Juridical deposition taken at Consuegra on April 20th,
1634, for the Cause of Ven. Anne of Jesus.

" Uno de los confesores de ñros Religiosos muy siervo de Dios y
ançiano las vezes que nos benia a confesar tenia traça para
enterarse y saber todo lo q pasaba en la Consulta y asi nos
daba abiso y decia q deseaba se pusiese remedio. . . ." Maria
de la Encarnacion. Dep. Consuegra, 1635 (fragment of the copy
authenticated by His Eminence Cardinal Deschamps, Arch. of
Malines, on December 21st, 1877. Arch Carm. R., Brussels).

75. " Biniendo un dia abisitarnos a el locutorio ñro padre
fray Nicolas de Oria tratando de su consulta y qual gran bien
era para ñra religion este modo de gobierno, mostrando gran
contento de averlo establecido, le dixo ñra venerable Madre :
Padre ñro yo temo que los padres consultores nos an de mudar
muchas cosas de las leyes y constituçiones que ñra santa madre
fundadora nos dejo. VR no le consiente pues bernos por
experiençia quam bien se procede en estas casas, guardando
loque ñra santa nos enseñó. A estas razones se alteró tanto,
y dixo ; Jesus madre no tema VR que no sera cosa de importancia
si se mudare algo. A este replicó ñra venerable madre ; Pues
ñras constituciones estan ya autoriçadas por el nuncio de su
santidad, para que tengan mas firmeza, si a VR le parece, no
seria bueno pedir breve a el sumo Pontifice en que nos, las
confirmase. Y ñro padre fr. Nicolas respondió a esto : bonisimo
Mᵉ aqui no me acuerdo si entremetieron otra platica, mas bien,
de que antes que el prelado se fuese ñra venerable le bolvio
segunda bez a ratificar y le dixo a el fin ; pᵉ ñro dijo VR qᵉ

seria bueno traer breve de Roma para lo que toca a ñras constituciones, y respondio que si y que si no ubiese quien fuese iria el a
pie y descalço, al fin dixo que si una palabra encareçida que no
me acuerdo ponctualmente qual destas fue, con esto se
despidió y a las que estubimos ally presentes a todo esto que
referido aqui, dijo ñra Venerable Madre Ana de Jesús ; hijas
sean me testigo de todo loque ñro p^e v^o g^1 me a dho. . . ."

This deposition, of April 20th, 1634, is given in full in the process of Anne of Jesus and in the reply to the Promoter of the Faith,
this conversation is called : *Momentosissimus dialogus* (No. 67).

Mary of the Incarnation also reported this famous conversation
with Doria in her deposition of 1635, already referred to (Arch.
C.R., Brussels). In a letter dated September 30th, 1625, she
again reports it and adds the following valuable details :

" Todo esto oymos yo, y otras dos Religiosas que estavamos
en el locutario que son ya muertas, que si no me acuerdo mal
fueron las madres Maria del Naçimiento y Maria de San
Joseph, y pienso que tambien estava presente la Me Catalina
de San Francisco, que ella y yo eramos rezien professas. . . ."
(Arch. C.R. Brussels).

76. St. Teresa on one occasion referred to Doria as *mogigato*.
We translate the word as " fearful," but Don Vicente de la
Fuente points out that in Castilian it means " hypocrite."
Escritos de Santa Teresa, Vol. II, note to Letter CCCLXXIII,
April, 1582. Greg., III, 301, note 1.

77. *Bull. Carm.*, Vol. II, p. 240.

78. *Ref.*, L. VIII, Ch. XXXV, § 5.

79. " . . . más para asegurar más su conçiençia tomo parecer
de los majores letrados y personas siervos de nro S. que entonces
se hallaron en Madrid y todo le dixeron le podia hacer consigura
conçiençia y que aviendolo dho su perlado aquellas palabras
no yba contra obediencia y con esto se determino de dar orden
en pedir y embiar por el breve escribiendo a su Santidad de Sixto
Quinto." Dep. April 20th, 1634. We read the following in the
reply to the Promoter of the Faith :

" Maximam etiam considerationem merentur ea, quae imme-
diate hace testis deponit tum de indubia eorum quae narrat
veritate, cum de prudentia insigni, qua Anna nostra in hac re se
gessit ad gravissimorum virorum maturum recurrendo consilium
antiquam quidquam agere inciperet. . . . Quis profecto in
hisce omnibus Servae Dei heroicam prudentiam non demirabitur,
nedum ipsam aliquam repraehensione dignam existimabit ? "
(No. 68). May God grant that the cause of Anne of Jesus may
succeed now that her friend and defender, John of the Cross,
is a doctor of the Universal Church. It is the wish of the whole
Carmelite Order.

80. *Ref.*, L. XIII, Ch. XXXV, § 6. If Mary of St. Joseph

had come to an arrangement with Gracian, it was before she received Doria's letter of August 15th, 1588, forbidding her to have anything to do with Gracian : " Sub precepto y so pena de excomunicación *latae sententiae.*" She herself states that she submitted. *Ramillete de mirra* (Burgos, 1913), pp. 160–161.

81. *Ref.*, L. VIII, Ch. XXXV, § 6.

82. *Ibid.*, Ch. XXXVII.

83. *Ibid.*, Ch. XXXVIII, §§ 1 and 2.

84. *Ibid.*, §§ 4 and 5.

85. Alonso, L. II, Ch. XXII. Jer., 696 and 697.

86. Mary of the Incarnation mentions only John of the Cross, " que nos diesen por Perlado y visitador de monjas a nro V^ble Padre Fray Juan de la Cruz q fue el primer descalzo y companero de ñ Santa Madre. . . ." (Deposition of 1635). The *Reforma* mentions John and Gracian (L. VIII, Ch. XXXV, § 5; Ch. XXXIX, § 3).

87. Quir., 98 ; Cyp., III, 83.

88. There is an inscription here to this effect : /Segun /tradición en este sitio/descansaba San Juan de la Cruz/cuando subia a la ciudad/Ave Maria Virgen/del Carmen e de San Juan de la Cruz/1747.

89. Arch. MS. of the Carmelites of Segovia.

90. *Ref.*, L. VIII, Ch. XLV, § 1.

91. " . . . Padre quiça saldra VR por provincial de esta provincia y el santo padre fray Juan de la Cruz la respondio Lo que acerca dello yo e visto estando en oraciones que me hecharan a un rincon. . . ." Me Maria de la Encarnacion. Seg. I. O., fo. 99.

92. " . . . Como un andrajo viejo le hecharan en un rincon. . . ." Maria de San José. Seg. P.A., fo. 28.

93. " . . . Como un trapo viejo de cocina y arrojado a un rineon. . . ." Maria de San Francisco. Med. I. O., fo. 20. " Como un trapo viejo hechado a un rincon. . . ." Elvira de San Angelo. *Ibid.*, 15. " En un rincon como un trapo viejo." Maria Evangelista. *Ibid.*, fo. 32. It was Mary of the Incarnation of Segovia who reported this fact to the Sisters of Medina whilst she was prioress of that convent, especially to Elvira of S. Angel. C. P., III, 491.

94. *Ref.*, L. VIII, Ch. XXXIX, § 4.

95. *Ibid.*, Ch. XL, § 5.

96. *Ibid.*, § 7.

97. Alonso. Seg. P.A., fo. 59.

98. Jer., 699.

99. Quir., 406 ; Cyp., 362. Alonso (Bk. II, Ch. XXIV) says that John went to Peñuela at the end of July.

100. Ger., III, 104 ; C.P., III, 489 ; Letter XVI, p. 175.

101. The brief *Salvatoris* did not require, as is commonly

said, that this commissary should be selected from the superiors (Ger., I, 119, in a note). It simply says : "Unum Commissarium Generalem ex Fratribus dictae Congregationis prudentia, aetate, pietate, ac scientia praestantem ad gubernium dictarum Monialium earumque Monasteriorum. . . . " *Bull. Carm.*, Vol. II, p. 282. The expedition to the Indies was a means of preventing John from becoming the nuns' superior. L. of Maria de la Encarnacion, November 18th, 1627 : " . . . y como querian desterrar a las Indias porque le pediamos las Monjas por nro perlado. . . ." Quir., 814 and 846 ; Cyp., III, 98 and 128.

102. J. Jœrgensen, *Saint François d'Assise*, pp. 342, 350, 380–381.

103. *Ref.*, L. VIII, Ch. LXXX, § 11.

104. *Ibid.*, Ch. XLV, § 4.

105. Eliseus of the Martyrs. Ger., III, 65.

106. *Ref.*, L. VIII, Ch. XLV, § 6.

107. " . . . y morirá, si fuere menester, por Vuestra Paternidad. Esto es, sin falta, verdad." L. to Gracian, February, 1580. Silv., VIII, 415 ; Greg., II, 519 ; Engl., IV, 13.

108. " . . . de aquel capitulo salio sin officio y penitenciado y le enbiaron a una cassa apartada de la provincia de Granada y quando el dicho siervo de Dios yba acumplir su penitencia. . . ." Velasco, Med., I. O., fo. 10. " . . . porque en el capitulo salio sin officio y penitenciado . . . venido del dicho capitulo par yr acumplir su penitencia. . . ." Elvira de San Angel. *Ibid.*, fo. 15. " Porque salio en aquel Capitulo sin officio y Penitenciado e ynbiado al Convento de la penuela. . . ." Maria de San Francisco. *Ibid.*, fo. 20.

109. L. to Maria de la Encarnacion of Segovia. Ger., III, 105. Letter XVII, p. 177.

110. " . . . y se encerraron, y estubieron hablando y consolando el uno al otro hasta muy de noche. . . ." Andres, 13482, J. 33.

CHAPTER XX

1. " . . . por esta estima y beneracion que esta testigo tenia del de hombre santo acavo con un pintor q una bez sinq el santo sabiese le retratase para que quedase retrato de persona tan santa despues de muerto y el pintor le hiço y esta testigo le hiço anadir estas palabras q el santo solia traer en la boca de ordinario Deus vitam meam anunciavi tibi posuisti lacrimas meas in conspectu tuo." Isabel de la Encarnacion. Jaen I. O., fo. 21. Quir., 371 ; Cyp., 331 ; Jer., 486. Catalina del Espiritu Santo. Granada P.A., fo. 18.

2. Quir., 858 ; Cyp., III, 139 ; Jer., 728 ; B.N.M. MS. 8568, fo. 445 ; Ger., III, 78.

3. Juana de Pedraza. Granada P.A., fo. 17.

4. Mother Anne of Jesus, at the request of Joanna of the Holy Ghost, the sub-prioress of Salamanca, had portraits painted, at Brussels, of St. John of the Cross, and sent them to her, at the end of 1616 or the beginning of 1617, as well as copper-plate : y la lamina con que se hicieron. The entire cost was 500 reals. Mother Joanna was to distribute them amongst the Fathers : a los Padres. (L. to Joan of the Holy Ghost, December 16th, 1616. Arch. C.R., Brussels.) In a letter, dated January 5th, 1624, Father Jerome of the Holy Ghost, of Toledo, writing to Mary of the Incarnation at Consuegra, states that he has received them from Mother Joan (Arch. C.R., Brussels). But, what proves that Anne of Jesus had actually carried into France, and subsequently to Flanders, the portrait painted at Granada during the ecstasy, and not another one, is the presence, on an engraving in the possession of the Carmelite Fathers of Bruges, of the scroll with the " Deus vitam meam annuntiavi tibi," of which Isabel de la Encarnacion speaks. And—we may also say—the striking resemblance of the countenance with that of the " cameo " in the possession of the Carmelite Convent of Troyes, which is said to be authentic. This " cameo " was first published in the *Études Carmélitaines* in January–April, 1920, and *Art Catholique* has reproduced it. Lastly, both the " cameo " and the Bruges engraving, bear an astonishing resemblance to the medallion reproduced as a plate in the life of the saint, by Jeronimo de San José, which appeared in 1641.

We read in the *Annales Congregationis Carmelitarum in Belgio*—in the account of the Foundation of the Convent of Discalced Carmelite Fathers in Antwerp (1618)—that, amongst the relics of this monastery there were " . . . particula ossis S.P.N. Joannis a Cruce *epusdem vera effigies*." And, a little later on the fact is mentioned that : " Joanne Baptista Gutieres signifer *cognatus germanus S.P.N. Joannis a Cruce* in habitu nostro," was buried in the church at the age of ninety-eight years, six months. . . . (Brit. Mus., Add. 17988, fos. 47 and 48).

5. See *The Miracle of Saint Hugh* in the Provincial Gallery at Seville.

6. Ger., III, 58 ; Alonso, L. I, Ch. XLII.

7. Luis de San Angel. Baeza P.A., fo. 50.

8. *Noche*, Ch. I. Ger., II, 78, 79.

9. " El convento de la soledad de la Peñuela. . . ." Alonso. Seg. P.A., fo. 60.

10. *Ref.*, L. III, Ch. X, § 1.

11. *Peregr.*, p. 208.

12. *Ref.*, L. III, Ch. LII.

13. *Ibid.*, L. IV, Ch. XXII, §§ 1 to 3.

14. *Ibid.*, § 4.

15. *Ibid.*, L. III, Ch. X, § 3.

16. Baeza I. O., fo. 103.

17. Quir., 804 ; Cyp., III, 88–89.

18. Diego of Jesus. Jaen P.A., fo. 115.

19. " . . . algunos ratos se ocupava, en escrivir unos libros espirituales que dejo escritos. . . ." Francisco de San Hilarion. Baeza I. O., fo. 48. ; Andres, 13482, B. I, 13, 49 ; D. 17. Quir., 806 ; Cyp., III, 91.

20. " The Rev. Father Provincial of the Discalced Carmelites, with his companion Father Joseph . . . came to lodge in this convent [of the Calced Carmelites] (at Rennes) and, having heard of the super-eminent holiness of our holy Brother, spoke to him ; Father Joseph, in particular, conversed with him at great length and asked him if he had seen the writings of Father John of the Cross. He said he had and that they were most excellent but that there was still a higher life than that. The treatises he had composed on the consummation of the subject in its object would show that what he said was true." MS. *Life* by Father Joseph of Jesus, who was an intimate friend of John of St. Samson and assisted him at the hour of death (Arch. Dep. of Ille-et-Vilaine : Collection Grande Carm., No. 18, p. 131). Quoted by Sernin de St. André in his *Vie du vénérable Frère Jean de Saint-Samson* (Paris, 1881), p. 191.

21. Diego of Jesus. Jaen P.A., fo. 115.

22. Quir., 807 ; Cyp., III, 92.

23. *Subida*, L. III, Ch. V. Ger., I, 288.

24. Maria de la Madre de Dios. Granada P.A., fo. 18.

25. Alonso, L. II, Ch. XXIX. Ger., III, 75.

26. *Ibid.*

27. Quir., 845 ; Cyp., III, 128 ; *Ref.*, L. VIII, Ch. XLVII, § 3.

28. Isabel de la Encarnacion. Jaen P.A., fo. 168.

29. *Ref.*, L. VIII, Ch. XLVII, § 4.

30. B.N.M. MS., 8568, fo. 445. Ger., I, p. xxix.

31. Quir., 858 ; Cyp., III, 139.

32. Quir., 854 ; Cyp., III, 135.

33. Jaen P.A., fo. 93.

34. Baltazar de Jesus. Ubeda P.A., fo. 280 ; Quir., 850 ; Cyp., III, 132 ; *Ref.*, L. VIII, Ch. XLVII, § 5, and L. VI., Ch. XLV, § 5.

35. Quir., 850 ; Cyp., III, 132.

36. Alonso. Seg. P.A., fo. 58.

37. Quir., 861 ; Cyp., III, 142. *Ref.*, Bk. VIII, Ch. XLVII, sec. 5. The *Libro negro de los capitulos de la orden* accuses Diego Evangelista of having transgressed his powers (Alonso, P.A., fo. 59). This abuse of power was discovered in May, 1594, by Elias of St. Martin and his definitors. " But, as he (Diego) was provincial of Andalusia, and as they wished to be merciful,

they condemned him to fast for ten days on bread and water, to receive two floggings for the space of a *Miserere,* and he was summoned to their presence to receive a severe reprimand." (Andres, 13482, D. 198).

38. Grégoire de Saint-Joseph, *Le P. Jérôme Gracien . . . et ses Juges, op. cit.,* p. 78.

39. Quir., 862 ; Cyp., III, 143.

40. *Op. cit.,* p. 77.

41. "El más intimo y de más confianza que tenia el P. Vicario General." Boneta. *Vida de Santos y venerables varones de la Religion de N.S. del Carmen* (Vida del V.P.F. Gerónimo Gracian de la Madre de Dios, Carmelita), Saragossa, 1680. See Greg., *op. cit.,* p. 77.

42. Amicitia aut pares invenit aut pares facit.

43. Greg., *op. cit.,* p. 78.

44. Luis de San Angel. Baeza P.A., fo. 55.

45. *Ref.,* L. VIII, Ch. XXXV, § 1.

46. Alonso, L. II, Ch. X. Quir., 813 ; Cyp., III, 97.

47. Juan Evangelista. Jaen I. O., fo. 6. Alonso, L. II, Ch. XXIX. Ger., III, 75.

48. Isabel de la Encarnacion. Jaén P.A., 168.

49. "Les llego nueba que El santo padre fray Juan hera muerto entonces El ynformante difinidor dixo si no fuera muerto le quitaran El avito y le hecharan de la Relision . . . aun despues de muerto el santo decia las mismas palabras y tanto que dos años despues de muerto El santo padre fray Juan aviendo pasado este difinidor ynformante a ytalia andubo alla ynquiriendo cosas contra el santo. . . ." Alonso, Seg. P.A., fo. 58.

50. Regestum P.P. Terasse, fo. 40 (Rome, Arch. Cal. Carm). Likewise, a deed drawn up by notaries, dated July 14th, 1505, in the State archives at Bruges (Charter, No. 5778).

51. Juan de Santa Ana. Malaga P.A., fo. 27. Alonso, Seg. P.A., 58 ; Ger., III, 108.

52. *Ramillete de Mirra,* p. 164.

53. Maria de la Encarnacion. L. of January 11th, 1626, and Dep. of April 20th, 1634, and of 1635.

54. *Ibid.*

55. Dep. of Hilary of St. Augustine, March 4th, 1627, and Dep. of Beatrice of the Conception. Arch. C.R. Brussels.

56. Maria de la Encarnacion. Dep. of March 2nd, 1622 (Arch. C.R., Brussels), and June 30th, 1633.

57. Maria de la Encarnación, July 24th, 1628, and Dep. of 1635.

58. Arch. C.R., Brussels.

59. *Ref.,* L. VIII, Ch. LVI, § 3.

60. *Ibid.*

61. L. to Gracian, February 17th, 1581. Silv., IX, 18. Greg., III, 98 ; Engl., IV, 122.

62. *Ref.*, L. VIII, Ch. LVI, § 8.

63. *Fund.*, Ch. XXIII. Silv., V, 203 ; C.P., IV, 34.

64. Andres, 13482, A. 7.

65. *Fund.*, Ch. XXIII.

66. See Ch. XIX.

67. Diego de la Concepcion. Jaen I. O., fo. 11. Inocencio de San Andres. Baeza I. O., fo. 136. Martin de la Asuncion. Ubeda I. O., fo. 71. Juan de la Madre de Dios. Jaen I. O., fo. 16. Alonso, Seg., P.A., fo. 64.

68. Fernando de la Madre de Dios. Ubeda I. O., fo. 75.

69. Quir., 816 *sq.* ; Cyp., III, 99 *sq.*

70. Alonso, L. II, Ch. XXIV. Ger., III, 76.

71. Alonso, L. II, Ch. XXVI.

72. Ger., III, 106. Letter XVIII, p. 178.

73. Jer., 741.

74. Alonso, L. II, Ch. XXIV. Ger., III, 76.

75. Quir., 805 ; Cyp., III, 89.

76. Diego de la Concepcion. Jaen I. O., fo. 10.

77. *Ibid.* When John arrived in Ubeda, Doña Maria Basan, sister of the Marquis de Santa Cruz, having already obtained the Provincial's consent, urged John of the Cross to come to Baeza ; he refused because he desired to be alone and forgotten. Alonso, Bk. II, Ch. XXVII.

78. Pedro de San José. Ubeda I. O., fo. 79. Ubeda was founded in 1587.

79. Juan de la Madre de Dios. Ubeda I. O., fo. 89.

80. Quir., 819 ; Cyp., III, 102.

81. Ines de Salazar says that it is seven leagues from Peñuela to Ubeda. Ubeda P.A., fo. 292.

82. Quir., 819 ; Cyp., III, 102.

83. *Saint Thomas d'Aquin, Sa vie,* by William de Tocco and the witnesses at the process of canonisation. Bk. VII (Paris-Toulouse, 1925), p. 126.

84. *Cántico,* canción IX. Ger., II, 523.

85. Sebast. of S. Hil. Jaen P.A., fo. 97.

86. Bartolomé de San Basilio. Jaen I. O., fo. 14.

87. Maurice Barrès. *Du Sang, de la volupté, de la mort.*

88. Fernando de la Madre de Dios. Ubeda P. A., fo. 200.

89. Ambrosio de Villareal. B.N.M. MS. 12738, fo. 662. Quir., 822 ; Cyp., III, 104–105.

90. Ubeda P.A., fo. 291.

91. Pedro de Ortega. Jaen I. O., fo. 11.

92. Ubeda P.A., fo. 292.

93. Jaen I. O., fo. 14 ; Quir., 835 ; Cyp., III, 117.

94. Francisco Garcia. Ubeda P.A., fo. 215.

95. Bartolomé de San Basilio. Jaen I. O., fo. 14.

96. Quir., 841 ; Cyp., III, 124.

97. Pedro de San José.   Ubeda I. O., fo. 79.

98. Quir., 830 ; Cyp., III, 112.

99. " En los dies del mes de Julio de mil y seis cientos y cuatro anos de parecio presente el hermano Bernardo de la Virgen Religioso lego Profeso de nuestra sagda Religion que ya ha dicho en esta información su dicho como en ella se contiene y en razon de lo que dixo del sto Religioso fray Jn de la Cruz y de su grande paciencia con sus trabajos y enfermedades dixo lo siguente debajo del precepto que se le ha puesto y del juramento que se le tomo dixo que siendo prelado del dicho P. fr Jn de la Cruz el P. fr Francisco Crisóstomo tenia muy grande repugnancia el dicho prelado con el dicho P. y era de manera que al parceer en todo lo que el podia hacerle molestia se la hacia aun en la enfermedad larga y penosa de que murió mandando que nadie le entrase a ver sin licencia expresa suya y entraba muchas veces en su celda y le decia siempre palabras, de mucha pesadumbre trayendole a la memoria cosas pesadas como vengandose y es el caso que siendo el dicho P. fr. Jn de la Cruz Provincial o Vicario Provincial no save por que le devio mortificar en algo que asi dice este testigo lo ha oido decir y por eso dio en mortificarle tanto que era cosa increible las cosas que acerca de esto pasavan y fue de manera que porque sabia el dicho P. Prior que este testigo que era enfermero del dicho P. fr. Jn de la Cruz le regalaba y acudia a sus necesidades le quito el ser enfermero con un precepto y viendo esto este testigo envio un propio al P. Provincial que entonces era el P. fr Antonio de Jesús el viejo el cual vino luego al puesto y reprendiendo al dicho P. Prior con palabras muy pesadas sobre el caso estuvo cuatro o seis dias en el convento regalando al dicho enfermo y mando que todos le visitasen le acudiesen en todo lo que fuese posible y a este dicho testigo le torno el oficio des enfermero y mando que acudiese al dicho enfermo con toda charidad y que si el dicho padre Prior no diese lo necesario que buscase dineros los que fuesen menester y le avisase que el lo pagaria todo en todas estas ocasiones de pesadumbre que tuvo el dicho enfermo que fueron muchas nunca jamas se le oyo decir una palabra contra el dicho Prelado antes las llevo todas con una paciencia de un santo. Esto añadio este dicho testigo a su dicho para el juramento que tiene hecho y precepto que se le ha puesto y se le ratifica en ello y de ello doy fe fr Bernardo de la Virgen fray Tomás de S. Joseph fr Pᵒ de Jh Mª." B.N.M. MS. 3537, fo. 162. ; Quir., 831 *sq.* ; Cyp., III, 113 *sq.*

100. Quir., 829 ; Cyp., III, 111.

101. Quir., 828 ; Cyp., III, 111.

102. *Cautelas.*   Ger., III, 3 to 5.

103. Quir., 833 ; Cyp., 115.

104. *Cautelas.*   Ger., III, 6.

105. *Avisos, ibid.*, p. 10.

106. Quir., 835 ; Cyp., III, 118.

107. *Avisos.* Ger., III, 11.

108. Luke of the Holy Ghost. Jaen P.A., fo. 158.

109. Alonso. Seg. P.A., fo. 60.

110. " Desde el talon para arriba de la carne." Fernando de la Madre de Dios. Ubeda P.A., fo. 201.

111. *Id.* Ubeda I. O., fo. 76.

112. Agostin de San José. Jaen I. O., fo. 13.

113. Juan Evangelista. Jaen I. O., fo. 6.

114. Alonso. Seg. P.A., fo. 60.

115. Jaen P.A., fo. 114.

116. Isaias i. 6.

117. Luke of the Holy Ghost. Jaen P.A., fo. 158. Ambrosio de Villareal. B.N.M. MS. 12738, fo. 662.

118. Jaen I. O., fo. 14.

119. Seg. P. A., fo. 60.

120. Quir., 826 ; Cyp., III, 109.

121. Alonso, L. II, Ch. XXIX. Ger., III, 75.

122. Ps. xxii. 7.

123. Pedro de San José. Ubeda I. O., fo. 79. Other witnesses mention this fact : Fernando de la Madre de Dios, P.A., fo. 202. Maria de la Cruz, Ubeda P.A., fo. 394. Bartolomé de San Basilio, Jaen I. O., fo. 13.

124. Jaen P.A., fo. 156.

125. Est autem extasim faciens divinus amor. Dionysius the Areopagite.

126. Jaen P.A., fo. 156.

127. Fernando de la Madre de Dios. Ubeda P.A., fo. 203.

128. Quir., 827 ; Cyp., III, 109.

129. Ambrosio de Villareal. B.N.M. MS. 12738, fo. 662, and Maria de la Cruz. Ubeda, P.A., fo. 402. The doctor also possessed a copy of *La Noche.* Andres, 13482, fo 37.

130. *Llama,* canción primera. Ger., II, 405.

CHAPTER XXI

1. Alonso. Seg. P.A., fo. 62. We shall follow, as far as direct testimony will permit, Alonso's account ; he resided for " a year and a half at Ubeda in order to question the religious and seculars who had witnessed his death " (*Ibid.*, fo. 62).

2. " . . . les dijo como la Madre de Dios del Carmen en el dia del sauado acudia con su aujilio y favor al purgatorio y como sacava de ally las animas de los Religiosos o personas que auian traydo su santo escapulario y le pareze a este testigo como que beya que el santo se regalaua con la memoria deste beneficio y ansi

le decian padre nuestro para el savado le a de llevar nuestro Señor a buestra Reverencia para que no baya a purgatorio o salga presto de ally con este favor de nuestra Señora y esto como hera cosa que acudia a su santidad no lo queria ojr." Bartolomé de San Basilio. Jaen I. O., fo. 15.

3. Alonso, Seg. P.A., fo. 62.

4. "Y diciendolelos que ally estavan como nuestro Señor se lo queria llevar bispera de savado que se reçava de nuestra Señora de quien hera muy devoto. . . ." Pedro de San José. Ubeda, I. O., fo. 79.

5. Bartolomé de San Basilio. Jaen I. O., fo. 15.

6. "Que solo ser su amigo era delicto." Quir., 868 ; Cyp., III, 148.

7. Alonso. Seg. P.A., fo. 62.

8. Luke of the Holy Ghost. Jaen P.A., fo. 160.

9. Diego of Jesus. Jaen P.A., fo. 116.

10. Quir., 835 ; Cyp., III, 117.

11. Jaen I. O., fo. 14.

12. Ubeda I. O., fo. 79.

13. Quir., 874 ; Cyp., III, 153.

14. Baeza P.A., fo. 55.

15. Alonso. Seg. P.A., fo. 62. Bernardo de la Virgen, in Quir., 822 ; Cyp., III, 105.

16. Sebast. of St. Hil. Jaen P.A., fo. 90.

17. *Ibid.*, fo. 95 ; Jer., 775.

18. Alonso. Seg. P.A., fo. 62.

19. Ines de Salazar. Ubeda P.A., fo. 292.

20. Alonso. Seg. P.A., fo. 62.

21. "Questo medesmo giorno hauendo duoi giorni prima ricevuto il Santissimo Sacramento per Viatico li domando affectuosamente al Patre Priore li portassero il Santissimo Sacramento per adorarlo, et disse (essendo io presente) molte cose de tenerezza et devotione al Santissimo Sacramento in modo tale que a tutti li circonstanti commosse a devotione et pigliando espeditione disse, gia Signor non vi vedero pui con l'occhi mortali." Diego of Jesus, Jaen P.A., fo. 117.

22. Quir., 876 ; Cyp., III, 155.

23. "Dico che tre hore avanti poco piu o meno che morisse il detto servo de Dio l'intese dire che moriva molto consolato perche Dio l'haveva concesso quello che a sua divina Maësta dimandava che erano tre cose che morisse non essendo Prelato et in luogo ove non fusse conosciuto et con molti travagli, et cosi l'ho inteso della bocca di detto Servo di Dio." Sebastian of S. Hilary, Jaen P.A., fo. 93. Juan Evangelista, Malaga P.A., fo. 37.

24. Alonso. Seg. P. A., fo. 63.

25. Francisco Garcia. Ubeda P.A., fo. 216, 217, and I. O., fo. 35.

26. Pedro de San José. Ubeda I. O., fo. 79.

27. "... binieron a la dha zelda como catorce o quince rreliziosos del dho convento que se prebenian para ir a maitines y entrando los dhos rreliziosos en la dha celda fueron colgando los candiles que traian en la pared della. . . ." Francisco Garcia. Ubeda P.A., fo. 217 ; Alonso, Seg. P.A., fo. 63. "No tenia otro descanso en los dolores sino que se asia de un cordel que estaba colgado de una viga. . . ." Ambrosio de Villareal. B.N.M. MS., 12738, fo. 662.

28. Fernando de la Madre de Dios. Ubeda P.A., fo. 206.

29. Francisco Garcia. Ubeda I. O., fo. 35.

30. The whole point to be determined is this : were the Penitential Psalms and the Recommendation of a departing soul said at one and the same time ? According to Francisco Garcia, it would seem so. Quiroga and Jeronimo should then be amended. According to Alonso, the religious, at the saint's request, had gone off to rest, and it was before they returned that he recited the psalms with some of the assistants. Quiroga says that the psalmody was interrupted by a reading of *los Cantares*. Alonso and Jeronimo say that it was the Recommendation which was interrupted for *los cantares*.

31. "Estando este testigo en la debozion y contemplazion que tiene dho bio como del techo de la dha zelda hasta los pies de la cama del santo bio un glovo de luz este testigo que con aber dentro dela dha zelda mucha luz encendida asi candiles como belas solo parezio a este t° que luçia el dho glovo y escureçia a las demas luzes. . . ." Francisco Garcia. Ubeda P.A., fo. 127 ; Quir., 884 ; Cyp., III, 162.

32. *Ibid.*

33. Pedro de San José. Ubeda I. O., fo. 79 ; Andres, 13482, fo. 62.

34. Diego of Jesus. Jaen P.A., fo. 117, and Juan Evangelista, Jaen I. O., fo. 6.

35. Alonso. Seg. P. A., fo. 62.

36. Fernando de la Madre de Dios. Ubeda P.A., fo. 206.

37. Alonso. Seg. P.A., fo. 63.

38. Diego of Jesus. Jaen P.A., fo. 117, and Francisco Garcia. Ubeda P.A., fo. 217.

39. Bartolomé de San Basilio. Jaen I. O., fo. 15.

40. "Et in questo instante tenendolo io abbracciato senza ch'avesse conosciuto ch'avesse spirato, viddi repentinamente un grande splendore sopra il letto del servo de Dio a foggia d'una sphera che resplande come il sole, et la luna et le lumi che stavano sopra un altare et due candele che stavano nella cella rimassero come si fossero circondate di nebbia in modo tale che pareva che non rendevano lumi, et tornando a mirare o guardare al servo de Dio quale io teneva nelli bracchi veddi et

conobbi che era già morto, et disse alli circostanti, Nostro Padre se ne é ito con questa lume al cielo, et volendo il Padre fratre Francisco . . . et fratre Mattheo .·. . et io stendere et componere il corpo del servo de Dio santissimo una fragranza d'odori suavissimi che usciva del corpo del servo de Dio. . . ." Diego of Jesus, Jaen P.A., fo. 117.

41. Francisco Garcia. Ubeda P.A., fo. 217.
42. *Llama.* Canción primera. Ger., II, 404.
43. Diego of Jesus. Jaen P.A., fo. 117.
44. Alonso. P.A., fo. 63.
45. Diego of Jesus. Jaen P.A., fo. 117.
46. Fernando de la Madre de Dios. Ubeda I. O., fo. 76.
47. Luke of the Holy Ghost. Jaen P.A., fo. 160.
48. Ines de Salazar. Ubeda P.A., fo. 293.
49. Quir., 894 ; Cyp., III, 170.
50. Sebast. of S. Hil. Jaen P.A., fo. 96.
51. Fernando de la Madre de Dios. Ubeda P.A., fo. 207.
52. " Et diedde l'anima al Signore con molta pace et senza alcuna agonia diquelle che in quell'hora sogliono morono et il volto suo resto molto lieto." Luca dello Spiritu Santo. Jaen fo. 160.
53. " La cui faccia resto bellissima et con particolare biancura non di difonto, non ostante che de prima haveva la faccia pallida et bruna." Diego of Jesus. Jaen P.A., fo. 117 ; Quir., 880 ; Cyp., III, 158.
54. Canción XXI. Ger., II, 563.
55. Constança Rodriguez. Med. P.A., fo. 75.
56. Tomas Perez de Molina. Med. I. O., fo. 24.
57. Sebast. of S. Hil. Jaen P.A., fo. 96. Don Luis was a priest. Cf. L., September 21st, 1591. Ger., III,106. L. xviii, p. 178.
58. Diego of Jesus. Jaen P.A., fo. 118 ; Quir., 935 ; Cyp., III, 207 *sq.*
59. *Llama.* Canción primera. Ger., II, 104.
60. This Father had been his confessor for twenty years. For the last eight years of his life, Francisco went to confession to the master of novices of the Carmelite Fathers of St. Anne, Francisco del Barrio. Vel., Bk. II, Ch. VII.
61. Quir., 947 ; Cyp., III, 218.
62. " Calle hiza, no lloras, inviara ella por me e me vera." Tomas Perez de Molina, already mentioned, fo. 24. Bernardo de Jesus, Seg. I. O., fo. 108. Alonso says that it was at Madrid John pronounced those words, when bidding goodbye to Doña Ana's brother (Bk. II, Ch. XXIV). Francisco de Yepes himself reports these facts (B.N.M. MS. 8568, fo. 375) but states that the words were uttered in Granada. As he heard it from a " Criada de una senora," and as Alonso heard it from another source, we prefer to rely on the firm testimony of Bernardo de Jesus, who knew the saint in Segovia.

63. Constança Rodriguez. Med. P.A., fo. 75.

64. "Llevando les dichas llaves, la dicha carta, la dicha reliquia del dicho braço." Tomas Perez de Molina, fo. 24.

65. Quir., 946 ; Cyp., III, 217.

66. When Francisco arrived in Segovia he told the Fathers that he had the saint's arm. (He had placed it for safety with the Carmelite nuns, and afterwards in the chapel of Our Lady of Fuencisla.) But as a difficulty was made about showing him the body, he set off with his precious burthen for Olmedo. He began to fear, on the way, that he might be pursued and the relic taken from him. At last, he showed it to a Jesuit who was his confessor, by whose advice and with Ana de Peñalosa's consent, it was given to the Carmelite nuns of Medina del Campo, where it is still venerated to-day. Francisco de Yepes, B.N.M. MS. 8568, fo. 375, etc., and Tomas Perez de Molina, already mentioned, fo. 24.

Francisco bequeathed the miraculous portion to Constança Rodriguez. There were apparitions, especially of the Virgin of Carmel and the Infant Jesus. This is Francisco's own account of what happened : "Andaba mucho tiempo suplicando a nuestro Señor que antes que yo saliese de este mundo, ordenase que viese yo a mi hermano : tenia yo esta carne que he dicho puesta en un agnus dei con sus viriles, el cual tenia de ordinario en un altar, y las fiestas lo tomaba de alli con la mayor reverencia que podia y besandolo me lo ponia al cuello Un dia de una fiesta principal a doshora y sin pensar tal cosa vi en ello clara y distintamente tres figuras, una de la Virgen nuestra Señora con el habito del Carmen y su hijo precioso en los brazos, que es la segunda, y la tercera otra que se me dio a entender era de mi hermano, y que por la gran devocion que a la Sacratissima Virgen tuvo ha querido Dios que en su carne vea yo estas figuras las cuales desde entonces siempre veo todas las veces que la miro, ya cerca de cuatro años que pasa esto. Ahora, de un mes a esta parte veo en la misma carne demas de estas figuras dichas, un crucifijo clara y distintamente, como si alli le hubieran pintado, no es mas largo que cuanto cabe alli." B.N.M. MS., 12738, fo. 613 sq. Francisco de Jesus, Med., Process of the Relics, 1615, fo. 11. Louis de la Trinité, Le Directeur d'âmes, p. 189, in the special number of La Vie Spirituelle devoted to the saint.

The three miraculous apparitions in the saint's flesh were painted by Pedro de Soria, an artist of Medina, during the process, and an official document of Don Juan Vigil, Bishop of Valladolid, dated July 24th, 1615, commands Diego Diaz, another painter of Medina, to make copies of them. B.N.M. MS., 12738, fo. 1240.

67. Francisco de Yepes died on the last day of November, 1606, as a tertiary of Mount Carmel, at Medina, aged seventy-seven.

This saint, whose knees were as hard as those of a camel (Vel., Bk. IV, Ch. V), who was so " perfect, loyal and truthful . . . that the nobility selected him as godfather to their children, despite his poverty and lowly state " (Don Luis Osorio, Med. P.A., fo. 87), " was buried with the greatest solemnity, as a prince might have been, without any fees. . . . His habit was cut into pieces and relics were cut off from his body " (Doctor Alvaro del Marmo, Med. I. O., fo. 7). His wife, Ana Isquierda, had died on August 1st, 1606, " old, blind and deaf." She, too, was a Carmelite tertiary (Vel., Bk. II, Ch. VII).

68. Tomas Perez de Molina, fo. 24.

APPENDIX

It gives me great pleasure to record, just as this work is appearing, my entire agreement upon the principal points in the Life of John of the Cross, with the illustrious editor of our saints' works. Father Silverio de Santa Teresa has just published the two first volumes of the critical edition of the writings of the mystical Doctor, containing important introductions and the text of the *Subida* (according to the hitherto unpublished Alcaudete text) as well as that of the *Noche*.

Amongst the Introductions is an abstract of the saint's life from the standpoint of his works. In all that concerns his studies at Salamanca and the influences he must have felt there (Ch. II) ; in all that regards his trials at Toledo and the still more painful ones at Madrid, Father Silverio's position is the same as my own. What I have written of John's desire to return to Castile because he was " satiated with suffering " (cf. Ch. XV) corresponds—I hope—with the Father's wish expressed on page 107. He, who has been dealing for so long with the works of Teresa, insists, as I have tried to do, on her esteem and affection for John of the Cross. My fuller documentation allows me to emphasise certain unpublished traits that confirm this supernatural friendship. Father Silverio, very fortunately, has saved one exquisite detail from oblivion (page 122) which I hasten to quote as I finish this book.

On one occasion Teresa, going to confession to John, told him that it seemed to her that she had not been treating him with proper respect owing to the affection she bore him. The saint, pretending to become grave, said, as soon as she had finished speaking : " *You should correct that, my child.*" Teresa gave a delightful account of the incident to her nuns.

INDEX OF NAMES OF PERSONS
MENTIONED IN THE TEXT AND NOTES

PRINTED IN GREAT BRITAIN BY THE WHITEFRIARS PRESS LTD.
LONDON AND TONBRIDGE